J. K. LASSER'S™
PERSONAL INVESTMENT PLANNER

by
Judith Headington McGee, CFP
and Jerrold Dickson

PRENTICE
HALL
PRESS

New York   London   Toronto   Sydney   Tokyo   Singapore

ACKNOWLEDGMENTS

We wish to thank the following friends and colleagues for helping to make this book possible:

Marv Tuttle	Robert E. Cole	Charles Brandes	Ronald Brock, JD
Michael Vitkauskas, CFP, Money Tree Software	John A. Watson	Avery Neumark, CFP	Judy Hawkins
	Nic Pilger	Jacob Bernstein	Paul Pennington, CFP
Venita Van Caspel, CFP	Luke V. McCarthy	David L. Biehl	Peter Weston
Allan Feldman, CFP	Colin (Ben) Coombs, CFP	R. E. McMaster	Betty Jones, CFP
Jeremy Black, CFP	Gary Krat	James McKeever	Al Jeanfreau, CFP
Loren Dutton	Allen Peterson, II	Robert Prechter	Bailard Biehl &
Andy Rich, CFP	Mitchell T. Curtis	Martin Weiss	Kaiser Inc.
Judith Cowan Zabalaoui, CFP	Diane P. Blakeslee, CFP	David Martel	Sybil Tresch
Brenda S. Payne	George Cranmer	Robert Irwin	Joan McCoy-Collins

J.H.M./J.D.

 PRENTICE HALL PRESS

Simon & Schuster, Inc.
15 Columbus Circle
New York, NY 10023

A J.K. Lasser Book
Published by Prentice Hall Press
J.K. Lasser, the J.K. Lasser Institute, Prentice Hall Press,
and colophons are trademarks of Simon & Schuster, Inc.

Manufactured in the United States of America

1 2 3 4 5 6 7 8 9 10

ISBN   0-13-508417-2

Publisher's Note: *J.K. Lasser's Personal Investment Planner* is published in recognition of the great need for clarification of personal financial and tax matters for millions of men and women. We believe the research and interpretation by the authors and the J.K. Lasser Institute to be authoritative and will be of general help to readers. Readers are cautioned, however, that this book is sold with the understanding that, although every care has been taken in the preparation of the text, the Publisher is not engaged in rendering legal, accounting, financial, or other professional service. Readers with specific problems are urged to seek the professional advice of a certified financial planner, an accountant, or a lawyer.

Production Services by BMR of Mill Valley, CA
Index by Susan DeRenne Coerr/Indexing of
Interior Art by David Gross

Page Layout by Suzanne Gepp
Project Management by Lisa M. Labrecque
Proofreading by Mary Beth Bullock

CONTENTS

PREFACE

As we enter the 1990s we are challenged to manage our money and investments with even greater skill than before. During the 80s we have learned some difficult lessons. We experienced the unprecedented stock market crash of 1987 and tax reforms that have changed our approach to handling money. We saw foreign investors take bigger slices of American property and securities. We learned, too, that financial security and independence could not be taken for granted.

Reaction to *J. K. Lasser's Personal Investment Planner* has been gratifying. Our goal is to help readers find financial guidance, information, and inspiration. Most of all, this book is designed to be easy, not overwhelming. It can be used in various ways: as a self-teaching handbook; as a reference book; and as a professional's desk book for help with clients.

Professional financial planners are using *J. K. Lasser's Personal Investment Planner* in adult education programs as a text. Professional financial planners, colleges, and professional groups need reliable, up-to-date, and comprehensible reference materials. To them good advice is not just good advice—but a means of earning a living.

We thank the many people who wrote, called and shared with us their opinions about this book. Professional planners continue to help freshen the materials and their help is most appreciated. We trust you'll find *J. K. Lasser's Personal Investment Planner* to be, like the economy, a fascinating and profitable vehicle for reaching a better life.

WINNING THE GAME OF GAIN

In the past, financial planning was played like a game of football. The coach (you or your advisor) could sit on the sidelines and watch the action (your assets at work) and send in plays or substitutions between downs. However, with the advent of programmed trading, instantaneous global communication, and a wider-than-ever range of innovative financial products, anyone who makes his or her next call based on the previous play is bound to be outscored.

Today, the game of gain is more like basketball or soccer. The ball (your asset in the investment market) is in constant motion, reacting to forces no single player can control. To come out ahead when the final whistle blows (that is, to have the funds you need for retirement, a child's college education, or other major financial goal), you've got to establish a winning game plan in advance. Preparation and mastery of fundamentals is as important to gaining superior returns and building net worth as it is to winning athletic trophies.

PUT YOURSELF IN THE WINNER'S CIRCLE

Each year, thousands of people discover that sacrificing their financial future for the sake of "earning a living" today is no virtue, and that concern for building net worth is no vice. Learning to use the right financial tool to achieve your personal goals is now as necessary to a rewarding life as attaining a college degree or finding the right vocational training. "Earning a living and creating a better life" has always been the American creed. "Preserving what you have and passing it on to those you love" will be added to America's economic cheer for the 1990s.

When you begin a financial plan, you make a fundamental and, we think, beneficial change in your life. You are no longer content to "speculate" or "get by" or just "do the best you can"; you take control of the earning, saving, investing, and spending cycle and aim it at something specific. You become suddenly aware of factors that may have troubled your financial health for years—risk, return, inflation, and a dozen others—and finally understand them. Armed with new knowledge, new skills, and the confidence that follows success, you act decisively (rather than react passively) in a complex economic world.

NEW TOOLS FOR FINANCIAL SUCCESS

In this edition, you'll find a number of features, valuable ideas, investing techniques, and specific product recommendations for the 1990s. For example, you'll discover:

- Your personal financial index—the combination of your investor type and financial situation that indicates which financial products are right for you
- A new chapter on teaching children about money
- Extensive updating of our retirement and postretirement money management chapters with special attention given to the new Social Security changes
- New tools in the appendices to help you coordinate your chapter reading with practical steps to your own financial plan
- An updated survey of all the popular (and many of the unusual and highly specialized) investment vehicles available for making your short- and long-term financial goals a reality
- New information on Asset Allocation Strategies in terms of the current economy and your own investment policy.

GETTING AHEAD IN THE 1990s

Looking forward to the 1990s, we anticipate that interest rates will remain somewhat stable as the Federal Reserve keeps the economy in check. We see a stronger demand for government bonds partially as a result of the attractiveness of the United States as a safe harbor for foreign investors.

Smaller investors have begun to rejoin the market. The Tax Reform Act of 1986 changed the way many investors looked at real estate. As 1990 comes to a close, many banks have tightened lending practices for developers. Real estate will be precarious in some parts of the country. President Bush has set a moderate policy both fiscally and monetarily. We see the administration's leadership continuing in a cautious mode, but pressures for covering the deficit will continue to plague both Bush and Congress. As we predicted in our last edition, President Bush backed away from his campaign promise of no more taxes in June 1990.

Good money managers set an investment policy for the long term by reallocating their investments through permanent asset allocation principles. It is proven that the best returns along with the most acceptable risk tolerance levels are the result of these strategies. You can protect your resources over time and receive good returns by diversifying your holdings over six basic asset categories: (1) cash and money market instruments, (2) domestic equities, (3) domestic fixed-income, (4) real estate, (5) international securities, and (6) precious metals and other tangibles. In Part III of this book, you'll find a thorough description of the investment vehicles comprising each asset category; and in Part IV, a look at the prospects for the investment markets in the decade of the '90s. How will financial events such as the S&L fiasco, the freeing of Eastern Europe, the unification of Germany, and the 1992 dropping of trade barriers among Common Market countries affect the markets?—along with recommended allocations for each category.

In the meantime, our entire team of contributors, editors, reviewers, and—above all—users of this book will be hard at work gathering information, tips, and new ideas for the next edition of *J. K. Lasser's Personal Investment Planner*. We're pleased you chose us to be your guides to increased net worth and a brighter future.

Judith Headington McGee, CFP

Jerrold D. Dickson

INTRODUCTION

J. K. Lasser's Personal Investment Planner, the only self-assessment, financial planning, and investment advisory book of its kind, will help you build and keep net worth NOW AND IN THE FUTURE. No other single volume gives you all of these:

- Up-to-date professional advice on how to establish and implement your own comprehensive financial plan
- A complete guide to 68 investment opportunities, along with up-to-the-minute information on their prospects for the 1990s
- All the basics of money management and investment strategy—plus tips for making financial decisions the way the pros do
- Insights into your money-related needs, goals, values, and investing behavior—including your *Personal Financial Index,* which guides you to investments that are right for your money management style and financial situation
- Advice on allocating your resources in a way that fits your needs and priorities, and optimizes your portfolio's safety and return.

In short, this book addresses the *heart* (Part I—how you feel about money and making money-related decisions), the *head* (Parts II and III—knowledge about financial planning and investments), and the *hands* (Part IV—how to implement your program) of total financial planning.

If you are an experienced money manager, this book will help you accomplish your financial goals more quickly and cost effectively—saving thousands of dollars in unnecessary fees, disappointing investments, and inappropriate financial products. If you're only beginning to build your wealth, this book will give you the facts and confidence you need to build a sound, defensive financial base for future offensive, wealth-creating investments. Although this book is no substitute for personalized legal and tax counseling or professional financial planning and investment advice, *J. K. Lasser's Personal Investment Planner* will help you deal with all financial professionals—from planning advisors to product salespeople—more knowledgeably and effectively.

YOUR KEYS TO MORE EFFECTIVE MONEY MANAGEMENT

Throughout this book, you'll find the symbols that appear on page ix near critical parts of the text. They are your reminders to take certain actions or seek advice from outside counselors in matters that are crucial to your financial health.

Throughout this book, too, you'll encounter various lists of top-performing investments, lists of special vehicles (such as mutual funds that invest for special objectives); and charts showing the general characteristics of specific investment vehicles. Although we've tried to make these lists as complete and timely as possible, seek the advice of your own financial advisors before making any specific investment.

About the Authors

Judith Headington McGee, CFP is an independent financial advisor with offices in Portland, Oregon and Seattle, Washington, and has served a professional clientele for over 16 years. A NASD registered principal, and prominent member of the financial planning community, Ms. McGee is a well-known speaker and frequent radio and television talk show host and guest. She is a leading advocate of consumer education, and is a teacher, writer and lecturer on financial planning and investment principals throughout the country. She is a former member of the board of directors of the Institute of Certified Financial Planners and is past national president of the ICFP Educational Foundation. She welcomes questions from readers and can be contacted at 4900 S.W. Meadows Road, Suite 100, Lake Oswego, Oregon 97035.

Jerrold D. Dickson is president of Econalyst Research, Ltd, an investment consulting firm in San Francisco. A registered Commodity Trading Advisor (CTA), he manages futures accounts for individuals and acts as a consultant to various institutions. Mr. Dickson is the past editor of a number of investment advisory newsletters including *The Dickson Letter, You & Your Money,* and *Futures Truth.* A frequent speaker at investment conferences, in 1989 Mr. Dickson completed a 4-week seminar tour of the Far East on computer assisted technical analysis for CompuTrac.

Other contributors are Ronald L. Brock, JD, a member of the NASD and IAFP; and Robert Irwin, author of more than a dozen investment and real estate works; and Don Adair, a freelance writer and consultant to financial services firms.

Let Us Know How We're Doing

Each edition of *J.K. Lasser's Personal Investment Planner* brings you new concepts, products, and methods from the world of personal finance—and some of our best ideas come from our readers.

If you have any comments or suggestions for improving this book, or any experiences you'd like to share with our readers, please write to *J. K. Lasser Institute, Simon & Schuster Reference Division, 15 Columbus Circle, New York, NY 10023.* We'd like to hear from you.

J. K. Lasser's Personal Financial Keys

These symbols are your keys to safer, higher-performing investments and more efficient money management.

 This is the symbol for *investment strength*. It tells you how that particular investment vehicle adds growth (capital appreciation), current income, inflation protection, liquidity, or tax shelter benefits to your personal portfolio.

 This symbol represents *investment risk*—your warning that one or more characteristic weaknesses of that investment type may be at work in your portfolio. These risks include business failure, market (asset price) volatility, interest rate fluctuations, inflation losses, deflation losses, and loss of principal (or profits) due to asset illiquidity.

 This symbol marks every J. K. Lasser *money management tip*—hints for more efficient and effective portfolio management.

Money Management Tip

 When time is of the essence, you'll see this symbol—your reminder that the timing of the action or decision in question is *critical*. Areas requiring quick reaction include market timing opportunities, special trading techniques, and calendar (tax-related or investment) deadlines.

Time Sensitive

These symbols remind you that the investment vehicle in question is extra sensitive to a market's *investment environment*—of significance to both "bullish" offensive- and "bearish" defensive-minded investors.

 This symbol appears wherever the investment vehicle has important *tax consequences*—for ordinary income or capital gains, or to flag useful tax-exempt or tax-deferred investments.

Tax Consequences

 This symbol is your reminder to *record this information* for future financial planning or tax-reporting purposes.

Record This Information

 This symbol appears whenever independent professional advice (CPA, attorney, tax preparer, or other) is critical to making an informed financial decision.

Professional Advice

 This symbol tells you to take extra precautions (examine a deal more closely; do more homework about the market, the economy, or your own investment objectives; or read the fine print of the contract or prospectus) when you encounter the problem or opportunity described.

Look At This:

 This symbol marks the asset allocation percentage limit appropriate to risk-sensitive or risk-averse investors.

Risk Sensitive

 This symbol marks the asset allocation percentage limit appropriate to risk-tolerant investors.

Risk Tolerant

Your Personal Financial Index

In Part I, you'll discover which of J. K. Lasser's four basic investor types fits you best and how your personal financial situation (tax status and goals) influences your money-related decisions. After that, you'll find customized planning and investment advice wherever your symbols appear.

Type I

Type I investors don't mind taking risks and prefer to manage their own investments. Type I's often seek out high-growth stocks, owner-operated commercial real estate, and individual options accounts.

Type II

Type II investors are also risk tolerant, but prefer to pay brokers or investment advisors to manage their portfolios. Type II's often favor such vehicles as aggressive growth mutual funds and managed options accounts.

Type III

Type III investors prefer to supervise their own portfolios of safer investments. They feel comfortable with such vehicles as switching funds, short-term CDs, and group real estate investments.

Type IV

Type IV investors prefer to "buy and hold" long-term vehicles or pay someone else to manage their portfolios of safer investments. They feel comfortable with such vehicles as balanced mutual funds, REITs, and long-term U.S. Treasury issues.

A
High Taxes
High Expenses

Situation A planners have a high tax liability and high current expenses. This situation calls for investments that yield good, tax-sheltered current income, such as tax-free municipal bonds.

B
High Taxes
Low Expenses

Situation B planners are able to defer their goal-related spending but expect to have a high tax liability when those investments are drawn down. This situation calls for investments that yield tax-sheltered capital gains, such as zero-coupon bonds.

C
Low Taxes
High Expenses

Situation C planners are in lower tax brackets (or have plenty of tax shelters) and need spendable income now. This situation permits investment in a wide range of vehicles that yield ordinary taxable income, such as high-dividend common stocks.

D
Low Taxes
Low Expenses

Situation D planners are also less sensitive to taxes and can afford to let their investments appreciate over time. This situation calls for vehicles that yield long-term capital gains, such as equity growth mutual funds.

PERSONALITIES AND LIFESTYLES

Can you picture a world filled with money but no people? Of course not — people earn, save, invest, and spend money to satisfy human wants and needs. In Part I, you'll learn more about yourself as a breadwinner and investor, and see why people who ignore the human side of financial planning often finish second best.

CHAPTER 1

YOUR FINANCIAL ATTITUDES AND VALUES

A GLANCE AHEAD

In this chapter, you'll discover

- *Why people in the coming decades will be less economically secure than previous generations*
- *How your attitudes about earning, saving, investing, and spending affect your wealth-building potential*
- *How financial planning is the only reliable way to increase your personal net worth—the money muscle you need to get the things you want.*

THE ECONOMICS OF PERSONAL FINANCE

Regardless of whether the Federal Reserve is successful in engineering a "soft landing" (slow—below 2%—annual GNP growth) and avoiding a recession (negative growth), the long-term picture for the U.S. economy is generally one of more stable growth over the next two decades than has been the experience of the last thirty years. However, there have been some significant changes in that time.

Two-income households are now the rule, not the exception. Home ownership is a more distant dream than every for young families. Health care and college costs have outstripped inflation. Mergers, acquisitions, foreign competition, and rapidly changing technology all contribute to less job security than in days past.

It's an economy that will reward those people who understand their goals and build their assets accordingly. It will punish those who think that tomorrow—inevitably—will turn out like today.

Your task as breadwinner and investor in this environment is to develop an offensive plan that builds, and a defensive plan that protects, your personal *net worth*—the best measure of anyone's ability to live a secure and comfortable life. To begin that process, you must take a new look at an old problem most Americans wish would simply take care of itself: money—and what it *really* means to you.

Taking Your Money Personally

Money—or the lack of it—has always played a big role in the way we Americans define ourselves. We value educated, successful people, yet despite the increased demand, college costs are growing beyond the reach of all but the wealthiest (or brainiest) Americans. We value our leisure time and the nonmaterial side of life, yet we regularly subordinate our personal interests to the endless treadmill of "earn and spend"—seldom remembering to pay ourselves first (save and invest) from the product of our labor. Money is the fuel for our society and a tool to help you achieve your goals. It fires the engine of our economy, creating opportunities and wealth. It greases the whéels of industry, creating jobs and life-enhancing products. It enables charities and public sector agencies to serve and assist us. Like it or not, money is the very "mother's milk" of a healthy and rewarding life.

Of course, what's true on a national scale is doubly true for individuals, couples, and families. We may earn and spend our money in a million different ways, but there are still only a few basic wants and needs.

Money as Power. Because of its ability to satisfy desires (achieve goals and mitigate or avoid calamities), a wealthy person has options that poor people lack—a fact that will come as a surprise to no one. But when that wealth is held by one person in a relationship (an employer versus an employee, one spouse versus another, a government official versus a needy citizen), that person can control the quality and direction of that relationship—at least to the extent that the other person feels dependent on the things that money can buy. From this perspective, money is more than a medium of exchange for goods and services—it is the vehicle of freedom itself.

Money as Magic. In a sophisticated, developed economy, money's ability to transform one thing into another seems to fulfill the alchemist's dream of turning base matter into gold. When your wealth is enough, your ability to transform life's raw materials (time, talent, energy, and good health) into pleasure, prestige, and security is virtually unlimited.

Money as Emotion. When it comes to expressing your feelings, money can help even the most inarticulate voice sing out with affection. From purchasing a ready-made greeting card to bestowing yachts, diamonds, and vacations on a loved one, using money has become, for some, the virtual language of love.

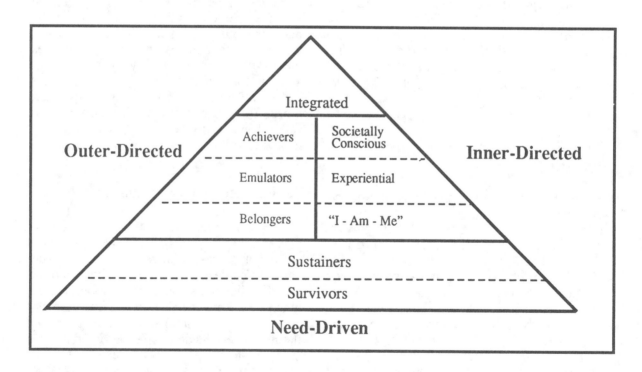

Figure 1-1 The VALS Categories

Money, Values, and Lifestyles

In his book *The Nine American Lifestyles,* SRI International researcher Arnold Mitchell describes how cultural values, beliefs, and personal drives combine with economic privilege or necessity to form a portrait of American society. This typology, called "VALS" for the comprehensive "values and lifestyles" questionnaire used to gather Arnold's data, has rapidly become the basis for many marketing and financial decisions made throughout America. Here is a brief look at the nine VALS categories. Do you recognize yourself in one of them?

The Need-Driven Groups. Although they comprise a relatively small percentage of the total population (around 11%), the VALS *Survivors* and *Sustainers* receive a lot of press and reflect many people's worst fears about a depressed financial future. Survivors tend to be old (their median age is 65), female (women live longer than men), and desperately short of income—living from one paycheck (or relief check) to another. Although almost half of all Survivors own their homes, the houses are sometimes hovels and only a handful have assets in excess of $50,000—few of which contribute to their sorely needed income. Financial planning for Survivors tends to center around the concerns of the poor and elderly—meeting living expenses and those medical costs not covered by federal or private insurance.

Their younger, more numerous counterparts, the Sustainers, experience many similar problems, but, unlike Survivors, they have hopes of improving their condition. Because they seek to rise above their economic hardships (many are from disadvantaged minority groups), they view money as a tool for social mobility—sometimes getting in over their heads in debt when they try to move too fast. Although they, too, live from paycheck to paycheck, their ability to earn and expand that income is significantly greater than the fatalistic Survivors. For these people, financial planning—learning to manage and build what few resources they have—can mean the difference between entry into the sunshine of the American middle class or another generation of poverty.

The Outer-Directed Groups. Above this economic "underbelly" of American society, the VALS typology splits into two segments: one inner-directed (concerned with personal and societal development) and the other outer-directed, composed of those more concerned with material wealth and status.

At the base of the outer-directed segment, the *Belongers* resemble what most people might call the traditional blue-collar or "lower-middle" class. They prefer to live in small towns or rural areas in the company of like-minded citizens who reflect traditional, conservative values. Church or family ties provide their strongest sense of community, and as a rule they tend to like things pretty much the way they are—and "always have been." Financially, they are conservative spenders, avoiding consumer debt, and believe in building net worth throughout their lives—a whopping 82% own their own homes, with almost a third of those holding no mortgage! For Belongers, financial planning offers a way to keep what they have earned and preserve their treasured lifestyle for the generation that will follow.

Just above the Belongers on the VALS hierarchy are the youthful (median age under 30) *Emulators:* those who admire, pursue—but have not quite reached—life in the economic fast lane. Emulators tend to be hard working and ambitious, prefer urban life, and fill the many clerical, service, and crafts jobs that lie just below the really remunerative professional positions to which they ultimately aspire—hence the name Emulator. Although their incomes are significantly higher than the need-driven types, they teeter on the edge of insolvency because of their drive to live—or at least appear to live—the good life. Financial planning for Emulators involves learning the basic disciplines of saving and investing—not just for security, but for the additional education, social mobility, and luxuries their values and lifestyle demand.

At the top of the outer-directed groups sit the objects of all this emulation, the VALS *Achievers*—the very model for the American dream. Achievers comprise the heart of the American middle and upper-middle class: their median age lies well above aspiring Emulators and well below the less ambitious Survivor and Belonger groups. They tend to have solid marriages, children of all ages (including those in college), and just under a third of them boasting at least some college themselves. They tend to be economically and politically conservative, distrust too much government or "social engineering," and are optimistic about the power of free enterprise to solve just about any kind of problem. Their average incomes are higher than any other group, and they participate in the full range of financial and investment activities—including liberal use of debt to increase or sustain their chosen lifestyle. Eighty-seven percent own their own homes (including townhouses and condominiums)—the highest of any VALS group. About a third of all Achievers regard themselves as "financial experts"—a proportion, curiously enough, exceeded only by Sustainers, whose ideas about making and handling money undoubtedly reflect the lessons learned on meaner streets than Wall Street. Still, it's an example of how initial self-perceptions are not always best when it comes to the emotional subject of money. Financial planning for Achievers, consequently, is less an option than a necessity. Not only do they have more assets to employ and protect, but—by virtue of their investing and spending power—the rest of the economy depends heavily on their success as well.

The Inner-Directed Groups. Parallel to the outer-directed Belongers, the first rung on the ladder of inner-directed lifestyles is the youngest of all (median age, 21 years), the *I-Am-Me* group; so-called because of its preoccupation with self-identity in a world that seems busy with other things. Although I-Am-Me's tend to hold lower-paying jobs, they view this situation as transitory, as if fate (if not their own effort) will eventually lift them to a higher quality of life—possibly because many grew up in the households of materially successful Belongers or Achievers. They tend to be socially aware, yet, because of their preoccupation with self, unengaged by social issues. They are spenders, rather than savers, and are ambivalent about financial security—probably because of their youth. Financial planning for people in this youngest, more intelligent, but some-

what alienated group means defining their career and life goals and moving forward in a way that will allow them to enjoy the fruits of their labor as they earn them—and discover who they are along the way.

Slightly older than the I-Am-Me's are the VALS *Experientials* with a median age of 27. These individuals are well educated (38% are college graduates), politically liberal, and prefer to live in the West—mostly in small towns or suburbs. Although they are moderately concerned with money, their predominantly professional or other well-paying jobs allow them to focus on the less material aspects of life. As the name implies, Experientials are interested in experiencing first hand what life has to offer. They are more confident than the less mature I-Am-Me's, and tend to be active in social and political issues. Financially, they respect the freedom money gives them and are pragmatic, if unstudied, money managers rather than big spenders or investors. For Experientials, financial planning means learning to make full use of a wider variety of financial markets—from individual stocks and bonds to mutual funds and real estate investments—as these are the appropriate vehicles for the financial independence their values and lifestyles demand.

Capping the inner-directed groups are the highly educated (58% are college graduates), liberal, and affluent VALS *Societally Conscious* group—the group with the highest number of intellectually oriented, professional, or technical occupations. Although they have benefitted greatly from the current socio-economic "system," they tend to believe that our system needs repair and subscribe to views that most other groups would consider "progressive." Although their income and assets are often substantial, the Societally Conscious are not strongly motivated by material gain or the status normally given to wealth. For them, money is a tool for achieving personal and societal objectives. Consequently, their financial plans must reflect unusual flexibility—a balance between income and growth and the capability to shift assets quickly when a need or opportunity presents itself.

The Integrated (Combined Inner- and Outer-Directed) Group. At the top of the

VALS hierarchy stands the emotionally, intellectually, and financially mature *Integrated* group—a scant 2% of the American population. This group has managed to combine and balance the outer-directed groups' striving for material success with the inner-directed groups' concern for social harmony and personal self-fulfillment. Obviously, such a rare and elusive group is difficult to pin down (even with the aid of the complex VALS questionnaire), and estimates about its composition, demographics, attitudes, and financial habits are still little more than conjecture. The VALS researchers, however, were able to make two startling conclusions about this most amazing and impressive group:

First, *Integrateds seem to be the ultimate destination of all VALS types.* As you may have noticed, the VALS typology formed not only a hierarchy (beginning with a bottom layer of disadvantaged, need-driven groups and ending with a group that has achieved concurrent material and psychological maturity), but it suggests paths of growth toward that destination. Thus, a Sustainer might pull him- or herself into the ranks of Emulators, accumulate enough wealth and success to become an Achiever, then seek to balance an overly material lifestyle with the inner-directed pursuits of the Experiential or Societally Conscious. When the pendulum has swung too far in the direction of self-actualization (suppose, for example, that the person begins to suffer financially from these expensive and less remunerative pursuits), a new respect for economic achievement will assert itself—but in harmony with that person's new inner-directed insights. Thus the long-sought, if hazily defined, goal of becoming a truly integrated person will have been achieved.

Second, *a surprising number of both inner- and outer-directed people view themselves as already belonging to the Integrated group.* A curious result of ongoing VALS research is the number of people who, when queried during seminars, identify themselves with the Integrated group—even though they clearly belong to other VALS types. This convinced Arnold—as it convinces many others—that people *do* generally aspire to a balanced life: one that permits personal fulfillment and societal contribution within the framework of financial security and material comfort.

This very natural human desire to eventually "have it all"—to live a balanced, secure, productive, and rewarding life—is what successful financial planning, and this book, are all about.

Ways and Means of Attaining a Desired Lifestyle

The uncertainty following the stock market crash of October 19, 1987—Black Monday—has given way to a new pragmatism, if not optimism, about personal and institutional investing. As shown in Figure 1-2, domestic equities—despite periodic stumbles—still deliver excellent long-term value. By the end of June 1989, NYSE issues had more than doubled their 1987 closing prices, although many winners benefitted from takeover moves that bolstered their component stocks. Markets for fixed-income investments, such as bonds and bond funds, will be strong as long as inflation stays low. The October crash ushered in an era of declining interest rates and bullish bond markets.

Internationally, the Japanese economy has staved off recessionary pressures despite a rising yen—at least for the present. The significant European economies, notably Britain and West Germany, continue to boast gains in real output. At home the Republican administration, has successfully engineered a steady rise in GNP with moderate inflation through 1990. More burdensome are the twin deficits of the federal budget and the U.S. balance of payments. Although the depreciating dollar has helped U.S. goods become more competitive overseas (boosting domestic production and exports), the structural budget deficit will saddle the new U.S. president—and the national economy—well into the 1990s.

What does this mean to the personal financial planner?

First, it means that while our personal financial health has always been tied to a robust national economy, that well-being is now equally dependent on financial, product, and service markets throughout the world. Need-driven, outer-directed, inner-directed, and well-integrated breadwinners and investors must now think in terms of global mar-

Figure 1-2 The Personal Investing Environment

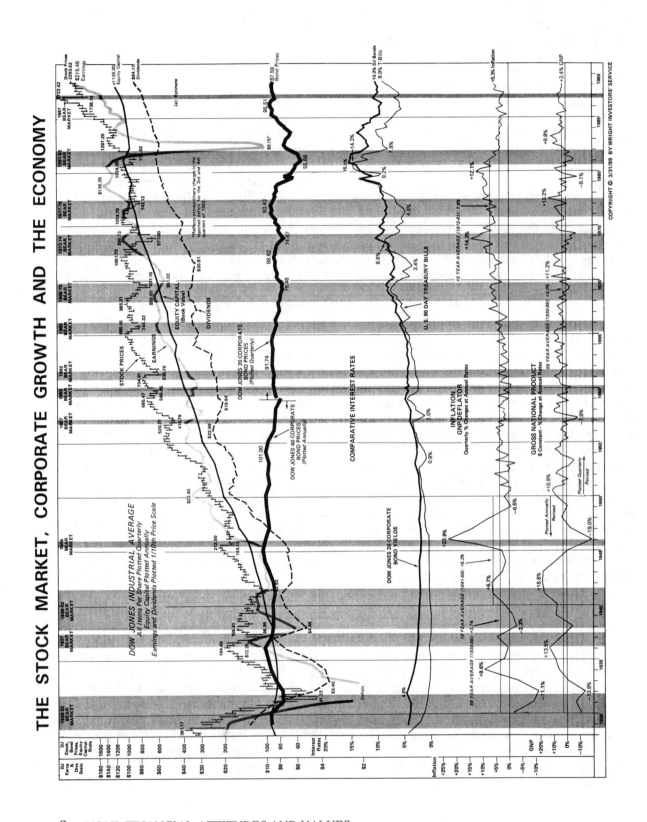

kets, multiple asset categories, and assets that assume both offensive and defensive postures in a personal portfolio, as well as the satisfaction of personal wants and needs.

Second, it means that most of the responsibility for this new and highly customized strategy lies with *you*—the breadwinner and investor—and no one else. You must sift through the veritable avalanche of financial product and service information and screen out the nuggets that apply to you: your needs, your plans, and your aspirations. No government agency, no university professor, no broadcast financial guru, no storefront financial planner is going to do this for you. Only *you* can diagnose your own true wants and needs, money-related attitudes, earning capabilities, and investment resources. Only then will you be ready and able to devise and implement the wealth-building and wealth-protecting plan that's right for you.

FOUR STEPS TO MASTERING YOUR FINANCIAL FUTURE

This book is divided into four parts, each of which is crucial to designing and implementing a comprehensive and successful financial plan. Because your lifestyle, goals, and values will place you in a different position from other readers, you may use the book in the way that suits you best: as a textbook on both the fundamentals and advanced concepts of financial planning, or as a reference encyclopedia for "a la carte" investment decisions.

If you are a novice money manager, you may want to read the book straight through, skipping only those parts that deal with sophisticated investments, advanced trading techniques, or specialized products aimed at the needs of wealthier or more experienced investors. If you are a reader who already has substantial assets and experience in financial markets, you may read only those chapters that apply to the investment opportunities or asset allocation decisions you currently face. Regardless of your experience, you'll want to use J.K. Lasser's *Personal Financial Keys* and *Personal Financial Index*, found throughout this book, to speed you on your wealth-building journey.

Part I: Personalities and Lifestyles

In Chapter 2, you'll learn the reasons why most successful people eventually turn to financial planning to take control of their lives and how those different situations lead to different needs, goals, and outcomes. You'll see how individual personalities affect one's ability to take, or avoid, the risks that are part of every financial decision and how certain investment vehicles fit some personalities better than others. You'll also discover your investor type—a tool that will help you use the rest of this book more effectively and efficiently.

In Chapter 3, you'll see how spending needs and asset growth tend to follow predictable patterns over the course of a lifetime and how your personal financial plan can—and must—reflect reality at every stage of life. You'll discover that the wealth-building, wealth-protecting, and portfolio management tools that are right for you depend as much on your personality, tax status, and goals as the ups and downs of specific markets. To help you match your investor type to specific investment opportunities, you'll determine which of the four basic financial situations influence your investment decisions.

Part II: Money Management and Investment Strategies

In Chapter 4, you'll explore every side of financial planning—from short-term cash management to long-range retirement and estate planning. You'll understand and compute your current net worth and find the strengths and weaknesses of your present financial position. Most important, you'll discover the secret of *multiple asset allocation*—investing in a carefully chosen mix of financial markets that, by responding *independently* to world economic forces, help ensure the steady growth of your portfolio.

In Chapter 5, you'll master the interdependency of time and money: the mechanics of investing and the cyclical nature of financial markets. You'll learn how to plan investments in a way that makes time work for you and avoids the ravages of inflation—regardless of your earning capacity and desired lifestyle. You'll examine the differences between, and strengths and weaknesses of, debt and equity instruments and how to construct offensive and defensive segments of your personal portfolio.

In Chapters 6, 7, and 8, you'll look further into the future to learn the do's and don'ts of pre- and post-retirement and estate planning—*before* your heirs and dependents are required to solve those problems for you.

In Chapter 9, you'll discover ways to help your college-bound dependents meet the high cost of higher education: from little-known scholarships and financial aid resources to investment vehicles that pay *what* you need *when* you need it for transportation, books, living expenses, and the spiraling cost of tuition.

In Chapter 10, you'll review the opportunities and pitfalls of the new era of "tax reduction and simplification" and see if you are really one of those who'll benefit from— or pay higher taxes because of—this often misunderstood legislation.

Part III: Investment Guide to 68 Product Opportunities

Here's where you'll get to the very heart of your wealth-building plan: designing your multiple asset portfolio from an extensive menu of investment vehicles—analyzed and presented in a way that reflects your own investor type, financial situation, goals, and investing attitudes.

In Chapters 11 through 16, you'll explore the six basic asset categories: near-money instruments, such as money market funds and short-term certificates of deposit; domestic (American) stocks; fixed-income investments, such as American Treasury issues and corporate bonds; real estate (both individual and group investments); international securities that tap the breadth and depth of the new global economy; and tangibles and precious metals. In addition, you'll learn which investments the experts pick as the best performers for growth, income, and safety in the 1990s and how to establish the multiple-asset allocations that will build and protect your portfolio.

In Chapters 17 and 18, you'll learn about special (and often high-risk) investing techniques, such as stock market options and commodity futures, that can increase your overall gains through profits from short-term trading. You'll also discover those exotic, one-of-a-kind investments—such as motion picture limited partnerships, and oil and gas investments—that can provide both tax and wealth-building benefits to the right kind of investors.

In Chapter 19, you'll see if the tried-and-true route to retirement security through purchased annuities is right for you; and which forms of insurance—from standard term and whole life to the newer universal policies— will protect your assets and your loved ones best.

In Chapter 20, you'll take a look at your home as an investment, weigh the emotional versus economic factors of home ownership, and discover ways to use and protect the equity you've established.

Part IV: Establishing and Executing a Financial Plan

In this last section, you'll learn the techniques and short-cuts of putting—and keeping—your financial house in order.

In Chapter 21, you'll learn to evaluate a prospectus (the legal description of a security) the way the pros do and find out that what isn't said is often as important as the information the investment company provides.

In Chapter 22, you'll find ways to get your own comprehensive financial plan under way: from locating specialist advisors to keeping appropriate records and coordinating the contributions of tax preparers, financial planners, family attorneys, and family members.

In Chapter 23, you will explore more fully the logic behind multiple-asset allocation as a wealth-building and wealth-protecting strategy. You'll learn where and when to use market timing and special investing techniques and when it's best to leave such methods to the experts. A special section of this chapter also reviews the latest money-management software and shows you just what your home computer can and cannot do in your quest for increased wealth.

In Chapter 24, you'll learn the importance

of teaching your children about the values and uses of money at an early age.

Finally, in Chapter 25, you will learn why it is important to have at least a passing understanding of the economic implications of critical events that will shape financial markets for years to come. These include the huge S&L bailout domestically, the emerging free trading European economy, the unification of Germany, the rising budget deficit in the U.S. and other similar events. You will learn how the "smart money" set (institutional and the super-rich investors) prepare for the 1990s.

Use that knowledge to make your own asset allocations.

Afterword: Making Use of What You've Learned

In the back of this book, you'll find even more tools for implementing and guiding your personal financial plan. In addition to extra forms for collecting and analyzing financial data, you'll find a complete glossary of terms used in personal finance as well as a year-at-a-glance financial planning calendar showing key dates that will help you meet your tax and investment deadlines.

Notes

_____

_____

_____

_____

_____

_____

_____

_____

_____

_____

_____

CHAPTER 2

YOUR PERSONALITY AND FINANCIAL BEHAVIOR

A GLANCE AHEAD

People sometimes say one thing and do another—an expensive habit when the subject is money. In this chapter, you'll learn

- *How financial phobias and negative money feelings can undermine your wealth-building plan*
- *Why money-related homilies and folk wisdom—however beloved—make poor financial planning strategies*
- *About your own investing attitudes and behavior—your J.K. Lasser Investor type—and how to make those habits work for you throughout the rest of this book.*

Some people know how to get along with their money. They know how to get it and how to put it to work. They create financial strategies and stick with them. They know when to take financial risks and when to leave them alone. Their wealth just seems to grow, effortlessly. Just as importantly, they seem to know how and where to spend their money for maximum satisfaction. Others—the vast majority—only muddle through.

Why do some of us seem so comfortable with money while others are so clumsy? Obviously, it's not a question of intelligence—many very bright people are hopeless money managers. Background and upbringing can play a role, though not the only one. Apti-

tude and attitude are important too, although their influence, too, is limited.

The bare fact is that people do or don't do well with money for many complex reasons: emotions, attitudes, personality types, intellect—all can play a role.

Although there's no single way to turn poor money managers into good ones, there are many ways to make virtually any money manager better—to understand and modify the behavior that keeps him or her from achieving financial goals.

IN SEARCH OF THE RATIONAL INVESTOR

As long ago as the 1950s, economist Harry Markowitz established a theory for managing investment risk. Markowitz's landmark work came to be known as *modern portfolio theory,* and its underlying principles guide the multiple-asset allocation strategy that you'll use later in this book.

Using modern portfolio theory and multiple-asset allocation, investors can optimize risk and reward for long- and short-term paybacks. The concepts are time-tested, and everyone—big investors and small—can benefit from using them. Unfortunately, most investors don't.

The reason is quite simple: most people just aren't rational about money.

DISGUISING FINANCIAL PHOBIAS

Effective money management begins with intelligent household spending and progresses to offensive and defensive investment strategies, prudent tax, estate, retirement, and insurance planning, and more. These elements join like links in a chain. If any one is too weak or underdeveloped, the entire system can fail—sometimes catastrophically. No wonder some people find the whole process simply too intimidating to contemplate.

Families that spend money capriciously never develop any real fiscal muscle. They get off on the wrong foot at once and never catch up with the crowd. Some people get further down the path toward security and wealth, but fall into well-worn planning potholes—inadequate insurance or incomplete wills.

Others ignore the tax implications of their financial actions and literally give away much of their wealth. Some commit these fiscal sins out of an inability to face life's realities: the inevitability of death and taxes. Others become hypnotized by one or a few financial products or markets at the expense of all the others. Despite their sincere intentions, they never get ahead and can't understand why they don't.

Foremost among these all-too-human financial foibles is the investor who tries on a money management investment strategy that doesn't fit his or her investment and spending temperament.

BUILDING A MONEY MIND AND MONEY MUSCLES

Creating a more rational investment temperament is like building a stronger body: a portfolio needs room to grow, make mistakes, and develop its muscles. It requires care and feeding. It needs nurturing by someone who understands the ways of markets and its owner's point of view.

How Money Managers Go Wrong

Money managers go wrong when they use investing strategies with which they aren't completely comfortable. Sooner or later they begin tinkering—out of worry or impatience—and that's when a portfolio loses its ability to grow.

Without realizing it, they trade away their assets until they end up with a few stocks or bonds that started out with lots of company, but end up as orphans to be cashed in as soon as the first kid's college tuition comes due. What began as a grand scheme to build net worth becomes a discouraging exercise in complacency or anxiety.

Other underdeveloped investors become hyperinterested in their portfolio. They buy and sell on impulse—victims of hot tips or the movement of "the herd." They take bad advice and when it doesn't pay off, try to reposition themselves by selling losers and acquiring winners—buying high and selling low—the cardinal sin of all investing. Invariably some irrational attitude or emotional foible interferes between themselves and profit, and their financial mind- and body-building program is undone.

How Money Managers Go Right

The key to successful money management is self-understanding. To be truly effective, your financial strategy must reflect who you really are, not who you would like to be and not who someone else thinks you should be. If your strategy doesn't fit your personality, you will unconsciously sabotage it. The irrational bad decisions of the many are what make big profits for the few.

If this were a perfect world, we all would be free of emotional stumbling blocks. If it were simply a better world, we would recognize where we went wrong and smooth things out—we would all be perfect money managers.

But that isn't going to happen. And investors tend more to repeat than to learn from their mistakes; smart money managers avoid those mistakes to begin with. On the path toward this more rational, reality-based money management, everyone else gets stuck. When the barriers are shown in sharp relief, the financial path around them is much clearer and easier to take.

Overcoming Negative Money Emotions

Many people are simply too prejudiced against money to use it effectively. Negative attitudes based on traditional religious or cultural values ("Money is the root of all evil") stunt some people in their growth toward financial maturity; others grow up in families where attitudes of defeat and failure in business or as employees linger into adulthood. Psychologists tell us that schoolchildren who do poorly at math may grow up with an aversion to money. Sometimes, the simple fear of the unknown—the often arcane and threatening world of banks and brokers—can make otherwise competent people indecisive and ineffectual with their money. Here's an example with which you may be familiar.

Money and the Devil

As a child, Bill got contradictory messages about money. He was expected to go to college to escape the working-class background of his family. He was also taught *not* to trust people with his money. "It is easier for a camel to pass through the eye of a needle than for a rich man to go to heaven," his mother told him. The idea stayed with him into manhood.

For many reasons, Bill's professional life was a series of false starts and financial stumbles. His jobs left him unsatisfied, and immediate expenses seemed to absorb all his income. Despite his hard work and long hours, he could never put any money away. He was intelligent and skilled, but everything he did with money was a struggle. "I felt like I was always floundering in quicksand," he said later. "Just thinking about money wore me out."

Circumstances (a hard-won promotion and a desire to marry and start a family) eventu-ally forced Bill to take a good, hard look at himself. With the help of a knowledgeable financial advisor, he began to identify some of the issues that kept him fiscally trapped in the past. As he told the advisor about his goals for a home and family, he began to relive the negative money feelings of his childhood. In ways he couldn't understand, money always evoked feelings of inadequacy, disappointment, and failure. From parents who had sometimes displayed their own bitter feelings about the wealth of others, he learned that success somehow made people unworthy. Money was a kind of taint—to be disposed of as fast as you got it.

"One day," Bill said, "it occurred to me that the bad feelings I had as an adult were the same feelings I had as a little boy. Every time I started to get ahead, my mother's voice told me to toss it away. It's as if I had to wear my childhood clothes for the rest of my life! Those feelings just didn't fit anymore."

Bill's story is true—and it's typical of many stories heard every day by financial advisors. When people who fail with money want to know why, they invariably discover underlying emotional answers.

Money and Loneliness

Financial professionals see people all the time—usually women—who give their money away. Such "loans," as they call them, are to someone they care about—and for the best of reasons. These victims (you can't call them lenders) just can't say no, even when it's the right answer. The outcome is usually the same: if someone doesn't intervene, the victims run themselves bankrupt.

Often, divorced or widowed women use money as a surrogate husband. They keep it close to them for security, feeling compelled to hang onto anything that reminds them of better, stabler times. Although making wise money decisions always involves some risk, even the slightest risk upsets the fragile sense of security these victims work so hard to maintain. For them, money represents far more than the things that money can buy.

"I've lost so much already," said Rose, a tearful widow. "Between my loans to Teddy's (her son's) business and the cost of just getting through the month, I couldn't stand to lose anything more." Yet Rose loses money everyday: her funds sit in a low-interest savings account, but her fear won't let Rose do anything else.

Money and Relationships

Some people squander money by using it as

a vehicle for personal power. They buy friendships and allegiances, hoping to control the actions of others. This is usually the by-product of insecurity—a common syndrome in our society—and if this substitution of money for self-worth continues long enough, both elements lose their value.

Take the case of Carl, for instance: the hard-driving president of a newly established service firm in a large midwestern city. An enthusiastic but inexperienced entrepreneur, Carl tried to combine the kind of charismatic leadership style he admired in other chief executives with a liberal salary and benefits policy for his staff. For the first 18 months, Carl's ideas about money and management seemed to pay off. The staff performed well, and he got a real emotional charge from the inspirational "kickoff rallies" he held every Monday morning.

Unfortunately, Carl's company had been riding the crest of a soon-to-poop-out local business cycle. As orders dwindled, Carl found his staff less anxious to attend his morning sermons. They wanted more say about company operations. They complained privately about Carl's "rah-rah" management style, and he became the butt of office jokes. Naturally, Carl turned to the other half of his "winning" motivational plan to make up for what his personal charisma lacked. He gave big raises to loyal workers (meaning those who kept their mouths shut) and cut off the bonuses from those whom he felt were "backsliders" and "not on the company team." One by one, the more aggressive, independent-minded employees dusted off their résumés and found employment elsewhere.

Soon, Carl discontinued his Monday morning rallies altogether and depended almost exclusively on written memoranda and announcements of bonus and equity-sharing awards to get his message across. By the end of the company's third year in business, Carl found he had purchased the finest staff of overpaid "yes people" that money could buy—but he could count few true friends (and virtually no high producers) on the company's payroll. Business picked up as the local economy improved, but Carl was so discouraged that he sold the company at a loss and accepted a salaried administrative position with a larger competitor. It took several years for Carl to overcome his bad experience and again take an interest in rebuilding his personal wealth or risk his feelings on new, intense personal relationships. For Carl, money alone proved to be a poor way to influence the people on whom his self-esteem and success ultimately depended.

Of course, the issues of spending for pleasure versus security is as old as money itself. Even for a single individual, life can be a juggling act as he or she tries to balance the desires of today with the needs of tomorrow. And when two individuals join together in a common household, that juggling act can become a three-ring circus.

THE DOUBLE-EDGED SWORD OF MENTAL ACCOUNTING

Learning to discipline ourselves—as individuals and as couples—can require some mental gymnastics. Trying to protect yourself from the uncontrollable urge to buy a new car, for example, you might do the obvious—earmark some of your money for security purposes, such as retirement or a cash pool for layoffs or emergencies, and some for spending for capital investments (like cars) and everyday expenses. We create what some experts call "mental accounts." This phenomenon works as follows.

Arthur was wise and respectably rich: his net worth amounted to over $7.5 million, mostly made in the past three years. His wisdom lay in this: he put $1.5 million into U.S. Treasury bonds and gave them to his wife with the following request: "Barbara, these securities are now yours. They represent as much income as we will probably ever need for the rest of our lives. However, I will continue to speculate and try to make more money. But if, by any incredible chance, I should ever come to you and beg for these bonds again, under no circumstances should you give them to me. Instead, get your brother, the psychiatrist, on the phone, for you will know that I've gone crazy."

Arthur—like many other red-blooded, emotional investors before him—broke his solemn, rational vow. His many speculations "went south," and he saw no option but to call on his wife for the $1.5 million to protect the other $6 million. Fortunately, Barbara neither gave him the bonds nor called a psychiatrist. She simply complimented him for putting the money where he couldn't get to it in an emotional flurry. He was imposing discipline on himself, with her as a backup. His speculative bankroll took a beating, but their nest egg stayed intact.

That's exactly the same logic we use when we make automatic salary deductions to fund a pension plan or pay every month into a whole-life insurance policy to build cash value. Both are savings tools, and both depend first on discipline—and later, mechanical safeguards—to keep those savings in the nest. From this perspective, "mental accounting" is a wise and productive idea.

In the investment world, however, all dollars are used for building wealth. By their nature, speculative dollars are subject to more risk than other, "safer" money. The traditional prudent investor knows that if worse comes to worst, the safe account will still be there. This strategy—Arthur's strategy—protects people from squandering everything on impulse.

That sounds good from an emotional point of view, but it leads to a major investing paradox. The purpose of financial planning is to build net worth—your financial bottom line. To be truly effective in this effort, you must consider all assets and all liabilities as working together in one pot. Segregating them mentally into "safe" and "speculative" accounts only dilutes your wealth-building power. The law of risking markets says eventually you'll lose, just as the law of safe investments says you'll make only pennies on every dollar.

Mental accounting, therefore, may protect important money from our worst impulses, but it inhibits financial growth.

For example, some people borrow from a bank at high interest to pay for a car, rather than "loot" a child's college education fund that pays 5% less than what they are paying for the loan. Their net worth, in the end, suffers from such false economy.

Of course there's only one reason for such a decision—the emotion-driven fear that they won't be disciplined enough to pay back the college fund. Overcoming such parent-child reasoning can be an expensive

lesson: using the bank as a "parent" costs them 5% a year—an amount they might easily make up, even as undisciplined consumers. In personal finance, such rational and irrational thinking are all-too-common bedfellows.

MULTIPLE-ASSET INVESTING: SATISFYING EMOTIONAL AND FINANCIAL NEEDS

If mental accounting costs, rather than saves you money, how can human emotional foibles be made to serve your wealth-building plan? The best way to minimize risk—the technique used in modern portfolio theory and multiple-asset allocation strategies—is the diversification of investments. This is the opposite of the go for broke, "all eggs in one basket" strategy used by many individual investors.

Because there's no "win, place, or show" competition in the world of investing, investors can, and should, spread their money across a variety of asset categories—from money market investments, stocks, and bonds, to real estate, foreign securities, commodities, and precious metals. The category mix should be adjusted periodically to respond to significant shifts in the market, but should not be tinkered with in an attempt to benefit from short-term fluctuations. Research shows that asset diversification results in better long-term gains than any other strategy (see Figure 2-1).

The process of mental accounting, however, leads the investor to separate asset categories by risk in his or her head and apply different investment criteria for each account. The success or failure of each category is then judged entirely on its own standards as high- (or low-) risk/reward investment—not a part of an integrated, wealth-building multiple-asset portfolio. The portfolio is not perceived as a fluid, united whole (with the potential for synergistic growth among the parts) but as a rigid, stratified structure with competing—not complementing—parts. Such an investor might adopt a buy-and-hold strategy for mutual funds in his or her bond portfolio and trade in speculative stocks vigorously, reasoning that the two groups intrinsically satisfy different needs. Because different criteria are used to judge the success of each category, investors apply different strategies to each. The result is that the parts of the portfolio look as if they were controlled by entirely different investors. This is not the route to a high-performing (or even consistent) wealth-building portfolio.

To be sure, this "safe" versus "speculative" strategy does what it is supposed to do—accommodates our emotional need for certainty as well as gain, and segregates money we can't afford to lose from money with which we are willing to gamble. But it also prohibits complete diversification, be-

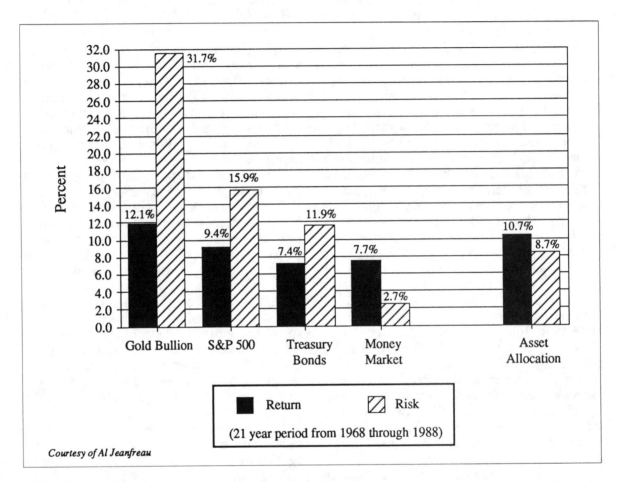

Courtesy of Al Jeanfreau

Figure 2-1 This graph shows compound rates of return for Gold Bullion, the Standard and Poor's 500 stocks, Treasury Bonds, and Money Market accounts. Those four indices are shown separately and then included in a fixed-mix portfolio using Asset Allocation principles. The four market indices and the asset allocation model are shown from 1968 through 1988, a twenty year period of time. Each rate of return bar is accompanied by a bar measuring that market's risk/volatility (standard deviation) for the same period of time. RETURN is on the right and RISK on the left.

Note that Gold Bullion has a return of 12.1% but an extremely high "standard deviation" or risk/volatility factor. The rate of return of the fixed-mix portfolio was surpassed only by the rate of return of gold bullion. However, the fixed-mix portfolio experienced the second lowest degree of risk/volatility, while gold experienced the highest degree of volatility.

cause the boundaries between the accounts are emotional, not rational, and inhibit the growth a combination of markets can deliver.

A CATALOGUE OF EMOTIONAL ILLUSIONS

Beyond mental accounting, a number of emotional barriers appear like irrational camouflage to obscure our view of investment reality. When we are caught in the spell of such illusions, a wrong decision may seem unimpeachably right.

The "Hot Hands" Fallacy

An investor (or investment forecaster) who, like a successful racehorse handicapper, usually picks the winners, is said to have "hot hands"—a Midas touch with the market. The "hot hands" illusion is so compelling that even authoritative sources commonly use it to predict the future behavior of stocks and funds and even the performance of financial advisors.

The concept is predicated on the appealing notion that past—especially recent—performance predicts future results. Hot-handers regularly ask, "Which brokerage firm has the hottest five-year record? Which mutual fund has posted the best return to date? Which tip sheet has the highest percentage of winners?" The supposition is that those which have performed the best are good bets for the future.

Unfortunately, hot streaks, like points on a scoreboard, don't say anything about the next play—about the secret to investing success. The performance of any investment or investor over a five- or six-year period (apart from cyclical effects) says little about next year's return.

For example, in 1979 the Wall Street Fund had the hottest five-year record around. But in 1980 it began a slide that put it at the bottom of the mutual fund heap in the next four-year period.

Or take the case of Joe Granville. In the late 1970s and early 1980s, Granville's successful stock market predictions made him look like the Jeanne Dixon of the market.

But when Granville advised investors to divest themselves of stocks on the eve of one of the greatest and longest-lasting stock market rallies in history, people stopped paying for his advice.

The Law of Small Numbers

We are conditioned to believe that when a coin is tossed ten times, it will land on "heads" 50% of the time and "tails" the other 50%—but that simply isn't true. The mathematical "law of large numbers" on which this statistic is based depends on hundreds or thousands of tosses. In small samples, disproportionately large runs in either direction can occur.

In fact, the 50–50 logic applies only to the *very next toss* of the coin. Only in a very large sampling will the "law of large numbers" take over and the true probabilities begin to exert themselves.

Of course, skill, along with luck, is involved in picking the best funds—but many highly skilled men and women operate on Wall Street, all with access to the same information at the same time, and no single firm—or individual—has yet demonstrated a clear, systematic superiority in the ability to pick winners in the long run. In modern portfolio theory, the "random walk" of stock prices means that no one trader has a systematic advantage over another—no matter how good his or her track record.

Is Seeing Truly Believing?

Emotional illusions can be just like optical illusions: once your senses are fooled, close scrutiny only supports the idea that the thing is just what you think it is not. Three "errors of attribution" can lead us to see a predictable pattern in a set of random events, and it's important for money managers of all personality types to know exactly what they are.

The Illusion of First Impressions

When we form a first impression (explain psychologists Hillel Einhorn and Robin

Hogarth), we have a natural tendency to look for, and find, evidence that supports our original conclusion. In this manner, first impressions become strong convictions. In the world of investing, a favorable emotional impression—from adopting a parent's prejudice to developing an affinity for a company's logo, products, or industry—can keep an investor "sold" long after the accounting ink has turned red.

The Illusion of Control

The illusion of control leads you to believe that you have a greater effect on the outcome of an event than in fact you do. Witness (says psychologist Ellen Langer) the gambler's tradition of throwing the dice physically harder for high numbers and softer for lower scores. Many investors establish similar routines and rituals, which they hope will sway the odds in their favor. Rationally, of course, the actions of one investor have no influence on the larger economic world that governs the movement of prices. Only recently, with the advent of large institutional investors and computer-triggered trading, has it become possible for the actions of one block of shares to affect the value of the rest. Beyond that, the rituals and formulas of small investors still count even less than do a magician's smoke and mirrors.

The Hindsight Fallacy Illusion

After an event has taken place, says psychologist Baruch Fischoff, many investors mistakenly believe that it was not only predictable but also inevitable. In other words, the event becomes self-evident after its occurrence, and investors are quick to convince themselves they knew that it was certain. This 20/20 hindsight gives investors exaggerated confidence in their own ability to predict what's going to happen next—often with disastrous consequences.

Blinded by any or all of these illusions, investors easily convince themselves that a "sure thing" is out there for the taking. They abandon common sense, their own experience, and rational strategy to pursue riches with the same fervor as a gambler with a foolproof "system." The only proof of the fools, unfortunately, is in the way the system takes them for all they're worth.

THE EMOTIONAL BOTTOM LINE: RISK VERSUS REWARD

Some people parachute from airplanes; others climb cliffs, shoot river rapids, or drive race cars—all for the sake of a thrill.

And then there are those who like to take chances with money—financial thrill seekers—the ultimate in adventurous living. Intuition may tell you that these physical and financial thrill-seekers should be the same people—but, interestingly enough, that's not the way it turns out. Financial advisors know that people who seek physical thrills tend to be no more or less carefree with their money than anyone else. Financial risk takers, it seems, get all the kicks they need taking chances with their assets. What's more, clear personality characteristics distinguish these fiscal daredevils, and you should learn to recognize one if you meet one—even in the mirror.

"The No. 1 goal in life of fiscal risk takers is to be successful," says Dr. Frank Farley, a University of Wisconsin psychologist who has done ground-breaking research into the thrill-seeking personality. "For the high financial risk takers, investments are a major focus in their lives, practically an obsession." Conversely, people who structure their lives to avoid financial risk tend to place a priority on happiness.

Said another way, taking financial risk seems to offer these investors the same stimulation and promise of big emotional rewards that physical risk taking does for others. Still, we should draw a distinction between what Farley calls "high financial risk takers" and more circumspect investors who are willing to assume some, if more reasonable, amounts of risk. The first type gets a charge out of going for greatness in one bold stroke. The second type knows that luck is an unavoidable element of every investment strategy and plans a balanced program of risk and rewards.

This ability to gauge your own tolerance for (and manage) risk is a key issue in developing a personal financial plan. You don't have to be a high roller to benefit from risk; in fact, the ability to assume *reasonable* risk is a sign of a healthy financial personality.

Profile of the Healthy Risk Taker

Experience shows that people who accept reasonable risk tend to be capable money managers. They are confident they can develop money-making ideas and can follow through on their investments. They spend an appropriate amount of time reading about money and investing, and have the personal leadership skills to communicate with and direct their financial partners and advisors.

Dr. Julian Rotter, a University of Connecticut psychologist, has uncovered an important clue to the ways people approach risk.

"If you think life is controlled by luck," says Dr. Rotter, "you'll either play your investments very safely or get enticed by a long shot, like the lottery. It's the people who think they have more control over destiny who will take risks when it seems the right thing to do."

This parallels the distinction that decision theorists make between risk and uncertainty. An "uncertain" decision is one in which the outcome cannot reasonably be estimated, like playing the Irish sweepstakes—the province of the lucky thrill seeker—or betting on an election. More rational players prefer "games" like the stock market, where risks can be reasonably assessed and measured.

Like everything else in life, risk and uncertainty—luck and judgment—have their qualitative as well as quantitative components. Do you wake up in the morning feeling like things will go your way? Are you confident of the job you're doing at work and feel secure as a result? Does it seem that when you put effort into a project, things usually turn out right?

Or do you have the sense that no matter what you do, nothing good will happen? Does it seem that getting and keeping a job has more to do with other peoples' actions than your own? Do you feel there really is hardly *anything* you can do about a situation to control its outcome?

Some people prefer to take a loss on a good risk than to be idle in perfect safety. Others hate loss so much that they will pass up a very good opportunity on the chance of a small loss.

RISK AND YOUR INVESTMENT STRATEGY

Don't let anybody fool you: risk is always part of the picture when you invest. Even people who bury their money in a tin can run risks: they could forget where it's buried, someone else might discover it, or natural elements could damage it. Worse, as long as it stays in the ground, every dollar loses value to inflation.

Most often, the fear of risk is founded on ignorance, and education is the best antidote. You'll read a detailed discussion of risk and one of the best available strategies to minimize its effects in Chapter 23—our approach to asset allocation. But right now let's explore the major areas of investment risk; after that, you'll have a chance to assess your attitudes about this most important financial phobia.

Purchasing Power Risk

In a word, purchasing power risk means *inflation* and it's a prime enemy of your portfolio. If your investments don't grow faster than the rate of inflation, you're losing money. Being philosophical about inflation won't help either—you've got to account for it in the rate of return you seek or accept for your investments. The worst thing you can do about inflation is nothing: if you stick your money in a mattress, kiss its purchasing power goodbye. You'll learn about hedging against inflation in Chapter 5, "Time and Your Money."

Market/Liquidity Risk

When it comes time to draw down your investment, will a ready market exist? A perfect example of the harsh reality of market risk is a homeowner trying to sell a house in a glutted market, or an investor trying to make a profit on diamonds purchased during

10 Highest-Risk Investments

1. Futures
2. Options
3. Short selling
4. Collectibles
5. Diamonds
6. Leveraged contracts
7. Oil drilling limited partnerships
8. Mutual funds—option buying
9. Options on futures
10. Strategic metals

10 Lowest-Risk Investments

1. Treasury bonds
2. Credit union accounts under $100,000
3. Passbook savings under $100,000
4. Certificates of deposit under $100,000
5. Unleveraged residential real estate (your home)
6. Corporate bonds rated AA or higher
7. NOW and super-NOW accounts under $100,000
8. Government agency notes held to maturity
9. T-bill money market funds (buy only T-bills)
10. Annuities issued by highly-rated companies

the great diamond boom of the 1970s. The appraised value of your home or your diamonds doesn't count for much if there's an excess supply and no one wants to buy them.

Business Risk

Many investments depend on the proper management of the business that underwrites the investment. A declining balance sheet or income statement that reads red will bode ill for investors.

Interest Rate Risk

Interest rates rarely stay put for long. As they rise and fall, they may affect the value of your investments. Interest rate risk most directly affects fixed-income investments, such as bonds. As interest rates rise, the price of old bonds falls. Conversely, as interest rates fall, old bonds become more desirable. Thus, the longer term the bond, the more "volatility" its value may have as interest rates fluctuate over time.

Strategies exist to minimize these risks, and you'll find them throughout this book. The bottom line is that investors must be aware of their own feelings about the different kinds of risk and take them into account when making financial plans.

Active Versus Passive Money Managers

Active money managers want to control, or at least to participate in, decisions affecting their finances. They tend to believe that by intervening in the course of an investment, they can make a difference in total return. They often engage in short-term market timing and frequently rely on economic forecasts. At minimum, these active money managers want the ability to move their funds around among various investment categories in anticipation of changing economic conditions.

Examples of an active money manager are an individual with a personally managed portfolio of individual stocks, and someone with shares in a mutual fund that features switching privileges.

Passive money managers are "passive" not because they are disinterested in their money, but because they lack either the time or expertise to make and implement money-related decisions. (True, people whose personal value system discounts the role of money in life will probably also be passive money managers, but they are unlikely to be readers of this book!) Passive money managers may or may not believe in the power of market timing and economic forecasting to add value to an investment; but if they do believe in such techniques, they are willing to pay someone else (a broker or fund sponsor or advisor) to make those decisions for them. If they do not believe in such techniques, they tend to "buy and hold" investments and keep their money parked in a specific vehicle for a very long time.

It's important to note, too, that although many passive money managers prefer conservative investments, others are great risk takers. They are "passive" only because they lack the time or expertise to make the aggressive investments they prefer. These investors are willing either to buy and hold speculative vehicles or to pay others to make trading decisions on their behalf.

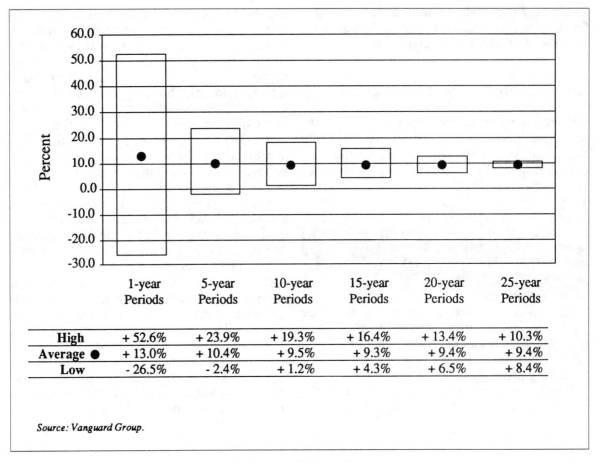

	1-year Periods	5-year Periods	10-year Periods	15-year Periods	20-year Periods	25-year Periods
High	+ 52.6%	+ 23.9%	+ 19.3%	+ 16.4%	+ 13.4%	+ 10.3%
Average ●	+ 13.0%	+ 10.4%	+ 9.5%	+ 9.3%	+ 9.4%	+ 9.4%
Low	- 26.5%	- 2.4%	+ 1.2%	+ 4.3%	+ 6.5%	+ 8.4%

Source: Vanguard Group.

Figure 2-2 This chart shows the relativity of risk and time.

In the chart, money invested in the stock market for a one-year period could have realized a loss of as much as 26.5% or realized a gain of as much as 52.6%. The one-year market average was 13.0%. The 20-year periods studied shows no loss, but a low return of 6.5% and a high return of 13.4%, with the average return being 9.4%. Note that the average return of 9.4% was fairly consistent from the 10-year through the 25-year periods.

Discovering Your Investor Type

Instructions: In front of each item below, enter the number from the following scale that best reflects your answer. If you do not currently invest, imagine how you might feel or behave in the situation described.

Very Much *Like Me*		*Sometimes* *Like Me*		*Not Like Me* *at All*
5	4	3	2	1

_____ 1. The money I invest should earn superior returns, even if I stand a chance of losing some or all of my principal.

_____ 2. I take the time to learn about an investment before I put down my money.

_____ 3. I don't mind making a quick investment decision if the payoff is high enough.

_____ 4. Financial recordkeeping is a chore, but it's important that I do it myself.

_____ 5. My motto is "Don't worry, it's only money."

_____ 6. I believe that nobody looks after my money as well as I do.

_____ 7. I believe in the old saying "Nothing ventured, nothing gained."

_____ 8. My motto is "If you want something done right, do it yourself."

_____ 9. I never second-guess a spending or investment decision after I've made it.

_____ 10. I believe in the saying "An investor who runs with the herd is bound to get trampled!"

_____ 11. I don't mind taking big risks when the reward is great enough.

_____ 12. I like to draw my own conclusions about spending and investing.

_____ 13. Most investments are a crap shoot anyway, so why not bet high and enjoy the game?

_____ 14. I'm pretty good at interpreting information about the economy.

_____ 15. If I know enough about an investment and can afford the possible losses, I'm willing to take a chance.

_____ 16. I have trouble trusting experts with my money.

Scoring Your Answers

To discover your investor type, add the numbers you entered for each odd-numbered item and enter the sum in Space A below. Now add the numbers you entered for each even-numbered item and enter that sum in Space B.

A.   Total for odd-numbered items: _____

B.   Total for even-numbered items: _____

If your total for A and your total for B above are *both* greater than 24, you are a Type I investor. If your total for A is greater than 24 but your total for B is 24 or less, you are a Type II investor. If your total for A is 24 or less, but your total for B is greater than 24, you are a Type III investor. If your total for A is 24 or less, *and* your total for B is also 24 or less, you are a Type IV investor. Enter your investor type in the space below and go to the next page.

    I am a Type _____ investor.

The Investor Types Explained

These investor types will give you a good clue about your tolerance for risk and the most appropriate ways for you to manage your money and your investments. Accompanying each description, you will notice a symbol that corresponds to that investor type. Look for your symbol throughout this book: it marks the financial strategies and specific investments that are most appropriate to your money-related attitudes and behavior.

Type I: Risk Tolerant/Active. These in-vestors prefer to manage their own high-potential investments and make timing or reallocation decisions themselves, as symbolized by the risk-taking climber. They typically prefer to own portfolios of individual high-growth stocks, operate their own income property, and maintain individual options or future accounts.

Type I

Type II: Risk Tolerant/Passive. These in-vestors prefer to pay someone else to make market timing and reallocation decisions for their speculative or high-growth vehicles. They are represented by risk-taking climbers following an experienced leader. This type of investor often feels comfortable with aggressive growth mutual funds, hedge funds, and managed options accounts.

Type II

Type III: Risk Averse/Active. These in-vestors prefer to supervise their own portfolio of safer investments. Their symbol is the investor relaxing in the safety and comfort of a backyard lounge chair. They feel comfortable with switching funds, short-term CDs, and more liquid group real estate investments.

Type III

Type IV: Risk Averse/Passive. These in-vestors prefer to pay someone else to manage a portfolio of safer investments or buy and hold investments of long duration. They are depicted by a comfortable, lounge-chair investor being waited on. They feel comfortable with balanced mutual funds, REITs, and debt instruments such as long-term U.S. Treasury issues.

Type IV

Solving the Rest of the Puzzle

Understanding your own attitudes about risk and discovering your investor type will help you establish satisfying financial strategies and select the vehicles that suit you best—but that's not the whole picture. Equally important is your financial situation: your tax status and financial goals. These needs dovetail with your investor type to form your "personal financial index"—a way to customize each financial decision. In Chapter 3, you'll assess your financial situation and learn how it interacts with your investor type to help you create a total financial plan.

CHAPTER 3

LIFESTYLES AND FINANCIAL LIFE CYCLES

A GLANCE AHEAD:

In this chapter, you'll take the first steps toward financial independence. You will learn

- *How to determine your present financial situation*
- *About the stages of your financial life: accumulation, preservation, and distribution*
- *How your current stage affects your money management strategies*
- *How goal setting provides a practical strategy for changing money behavior*
- *How to set long- and short-term financial goals.*

INVESTING NEEDS VERSUS SPENDING DESIRES

Like fingerprints and snowflakes, no two investors are alike. We each have specific needs and circumstances that set us apart from all other money makers, money spenders, and money managers.

Some people are saddled with debt and feel bound to lighten that burden before they feel capable of creating a cohesive investment strategy. If you're in that situation, turn now to Chapter 4 and discover the principles of household cash flow and income management. ("Budget" may seem like a "four-letter" word, but it's the key to success for most money managers. Reducing debt and attaining that first investable sum is not as hard as it sounds.)

Other people are concerned with taxes: they need to switch some investments from taxable to tax-free (or tax-deferred) vehicles, or find investments that complement the low-bracket (or tax-sheltered) income they already enjoy.

Other factors you must consider when developing your overall financial strategy are your current and future spending needs. Do you need investments that produce cash now for living expenses or for later goal-related spending? From this perspective, financial planning is really no more than balancing your current versus future spending goals and obligations.

Discovering Your Financial Situation

In determining your investor type, you gauged your tolerance toward risk and the level at which you want to be involved in financial decision making. Now it's time to learn about two remaining factors that influence the kinds of investment vehicles that are right for you.

First, how sensitive are you to taxation when it comes to computing the return you need on your investments? *Tax-sensitive* investors are typically in high-income tax brackets and seek ways of minimizing taxation on marginal returns, usually through tax-sheltered, tax-exempt, or tax-deferred investments.

Tax-insensitive investors are in lower income tax brackets or have plenty of shelters or other ways of offsetting taxable income.

Their investing strategies can focus on generating current income and growing investment capital.

An investor who needs cash for immediate spending is said to be *income-oriented* and tends to look for vehicles that produce regular distributions without reducing the principal sum.

Investors who are able to defer spending, or those who desire to spend a certain amount of money at some future date for a certain goal (such as college tuition or a new automobile), are *growth-oriented* investors and they tend to seek investments that forgo distributions in order to build value over the long haul.

Some investments provide the potential for both income and growth (such as divi-dend-paying stocks), and some investments offer tax advantages as well as growth (such as tax-deferred annuities and zero-coupon bonds), but most investment products are designed to appeal primarily to one type of investor or the other. Therefore, and because many investors have both growth and income objectives, it's not at all uncommon to invest in a number of vehicles that deliver both kinds of return.

As you can see, your financial situation is as important to your total plan as your tolerance for risk and your money management style. The accompanying questionnaire can help you complete your inventory of the "raw materials" you bring to your wealth-building efforts.

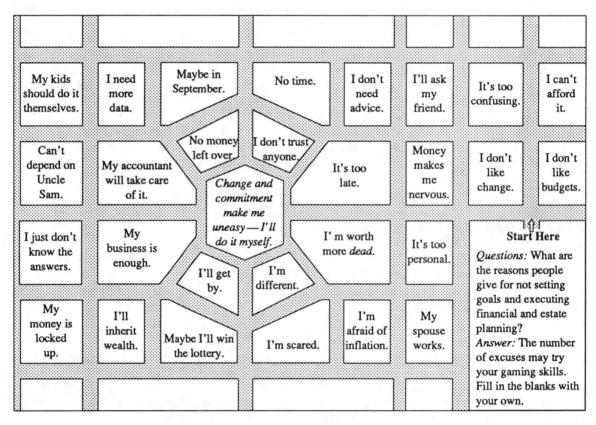

Figure 3-1 Remember that most people procrastinate because of the F.U.D. Factor: fear, uncertainty, and doubt.

Determining Your Financial Situation

Instructions: In front of each item below, enter the number from the following scale that best reflects your answer:

Very Much Like Me		Sometimes Like Me		Not Like Me at All
5	4	3	2	1

_____   1. I usually owe more taxes when I file my income tax returns.

_____   2. I have trouble meeting my current living expenses.

_____   3. I am in or near the top federal income tax bracket.

_____   4. I need cash *now*, not many years in the future.

_____   5. I pay more taxes than most people in my income bracket.

_____   6. Most of my financial goals lie in the next few years, not 10 to 20 years down the road.

_____   7. I have few, if any, tax-sheltered investments.

_____   8. I am retired now, or plan to retire within the next 12 months.

_____   9. Each year I seem to earn more money and pay more taxes, but have less to spend for myself.

_____   10. I have plenty of insurance or other assets in case I need cash for emergencies or goal-related spending.

Scoring Your Answers

To determine your financial situation, add the numbers you entered for each *odd-numbered* item and enter it in Space I below. Next, add the numbers you entered for each *even-numbered* item and enter it in Space II.

I. Total of odd-numbered items: _____

II. Total of even-numbered items: _____

If your total for I and your total for II are both more than 15, you are in Financial Situation A. If your total for I is more than 15 but your total for II is 15 or less, you are in Financial Situation B. If your total for I is 15 or less but your total for II is more than 15, you are in Financial Situation C. If your total for I and II are both 15 or less, you are in Financial Situation D. Enter your financial situation letter in the space below and go on to the next page.

I am in financial situation _____ .

The Financial Situations Explained

A
High Taxes
High Expenses

Situation A—Tax-sensitive, income-oriented investors: These people have a high tax liability and also have high current expenses. They need money right now to help meet their financial obligations and near-term spending goals. This situation calls for investments that yield good, tax-sheltered current income, like tax-free municipal bonds.

B
High Taxes
Low Expenses

Situation B—Tax-sensitive, growth-oriented investors: These people are able to defer goal-related spending until a later date, but expect to have a high tax liability when that investment is drawn down. This situation calls for investments whose objective is tax-sheltered capital gain, such as zero-coupon bonds.

C
Low Taxes
High Expenses

Situation C—Tax-insensitive, income-oriented investors: These people are in lower tax brackets (or in higher tax brackets with plenty of shelters) and need spendable income now. This situation allows such investors to choose from a wide range of instruments producing ordinary taxable income, such as high-dividend common stocks.

D
Low Taxes
Low Expenses

Situation D—Tax-insensitive, growth-oriented investors: These people are in lower tax brackets (or in higher brackets with adequate shelters) and seek a good return on investments that can be left to appreciate in value over time. This situation calls for investments that may be liquidated in the future for taxable capital gain, such as equity growth funds.

The Case of the Well-Rounded Investor: Your "Personal Financial Index"

In the same way most of us naturally seek to balance our lives, like the VALS Integrated group, we should attempt to balance the requirements of our financial situation with our investor preferences. Throughout the rest of this book, you'll find your personal investor symbols matched with your financial situation letter wherever financial services, investment products, or a money man-

agement activity suits your particular needs. Because your risk tolerance or desire to manage your investment actively may vary with certain vehicles, you'll want to inspect the text whenever you see *either* symbols or letters, not just when they're together—although the matched letter and symbol will always be your best guide to a completely tailored product or service.

Suppose, for example, that you're a Type II investor in Situation B. You are primarily interested in tax-sheltered, tax-exempt, or tax-deferred investments, managed by someone else, that can deliver long-term growth—and you're not too concerned about the risk such investments encounter while they do it. You'd therefore look for the Type II icons *and* B letter code together for the best possible investment or service opportunities, but you *may* be interested in *any* product marked with the B code, because your risk tolerance or desire to manage the investment yourself may depend on that product's asset category or your experience in that industry.

The main idea here is to let your *Personal Financial Index* guide you to—and not force—the money-related decisions that are right for your needs, lifestyle, and position on the financial life cycle.

THE STAGES OF LIFE

Our lives tend to pass through a few distinct and fairly well-defined phases, and each brings with it unique opportunities and responsibilities. Effective money managers know that age and outlook play a big role in the way their financial plans are structured.

- Doug and Cynthia, Type I, Situation B planners, are just getting started. They've decided to postpone having children, but they are starting a fund for a planned-for child's education. If they choose to stay on career tracks that make having children too burdensome, they'll use the education fund for retirement. They are trying to decide whether to buy a home or rent and want to know what type of investment profile best suits their needs.
- Jim and Jean are in their early 40s and have a household income of around

$80,000. In two years, their oldest daughter, Sara, will leave for college; her two brothers and a sister have decided to go to college, too. The Smiths put some money away for education, but not enough. Now they have 24 months to prepare for the shock of college tuition and Sara's living expenses. Here is a case of two Type IV planners shifting from Situation B to Situation A in the very near future.

- Bill, a Type III money manager, hopes to retire from his job as plant foreman in 10 years. He and his wife Rose own a piece of riverfront property, on which they haven't built yet. Their children are grown and Bill and Rose are in good health, but aside from the land and the family home, they don't have many assets. They don't want to lose what they have, but they feel they need to implement a fairly aggressive financial strategy in order to be ready for their Situation C retirement.

Their values and lifestyles are all from mainstream America, yet they have unique goals, values, and financial needs. Just as your view of the land around you shifts when you walk to a different spot, your perception of finance, and your financial situation, changes with your age and your circumstances.

Most people progress through distinct financial stages: the *education* (Situation D) years, the *accumulation* (Situation B) years, the *preservation* (Situation A) years, and the *distribution* (Situation C) years. On paper, as in real life, these situations are not segregated by clear boundaries; rather, they overlap as we gradually grow from one phase into the next.

The Education and Accumulation Years

In all societies, youth is the time for learning. By the time young people in our culture have reached their mid-20s, they are expected to have learned the skills they need to support themselves. They are no longer financially dependent on their parents; they have made their first self-supporting steps into the world.

Life's next decade should be devoted to establishing a career and laying the groundwork for future financial security. Needless to say, the education process continues—in the laboratory of life if not in the classroom. During these years, young people should learn the basics of household financial management and begin taking the first steps toward defining their financial strategies. One great joy of this stage of life is that money put aside now has time to build to far greater value than like amounts invested later: the 25-year-old who begins investing $2,000 a year in an IRA at 10% annual interest will see that sum grow to $973,703 at age 65; postponing the IRA by 10 years reduces earnings to $361,887.

The years between 25 and 35 are pivotal to future success. During them, you should build a sound financial base; except for the fortunate few who came into the world well positioned, it's not generally a good time for speculation. Regardless of your investor type, your efforts should be focused on building a good savings program, acquiring a home, preparing for the education of children, establishing a long-range financial plan.

This also is the time when some people begin to develop entrepreneurial skills; if you want to start your own business, do it now. Don't wait until you are too entrenched in someone else's enterprise to seek your own financial fortune.

Establish credit and protect it during these formative years; use leverage prudently to develop net worth. Don't be afraid of debt—leverage will get you into your first home or get your business on its feet—but don't abuse consumer credit. Remember: use debt for assets that appreciate (grow in value over time), not for those that depreciate, or become less valuable. Learn to save for a new refrigerator instead of opening a revolving charge account.

While this is a time for caution, don't let fear paralyze you; there is still time to rebound from mistakes.

The Accumulation and Preservation Years

As you move into your 40s and 50s, you

should be in a position to capitalize on the base you carefully built in the preceding decade. By now, most people are ready to prepare seriously for the retirement years by putting a full-scale multiple-asset investment program into place.

These years can be a mixed bag. The earning power we have generated may be offset by the expense of helping children get educatedand established. Some people who have accumulated net worth may use it as a cushion while they prepare themselves for a career change, or they may invest it in a new business venture.

Most people, though, should use these years to prepare for a comfortable retirement. During the early years of this phase, even risk-averse people tend to be fairly aggressive with a portion of their assets so that the accumulation process is accelerated. They can take advantage of good credit to move quickly when an outstanding business or investment opportunity presents itself.

Later, as they approach the age of retirement, most people grow more conservative and reduce financial risk and debt. They get their house in order for the golden years by gathering and consolidating their assets. Those who plan to work right through the retirement years may stay aggressive, but most people are beginning to look for stability.

The Preservation and Distribution Years

The goal of the accumulation years was to stimulate the growth of your assets so they pay off in regular income at retirement. With retirement comes a continued shift to the preservation mode. People tend to reduce the number of investments they hold; they look for less complicated and more liquid investments. Good money managers of any type aim to preserve what they have by reducing risk and debt, and they begin to prepare their affairs for the time when they will no longer be able to care for themselves.

They also look ahead to the responsible distribution of their assets. Most people like to leave something for their families, and many leave assets to their church or a favorite charity; there's a good feeling when you can leave something behind as a way of making the world a better or more comfortable place.

The successful completion of each phase results from good planning, self-discipline, and the mastery of appropriate skills. Part II describes specific tools and strategies to accomplish the goals of each of your life's financial stages.

MAKING IT WORK

All people have visions of how they would like their life to be; for most people, comfort and financial security are a big part of the picture. Need is one of life's least pleasant realities, and we are reluctant to imagine ourselves burdened by poverty—especially in old age. We know we don't need millions, but we want to know our everyday dreams of comfort and peace of mind can come true.

Learning how to transfer that vision to reality can be tricky. In fact, it's almost like magic, since it means making something intangible (an idea) into something concrete (reality).

But getting from here to there may require that you learn some new skills and apply them consistently—but these tasks are well within the reach of even the most inexperienced or reluctant money manager.

Planning for Success

Every expert on getting ahead will tell you that success is a habit. It's not a mystery; it's a way of life built up with attitudes and skills you can learn and practice. The biggest hurdle most of us face is not believing we can do it. Although complicated discussions about fear of failure (and of success) are best left to the psychologists, we've coached enough fledgling money managers to know that success is seldom an accident.

Successful individuals—like successful companies—use a planning process that forces them to prepare for the future and to review periodically their progress against those goals. In the corporate world, this process is called *strategic planning*. For individuals, any plan that is comprehensive, long-ranging, and specific, will accomplish the same objective.

Whatever you call it around your house, your plan should do the same thing for you that strategic planning does for General Motors or the neighborhood bank—it should give you a basis for making both near- and long-term financial decisions. Such a plan assures you that as time passes, your career and life actions complement one another and fit into a cohesive pattern designed to get you from where you are to where you would like to be.

Successful plans are composed of *goals* and *objectives*.

Goals

A goal is a desired state of being, represented by an activity (lifestyle) or an acquisition. Goals work in three time frames: near-term, mid-term, and long-term. A typical long-term goal might be your desire for a comfortable retirement, with time and money enough for travel and recreation as well as resources adequate to meet your health care and housing needs. Mid-term goals might include providing a college education for the children, a vacation to Asia, and the purchase of a new home. Short-term goals—generally meant to include those you hope to accomplish within the next year to 18 months—might include a new car, a family vacation to Disneyland, or a new piano for the sitting room.

Objectives

An objective is a concise statement of the actions you will take to achieve your goals. Often, each goal will require several action statements.

How to Define a Goal

All goals have three common elements:

1. They must be well defined and understood by everyone who will be affected by them.
2. They must be specific and measurable.
3. They must be time-dated.

Finally, goals and the objectives (the action statements) that will achieve them must be put in writing: writing a goal forces you to be concrete and literal; plus, you're much less likely to forget a task or slip a deadline when your objective is on paper.

Two Important Attributes: Price and Priority

Each goal you write must be assigned a dollar value and a priority.

Pricing a goal doesn't need to be an elaborate process; in fact, if you complicate it too much you may get discouraged and not complete the job. Resist the temptation to try to account for inflation (inflationary factors are discussed in a later chapter); instead, price your goals in today's dollars and let your choice of investments handle inflation for you.

When ranking your goals, be flexible. Since buying a new car and funding the children's education can seem as important as contributing to a retirement nest egg, it may be helpful to categorize goals by time horizon and rank them accordingly. You must be careful not to defer long-term goals indefinitely in order to achieve short- and midterm objectives. There will always be a multitude of "good causes" clamoring for your resources; unless you give your long-term goals a high priority, you are almost certain to find them always bumping along at the bottom of the list—and retirement will find you unprepared.

Why People Don't Set Goals

Three common myths keep many of us from setting goals:

1. Plans are a waste of time. Some people are afraid a plan will lock them into a direction with which they may later become uncomfortable, or prevent them from reacting to an unanticipated need. To keep their options open, they don't plan—and wind up reacting, instead of acting, in a turbulent financial world.
2. Executing a plan is too difficult. To some people, anything short of 100% ac-

complishment seems like failure. Because they are so afraid to fail, they don't plan—and wind up accomplishing less than they'd intended.

3. *A plan will force me to forgo immediate pleasures.* Other people are afraid a plan will impose endless sacrifices on the altar of distant—and unachieveable—future rewards. By living only for today, these people impoverish the many other "todays" that constitute their future.

As you can see, these rationales are only excuses for not planning. What follows are ways you can turn your own irrational fears into a rational financial plan.

Accept the fact that circumstances change. Economic conditions change and people change—what you want at 40 may be entirely different from what you wanted at 25, or will want at 60—so a good plan must bend accordingly. A good plan will never lock a bad decision in or a good opportunity out. In fact, successful organizations assume unpredicted changes will occur—your family should do the same.

Jim had worked for 20 years as a machine shop sales manager when his boss called him in one day and made an offer: "You've been a good employee and you know the business as well as I do. My wife and I have decided to sell the company and retire before we're too old to enjoy it. If you're interested, I'm willing to make you vice president and let you begin a phased buy out that will give you controlling interest in the company within 10 years, when I'm 60. What do you say?"

Jim's boss proposed a phased acquisition plan that would cost Jim a sizable chunk of his income over the next decade, but when all was said and done, would deliver to Jim a thriving business. Jim and his wife, Gay, Type IV investors in Situation B, had been careful planners but their plans had not included the purchase of a business. Before they could accept the offer, they needed to know how their overall financial plan would be affected.

That evening, Jim and Gay sat down and talked through their goals, trying to decide which ones could be delayed or eliminated. They discovered that their long-term plans would be enhanced by the purchase of the business. By becoming equity partners, they might actually enjoy more options and a far more comfortable retirement than they had imagined.

Their mid-term goals were hardest hit. The purchase of the machine shop would probably cost them the new home they desired, and Gay would have to work for another few years before returning to school for her advanced degree. Their long-awaited trip to Europe, too, would once again be deferred for "a more important" cause.

On the other hand, they decided their children's college funds would be unaffected (a lump sum having been invested 10 years before), they still could afford a replacement for Gay's aging car, and the old house could be painted and improved as planned—but now to enhance its liveability, not its resale value.

Ultimately, Jim and Gay chose to accept the offer. The promise of long-term financial and employment security offered by the machine shop option felt like a good choice, even though it represented some short-term and mid-range sacrifices.

You may face decisions of equal magnitude during your life—but will you be as prepared as Jim and Gay to make rational decisins based on self-knowledge, current needs, opportunities, and future plans?

When an unexpected event or opportunity forces us to examine our goals and priorities, a well-crafted plan is not an albatross, but wings to help us soar past doubts and guesswork to higher-quality decisions.

A plan represents your needs and wants, but it is not the Ten Commandments. If you set 10 goals and reach six of them, aren't you better off than if you hadn't reached for any? People who say, "I can't," are usually right. People who say, "I'll try," at least have a chance to succeed.

A good plan provides some immediate paybacks. Chapter 4 gives you planning techniques that allow you to enrich your life in the "here and now" even as you prepare for the future. Suffice it to say at this point that effective financial planning actually increases income for current spending while marshalling resources for future growth. If Jim and Gay had felt they must sacrifice everything today in order to achieve a long-term goal, they might well (and wisely!)

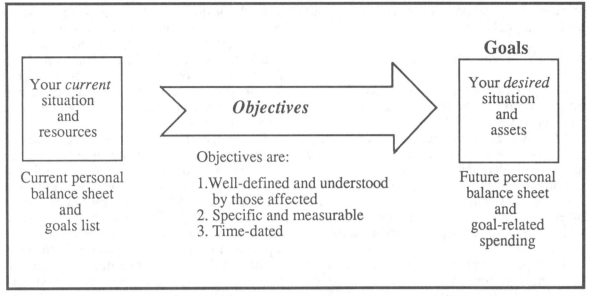

Figure 3-2 The Strategic Financial Planning Process

have declined the boss's offer.

GOALS VERSUS WISHFUL THINKING

Goals not solidly rooted in reality are just pipe dreams. Your goals must be built on a realistic assessment of your current financial situation, where you would like to be, and when you would like to be there. They must take into account your age and your ability to tolerate risk: the odds of actually achieving the results you have in mind.

Factoring all the necessary conditions into that equation is not a science, but you should know enough about yourself by now to have a good idea about the direction your financial plans should take.

At the end of this chapter, you'll find a goal-building worksheet with examples from Jim and Gay's goals list. Using this form, try listing and ranking some of your key financial goals. It may be difficult at first, but if you stick with it and use your family and friends as goal-definition resources, you'll almost certainly develop a list that's both meaningful and feasible as the basis for your personal financial plan.

Remember to keep your goals specific, time-bounded, and clear. Give them each a due date, a current dollar value, and a rank

or priority that fits your resources as well as your desires.

Reviewing the Plan

Some people mistakenly believe that plans are chiseled in stone. In fact, plans must adapt to all kinds of changes, or they have no value.

Not once in the history of the world have economic conditions stood still: economic forces roll along in gigantic cycles that absorb all manner of disruptions, including war, famine, and political upheaval. In everyday terms, interest rates and inflation are two of the macroeconomic factors most likely to affect an individual plan. On a more personal level, illness, disability, or the loss of a job are just a few of the events that can throw a monkey wrench into any plan. Although there are ways to accommodate almost any exigency, good money managers know they must revise their strategies when circumstances change.

An occasional review will help you keep your plan in line with your changing priorities, and a review may show that (1) you need to make a renewed effort, or (2) you're doing better than you thought. A review is a rejuvenating experience that can stimulate your thinking and help you develop even more effective strategies for arriving at your long-term goals.

A Goal Accomplished

If a plan is a road map, goals are destinations, and objectives are signposts, what happens when you arrive?

Effective financial planners know that goals give life purpose and direction, so they never stop planning—no matter how many important goals they've accomplished. Goals flow into one another; as one is reached, another presents itself. Accomplishing one goal is merely the trigger for setting another.

Some people believe that reaching a major goal entitles them to enter a state of grace where they will never again be touched by struggle or difficulty. But reaching a goal is like climbing a mountain: you can appreciate the height you've achieved, but the next peak—the one that looked unattainable from the ground—now beckons. Your new goal has presented itself and if you are alive and growing you will learn the skills you need to take you to new achievements.

Building a plan that accommodates several important goals in many time frames can seem overwhelming when you're standing at sea level looking up at mountain peaks, but the skills are available to you when you've committed yourself to making the climb. In succeeding chapters, you will learn the principles and techniques that can pull all those needs and desires into one neat package, and provide the fiscal muscle power you will need to accomplish them.

Jim and Gay used this goal-setting format to create priorities and evaluate opportunities. It's a simple and effective way of taking that first step toward turning your dreams into reality.

Go To...

Go to Appendix B, pages 490 through 495, to complete your *Money Management Attitudes Sheets*.

Financial Goals Worksheet

Name: Jim and Gay Stewart

Month/Year: October, 1990

Priority	Goal	Objective		Date	Dollars Needed
1	Sufficient income for comfortable, secure retirement	Continue monthly contributions to investment portfolio		Ongoing	$1,000/ month
1	College education for kids	Start Growth Mutual Fund		9/92–9/98	875/ month
4	Home Improvement Deck and Hot Tub	Get bids Hire contractor	3/15/91 4/2/91	6/31/91	5,000
2	Buy new house	Contact realtor Meet with lender	12/10/93 1/15/95	8/31/95	2,500/ month
2	Gay: advanced degree	Contact admissions director Obtain transcripts		9/15/95– 6/20/97 3/15/95– 4/1/95	12,000
4	Australia trip	Establish trip fund		6/15/93 Ongoing	7,000 300/ month
4	Replace Gay's car	Save in Put & Take account for 50% down payment		1/15/91	12,000 300/ month

Notes

PART II

MONEY MANAGEMENT AND INVESTMENT STRATEGIES

Even the finest automobile is useless without roads, fuel, and a competent driver. Similarly, wealth means little if you don't know how to acquire it, protect it, and use it as a vehicle for a more secure and rewarding life. In Part II, you'll discover the un- *derlying principles of effective financial planning, learn how to make time and the new tax laws work for you, and see how to preserve more of your assets for college expenses, your retirement, and your heirs.*

CHAPTER 4

WHAT IS FINANCIAL PLANNING?

A GLANCE AHEAD

In this chapter, you'll survey the general principles behind effective personal financial planning including

- *Facts and myths about money management*
- *How to measure your net worth and track it from year to year*
- *How to build discretionary income for investing and for enjoying the finer things in life.*

FINANCIAL PLANNING: FACTS AND FICTIONS

People often equate income with wealth: the more someone makes, the wealthier he or she appears to be.

In truth, income has less impact on financial net worth than most people think. It's one of many economic fallacies promoted by a society that is more concerned with increased consumer spending than building wealthy citizens. Your job as an effective financial planner is to overcome a lifetime of such prejudices and to learn the skills and habits of a successful money manager.

The Main Goal of Financial Planning

How many times have you said, or heard someone say, "No matter how much I make, I always seem to spend it all"?

The great tragedy in our society is that many of us will reach our senior years unnecessarily impoverished. Literally millions of dollars will have passed through our hands in a lifetime, yet we will have failed to put any of it aside. We may survive, but dependence on Social Security and Medicare is no picnic. To make matters worse, few of us will have pensions sufficient to fill the gap.

The bad news is, in order to enjoy a secure and rewarding financial future, you've got to prepare today. The good news is you can begin with far less than you think— provided you start right now. If you want to take an early retirement; enjoy first-quality medical care, travel, and leisure; send your children to good schools; have a home on the beach; and have the other, innumerable benefits of a quality life, you have to make a plan.

A financial plan is a map of the road to success. It tells you how to get from where you are now in terms of assets and potential, to where you want to be—next year, five years, or 20 years in the future. Financial planning is a process that reflects who you are, where you want to go, and how you want to get there. In short, it encompasses all the economic factors that affect your progress through the many stages of life.

Financial planning helps you manage your income so that you will accumulate the money you need to invest. It encourages (indeed, requires) practical goal setting and realistic risk assessment and management. It gives you a framework for investment strategies and the resources and capabilities you need to profit from the changing economy.

If your ultimate goal is a healthy financial maturity, the best way to achieve it is through a healthy—and muscular—financial plan.

How Financial Planning Works

Financial planning attacks the barriers to your future well-being simultaneously. First, it gives you a clear snapshot of where you are. This includes guidelines for a budget that will help you find the money you need to begin investing.

When you have mastered your current financial circumstances, planning then helps you establish strategies to achieve your goals.

Figure 4-1 illustrates the various components of a personal financial plan and how they interact at any given time.

Cash In. This component consists of your paycheck, your income from rents, child support, gifts, inheritances, and interest and dividends you receive from investing. It's all the cash you receive within a given period of time.

Inexperienced money managers often make the mistake of thinking that there are different "cash ins" for each purpose. For example, they believe that dividends go only toward stock investments or rents go only toward new housing or other real estate investments. In a sound financial plan, however, all income is considered "cash in" and, consequently is fair game for the best mix of investments.

Cash Out. This component is your expenditure of income. The two biggest categories are usually living expenses and liabilities such as taxes and mortgage payments. What's left over is discretionary income, and building this resource is an important objective of any financial plan.

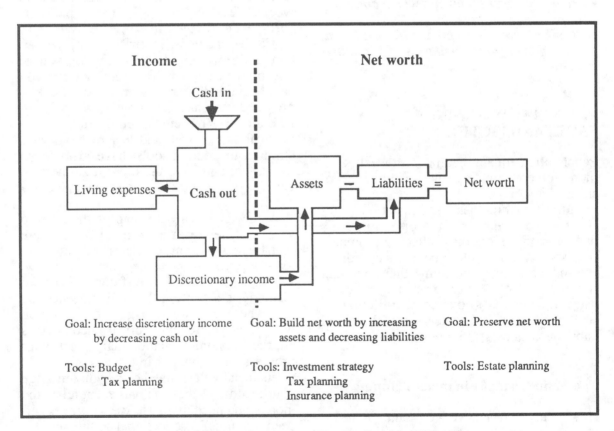

Figure 4-1 How Financial Planning Works (Understanding Net Worth)

Discretionary Income. This component is the money left after paying living expenses and liabilities. You can spend it on entertainment or travel, give it away, or invest it for the future—anything your heart desires. If you invest it, however, it builds your asset base, which in turn can build more discretionary income and—ultimately—net worth.

Liabilities. Your liabilities include taxes and debt, such as mortgages and all the interest on all loans.

Assets. Your assets are what you own, even if someone else (such as a bank) has a claim against them. Assets may be productive or nonproductive. Productive assets generate income in the form of dividends, interest, rent, or other cash payments that flow back as "cash in." Nonproductive assets are those that, while possibly appreciating in value (such as your house), do not contribute to "cash in" until they are sold.

Net Worth. Your net worth reflects the assets you own "free and clear"—your wealth at any given moment. Building and preserving net worth is the ultimate objective of all financial planning. To calculate your net worth, subtract all your liabilities from all your assets. We'll show you how to do this shortly.

STRATEGIES FOR INCREASING NET WORTH

The basic goals of a financial plan are to

1. Increase discretionary income by increasing cash in and, where possible, decreasing cash out, consistent with a desired lifestyle
2. Build net worth by developing effective tax and investing strategies
3. Preserve existing net worth with effective tax, estate-planning, and insurance strategies.

Measuring Where You Stand Today

A map of a strange city is useless unless you first know where you are. Similarly, your financial plan cannot proceed without a realistic understanding of your net worth—your balance of assets and liabilities—as they exist today. In financial planning, this "road map" is called the *personal balance sheet*, and it reveals important facts about your current fiscal status.

Your Personal Balance Sheet. Your balance sheet is very much like stopped action on a videotape. If you hit the "pause" or the "freeze frame" button on a VCR, the picture suddenly halts so that you can examine one frame at a time. A personal balance sheet is one "frame" of your financial life.

Of course, this single picture changes as often as your financial situation changes. By following its progress from one period of time to another, you can see if your net worth is growing or declining.

It doesn't take much time or work to create a personal balance sheet—and the reward is vastly greater than the effort. Simply create two columns, side by side, on a blank sheet of paper. In the left-hand column, list all your assets, starting with your most liquid assets, such as cash, and move downward through long-term assets—those that would take a lot of time and trouble to sell off, such as your house or a business. In the right-hand column, list all your liabilities, progressing again from current (outstanding bills) to long-term debt, such as a home mortgage. Figure 4-2 gives you an example of a typical personal balance sheet.

Personal Assets. Here are the elements of the asset side of the balance sheet, beginning with current (liquid) assets.

1. *Cash.* This element includes not only cash but items that can be quickly turned into cash, such as savings and money market accounts, certificates of deposits (CDs), contracts or notes receivable, and the cash value (if any) of your life insurance policies.
2. *Marketable securities.* Your marketable securities are stocks, bonds, mutual funds, and other investments that can be sold quickly. (Restricted stock is an example of a nonmarketable security, since it can't be sold until a specified time. Include that kind of investment under long-

PERSONAL BALANCE SHEET

Name_____   Date_____

ASSETS
Cash on hand _____
Checking accounts_____
Savings accounts _____
Money market funds _____
Life insurance cash values _____
Notes/accounts receivables _____
Annuities _____
              TOTAL:_____

MARKETABLE SECURITIES
Stocks_____
Bonds _____
Government securities_____
Mutual funds _____
              TOTAL: _____

TOTAL CURRENT (LIQUID) ASSETS:

PERSONAL PROPERTY
Automobiles _____
Household furnishings _____
Art / antiques / collectibles _____
Clothing, furs _____
Jewelry _____
Other possessions _____
              TOTAL: _____

REAL ESTATE
Residences _____
Other properties _____
              TOTAL: _____

PENSIONS
Vested pension benefits _____
IRA/Keogh _____
Tax-sheltered annuity _____
              TOTAL: _____

LONG-TERM ASSETS
Equity in business _____
Pending inheritance _____
Limited partnerships _____
              TOTAL: _____

TOTAL ASSETS: _____

LIABILITIES (current balance and interest rate)
Mortgage (residence) _____
Mortgage (other) _____
Autos _____
Charge accounts _____
Education loans _____
              TOTAL: _____

TAXES: Due within 12 months
Federal taxes _____
Property taxes_____
Social Security _____
              TOTAL: _____

TOTAL LIABILITIES _____

TOTAL NET WORTH _____

TOTAL LIABILITIES AND NET WORTH _____

CURRENT RATIO _____

NET WORKING CAPITAL _____

DEBT-TO-EQUITY RATIO _____

CASH FLOW:

MORTGAGES (monthly payments)
Residences _____
Other properties _____
              TOTAL: _____

OTHER LOANS (monthly payments)
Auto Loans _____
Charge accounts _____
Other _____
              TOTAL: _____

NOTE: Assets shown at fair market value.

Figure 4–2 Personal Balance Sheet

Go To...

Appendix C for your Balance Sheet and Income Statement worksheets.

Disability Income Insurance

Insured	Policy Number	Plan	Company	Issue Date	Monthly Income Benefit	Elim. Period	Benefit Period	Annual Premium
_____	_____	_____	_____	_____	_____	_____	_____	_____
_____	_____	_____	_____	_____	_____	_____	_____	_____
_____	_____	_____	_____	_____	_____	_____	_____	_____

Life Insurance

Insured	Policy Number	Ownership	Beneficiary	Cash Value	Face Amount	Cost per $1,000	Annual Premium
_____	_____	_____	_____	_____	_____	_____	_____
_____	_____	_____	_____	_____	_____	_____	_____
_____	_____	_____	_____	_____	_____	_____	_____

Financial Resources / Cash Reserves (passbook, certificates of deposit, etc.)

Bank	Branch	Amount	Interest Rate	Term	Date Due
_____	_____	_____	_____	_____	_____
_____	_____	_____	_____	_____	_____
_____	_____	_____	_____	_____	_____

Real Estate   (residence, second home, industrial, commercial, land)

Type	Original Cost	Current Value	Date Acquired	Mortgage	Mortgage Rate	Principal & Interest Payments	Property Tax	Equity
_____	_____	_____	_____	_____	_____	_____	_____	_____
_____	_____	_____	_____	_____	_____	_____	_____	_____

Stocks   (common, preferred, options, mutual funds)

Shares	Name of Company	Date Acquired	Cost	Current Price per Share	Value	Dividend	Yield
_____	_____	_____	_____	_____	_____	_____	_____
_____	_____	_____	_____	_____	_____	_____	_____
_____	_____	_____	_____	_____	_____	_____	_____
_____	_____	_____	_____	_____	_____	_____	_____

Bonds (government, municipal, corporate)

Number of Bonds	Name of Company	Coupon	Date Acquired	Maturity Date	Cost	Current Price	Current Value	Current Income
_____	_____	_____	_____	_____	_____	_____	_____	_____
_____	_____	_____	_____	_____	_____	_____	_____	_____
_____	_____	_____	_____	_____	_____	_____	_____	_____

Keogh, IRA   (circle one)

Grantor	Trustee	Trustee Address	Account Number	Value of Account	Investment Vehicle	Rate of Return
_____	_____	_____	_____	_____	_____	_____
_____	_____	_____	_____	_____	_____	_____

term assets.)

3. *Personal property.* Your personal property includes cars, furniture, clothing, and other nonproductive personal property. They could be sold for cash if necessary; otherwise they don't produce income.
4. *Real estate.* Use current market values and include your home as well as any rental properties.
5. *Pension.* Include IRA/Keoghs as well as annuities.

Personal Liabilities. Here are the elements of the liability side of the ledger—claims against your personal assets.

1. *Current debts.* Your current debts are debts such as payments on your mortgage, on credit cards, and education loans *that are due within the next 12 months.* List the interest rate you are paying on each to determine which area of debt is most heavily burdened with interest payments.
2. *Taxes.* Include all taxes due in the next 12 months. List city and state taxes as well as federal and Social Security taxes.
3. *Long-term liabilities.* Includes the balances of all loans, including balloon payments. List any other long-term commitments.
4. *Long-term assets.* Include anything that can't be converted into cash within the next 12 months or that does not have a ready market value. Include limited partnerships.
5. *Total assets.* Your total assets are the sum of both short- and long-term assets.

Analyzing Your Balance Sheet. You now have a snapshot of your current financial position. If you're already familiar with the balance sheet, you can quickly tell what your net worth is, if your financial position is healthy or ailing, and how much cash or cash equivalents you have to meet emergencies or capitalize on new opportunities.

If you are new to balance sheets, here's how to analyze yours.

Net Worth. Your net worth is the difference between total assets and total liabilities—and it *is* possible to get a negative number if you owe more than you own. Subtract your total liabilities from your total assets to compute this value.

People often are surprised when they see their actual net worth in black and white. Some people tend to underestimate how well they've done, while others are reminded of how far they have yet to go.

Knowing your net worth gives you a reference point for future decisions—a foundation for subsequent financial planning. If you update the numbers every six months and recalculate your net worth, you can tell whether you are winning, losing, or tied in the game of wealth. Comparing balance sheets over a longer period of time can tell you if you are reaching your financial goals.

Measuring Your Financial Health

Time Sensitive

Health is something we usually associate with our physical bodies, but it is also relevant to finance. Having a healthy balance sheet generally means that your current assets exceed your current liabilities—that there is enough money coming in to meet your short-term debts. An unhealthy situation exists when current liabilities exceed current assets because an interruption of that income stream could result in insolvency and possibly even bankruptcy itself.

To determine your fiscal health, you need to compute two simple ratios—your *current ratio* and your *debt-to-equity ratio.*

Current Ratio. The current ratio is the relationship of your current assets to current liabilities. To obtain it, simply divide the sum of your current assets by the sum of your current liabilities. For example, let's take the balance sheet of Robert, owner of a successful restaurant.

Robert is typical of many entrepreneurs—he's an active manager of his own money, and he's not afraid to take a well-considered change. He fits our Type I Investor profile "to a T." With his high income, he is tax sensitive and his portfolio is growth oriented:

Total current assets	=	$250,789
Total current liabilities	=	$78,426
$250,789 ÷ $78,426	=	3.19

This calculation yields a current ratio of 3.19, which means that Robert has more than three times the assets needed to meet his current liabilities—a very healthy financial situation. A ratio of 1:1 or better is satisfactory, but if the ratio is less than 1:1 it means your liabilities are outrunning your assets.

Debt-to-Equity Ratio. Your debt-to-equity ratio influences your ability to acquire new financing. Banks use this ratio to calculate the assets you could use to cover losses in the event of a personal financial setback. The lower the debt ratio, the better bankers like it. However, too low a debt ratio may mean that you have too much nonproductive cash. Too few investments mean that your money isn't working hard enough for you.

Determine your debt-to-equity ratio by dividing your total liabilities by your net worth.

Robert's total liabilities are $422,567, and his net worth is $1,465,000.

$422,567 ÷ $1,456,000 = 0.2902

Robert's balance sheet shows that his debts are less than 30% of his net worth—a robust financial condition.

Net Working Capital. Net working capital is the money you have available for new investments or other spending. It is a short-term measurement of your financial strength—your "muscle" to get the things you want. Because some of it may be in the form of life insurance cash value or stocks you don't want to sell, the entire amount may not be fully available to you now. However, net working capital represents potential spending or investing resources you could obtain by converting everything to cash and paying off your current liabilities.

To find your net working capital, subtract your total current liabilities from your total current assets. For example, Robert's total current assets are $250,789 and his total current liabilities are $78,426. Subtracting the second amount from the first gives Robert a net working capital of $172,363— certainly enough to accommodate a wide range of unforeseen problems or opportunities.

Using the Financial Ratios. These formulas are not complex, and they can be easily computed each time you update your personal balance sheet. If you have a computer with spreadsheet capability (such as Lotus 1-2-3 or Excel), you can quickly configure the sheet so that each time you enter new figures, the computer automatically recalculates your ratios.

Money Management Tip

Checking the ratios, as well as your net worth, will give you an immediate fix on your financial position. You can then compare your ratios every six months to see how you are progressing toward your financial goals.

ONE FAMILY TAKES A LOOK AT ITS FINANCES

One evening, as she labored long into the night over the family checkbook, Susan Lewis realized that she'd finally had enough. Each month, it was harder to pay the bills. She either robbed one account to pay another or had to ask her husband, Bill, to write a check against their personal line of credit. She was able to get the family through each month in this rag-tag fashion, but Susan knew it would just catch up with them one day.

Bill had worked his way up to regional sales manager for a yard-supply company and his $69,000+ salary allowed them to live well in a mid-sized Northwestern city. They dined out and traveled often—but their debts had simply become overwhelming.

The Lewises were like a lot of other people: there was nothing wrong with their lifestyle—provided they made another $10,000 a year! The personal line of credit—used to finance furniture, travel, and unexpected bills—had silently soared to more than $12,000. Instead of buying a car he could afford, Bill borrowed $16,000 from his pension account and bought a car he thought would look "just right" in the sales manager's parking slot. For her part, Susan just couldn't say "no" to a good clothing sale. The result was not unmanageable, but unmanaged debt, and despite sincere and repeated efforts, they couldn't drive it down.

Still there were a couple of bright spots on the Lewises' financial horizon. Despite the fact that he had borrowed from it to buy a car, Bill's pension fund was still growing and was now worth over $42,000. Bill's mother had also salted away some money for their two children's educations, and the Lewises had some equity in their home.

After her long and mostly sleepless night, Susan made an appointment with Shirley Lee, a financial planner who had been recommended by a friend. During her first meeting with Lee, Susan talked about the difficulty of breaking the Lewises' well-established patterns of spending.

Susan told Lee, "It makes me sick to see the balance on our personal line of credit go up instead of down, but it seems like something 'worthwhile' always comes up."

"I know it's small consolation," Lee told her, "but I see lots of couples with stories just like yours. Even with the best intentions and a healthy income, they go deeper in debt every year. Usually, they don't see the evidence in front of their face until the situation is really desperate."

"Well, I guess we're not desperate yet," Susan said, "and that's why we've got to get things turned around."

"I want you to do two things before you return next week," Shirley Lee said. "I want you and Bill to fill out an income statement and a personal balance sheet. Together, they will give us a clear picture of where your finances are right now. Only after we know that can we find rational ways to reduce your debt and build a base for future investing."

Why Financial Planning?

As Lee explained it to Susan, the purpose of financial planning is to help avoid disasters and build your personal wealth. It can help families like the Lewises out of a hole but it's equally valuable for people who are in good financial shape and want to do even

Figure 4-3 The Lewises' Income Statement

	Year-End 1991	% Annual Income
Annual Income		
Salary & wages	69,447.00	99.71%
Interest & dividends	200.00	0.29%
Capital gains	0.00	0.00%
Other investment income	0.00	0.00%
Other	0.00	0.00%
Total	**$69,647.00**	**100.00%**
Less Taxes		
Federal	10,298.00	14.79%
State	0.00	0.00%
Social Security	3,970.00	5.70%
Total	**$14,268.00**	**20.49%**
Total Annual Disposable Income:	**$55,379.00**	**79.51%**
Monthly Disposable Income:	$ 4,614.92	
Committed Expenditures		
Housing (incl. mortgage)	9,600.00	13.78%
Transportation	1,400.00	2.01%
Medical / dental	900.00	1.29%
Household repairs	600.00	0.86%
Insurance	1,750.00	2.51%
Utilities	2,400.00	3.45%
Misc. debt repayment (P & I)	11,592.00	16.64%
Housekeeper	1,200.00	1.72%
Other	500.00	0.72%
Total	**$29,942.00**	**42.99%**
Manageable Expenditures		
Food	4,800.00	6.89%
Clothing	6,000.00	8.61%
Travel / entertainment	8,000.00	11.49%
Household furnishing	2,050.00	2.94%
Contributions / gifts	1,200.00	1.72%
Education	0.00	0.00%
Personal allowances	1,800.00	2.58%
Misc.	1,200.00	1.72%
Other	500.00	0.72%
Total	**$25,550.00**	**36.68%**
Total Annual Expenditures:	**$55,492.00**	**79.68%**
Monthly Expenditures:	$ 4,624.33	
Annual Net Income	**$113.00**	**–0.16%**
Monthly Net Income	$ 9.42	
Less Amount to Savings (Ann.)	$0.00	0.00%
Less Amount Investments (Ann.)	$0.00	0.00%
Balance Annual Net Income Available	$113.00	–0.16%
Balance Month Net Income Available	$ 9.42	

Assets		%
Cash:		
Cash on hand	100	0.04%
Checking accounts	50	0.02%
Savings accounts	2,200	0.84%
Money market funds	700	0.27%
Life ins. cash value	0	0.00%
Notes/acc. receivables	0	0.00%
Total	$3,050	1.17%
Marketable Securities:		
Stocks	0	0.00%
Bonds	0	0.00%
Government securities	0	0.00%
Mutual funds	0	0.00%
Children's education	25,750	9.89%
Total	$25,750	9.89%
Total Current (Liquid) Assets:	$28,800	11.06%
Personal Property:		
Automobiles	16,000	6.14%
Household furnishings	30,000	11.52%
Art, antiques, collectibles	2,000	0.77%
Clothings, furs	2,000	0.77%
Jewelry	4,000	1.54%
Other possessions	10,500	4.03%
Total	$64,500	24.76%
Real Estate:		
Residences	125,000	47.99%
Other properties	0	0.00%
Total	$125,000	47.99%
Pensions:		
Pension benefits	42,195	16.20%
IRA/Keogh	0	0.00%
Tax-sheltered annuity	0	0.00%
Total	$42,195	16.20%
Long Term Assets:		
Equity in business	0	0.00%
Pending inheritances	0	0.00%
Other	0	0.00%
Total	$0	0.00%
Total Assets	$260,495	100.00%

Liabilities and Net Worth		%
Current Debts: (Due within 12 months)		
Mortgage	9,600	8.61%
Utilities	2,400	2.15%
Charge accounts	300	0.27%
Insurance premiums	1,750	1.57%
Education	0	0.00%
Total Loan pmts. due	11,592	10.40%
Other	0	0.00%
Total	$25,642	23.01%
Taxes: (Due within 12 months)		
Federal	10,298	9.24%
State taxes	0	0.00%
Social Security	3,970	3.56%
Total	$14,268	12.80%
Total Current Liabilities:	$39,910	35.81%
Mortgages: (Prin. due within 12 months)		
Residences	49,123	44.08%
Other properties	0	0.00%
Total	$49,123	44.08%
Other Loans: (Prin. due within 12 months)		
Auto	0	0.00%
Pension loan	9,596	8.61%
Home improvement	0	0.00%
Life insurance	0	0.00%
Other PLC	12,820	11.50%
Total	$22,416	20.11%
Total Liabilities	$111,449	100.00%
Total Net Worth	$149,046	
Total Liabilities Net Worth	$260,495	
Current Ratio	0.72	
Net Working Capital	($11,110)	
Debt-To-Equity Ratio	74.77%	

Remarks
Assets shown at fair market value

Figure 4-4   The Lewises' Balance Sheet

Go To...

See Appendix C for your personal income statement/ balance sheet.

better.

An income statement and personal balance sheet (see Figures 4-3 and 4-4) are the primary tools employed by Lee and most financial planners. Together, they show exactly where a family's finances stand at a given moment in time. The balance sheet compares assets and liabilities, and the income statement shows how much money comes in and goes out every month.

At home after her meeting, Susan went to work on her family's income statement. Although it's no more than a simple accounting of income and expenses, her income statement revealed some overlooked facts about her family's finances. The number that jumped out at her was the $11,592 they paid each year against loans—a $966 monthly commitment. Over the years, the small increases to this monthly total didn't seem like much, but for Susan, seeing the annual commitment in black and white came as a shock.

At the bottom of the income statement, Susan saw why the family finances seemed to have run aground. Despite an annual disposable income of more than $55,000, she and Bill had a negative monthly income of ($9.42) after all expenses. No wonder their financial future seemed trapped in shallow water!

With that discovery behind her, Susan went to work on the family's balance sheet. It was even more revealing.

The Lewises' Financial Ratios

As Lee instructed her, Susan determined her family's net worth by subtracting their liabilities from their assets, arriving at $149,046.

"I don't know what to make of this," she told Lee during their next appointment. "$149,046 sounds like a lot to me, and I'm sure it would have been a lot for my parents—but is it really so much today?"

"Your net worth represents all the things you have accumulated over the years," Lee told her. "It reflects the money in Bill's pension fund and the amount you've saved for the kids' education. It also shows that you have some equity in the house," Lee said. "But your financial ratios will really tell the full story." Lee divided the Lewises' current assets ($28,800) by their current liabilities ($39,910), for a current ratio of 0.72:1.

"That number is a way of expressing your ability to pay your debts," her planner said. "You have only 72 cents of current assets to cover each dollar that creditors claim against those assets. A healthy current ratio should be at least 1:1 or greater, or you'll have trouble making your important payments every month. At 0.72:1, your ratio says that you have too many debts for the level of assets you own. As our first order of business, we'll need to get that ratio up."

Then Lee calculated the Lewises' debt-to-equity ratio, which expresses the relationship between their net worth (wealth) and their total liabilities. Banks use this number, arrived at by dividing total liabilities by net worth, to calculate credit worthiness. Too much debt—too big a ratio—invariably results in a loan rejection. Predictably, the Lewises' debt-to-equity ratio exceeded that required for good financial health.

"At almost 72%, it's a good thing you don't have to borrow any money," Lee told Susan. "This means you're already way too leveraged and you have no fiscal flexibility. Of course, you know that when you pay the bills every month."

Finally, Lee showed Susan the Lewises' net working capital, another important—and for them, discouraging—number. "Basically, this says you have no money for short-term use. You don't have extra money to pay unexpected debts, meet family emergencies, or take advantage of new opportunities. By all means, we have to build some working capital for you."

"How?" Susan asked. "Bill works as hard as he can and I don't want to go back to work until the children are older!"

"That's our next financial planning lesson," Lee told her. "It will mean putting some controls on your spending, devising a strategy to save as much as we can on your tax bill, and establishing a good investment plan that will begin to put dollars into your pocket instead of taking them out."

"But the most important thing now is to get Bill involved, too. Financial planning for families only works if both partners are committed to it."

As it turned out, Susan's persistence paid off. She convinced Bill of the need to get their finances under control; Lee came up with some creative solutions to their problems—including refinancing their home mortgage at a better rate with lower monthly payments. Together, they got the Lewises out of debt and on the road to financial stability.

"We bless the day I met Shirley," Susan said afterward. "And the first lesson was the best. When I saw our financial facts of life laid out on our first financial statement, I finally got the message: If you're going to get anywhere in life, you've got to take control!"

PREPARING A FINANCIAL PLAN

Once your balance sheet is complete, you can move forward to develop a comprehensive financial plan. Remember, a financial plan is like a living organism. It may possess fixed goals such as long-term growth, but it may also require changing strategies to achieve them. The purpose of any financial plan is to increase and preserve net worth, which, as you have seen, is the best true measure of your financial health.

Net worth is built by (1) increasing the amount of resources you have available for investment, and (2) properly allocating those resources into asset categories and investment vehicles that fit your investing personality, lifestyle, stage of life, and personal goals. You'll begin by increasing the resources available for asset building.

Building Discretionary Income

Discretionary income is the key to increased investing power. Unless you win a lottery or inherit a fortune, you can and must find practical, day-to-day ways to make money available for building your asset base.

Of the several options available, all revolve around increasing your flow of cash. Cash flow, of course, can be positive or negative. Positive cash flow—a continuous, incoming stream of dollars—contributes to discretionary income. Negative cash flow diminishes it.

One way to build discretionary income is to earn more money and for people with high income potential, building one's value as a breadwinner is an important component of a healthy financial plan. For nonearned income, you can increase the contribution made by your productive assets—those that generate interest or dividend income. You can control your expenses by reducing the drain on current income. This control automatically puts more dollars in the investment kitty.

As you learned at the beginning of this chapter, your income does nothing to contribute to net worth unless you keep enough of it to build your assets. Since most of us have a tendency to spend as much as we earn, good financial planning often begins with good budgeting.

Budgeting for Fun and Profit

If you wait to plan or invest until you've finally saved some money, you've missed the entire point: *Financial planning not only uses your money effectively, it also helps you get that money in the first place.* The money you need to start an investment strategy almost always can be found among existing assets and income. Budgeting is the process that helps to uncover it.

Every fit and healthy person knows that a sound diet and exercise program perpetuates itself because you feel better every day— you are tangibly rewarded as you go along. A good budget produces tangible, immediate results too, and that's encouraging. Bad budgets produce more pain than reward, which is why so many of them are so quickly abandoned by so many people.

A basic "low-pain" budget is built on a time-tested formula we call the 10/20/70 plan. It is amazingly simple, yet more effective than budgets that are much more complicated. It works by helping you put your money into three separate "accounts." Here's the first element, or account, of the 10/20/70 budget. (See Figure 4-5.)

The Put-and-Keep Account

Each month, write your first check to yourself, for 10% (or more) of your after-tax earned income. It must be the first commitment you make after the charitable or religious contributions to which you have committed yourself.

This 10% goes into an account to which you will continually add for investment funding. Consequently, you never spend those dollars, but manage them over time in diversified investments. It's called your "put-and-keep" account because once you put it there, you will never touch it. It is used to build, and to keep building, your asset base.

There's nothing new about paying yourself first. In the past, people called their put and keep accounts their "savings" and kept them in passbook accounts, which earned very little interest. Whenever they needed something expensive, they would use this money. After a while, they rightly got the feeling that they were never getting ahead.

Your put-and-keep account isn't the savings account of yesteryear. It's money that you accumulated to invest for long-term security and future income needs when your earning power will be reduced. It's even possible to defer taxes on this money through real return annuities and cash value life insurance contracts—vehicles you'll learn about later in this book. If necessary, impose some discipline on yourself by setting up an automatic payroll deduction or automatic bank draft to make sure that 10% of your total income is invested in

your put-and-keep account. Once the habit is established, it can help make you wealthy faster than you think.

How Your "Keep" Account Will Be Structured. The cash flow you tap to build net worth will be earmarked for eventual short- or long-term spending (such as retirement) or for the logical and orderly transfer of your estate to your heirs. How you structure the assets that achieve these goals is greatly influenced by your tolerance for risk and by the other components of the offensive and defensive segments of your portfolio.

Just what is a portfolio, and how does it relate to your financial plan? A portfolio is nothing more than a collection of investments, although some financial planners break the collection down into portfolios of similar or complementary investments. Your portfolio will always require attention, even if you are the most passive investor. To start, you have to allocate funds to several basic asset categories, choosing appropriate investment vehicles (and specific securities) in each. You then have to rebalance that portfolio periodically (usually once a year) by transferring profits from the asset categories that did well to those whose time has yet to come. If you are an active portfolio manager, you will be trading individual securities within each asset category in hopes of adding marginal profit to the general profits delivered by market growth—but handsome

The 10/20/70 Budget

10% (or More)	20%	70% (or Less)
Put-and-Keep	*Put-and-Take*	*Living Expenses*

This is your wealth accumulation account. Use for long-term needs. (Never use for consumer spending.)

Retirement capital

Tax-planning dollars

When invested, these are your wealth-building accounts:

   Mutual funds
   Stocks
   Bonds
   Limited partnerships
   Pension funds
   I.R.A.
   Land
   Real estate
   Oil/gas
   Etc.

This is your spending account. Use a bank account or credit union close to you so that it can be used for withdrawals easily.

Preplanned consumer spending

   Education
   Furniture
   Travel and fun!

New car

Dreams . . .

Debt reduction if off budget (list)

_____
_____
_____
_____
_____
_____
_____
_____

This account reflects your absolute needs. Use your personal checking account.

Fixed expenses

   House payment
   Medical and dental
   Food
   Utilities
   Car expenses
   Property taxes
   Home maintenance

   Insurance
      Home
      Auto
      Life
      Medical
      Etc.

   Career improvement
   Day care expenses

   Children's allowances
   Wife's allowance
   Husband's allowance

   Clothing
   Charity/contributions

   Miscellaneous debt

Figure 4-5 The 10/20/70 Account

long-term profits don't depend—and should never depend—on "market timing" or other short-term trades.

Money Management Tip

Eventually, you will invest a portion of your put-and-keep funds into each of the six basic asset categories identified in Part III: (1) near-money and money market investments; (2) U.S. equities, or individual stocks or stock market mutual funds; (3) U.S. fixed-income or interest-bearing debt investments, such as Treasury bonds, Treasury notes, and municipal or corporate bonds; (4) real estate investments, either in individual properties or group investments, such as limited partnerships or real estate investment trusts (REITs); (5) international securities, such as international mutual funds; and (6) precious metals and tangibles—stock in mining companies, metal bullion, or coins.

If you wish to manage your put-and-keep account actively, you will eventually use the special trading techniques that try to profit from short-term fluctuations in the market prices of these basic assets, typically using options and futures. If your financial plan involves unusual tax or personal situations, you may even be a candidate for some of the so-called exotic investments, such as precious gems, strategic metals, collectibles (like art), or a whole range of special-venture limited partnerships, but these techniques are for the sophisticated investor—a novice shouldn't try them.

Put-and-Take Account

When your investment account is taken care of, you will place the next 20% of your after-tax earned income into your put-and-take account. This account stores the kind of money you need for emergencies or big-ticket expenditures such as vacations, new car down payments, and home improvements. The money placed here is meant to be saved until it's needed. If you use it for dinners in nice restaurants, you won't have it for the things you really want.

The put-and-take account can also save marriages. Many couples have different ideas about how money should be spent—most all marital disagreements begin over money-related issues. A lot of this friction can be eliminated by dividing some of your put-and-take money into separate "his" and "hers" *subaccounts*. Each spouse then spends his or her money independently, without argument or justification.

One husband called his put-and-take kitty his "toy" account. His wife placed approximately 5% of their budget in this subaccount—enough that by the end of the year her husband had not only bought all the "toys" he had in mind, but had enough money left over to buy his wife and children special gifts. Not only did this family reduce their level of tension about money, but the amount they *did* spend had never before given so much happiness and satisfaction.

Another couple targeted a trip to Japan as a three-year goal. They named their put-and-take account "Japan" and even began a contest over who could contribute the most after their basic 10 and 20% deductions had been made.

To keep them productive, you can invest your put-and-take dollars in short-term money market accounts or money market checking accounts for reasonable returns without diminishing liquidity. Chapter 11, *Cash and Money Market Instruments,* presents some other vehicles for liquid, short-term investments.

Living Expenses

You should earmark 70% of your monthly income for living expenses. This percentage includes money for the mortgage payment, taxes, and daily living expenses—plus a fudge factor for unforeseen but non-emergency expenses. Any funds not spent in these categories will be channeled into your put-and-keep or put-and-take accounts at the end of the month, the year, or on a quarterly basis.

With this low-pain 10/20/70-plan budget, you control your money instead of it controlling you. Your budget helps you redirect the money that flows into your household every month and apply it to the things that will support your desired lifestyle, and also build discretionary income. It provides a framework not only for managing your income—

wages, salaries and commissions—but also for managing the capital that is generated by your assets.

Asset Management

You have two kinds of assets—productive (adds money to your income stream) and nonproductive. By increasing your productive assets, you can generate income that contributes to the cash flow that actively builds net worth.

Nonproductive assets are those intended for personal enjoyment. They may include jewelry, personal property, furniture (including antiques), cars not used in business, clothing, and even your home—if you do not intend to sell it to obtain retirement funds.

Productive assets are those that pay interest, dividend, rents, or royalties. One of the advantages of the 10/20/70-plan budget is that you may find it reduces your need to generate income through investments. If you can afford to reinvest your interest and dividend payments, your net worth will grow faster. Of course, your put-and-keep account does not depend on these asset management decisions. It will keep on chugging along, adding a solid 10% or more of your income each month to your net worth-building muscle.

Controlling Cash Flow

Your 10/20/70 budget can also help in yet another important way: to analyze and gain greater control over the two important elements of cash flow.

You already know that cash flow is nothing more that the difference between money income and outflow. The higher the income-to-outflow ratio, the better your potential financial health—although *what* you do with that surplus is often as important as the surplus itself.

Just looking at the total cash flow, for example, is not particularly helpful, from a planning point of view. To gain control over it, you need to know its components and assign a weight to each, starting with the income side.

Linda, an attorney and Type II Investor in Financial Situation B, had a total income of $70,000. Of that total, $50,000 came from her law firm salary and the remainder from dividends, interest payments, rents, and other investments. To determine what percentage of her total income is generated by professional earnings, she divided the total cash ($70,000) into her salary ($50,000). This year, her wages represented 71% of her cash flow income.

This calculation gave her a handle on how well her investments are doing—what contribution they were making to her total wealth-building potential. This became particularly important as Linda contemplated her future and began to see the need—and advantages—of income produced from non-work sources.

Still, your budget—or anyone's budget—won't be workable if you can't get a handle on the 70% that goes to monthly expenses. To determine how expenses influence cash flow, and how well yours conform to the norm for your lifestyle, you can apply some simple tests. The best example is your mortgage: is it proportional to the rest of your income/expense posture?

Case Study 1: The Reasonable Mortgage Payment. Linda's annual expenses happened to be $56,000, and her mortgage payments were $18,000 annually. By dividing her expenses ($56,000) into her mortgage payments ($18,000), she learned that her mortgage represented 32% of her total expenses. Most lenders consider this amount reasonable, although criteria for "reasonableness" can differ greatly from lender to lender, region to region, and the method by which a person's primary income is earned—including the other ratio tests for financial health.

Case Study 2: The Unreasonable Mortgage Payment. Now suppose Linda's adjustable-rate mortgage increased her payments to $29,000 annually. Her mortgage now represents 52% of her total expenses. Such a percentage is of far more concern to her lenders because it may indicate she is overleveraged—owes too much money in comparison to the income she has available to service her debt.

The Bottom Line: A Livable Mortgage Payment. When mortgage payments are as

Money Management Tip

high as the one in Linda's second case, the money to pay them may have to come from her discretionary income. In fact, imbalance in any debt component can set up negative cash flow—more cash going out than coming in—and deplete discretionary income. In such circumstances it's virtually impossible for Linda or anyone in her situation to put aside anything for the future. You should apply this same analysis to all debt components on the liability side of your balance sheet, including insurance, car expenses, and your food budget. When you subject your monthly expenses to this kind of scrutiny, you will probably find "financial fat" that can be trimmed without too much pain—or risk to your wealth-building discretionary income. (See Figure 4-6.)

THE SATISFACTIONS OF FINANCIAL PLANNING

The first comment most financial planners hear from new clients is that for the first time, the clients finally know they have control over their money. They are no longer subject to the unexpected and uncontrollable twists of everyday life and are putting money into the bank, rather than taking it out.

No matter how insignificant the amount may seem, every dollar you put into your put-and-keep account contributes to your financial wealth. All you need to keep even a modest sum growing is that greatest of all allies to any investment—time.

Note: For help with credit trouble call the National Foundation for Consumer Credit (301-589-5600). A credit consumer counselor will review your debts and your income and will help set up a payment plan.

Figure 4-6 Appropriate Spending Levels

Do you know how much you should spend each month on essentials such as housing, food, transportation, and clothing? How much should you allocate to hobbies and entertainment, vacations and gifts? Using your net income as a base, these percentages may serve as a general guideline.

Percentage of Net Income

Expense	Single, no Children	Single, with Children	Married, no Children	Married, with Children
Housing	20–25	20–25	25–30	30
Loan payment	13–15	13–15	15–17	13–15
Food	10–15	10–15	10–15	10–15
Hobbies/entertain.	9–16	9–14	9–14	8–14
Child care	0	8–10	0	8–10
Out-of-pocket	8–12	7–10	7–10	5–8
Transportation	7–10	7–10	7–10	7–10
Utilities/phone	5–10	6–11	8–12	6–11
Clothing	3–10	4–10	8–10	4–10
Savings	5–7	5–7	5–7	5–7
Pension	5–7	5–7	5–7	5–7
Medical	3–5	4–7	7–10	7–10
Education (including student loan payments)	3–5	5–7	3–5	5–7
Gifts/contributions	2–10	3–10	3–8	4–10
Vacation	3–7	3–7	3–7	3–7
Insurance	1–3	3–5	3–5	3–5
Personal care	1–3	2–4	2–4	2–4
Dues/subscriptions	1–3	1–3	1–3	1–3
Alimony, Child Support	0-4	0-4	0-4	0-4
Mystery Cash (?)	1%	1%	1%	1%

Source: Financial Strategies, Inc.

Spending Levels Worksheet, Appendix C, page 505.

Go To...

CHAPTER 5

TIME AND YOUR MONEY

A GLANCE AHEAD

Time heals all wounds, as the saying goes—even an anemic pocketbook; and that's the miracle of effective money management. The inner workings of time and money can turn a handful of dollars into true wealth. All it takes is commitment, patience, and knowledge of a few financial basics.

In this chapter, you'll discover

- *The power of compounding to double, triple—even quadruple—any investment*
- *How present value theory can help you assess the worth of your investments*
- *Why inflation is the number one enemy of future spending power and how your real (after-inflation) returns can be increased*
- *The time-related risks that can keep your investments from producing top returns*
- *How the time-tested technique of dollar-cost averaging can build your put-and-keep account.*

HOW COMPOUNDING REALLY WORKS

The amount of put-and-keep dollars you set aside each month may seem too small to do much good, but that's because you see your investment "frozen" at the moment of its birth—like the snapshot of a baby that has a lot of growing to do. When you learn to visualize those dollars compounded over many years, you will see them as an ocean, not a few meager drops in the bucket.

Time is the powerhouse that turns dollars into fortunes. At the root of its power is the concept of compound interest, a powerful financial tool available to everyone. Interest makes money grow, and compound interest makes it grow fastest of all. Here's how.

Simple Versus Compound Interest

"Simple" interest is the basic interest charged on any amount of money loaned. If you loan $10,000 at 10% simple interest per year, each year you will receive $1,000 back on your money. At the end of five years, you will still have your original $10,000 plus five yearly interest installments of $1,000 each, for a grand total of $15,000.

"Compound" interest pays interest-on-the-interest as well as on the principal. Interest accrues periodically—it may accrue daily, weekly, monthly or quarterly—and, as it accrues, it is added to the principal and future interest is computed on this total. Thus you end up receiving interest not only on your principal, but on previous interest as well. $10,000 loaned out at 10% compounded annual interest yields $16,105 after five years, a bonus of $1,105 over simple interest.

Of course, if you were to set aside $1,000 each year and add it to your $10,000 principal, the rate of growth would be even faster.

Figure 5-1 shows how compounding

Years	5	10	15	20	25	30
7%	6,153	14,783	26,888	43,865	67,676	101,072
8%	6,335	15,645	29,324	49,422	78,954	122,345
9%	6,523	16,560	32,003	55,764	92,324	148,574
10%	6,715	17,531	34,949	63,002	108,181	180,942
11%	6,912	18,561	38,189	71,265	126,998	220,912
12%	7,115	19,654	41,753	80,698	149,333	270,292
13%	7,322	20,814	45,671	91,469	175,850	331,314
14%	7,535	22,044	49,980	103,768	207,332	406,736
15%	7,753	23,349	54,717	117,810	244,712	499,956
16%	7,976	24,732	59,924	133,840	289,087	605,161
17%	8,206	26,199	65,648	152,138	341,761	757,503
18%	8,441	27,755	71,938	173,021	404,272	933,317
19%	8,682	29,403	78,849	196,845	478,430	1,150,386
20%	8,929	31,149	86,441	219,859	566,374	1,418,256
21%	9,182	33,001	94,780	255,017	670,632	1,748,630
22%	9,441	34,961	103,934	290,346	794,164	2,155,837
23%	9,707	39,237	113,982	330,640	940,464	2,657,402
24%	9,979	41,565	125,010	376,464	1,113,628	3,274,734
25%	10,258	37,038	137,108	428,680	1,318,487	4,033,865

Figure 5-1 The effects of compound interest on $1,000 invested per annum.

works when $1,000 is invested annually at different interest rates over a number of years. A mere $1,000 invested annually at 10% compounded interest over 30 years yields an impressive $180,942!

The "miracle of compounding" can be seen even more clearly in Andrew Tobias's book, *Money Angles*. Tobias notes that Benjamin Franklin's will, leaving 1,000 pounds sterling each to the cities of Boston and Philadelphia, with instructions that the cities lend it at interest to worthy apprentices, exceeded $3 million 192 years later.

That's the power of compound interest!

The Rule of 72. Unfortunately, one of the problems with compounding is figuring out just how fast your money is growing. You can look it up in tables or compute it with alegbra yourself, but mathematical shorthand provides a quicker answer. It's called the rule of 72.

To determine how long any amount of money invested at a compound interest basis will take to double, simply divide the interest rate into 72. If you're receiving 10% interest, for example, your money will double in 7.2 years:

Rule of 72

Years to double money = $\dfrac{72}{\text{Rate of return}}$

$$72 \div 10 = 7.2$$

Here are some common interest rate calculations using the rule of 72:

Rule	÷ Interest	=	Years
72	20	=	3.6
72	15	=	4.8
72	12	=	6.0
72	10	=	7.2
72	7	=	10.3
72	5	=	14.4
72	3	=	24.0

The Present Value of Money

Compounding interest has an attractive effect on the value of money—it makes money worth more tomorrow than it is today.

Years to payment date	2%	4%	5%	6%	8%	10%
1	$.9804	$9615	$.9524	$9434	$.9529	$.9091
2	.9612	.9246	.9070	.8900	.8573	.8264
3	.9423	.8890	.8638	.8396	.7938	.7513
4	.9238	.8548	.8227	.7921	.7350	.6830
5	.9057	.8219	.7835	.7473	.6806	.6209
10	.8203	.6756	.6139	.5584	.4632	.3855
15	.7430	.5553	.4810	.4173	.3152	.2394
20	.6370	.4564	.3769	.3118	.2145	.1486
30	.5521	.3083	.2314	.1741	.0994	.0573
40	.4529	.2083	.1420	.0972	.0460	.0221
50	.3715	.1407	.0872	.0543	.0213	.0085
60	.3048	.0951	.0535	.0303	.0099	.0033
80	.2051	.0434	.0202	.0095	.0021	.0005
100	.1380	.0198	.0076	.0029	.0005	.0001

Figure 5-2   Present value of a single $1 payment to be collected at a future time, at specified compound rates

Years	2%	4%	5%	6%	8%	10%
1	$ .98	$ .96	$ .95	$ .94	$ .93	$ .91
2	1.94	1.89	1.86	1.83	1.78	1.74
3	2.88	2.78	2.72	2.67	2.58	2.49
4	3.81	3.63	3.55	3.47	3.31	3.17
5	4.71	4.45	4.33	4.21	3.99	3.79
10	8.98	8.11	7.72	7.36	6.71	6.15
15	12.85	11.12	10.38	9.71	8.56	7.61
20	16.35	13.59	12.46	11.47	9.82	8.51
30	22.40	17.29	15.37	13.76	11.26	9.43
40	27.36	19.79	17.16	15.05	11.92	9.78
50	31.42	21.48	18.26	15.76	12.23	9.92
60	34.76	22.62	18.93	16.16	12.38	9.97
80	39.74	23.92	19.60	16.51	12.47	9.99
100	43.10	24.50	19.85	16.62	12.49	9.99
Forever	50.00	25.00	20.00	16.67	12.50	10.00

Figure 5-3   Present value of a $1 annual payment for specified numbers of years invested at various rates

In fact, the basic premise of any investment is that the money you invest today will be worth more in the future. For this and other reasons, it's helpful to know the present value of a sum of money you'll receive (or need) in the future. For example, if you wish to receive a dollar 10 years from now, how much would you have to invest today if the investment promised "10% interest, compounded annually?"

As Figure 5-2 shows, $1.00 received 10 years from now is "worth" $.3855 invested at 10% interest, compounded annually. If this was a financial product promising $1,000 in 10 years, you would expect to invest no more than $385.50 under these terms to get that crisp $1,000.

Present value tables also can be used to determine the present value of a sum of money received at regular intervals over time, as shown in Figure 5-3. For example: if I receive $1.00 per year for 10 years at 10% compounded interest, the present value of that $10 is $6.15.

Knowing the present value of a future investment return can be of real help when it's time to evaluate the "cost" of specific investment opportunities, or what sort of return rate and holding period will be needed to turn the amount you have into the amount you need for goal-related spending. Is it better to take a lump sum payment on retirement, for example, or carry a long-term annuity? Should you invest an inheritance in a particular vehicle, or use it to make a down payment on a house? Present value theory not only illustrates the real power of compound interest, it can help you make many nuts-and-bolts investing decisions.

See Appendix E for expanded present value and future value tables.

Go To...

INFLATION—THE ENEMY OF WEALTH

Just as compounding builds wealth, inflation tears it down. Compounding interest gives you more dollars, but inflation makes them worth less when you receive them. Inflation can rob you of everything you hope to gain through the use of compounding, and every

investor should know how to hedge against it.

Before 1970, few people in this country worried much about inflation. Of course, stories had been told of great inflationary periods, like post-World War I Germany, when 500,000 German marks bought one loaf of bread, or the hyperinflation that racked many Central and South American countries in the 1960s and 1970s. But those were distant experiences until, in the late 1970s, inflation took this country by storm. Soaring well into double digits, the menace of inflation finally got our attention.

Although rebuffed by the monetary recession of the early 1980s, inflation is always a threat. Unless you hedge against it in your investments, you run the risk of earning high interest rates—but at very low *real* (after-inflation) rates of return.

The Real Rate of Return

Look At This:

When calculating your return on an investment, be sure to consider the real rate of return—the true measure of your investment's future purchasing power.

To find the real rate of return, you must know two things: (1) the nominal rate of return (the interest paid), and (2) the annual rate of inflation. The nominal interest rate is easy to find; it's the interest you are getting from the borrower.

The rate of inflation is measured by the CPI (Consumer Price Index) published by the federal government, although more sophisticated investors tend to follow the WPI (Wholesale Price Index). To find the approximate real rate of return, simply subtract the annual CPI or WPI from the interest rate you are receiving. The results might surprise you.

Suppose, for example, you have $10,000 to lend. You get 10% compound interest and think you are doing well. But real rate of return is only relative. If inflation is 9%, your real rate of return is just 1% (10 − 9 = 1). Not such a great investment!

Are Inflation Worries Realistic?

If you are like a great many people, you may

feel that worrying about inflation is a waste of time. They feel that inflation is waning, that the double-digit inflation of the late 1970s was an anomaly. It won't return, and there's really no reason to worry about inflation for another 40 years. Such thinking will probably get you in trouble.

The truth is that inflation has specific economic causes, and those causes often recur. Inflation *will* return again. The question is only when. Here are two economic theories that may convince you.

Money Supply Theory.   In the 1500s, when Europe was getting huge shipments of gold from South America, a finance minister warned the Spanish queen that the arrival of new gold would cause a terrible inflation. Everything would become more expensive, and nobody would be better off. The queen laughed. How could more gold be bad? Gold was money. It was struck into coinage as soon as it arrived. More money meant more wealth. Who would be hurt by that?

Very soon afterward, however, the minister's warning proved true. Spain experienced a terrible inflation. The more money Span-

iards made, the more things seemed to cost. The queen summoned the minister—but now she was speaking as a student of economics, not a monarch. "Why did this happen?" she asked.

"It is simple," the minister explained. "When gold coins were scarce, everyone hoarded them. They were precious. Hence, they bought many goods and services. But when gold from South America resulted in tens of thousands of new gold coins, each became less precious. People thought less of them and asked for many when before only a few were needed."

The queen realized she too was as guilty of this "inflationary psychology" as anyone else. "Easy" money—the expansion of the money supply—did not produce more goods and services; it simply increased the medium used for exchange. With the same number of Spaniards and products available, the only thing that could increase was prices.

In this country, something similar happens. When the federal government creates more money (through an expansion of credit, bank deposits, or printing paper money), the value of that money as a commodity de-

Two Kinds of Inflation

The inflation of the late 1970s provides an excellent example of two kinds of price instability—*money supply* and *price shock inflation*. The huge overnight increase in the cost of oil is a textbook example of price shock inflation; but the worst inflation in recent U.S. history had a strong money supply component too. Because the Vietnam war drained resources away from President Johnson's Great Society programs, the government tried to pay for both without raising taxes. The only way to do that was to create new money, and the resulting surge in the money supply spurred not only increased borrowing and consumption, but the *expectation* that such a condition would go on indefinitely. Consequently, people demanded more and more money for products and wages even though both productivity and output increased at a much slower rate. When the OPEC price shock occurred in the 1970s, the United States was vulnerable to this inflationary "double whammy."

Similar occurrences can happen with any commodity when cartels or other forces, such as trade quotas, act to control the free market. Commodity prices have been dropping steadily, or increasing at a very slow rate, since 1980. However, in the late 1980s there were periodic signs that inflation may once again return to higher levels as commodity prices climbed faster than GNP growth.

creases just as the increase in gold in early Spain devalued gold coins. Too many dollars mean less buying power for each of them—and that is the definition of inflation.

It's the job of the Federal Reserve to control the money supply so that enough enters the economy to spur growth, but not so much as to cause inflation. That, at least, is the plan—but plans don't always work out.

During 1986 and 1987, the money supply rose at such alarming rates that many people began to predict a return of inflation. But it is not that simple. To make an intelligent guess, you need to understand, like the Spanish queen, the psychology that tends to drive people's expectations about prices.

"Price Shock" Inflation. In addition to money supply inflation, economists today recognize inflation caused by commodity shortages. When there was a worldwide shortage of oil in the 1970s, the Organization of Petroleum Exporting Countries (OPEC) cartel used it as an excuse to multiply oil prices by a factor of 8 (from $5 a barrel to $40). By prolonging that shortage through intentionally low production, OPEC kept oil prices high long after any physical shortage had disappeared.

Since oil is used both as a product and as a fuel to power vehicles that move products, the price of virtually every commodity in the country shot up. The inflation of the late 1970s and early 1980s was caused, in part, by the shock of that oil price increase.

Price Inflation...a 1908 Example

- In 1908 a loaf of bread was 4 cents...
- A gallon of milk was 32 cents...
- A pound of butter was 33 cents...
- A gallon of gasoline was 7 cents...
- A new Ford was $825...
- A new house was $3,395...
- Annual income was $1,111...
- An ounce of gold was $20.67...
- An ounce of silver was 61 cents...
- An ounce of copper was 13 cents...
- The Dow Jones Index was $87.67...
AND...there was no income tax until 1913!

(Courtesy of LeMaster & Daniels, CPAs)

PUTTING TIME ON YOUR SIDE

If we accept the fact that inflation is likely to be an on-again/off-again phenomenon, we must have some strategy that allows us to invest and gain reasonable *real* returns.

Unfortunately, virtually all financial markets respond to inflation. The stock market generally falls in value after an extended bout of inflation. Most companies eventually find ways to fortify the prices of the stocks. The commodity market, typically, rises at once. The bond market falls as interest rates rise (in response to inflation) because the value of older bonds (issued at lower rates) diminishes.

Of course, inflation isn't the only factor affecting these markets. The health of the economy (growth of GNP), the size of the national debt, the foreign trade imbalance (export of U.S. jobs and dollars), and other factors also are involved. However, over the long term, inflation tends to affect financial instruments adversely.

How does one "put-and-keep" money safely in an economy that, over the years, will see prices shoot up and down? How do you build wealth steadily when there are periods during which inflation will rob you of your money's buying power?

The answer is to let time work *with,* and not against you. If you assume that over the long haul, even with the ups and downs of inflation, overall market trends will be up—as historically they have been—you can put time and the overall power of the economy on your side. As markets move up and down in response to inflation and other factors, inexperienced investors typically move their money impulsively. When a market is high, such investors imagine that everyone is making money, and they jump in and "buy high." When a market is low, they think that everyone is going broke, and they bail out, selling when asset prices are low. As a result, these impulse investors have the worst of both worlds: they buy high and sell low—the cardinal sin of all investing.

It's usually impossible to say when high prices are "too high" and when low prices are "too low." It is very easy to say how the market did yesterday or what the rate of inflation was last month. But how do we know what either will be tomorrow? Trying to an-

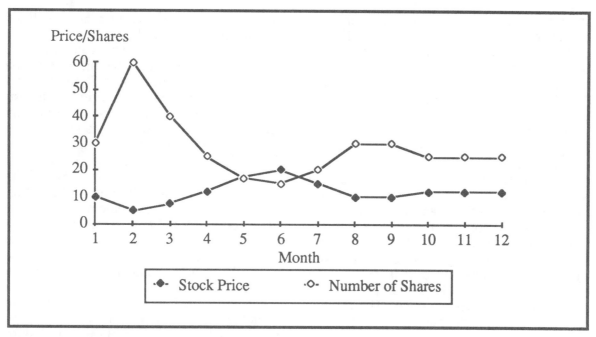

Figure 5-4 Dollar-cost averaging

ticipate trends and move investments around accordingly can end up being the most expensive lesson you've ever learned in the futility of amateur financial fortunetelling. Market timing can ultimately wear down the most determined investor, finally sending him or her to the sidelines with a near-empty put-and-keep account suitable only for savings accounts, savings bonds, or one last night on the town.

Winning Through Dollar-Cost Averaging

Money
Management
Tip

Fortunately, there is a solution that puts time back in your corner. It works in virtually any market, and while its results on any given day may not be spectacular, over the long run it almost always turns up a winner. It's called *dollar-cost averaging* and it's been called the greatest investing tip of the century.

Dollar-cost averaging began in the 1920s as a way to keep up with the then skyrocketing price of stocks. Although it's tempting to say that averaging ignores market cycles, it's more accurate to say that averaging plays

right through them.

Figure 5-4 shows what dollar-cost averaging does. It flattens out the day-to-day and month-to-month see-saw of market prices so you can take advantage of a long-term upward trend.

How Dollar-Cost Averaging Works. The principle is simple: each month (or every six months or at whatever period is comfortable for you), invest a constant amount of money—come rain or shine, even if the market is in the doldrums. Suppose you have $300 a month of your put-and-keep money to invest in stocks. You decide to put the money into XYZ Mutual Fund—a growth fund. Initially the shares sell for $10 apiece. You buy into the fund, getting 30 shares the first month. The next month you buy another $300 worth, although the actual number of shares you buy will depend on the current price per share. Six months later, you discover that the fund has soared. The market has turned up, and the fund took advantage of it. Now the shares are selling for $20 apiece. If you buy $300 worth again, you will only be able to get 15 shares. You are now faced with a decision—and a temptation. Because the market is up and the fund has done so well, your natural impulse is to put more money in—to raid your other investments and spend $600, for example, this month. But because you are working on a dollar-cost plan, you resist the impulse and buy only the same $300 worth of the fund. You buy more shares of a winner, but fewer than before because the price is high.

Now suppose that nine months after you bought into the fund, things have taken a turn for the worse. The fund is now back to $10 per share. Your urge is to bail out—to sell before the stock drops lower. However, you resist the impulse and again buy your standard $300 worth of the stock. This time you end up with 30 shares. You bought into a "loser" when the price was low and consequently bought more shares than before.

After a year you take a look at your investment. How have you done? The following chart describes your stock purchases.

Twelve-Month Chart of Investments with Dollar-Cost Averaging

Month	Amount Invested	Stock Price	Shares
1	$300	$10.00	30
2	300	5.00	60
3	300	7.50	40
4	300	12.00	25
5	300	17.50	17
6	300	20.00	15
7	300	15.00	20
8	300	10.00	30
9	300	10.00	30
10	300	12.00	25
11	300	12.00	25
12	300	12.00	25
Totals:	$3,600		342

Average cost per share $10.53 ($3,600 ÷ 342)
Average price per share $11.91 ($143.00 ÷ 12)

Have you lost money over the year or made it? After all, the stock went as high as $20 and as low as $5. Your natural impulse would have been to buy at $20 and sell at $5. But, instead of buying high and selling low, you steadily bought $300 worth of stock per month regardless of the price. How well did this strategy serve you?

At the end of the year, you have 342 shares. At $13 per share, that means that you have $4,446 for earnings of $846. That's a little over 24% on your original investment—not too shabby—and considerably better than you would have done following your "normal" investor instincts.

Some people, of course, point out that you could have made much more by selling when the stock was at its high of $20. Yes, you could have. But remember too, the whole point of dollar-cost averaging is to come up with a plan that allows you to win *regardless* of market cycles. You might have sold when the mutual fund stock was at $20 and made a killing. But you might just as easily have sold when it dropped down to $5 and lost a lot. The point is, you can't really tell which time is the right time to buy or sell. Who knows when high is "high enough" and when low is "too low"? Thus, by buying steadily and using time as your ally, you break through the crests and troughs and end up with a very healthy profit.

The Logic Behind the Numbers. The reason it all works is mathematical. With a dollar-cost averaged investment of $300 per month, you bought more shares of XYZ Mutual Fund when the price was low and fewer shares when the price was high. Thus you were buying more at the low end and less at the high end. It's easy to see why you came out on top: you bought low and although you did not "sell high," at least you did not spend more money "high" than you should have. Another way to gauge the value of dollar-cost averaging is by looking at the average cost per share of the fund. The average price per share during the year was roughly $11.91. But your average cost per share was only a little over $10.53. Again, a recipe for winning in any market.

Of course, there is one more factor to consider. Earlier, you learned that dollar-cost averaging allows you to break through the ups and downs of the market to take advantage of its generally upward trend. The fact that your cost per share is lower than the average price per share means you are in a good position to make a profit. When you want to sell, the price of the stock at that time must be higher than your average cost. In the preceding example, you invested $3,600 to acquire 342 shares. To make a profit, you would have to receive a price per share of more than $10.53—but this probably won't be difficult.

Like most investment concepts, dollar-cost averaging must be practiced consistently. Since the success of the technique depends on buying more shares when prices are low, you must resist the impulse to stop buying when the market drops.

And, just as important, you must be willing to wait out the peaks and valleys of the market, which means you must consider your dollar-cost averaging account to be illiquid. If you're forced to sell before you're ready, you could take an unnecessary loss.

Sometimes it happens, too, that a stock falls and never comes back up. This problem can be avoided by proper diversification, such as investment in a no-load mutual fund, where no single stock can penalize you excessively and you can afford to make small share purchases regularly without running up broker commissions fees, as in the case with single stocks.

Finally, you must be prepared to stick with the program for at least five years. This period gives the strategy the time it needs to ride out a normal business cycle and deliver the kind of growth that is inherent in the market.

Time Diversification Theory and Dollar-Cost Averaging

Money
Management
Tip

"Time diversification" is one of the newest ideas in modern portfolio theory—it embraces the twin concepts of dollar-cost averaging and multiple-asset allocation. Time diversification theory holds that to reduce risk and maximize total return, investments should be held through a complete market cycle, which usually lasts at least four to six years. Recent academic evidence suggests that when it comes to reducing total risk, time diversification is more important than the traditional diversification of buying many different securities. Thus, it gives you further guidelines for deciding how long is

"long enough" to hold your investment.

SELECTING YOUR BASIC INVESTMENT STRATEGY

Once you have made your commitment to invest a consistent amount of money each month in your put-and-keep account, you must decide where it should be invested. Should it be in stocks, bonds, commodities, or something else?

You need a basic strategy that unites the time factors of investing to investments you'll choose. The first task is to match your portfolio to the time available and your financial goals. Are you in the stage of life where you want to build wealth, or do you need to preserve it and invest for current income? One calls for an offensive investing strategy; the other implies a defensive strategy. Neither, however, negates the value of multiple-asset investing or dollar-cost averaging. Most investors should build elements of both tactics into their portfolio strategies.

Defensive Players

Risk Sensitive

Defensive players use their money to protect existing assets. They are most concerned about not losing what they already have. They do not want to risk giving up their hard-won principal.

Unfortunately, too many people think they must be defensive players. They remember the hard work it took to acquire their put-and- keep money. At parties, they tend to repeat stories about this person or that who lost his or her shirt in the market, or who got wiped out by a chancy investment. Defensive players basically distrust all investments and consequently distrust their own ability to succeed in investing. "Never mind shooting for big profits—just take the money and run!" seems to be their motto.

Many kinds of investments are suitable to defensive players and the defensive segment of any portfolio. Generally speaking, debt-based assets provide the benefits of safety and income. Many debt-based investments are "stable" (they offer no growth), but they are dedicated to preserving principal. Debt assets include T-bills, CDs (certificates of deposit), money market accounts, and insurance plans. More aggressive debt assets include trust deeds and notes, direct loans, and commercial paper. Having large cash reserves is also a defensive play because it keeps you out of other markets, and hence keeps you immune to all risks but inflation.

The big advantage of debt-based assets is that the principal is always protected, sometimes by government insurance or other guarantees.

The big drawback to debt is that should inflation rise while you are locked into a fixed-income asset, it can undercut the buying power of both the dollars you are earning and those you are protecting. The cruel part of debt assets is that during periods of intense inflation, the defensive players who can afford it least—the elderly and those on fixed incomes—can end up with dollars that are worth only half as much as when they began.

Offensive Players

Risk Tolerant

Offensive players don't worry too much about keeping what they have—their goal is to get more! They think of their current money as a tool to build a bigger asset base. Offensive players are always "in the market" and keeping their eye on the bouncing ball—market prices and new opportunities.

Equity-based assets are usually the best play here. They offer growth—the rapid increase of principal—that is generally unrelated to interest (unless that interest rate gets too high). Equity-based assets can make money quickly, but they can lose money just as fast. Even with mutual funds and dollar-cost averaging, if you buy into a fund that eventually bottoms out at a price far lower than your average cost, you will end up losing money.

Typical equity investments include publicly traded stocks, stock options, real estate, equity-based mutual funds, and certain tax shelters left over after the 1986 Tax Reform Act, including domestic oil and gas. They also include commodities, bullion, and rare coins.

When you buy an equity investment, your main objective is to make money—to experience capital gain. You are on the offensive. You are specifically looking for growth. The typical questions you will ask yourself are

- *"How good is the market for this type of investment?"* Not all equity issues are easily traded.
- *"Is there liquidity? Can I get out after I make my profit?"* Stocks, for example, are highly liquid. Stock options, however, tend to be slightly less liquid. Bullion is extremely liquid. Rare coins are more limited in liquidity. And real estate should always be considered a long-term investment.
- *"Are my assumptions about growth realistic?"* You don't expect stocks in general to soar during a recession; you'll have to look for particular stocks or wait until the business cycle picks up. And you won't see commodities doing well during *dis*inflation. Existing bonds are going to do well when interest rates are falling and do poorly when rates are rising. You have to realize that, over time, the general road "up" is not without its potholes.
- *"Can I trade, or may I buy and hold the investment?"* Is it something that takes constant attention, such as investing in commodities, or can you sit back and check in every six months or so?

Toward a Combined Investment Strategy

Most of us are neither defensive nor offensive players exclusively. How we "play the markets" tends to be determined by our positions in life, goals, and other elements of investor personalities, as discussed in Part I of this book. The traditional view of the investment life cycle is that at the beginning we *accumulate,* in the middle we *protect,* and at the end we seek to *dispose* in an orderly and efficient manner. Younger people are typically attuned to spending and to accumulating wealth. They have little, are more likely to take risks, and are often hungry to get more. They have time to recover from the mistakes, so they tend to be offensive equity players.

As people get older, they tend to become more conservative. Those who have accumulated some wealth are anxious to protect it. They tend to shift their strategy to the defensive, and debt assets play a larger role in their portfolios.

Of course, not all assets acquired during the accumulation stage are or should be offensive. It is important to build a solid financial base on which a more aggressive investment strategy can be pursued. Such a pyramid starts with the construction of a sound, conservative, defensive foundation; moves to the middle of the structure containing assets of different traits; and, finally, peaks at the apex of aggressive, growth investments. A typical financial pyramid might look something like this:

LIFETIME FINANCIAL PYRAMID

Greater
Risk

Rare Coins
Art and Stamps
Bullion and Jewels
Speculative options
(unrecovered)
Stock, R&D, commodities,
bare land
Investment in commercial
and residential real estate
Mutual funds, stocks in utilities
and solid companies
Investing in bonds and annuities and
owning your own home
Opening a savings account, establishing an IRA,
and buying life insurance

The pyramid suggests that you begin defensively by first building a base that includes savings, retirement account, insurance, and your own home—all defensive strategies. Only when you have accomplished this, should you become more aggressive. When you have developed sufficient net worth to satisfy your basic financial needs, you can take on riskier and riskier investments, as represented in the upper levels of the pyramid.

Ultimately, the strategy—or mix of strategies—you choose to follow should depend to a great degree on your level of comfort with risk. As we have seen, some people are comfortable only when they have all their bases covered; others are always out there scrambling for more even after they have acquired considerable wealth.

Your goal should not be to select a model artificially and then force yourself to fit it. Rather, it should be to find a model that best suits your own investing personality, lifestyle, values, and goals.

Alternatively, many contemporary financial advisors suggest that a mix of offensive and defensive investments are desirable from the earliest possible date. Thus your more offensive equity investments have more time to weather market cycles and grow, and even defensive debt investments can be of longer duration—allowing the power of compounding to work its magic. This is the essence of the multiple-asset allocation philosophy you'll encounter throughout this book, and understanding its offensive, defensive, and time-related components is important to your financial success.

Notes

_____

_____

_____

_____

_____

_____

_____

_____

CHAPTER 6

PRERETIREMENT PLANNING

A GLANCE AHEAD

Americans are retiring younger, healthier, and more active than ever. And they're living longer: most of us can expect to live 25% to 30% of our life spans after we have formally retired. That's changing the way we plan for our older years. In this chapter, you'll discover

- *How the new retirement era is affecting millions of Americans*
- *How to decide if early retirement is right for you*
- *Why the Social Security system may let you down when you need it most*
- *How much money you'll need to retire*
- *How to make Keogh and corporate retirement plans work harder for you*
- *Why an annuity may be your passport to retirement security*
- *When a lump-sum pension payment is right for you.*

THE NEW RETIREMENT ERA

On the first Monday morning after Bill's retirement, nothing much had changed, especially for his wife Joan. Bleary-eyed, she reached across his slumbering body to turn the clock radio off.

"Come on, sleepy-head, time to walk," she said. As always, he grumbled and moaned before swinging his legs out of bed.

Mornings had been a customary and comfortable routine for Joan and Bill. Over the past 10 years, they had risen together, had a cup of coffee, and taken a brisk walk. As a two-career family, they found morning was the one part of the day they could control, and their morning hikes gave them a chance to spend some quality time together before tackling the cares of the world.

After their walk, a shower, and a quick breakfast, Joan would leave for work. She felt odd leaving Bill behind today. This morning, Bill had scheduled a celebratory round of golf with an old friend, Hank, a fellow former engineer who had retired from a competing firm some months earlier.

The sun was low on the horizon, and the grass was still damp with dew when the two men teed off.

"Welcome to the wonderful world of retirement," Hank said flatly, steering the cart in the direction of Bill's ball. "I sure as hell hope you enjoy it more than I have!"

Bill looked over at his friend. "I fully intend to enjoy it. Why—haven't you?"

"I *hate* it," Hank said. "It's nothing like I thought it would be. The plain and simple truth is, having too much free time on your hands is worse than not having enough."

He stopped at the spot where Bill's ball lay nestled in the coarse grass on the edge of the fairway. "You know how they kid you about not knowing what to do with yourself when you retire? Well, it's true."

Bill's fairway shot hooked to the left of the green and landed in a sand trap. This was not the way he had envisioned his inaugural retirement game starting out. He climbed back into the cart.

"You and Mary just got back from a couple of weeks in Mexico," he grumbled. "I thought traveling and golf were going to keep you busy for life!"

"You can't travel all the time, old buddy, and you can't play golf every day. I miss seeing people, solving problems, and doing something productive. I guess I just miss my job."

Bill watched Hank chip his second shot to within a foot of the cup.

"Nice to see all those idle days on the green weren't wasted," Bill said. "So what are you going to do?"

"I've already done it. Last week I talked to the partners at my old firm about taking on some special projects as a consultant. I go in this afternoon to pick up my first assignment."

Bill replayed his conversation with Hank in his head for the rest of the day—especially when he settled into his favorite TV chair for a long-awaited baseball telecast. He had always liked his work, but there was no denying it—he had looked forward to retirement, too. Could life after work really be as bleak as Hank painted it?

The first pitch was a strike, and Bill's cheer of "all right!" echoed through the empty house. As the first day of retirement stretched out before him, uncluttered and relaxed, Bill decided things would probably work out just fine. "Then again," he thought, "Hank is no dummy. . . ."

RETIREMENT: THE ROLE-LESS ROLE

Hank discovered what millions before him have learned: for some people, retirement isn't all it's cracked up to be.

Retirement planning used to mean putting enough money aside in good investments to live out your remaining years comfortably. Now it means much more.

America is changing. It's growing older. According to numbers compiled by the Administration on Aging (AoA), the number of Americans 65 and older increased by 21% between 1980 and 1989 to 5.8 million while the under-65 population grew just 5%.

We're living longer, too. A person in good health who reached age 65 in 1989 could plan to live another 17.2 years. And the 65–74 age group was 8.5 times larger than it was in 1900; the 75–84 group had grown 13 times; and the 85+ group multiplied 24 times.

That trend is expected to continue as medical science finds ways to extend our lives. And when the baby boom generation jogs and cycles its way into old age around the year 2010, it will accelerate. By the year 2030, those of us 65 and older will number about 65 million, two-and-a-half times more than the same population in 1980.

At the same time that we're growing older, we're retiring earlier. As a culture, we have decided it would be nice not to force our senior members to work all their lives to avoid poverty—a philosophy that led to the creation of the Social Security system in 1935. Social Security makes it possible for millions of people to quit working as early as age 62.

People quit working for other reasons, too. One big reason has been the advent of financial planning, which has helped many ordinary people prepare for a comfortable retirement. Many companies are offering their employees attractive early retirement packages, to open up room for younger personnel or simply to reduce their payroll costs.

At the turn of the century, nearly 70% of all men over 65 still worked. By the mid-1980s, only 20% of all men over 65 were still in the work force, a 50% drop in 85 years. The effects of pension plans and early retirement programs on the employees of large companies are equally startling. In 1986, only 3% of those employees worked beyond 65; just 5% actually made it to 65.

Only eight years earlier, in 1978, 19% of the large-firm employees with vested retirement rights were still on the job at age 65. That's a drop of 14% in less than a decade.

The net effect is that, as a society, we tend to live longer after formal retirement than any previous generation. Many of us will live 25% or 30% of our life spans after we retire.

This generation of younger, healthier, and

more active retirees is entering a new world full of both opportunity and peril. As our life spans increase, we risk more years of physical degeneration, so the issue of long-term health care becomes significantly more important—an issue discussed thoroughly in Chapter 7.

On the other hand, many people with the prospect of another 20 or 30 years of life retire only to a second career. Some of them need the money for survival, but many have learned the hard way that even retirees can't live on bread alone.

Consider Bill's friend Hank. Long an important, contributing member of a dynamic firm, he suddenly found himself in retirement and at a loss for stimulating activity. It's a common experience. Our work environments tend to provide us with our sense of self. Most of us receive stimulation and recognition from work; when we retire to inactivity, that important emotional charge is missing.

Retirement is hard even on a spouse who has been at home during the work years. Suddenly everything changes: all the routines are new and additional responsibilities are created. For many wives, a retired husband seems like a grown-up child who has come home to live.

Add to that the fact that society expects (and demands) so little of its older citizens, and it is clear why the retirement years can be so difficult. Some sociologists refer to retirement as the "role-less role," since our youth-oriented culture makes so little room for its older members—people who, in other cultures, often enjoy a privileged status.

In Chapter 7, we examine more closely the pros and cons of postretirement careers. In many cases, a retired person's finances demand a return to work—but in increasing numbers they are trying to find a new role in life as well.

HOW TO CALCULATE WHAT YOU'LL NEED FOR A COMFORTABLE RETIREMENT

Most people find that they need about 70% of their preretirement income to live as comfortably in retirement as before. Unfortu-

nately, average income during this period drops about 50%.

Retired people who live comfortably typically have three major sources of income: Social Security, an employer-sponsored pension plan, and their own retirement investment program. Like a three-legged stool, when all three components are in place retirement is stable and comfortable. When one leg is missing, however, the resulting balancing act can be far from amusing.

Self-employed individuals or employees lacking a company-sponsored pension plan have to double their own retirement-planning efforts. As you will see, the laws provide the self-employed with special retirement-planning investment opportunities—but the discipline and the effort to take advantage of them must come from the individual.

CAPITAL NEEDS ANALYSIS: HOW MUCH IS ENOUGH?

Money Management Tip

A capital needs analysis is a tool to help you determine how much money you will need in order to retire with a suitable lifestyle. It can help you determine whether your expectations are realistic and if an early retirement is possible.

Ruth and Fred are a one-career couple who would like to retire when Fred is 62 and Ruth is 59, an event that's 22 years away, in the year 2012. They estimate that their dream retirement will require a monthly income (in current dollars) of $3,500. Adjusting for an assumed annual 5% rate of inflation, they will need $10,238 per month in the year 2012. (See Figure 6-1.)

They anticipate that Ruth's pension plan will provide them with $2,076 in the year 2012, leaving a shortfall of $8,162. Given their life expectancies at ages 62 and 59, and without considering Social Security, they will need to retire with an accumulation of $1,410,603.

Figuring Social Security income at a potential $2,352 per month, or $406,455 over their remaining life span, they will need to accumulate $1,004,158 in investments and

- Age when you want to be financially independent **62**
- Your present age **40**
- Working years remaining **22**
- Income desired per month at 62 .... $ 3,500
- Adjusted for inflation at 5.0%, you need .... $ 10,238
- Less: Retirement plan income plus increases .... (2,076)
  - Other retirement income sources 0
  - Shortage (or surplus) .... $ 8,162
- Capital required to make up income shortage .... $ 1,410,603
- Less potential Social Security of $2,352 per month
  at age 62 or discounted to age 62 is equal to .... $ 406,445
- Personal capital needed to make up income shortage .. $ 1,004,158

Capital available from	Present Value	Growth Rate (%)	Future Value
Life insurance net values	$ 0	3.00%	$ 0
Saving and fixed assets	29,954	5.76%	102,690
Stocks and mutual funds	36,553	8.00%	198,722
Real estate equity	21,344	2.00%	32,997
Partnerships	20,000	8.00%	108,731
Other investments	0	0.00%	0
Retirement plans	0	0.00%	0
Monthly additions	500	8.00%	358,394
	$107,851		$801,534

Capital shortage (capital required less future value) $202,625
Present estimated average rate of return is 6.19%.
In order to reach your goal, you would have to increase the average
rate of return on your present capital to 9.69%.
Or you would need to deposit additional funds each month in the
amount of $371 at 6%, $214 at 10%, $99 at 15%.

Figure 6-1   Fred and Ruth's Retirement Capital Needs Analysis

savings to retire in the year 2012 with the desired income.

By carefully using their resources and inheritances from Ruth's family, she and Fred have built a portfolio worth about $107,851 in 1990 dollars. Given the portfolio's current rate of growth, their investments will be worth $801,534 in 2012, a shortfall of $202,625 from the needed $1,004,158.

How can they make up the difference? They have two traditional ways to try: they can reorient their portfolio for higher growth, or they can increase the amount of money they set aside each month.

Notice that the estimated average rate of return on their investments is 6.19% after tax. If they can shift some of their assets into more productive investments, and increase their rate of return to 9.69% after tax, they can meet their goal.

But Fred and Ruth, Type IV investors (see Chapter 2), prefer to maintain a rela-

- Age when you want to be financially independent **65**
- Your present age **40**
- Working years remaining **25**
- Income desired per month at **65** $ 3,500
- Adjusted for inflation at 5.0% you need $ 11,852
- Less: Retirement plan income plus increases (2,852)
    Other retirement income sources 0
    Shortage (or surplus) $ 8,987
- Capital required to make up income shortage $ 1,396,600
- Less potential Social Security of $3,190 per month at age 65 or discounted to age 65 is equal to $ 495,669
- Personal capital needed to make up income shortage $ 900,931

Capital available from	Present Value	Growth Rate (%)	Future Value
Life insurance net values	$ 0	3.00%	$ 0
Saving and fixed assets	29,954	5.76%	121,476
Stocks and mutual funds	36,553	8.00%	250,332
Real estate equity	21,344	2.00%	35,017
Partnerships	20,000	8.00%	136,970
Other investments	0	0.00%	0
Retirement plans	0	0.00%	0
Monthly additions	500	8.00%	475,513
	$107,851		$1,019,308

Capital shortage (capital required less future value) –$0
Present estimated average rate of return is 6.19%.

Figure 6-2   Fred and Ruth's *Alternate* Retirement Capital Needs Analysis

tively conservative investment mix, increasing their monthly contributions instead. Assuming they make 6% on that additional investment sum, they will need to raise their monthly contributions by $371. If they use a more aggressive investment tool and receive 10% on their money, they need to set aside only an additional $214; and if they can find an investment that returns a whopping 15%, their monthly increase need only be $99. Careful investors like Fred and Ruth will be more comfortable finding the extra $371 in the budget each month and counting on only the 6% after tax return.

Notice in Figure 6-2 what happens if Fred chooses to continue working to age 65. Without increasing their monthly savings or reallocating their resources, they will have more than enough capital at retirement to live the way they want, even with the effects of inflation figured in.

SOCIAL SECURITY: WHO'S SECURE AND WHO'S NOT?

It's no secret that Social Security won't pay for a comfortable retirement. If you have prepared for your retirement, Social Security will provide a supplementary income, but no more. Those who must rely on Social Security soon wish they had other resources. On the other hand, there are reassuring indications that the Social Security system is back on solid ground and that benefits—no matter how paltry—will continue to be paid well into the 21st century.

The size of your Social Security benefits is relative to how much you paid into the system during your working years. If you made at least the maximum Social Security base salary for the past 29 years, $51,300 in 1990, you are entitled to the maximum benefit of $11,700 in 1990. Social Security has an automatic escalator and the base wage changes every time an automatic increase becomes effective.

If your spouse doesn't collect his or her benefits, that person will usually receive a sum totaling about 50% of yours—in 1990, the two of you would receive in the neighborhood of $17,500 from the Social Security system.

If you are 45 or older, the Social Security Administration can give you an estimate of your monthly payments, or you can figure it yourself using a booklet called "Your Social Security Retirement Check"; it's available at your local Social Security office.

The Social Security Administration is a large organization, and mistakes can occur. Every now and again, people discover that they have not received full credit for all the years they have worked. You should periodically confirm your earnings record by contacting the local Social Security office and requesting Form SSA-7004, "Request for Statement of Earnings." (See copy in Appendix D.)

Look At This:

Once you have completed and returned Form SSA-7004, the Social Security Administration will send you a "Summary Statement of Earnings." If you request it, the administration will also send a statement of the number of quarters you have fulfilled and an estimate of the amount of your monthly check were you to retire immediately. *This will only be an estimate:* there is a recording lag time of two years, so your summary won't be precise.

Any mistakes should be reported directly to your local Social Security office. They'll need to see a copy of your W-2 form from the year in question.

The Future of Social Security

Much has been made of the crisis brewing within the Social Security system. Too few workers are supporting too many retired persons. The current surplus has been lent, in large part, to the Treasury Department to help finance our huge national debt. As the baby boom generation begins to retire in the second decade of the next century, the disparity will be even more pronounced and the pressure to raise taxes to pay back funds to the Social Security administration will be great.

But the picture is actually brighter than it appears on the surface. The increase in Social Security taxes created a surplus in the Social Security retirement and disability trust which had reached $58 billion in 1989. It's projected to hit $11.8 trillion by 2030, exactly when the baby boomers are expected to begin to withdraw their benefits. Resources will be depleted by 2046. If the Treasury Department continues to be the planet's most reliable debtor, the trust fund should be secure. However, the most pessimistic assumptions call for the Disability Insurance Fund to face trouble in about 10 years. But, any long-term problems are about 40 to 60 years off, giving plenty of time to make any needed adjustments.

Since 1990, employers and employees each contribute over 7.65% (6.2% for FICA and 1.45% for Medicare) of personal earnings to Social Security each year; self-employed people pay a net of 15.3% (12.4% OASDI and 2.9% Medicare). Since 1989, an individual taxpayer may deduct one-half of self-employment tax paid from his gross income.

Another factor should also ease some of the pressure on the system. In the year 2003, the official social security retirement age will rise to 67, reversing a trend that's been going in the opposite direction for 50 years.

Despite the new-found financial health of the Social Security system, it's still vulnerable—primarily to political pressures.

Medicare's hospitalization insurance fund is falling short. Some people feel that projected shortfalls should be combatted with funds from the Social Security surplus; other people support new taxes.

Finally, there's the continuing specter of the federal deficit. The Social Security Administration lends its surplus to the Treasury—at interest—so that deficit public programs can be funded without raising taxes. It's a convenient solution to a tricky problem, but there's the danger that current benefit consumption will outstrip Social Security's income abilities and deplete the hard-earned surpluses. Then taxes will have to be raised to repay not only the Treasury debt, but the retirement needs of the baby boom generation as well.

The American Association of Retired Persons (AARP) tells its members that they can expect a stable Social Security for at least another 35 years—after that, they say, it's anybody's guess. Only wise decision making on the part of our leaders and constant voter surveillance can assure the future of Social Security.

New changes that affect retirees and income taxes on the money they earn begins in 1990. Retirees collecting Social Security benefits ages 65 through 69 will have benefits increased. Prior benefits were cut $1.00 for every $2.00 a retiree under age 70 earned over the earning limit of $8,880. Now a retiree is cut $1.00 for every $3.00 of earnings over the limit. A retiree over age 70 may earn any amount without being penalized.

For updated information you may call the Social Security General Accounting Office at (202) 275-6241 or call Social Security information at 1-800-234-5772.

YOU AND YOUR PENSION PLAN

As the song says, "The times they are a'changing."

It's too soon to say goodbye to traditional pension plans in which employers guarantee specific, defined benefits, but the handwriting is on the wall. Conventional pension plans are rapidly being replaced by so-called capital accumulation plans, which offer employees no guarantees but increase the potential rewards.

In a traditional pension plan, employee benefits are guaranteed and paid for by the employer. The employer establishes and runs the plan, and makes all pertinent investment decisions. The earnings grow tax-deferred within the plan; when you retire, you will be taxed on your benefits, but hopefully at a lower tax rate than the one you pay now. If the employer goes into bankruptcy, the Pension Benefit Guaranty Corporation picks up the benefits to a limit of $2,028.41 (1989) a month. No muss, no fuss, and no bother for the employee.

With the new capital accumulation plans— including profit sharing, thrift, and 401(k) plans—the employer creates a tax-free investment account for the employee and promises to contribute a specified sum at regular intervals. You have the opportunity of making contributions, too—together, you and your employer may contribute up to 25% of your wages up to $30,000 per year.

In a 401(k) plan, a portion of your contribution (up to the deduction limit) is not included in your income for tax purposes. The deduction limit is indexed annually for inflation. The remaining amounts contributed are tax-deferred. In addition, you may be responsible for making key decisions about how the money in your account is invested.

Benefits in a traditional pension plan are based on the number of years you worked for the employer and the size of your salary. Normally, the size of your pension is calculated by multiplying a percentage of your salary by the number of years you put in. The percentage of salary used for the calculation may range from 1% to more than 2%, depending on whether the plan bases its calculation on all the years you were employed, or on the income you received during the three to five years in which you received the greatest amount of compensation.

Depending on your contribution level, the contributions of your employer, and on how well your underlying investments fare, your earnings within a capital accumulation account are potentially unlimited—and they can earn you a big tax break. Many employers are willing to match your contributions, most often with contributions of stock or profit sharing: some will contribute 50 cents for every dollar you contribute; others match dollar for dollar; and a few companies contribute two for one.

Needless to say, because big employers like getting rid of the obligations that accompany guaranteed pension plans, the growth of capital accumulation plans has been phenomenal. In 1983, less than 2% of large and medium-size employers offered 401(k) plans; in 1988, 82% have them. However, since 1989 the number of companies offering 401(k) plans has fallen from the 1988 numbers. The Employee Benefit Research Institute says that when today's 50-year-old workers retire, capital accumulation plans will be paying out as much retirement income as conventional plans.

From an employee's point of view, each concept has competing strengths and weaknesses. Clearly, the biggest factor limiting the size of a traditional pension is job hopping. When you leave a job where you are enrolled in a pension plan, your earnings are frozen at the date of your departure. In the past, employers were required to vest employees at 10 years.

New vesting rules exist which mandate when employees are entitled to part or all of an employer's contributions to his/her pension. They apply *only* to plan years beginning after December 31, 1988. Employee vesting in benefits accrued up to that date is governed by the old rules, which favored the employers more.

The new rules, part of the Tax Reduction Act of 1986, offer employers two alternatives: provide 100 percent vesting to employees after five years of service, with *no* vesting before then; or use a seven-year option, with 20 percent vesting after three years' service and an additional 20 percent after each successive year of employment until 100 percent vesting is reached at the end of seven years.

These vesting standards apply only to the *employer* contributions. Employee contributions are vested in full immediately. Consequently, employees who change jobs will find it easier to become vested in more than

A 401(k) plan (see Figure 6-3) is a voluntary retirement investment program sponsored by your employer. Known as a "capital accumulation plan," 401(k) plans have become enormously popular in recent years, partly because they allow employers out from under the obligations of traditional pension plans in which the employer shoulders responsibility for guaranteeing pension plan benefits; partly because they allow for exceptional growth of assets; and partly because they allow employees to make tax-deferred contributions into their own retirement programs.

Your contributions are made by deferring a portion of your salary into the plan, and your employer may make contributions as well. Together, you may contribute as much as 25% of your salary, with a maximum contribution of $30,000. Taxes on all the earnings, profits, and dividends within a 401(k) plan are deferred, and taxes on the contribution (up to the deduction limit) are deferred also. The deferral limit was $7,979 in 1990 and is adjusted by the cost of living annually.

You may begin taking your 401(k) benefits at age 59½ (there is a penalty for taking them sooner). You *must* begin taking them by 70½.

In these examples, a 401(k) plan is compared to any taxable investment earning the same interest rate—in this case, 8%. Notice the advantage of the tax deferral allowed with the 401(k): although the same annual contribution—$6,000—is made in either case, the net deduction for the taxable investment, assuming a 28% tax rate, is $4,320 a year, lowering the real rate of return to 5.76%.

one plan, but may find that no one plan pays much in real dollars at the time they retire. On the other hand, pension plan payments are guaranteed, and you don't have to worry about managing your account.

If you're enrolled in a 401(k) plan, you cannot withdraw funds before age 59½

Type IV

without paying a 10% income tax penalty on top of whatever taxes you pay on your withdrawals. 401(k) plans can, however, be treated as IRA rollovers and managed personally in a variety of ways. The rollover provision gives you the ability to continue managing your own money. Most people continue the deferral of taxes until retirement or age 59½.

Should you decide you need money out of a plan before age 59½, the I.R.S. has pro-

Type I

vided some loopholes: (1) Withdrawals for death, disability, and to pay for catastrophic medical expenses (in excess of 7.5% adjusted gross income) or "hardship." At age 70½, the savings must start to be distributed and in most cases, further contributions are no longer permitted.

(2) You may also be able to avoid the 10% penalty at any age if you receive substantial equal period payments (at least annually) over your life expectancy, or over the joint lives of yourself and your beneficiary. Should you change the payout distribution before age 59½, you may pay a recapture penalty tax applying to all amounts received prior to age 59½. This penalty may also apply if equal payments are not received for at least five years.

(3) Another exception is a distribution paid to an alternate payee because of a domestic relations court order. No penalty is assessed, but the receeipient will pay income tax if the proceeds are not used as an I.R.A. rollover.

(4) Dividend distributions from an employee stock ownership plan (ESOP) as well as certain other ESOP distributions, are exempt if most of the plan assets have been invested in employer stock for five plan years.

(5) Another exception may be available to you if your pension plan document allows early retirement after age 55 and you terminate service by reason of early retirement under the plan. The distribution can be a lump sum or another form of receipt as you may direct. If you elect a lump sum distribution you will be fully taxed, but exempt from the 10% penalty. Your 1099 will reflect what type of distribution you received: A premature distribution; death or disability; or a regular distribution under the plan.

For more information, two J.K. Lasser books are available: *How to Retire Prosperously*, by C. Colburn Hardy, and *J.K. Lasser's Your Income Tax* (updated regularly), both published by Simon & Schuster, Inc.

How to Use a Capital Accumulation Plan

Your goal with a capital accumulation retirement plan is to create a substantial body of

Money
Management
Tip

investments that has both safety and growth. The trick is to create a diversified but conservative portfolio from among the available offerings. Choosing from only the safe side of the list may not produce satisfactory returns, and picking only from the growth side subjects your retirement fund to market swings. If your employer's stock is indeed among the options, resist loading up too heavily; your future already depends largely on your employer's fiscal well-being—no need to tie up your pension funds there, too. Many employers offer stock as their share of a 401(k) contribution, but if your holdings in the stocks of your employer exceed 10% of your retirement portfolio, you should consider converting some shares to other investment choices.

Think of your holdings in a capital accumulation account as a part of a coordinated investment strategy.

For example, if you have a substantial investment portfolio in addition to your capital accumulation plan, concentrate on safe, income-producing tools within your retirement

	Without 401(k) Plan	With 401(k) Plan
Your contribution	$6,000	$6,000
Employer contribution	0	0
Tax rate	28.00%	0
Income tax	$1,680	0
Net deposit	$4,320	$6,000
Interest rate	8.00%	8.00%
After-tax rate	5.76%	8.00%

Age	Without 401(k) Plan Contribution	Without 401(k) Plan Year-End Balance	With 401(k) Plan Contribution	With 401(k) Plan Year-End Balance
40	$4,320	$ 4,569	$6,000	$ 6,480
41	4,320	9,401	6,000	13,478
42	4,320	14,511	6,000	21,037
43	4,320	19,916	6,000	29,200
44	4,320	25,632	6,000	38,016
49	4,320	59,546	6,000	93,873
54	4,320	104,420	6,000	175,946

NOTE: The following figures are for retirement selected at age 62.

Summary At Age 62	Without the plan	With the plan
Before-tax earnings	$132,000	$132,000
Income taxes paid	36,960	0
Net plan contributions	95,040	$132,000
Retirement balance	$192,608	$359,360
Gross monthly income	1,545	2,883
Average income tax (28%)	(231)	(807)
Net monthly income after tax	$ 1,314	$ 2,076

Projections based on life expectancy of 22 years with principal and interest paid out in level monthly installments.

Figure 6-3 The 401(k) Plan and how it works

Figure 6-3 continued

	Without 401(k) Plan	With 401(k) Plan
Your contribution	$6,000	$6,000
Employer contribution	0	0
Tax rate	28.00%	0
Income tax	$1,680	0
Net deposit	$4,320	$6,000
Interest rate	8.00%	8.00%
After-tax rate	5.76%	8.00%

	Without 401(k) Plan		With 401(k) Plan	
Age	Contribution	Year-End Balance	Contribution	Year-End Balance
40	$4,320	$ 4,569	$6,000	$ 6,480
41	4,320	9,401	6,000	13,478
42	4,320	14,511	6,000	21,037
43	4,320	19,916	6,000	29,200
44	4,320	25,632	6,000	38,016
49	4,320	59,546	6,000	93,873
54	4,320	104,420	6,000	175,946

NOTE: The following figures are for retirement selected at age 65.

Summary At Age 65	Without the plan	With the plan
Before tax earnings	$150,000	$150,000
Income taxes paid	42,000	0
Net plan contributions	$108,000	$150,000
Retirement balance	$242,356	$473,726
Gross monthly income	2,035	3,979
Average income tax (28%)	(284)	(1,114)
Net monthly income after tax	$1,751	$ 2,865

Projections based on life expectancy of 20 years with principal and interest paid out in level monthly installments.

program. That allows you to orient the remainder of your portfolio toward growth-oriented stocks. If the stock market falters, you can write off the capital losses on your tax return, while losses inside your sheltered pension plan can't be written off.

If your capital accumulation account comprises the bulk of your investment program and you are 10 years or more from retirement, keep one-half to two-thirds of it in a growth-oriented fund and the remainder in fixed-income instruments. When you have a choice between two products in a single category, use both for diversification.

As retirement approaches, begin orienting your account toward the income side: transfer at least two-thirds of the assets into the income fund. This process will be gradual, as most plans limit the amount of funds that can be transferred in a single transaction, and curtail the number of transactions that can take place in a year.

EARLY RETIREMENT: YES OR NO?

On a hot Friday afternoon in August, Franklin's intercom buzzed. It was Jim, Franklin's boss, senior vice president and head of eastern sales for the large paper company where Franklin had worked for 17 years. "We need to talk, Franklin. Do you have a few minutes now, or can we arrange a time?"

Franklin felt lightheaded; his stomach suddenly churned. The rumor mill had been working overtime recently with speculation about massive layoffs. Jim had made several trips to corporate headquarters in the past few weeks and refused to discuss even with his closest associates the subject of the meetings.

"I'll be right down," he said. Grimly, he thought of the old Indian saying: "Today is a good day to die."

Death? Hardly, but at age 56 the axe could certainly be the death knell to his career. It would change a few plans.

"Sit down, Franklin," Jim said genially as Franklin entered. A faint smile crossed his face. "Listen, you can relax. It's OK. I know there've been rumors about cutbacks and I haven't helped things by being secretive. You're going to walk out of here with your job intact, so relax."

Franklin felt his blood pressure drop and the knots in his stomach unravel. Jim leaned back in his chair and continued.

"As you know, Franklin, we've been under a certain amount of pressure these past two years. Sales are up—in fact, your department has been among the leaders this year— but our margins are down and we have to economize. Atlanta has asked all senior managers to find ways to trim expenses."

Franklin nodded. At that instant, he knew what was coming next.

"For the last six weeks," Jim continued, "we've been meeting with the pension committee. We've tried to structure an early retirement program that we could offer to several key personnel throughout the organization, such as you."

He picked up a gray folder. "This is it; I think it looks good. I'm wondering if you'll take a look at it over the next few days and see if you think it represents a fair offer. It's for six years early."

A thousand conflicting feelings swarmed through Franklin's head. He enjoyed his job—always had—but still, the thought of retiring six years earlier than planned . . . he had to admit it sounded attractive.

But what if the "early out" wouldn't support him and Katherine the way they had envisioned? If it didn't and he turned down the offer, would he be out the door anyway in six months with an inferior settlement?

"Do you want my comments on the plan or my answer as a beneficiary?" he asked.

"Maybe both. It depends on how strongly you feel about what we've offered. I want you to know that I have no plans to cut you loose. You've been a valuable part of our sales team. On the other hand, I can't give you any guarantees.

"If push comes to shove and Atlanta gets tough, I can't say how many people we'd have to lay off around here. Anyway—take a look; see what you think."

Franklin left Jim's office with the gray folder and a queasy stomach. It hadn't been the disaster he'd feared, but he still had a feeling the outcome wouldn't be good. One thing for certain, early retirement was now no longer a pipe dream, and he and Katherine would have to decide if they could live on what the company offered.

Evaluating an Early Retirement Offer

For better or worse, Franklin's predicament is not an uncommon one: thousands of employees of all kinds of companies are given early retirement offers every year for a variety of reasons. Very few of them know how to evaluate the offer, although many of them recognize the underlying threat and realize that the offer they get today may be a lot more attractive than the one they get in six months.

At the bottom line, most early retirement offers fall short of offering employees what they would receive if they waited until normal retirement age to begin collecting benefits. Most companies calculate benefits using a formula based on earnings at retirement multiplied by the number of years employed, so most of a pension's value is accrued after the employee reaches age 55.

Some plans use a "final pay" formula, which bases benefits on your salary during your highest-paid years multiplied by the number of years you served. Others use your average income over the duration of your employment, although many plans adjust the numbers to be more competitive with final-pay plans. In effect, figuring the value of an early retirement offer is roughly the same as calculating the cost of an annuity of the same amount and duration. (See our discussion of insurance products in Part III.)

Franklin scheduled a visit to the employee benefits department. Using insurance company actuarial tables, the benefits manager determined the monthly payments to which Franklin's pension settlement would entitle him. Now Franklin could calculate how much additional money he would need to make up for the shortfall.

At the time of the offer, six years before Franklin's intended retirement date and after 17 years of employment, the company offer showed a pension reserve of $171,000.

Given his $72,500 salary, and assuming annual raises of 7% and earnings within the pension plan of 7.5% per year, that reserve would grow by $209,000 to $380,000 in six years.

Calculated in today's dollars, Franklin's final pension reserves of $380,000 are worth $243,000. So the real shortfall is the difference between the offer of $171,000 and to-day's value of the original reserves ($243,000 – $171,000), or $72,000.

In order to compensate Franklin for the difference, his employer would have to sweeten the early retirement offer with a $72,000 bonus—roughly one year's pay. The offer referred to the possibility of such a bonus in the case of voluntary early retirement; Franklin suspected that, at minimum, the bonus clause would be stricken from the agreement if he failed to accept the current offer.

Even with the bonus, Franklin would be forced to begin living off the proceeds of his pension six years earlier than he intended. Taking into account his present age (56) and the current value of his pension reserves, his monthly early retirement check would total just $1,425, a significantly lower sum than the $3,667 he would have received at full retirement.

On the other hand, he was healthy and had plenty of energy. Perhaps an early retirement would free him to consider a second career. Perhaps his employer would consider the possibility of project assignments, or he might become a consultant. Franklin's wealth of knowledge about his industry could be worth a lot to other companies. In the next chapter, we discuss the growing phenomenon of second careers, a consideration of special value for workers who have taken an early retirement.

In a typical pension plan, the value of the pension generally quadruples in the decade between 55 and 65. For that reason, many financial planners recommend that you stay at work as long as possible. If, like Franklin, you don't feel that you have that option, you will be forced to find ways to compensate. In Franklin's case, simply knowing the value of next year's salary to his overall retirement needs enabled him to evaluate his employer's offer more accurately and completely.

Money Management Tip

Other Pension Options

Self-employed individuals and the owners and employees of small, unincorporated businesses have the same needs at retirement as anyone else—but they don't have a big company with deep pockets that is able to share the load. All pension contributions come directly from their own pockets. A variety of programs can help.

Individual Retirement Accounts (IRAs). The use of an Individual Retirement Account is not limited to self-employed individuals. The 1986 Tax Reform Act (TRA) diminished their value for people who have another tax-sheltered retirement plan, but an IRA still makes sense for many people — especially if they are self-employed.

Almost anyone may still open an IRA account and make IRA contributions of up to $2,000 annually. Tax on the earnings in the account will be deferred until retirement, but you may only deduct your contributions if you are not enrolled in another tax-deferred plan.

Individuals with adjusted gross incomes of less than $25,000 and couples who file jointly with less than $40,000 income may still claim their contributions, even if they are covered elsewhere—up to $2,000 for an individual and $2,250 for a spousal IRA. Partial deductions are allowed on incomes between $25,000 and $35,000 for singles, and $40,000 and $50,000 for couples filing jointly.

For every $1,000 increment in those ranges, your maximum deductible IRA contributions will be reduced by 10%.

There's a $200 floor, which means if your adjusted gross income is within $2,000 of the top of the range, you can deduct up to $200 even if the calculations would otherwise permit less.

The rules for IRA withdrawal were unchanged by the 1986 Tax Reform Act: withdrawals are permissible at age 59½ and mandatory by age 70½. If you must withdraw funds from your IRA early, you will pay a penalty that equals 10% of the value of the withdrawal, unless you make substantially equal withdrawals, following strict guidelines established by the IRS, over a period of at least 5 years. As distasteful as that may seem, you might pay less for such early withdrawal than if you were to borrow a like amount from a bank.

Don't underestimate the value of an IRA, even if you are unable to deduct your contri-

butions. Because tax on earnings is deferred and your money may grow at a compounded rate, an IRA may still make sense for you.

Figure 6-4 shows the value of a taxable $2,000 annual IRA contribution versus a taxable investment of the same size, assuming that both earned 10% a year:

B

High Taxes
Low Expenses

If you took out your money after...	10 Years	20 Years	30 Years
Nondeductible IRA	$22,614	$76,528	$214,491
Taxable Investment	21,772	66,215	156,938
The IRA Advantage	**842**	**10,313**	**57,553**

Includes 28% tax on earnings

Figure 6-4
Non-Deductible IRA vs. Taxable Investment

Keoghs. A Keogh is a plan designed to offer the self-employed and owners of unincorporated business the same benefits as a corporate pension plan. A Keogh plan allows an individual to make contributions of up to 25% of compensation, or $30,000, and the entire contribution is deductible. Under a 401(k) plan, by comparison, an individual may defer no more than 15% of compensation, and only the first $7,979 (limit changes annually) is deferrable.

OTHER RETIREMENT PLAN OPTIONS

Despite the wide use of Keogh, company, and insurance-based pension plans, other means for a secure retirement are available.

SEP-IRAs

A self-employed individual or the owner of a small business who doesn't want the cost or administrative burden of a qualified retirement plan may choose to establish a simplified employee pension plan (SEP-IRA). Under a SEP plan, employees establish their own IRAs, to which the company may make contributions. The company eliminates the headaches of managing a more complicated plan, and retains the ability to make tax-sheltered contributions to its employees' retirement plans. SEP contributions are limited to 15% of compensation or $30,000, whichever is less, and do not require the special IRS 5500 form as do other pension plans. However, the 1986 Tax Reform Act added one more advantage to SEP-IRAs, called the SAR-SEP.

SAR-SEPs

The SAR-SEP provision allows the employee to elect to make a separate, nondeductible contribution to his or her SEP-IRA, subject to the 15%/$30,000 limit. This separate contribution may not exceed $7,979 (1990) and is funded via a payroll deduction. The contribution is not counted as taxable income to the employee.

Door 1 and Door 2: Lump-Sum Payments Versus Annuities

Nothing can strike terror in the heart of a retiree like deciding how to take the proceeds of a retirement plan. The choice is irrevocable: once made, you can't call it back. The only answer is do your homework ahead of time.

Essentially, there are two choices: you take your pension in the form of a monthly check, or in a lump sum. If you have been employed by a large company throughout your career and have a traditional pension, you probably don't have a choice—most pension plans pay out proceeds in the form of a monthly annuity, meaning equal payments for the rest of your life. Only about 20% of all conventional plans allow you to take a lump sum.

If you have a capital accumulation plan, you do have a choice. Most pay benefits as a

lump sum, but allow you to convert to a monthly annuity if you prefer. Of course, if you are not allowed the option, you can always take your lump sum and convert it by purchasing an annuity from an insurance company.

The same holds true for holders of IRAs, Keoghs, SEP-IRAs, and SAR-SEPs.

Life is full of risks, and so is this choice. An annuity guarantees funds until you die; it's safe, secure, and trouble free.

An annuity is a fixed-income instrument however, and inflation will steal its buying power over time. If an annuity and Social Security are your only sources of retirement income, your real income will diminish with time. If you take your money in a lump sum, you can invest at least a portion of it in a growth fund and—assuming all goes well with your choice of investments—your income should keep up with inflation.

Taking a lump sum has its risks, too. Under an annuity, the pension payments are scheduled to stop at the end of your life or your spouse's life if he or she outlives you. But the amount of each monthly payment is based on actuarial tables, so if you outlive your life expectancy, your annuity will ultimately pay out more than the actual reserves in your account.

If you had a crystal ball, and could tell how long you would live, you would know to choose one annuity for a long life span, another annuity for a shorter one. Don't overlook the fact that annuities are based on unisex life expectancy tables. Because women typically live longer than men, an annuity could turn out to be a bargain for a woman.

There is also the matter of your heirs. An annuity spends itself out, and nothing is left over after you die—although in some cases an annuity will provide your spouse with income if you die first. If you believe that you can invest your lump sum prudently, you'll keep control of your invested money and experience some growth as well as income. With good money management, you'll probably do better than annuitizing.

Annuity Options

You can choose to invest your retirement funds into one of three basic types of annuities.

Life-Only. Life-only annuities pay monthly benefits until your death. They pay the highest monthly sum.

Joint and Survivor. Joint and survivor annuities continue to pay your spouse a monthly check even after your death. To pay for the extended period, the amount of income you receive during your lifetime is reduced by 10% to 15%.

Life- and Period-Certain. Life- and period-certain annuities pay benefits until your death, or for a predetermined number of years, whichever is longer. Life- and period-certain policies reduce income as well, by about 10% to 15%.

Look At This:

You have the option of choosing a life-only annuity and buying a life insurance policy to cover your spouse upon your death. If you buy right—find a level-premium whole life policy with minimum cash value buildup and a face value that decreases over time— you can collect the highest possible annuity benefits during

your lifetime and leave your surviving spouse with a comparable income. Because federal law prohibits you from selecting a life-only annuity without the written consent of your spouse, be sure to have a waiver signed if you choose the latter option.

How to Take a Lump Sum

A lump-sum payment puts you in total control of your money. Greater risks and opportunities attend this choice, and a lump sum can bump your income into a higher tax bracket, so careful planning is in order.

In many cases, a lump-sum payment represents only a portion of your total pension reserves. If it is at least 50%, you can roll over the proceeds into a rollover IRA account within 60 days. In the IRA, your money will compound tax-free until you begin taking withdrawals. You must begin taking withdrawals by the time you are 701/2 and they will be taxed at that time as ordinary income.

A second strategy uses a special consideration developed by the IRS called *forward averaging*; it may be used only once. You may use forward averaging if (1) you receive the entire balance of your pension assets at one time (2) you have been enrolled in the plan at least five years; and (3) you are 591/2. An exception is made for people who turned 50 by 1986 (born before January 1, 1936); they don't have to wait until they are 591/2 and they can select either five or ten-year forward averaging.

Using forward averaging, your lump sum is taxed as if it were your only income over a 5- or 10-year period. If you select five-year forward averaging, your money is taxed

Lump-Sum Distribution	Five-Year Averaging (using 1989 rates)		Ten-Year Averaging (using 1986 rates)	
	Federal Taxes Due	Tax as Percent of Distribution	Federal Taxes Due	Tax as Percent of Distribution
$ 20,000	$ 1,500	7.50%	$ 1,100	5.5%
50,000	6,900	13.80	5,875	11.7
100,000	15,943	15.94	14,474	14.5
200,000	43,943	21.97	36,924	18.5
500,000	140,000	28.00	143,680	28.7

Figure 6-5   Examples of Forward Averaging

at the rate applicable in the year you receive the distribution; ten-year averaging uses 1986 rates.

Figure 6-5 illustrates the results of both five- and ten-year forward averaging.

Since you can use forward averaging only once, you should carefully consider whether or not you should exhaust your privilege if you are going to receive another distribution later. See your tax advisor for help because tax rules change.

TAKE A GOOD LOOK AHEAD

If you are typical, you will live another 20 or 30 years past your retirement. Chances are good that you will be healthy and active for most of that time, and the future holds many possibilities: you may choose to go back to work, to move to another part of the country, or to start a new business.

It is important to take a good look ahead at your expected cash flow during this peri-od. Figure 6.6 illustrates the disastrous results of not making the proper decisions regarding the timing of retirement, retirement income sources, living expenses and investments. In the example, a prospective retiree was looking forward to an early retirement at age 55 with $500,000 in retirement assets (expected to grow at 10% annually) and social security payments expected to begin at age 62. The analysis shows how $40,000 in annual living expenses, inflation and income taxes eat away at that seemingly considerable retirement fund until it is gone as early as age 72. The retiree would then be forced to live on social security alone with a dramatically changed lifestyle, having gone from financial independence to total government dependence in only 17 years.

The decisions you make today will play a big role in determining which of many options are realistic. Make wise choices today, and you will reap the benefits for the remainder of your life.

	Five-Year Averaging (using 1989 rates)		Ten-Year Averaging (using 1986 rates)	
Lump-Sum Distribution	Federal Taxes Due	Tax as Percent of Distribution	Federal Taxes Due	Tax as Percent of Distribution
$ 50,000	$ 7,200	14.4	$ 7,112	14.2%
100,000	16,500	16.5	16,132	16.1
200,000	39,143	19.57	37,847	18.9
500,000	122,218	24.44	130,576	26.1

Figure 6-6 Examples of Combined Preferential Capital Gain Treatment and Forward Averaging

Notes

_____

_____

_____

_____

_____

_____

_____

_____

_____

_____

_____

_____

CHAPTER 7

POSTRETIREMENT PLANNING AND MONEY MANAGEMENT FOR YOUR LATER YEARS

A GLANCE AHEAD

Longer life spans and earlier retirements are extending the retirement years. Many Americans are finding that sound financial planning enhances the quality of life in later years. In this chapter, you'll learn

- *How your financial attitudes can change with age*
- *How second careers have become an important part of retirement planning*
- *How to satisfy your increasing health care needs*
- *How to make important decisions about where to live.*

HOW TO SELL A DONKEY

Once upon a time, on a bright and sunny morning in a mountain village in southern Europe, where the ocean glistens in the distance and village elders gather to exchange the news of the day, one older man decided to sell his donkey at market. He and his grandson, with whom he planned to share the profits, groomed the animal, and the three of them set off together for the town in the valley.

After a short while, they encountered some strangers along the wayside.

"Look at that silly pair," said one onlooker. "There they go, scrambling and stumbling down the path, when they could be riding comfortably on the back of that sure-footed beast." The old man listened and thought the onlookers to be right. He and the boy got on the donkey and continued their descent.

Soon they passed another group of loiterers gossiping by the road.

"Look at that lazy pair," one man yelled, "breaking the back of that poor donkey."

The old man thought that too made sense. So he dismounted while his grandson rode on.

In a while, they heard another comment from a passerby.

"Look at that disrespectful child—he rides while the old man walks!"

"Surely he is right," thought the old man. "My grandson is young and strong; I am old and growing weary of this journey."

So the grandson got off and walked while the grandfather took his place on the back of the donkey.

It should come as no surprise that there was yet one more observer who took offense at even this arrangement. "What a mean old man," he grumbled, "riding at his ease while the poor child must try to keep up on foot. And the donkey will be so worn out from its long journey down the mountainside that no one will want to buy it."

Imagine the old man's confusion. Dejected, the old man sat with his grandson and the donkey by the side of the trail and thought for a long time about what he had done.

Late in the afternoon, long after all the sellers and the buyers had gone home for their evening meal, the party of three made its way into the market.

What a sight! The townspeople say they had never seen such a thing before, nor have they since: the old man and the young man gasping for air and struggling across the cobblestones with the donkey, suspended by his bound feet, hanging from a pole between them!

Aesop told that story more than 2,500 years ago. It has special meaning to anyone contemplating retirement today, because at retirement there is no shortage of people willing to give you advice. And most of it is contradictory.

At such times remember the moral of Aesop's story: you can't make everyone happy; if you try, you will only lose sight of your own needs.

There is only one solution for this dilemma—you must educate yourself about your own real retirement needs, because no one knows your own goals and aspirations better than you, nor is anyone more qualified to decide how to achieve them.

Type IV

C

Low Taxes
High Expenses

TIME AND YOUR CHANGING ATTITUDES

As we grow older, most of us tend to become more cautious. It seems easier, and less risky, to do things the same way we always have done them. In many cases, this conservative approach is not bad but often it's not best.

Too many older people stay in family homes simply because they're afraid of change. Others refuse to get out of an investment that no longer makes sense and into one that does. Some people grow so wary of outsiders that they won't take any advice—which makes no more sense than indiscriminately taking advice from everyone.

Our arteries tend to harden as we grow older. Sometimes so do our attitudes about money. But it's good to stay open to new ideas and opportunities: in the dynamic world of investing and financial planning, where concepts and strategies are always evolving, flexibility is the key to survival. Competition in the financial markets stimulates development of important new products almost daily. Older investors can miss good opportunities by becoming "fixed" on a mix of comfortable-feeling investments and financial products and refusing to consider alternatives.

For example, the insurance industry is awash with new products that offer safety, growth, and tax-deferred earnings. One example is a product called one-year annuities. These renewable, one-year annuities have many attributes that make them suitable for older people, including safety of principal, liquidity, and guaranteed growth. For tax purposes, the earnings are tax-deferred until you begin taking withdrawals, and they are probate free.

One-year annuities may be appropriate for conservative investors, for older investors with bank CDs or bonds coming to maturity, and for those who are considering gift giving as part of their estate-planning strategy. Don't become so inflexible that you cannot bend toward new ideas. Seek out vehicles that match your investor type and your own evolving financial situation.

THE IMPACT OF INFLATION				
Inflation (%)	Today's Cost	5 years	10 years	20 years
5%	$1,000	$1,276	$1,630	$2,653
8%	1,000	1,469	2,159	4,661
10%	1,000	1,611	2,594	6,727

Recognize that you must not discount the impact of inflation when planning retirement. The value of your money and its future purchasing power is in direct relationship to inflation.

TEST YOUR FLEXIBILITY QUOTIENT

The following short quiz will help you determine how open you are to new concepts. If you're retired, or nearing retirement, check your Flexibility Quotient. Mark each item *T* for *True*, *F* for *False*.

1. When it comes to investment ideas and products, there's nothing new under the sun.   T___ F___

2. I have a trusted group of friends and advisors whose counsel makes sense to me.   T___ F___

3. Once I have hit on a concept that works for me, I tend not to examine alternatives.   T___ F___

4. My motto is "You can't teach an old dog new tricks."   T___ F___

5. When my spouse reads me something he or she thinks I will find informative, I usually listen closely.   T___ F___

6. I usually feel that someone who wants to present a new financial idea is only after my money.   T___ F___

7. I think it's exciting to learn about fresh concepts and ideas.   T___ F___

8. I have often thought that it would be interesting to take a few college courses when I'm retired.   T___ F___

9. I have a wide circle of friends and acquaintances, and I enjoy socializing with them.   T___ F___

10. Routine is preferable to change.   T___ F___

Scoring the Flexibility Quotient Quiz

There are no right or wrong answers to the Flexibility Quotient Quiz; it only indicates how you approach new ideas and challenges.

Count the number of *True* responses you gave to Questions 2, 5, 7, 8, and 9. Three or more such answers indicate that you generally are open to new ideas and change. Your responsiveness to fresh thinking may help you adapt to changing circumstances, just be careful to avoid change for change's sake alone.

Now count the number of *True* responses you gave to Questions 1, 3, 4, 6, and 10; three or more means change may not be your cup of tea. Although there is nothing wrong with sticking with tried and true investments, you may be missing out on some good opportunities.

BIG PAYOFFS FOR BIG DECISIONS

The significance of the decisions you make at retirement may be proportional to the amount of advice you receive, for some truly major choices lie ahead, and how you respond to them can make significant differences in the quality of retired life you enjoy. Generally, these decisions can be lumped into three categories: career, health care, and housing.

Postcareer Careers

What's a discussion on careers doing in a chapter on retirement? Simple: for a variety of reasons, many of which have nothing to do with money, some retirees are choosing to work after they have formally retired.

True, many retirees depend on the money a second career or a part-time job brings in. But an increasing number of people—especially early retirees—also believe that "doing nothing" for the rest of their lives would be unfulfilling at best and boring (if not downright hazardous to their health) at worst.

"My sense is that people reenter the work force for one of two reasons," said James M. Thompson, manager of Consumer Affairs at the American Association of Retired Persons. "They do it either because they desperately need the funds, or they go back for personal satisfaction."

As Alex Comfort, author of *The Joy of Sex,* put it: "The right time for retirement? About two weeks."

"Work reinforces people's sense of purpose and accomplishment," says Letitia Chamberlain, director of New York University's Center for Career and Life Planning. "It also gets them out of the house and involved with others."

The upshot of all this is that many people are choosing to start over—with second careers, part-time jobs, and home-based jobs. For the first time in their lives, a significant number of them get to be their own bosses, and they love it. They get to name their own hours, work as much or as little as they please, and choose when and for whom they work.

For those who are willing to put off retire-ment, the Social Security Administration actually pays a little bonus: if you wait until you're 70 to begin claiming benefits, you'll receive an extra 3% every month.

On the other hand, if you've spent a lifetime working toward retirement, and your golden years are well planned, who can blame you for wanting to take some well-deserved years off?

There is also the possibility that you might lose money by going back to work—especially if you have done well and accumulated a good nest egg. The loss-to-earnings ratio is $1.00 to every $3.00 earned over the Social Security earnings limit for those ages 65 to 69. Over 70, there's no penalty no matter how much you earn. The Social Security earnings limit is adjusted annually according to average earnings.

The IRS can bite, too, if you earn too much. If the total of your adjusted gross income, the nontaxable interest you earn, and half your Social Security benefits exceeds $32,000 ($25,000 for singles), you'll pay federal tax on up to 50% of your Social Security benefits.

And, your extra income could bump you into a higher tax bracket and you'll have to continue to pay Social Security withholding.

The Work Choices. Just like first careers, second careers come in a wide range of colors: from the vivid and breathtaking to drab and predictable black and white. You can work for yourself or for someone else; you can continue to work in the field you've become accustomed to or you can make a change to something completely different; you can work full-time or earn those extra dollars on a part-time basis.

Some innovative companies are beginning to allow their employees to take a trial retirement, just to see how they like it. These employees typically have six months to try retirement on for size, with the option of returning to their original jobs at the end of the experimental period.

Other companies are willing to take senior staff back as consultants. One former banker made nearly as much as a consultant developing new products for his former employer as he had made as an enrolled employee.

Some retirees don't embark on a second

career until the idle hours of an unplanned retirement start to weigh too heavily on their hands. But if you know ahead of time that you want to work, early planning in that direction can help smooth the transition—financially and emotionally. A second career may give you the opportunity to do something you really enjoy—something you dreamed of doing the first time around. But without good research and proper planning, you may find yourself back at the same old grind.

Two publications, available at your library, can be helpful in making a decision: *The Occupational Outlook Handbook*, and *The Encyclopedia of Careers and Vocational Guidance*. Career counselors at the local community college are a good source of information, too, and can be especially valuable if your second career will require retraining or special academic degree. Talk with friends and acquaintances—or even strangers—who are doing work that appeals to you. Don't let "hardening of the attitudes" keep you from a career you might enjoy.

The American Association of Retired Persons (AARP) sponsors *AARP Works,* a series of career development and job search workshops for retirees. Or write for AARP's "Working Options" (D12303) guide for additional job search tips. Request a single copy from Working Options, AARP Fulfillment, P.O. Box 2400, Long Beach, CA 90801. You can get information from Worker Equity Department, AARP, 1909 K St. NW, Washington, DC. Also, seven states—Arkansas, California, Massachusetts, Michigan, Nebraska, New York, and Vermont—host "Operation Able," a service that helps seniors find work.

Many smaller communities, too, have counselors that specialize in career changes, and big companies often help retiring personnel with career counseling. Solutions to your postretirement, postcareer career may be nearer than you think.

Starting a Business. Before you start a new business, remember that two-thirds of all small businesses in this country fail within the first five years. Yes, you may have lots of experience and a burning desire to succeed, but do you have (and are you willing to risk) the funds needed to get you through the first tough years? Do you really want to work the 12- to 15-hour days a new business usually requires?

Even more importantly, are you certain a market exists for your product or service? Every year, thousands of new businesses fail simply because there are too few customers. Market research is a sometimes costly, but always important, part of any new venture.

The next step is a business plan, including (first and foremost) a realistic projection of your cash flow needs. Don't forget to figure in the costs of promoting your new business: you can spend a fortune on equipment, inventory and a location—but if no one knows you're there, you probably won't survive.

You must also assess your own character: Are you truly a calculated risk taker and entrepreneur? What fun is retirement if you wind up lying awake at night worrying about your "new baby," the business? Perhaps one of the other alternatives to starting from scratch would suit your postretirement career a little better.

Buying a Business. One popular alternative to starting from zero is to use a portion of your lump-sum retirement assets to purchase a going concern—a business that has already weathered those first few turbulent years. But before you buy any business, make certain you understand its financial position inside and out. A business in decline can be a good value for a shrewd operator willing to put in the hours and capital needed to turn it around. Or it can simply turn out to be a white elephant in a bad part of the investment jungle. You might be buying a stable client base, or you could be saddled with unhappy customers who want you to fix the problems the old owner left behind.

If the business involves fixed assets, such as buildings, find out about property rights and easements and the potential for changing utility assessments. In other words, don't buy a business with your hard-earned nest egg until you are absolutely certain it's right for you.

Buying a Franchise. A good franchise, bought at the right price, can be your ticket to self-fulfillment and security; but it can also lead you to financial and emotional ruin.

Again, thorough research before you invest is vital. What are the terms of the franchise agreement? Are the sales quotas and other franchisee demands reasonable? Do you truly have a chance to build a stable business, or will your franchise fees simply make you the hard-working "employee" of a big company and victim of its lawyers? What protections exist to prevent revocation of your franchise at the whim of the franchiser? How much say does the franchiser have in how you staff and run your operation? And, most importantly, does the franchiser control or limit your compensation?

Buying a franchise doesn't exclude you from the need to do good market research and to develop a business plan. What works terrifically in other markets may fall flat on its face in your local area. The key idea behind franchising is to add your own value to someone else's good idea and resources, not to make the franchiser rich at your expense.

Starting a Home-Based Business. One way to limit your exposure to financial loss and control the hours you spend at work is through a home-based business, although it may be no less demanding than any other enterprise.

One of the first things anyone should think of when considering a home-based business is his or her personal tax situation.

Professional Advice

For years, declaring that you operated a home business was a good way to get another income tax deduction. But the IRS has tightened its regulations: now you can't declare a home office deduction unless you actually earn income from the enterprise. There are other restrictions, as well, and you should check with an accountant to see if what you have in mind qualifies.

Remember that having a home-based business may result in certain unanticipated expenses. You'll want insurance on your business equipment, and you need to insure yourself against personal injury liability in case a client or vendor is injured at your home or sues you for damages resulting from use of your products or services.

You must also understand zoning issues; be certain you have adequate parking, observe signage ordinances and residential business limitations; and secure all necessary local business licenses.

In short, opening a home business may give you better working hours and limit your potential for losses, but will not be without its own costs and potential hazards.

If you do choose to go into business for yourself, the Small Business Administration operates the Service Corps of Retired Executives (SCORE) to help entrepreneurs of almost every type get started. You can find their number in the phone directory under "U.S. Gov't./SBA/SCORE," or call 1-800-368-5855.

The Unhealthy Facts About Health Care

First, the good news: the odds against contracting a disease or disability that would require a lengthy stay in a nursing home or convalescent facility, or one that would require you to employ nursing care at home, are in your favor.

Now the bad news: if the need does arise for long-term health care, it will probably break you—unless you are very well off, or have had the foresight to buy long-term health care insurance or make other provisions specifically for this purpose.

Until a few years ago, you were most likely to be disabled by diseases such as strokes, cancer, and heart disease. But today, with the major advances medicine has made against crippling diseases, you are more likely simply to outlive your ability to care for yourself.

Accordingly, your chances of needing long-term health care increase dramatically with age. Just 5% of the population aged 65 to 84 live in nursing homes, but that number jumps to 22% of those 85 and older. An additional 20% is able to stay at home only with the assistance of nurses, housekeepers, and meal-delivery programs. And the expenses for even modest services are shocking. The best estimate is that over $50 billion will be spent on long-term health care annually, and that half of that amount will be paid for by the elderly themselves—and by their families.

For example, the average cost of nursing home care for a year is $25,000 to $30,000, and—like all important costs—rises with inflation. Half the couples over 65 with one spouse in a nursing home are impoverished within six months. Seventy percent of all single nursing home patients over 65 run out of money in just 13 weeks.

If you are fortunate enough to live at home, your care may range from $30 to $50 a day.

Medicare pays for only about 100 days of care per admission and less in many cases. It only covers care in skilled nursing homes. So-called Medigap policies also fail to cover long-term care in any significant way. When Medicare runs out, couples are forced to "spend down" their assets to the point of impoverishment. Then they are picked up by the state-run Medicaid system—"welfare" as it's known to most of us. When that happens, the patient can be moved to less expensive accommodations within the facility, or to another, less commodious facility altogether. Non-Profits by mission may have more charitable care.

How to Avoid Disaster

For most people, there are two ways to ensure against having to pay for long-term health care out-of-pocket: you may purchase long-term care insurance; or you may join a comprehensive life care facility.

A third option—specialized health maintenance organizations that include long-term care—is still underdeveloped, but as the population continues to age, prepaid long-term health plans will probably continue to grow.

Long-Term Health Insurance. In light of its tremendous future, as well as present demand, the insurance industry has developed comprehensive long-term health care coverage. As it stands now, 100 commercial carriers offer some form of long-term coverage. New products being developed include long-term care riders with life insurance policies.

Long-term care is defined as up to lifetime coverage in either a nursing home or in the home of the insured. A survey conducted by the Government Accounting Office disclosed that policy costs range from as low as $200 a year to as high as $7,000, depending on age, health condition, and coverage. If

you wait until you're 70 or older to buy coverage, you can plan on paying at least $1,000 a year; in most cases, a person nearing 80 shouldn't have to pay more than about $3,000 for a policy with good coverage. Average annual cost of long term health care insurance: age 50—$350/year; age 65—$1,000/year; age 80—$3,000/year.

Coverage options are changing virtually every week as the industry matures, but existing plans offer anywhere from six months to lifetime of coverage and pay up to $100 per day.

Unfortunately, almost all policies mandate a fixed per-day coverage limit. Some carriers are beginning to offer an inflation provision, but there is a surcharge for the option—usually amounting to about 1% additional cost per year for each additional 1% of benefits.

If you're willing to pay for a top-of-the-line policy, you will be paid benefits for an unlimited number of days for each nursing home stay and unlimited days for your cumulative stays. Less expensive policies limit the number of days per stay and the total number of days allowed cumulatively for all stays. To receive benefits for a repeat stay, you must in some cases have been out of a nursing home for at least 180 days.

Although insurance is regulated on a state-by-state basis, and not all policies are available in every state, a full range of options should exist wherever you live. If you opt for a long-term health care policy, the following guidelines can make the difference between a good policy and one that is bound to cost more than it pays.

1. Avoid policies that require hospitalization before benefits are paid. Some diseases, such as arthritis and Alzheimer's disease, may never require a hospital stay, but are as debilitating as any other serious problem.
2. Avoid policies that restrict the type of services covered. The best policies provide equivalent coverage for care at home, at an adult day-care center, or at a nursing home. Nursing home care should be provided in three categories: (1) in skilled homes where care is prescribed by a doctor and administered 24 hours a day; (2) in intermediate homes where you can re-

ceive rehabilitative therapy and less intensive nursing care; and (3) in custodial homes, which offer assistance with routine activities.

Coverage should not be skewed toward one form of care over the others, so as not to influence your choice of care. Be careful of policies that provide for all three types of care but limit the type of facility that may be used. Some policies exclude custodial care, which might not seem to be a major drawback, except that most patients need only limited amounts of skilled care, while recuperation requiring custodial care can stretch on for months. Home health care may be the wave of the future.

3. Avoid policies that carry exclusions for illnesses like "organic brain disease," which is insurance company language for Alzheimer's disease.

4. Avoid any policy that allows the company to cancel your insurance because of age or deteriorating health.

5. Avoid any policy that allows the company to raise your premiums unless it also raises the premiums of every other policyholder in your area.

6. Most policies mandate a waiting period, and benefits don't begin until the waiting period requirement has been satisfied. If you feel you can afford to select a longer waiting period, you may be able to cut your premiums by as much as 30%. Expect to serve a six-month waiting period before receiving benefits for any preexisting condition; companies are under no obligation to cover you for a preexisting condition or may choose to limit the coverage granted for treatment that results from the condition.

The waiting period provision is applied for each repeat nursing home stay.

7. Finally, you must decide between long-term coverage and coverage of a shorter duration. Statistically, many people die within a year of entering a nursing home, so in many cases benefits that extend beyond 12 months may be wishful thinking. On the other hand, if you contract a disabling disease that drags on, you will bless yourself for having had the foresight to buy the extra coverage. It's a gamble, true, but your previous health history and the health history of key family members may give you some clues about which policies may be right for you.

Long-term health care insurance is so new and so complex that even most agents are hard-pressed to understand all the details, so be certain that what you are promised is down in writing. Don't let an agent slide by with a vague promise or assurance that "everything is covered." At the end of this section, you'll find a list of publications with good information on long-term health care insurance.

The insurance industry is addressing the issue of long-term health care, and good solutions are now here and prior to age 50, many of these products will be tied to life insurance coverages. More new options will be available as state insurance commissioners approve them.

For more information on long-term care insurance and long-term care:

1. American Association of Homes for the Aging
1129 20th Street, N.W., Suite 400
   Washington, DC 20036
Telephone: 202-296-5960
Brochures describing continuing care retirement communities.

2. *Before You Buy: A Guide to Long-Term Care Insurance*
Single copies available free from the American Association of Retired Persons Health Advocacy Services
1909 K Street, N.W.
Washington, DC 20049
Telephone: 202-872-4700

3. American Health Care Association
1202 L Street, N.W.
Washington, DC 20005
Telephone: 202-842-4444
Various pamphlets about long-term care facilities.

4. Council of Better Business Bureaus
4200 Wilson Boulevard, Suite 800
Arlington, VA 22203
Telephone: 703-276-0100
Written materials on home care and nursing homes.

Long-Term Care Policy Checklist

Policy A Name: _____

The following checklist will help you compare policies you may be considering.   Policy B Name: _____

	Policy A	Policy B
1. What Serves are covered? ■ Skilled care ■ Intermediate care ■ Custodial care ■ Home health care ■ Other care		
2. How much does the policy pay per day for? ■ Skilled care ■ Intermediate care ■ Custodial care ■ Home health care ■ Other care		
3. Does the policy offer a means for increasing benefits to account for expected future costs? If so, how? Is there an additional Premium?		
4. Does the policy have a maximum lifetime benefit? If so, what is it? ■ Nursing home ■ Home health		
5. Does the policy have a maximum length of coverage per "spell of illness" of maximum benefit period? If so, what is it? ■ Nursing home ■ Home health		
6. How long do I have to wait before preexisting conditions are covered?		
7. Is Alzheimer's disease covered?		
8. How many days is the elimination or deductible period before benefits?		

9. Does this policy require:
■ Physician certification of need
■ A functional assessment
■ A prior hospital stay for
  ■ Nursing home care
  ■ Home health care
■ A prior nursing home stay for home health care
■ Other		

10. Can the policy be cancelled?		
11. Will the policy cover you if you move to another area?		
12. What is the age range of enrollment?		
13. What does the policy cost? ■ per month ■ per year		

Source: *The Consumer's Guide to Long-Term Care Insurance*, Health Insurance Association of America.

5. National Consumers League
   Suite 516
   815 15th Street, N.W.
   Washington, DC 20005
   Telephone: 202-639-8140
   Consumer's guide to life care communities has health and ambulatory fact sheets on Medicare.

6. Health Insurance Association of America
   1025 Connecticut Avenue, N.W.
   Washington, DC 20036-3998
   Telephone: 202-223-7780
   Pamphlet: *The Consumer's Guide to Long-Term Care Insurance*

ALERT: Actuaries calculate that by year 2000 more than eight million Americans will be 65 years old or older, an increase of 56% over 1980. As people live longer, the need for long-term medical care increases. New news for seniors is living benefits in life insurance policies. Watch for intensive marketing by insurers on policies known as: ASSURED CARE, CARETAKER, SAFEKEEPER and others. These life insurance policies provide for living benefits to pay for medical bills, or long-term care. Policies are not the same. Some are customized and you'll need some research to decide if they are for you. CONSUMER RESOURCE: Health Insurance Association of America.

Life Care Communities. For the price of a hefty entrance fee and additional monthly fees, older senior citizens can receive perpetual housing and health care at a life care community.

Life care communities have been rocked by fiscal mismanagement—about 40 communities closed their doors between 1975 and 1985—but the concept seems to have landed on its feet and now about 700 life care communities operate in 45 states, double the number in operation a decade ago.

Designed to cater to the needs of those 75 and older, life care communities offer a variety of living accommodations as well as several health care options.

You'll pay a hefty entrance fee, ranging from $29,000 for a studio apartment to more than $112,000 for a 2 bedroom apartment, and monthly fees of $700 to $1,100 per person, to live in an all-inclusive community. But in return you'll receive full medical and support services, including physical therapy, home care if you need it, and housekeeping. Most all-inclusive communities will refund a portion of your entrance fee if you leave, or turn it over to your estate on your death. There's a price for the privilege, however: entrance fees at refunding communities are typically twice those of nonrefunding communities.

You'll pay less to live at a community with a modified continuing care contract. Most charge an entry fee that ranges from $27,000 to $85,000, as well as a $650 to $750 monthly fee, for full residential and limited medical and support services. You may receive 50 or 60 days of nursing home care as part of your agreement, or a discount on the services of the community-owned nursing home.

Some communities offer a fee-for-services contract, in which residents buy apartment space and pay for medical and support services as needed. By combining a fee-for-service community with long-term care health coverage, you can create a cost-effective package of residential, medical, and support services. Expect to pay $21,000 to $56,000 in entry fees and monthly fees of $570 to $690.

Look At This:

Choosing the type of long-term care you'll need for the last years of your life can be one of the most important decisions you'll make. Before entering a life care community, be absolutely certain that it can do the things it promises to do. Understand your contract down to the fine points, and check out the fiscal stability of the organization. A life care community must provide you with a prospectus, actuarial reports, balance sheets, and financial statements. If you don't understand them, find someone who does. Consult with authorities at the local agencies on aging, the Better Business Bureau, your state's consumer protection office, and with current residents of the facility you're considering. Your state attorney general's office can inform you about regulations governing the financial operation of life care communities. You can't do too much homework; a mistake now could undo years of hard work and saving.

HOUSING CONSIDERATIONS

Take a moment to review these lists. They may help you make a more informed housing decision.

What Is Important to You?

	Very Important	Moderately Important	Not Very Important
1. Staying in your present home	☐	☐	☐
2. Living near your friends	☐	☐	☐
3. Living near your family	☐	☐	☐
4. Living near your place of worship	☐	☐	☐
5. Access to public transportation, stores, and community services	☐	☐	☐
6. Having home maintenance services available	☐	☐	☐
7. Privacy	☐	☐	☐
8. Keeping housing costs to a minimum	☐	☐	☐
9. Having in-home companionship	☐	☐	☐
10. Keeping your pets, your own furnishings, and other personal items	☐	☐	☐
11. Feeling secure in your home and neighborhood	☐	☐	☐
12. Living in a homelike environment	☐	☐	☐
13. Having numerous activities available to you	☐	☐	☐
14. Having a large amount of living space	☐	☐	☐
15. Knowing that health care services are readily available	☐	☐	☐

Assistance: Do You Need or Anticipate Needing Assistance with the Following?

	Now	Within 1 Year	Within 3 Years
1. Preparing meals	☐	☐	☐
2. Transportation	☐	☐	☐
3. Light housekeeping	☐	☐	☐
4. Medical care	☐	☐	☐
5. Bathing and personal care	☐	☐	☐
6. Home maintenance	☐	☐	☐
7. Getting around the house	☐	☐	☐
8. Overcoming loneliness or isolation	☐	☐	☐

Financial Considerations

1. What percent of your income do you currently spend on housing? (A general rule of thumb is that approximately 30% of one's gross income can be spent on housing, including utilities.) _____

2. Does the amount you presently spend on housing provide minimal, adequate, or comfortable accommodation? _____

3. What is your anticipated budget for housing over the next five years? _____

4. Do you expect your income to increase or decrease over the next five years? _____

5. Would you consider changing your housing arrangement to adjust to any change in income? _____

6. Would an arrangement that brought in rental income from an accessory apartment or a housesharer be worth the modification costs? _____

7. Would the financial benefits of living with others be worth adapting to a new living arrangement? _____

8. Would you be eligible for an arrangement that offers subsidized rents? (Income limitations vary across the country, so check with your local housing authority.) _____

9. If you need minimal health care services under a physician's care, have you considered the cost difference between home health care and moving into a nursing home? _____

10. What is the possibility of receiving Medicare, Medicaid, or private insurance reimbursement for any of the health care services that you need? _____

Decision Making

Keep the following questions in mind as you read through this chapter. When you have finished, you may want to refer back to this section for help in your decision making.

- What could force you to give up your present home?
- What would allow you to stay in your present home?

	Yes	No
1. Have you carefully reviewed all the options available to you?	☐	☐
2. Have you learned enough about the available providers in your community?	☐	☐
3. Have you talked to other older consumers about their experiences?	☐	☐
4. Have you discussed the options with members of your family? With friends?	☐	☐
5. Are you confident that the provider you have selected offers services that will meet your needs?	☐	☐
6. Have you determined the prospective costs and benefits of each housing option?	☐	☐
7. Is there a waiting period for the housing service you want, and, if so, when should you put your name on the waiting list?	☐	☐

Source: Reprinted with modifications from AARP Workbook, "Your Home, Your Choice," 1985.

The American Association of Homes for the Aging will provide you with a list of facilities that it has accredited. Write the association at 1129 20th St. NW, Suite 400, Washington, DC 20036, or call (202) 296-5960.

Housing Those Long-Term Dreams

Logic and emotion often tangle when making decisions about where you'd like to live out your senior years. For many people, moving from the family home is inconceivable.

"All my memories are here," says Mary, a spry 74-year-old whose two-story, four-bedroom family home is just now becoming too much to handle. "My family has lived in this house since it was built; I can't just sell it to strangers, but I don't want to end up like those old people who live in a corner of their house while the rest of it falls apart."

Like thousands of older Americans, Mary has to make some hard decisions about housing. Her house on the outskirts of a small city in the Northeast has been appraised at more than $175,000; in a strong real estate market, she could make enough from the sale of her home to live comfortably for the rest of her life. Although she lives rent free, staying in the family home might become a real problem—and a real hazard—as she grows older.

Fortunately, Mary is healthy and still capable of making a sound decision. But in too many cases, decisions about housing are put on hold until a crisis arises, until keeping up the old house has depleted existing resources, or until someone who cares finally realizes that the house is simply too much for the older person to cope with.

Fortunately, there are numerous housing options for seniors. Planning at an early age to make the right choices later can help you take advantage of the choices that are right for you.

How to Make a Smart Decision. The American Association of Retired Persons in cooperation with the Federal Trade Commission has prepared a helpful booklet, "Your Home, Your Choice," which includes an excellent set of questionnaires designed to help

you make a logical decision about housing.

The accompanying checklist is reprinted with modifications from "Your Home, Your Choice," which is available by writing the AARP, Consumer Affairs—Program Department, 1909 K Street, NW, Washington, DC 20049.

Selling the Family Home. Many retirees discover that the family home is their key to financial stability. Often the mortgage is paid in full, and the home has increased in value. By selling, they are left with enough cash to move into a smaller place and salt some away in safe, income-producing investments.

"We did a study a few years ago and we found that 80% of the older population own their own homes," said AARP's Jim Thompson. "And 70% of them own them debt-free. The value of the home equity that they sit on is tremendous."

The average equity of homes owned by older citizens is said to be about $50,000—that's a lot of buying power. But because they live on fixed incomes, most senior citizens don't qualify for home equity loans—so in order to capitalize on that equity they must sell.

The experts say that's usually the best bet even if you have enough income to live comfortably without selling the house. The costs in time and energy of maintaining a home can take a heavy toll on the resources of a senior citizen.

Before you decide to sell in order to trade down, it's wise to consider several factors. First among them, of course, is the amount of profit you anticipate making in the trade. Sometimes you can't make enough to make the trade worthwhile. Don't forget to factor in the reduced costs of maintenance and utilities of a smaller home.

There are tax considerations, too. People 55 or older can exclude from taxes up to $125,000 of the capital gain from the sale of a house. If the gain exceeds $125,000, the balance can be deferred by investing in a new home. You must have lived in the home for a total of three of the last five years in order to claim the exclusion, however. There's an exception—if an owner is moved to a state licensed care facility (including a nursing home) and the home is sold after September 30, 1988, the seller will qualify for the $125,000 inclusion if he or she has used the residence for at least *one* of the *prior* five years.

You should try to pay cash for the new house or keep your mortgage payments as low as possible. Don't put all your cash into a home, though—you need to set aside enough to cover emergencies.

Senior citizens who must borrow for a new home are well advised to stay away from variable-rate mortgages: when you're on a fixed income, an increase in mortgage payments can spell trouble.

Some people have discovered that they can facilitate a transaction by loaning the buyer of their home part of the purchase price. Interest payments on the loan pay better than an equivalent amount of cash in conservative investments. A word of caution: be sure to get at least a 20% down payment to protect your principal if the buyer defaults. A down payment of that size will help ensure that the purchaser, in fact, doesn't take a walk.

If you don't want to burden yourself with the cares of another house, renting can be a good option for senior citizens. You probably won't do as well financially in the long run, but renting can be ideal for people who want cash for traveling, entertainment, and other lifestyle expenses.

If your choice is to stay at home, but you don't think you can afford it, a number of creative financing solutions are possible.

Reverse Mortgages and Term Reverse Mortgages. Under the terms of a reverse mortgage, the homeowner borrows a monthly income that is paid back by the estate when the homeowner moves or dies. With the most popular reverse mortgage, the Individual Reverse Mortgage Account (IRMA), the lender receives a portion or all the value of your home, plus appreciation earned during the term of the loan.

If you outlive your statistical life expectancy, the total of the loan may exceed the value of the house. On the other hand, if you die shortly after taking the loan, your estate must repay the lender for the monthly checks you received, plus interest and appreciation.

"Reverse mortgages are home equity con-

version, as opposed to home equity loans, and that's an important distinction that has to be made," Jim Thompson has said. "Reverse mortgages have great potential and they're being written with all the right consumer protections."

Thompson says that although reverse mortgages are the wave of the future, "Only about 1,500 reverse mortgages have been written in the country; the financial institutions are not buying into the idea because it is a strange animal to them."

Thompson feels that a demonstration project planned by the Department of Housing and Urban Development will do for reverse mortgages what a similar project did for the 30-year mortgage years ago.

A term reverse mortgage pays a monthly amount for a fixed period of time, usually seven years, at which time the loan must be repaid. This generally makes sense only in certain cases, such as when a senior citizen is on a waiting list for a nursing home or care community and needs additional monthly income temporarily.

Sale-Leasebacks. Money seems to go in a circle in a sale-leaseback agreement, and that, in effect, is just what it does. The homeowner sells the home to a buyer who makes a down payment of 10% to 20% and agrees to make monthly payments for a fixed period of time, often 15 years. The seller becomes a renter, and pays the buyer a monthly rent.

Unfortunately, the income to the seller/renter remains constant, while the rent may increase. It's wise to invest at least a portion of the down payment in a safe, income-producing product that will help offset rent increases and give you some safety in the event that you outlive the mortgage.

Many older people arrange sale-leaseback arrangements with family members, but your local bar association or real estate board should also be able to help you find a willing investor.

Giving It All Away. Many charitable organizations will accept your house as a gift and compensate you with a lifetime annuity. You own the house until you die, at which time it becomes the property of the organization.

House Sharing. Mary, the 74-year-old in our earlier example, finally hit on a simple solution to her problem: she found someone with whom to share her home.

"We hit it off right away," Mary said. "Jill is 10 years younger than me, and just loves to do the gardening that hurts my back so. She's also a wonderful cook, and we've had a great time showing off our recipes to each other."

House sharing is an increasingly common solution for older people who would prefer not to leave their homes but aren't able to go it alone any longer. Obviously, many personal issues need to be carefully considered— living with a roommate can be a tricky business after years of being alone or living with a spouse—but when it works, everybody wins.

Accessory Apartments. Accessory apartments are an elaboration on the house-sharing theme. Many older homes can easily be modified to create a separate living space that can be rented out. Legal and zoning limitations may affect your plans, and you must think carefully about whether you really want to be a landlord, but accessory apartments have enabled many a senior citizen to stay put.

For those who are simply unable for whatever reasons to remain at home, a number of options exist short of nursing homes.

Elderly Cottage Housing Opportunity. Elderly Cottage Housing Opportunity (ECHO) is a program in which special zoning variances are granted enabling a family to put a portable building behind its house for an elderly or disabled relative. Generally, the variance has a termination date, because the intent of the program is to provide temporary housing for semidependent family members.

Board and Care Homes. Distinguished from standard boarding homes because of the personal services they provide, board and care homes can be a good compromise between the independence of living alone and the more restrictive conditions of other live-in facilities. Known also as "sheltered housing" and "residential care facilities," board and care homes usually include room, board, utilities, housekeeping, and laundry for a monthly fee. Many homes provide additional services, such as bathing and grooming, for an additional fee. Meals often are shared, and many homes try to provide for social, recreational, and personal needs.

Staff members take personal responsibility for tenants, and check in regularly to see how things are going. Board and care homes often strive for an intimate, family-like atmosphere.

Licensing requirements vary from state to state, so in some states you may encounter considerable diversity in the quality of care, cleanliness, and safety and health standards.

Congregate Housing. Congregate housing provides a more intense level of personal service; the staff of these facilities often includes social workers, counselors, and nutritionists. Services may include housekeeping, transportation to shopping, and other activities and entertainment. Meals generally are provided, although many facilities may include kitchenettes so tenants can prepare their own light meals.

Rates often are subsidized by federal programs, and most congregate care facilities are sponsored by nonprofit organizations or government agencies.

SUMMING UP

Art Linkletter titled his popular book *Old Age Is Not for Sissies,* and he's right. Aging can be tough. It takes foresight, wisdom, and lots of good planning to make your senior years golden. Learning to deal with the ins and outs of senior jobs, health care, and financing is a task requiring a flexible mind and plenty of patience—but the consequence of good planning can be a very good life.

And, once you've arrived comfortably in your later years, the trick is to figure out how to preserve what you so carefully have accumulated to meet your long-term needs and perhaps pass along to those you love the most. That's called estate planning, and it's the subject of another—and very important—chapter.

CHAPTER 8

ESTATE PLANNING

A GLANCE AHEAD

A lifetime of careful planning and wise investing can be seriously compromised by a failure to plan for the efficient distribution of your estate. The tax collector will gladly take from your heirs any amount you leave unprotected. In this chapter, you'll discover

- *The importance of estate planning to your wealth-building and wealth-preserving plan*
- *The tools available for the orderly transfer of wealth*
- *The tax consequences of the estate-planning techniques you choose.*

ESTATE PLANNING SHOWS YOU CARE

The primary purpose of estate planning is to pass your wealth on to your heirs while minimizing tax liabilities and saving them the burden of making troublesome (and often costly) decisions after your death.

If you die without a will, your heirs' inheritances will be determined by state law. Your assets will be divided according to a pre-arranged formula that may not reflect your wishes at all. Normally, one-half to two-thirds will be given to your children, the remainder to your spouse. There are no provisions for your favorite charities, your church, or to those close friends you may care to remember.

And simply writing a will is not enough if you want to protect the interests of children, a disabled dependent, or anyone who is not likely to manage effectively the assets you leave behind. Today, a variety of trust plans are available that give you a say in how your assets are used following your death— and they're not just for the very rich.

Finally, it helps to know the ins and outs of estate tax law, for when it comes time to settle your estate, unless you have done some careful homework, the process of probate will virtually eat your assets alive. If your estate is valued at $600,000 or more, estate taxes start at 37%. (Don't laugh: with the equity in your house, your life insurance policies, retirement benefits, any business interests, and your investment portfolio, you'll see that $600,000 isn't really so high.) The graduated rate swells to a frightening 55% on estates of $3 million or better (see Figure 8-1). You don't have to be among the ranks of the patricians to see how a little estate planning now can go a long way toward conserving your holdings when it counts the most.

Put them all together, and you end up with an estate plan through which your assets are distributed in an orderly, efficient fashion—and in exactly the way that you want them distributed.

WILLS AND WILL SUBSTITUTES

Seven of 10 adults have life insurance, but only three of 10 have wills. Even many lawyers don't have wills! For some, it's

UNIFIED GIFT AND ESTATE TAX RATE SCHEDULE
(Decedents Dying and Gifts Made in 1984-1992)

(A) Amount Subject to Tax Equal to or more Than—	(B) Amount Subject to Tax Less Than—	(C) Tax on Amount in Column A*	(D) Rate of Tax on Excess over Amount in Column A %*
$ 0	$ 10,000	....	18
10,000	20,000	$ 1,800	20
20,000	40,000	3,800	22
40,000	60,000	8,200	24
60,000	80,000	13,000	26
80,000	100,000	18,200	28
100,000	150,000	23,800	30
150,000	250,000	38,800	32
250,000	500,000	70,800	34
500,000	750,000	155,800	37
750,000	1,000,000	248,300	39
1,000,000	1,250,000	345,800	41
1,250,000	1,500,000	448,300	43
1,500,000	2,000,000	555,800	45
2,000,000	2,500,000	780,800	49
2,500,000	3,000,000	1,025,800	53
3,000,000	....	1,290,800	55

* Before credits and phaseout of graduated rates.

Figure 8-1   Estate Tax Rate Schedule (1984-1992)

one way of refusing to confront mortality. For others, making a will just seems like a lot of unnecessary trouble and expense.

In the parlance of wills, the word *probate* means "prove." The process of probate is designed to assure that your will is valid and that your property is distributed according to your wishes.

Most states have passed probate simplification legislation in recent years, making it easier for family members to handle probate by themselves. Fortunately, making a will is a simple thing and a will that resolves even a single family

Money Management Tip

dispute may be worth its weight in gold, let alone the relatively few legal hours it costs to prepare. Dying without a will —"intestate"—leaves your estate open to dispute. (See Figure 8-2.) This means beneficiary wrangling in the worst cases, and confusion and ambiguity in the rest.

A will is simply a legal statement describing how you want your assets distributed at your death. It names your beneficiaries (those who are to receive your assets) and an executor (a person who has agreed to act on the behalf of your estate).

Most families feel they can get by without a will because of the laws of joint ownership. But in a childless marriage, for exam-

PROBATE COMMISSION
(Based on Value of Estate)

First 15,000	4%		
15,000 to 100,000	3%	Example of $500,000 estate:	
100,000 to 1,000,000	2%	Attorney	$11,150
1,000,000 to 10,000,000	1%	Executor	$11,150
10,000,000 to 25,000,000	0.5%	Total	$22,300
over 25,000,000	Set by court		

The above schedules apply to both attorney's fees and Executor fees.

Figure 8-2 The Consequences of Dying "Intestate"

Man Dies Leaving (His property if he makes no will goes to →)	COMMUNITY Property States					SEPARATE Property States				
	His wife	His only child	His children	His parent or parents	His brothers and sisters	His wife	His only child	His children	His parent or parents	His brothers and sisters
Wife and child	All	None				Half	Half		None	None
Wife and children	All		None	None	None	One-third		Two-thirds	None	None
Wife no children but parents	All			None	None	Half			Half	None
Wife no children no parents	All				None	Half				Half
Wife no children no immediate family	All					All				
No wife but children	No Community Property							All		
No wife no children but parents	No Community Property								All	
No wife no children no parents	No Community Property									All
No wife no children	See Probate Code Section					See Probate Code Section (Property from a Predeceased Spouse)				

ple, an estate that passes to a wife on the death of her husband may pass automatically to her family at her death, leaving the husband's family with nothing.

When the parents of minor children die intestate, the family's property is divided among those children, but the court appoints the guardians who will determine, with the approval of the court, how and when the estate is to be spent on behalf of the children. Without a will, the parents have no say in the matter. A guardian represents the child's interests in court, but may be insensitive to the priorities of the parents. In some cases, a court will direct the children to live with relatives in another state, although the parents would have preferred to have their children remain in the community with friends.

A will also protects older people who may rely on younger members of their family to take care of legal and bookkeeping chores. Without a will, the person who has been kind enough to manage an elder's finances may confiscate those assets upon the elder's death. A suit may be filed, but if the estate is worth only a few thousand dollars, it's hardly worth the time and effort.

These examples show the many unexpected twists and turns that state probate laws may take. It's best to hire a lawyer to prepare your will; from experience, he or she knows how to protect your interests against unforeseeable problems. A couple with relatively straightforward requirements can expect to pay from $200 to $400 for a pair of wills. The few extra dollars you may spend today could be worth a fortune to your heirs.

At the very least, you should write up a "holographic" will. Written in your own hand, dated, and signed by you, a holographic will is legally inferior to the "real thing" (more difficult to enforce if contested), but offers some hope, at least, that your estate will be dealt with as you see fit. A "holographic" will may not be legal if it isn't witnessed by two legal age adults. State laws

HOW LONG WILL YOU LIVE?
1980 Commissioners Standard Ordinary Mortality Table
(Life expectancy, years)

Age	Male	Female	Age	Male	Female	Age	Male	Female	Age	Male	Female
0	70.83	75.83	25	47.84	52.34	50	25.36	29.53	75	8.31	10.32
1	70.13	75.04	26	46.93	51.40	51	24.52	28.67	76	7.84	9.71
2	69.20	74.11	27	46.01	50.46	52	23.70	27.82	77	7.40	9.12
3	68.27	73.17	28	45.09	49.52	53	22.89	26.98	78	6.97	8.55
4	67.34	72.23	29	44.16	48.59	54	22.08	26.14	79	6.57	8.01
5	66.40	71.28	30	43.24	47.65	55	21.29	25.31	80	6.18	7.48
6	65.46	70.34	31	42.31	46.71	56	20.51	24.49	81	5.80	6.98
7	64.52	69.39	32	41.38	45.78	57	19.74	23.67	82	5.44	6.49
8	63.57	68.44	33	40.46	44.84	58	18.99	22.86	83	5.09	6.03
9	62.62	67.48	34	39.54	43.91	59	18.24	22.05	84	4.77	5.59
10	61.66	66.53	35	38.61	42.98	60	17.51	21.25	85	4.46	5.18
11	60.71	65.58	36	37.69	42.05	61	16.79	20.44	86	4.18	4.80
12	59.75	64.62	37	36.78	41.12	62	16.08	19.65	87	3.91	4.43
13	58.80	63.67	38	35.87	40.20	63	15.38	18.86	88	3.66	4.09
14	57.86	62.71	39	34.96	39.28	64	14.70	18.08	89	3.41	3.77
15	56.93	61.76	40	34.05	38.36	65	14.04	17.32	90	3.18	3.45
16	56.00	60.82	41	33.16	37.46	66	13.39	16.57	91	2.94	3.15
17	55.09	59.87	42	32.26	36.55	67	12.76	15.83	92	2.70	2.85
18	54.18	58.93	43	31.38	35.66	68	12.14	15.10	93	2.44	2.55
19	53.27	57.98	44	30.50	34.77	69	11.54	14.38	94	2.17	2.24
20	52.37	57.04	45	29.62	33.88	70	10.96	13.67	95	1.87	1.91
21	51.47	56.10	46	28.76	33.00	71	10.39	12.97	96	1.54	1.56
22	50.57	55.16	47	27.90	32.12	72	9.84	12.26	97	1.20	1.21
23	49.66	54.22	48	27.04	31.25	73	9.30	11.60	98	0.84	0.84
24	48.75	53.28	49	26.20	30.39	74	8.79	10.95	99	0.50	0.50

CHECKLIST TO HELP YOUR LAWYER
WRITE YOUR WILL

1.   Your legal name.
2.   Address of your permanent residence—if you have more than one, give the address of each residence and the time spent there.
3.   The date and place of your birth.
4.   Your Social Security number.
5.   Your spouse's name, date, and place of marriage and place where marriage license is kept—name of former spouse if previously married.
6.   If you are divorced, give place, whether the divorce was contested, who brought the action. Give all the details of a separate agreement or court action.
7.   Give a copy of a prenuptial agreement if you entered into one.
8.   List the names, addresses, and ages of your immediate relatives. Indicate if they are incompetent.
9.   List the names and addresses of others you intend to make beneficiaries.
10. If you are the beneficiary under a trust, show the document to the lawyer.
11. Do you have a power of appointment under someone's will or trust? Explain.
12. Give the name and address of your accountant.
13. State the place where copies of your income tax and gift tax returns are kept. Give the name of the tax preparer, if any.
14. Name and address of your employer—do you have an employment contract or special agreement? Explain.
15. Are you entitled to a pension, profit-sharing plan, stock options, any other employment benefits? Explain.
16. List life insurance policies:
     a. Owned by you on your life
     b. Owned by others on your life
     c. Owned by you on lives of others
     d. Annuity policies, names of beneficiaries, loans if any.
17. Do you own real estate? State present value, your cost basis, mortgages if any, and whether you own property yourself or jointly with someone else.
18. List your assets showing the respective values and cost basis.
19. List all debts owed to you and the nature of the debt.
20. List amount of your debts to others, give names and addresses of persons to whom you are indebted.
21. Make a list of the names and addresses of those persons you wish to serve as executors, trustees, guardians.

Used through the courtesy of Paul Pennington, CFP, Sacramento, CA.

vary on the acceptibility of a hand-written will.

Will Substitutes. Certain legal arrangements—particularly property titles—have the effect of becoming "will substitutes." For instance, by holding property under "joint tenancy with right of survivorship," you are guaranteed that your property will pass directly to your spouse, or other beneficiary, without probate.

Virtually all states have adopted "community property" legislation, or some equivalent thereof. Community property statutes deem each spouse as equal partners in jointly owned property; under the provisions of most states, ownership normally passes to one spouse at the death of the other, although one partner may will his or her share to heirs.

In "severalty" states, where there is no community property, "tenancy by entirety" provisions limit each spouse's right of ownership to just half the estate. Both partners must agree if the property is to be sold, and it must be sold in its entirety. On the death of one spouse, his or her survivor receives the entire title.

"Tenancy in common" is an ownership arrangement that may involve a husband and wife, or any other group of people. Each co-owner has individual title to his or her undivided interest (equal right of possession), and may pass on the interest separately. Should any co-owner die, his or her interest in the property must pass by will to the heirs, unless there is no right of survivorship.

Husbands and wives are most often the partners in a "joint tenancy" agreement. Although any number of people may use the strategy, its major purpose is to create an iron-clad agreement that jointly owned property will bypass probate, bypass your will, and pass to the surviving partner. Although all joint tenants have equal ownership and rights of possession, there is only one title to the property. When one co-owner conveys his or her interest, the joint tenancy is broken (except when the property is community property and joint tenancy is a legal convenience) and is replaced by a tenancy in common with the new purchaser. When a joint tenant dies, the surviving spouse (or other

joint tenants) gains the property automatically by right of survivorship.

Joint tenancy is often used by couples who own real estate, and is very useful when

Look At This: the estate is relatively small. It provides for the smooth transfer of ownership and helps cut estate administrative costs and state inheritance taxes. The surviving spouse takes immediate control of the asset, which, if it had been used to secure the deceased spouse's debts, may not be seized by creditors.

But if the joint tenant is not a spouse, a gift tax may be levied on the transfer of the property. Also, the decedent may not dispose of the property in any other way, despite the provisions of his or her will. In some cases, estate executors have faced cash shortages because much of the property was tied up in joint tenancy arrangements, and couldn't be sold.

Finally, joint tenancy subjects the property to double taxation (once at the first spouse's death and again at the death of the second spouse). Because the surviving spouse gains title to the property, and not a trust, the property will be taxed again as part of his or her estate.

CHOOSING YOUR EXECUTOR

The executor of your will is more than a ceremonial office holder. The person you choose should have good judgment and some experience with financial matters. An executor's tasks are many and varied, and run from such simple duties as taking inventory of your safe deposit box and obtaining your income tax and canceled check records for the past three years, to making some very substantial decisions about the valuation and tax elections of your estate.

Your executor should either be a responsible member of the family or a professional, such as a lawyer, accountant, or financial adviser. If no suitable family member is available, or if there is contention or rivalry among family members, it's better to avoid the potential for conflict and go outside the family. Some who leave large estates select co-executors representing each specialty. If you select professionals, you should expect to pay between 3% and 5% of the estate value for their services.

Naming your spouse as the executor of your will subjects him or her to having to make legal and financial decisions in the wake of your death—a difficult time for loved ones to make objective, pragmatic decisions. This is especially true when a closely held business is involved; and business, as the saying goes, is business. It must proceed as usual, without missing tax deadlines, payrolls, or income-generating operations on which the family depends.

Acting as executor of a will also carries legal responsibilities. A nonprofessional who decides to settle a tax payment out of the proceeds of the estate, but mistakenly forgets to pay, will be personally liable for all charges, including penalties and interest, when the IRS comes to collect. And if the spouse who acts as executor elects not to collect a fee, which would be taxable income, the IRS may assign one anyway and levy a tax against a portion of the normally tax-free inheritance.

Family members commonly make other mistakes as well. Many widows move at their husband's death and destroy their husband's records. If the IRS chooses to audit the estate, the widow might face criminal action for destroying tax records.

Whomever you select as your executor, make sure he or she understands the job's scope and nature before naming that person in your will. And designate a substitute on the off chance that the person you select may die, is incapacitated, or otherwise turns out to be unable to perform his or her responsibilities.

Should none of your executors be able to do the job, the court will assign an executor who likely will have no interest in your estate other than the fees it will generate. It's often best, then, to name a law firm to back up your primary and alternate executors.

ARE YOUR HEIRS PROTECTED?

Among your major estate-planning goals are the security and well-being of your heirs. Simply creating a will and naming an executor is no guarantee that all the decisions made will be in the best interests of those you love.

A trust is a tool that allows you to create a pool of inheritance assets that can only be used in the way you dictate. In some cases, the assets in a trust become the property of your heirs and are no longer taxed as part of your estate. In all cases, a trust can protect your heirs from the mismanagement of their funds, either by you, by the courts, or by themselves.

A trustee, appointed by you, is responsible for watching over the trust and making sure that your wishes are carried out.

Most people make the mistake of thinking that trusts are the exclusive domain of the wealthy, but anyone with assets to pass on—particularly to children or others who are unable or unlikely to make good decisions—can establish a trust for as little as $250.

There are two basic types of trusts: *inter-vivos* (or living) trusts, and *testamentary* trusts. A testamentary trust is created by your will and comes into being on your death; a living trust operates while you are alive.

Living trusts come in two forms: revocable and irrevocable. You maintain control of a revocable trust: you may cancel it, change its provisions, and in some cases serve as its trustee. You even get to keep the income it produces. But because the assets within the trust remain under your control, they remain part of your estate and are taxed as such, although they escape certain estate administration costs and bypass probate. Trusts are useful when you would like a capable, discreet third party to manage your assets, even after your death or disability.

You may not alter or terminate an irrevocable trust. The property is legally transferred to your heirs and is out of your control. It is no longer part of your estate and is excluded from estate tax calculations, although you may pay a gift tax on the assets when you establish the trust.

THE LIVING WILL

Thirty-eight states and the District of Columbia (see list below) have passed laws authorizing residents to provide instructions to family and physicians about what should be done, or not done, in the event they are unable to make or communicate a decision about their medical treatment. These instructions have become known as The Living Will. They are concerned with the extent of treatment when a person is terminally ill. It does not always provide the ultimate solution to the question of medical procedure during these difficult times, but can help medical personnel and family.

It can help a family group with different feelings and impressions of how the ill member of the family feels about death. It helps the physician know the ill member's wishes.

The living will is usually for just one medical treatment decision, but can be extended to designate the disposition of vital organs after death as well. The sample living will gives some idea of what they are like as a document. They need not be complicated, but you should use an attorney in any legal matter for advice.

Two organizations will give you information about your specific state: Concern for the Dying, 250 W. 57th St., New York, NY 10107 (telephone: 212-246-6962), and Society for the Right to Die, 250 W. 57th St., New York, NY 10107 (telephone 212-246-6973).

The Living Will is not always adhered to by hospitals and some states don't recognize it. However, most advisors agree that it is better to leave such instructions than to have nothing at all. It's recommended that you give copies to your lawyer, clergyman, and the person to whom you give your power of attorney. The living will can be revoked easily at any time.

States Permitting Living Wills

The following have some form of law authorizing a patient to make his or her own decision about dying:

Alabama	Illinois	North Carolina
Alaska	Indiana	Oklahoma
Arizona	Iowa	Oregon
Arkansas	Kansas	South Carolina
California	Louisiana	Tennessee
Colorado	Maine	Texas
Connecticut	Maryland	Utah
Delaware	Mississippi	Vermont
District of Columbia	Missouri	Virgina
Florida	Montana	Washington
Georgia	Nevada	West Virginia
Hawaii	New Hampshire	Wisconsin
Idaho	New Mexico	Wyoming

If your state has a living will law, we recommend that you obtain information about it. Otherwise, you might want to use the form printed on page 113.

Courtesy: Modern Maturity magazine.

Living Will
DECLARATION

Declaration made this day of _____ 198____

I, _____, being of sound mind, willfully and voluntarily make known my desires that my dying shall not be artificially prolonged under the circumstances set forth below, and do declare:

If at any time I should have an incurable injury, disease, or illness certified to be a terminal condition by two (2) physicians who have personally examined me, one of whom shall be my attending physician, and the physicians have determined that my death will occur whether or not life-sustaining procedures are utilized and where the application of life-sustaining procedures would serve only to prolong artificially the dying process, I direct that such procedures be withheld or withdrawn, and that I be permitted to die naturally with only the administration of medication or the performance of any medical procedure deemed necessary to provide me with comfort, care, or to alleviate pain.

In the absence of my ability to give directions regarding the use of such life-sustaining procedures, it is my intention that this declaration shall be honored by my family and physician(s) as the final expression of my legal right to refuse medical or surgical treament and accept the consequences from such refusal.

I understand the full import of this declaration and I am emotionally and mentally competent to make this declaration.

Signed _____

Address _____

I believe the declarant to be of sound mind. I did not sign the declarant's signature above for or at the direction of the declarant. I am at least 18-years of age and am not related to the declarant by blood or marriage, entitled to any portion of the estate of the declarant according to the laws of interstate succession of the _____

or under any will of the declarant or codicil thereto, or directly financially responsible for declarant's medical care. I am not the declarant's attending physician, or an employee of the health facility in which the declarant is a patient.

Witness _____

Address _____

Witness _____

Address _____

Before me, the undersigned authority, on this ____ day of _____ 198 _ personally appeared _____ and _____ , known to me to be the Declarant and the witness, respectively, whose names are signed to the foregoing instrument, and who, in the presence of each other, did subscribe their names to the attached Declaration (Living Will) on this date, and that said Declarant at the time of execution of said Declaration was over the age of eighteen (18) years and of sound mind.

[Notary Public Seal]

My commission expires:

_____
Notary Public

Check requirements of individual state statute.

SAMPLE FORM IS FROM *A MATTER OF CHOICE*, PREPARED FOR THE U.S. SENATE SPECIAL COMMITTEE ON AGING.

YOUR WILL NEEDS TO BE AMENDED IF...

Use this checklist to determine if a material change affects your estate planning and you need to see your attorney for a will review:

____ Review of will has not been done for at least twelve months.

____ You have not "signed" and "executed" your will or trust documents.

____ You want to change the dollar or assets given to beneficiaries.

____ You want to remove a beneficiary.

____ Change in life insurance to surviving spouse or change in income amount.

____ Change in your marital status of yourself or another beneficiary.

____ New birth in your family.

____ Change in health since last review.

____ Change in guardian, trustee, or executor designations.

____ Will was written prior to 1981.

____ Change in residency…new state laws may apply.

____ Change in type of property bequested.

____ Add new successor guardian or trustee.

____ New property purchased or acquired in another state other than home state.

____ New tax law changes since the last review.

____ You are more successful and a simple will may not be adequate estate planning.

____ Assets are illiquid and the estate faces problems with cash.

____ Other personal concerns that affect planning and your will.

If you have checked any of the above, call your attorney and review your documentation. Your financial planner should be included in the update process as titling and beneficiaries are very important to estate planning and need to be considered at this time.

LIFE INSURANCE
AS AN ESTATE BENEFIT

Many of us like to joke about life insurance salespeople, but few financial service professionals have done more to get people to think— and do something—about the far end of life's cycle.

Money Management Tip

For the sake of your heirs, make insurance planning an integral part of your estate-planning process—even if you have sufficient assets to ensure the long-term well-being of your loved ones, insurance proceeds can provide them with ready cash on your death and in many cases it is income and estate tax free.

But the primary purpose of any type of life insurance is to replace your income when you are gone. Figure 8-3 shows a tool commonly used by financial planners to determine the amount of insurance required to replace the income of a family's primary wage earner: a Survivor Estate Capital Needs Analysis. This tool provides a systematic method of calculating assets and expenses to determine the needs of survivors. As you can see, certain assumptions must be made when buying insurance even though they may prove later to be a little (or a lot) off base. One shouldn't, for example, assume that a young wife will remarry, or that her income will be sufficient to continue to make the mortgage payments, although these events may, in fact, occur. Insurance is a defensive tool; it should be considered a safe harbor for your survivors.

This Survivor Estate Capital Needs Analysis was developed for Dave, 35, and Carol, 32, and their two young children, Paul and Ashley. If Dave were to die next week, Carol could plan on having the children at home for another 17 years, at which point she would be 49. Since Carol anticipates working until she is 62, a period of 13 years will lapse between the time the youngest child leaves home and Carol retires. Assuming a life expectancy of 78 based on actuarial information, Carol must provide for 16 years of post-retirement income.

Carol feels she would need a monthly income of $4,000 to support herself and the children until they are ready to leave home. Social Security will pay monthly survivor's benefits of $1,586 for the 15-year period while both children are dependents, and $1,058 for the two years when just Ashley is at home. Carol earns $1,800 a month as an executive secretary, leaving a monthly income shortfall of $614 while both children are at home, and $1,142 when Dave's Social Security benefits end.

When the youngest child leaves home, Carol feels her monthly income needs will fall to $3,500, but, without Social Security payments, her income shortage will actually rise, to $1,700. At retirement, her needs will continue to decrease but her income will be cut dramatically.

By annualizing those numbers, we can see that Carol will need a total of $347,291 to compensate for the loss of Dave's income. Plus, she must consider additional capital requirements, such as the cost of Dave's funeral, an education fund for the kids, $5,600 worth of debts, and an emergency reserve of $10,000. Ideally, insurance coverage should also pay off the mortgage which, in Dave and Carol's case, totals $38,000.

Carol has a total capital need of $495,891, which is offset by about $36,000 in liquid assets and Dave's IRA, and a $100,000 insurance policy on Dave's life.

Bottom line: it's clear that Dave will need to purchase additional insurance with survivor's benefits paying $359,571 to insure Carol adequately in the case of his death.

Try this exercise for yourself and see if your coverage is truly in line with your needs. You may be pleasantly—or unpleasantly!—surprised by what you find.

Income Capital Needed:	Two or more children	One child	Pre-retirement	After retiring
Number of years	15	2	13	16
Income desired	$ 4,000	$ 4,000	$ 3,500	$ 3,200
Less: Social Security	1,586	1,058	0	1,058
Employment/etc.	1,800	1,800	1,800	0
Income shortage	$ 614	$ 1,142	$ 1,700	$ 2,142
Capital required *	$ 88,911	$ 16,825	$ 130,711	$ 110,844

Total income capital required for income shortage.............................. $ 347,291

Plus immediate capital requirements:

Final expenses..................................	$	5,000
Emergency reserves..........................		10,000
Education fund.................................		90,000
Debts...		5,600
Taxes...		0
Mortgages..		38,000

Total immediate capital requirements.................................... $ 148,600

Total survivor capital required... $ 495,891

Present assets available......................	$	34,320
Insurance cash value net of loans..........		0
Retirement plan death benefit..............		2,000

Less capital available... $ (36,320)

Shortage to be provided by life insurance.. $ 459,571

Existing personal insurance................	$ 100,000	
(excluding cash value)		
Existing group life insurance..............	0	

$(100,000)

Less existing life insurance death benefits.. $ 359,571

Net additional life insurance coverage needed...

OR

0

Surplus life insurance coverage at this time...

Assuming earnings on investment capital of 9% with an annual inflation rate of 5.00%

Figure 8-3 Survivor Estate Capital Needs Analysis for Dave and Carol Hern

BLUNTING THE TAX COLLECTOR'S BITE

Your estate is vulnerable to two kinds of financial attacks at your death: probate costs and taxes. The probate process manages the distribution of your estate and covers only the assets that are in your name, and that pass through your estate's executor and the courts. Life insurance proceeds, assets in a living trust, and jointly owned property all bypass the probate process and go directly to your heirs.

Taxable assets include all property in your name, large gifts made during your lifetime, the face value of insurance you own or on which you have incidents of ownership, half of all jointly held property and property within revocable trusts.

Your goal is to manipulate your assets so that they will legally escape as much probate and tax cost as possible. Several tools allow you to do that.

First, Uncle Sam allows your estate's executor to deduct all your debts, estate costs, and funeral expenses from the final bill.

Second, the unified credit provisions of the tax code allows you to exclude from federal gift or estate taxes up to $600,000 in assets and taxable gifts. You may also make tax-free gifts of up to $10,000 a year to any number of persons you please, and couples can give up to $20,000. You may also make unlimited gifts to charity and may even pay someone else's health and education bills—and it's all free from taxes.

Look At This:

But (third) the biggest single exclusion—and the biggest estate-planning trap—is the unlimited marital deduction that permits you to pass on everything you own to your spouse, tax-free and free of probate. The catch is this: those assets may not be passed on again without being subject to probate and a tax assessment.

Say a husband dies, and his wife is left with an estate of $1.2 million. By the terms of the unlimited marital deduction, she does not pay taxes on her inheritance. But, when it's time for her to pass on the assets to her heirs, she may protect only $600,000 of those assets under the unified credit. Her heirs are stuck with a tax bill on assets of $600,000.

Bypass, Family, or Credit Shelter Trust

With proper estate planning, the entire $1.2 million could have passed on to the children free of taxes. The couple should have set up a revocable trust into which $600,000 of assets would have gone to his children or heirs at his death. This is called a *bypass*, *family*, or *credit shelter trust*, and the income earned on the assets is used by the wife until her death. Each year she also can tap up to 5% of the assets, or $5,000, whichever is greater. The trustee is authorized to provide her with whatever additional principal is necessary for basic support and medical bills. Whatever remains at her death passes on tax-free to the children, since the unified credit was used to establish the trust on the first death.

She also passes on to the children, tax-free, her $600,000, using the unified credit provision at her death.

QTIP Trusts

QTIPs (Qualified Terminal Interest Property Trust) are often used by two-marriage families, where one spouse wants to make sure that the children from the first marriage receive a portion of his or her assets after the death of the second spouse. In a QTIP, the income from the trust's assets is paid to the surviving spouse. He or she may take 5% of the assets or $5,000. The remainder passes on to the children of the first marriage, or to whomever the original spouse has designated in the will.

General Power of Appointment Trust

This trust gives the surviving spouse the right to name the eventual heirs of your assets. From a tax standpoint, it works the same way as a QTIP.

Charitable Remainder Trusts

You can remove assets from your taxable estate and continue to receive the income by establishing a charitable remainder trust and giving the assets to your favorite charity. (See Figure 8-4.)

With a charitable remainder trust, for example, you receive an amount determined each year by multiplying a fixed percentage that you select when you create the trust—usually 7% to 9%—by the market value of the trust's assets. When you die, the payments end or a beneficiary that you name—usually your spouse—can continue to receive the income from the trust. At that person's death, the property goes to the charity. For economic reasons, most charities accept charitable remainder trusts in amounts of $25,000 or more.

You can get nearly the same results by gifting the charity and buying an annuity from it. A charitable remainder annuity trust is a good way to give to your favorite charity, earn some income, and remove a fully appreciated and unproductive asset from your portfolio, thereby saving estate and income taxes. If you were to sell the property and reinvest the proceeds for higher income, a taxable gain would result. But the annuity will pay you 7% to 9% a year, and when the charity sells the property, no tax is due.

Here's another option if you don't have much to give. Some larger tax-exempt organizations issue charitable gift annuities for a minimum contribution of $1,000 and pay a fixed amount each year for the rest of your life. The older you are, the higher the payment: a 50-year-old would receive 6.5%, while a 90-year-old is paid 14%. You could get a better return somewhere else, but a charitable gift annuity entitles you to an income tax deduction and an estate tax exemption, as well as providing a benefit to a cause or institution that you value.

Life Insurance Trusts

You can combine the benefits of insurance and trusts by creating "funded" or "unfunded" insurance trusts—a trust that owns the insurance policy on your life. (See Figure 8-5).

You establish a funded trust by irrevocably transferring the life insurance policy plus enough money (or assets capable of producing enough money) to pay the policy's premium.

An unfunded trust holds the policy only, and the premiums must be paid by you or your beneficiary.

Either way, the trust removes the life insurance benefit from your taxable estate, minimizing your federal tax exposure. When you die, the proceeds go into a trust untaxed, and normally your spouse receives income from the trust for life. Your trust agreement specifies the heirs to whom the assets will go next.

Professional Advice

Although the transfer of both the policy and the payment of its premiums constitute a gift and are subject to gift tax, the costs are usually less than the $10,000 annual gift tax exclusion, and no tax consequence results. Your tax advisor can tell you about other tests your irrevocable life insurance trust must meet and whether a funded or unfunded trust will work best for you.

But you must be aware that if you die within three years of creating an irrevocable life insurance trust, the proceeds of the policy go into your estate for taxation. Ask your attorney to include a clause that directs the life insurance to your spouse or into a trust at your death. The trust is part of your spouse's estate.

DURABLE POWER OF ATTORNEY

An "attorney" is someone legally entitled to conduct business on your behalf. If the power of attorney is limited, the person can conduct only that business specified in your agreement. If the power of attorney is general, the person's authority is much broader but still assumes you are competent to review and approve the person's decisions. If you become incapacitated, the "attorney-in-fact" can no longer handle your affairs. If the agreement contains what is known as "durable" language (made possible by passage of certain recent state laws), it allows the attorney-in-fact to make decisions regardless of your competence. As you can see, this "durable" feature has enormous implications in estate planning because it can prevent an unwanted court-appointed guardianship in case you are incapacitated or disa-

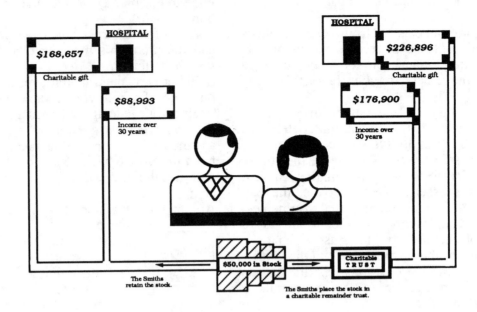

Figure 8-4 By participating in a charitable remainder trust, this couple increases their benefit package by more than 56%.

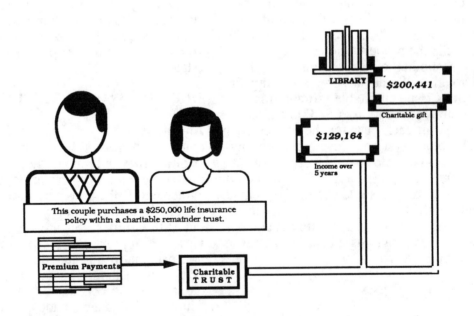

Figure 8-5 By purchasing a life insurance policy within a charitable remainder trust, you may produce significant survivor income and benefit a favorite charity.

bled.

In essence, the durable provision assumes you should be able to specify in advance the person you want to make critical decisions regarding your medical care, well-being, and wealth should you ever become incapable of making those decisions for yourself. Especially helped by this option are elderly people who fear senility in the closing stages of life, people with debilitating or degenerative diseases, people in dangerous occupations where sudden incapacity through accidents is a real possibility, or people facing major medical treatment the outcome of which might render them temporarily or permanently incapacitated.

For example, Helen, age 62, is scheduled to undergo exploratory surgery next month. She has been advised of the risks of the operation and the slight chance of her mental incapacitation as a result of the procedure. She consults her family attorney and is advised that her state has passed a law authorizing the addition of "durable" language to a general power-of-attorney document. She asks her adult daughter to act as attorney-in-fact, in an agreement that includes the words "this power of attorney shall become effective in the event of the disability or incapacity of the principal." Helen's operation goes well, and her recuperation is much quicker owing to the fact that she had no worries about how her affairs would have been handled had she survived the surgery with diminished mental capacity.

Because a will only becomes operative at your death, it is not the appropriate vehicle for granting a durable power of attorney. Consult your family attorney for the language necessary to create this important part of your estate preservation plan. (See Figure 8-6.)

FAMILY BUSINESS ORGANIZATIONS

Lawyers, physicians, dentists, and entrepreneurs have long seen the wisdom of structuring the ownership of certain assets through a family or professional business. The key idea, as it is with a trust, is to separate, for purposes of tax reduction or managerial control, income- or wealth-producing assets from the single individual who would otherwise face a higher-than-necessary income or estate tax liability. Although no single form of ownership is perfect for all assets, individuals, and situations, those available are quite flexible and may serve your estate-planning needs admirably.

General Partnership

In this form of business, all general partners exercise managerial control over the asset and share total liability for the business's operation. The terms of the general partnership agreement govern the actual workings of the partnership and, for estate-planning purposes, should state explicitly who takes over the managing partner's duties if the principal partner dies or becomes disabled. Although the partnership must file a tax return, the individual partners are each responsible for paying their own taxes and there is no inherent double taxation, as with a corporation (to be discussed shortly).

The drawback to a general partnership as an asset-holding vehicle, of course, is that all partners have legal managerial control and unlimited liability. This agreement may not be suitable for family businesses involving children or an inexperienced spouse or other nominal general partners.

Limited Partnership

A limited partnership consists of at least one general partner (who assumes managerial control and liability for the business) and a specified number of limited partners, whose liability is limited to the value of their share of the assets and who take no active part in running the business. In a family business, the general partner is usually the principal breadwinner and the limited partners are dependents (spouse and children) or other relatives. For estate-planning purposes, the partnership agreement should spell out the procedure for the orderly succession of a new general partner should the current general partner die or become disabled. As with the general partnership, there is no inherent double taxation.

Corporation

A corporation is a legal entity that operates in perpetuity; that is, it does not depend on

FOR HEALTH CARE*

I, _____, hereby appoint:

Name_____

Home address _____

Home telephone number _____

Work telephone number _____

as my agent to make health care decisions for me if and when I am unable to make my own health care decisions. This gives my agent the power to consent to giving, withholding, or stopping any health care, treatment, service, or diagnostic procedure. My agent also has the authority to talk with health care personnel, get information, and sign forms necessary to carry out those decisions.

If the person named as my agent is not available or is unable to act as my agent, then I appoint the following person(s) to serve in the order listed below:

1. Name _____
   Home address _____
   Home telephone number _____
   Work telephone number _____

2. Name _____
   Home address _____
   Home telephone number _____
   Work telephone number _____

By this document I intend to create a power of attorney for health care which shall take effect upon my incapacity to make my own health care decisions and shall continue during that incapacity.

My agent shall make health care decisions as I direct below or as I make known to him or her in some way.

(a) Statement of desires concerning life-prolonging care, treatment, services, and procedures:

_____
_____
_____
_____
_____
_____

(b) Special provisions and limitations:

_____
_____
_____
_____
_____
_____

BY SIGNING HERE I INDICATE THAT I UNDERSTAND THE PURPOSE AND EFFECT OF THIS DOCUMENT.

I sign my name to this form on _____

     (date)

My current home address:

_____
_____
_____
     (You sign here)

WITNESSES

I declare that the person who signed or acknowledged this document is personally known to me, that he/she signed or acknowledged this durable power of attorney in my presence, and that he/she appears to be of sound mind and under no duress, fraud, or undue influence. I am not the person appointed as agent by this document, nor am I the patient's health care provider, or an employee of the patient's health care provider.

First Witness
Signature _____
Home address _____
Print name _____
Date _____

Second Witness
Signature _____
Home address _____
Print name _____
Date _____

(At least one of the above witnesses must also sign the following declaration.)

I further declare that I am not related to the patient by blood, marriage, or adoption, and, to the best of my knowledge, I am not entitled to any part of his/her estate under a will now existing or by operation of law.

Signature _____

Signature _____

* Check requirements of individual state statute.

Source: Sample form is from a Matter of Choice *prepared for the U.S. Senate Special Committee on Aging.*

Figure 8-6   Durable power of attorney sample for health care only. Does not cover financial matters.

specific people for its organization, as with general and limited partnerships. It issues stock, which is the form and evidence of ownership. In "closely held" family corporations, family members (and perhaps one or two others, such as a family friend, attorney, or accountant) usually hold all the stock. Many family corporations are organized according to Subchapter S of the Internal Revenue code, which applies to small businesses—"small" with regard to the number of shareholders, not necessarily the value of its assets, which can be quite large. Shareholders' liability is limited to the value of the stock they own.

One big disadvantage to the family corporation, besides the cost of organization, is the double taxation of the income its shareholders receive. Because it is a separate legal entity, a corporation pays taxes on its income before it can distribute those earnings to its stockholders, who are taxed again when they declare that income on their personal returns.

Other forms of business are available, such as joint ventures, but those just described are the most widely used. Although your attorney and tax advisor should guide your decisions about the feasibility and desirability of assigning assets to a family business, the following general steps are recommended for everyone.

1. *Identify all assets that may be accounted for in a family estate plan.* Only then will you know which might be reasonably assigned to a family business.

2. *Obtain current fair market value of your assets, paying for independent appraisals when necessary.* It is important to establish asset value when ownership of a personal asset is transferred to the family business.

3. *When assets and their value have been identified, consider the tax consequences of doing nothing.* Avoid the false economy of continuing with the formation and maintenance of a family business just because you have made a tentative decision to do so. If you are not helped economically by the decision, it's foolish to pursue it.

4. *Compare the costs and benefits of alternate forms of ownership.* If a family business still seems like a reasonable asset-holding arrangement, explore the costs and benefits (*pro forma* analysis) of several alternative approaches. Don't form a Subchapter S corporation, for example, simply because it worked for a friend or relative in a similar situation. Different organizational, tax-reporting, and clerical costs are associated with each form of business.

5. *Be certain each family member involved is aware of what you're doing.* All relatives involved in a family business should understand their roles, obligations, liabilities, and the tax consequences of participation—especially if they file their own returns. In some cases, minor children may need to have their interest held by a custodian. Consult your legal and tax advisors about the requirements of the form of business you select.

A FINAL WORD ON YOUR FINAL ARRANGEMENTS

An orderly, efficient transfer of your wealth to your heirs is the ultimate act of love. Because the economy, tax laws, your resources, and the needs and capabilites (as well as the number) of your heirs will change over time, estate planning is not so much an event as an ongoing—indeed, a lifelong—process. Keep the people you love apprised of your activity and the location of important documents. Use the members of your financial planning team—your CFP, tax preparer, family attorney, and others—to make sure the efforts of a lifetime are not wasted when the people you love need them most.

LOVE LETTERS

Planners have found that often the grieving of adults is unrecognized. A loving thing to do is to leave individual letters in your legal papers to address your feelings regarding spouse, children, or others who may mourn your passing. A "love letter" might recall some of the fun you shared or some of the memories that gave you both pleasure.

Your love letter to your spouse may also include your personal feelings about possessions or investments: how you would want these items handled, or name the advisors on whom your spouse can count when help is needed.

CO-OWNERSHIP INTERESTS CHART

	TENANCY IN COMMON	JOINT TENANCY	COMMUNITY PROPERTY	TENANCY BY ENTIRETY
Parties	Any number of persons (Can be husband & wife)	Any number of persons (Can be husband & wife)	Only husband & wife	Only husband & wife
Division	Ownership can be divided into any number of interests, equal or unequal	Ownership interests must be equal	Ownership interests are equal. Managerial responsibility is in the husband (certain exceptions)	Whole title ,rests in both parties
Title	Each co-owner has a separate legal title to his undivided interest	There is only one title to the whole property	Title is in the "community". Each interest is separate but management is unified	Whole title rests in both parties
Possession	Equal right of possession	Equal right of possession	Wife's rights subject to husband's managerial prerogatives	Equal right of possession
Conveyance	Each co-owner's interest may be conveyed separately by its owner	Conveyance by one co-owner without the others breaks the joint tenancy except where it is community property held in joint tenancy merely for purposes of convenience	Both co-owners must join in conveyance of real property. Separate interest cannot be conveyed	One party cannot terminate the tenancy without the consent of the other party
Purchaser's Status	Purchaser will become a tenant in common with the other co-owners in the property	Purchaser will become a tenant in common with the other co-owners in the property	Purchaser can only acquire whole title of community; cannot acquire a part of it	Purchaser can only acquire whole title
Death	On co-owner's death his interest passes by will to his devisees or heirs. No right of survivorship	On co-owner's death, his interest ends and cannot be disposed of by will. Survivor owns the property by rights of survivorship	On co-owner's death, 1/2 belongs to survivor in severalty, 1/2 goes by will to decedent's devisees or by succession to survivor	On co-owner's death, the survivor has the whole title
Creditor's Rights	Co-owner's interest may be sold on execution sale to satisfy his creditor Creditor becomes a tenant in common	Co-owner's interest may be sold on execution sale to satisfy creditor. Joint tenancy is broken, creditor becomes tenant in common	Co-owner's interest cannot be seized and sold separately. The whole property may be sold on execution sale to satisfy creditor	Co-owner's interest cannot be seized and sold separately. The whole property may be sold on execution sale to satisfy creditor
Presumption	Favored in doubtful cases except husband & wife cases	Must be expressly stated in writing. Not favored	Strong presumption that property acquired by husband & wife is community	Strong presumption that it is tenancy by entirety if husband & wife hold in both names

CHAPTER 9

PLANNING FOR A COLLEGE EDUCATION

A GLANCE AHEAD

A college education is one long-cherished component of the American Dream. But escalating costs are putting this dream further and further away from millions of Americans. This chapter gives you some practical strategies for putting that dream back within your children's reach. You will learn

- *How to help your child select the right college*
- *Why college costs are rising so quickly*
- *What factors will affect college costs in coming years*
- *How the new tax laws affect the high finance of higher education*
- *New ways to pay those college bills.*

COLLEGE IS MORE THAN A FINANCIAL DECISION

Chuck and Lorie were thrilled the day they put Erin on the plane for her first year at college. Erin had worked hard to be accepted at Lorie's alma mater—a well-known women's college in the Northeastern United States—and Chuck and Lorie were pleased that Erin's bills would be paid by a trust fund they established before she was born. Although the trust fund covered the big expenses, Erin planned to work a few hours each week in the school cafeteria for spending money.

During her first weeks away, Erin's let-

ters were filled with longing for home. Her parents reassured her constantly, but could almost set the clock by her habitual Sunday evening phone calls.

However, Erin's letters became less morose as the semester wore on, and her phone calls grew less frequent. Chuck and Lorie agreed that she seemed to be settling in.

Erin came home for Thanksgiving in November. She spent the holiday seeing friends and visiting relatives. On Saturday, she announced she wasn't returning to school. She'd go to the local state college, she said, and preferred to stay close to home. Her parents—Lorie in particular—were stunned.

Many tears were shed that weekend, and angry words passed within the family. Chuck and Lorie finally prevailed, and Erin returned to complete the semester. Predictably, Erin was miserable. Her grades suffered and communication with her parents fell apart. Erin finished the semester but was so distraught she refused to go back to college in the spring. Finally, after working awhile as a sales clerk, Erin did complete her education—at the state college—and she's happily employed now (in the Northeast, ironically) by a large financial institution. She says she simply picked the wrong school at first.

"We're doing lots better now, but for a long time Mom was so upset that we just weren't comfortable around each other," she says. "I can understand why she was hurt; and to my Dad, that college fund was something he was truly proud of. My troubles at school must have seemed like rejection of all the hard work he went to in order to pay the private school tuition.

"The fact is, I just wasn't happy there. I never did feel like I belonged. I suppose I could have stayed, but I would have had to change myself as a person to do that. It just wasn't what college was supposed to be all about."

Erin and her family learned a couple of important lessons from their experience. First, selecting the right college is a crucial decision for which the student must be the final arbiter. Second, even though Mom and Dad may have sacrificed to make college a reality for their child, it's usually a mistake for them to dictate how and where that education takes place. Many families have been torn apart by conflicts over just these kinds of questions, and the high cost of higher education only seems to raise the emotional stakes.

Traditionally, sending a child to college is seen as an investment. In 1990, the average annual cost of attending a public four-year college was $6,600; the average for a private school was $13,700. Like any costly purchase, the choice of college on which this money is spent should be evaluated the same way you would evaluate any investment—by assessing the risks (emotional and otherwise) as well as rewards.

How to Choose the Right College

The best course is to begin talking about college early enough with your children so that there's no pressure on the decision-making process. If you as a parent have predetermined ideas about a school, try to be sensitive to any resistance you may hear from your children. Avoid using your control over the purse strings to force your child into a decision.

About 75% of all college students are able to attend the school of their choice; 20% settle for second choice.

Your children increase their chances for being accepted by the school they prefer if they are well prepared before the application process begins.

You can help your child make the right choice by asking the key questions:

1. What does your child like to do? What is he good at? Is your child more comfortable working with people, ideas, or machines? Does he relate better to hard, practical information or to softer, more esoteric subjects?

2. How will your child's personality and character influence the college experience? Is she organized or impulsive? Withdrawn or outgoing? Is he aggressive and does he deal well with new situations, or does he need a lot of support and structure?

3. What are your child's reasons for going to college? Does he love to think critically and analyze? Is he gaining a world view that would be complemented by a college experience? Or is he going to party, make new friends, and further his abilities in sports?

4. What are your child's goals? Realistically, what career choices will fulfill them and what sorts of schools accommodate these goals the best?

Encourage your child to begin setting personal and educational goals, saving money, and orienting him- or herself toward a higher education. If your child is in high school, the sophomore year is none too soon to begin talking with a counselor about existing opportunities and the kinds of high school coursework it will take to qualify for them.

The Rising Cost of a College Education

But, as important as it is, picking the right school is only half the problem; paying for it is the other half. The cost of a college education has far outstripped inflation in the 1980s. Between 1980 and 1986, total costs of private four-year colleges rose 90.2%; public school costs went up 67.1%. In the same time, the Consumer Price Index rose just 33.4%. 1988-89 colleges and universities raised average tuitions by 7%, marking the eighth straight year of higher increases than inflation. Private colleges rose 9%. The most expensive schools now cost $19,000/ year, including room and board. The freshman in the fall of 1990 will have a $100,000 sheepskin.

Why the exorbitant increases? That question has stimulated debate from Capitol Hill to the ivy-covered halls of academe. Critics charge educators with taking advantage of a political process that favors higher education: as long as state and federal governments subsidize student loan programs and other price supports, schools will continue to hike the bill.

Some people say the cost of recruiting has gotten out of hand as schools battle over a diminishing number of applicants—even though the number of high school graduates dropped 16% between 1977 and 1985, and college attendance was up 9% from a decade earlier. One expert says that colleges spend an average of $800 to recruit each freshman. Recruitment brochures, long the staple of the recruiting arsenal, are being supplemented with expensive audio and video productions.

The cost of providing student services is increasing, too. Social services, entertainment and recreational facilities, and other amenities are all part of the recruiting effort and offer students a broader range of experience—but at an unnecessary price to everyone, many critics say.

The size of faculties is growing faster than the student population as well. Many new faculty members are research-oriented rather than teaching-oriented—although college administrators are quick to say that these projects usually pay for themselves in government grants. Consequently, many of the new teaching positions have gone to lower-paid, part-time instructors, while tenured positions have been limited.

Keeping up with technological developments in the age of space is expensive. Science departments no longer run on bunsen burners and slide rules but require state-of-the-art computer and laboratory equipment. Libraries are hard-pressed to keep up with an expanding information base. Now more than ever, knowledge costs, as well as creates, a society's wealth.

The colleges claim that much of the rising cost is the result of increased demand for the school's own financial aid. In the 1985–86 school year, students received about $15.9 billion in federal aid (down about $1 billion from the 1970s), requiring colleges to pick up the slack, boosting their scholarship dollars by about $1.04 billion.

Unfortunately, much of that money is used to lure top scholars, rather than to provide assistance to the average students who may need it most.

PICKING UP THE COLLEGE TAB

As with any goal-related spending, the sooner you begin a program to pay for your child's education, the easier it will be. Fortunate indeed are the families with enough foresight (and resources) to begin a college investment program while their children are still in diapers. For the rest of us, college financial planning often begins after the student has entered high school.

But no matter when you start, you are better off with a plan rather than a random, catch-as-catch-can attempt to save more from current income. Sadly, since the 1986 Tax Reform Act became law, it has become much more difficult for families to invest for college. The TRA eliminated or modified many of the strategies once used to maximize the funds put aside for college, and you should know how these changes may affect your family.

College Planning After TRA

Tax Consequences

The 1986 Tax Reform Act was hard on students and on the families that support them. Loan deductions were cut, several helpful tax strategies were limited, and gift-giving provisions were slashed.

Hardest hit was a technique known as *income splitting*, in which the interest from income-producing property is assigned to the minor children of a family, and is therefore taxed at the child's lower rate.

Before the TRA, income splitting was commonly used to build education funds. Income from $500 to $1,000 is taxed at 15% or $75, whichever is less. And, any income of over $1,000 earned on such property is taxed at the parents' rate, unless the child is 14 or older, making long-term tuition building even more difficult.

Another tool once widely used to shelter assets for college funding, but now disallowed, is the Clifford Trust.

In this scheme, parents placed bonds or other income-generating assets into a special trust where earnings would be taxed at the child's lower rate. After 10 years and a day, the original investment returned to the parents and the child kept the earnings. After the TRA, all Clifford Trusts have been scrapped.

Fortunately, you are still allowed to transfer full ownership of property to your child, in which case the income is taxed at the child's lower rate. This is true of dividends, rents, and other forms of income, but you can no longer simply assign the income to the child—you must transfer the ownership.

Of course, you must be careful when transferring large sums. Transferring high value property may subject you to gift tax liability. You can avoid this liability by giving no more than $10,000 (or $20,000 for joint gifts from both spouses) to each child per year. You may also avoid tax on gifts over this amount by applying the unified gift and estate tax credit. An interest-free or low-interest loan to a family member may also subject them to income tax and you to a gift tax as well.

How Much Do I Need?

Not every American family can fully fund their children's education, but a good savings and investment program can help. Here's a tool that can tell you how much you'll need to invest, either in a lump sum today or in increments over the years.

Remember Dave and Carol from our insurance discussion in Chapter 8? Figure 9-1 shows the calculations used by their financial planner to determine how much it would cost to put Paul and Ashley through school.

Using $12,000 as the cost of one year of college in today's dollars and planning for 7% inflation, you can see that the total cost of funding a total of eight years of education between the years 1997 and 2005 would total $205,550. That's the amount of money Carol and Dave will have to come up with to fund the education of their two children fully. They already have a start of $8,000, but this seed money has a long way to go!

They have a choice: they can wait and pay it out of their pockets, in which case they'll pay the full amount in taxable dollars. However, if they can invest a lump sum today of $71,026 at 10% interest, they will end up with the necessary money and they can take advantage of some helpful tax breaks along

the way. Or, they can save and invest $694 a month and accomplish the same objective. The right hand column shows the lump sum necessary at a given future date to achieve the $205,550 total.

THE BEST WAYS TO FINANCE A COLLEGE EDUCATION

For most families, the college investment fund is sacred—it is never touched until the child is ready for school. Therefore, an ideal college investment is both safe and growth oriented during the accumulation period. The trick is to salt enough away to cover the ever increasing costs. How much will be enough 5, 10, or 15 years down the line? Because that's such an uncertain proposition, there's been tremendous response to new "guaranteed prepayment" programs such as those offered by several states and colleges.

College-Based Investment Plans. In a growing number of states, parents can invest in college- or state-backed investment plans. The parents prepay their child's education at today's prices, and the college, or the state, invests the money. The assumption is that the investments will yield sufficient income to cover the difference between today's costs and tomorrow's. If the plan doesn't yield the necessary profits, the sponsor would have to make up the difference. Illinois recently said, "Damn the torpedoes" and issued $90 million in such bonds anyway—and there was demand for over $270 million! In California, a budget-conscious governor vetoed similar legislation, citing the risk to the state treasury if the investments should fail to perform.

There are other problems as well. If the child chooses another school, or dies, or the family moves out of state, most programs return only the principal—the earning power of those early dollars has been wasted.

One bank, College Savings Bank in Princeton, New Jersey, now offers a prepayment program that uses certificates of deposit as the underlying investment tool.

To compensate for rapid cost increases, College Savings Bank charges an up-front premium that's about $3,000 higher than the average current tuition of a private school,

The table below illustrates the funds required for your children's education based on the following assumptions:

Annual education expenses (in today's dollars)............$ 12,000
Portion of expenses you plan to provide............... 100%

To help accumulate education funds you might consider use of savings or investment vehicles that could provide income tax advantages or growth opportunities. Consult with your attorney or tax advisor for details relating to the tax aspects of any program considered.

Client name   *Dave and Carol Hern*

Present year	1990
College fund balance	8,000
Annual college cost today	12,000
Percent paid by client	100
Inflation rate	7.00
Interest rate on fund	9.50
Number of years of college	4
First year of college	
1st child	1997
2nd child	2002

Year	Number of Children in School	Cost in Today's Dollars	Cost Inflated at 7%	Capital Need at 10.00%
1990	0	0	0	71,026
1991	0	0	0	78,129
1992	0	0	0	85,942
1993	0	0	0	94,536
1994	0	0	0	103,989
1995	0	0	0	114,388
1996	0	0	0	125,827
1997	1	12,000	19,269	138,410
1998	1	12,000	20,618	131,054
1999	1	12,000	22,062	121,480
2000	1	12,000	23,606	109,360
2001	0	0	0	94,330
2002	1	12,000	27,026	103,763
2003	1	12,000	28,918	84,410
2004	1	12,000	30,942	61,041
2005	1	12,000	33,108	33,108
2006	0	0	0	0
2007	0	0	0	0
2008	0	0	0	0
2009	0	0	0	0
2010	0	0	0	0
2011	0	0	0	0
2012	0	0	0	0
2013	0	0	0	0
Totals	8	96,000	205,550	1,550,793

You may meet future education cost by:

1. Investing capital now in the amount of $71,026

2. Monthly savings or investment deposits of   580

3. Combine present fund with monthly additions
   College fund balance   8,000
   Monthly additions needed   515

4. Paying educational expenses out-of-pocket   205,550
   (with taxable dollars)

Figure 9-1   Education Funding Analysis for Dave and Carol Hern

and the charge is less for a state-sponsored institution. The bank guarantees that earnings will cover the cost of college, although tuition must continue to rise significantly faster than inflation for the plan to make sense as an investment.

The bank offers a taxable short-term introductory rate of 8.27%, and your yield soon drops to a little more than 5%. Unless tuition outpaces inflation by about 4% a year, parents may fare better by investing the money themselves in more traditional tools.

In a case challenging Michigan's prepayment program, the IRS set up some relevant tests:

1. The money put into the plan is a taxable gift and must be reported to the IRS. But no tax is owed unless the value of your taxable gifts *and* the remainder of your estate exceed $600,000 either before or after your death.
2. No taxes are owed to the fund while it accumulates.
3. Your child will owe tax on the difference between the amount invested and the actual cost of tuition at the time she enters college. If you invested $4,000 and tuition is $16,000, she owes tax on $12,000 over four years, or $3,000 a year. The tax is paid at her (presumably lower) rate.
4. Most important, the court dealt a blow to the heart of the program by ruling that Michigan would have to pay federal taxes on the income earned every year on funds deposited by parents. This has slowed the program's growth and may force Michigan and other states to charge parents more money up front.

Other Investments for College-Bound Kids. If your state doesn't have a prepayment progam, your best bet is an investment that defers income until after your child turns 14.

There's a Catch 22 in the law, however: a child is generally not considered competent to administer his or her own property and if you exercise control over property you give to your child, the transfer might not be accepted as a gift by the IRS for the purposes of shifting income.

Government Bonds. You can choose from a range of bonds, from Series EE U.S. savings bonds to zero-coupon municipals. They produce no current income and pay a good yield at maturity. You can even time taxable interest earnings to arrive after your child's fourteenth birthday.

Type III

Type IV

By shopping around, you can find Treasury bills and other securities that have been stripped of their coupons and are being offered as college investment tools. They are sometimes called "CATS" or "TIGRS." At a current annual yield of 8.16%, a $5,000 investment would be worth $13,523 in 11 years. When registered in the child's name, the coupons or proceeds on the sale or maturity of a bond may be cashed or deposited in the child's name.

For a very young child the Series EE Bonds can be rolled over, if desired, without incurring current taxation by purchasing Series HH at maturity of the EE's. A new way to use EE Bonds since the Technical and Miscellaneous Revenue Act of 1988 applies to persons over 24 years of age and purchasing U.S. Savings Bonds after 1989. The bond interest is tax-free to the extent the funds are used for college tuition and fees. Taxes are due, however, on the amount of bond dollars redeemed that exceed college costs per year. The exceptions to this new regulation are complex but wholly usable for people with annual incomes of less than $60,000. At $60,000 adjusted gross income, the tax-free benefit begins to phase out and is completely out at $90,000 adjusted gross income for joint taxpayers.

Insurance. Many families are turning to whole or universal life policies, written in the child's name, which combine regular coverage plus a company-managed investment plan to fund college expenses.

In many cases, a company will write a policy in a child's name or recognize a child's ownership of a policy covering another person. You may need to appoint a guardian to cash in or borrow on a minor's insurance policy, but a gift of a policy (or an annuity) generally will be recognized as a gift for the purpose of income splitting.

Mutual Fund Shares.

Type III

D

Low Taxes
Low Expenses

Because mutual funds, such as stock market funds are professionally managed, they are ideal tools for a child's investment. Although they offer less safety than bonds and insurance policies, their long-term track record is good, and most funds will automatically reinvest the dividends on request. Example: dollar-cost averaging a growth mutual fund for the past 10 years would return approximately 15.6% compounded annual yield. This average includes the crash of October, 1987.

Some experts like equity mutual funds better than debt instruments because of their generally higher yield. They suggest investing in a broadly diversified, growth-oriented mutual fund until the child is three or four years away from college. At that point, the assets can be redistributed among the family of funds to include less volatile bonds and money market accounts.

Children's Custodial Accounts.

You may administer a bank, mutual fund, or brokerage account on behalf of your child by establishing a custodial account. This eliminates the need for trusts, which are no longer effective tools for splitting interest income.

A number of limitations are placed on the administration of the account, however, and the rules by which they are governed vary from state to state—although those differences generally don't affect federal tax consequences.

As long as the parent doesn't use the income from a custodial account to pay child support and provided the child is over 14, the income is taxable to the child at the child's rate. For children under 14, the income is taxed at the parent's rate.

Professional Advice

Gift tax and estate tax provisions in the law might saddle you with extra expenses when you set up a custodial account, so be sure to confer with your financial planner or CPA to make certain the transfer goes smoothly.

Home Equity Loans.

That old standby, the home equity loan, has probably financed more college educations than any other tool around; and even the 1986 Tax Reform Act didn't tarnish its luster. Interest on a loan made against the equity of your home is still fully deductible when the money is used for educational purposes. The loan, however, cannot exceed your cost basis—price and improvements.

If you have a good credit history, you can borrow between 80 and 85% of the market value of your home, minus the balance outstanding on your mortgage.

Look At This:

One note of caution: home equity loans subject you to foreclosure if you are unable to repay the loan on schedule, and your normal mortgage payments must still be paid. Be sure to read and understand the fine print in your contract, including balloon payments, upward adjustable rates, and other potentially nasty surprises.

Other Kinds of Financial Help

Each year, millions of dollars earmarked for college assistance go unused simply because no one asked for them. One estimate is that in 1986, about $9.5 billion was issued in public and private scholarships, but that another $6.6 billion went unclaimed—and only a fraction of that was reserved for students with high grades.

Clearly, resourcefulness pays dividends, so start your search for money early, and don't quit until you're convinced you've exhausted your alternatives.

Federal Aid.

The federal government provided more than $17 billion dollars in student aid in 1987. Although no one likes to deal with government red tape, a wealth of funding is available for those who qualify and persevere.

To establish eligibility for federal assistance, a family must pass a uniform needs test. "Need" is a relative term, and you may qualify based on a variety of conditions even if your income is $30,000 or higher, so don't be bashful about applying.

Beginning with the 1987–88 school year, award levels in federal programs were increased. Guaranteed Student Loans (GSLs) were boosted from $2,500 per year to $2,625 for the first two years, and to $4,000 for the next three. Graduate students may be eligible for up to $7,500 per year.

School Aid. In the past five years, individual schools have increased by 60% the amount of assistance they provide.

Many colleges now offer guaranteed tuition plans that may take several forms. Some will guarantee an entering freshman that his or her tuition will not be increased during their undergraduate years. Others will make that guarantee but require an upfront deposit—$2,500 is a typical amount. Another method of guaranteeing tuition is to allow families to prepay two, three, or four years of tuition at the freshman rates. Parent loans at favorable rates are also available through participating lenders if needed.

Look At This:
Some schools provide discounts when more than one family member enrolls—and it needn't be a sibling. Most allow you to pay in installments, although you need to ask about fees or interest charged on the outstanding balance.

State Aid. In recent years, states also have shouldered some of the burden for higher education programs. Many states have enacted teacher loan forgiveness programs to help ease the teacher shortage. A portion of the student loan is forgiven for each year the graduate teaches in secondary or elementary schools. The loan must be repaid in full, however, if the student doesn't become a teacher.

The dependents of deceased or disabled verterans, POWs, and MIAs may receive financial assistance in most states. Many states allow military personnel and their dependents assigned within the state to enroll in local institutions at the lower, in-state tuition fees.

To help offset the higher cost of a private college, some states offer awards to students planning to attend a private school within the state.

Help at Work. Many large companies offer some kind of assistance to the children of employees. You also are allowed to borrow from your pension plan, and may actually save enough in taxes to come out ahead—even after paying early withdrawal penalties!

ATTAINING THE DREAM

When there's a will, there's a way—and what could be more appropriate than giving the old college try to funding your child's education?

There are many ways to accumulate funds for a college education but, as in the case with most investments, the earlier you start the easier the task will be. Remember, too, that although your child is ultimately in the driver's seat regarding how and where that education is obtained, a parent's steady hand on the wheel will help make sure the journey is a happy one. For more information, read *The Right College Financial Aid Handbook 1991* (Arco Publishing).

CHAPTER 10

TAX PLANNING

A GLANCE AHEAD

Your tax return is a historical document; it reflects only what you did (or failed to do) to reduce your taxes in the preceding year. Consequently, tax savings begin on or before January 1 of the tax year—not 16 months later, when you prepare your return on April 15 of the following year and compute the tax you owe. In this chapter you'll learn basic tax planning objectives and how to apply them in different situations.

BASIC TAX-PLANNING OBJECTIVES

You can minimize or avoid taxes in any given year by eliminating income from taxable sources, deferring taxation to a later date (when you may be in a lower bracket or have more shelters), or by switching income from one tax status to another.

Earning Tax-Free Income

You can earn tax-free income by

A

High Taxes
High Expenses

1. Investing in tax-exempt securities. But before you invest, determine whether the tax-free return will exceed the after-tax return of taxed income.
2. Taking a position in a company that pays substantial tax-free pay fringes, such as health and life insurance protection.
3. Seeking tax-free benefits offered by scholarship arrangements.
4. Taking a position overseas to earn up to $70,000 of tax-free pay.

Deferring Income

You can defer income to years when you will pay less tax, through

B

High Taxes
Low Expenses

1. Deferred pay plans.
2. Qualified retirement plans, such as Keogh plans and IRA investments.
3. Transacting installment sales when you sell property.
4. Investing in Series EE U.S. savings bonds.

Income Splitting

Through income splitting, you divide your income among several persons or tax-paying entities that will pay an aggregate tax lower than the tax that you would pay if you reported all the income. Although the tax law limits income-splitting opportunities, certain business- and family-income planning can provide tax savings.

Tax-Free Exchanges

You can defer tax on appreciated property by transacting tax-free exchanges of such property.

Buying a Personal Residence Rather Than Renting

Homeowners are favored by the tax law. For example,

B

High Taxes
Low Expenses

1. Rather than rent, breadwinners can buy a home, condominium, or cooperative apartment. You may deduct interest and taxes. When you sell your house, you may defer tax on gain and, if you are 55 or over, take advantage of a $125,000 exclusion.
2. Homeowners can borrow on their home equity and fully deduct interest expenses.

TAX SAVINGS FOR HOMEOWNERS

Homeowners enjoy substantial tax benefits, such as the benefits of tax deferral on a home if sale proceeds are reinvested in a new home within two years, and the $125,000 exclusion for homeowners age 55 or over. Interest paid on home mortgages is also fully deductible, provided certain rules are followed. However, taxable sales of personal residences are subject to higher taxes because of the repeal of the capital gains deduction. Even so, your home may be a source of additional deductions—and of cash for investing or other use.

Tax Savings Through Home Equity Loan Deductions

The law distinguishes between mortgages incurred before October 14, 1987, and mortgages incurred on or after that date. If all your mortgages were incurred *before* October 14, 1987, the law is straightforward: you

may fully deduct all interest on debt secured by a principal or second residence. This is true for loans used to acquire a residence as well as for home equity loans made before October 14, 1987.

As for loans incurred after October 13, 1987, interest deductions may be available for debts of up to $1.1 million on a first or second residence. The actual amount in your case depends on whether you currently own a residence and on the amount of current home mortgage debt. As explained in the following paragraphs, the law distinguishes between (1) debt to buy, construct, and improve a residence and (2) debt secured by a residence where the loan proceeds are used for nonresidential purposes.

Qualified Residence Interest on Loans After October 13, 1987. The tax law calls fully deductible home mortgage interest "qualified residence interest." It is interest paid or accrued during a taxable year for either acquisition debt or home equity debt, which are discussed next. The debt must be secured by either a principal residence or a second home.

Acquisition Debt. Debt secured by a principal or second residence, and incurred in acquiring, constructing, or substantially improving that residence is called *acquisition debt.* Qualifying acquisition debt made after October 13, 1987, may not exceed $1 million, or $500,000 for married persons filing separate returns.

Generally, a debt qualifies as being incurred in buying, constructing, or improving a residence if you satisfy IRS tracing rules that prove the use of the loan proceeds for such residential purposes. Even if you cannot prove under the tracing rules that a loan was used to buy a residence, a loan will be treated by the IRS as incurred for buying a house to the extent you can show acquisition expenses within 90 days before or after incurring the loan. (Special construction loan and improvement loan rules are discussed later.)

Refinanced-acquisition mortgages are treated as acquisition debt as long as the refinanced amount does not exceed the principal amount of the acquisition debt immediately before refinancing.

If you incurred substantial loans prior to October 14, 1987, and later purchased a new home, your deduction for the mortgage for the new home may be limited. The $1 million limit for acquisition debt after Octrober 13, 1987, is reduced by the amount of outstanding pre-October 14, 1987 debt.

Acquisition debt is reduced by principal payments.

Home Equity Debt. Any debt secured by a personal residence, provided the debt does not exceed the fair market value of the residence less the amount of acquisition debt on the residence, is called a *home equity debt.* The total home equity debt may not exceed $100,000 ($50,000 if a separate return is filed by a married person). Interest on a qualifying home equity loan is deductible regardless of the way you spend the loan proceeds, unless it is used for buying tax exempts or for other prohibited purposes. If you have a principal residence and a second home, the total home equity loan limit for both houses is $100,000 (or $50,000 for a married person filing separately).

Example 1. You bought your house in 1984 for $200,000, subject to a mortgage of $150,000. In 1990, the mortgage principal is $120,000 and you plan to make a home equity loan. The fair market value of the house is $210,000. Interest on a home equity loan of up to $90,000 is fully deductible. A home equity loan may not exceed the difference between the fair market value of the house ($210,000) and the current acquisition debt ($120,000). If the value of the house exceeded $220,000, up to $100,000 could have been borrowed as a qualifying home equity loan.

Example 2. The market value of your house is $200,000, and the current mortgage is $160,000. You can make a home equity loan of only up to $40,000 ($200,000 - $160,000).

A loan may qualify as partially acquisition debt and partially home equity debt when part of it is used to refinance an existing acquistion debt. The refinanced amount is still considered acquisition debt. Debt in excess of the refinanced amount is home equity debt subject to the $100,000 ceiling.

Home Construction Loans. Interest on a home construction loan is fully deductible from the time construction begins, and for a period of up to 24 months while construction takes place. Within the 24-month period, the loan is considered acquisition debt subject to the $1-million ceiling provided that the home is a principal residence or second home when it is actually ready for occupancy. Furthermore, the loan proceeds must be directly traceable to home construction expenses, including the purchase of a lot, and the loan must be secured by the lot to be treated as acquisition debt. According to the IRS, if construction begins before a loan is incurred, the loan is treated as acquisition debt to the extent of construction expenses within the 24-month period before the loan.

Interest incurred on the loan before construction begins is treated as personal interest which is no longer deductible after 1990. (See Example 1 below). If construction lasts more than 24 months, interest after the 24-month period is treated as personal interest.

Interest on loans made within 90 days after construction is completed may qualify for a full deduction. The loan is treated as acquisition debt (subject to the $1 million ceiling) to the extent of construction expenses within the last 24 months before the residence was completed plus expenses through the date of the loan. (See Example 2 below.) For purposes of the 90-day rule, a debt may be considered "incurred" on the date a written loan application is made, provided the loan proceeds are actually received within 30 days after loan approval. If a loan application is made within the 90-day period and it is rejected, and a new application with another lender is made within a reasonable time after the rejection, a loan from the second lender will be considered timely even if more than 90 days have passed since the end of construction.

Example 1. On January 15, 1990, you borrow $100,000 to buy a residential lot. The loan is secured by the lot. You begin construction of a principal residence on January 1, 1991, and use $250,000 of unborrowed funds for construction expenses. The residence is completed on December 31, 1992.

The interest paid in 1990 is personal interest, which is only 10% deductible under the

1986 Tax Reform Act. It was paid before the 24-month qualifying construction period that started January 1, 1991, and ended December 31, 1992.

Interest paid in 1991 and 1992 is fully deductible, because the $100,000 loan is treated as acquisition debt for the 24-month construction period.

Example 2. Extending the facts of Example 1, in March 15, 1993, you transact a $300,000 mortgage on the completed house to raise funds. You use $100,000 of the loan to pay off the $100,000 loan on the lot, and keep the balance.

All the interest on the $300,000 loan is fully deductible because the loan qualifies as acquisition debt. Of the debt, $100,000 is treated as acquisition debt used for construction because it was used to refinance the original 1990 debt to purchase the lot. The $200,000 balance is also treated as a construction loan under the 90-day rule: it was borrowed within 90 days after the residence was completed, and construction expenses of at least $200,000 were incurred within 24 months before the completion date.

The Two-Residence Limit. The preceding rules for deducting residential mortgage interest apply to loans secured by your principal residence and one other residence. A principal residence may be a condominium or cooperative unit, a houseboat, or house trailer. If you own more than two houses, you decide which residence shall be considered your second residence; interest debt secured by the designated second residence is deductible under the above rules. Mortgage interest on loans to buy any other home will be subject to the limits for personal interest. A residence that is rented out for any part of the year may be designated as a second residence only if it is used for personal nonrental purposes for the greater of 14 days or 10% of the rental days. By making the designation you ensure that interest is fully deductible as residential interest. If you do not make the designation, part of the interest allocated to your personal use is personal interest that is 10% deductible in 1990 and not deductible at all after 1990, and interest allocated to the rental activity is treated as passive activity interest subject to passive loss limitations.

A married couple filing jointly may designate as a second residence a home owned or used by either spouse.

If a married couple files separately, each spouse may generally deduct interest on debt secured by one residence. However, both spouses may agree in writing to allow one of them to deduct the interest on a principal residence plus a designated second residence.

Home Improvements. Loans used for substantial home improvements are treated as acquisition debt. For example, say your current acquisition mortgage is $100,000. You borrow $20,000 to build a new room. Your qualifying acquisition debt is now $120,000.

If substantial improvements to a home are begun but not completed before a loan is incurred, the loan will be treated as acquisition debt (assuming the debt is secured by the home) to the extent of improvement expenses made within 24 months before the loan. If the loan is incurred within 90 days after an improvement is completed, the loan is treated as acquisition debt (assuming the debt is secured by the home) to the extent of improvement expenses made within the period starting 24 months before completion of the improvement, and ending on the date of the loan.

Refinancing Pre-October 14, 1987, Mortgage Debt. This debt is not subject to the ceiling of $1 million. If you refinance debt incurred prior to October 14, 1987, the refinanced amount remains pre-October 14 debt to the extent it does not exceed the outstanding principal immediately before refinancing. Any refinancing may not extend the term of the debt beyond the term of the acquisition debt immediately before the refinancing. In the case of acquisition debt such as a "balloon" note that is not amortized over its term interest on any otherwise qualified refinancing will be deductible for the term of the first refinancing of such acquisition debt, but not for more than 30 years after that first refinancing.

Tax Consequences of Selling Your Home

Because wealth building for more people involves buying or repurchasing (trading up) a home, we won't go into detail here about strategies for liquidating a personal residence. You'll find complete guidance for minimizing tax exposure from such transactions in *J.K. Lasser's Your Income Tax 1991* and later editions.

Most people may avoid or defer tax on all or part of a profit from the sale of a home depending on the owner's age:

1. *Age 55 or over.* If you are age 55 or over, you may elect to avoid tax on gain of up to $125,000. To claim this exclusion, you must (1) elect to avoid tax, (2) be age 55 or older on or before the date of sale, and (3) have owned and occupied the house as your principal residence for at least three of the five years preceding the day of sale.

2. *Under 55, or 55 or over but do not want to avoid the tax.* You may defer tax by (1) buying or building another residence for use as your principal residence, (2) buying or building within two years of the sale of your old house, at a cost at least equal to the amount you received from the sale of the old house, or (3) by making an even exchange (or pay additional cash) for a new principal residence.

If you sell your house at a loss, you may not deduct the loss. However, you may claim a loss (1) if you convert the house from personal use to some profit-making purpose before the sale, (2) if you sell a house acquired by gift or inheritance that you did not personally use but rather offered for rental or sale shortly after acquisition, or (3) if you sell stock in your cooperative apartment in which there were nonstockholder tenants when you acquired your stock.

You must report details of a sale on Form 2119, which you attach to your Form 1040. On Form 2119, you compute gain on the basis of a new residence and may make the election to exclude gain. If you do not qualify for tax deferral or exclusion, enter taxable gain from Form 2119 on Schedule D.

The IRS may tax you on the unreported gain from the sale of your residence during a three-year period that starts when you notify the IRS (1) of the cost of your new residence, or (2) of your intention not to buy one, or (3) of your failure to acquire a new residence before the required time limit. If you don't notify the IRS, you may be assessed the tax on unreported taxable gain at any time.

If you will receive some or all of the sales proceeds after the year of sale and you do not qualify for deferral or elect the exclusion, you must report your gain on the installment basis, unless you elect to report the entire gain in the year of sale.

TAX SAVINGS FOR INVESTORS

With the repeal of the capital gain deduction, the substantial tax benefits of realizing long-term capital gain are no longer available. Long-term capital gains are now subject to ordinary income tax rates. However, the distinction between short- and long-term capital gain remains effective, although the ordinary tax rates apply equally to both types of gains. Although capital gains are fully subject to ordinary income tax, the $3,000 limitation on deducting capital losses from other types of income remains as a substantial limitation on capital losses. If you have substantial capital losses, limited by the $3,000 rule, it will remain advisable to realize income from capital asset transactions.

As long-term capital gains, interest, and dividends become taxable at the same tax

---

WILL CAPITAL GAINS BREAK BE RESTORED?

As this book went to press, Congress was debating whether to restore an exclusion for long-term capital gains or to limit the tax rate on such capital gains to 20% or 15%. Another proposal would index capital gains for inflation. Supporters of cutting the rates on capital gains claim that doing so would increase government tax revenues as investors sell appreciated assets to take advantage of the lower rates.

Watch for developments in the capital gain area; it's possible that tax incentives for long-term investing may be put back into the tax law!

rate, your investment strategies should change. In holding securities, you will generally not pay as much attention to holding periods as with pre-1987 investments. Your test for judging the investment return will be the same for gains, interest, and dividend income, which is the net after-tax return over a given period. If the projected after-tax return on a stock held for investment will give only 5% over a two-year period, for example, an investment that will return net interest after tax of 7% during the same period should be the preferred investment, all other things being equal.

Investing in Mutual Funds

Many people buy a ready-made tax liability simply by investing in a mutual fund that has already realized significant capital gains during the year. With a mutual fund, the cost of your shares is based on the current value of its portfolio. At the end of the year, the

Money Management Tip

gains realized by the fund before your investment are distributed to you as a capital gain distribution. You then have to pay tax on the return of your own money. You also have to pay tax on the return of your own money if you invest shortly before the stock goes "ex-dividend"—not a wise move in any financial planner's book! However, an experienced fund advisor can tell you when to make your investment. You can postpone investing until after the stock goes "ex-dividend." You will not receive that dividend or pay tax on it, and your buying price will be based on an asset value that is reduced by the capital gain dividend distribution.

Identifying Specific Shares When You Sell

By providing the mutual fund with specific instructions to sell shares bought on a particular date at a particular price, you can determine whether profit or loss will result, based on the cost of the shares selected. If you do not specifically identify the shares being sold, the IRS applies a first-in, first-out (FIFO) rule that treats you as selling shares in the order you bought them. Alternatively, you can make the election discussed below for averaging the cost of your shares.

Averaging Cost for Sale of Mutual Fund Shares. A U.S. Treasury regulation sets rules for averaging the cost of purchases made at different times if only part of your holdings are sold. The election applies to open-end mutual fund shares held by an agent—usually a bank—in an account kept for the periodic acquisition or redemption of shares in the fund. Averaging avoids the difficult task of identifying the exact shares being sold where shares were bought at different times and prices. There are two averaging methods: single and double category.

Under the single-category method, all shares in an account are totaled. The basis of each share is the total basis of all shares in the account at the time of a sale or transfer, divided by the number of shares in the account. For purposes of determining the holding period, the shares sold or transferred are considered to be those shares acquired first.

Under the double-category method, at the time of each sale you divide all shares in an account into two classes: shares held long-term and shares held short-term.

Shares are deemed to be transferred from each class without regard to stock certificates. You may tell the agent from which class you are selling. If you do not so specify, the long-term shares are deemed to have been sold first. If the number of shares sold exceeds the number in the long-term class, the excess shares are charged to the short-term class.

IRS Publication Number 564 provides de-

Record This Information

tails of these methods. You choose to average on your tax return for the first taxable year to which you want the election to apply. Note on your return which method you have chosen. Keep records to support the average basis used on your return. The election applies to all shares of the particular mutual fund in which the election is initially made.

Reducing the Tax on Dividend Income

Because current tax law encourages investors to look for current income instead of shelters, minimize taxes as follows:

1. *Sell stock on which a dividend has been declared but not yet paid.* During the period a dividend is declared but not paid, the price of the stock includes the value of the dividend. If you plan to sell stock in this position and figure that the tax on the dividend reflected in the selling price will be less than the tax on the dividend received, transact the sale before the stock goes ex-dividend.

2. *Invest in companies that pay tax-free dividends.* Some companies pay tax free dividends. A list of companies that do may be provided by your broker. When you receive a tax-free dividend, you do not report the dividend as income as long as the dividend does not exceed your stock basis. A tax-free dividend reduces the tax cost of your stock; dividends in excess of basis produce capital gain.

3. *Invest in companies that pay stock dividends.* A stock dividend is generally not taxable income.

Real Estate Tax Planning

The current tax law has caused radical restructuring for many commercial real estate investments, as follows:

1. *Passive activity income or loss.* By law, income and losses of rental operations are treated as passive activity income and loss. This treatment has its advantages and disadvantages. The disadvantage is that losses are not deductible from salary, interest, and dividend income. The advantage is that rental income may be offset by other passive activity losses.

2. *Dealer or investor status.* Your status as a dealer or investor will affect how you deduct interest and whether you can use the installment sales method on sales of property.

3. *Leasehold improvements.* Leasehold improvements made by you as a lessee must be depreciated although the lease term may be shorter than the depreciation period.

4. *Tax credits.* Benefits from tax credits are available for rehabilitation and low income housing.

The ideal real estate investment should provide a current income return and an appreciation in the value of the original investment. As an additional incentive, a real estate investment may in the early years of the investment provide income subject to little or no tax. That may happen when depreciation and other expense deductions reduce taxable income without reducing the amount of cash available for distribution. This tax savings is temporary and is limited by the terms and the amount of the mortgage debt on the property. Mortgage amortization payments reduce the amount of cash available to investors without an offsetting tax deduction. Thus, the amount of tax-free return depends on the extent to which depreciation deductions exceed the amortization payments.

To provide a higher return of tax-free income, at least during the early years of its operations, a venture must obtain a constant payment of mortgage that provides for the payment of fixed annual amounts that are allocated to continually decreasing amounts of interest and increasing amounts of amortization payments—the buildup of owners' equity through mortgage reduction. Consequently, in the early years a tax-free return of income is high while the amortization payments are low. But as the amortization payments increase, nontaxable income decreases. When this tax-free return has been substantially reduced, a partnership must refinance the mortgage to reduce the amortization payments and once again increase the tax-free return.

For example, let us say a limited real estate partnership of 100 investors owns a building that returns an annual income of $100,000 after operating expenses are deducted, but before a depreciation deduction of $80,000. Thus, taxable income is $20,000 ($100,000 minus $80,000). Assuming that there is no mortgage on the building, the whole $100,000 is available for distribution. (Since the depreciation requires no cash outlay, it does not reduce the cash available for distribution.) Each investor receives $1,000. Taxable income being $20,000, only 20%

($20,000 ÷ $100,00) of the distribution is taxable. Thus each investor reports as income only $200 of the $1,000 distribution; $800 is tax free.

Now, suppose the building is mortgaged and an annual amortization payment of $40,000 is being made. Consequently, only $60,000 is available for distribution, of which $20,000 is taxable. Each investor receives $600, of which one-third ($20,000 ÷ $60,000) or $200 is taxed, and $400 is tax free. In other words, the $60,000 distribution is tax free to the extent that the depreciation deduction of $80,000 exceeds the amortization of $40,000—namely, $40,000. If the amortization payment was increased to $50,000, only $30,000 of the distribution would be tax free ($80,000 minus $50,000).

The tax-free return is based on the assumption that the building does not actually depreciate at a rate as fast as the tax depreciation rate. If the building is depreciating physically at a faster rate, the so-called tax-free return on investment does not exist. Distributions to investors (over and above current income return) that are labeled "tax-free distributions" are in fact a return of the investor's own capital.

The preceding advantages are available for investments made by you individually or in partnership with other associates. They are also available to investors in limited partnerships. However, before investing in a limited partnership, consider these disadvantages of this form of business:

1. Investors in limited partnerships are by law generally treated as receiving passive activity income or loss. Furthermore, as a limited partner, you may not take advantage of the $25,000 rental loss allowance, as you are not considered an "active participant." In view of the passive activity rules, if you and others join together to buy rental property, you should generally not organize as a limited partnership if losses are anticipated. Limited partnerships are advisable only if income is expected or where two or more investment activities will produce income and loss, which will offset each other.

2. Although limited partnerships are organized to prevent double taxation, which occurs in doing business as a corporation, there is a danger that the partnership may be taxed

as a corporation if its operations resemble those of a corporation.

Look At This:

3. Partnership operations do not provide for the diversification of investments or for the free transfer of individual interests. Investors may find it difficult to sell their interests because of transferability restrictions and a lack of an open market for the sale of their interests.

Investing in REITs. The tax treatment of real estate investment trusts (REITs) resembles that of open-end mutual funds. Distributions are taxed to the investors in the trust as ordinary income. Distributed long-term capital gains are reported by the investors as long-term gains. If the trust operates at a loss, the loss may not be passed on to the investors.

A REIT may not necessarily invest in equities. It may operate for interest return by providing loans to other real estate investors. Before investing, check the scope of the REIT's operations and current market conditions and projections.

Investing in REMICs. The tax law encourages the creation of "real estate mortgage investment conduits" (REMICs). A REMIC is formed to hold a fixed pool of mortgages. Investors are treated as holding a regular or residual interest. A corporation, partnership, or trust that meets statutory tests is allowed to be treated as a REMIC. In addition, a segregated pool of assets may also qualify as a REMIC as if it were an entity meeting the requirements.

A REMIC is not a taxable entity for federal income tax purposes. The income from the REMIC generally is reported by holders of regular and residual interests. However, a REMIC may be subject to tax on prohibited transactions and may be required to withhold on amounts paid to foreign holders of regular or residual interests.

The passthrough status of the REMIC applies regardless of whether the REMIC was formed as a corporation, partnership, or trust. For example, where a REMIC is organized as a partnership, the partnership provisions do not apply

A

High Taxes
High Expenses

to any transactions involving the REMIC or any of the holders of regular or residual interest. At the time this book went to press, the Treasury had released few regulations governing REMICs, so it important to look for new developments in this area. Income from a REMIC is reported on Schedule E.

Exchanging Real Estate Without Tax. You may trade real estate held for investment for other investment real estate and incur no tax until the time you sell the exchanged property at a price exceeding the tax basis of the property. A tax-free exchange may also defer a potential tax due on gain from depreciation recapture and might be considered where the depreciable basis of a building has been substantially written off. Here the building may be exchanged for other property that will give larger deductions.

The postponement of tax is equivalent to receiving an interest-free government loan in the amount you would have owed in taxes had you sold the property. With no part of your capital depleted by tax, you can reinvest the full value of your old property.

Although tax-free exchange has this major tax attraction, there are limitations on its use. The primary problem is bringing together suitable exchange properties and investors interested in trading. This difficulty may sometimes be overcome by brokers specializing in real estate exchanges. Another serious limitation attaches to exchanges dealing with depreciable property: the tax rule requires you to carry over the basis of the old property to the new property. A tax-free exchange is not desirable if the transaction will result in a loss, because you may not deduct a loss in a tax-free exchange. To ensure the loss deduction, first sell the property, then buy new property with the proceeds. Furthermore, if you trade property with a related person, tax-free treatment may be lost unless both of you keep the exchanged properties for at least two years.

Caution: The IRS has proposed new time limits for deferred exchanges and like-kind tests for business equipment. Additional Congressional restrictions on tax-free exchanges are possible. Check with your tax advisor before planning an exchange.

Timing Your Real Property Sales. Generally, a taxable transaction occurs in the year in which title or possession to property passes. By controlling the year in which title and possession passes, you may select the year in which to report profit or loss. For example, suppose you intend to sell property this year, but you estimate that reporting the sale next year will incur less taxes. You can postpone the transfer of title and possession to next year. Alternatively, you can transact an installment sale, giving title and possession this year but delaying the receipt of all or most of the sale proceeds until next year.

Money Management Tip

TAX SAVINGS AT WORK

Pay plans provide one of the few opportunities for deferring or sheltering income. The right plan for you, of course, will depend on your financial situation and near-term spending needs.

Pension and Profit-Sharing Plans

A company-qualified pension or profit-sharing plan offers these benefits:

1. You do not realize current income on the contributions your employer makes.
2. Funds contributed by both you and your employer compound tax free within the plan.
3. If you receive a lump sum, tax on employer contributions may be reduced by a special averaging rule.
4. If you receive a lump-sum distribution in company securities, unrealized appreciation on those securities is not taxed until you finally sell the stock.

When you are allowed to choose the type of payout from a qualified plan, make sure that you compare (1) the tax on receiving a lump-sum distribution with (2) the projected tax cost of deferring payments over a period of years or (3) of rolling over the distribution to an IRA account.

Caution: Check with your tax advisor about Congressional threats to limit special averaging for lump-sum payouts.

Cash or Deferred Pay Arrangements: 401(k) Plans

If your company has a profit-sharing or stock bonus plan, it has the opportunity of giving you additional tax-sheltered pay. The tax law allows the company to add a cash or deferred pay plan, called a 401(k) plan, which can operate in one of two ways:

1. Your employer contributes an amount to a trust account for your benefit. You are not taxed on your employer's contribution. Although there is no income tax, the contribution is subject to Social Security tax.
2. You agree to take a salary reduction or to

Money
Management
Tip

forgo a salary increase. The reduction is placed in a trust account for your benefit. The reduction is treated as your employer's contribution. In addition, your company may match part of your contribution.

In 1990, the law limited total salary reduction deferrals to $7,979. This amount is increased by cost-of-living adjustments. Taking a pay reduction may be an ideal way to defer income and benefit from a tax-free buildup of income.

Income earned on the trust account accumulates tax free until it is withdrawn. By law, you may not withdraw funds attributable to elective salary reduction contributions until you reach age 59½ are separated from service, become disabled, or in limited circumstances show financial hardship. Withdrawals are also allowed if the plan terminates or if the corporation sells its assets or its interest in a subsidiary and you continue to work for the buyer or the subsidiary. However, the hardship provision and age 59½ allowance do not apply to certain "pre-ERISA" money purchase pension plans (in existence June 27, 1974). Furthermore, hardship withdrawals may include only an employee's elective deferrals; the hardship withdrawal may not include employer contributions or income earned on the employ-

ee's elective deferrals.

If withdrawals are allowed before age 59½, such as for hardship, you are subject to the

Money
Management
Tip

10% penalty for premature withdrawals unless you meet one of the exceptions allowed. A lump-sum distribution may be eligible for special averaging under IRS rules. Lump-sum distributions exceeding $750,000 may be subject to the excess distribution penalty. If you are allowed to borrow from the plan, certain loan restrictions apply.

Finally, you should know that the law imposes strict contribution percentage tests to prevent discrimination in favor of highly compensated employees. If these tests are violated, the employer is subject to penalties and the plan could be disqualified unless the excess contributions (plus allocable income) are distributed back to the highly compensated employees within a specified time.

Saving Taxes on Insurance Plans

Company-financed insurance for employees is a common way to give additional benefits at low or no tax cost. For example, group insurance plans may furnish not only life insurance protection, but also accident and health benefits. Premium costs are low and tax deductible to the company while tax free to you unless you have nonforfeitable rights to permanent life insurance or, in the case of group term life insurance, your coverage exceeds $50,000. Even where your coverage exceeds $50,000, the tax incurred on your employer's premium payment is generally less than what you would pay privately for similar insurance.

Where you want more insurance than provided by the group plan, your company may be able to help you get additional protection through a split-dollar insurance plan. Under this type of plan, your employer purchases permanent life insurance for you. The company pays the annual premium to the extent of the yearly increases in the cash surrender value of the policy, and you pay only the balance of the premium. At your death, your employer is entitled to a part of the proceeds equal to the cash surrender value of the total premiums he or she paid. You have the right to name a beneficiary to receive the remaining proceeds, which under most policies are substantial compared with the employer's share.

You annually report as taxable income an amount equal to the one-year term cost of the declining life insurance protection to which you are entitled, less any portion of the premium provided by you.

Despite the tax cost, you may find the arrangement an inexpensive way to obtain additional insurance coverage with your employer's help. Split-dollar insurance policies entered into before November 14, 1964, are not subject to this tax on the employer's payment of premiums.

Educational Benefits for Employees' Children

The IRS has published guidelines under which a private foundation established by an employer may make tax-free grants to children of employees. If the guidelines are satisfied, employees are not taxed on the benefits provided for their children. Advance approval of the grant program must be obtained from the IRS and it must also meet a percentage test regarding the number of grants awarded versus the number of eligible children.

SAVING TAXES THROUGH FAMILY INCOME PLANNING

The law discourages income splitting among family members by

1. Reducing the difference between the lowest and highest brackets. When the range between tax brackets was 11% and 50% (and sometimes as high as 70%), there was an obvious incentive for diverting income from high breadwinner brackets to the lower brackets of dependents. The 18% spread between the 15% and maximum 33% tax brackets provided under current law may not offer the same motivation for such transfers.
2. Taxing investment income exceeding $1,000 of minor children under the age 14

at the top bracket of parents.
3. Repealing the income-shifting feature of short-term (10-year, or Clifford) trusts.

Although the tax-saving advantages of family income splitting have been eroded by these developments, certain tax savings are available.

Escaping Gift Tax Liability

Because family income planning generally requires the transfer of property, you must consider possible gift tax liability. The gift tax rates and credit are the same as those of the estate tax. However, gift tax liability may be avoided by making gifts within the annual exclusion of $10,000 (or $20,000 for joint gifts). Gifts over this exclusion may also avoid tax after applying the unified gift and estate tax credit described at the end of this chapter.

If you make interest-free or low-interest loans to a family member, you may be subject to income tax as well as a gift tax.

Unfortunately, to realize the full potential of income splitting, you must do more than make gifts of income: you must actually transfer property from which the income is produced. For example, you do not avoid tax on interest by instructing your savings bank to credit interest to your children's account. Unless you actually transfer the complete ownership of the account to your children, the interest income is earned on money owned by you and must be reported by you. The same holds true with dividends, rents, and other forms of income. Unless you transfer the property providing the income, the income will be taxed to you.

You may not split earned income; income resulting from your services is taxed to you. You may not avoid this result by setting up trusts to receive your earned income.

Custodian Accounts for Children

Custodian accounts set up in a bank, mutual fund, or brokerage firm can achieve income splitting, although certain tax consquences apply to each type of account. Trust accounts are considered revocable under state law and are ineffective in splitting interest income. Also, limitations are placed on the custodian. He or she may not take proceeds from the sale of an investment or income from an investment to buy additional securities on margin. Although the custodian should prudently seek reasonable income and capital preservation, he or she generally is not liable for losses unless they result from bad-faith, intentional wrongdoing, or gross negligence.

When the minor reaches majority (depending on state law), property in the custodian account is turned over to the child. No

Money Management Tip

formal accounting is required, although a separate bank account should be opened in which proceeds from sales of investments and investment income are deposited pending reinvestment. Such an account will furnish a convenient record of sales proceeds, investment income, and reinvestment of same.

Income from a custodian account is taxable to the child as long as it is not used by the parent who set up the account to pay for the child's support. Tax-exempt income from a custodian account is not taxable to the parent even when used for child support. Income from a custodian account in excess of $1,000 is taxed at the parent's tax rate if the child is under age 14.

When setting up a custodian account, you may have to pay a gift tax because transfer of cash or securities (above the $10,000 single, or $20,000 joint, annual exclusion) is a gift. If you die while acting as custodian of an account before your child reaches majority, the value of the custodian account will be taxed with your estate. This problem may be avoided if you appoint someone other than yourself as custodian.

Other Types of Investments for Minors

Because a minor generally lacks the ability to manage property, you may wish to control the property you give—although such active management may disallow the gift for income-shifting purposes. You could appoint a fiduciary for the child, but this will only add to the investment's cost. Alternatively, you might choose a property that does not re-

quire investor participation and that can be transferred to a minor, such as

1. *Bonds, which may be purchased and registered in a minor's name.* Coupons or the proceeds on sale or maturity of bonds may be cashed or deposited in a minor's name.

2. *Insurance policies written on the lives of minors.* These policies recognize the minor's ownership of the policy and may cover the lives of others. Depending on the age of the minor, state law, and company practice, it may be necessary to appoint a guardian for the purpose of cashing in or borrowing on insurance policies given to a minor. A gift of a life insurance policy or annuity will usually qualify as a gift of a present interest in property for the annual gift tax exclusion.

3. *Mutual fund shares that may be purchased and registered in the name of a minor.* The problem of management is minimized by the investment company's supervision of the fund. Most funds also provide automatic reinvestment of dividends in additional shares.

Other Income-Splitting Possibilities

Making a gift of appreciated property that will eventually be sold may reduce income tax. To shift the profit and the tax, the gift must be completed before the sale or before the donor has made a binding commitment to sell. By making a gift of interests in the property to several family members, it is possible to spread the tax among a number of taxpayers in the lowest tax bracket. Of course, the IRS may claim that the gift was never completed if, after sale, the donor controls the sales proceeds or has use of them. You should also remember that appreciation on property passed by inheritance will escape income tax: the heir takes a basis equal to estate tax value, usually fair market value at the date of death. Furthermore, appreciated property encumbered by mortgage may result in income tax liability to the donor when a gift of the property is made.

If you own a business, tax on your business income may be reduced if you can shift it to members of your family.

Business income may be shifted by forming a family partnership or by making your family stockholders in a corporation. Generally speaking, a Subchapter S corporation in which stockholders elect to report income may be used more freely than a partnership to split income. A minor child will not be recognized as a partner unless he or she is competent to manage the property, or unless control of the property is exercised by another person as a fiduciary for the child's sole benefit.

Life Insurance Tax Advantages

Insurance may provide tax-free accumulation of cash. During the time you pay premiums, the value of your contract increases at compound interest rates. The increase is not subject to income tax. In addition, when your policy is paid at death, the proceeds are not subject to income tax.

To shelter life insurance proceeds from estate tax, you must not have ownership rights. If you have an existing policy, you must assign your ownership rights, such as the right to change beneficiaries, the right to surrender or cancel the policy, the right to assign it, and the right to borrow against it. An assignment must occur more than three years before death to exclude the proceeds from your estate.

If you create a trust to carry a policy on your life by transferring income-producing property, the income of which is used to pay the premiums, you are taxable on the trust's income. Similarly, if your spouse creates the trust to carry the policy on your life, he or she is taxable on the trust's income. This tax rule does not apply to the trust funding of life insurance covering the life of a third party other than your spouse. For example, a grandparent transfers income-producing property to a trust to pay the premiums on a life insurance policy for a son. The grandchildren are named as beneficiaries. The grandparent is not taxed on the income earned by the trust on the transferred property because the trust purchased insurance on the son's life, not on the grandparent's.

The trust may receive insurance proceeds where there is a concern that the beneficiary may be unable to manage a

Look At This:

large insurance settlement. Insurance proceeds are not subject to income tax whether paid directly to named beneficiaries or to a trust.

More information on types of insurance policies available, their investment value, and their tax consequences, may be found in Part III of this book.

TAX SAVINGS FOR SENIOR CITIZENS

When you reach age 65, you receive an increased standard deduction allowance, provided you do not itemize deductions. If you or your spouse have reached the age of 65 on January 1, 1991, you claim the extra standard deduction amounts on your 1990 tax return. For tax purposes, you are considered to be 65 on December 31, 1990. You may also be entitled to a tax credit depending on the amount of your income and Social Security benefits. If you are age 55 or over and sold your principal residence at a gain, you may elect to avoid tax on up to $125,000 of profit, provided you meet certain tests and file an election, as discussed earlier in this chapter.

Tax Credits for the Elderly and Disabled

In 1990, the credit for the elderly is available mainly to people 65 or over who do not receive Social Security or Railroad Retirement benefits or people under 65 who are permanently and totally disabled and receive disability income. There is also an overall income limitation. The credit for elderly and disabled is combined with the credits for dependent care and mortgage credit certificates. The total credits may not exceed regular tax liability without the alternative minimum tax and self-employment tax and penalty taxes for premature retirement distributions.

Taxes and Social Security

Social Security benefits are not paid automatically. You must register at the local Social Security office three months before your sixty-fifth birthday to allow time for your application to be processed and to locate all necessary information. Even if you do not plan to retire at age 65, you must register to ensure your Medicare coverage. For each year past 65 that you delay retiring, your potential Social Security benefits increase.

If you are under 70, Social Security benefits are reduced by earned income (wages and self-employment income). For example, if you were 65 or older but under 70 in 1990, you could earn $9,360 without losing benefits. If you were under 65 for the whole year, you could earn $6,840 without losing benefits. These ceilings are subject to inflation adjustments. Once you earn more than these ceilings, benefits are reduced. After 1990, you will lose $1 in benefits for each $3 you earn above the earnings ceiling if you are between 65 and 69; $1 in benefits for each $2 of earnings above the ceiling if under 65.

For those age 70 or over, benefits are not reduced by earnings. You can work, earn any amount, and receive full Social Security benefits.

As long as you continue to work, regardless of your age, you will pay Social Security taxes on your earnings. You may also receive any amount of income from other sources than work (private pensions or investments, for example) without affecting the amount of Social Security benefits. However, benefits may be taxable if your income exceeds a base amount, so check with your Social Security office if this potential liability is significant for you. The maximum taxable amount is 50% of benefits.

There are two steps in figuring taxation of Social Security benefits: (1) deciding whether your income exceeds the base amount for your filing status, and (2) calculating the amount of benefits subject to tax. Your tax advisor or *J.K. Lasser's Your Income Tax* will show you how to make these computations.

The Social Security Administration has been criticized for not keeping up with workers' earning records. Don't risk a problem by ignoring your own record. Once every three years you should obtain from your local Social Security Office a form for requesting a statement of your earnings history. The Social Security Administration will provide an estimate of future benefits when it sends you the earnings statement.

Money Management Tip

SAVING TAXES IN OTHER SITUATIONS

Members of the armed forces stationed outside the United States and those returning from foreign duty, veterans of the Vietnam conflict, members of the reserves, and anyone receiving income from foreign sources all face special tax situations. Resident and nonresident aliens also face tax consequences for money earned in the United States. If you fall into one or more of these categories, consult your tax advisor or *J. K. Lasser's Your Income Tax* before filing your return to ensure you have taken advantage of every possible deduction, credit, and benefit—and met every obligation.

WHAT HAPPENS AFTER YOU FILE YOUR RETURN?

Although the time to minimize your taxes is *before* you prepare your return, your opportunities for savings (and potential for new liabilities) continue while the IRS examines your return.

First the IRS checks your return for arithmetic accuracy. If a mistake is found, you receive either a refund or a bill for additional tax. Naturally, the IRS looks first for errors that most typically result in a higher tax, such as reported medical expenses without the adjusted gross income limitation, or use of auto mileage for business travel that exceeds the allowable IRS rate.

The IRS also screens returns that claim refunds from tax shelters. If your return is selected for more thorough review, you will be notified by letter—although this may not happen for a year or two after you file. Your chances of being audited are greatest in the following circumstances:

- If you claim tax shelter losses
- If you report complex investment or business transactions without clearly explaining them
- If you receive cash payments in your work that the IRS thinks are easy to conceal, such as cash fees received by physicians or tips received by cab drivers and waiters
- If your business expenses are large in

comparison to income

- If your cash contributions to charity are large in relation to income
- If you are a shareholder of a closely held corporation whose return has been examined
- If a prior audit has resulted in a tax deficiency
- If an informer gives the IRS grounds to believe you are omitting income from your return

An examination may take place at a local IRS office or at your place of business or home if your return is complex and involves many outside records. If the questions can be cleared up by correspondence, you may not have to appear at all. If your return is complex, a large potential tax liability is involved, or if you are unfamiliar with how the return was prepared, it's advisable to have an experienced tax practitioner represent you during the examination. If you disagree with the examiner's findings, many appeal steps are possible, from an immediate interview with the examiner's supervisor (if the audit was conducted in an IRS office) to eventual litigation in Tax Court, federal district court, or U.S. Claims Court.

Notes

PART III

INVESTMENT GUIDE TO PRODUCT OPPORTUNITIES

In the deregulated and reregulated financial markets of the late 1980s, investment products change almost daily. In Chapters 11 through 20, you'll learn which products comprise the six basic asset categories over which you'll spread your wealth-building portfolio. In

Chapters 17, 18, and 19, you'll discover the advanced trading techniques and special investments that are tailored to unique portfolio needs. In Chapter 20, you'll find out how to maximize the value of your home as an investment.

CHAPTER 11

CASH AND MONEY MARKET INSTRUMENTS

Liquidity

Inflation

Ordinary Income

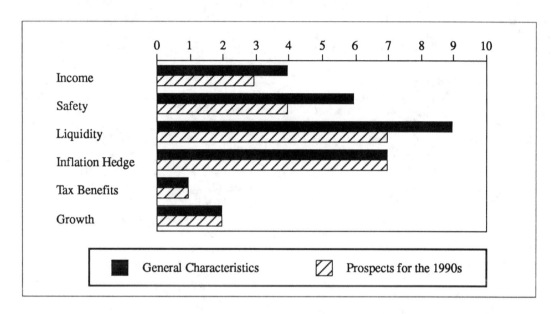

	0	1	2	3	4	5	6	7	8	9	10
Income											
Safety											
Liquidity											
Inflation Hedge											
Tax Benefits											
Growth											

■ General Characteristics   ▨ Prospects for the 1990s

Outlook for the 1990s

Low volatility

Record deficits will temper down move in rates

Rates will trend lower if recession occurs after initial increase

Minimal Inflation risk

Liquidity problems if recession develops leading to cash flow problems for corporate issuers

A GLANCE AHEAD

The collapse in oil prices in 1985 and 1986 left many wealthy Americans in the peculiar position of being "asset rich" and "cash poor." In the headlong rush to accumulate wealth, they failed to understand the importance of liquidity. All investments are ultimately valued in the terms of the cash they will fetch.

Cash provides the grease that enables the wheels of our increasingly complex economy to roll. The high inflation and interest rates of the late 1970s led to deregulation of the financial markets. A variety of new money market instruments developed to meet the demands of savvy investors who want their money earning market interest rates while

remaining liquid enough to take advantage of new market opportunities.

In this chapter, you'll discover the most important of these new products as well as updates on the more familiar savings alternatives. You'll learn

- *How money market instruments provide portfolio liquidity so you'll be prepared for*

    *Emergencies requiring immediate cash
    New opportunities
    Quick asset allocation adjustments*

- *How money market instruments can be used to earn more income on even your personal bill-paying accounts.*

PROSPECTS FOR THE 1990s MONEY MARKETS

Since the stock market crash of October 1987, investors have been cautious. Daily market swings have become more moderate as previously aggressive traders turned to more defensive investment strategies. Money market instruments play a very important role in this new environment.

While the stock market in 1990 surprised many analysts, ourselves included, we still rate the prospect of earning high double-digit returns like those of the 1982 through 1986 period to be low. The bond market was the immediate beneficiary of the October Crash and the subsequent reorientation of traders. However, that market has fluctuated widely since then.

Much money was pulled out of both stock and bond mutual funds following the crash. That money has flowed into money market instruments, notably money market funds. In fact, money market fund balances hit new highs throughout 1989 and the first half of 1990.

Many advisors recommend holding higher cash levels during these uncertain times. The consensus economic forecast for the 1990s is for slower economic growth, though only a few look for anything more severe than a mild recession.

Whereas the stock market tends to lead the economy, the money markets are most immediately affected by economic developments. Below, we detail both the pluses and minuses for the economy as of mid-year, 1990. These areas should be watched for clues on how aggressive you want to be in the various asset classes. When in doubt, use the money markets as a safe, liquid place to park your money.

The Economy. Following the massive stock market crash in October 1987, many economists projected an economic downturn for 1988 and 1989. The robust growth in 1988, and steady growth in early 1990, shows the limitations of such forecasts. The strong growth was fueled by a continued export boom that strengthened the manufacturing sector. Steadily improving employment prospects raised shaken consumer confidence. As consumers once again demonstrated their willingness to take on additional debt, domestic demand also increased, further benefitting the market.

Why didn't the stock market crash lead to recession, or even depression, as some expected? There are many theories. Perhaps the best explanation lies in equity statistics. Only slightly more than 20% of all U.S. families own stocks directly. Those who do own stocks tend to be the more affluent, with high net worth. That net worth usually is tied to home equity rather than stocks and bonds. Home prices for the most part were not hurt by the crash or since.

In addition, job and income growth was steady. Export demand did not diminish noticeably. Employment continued its upward path, though slowing somewhat in 1989 and early 1990.

Other positive developments include the sharp increase in productivity in the first quarter of 1988. Economists had been worried about the 1% decline in nonfarm productivity of the last quarter of 1987.

This business cycle is certainly not following the usual script. Typically, productivity falls off in the later stages of a recovery after strong gains at the beginning. By the summer of 1990, the recovery was already over 90 months old. That is about three times longer than average.

With good export demand and heightened consumer spending leading the way, the economy in 1989 proved the doomsayers wrong once again. By late 1989 though the manufacturing sector was showing signs of weakness.

Strong industrial growth strained plant capacity, with average factory utilization exceeding 80% by 1989. (Some industries, such as paper, chemicals, and base metals have utilization rates of over 90%!) As production pressures slipped, it moderated rising inflation fears. By June 1990 a Federal Reserve report on economic activity in 12 sectors of the country showed that only the West, served by San Francisco's Federal Reserve Bank, could be described as healthy.

Credit pressures caused by tough Federal Reserve policy led to softening in real estate markets in many parts of the country. This offset inflationary pressures from a tight labor market. When business seeks to expand capacity, it will require huge injections of capital.

The chief concern for money market investors is the expected level of interest rates. Interest rates are closely tied to two main factors: the demand for money, and the expected rate of inflation. When business is booming, businesses borrow money aggressively to expand. As businesses expand, employment prospects improve. This improvement leads to greater consumer confidence which, in turn, leads to further borrowing.

That scenario has been played out in the last six years of economic expansion. Corporate debt has risen over 120% in the 1980s. By the end of 1987, it had reached $1.9 trillion. Interest payments on this debt has also grown. It now accounts for over 20% of corporate cash flow.

As interest rates rise, some sectors in the economy will be hard hit. The already reeling construction business will be dealt another blow. Higher rates will also hurt new car sales, an important part of the manufacturing sector.

What to Watch

The sheer length of the current business expansion increases the odds that a recession may be just around the corner. It is important for investors to keep tabs on these developments. Although a recession will eventually mean lower interest rates, rates initially turn higher. As the odds of recession increase, you will want to move money from asset classes that will be hurt most (stocks, real estate, and inflation hedges) into money market instruments. Because of these increasing rates, you will want to minimize your bond investments, then buy more bonds as rates turn down in reaction to the slowing economy.

Every recession in the last 30 years has been led by increasing rates. Rates bottomed in June 1958 prior to the April 1960 recession. They bottomed in January 1963 for December 1969; January 1972 for November 1973; January 1977 for January 1980; and June 1980 for July 1981.

For the current expansion, rates bottomed in February 1987. Since then, rates on high-grade corporate bonds have been as high as 10.80% in October 1987. They slipped back to 9.17% in July 1988. By July 1990 they dropped to 8.55%. A move back over 9.25% will be an important warning signal.

Federal Reserve actions will be an important tipoff on interest rates and inflation. Rising inflation will lead to sharply higher interest rates. Unlike years past, when interest rates lagged behind the rate of inflation, today's markets react almost instantaneously. In fact, today's bond market tends to overreact to even a hint of resurgent inflation!

Bonds fall in price when interest rates (or inflation) rise. The Federal Reserve has been walking a fine line between inflation containment and economic stimulus. It is vital for you as an investor to know what the Fed is up to. There are many different ways to analyze Fed action.

The simplest method is to watch what it does, not what is said. To do so, monitor the federal funds rate. The fed funds rate is the rate at which banks loan overnight reserves among themselves. Those banks needing reserves to meet legal requirements borrow, while those with excess reserves do the lending.

In recent years, the Fed has targeted the federal funds rate for most of its actions. However, don't make the mistake of thinking the Fed will target an exact rate. Watch for a specific zone. As this update is being written, the Fed has kept the federal funds rates between 8.25 and 7.5%. Any sustained move beyond or below those limits will indicate the Fed has adopted a new policy.

A drop in the interest rate points to an easing of the money supply by the Fed. Look for lower interest rates in the short term, but this move would heighten the prospects for higher inflation down the road. Many analysts expect just this tactic by the Fed before the presidential elections.

A steady increase in the federal funds rate indicates tightening up by the Fed. This move will mean higher interest rates. The Fed has adopted this tactic a few times during this expansion in an attempt to head off an "overheated" economy. This move is a real possibility if inflation indicators rise sharply or if dollar weakness turns into a collapse.

Summing Up

The 1990s should not see markets as volatile as the recent past. The Bush Administraton and Federal Reserve Chairman Greenspan are working well together which gives the markets some stability. In uncertain times such as these, rĕly on money market instruments even more than usual.

After a peacetime economic expansion of record length, caution is the best policy. Remember, the real key to long-term investment success is to avoid the disasters. Transition years such as 1989 and 1990 are liable to spawn disasters for many investors.

Cash in the form of short-term money market instruments provide an important hedge against rising inflation and interest rates. Although bonds, real estate, and even stocks can be hurt by rising rates, your money market reserve will preserve its value. Remember, your money market allocation provides the liquidity to take advantage of emerging trends in other asset catagories.

Keep a minimum of 30% of your total cash equivalents in short-term U.S. Treasury bills or in money market funds that invest only in T-bills. More conservative investors should consider maintaining an even higher percentage of U.S. Treasury bills during the early 1990s. The problems in the banking and thrift industries will be exacerbated by an economic slowdown. Keeping a portion of your cash reserves directly in Treasury securities insures that you will not be inconvenienced by institutional failures.

INVESTING IN CASH AND MONEY MARKET INSTRUMENTS

Cash is legal tender for all transactions. Money market instruments are short-term investment vehicles that provide income to the owner of the cash in exchange for "loaning" the cash to another party for a short time. Money market instruments are frequently referred to as "cash equivalents" or "near-money investments." They have very short-term maturities, never more than 12 months, and typically are very liquid—very easily reconverted back to cash.

Cash itself earns no income. It has to be loaned at interest or invested in an apprecia-

Look At This:

tive security to grow. Cash is the last word in liquidity. In order to entice investors to forgo some liquidity an institution must offer to pay a reasonable interest in return. The less liquid the account becomes, the more interest the institution must pay. While the interest paid on cash and short-term debt varies widely, the value of cash itself varies only with the rate of inflation. When interest rates rise, the yields paid on cash and money market instruments also rise. Unlike long-term fixed income instruments, there is no risk due to principal if rates rise.

There are two types of near-money or cash equivalents: deposit accounts (such as passbook savings) and short-term debt called "paper" (such as commercial paper). Deposit accounts in federally chartered institutions are insured to $100,000. Short-term debt paper is typically not insured and pays higher in-terest. However, Treasury bills, short-term debt issued by the federal government is even safer than insured deposit accounts. They are backed by the full faith and credit of the U.S. government.

Risks

Although greenbacks can be lost or stolen, cash (demand deposit account) is very safe— although there are some risks. The principal risk is that of the bank's failure as a business. If your bank or money market fund fails due to malfeasance or simply poor business judgment, you may lose some or all of your uninsured principal. The short-term nature of money market instruments protects them from the heavy loss of purchasing power due to inflation, but interest rates typically rise more slowly than inflation in the early stages. Stocks, precious metals or real estate are better inflation hedges.

All investments are subject in part to political risk. The falling dollar of 1986 and 1987 diminished the purchasing power of the dollar relative to other countries' currencies. A change in tax laws or the regulatory environment may adversely affect the profitability of cash in your portfolio. The adverse affects of political events are less onerous for cash and money market vehicles than other assets simply because they are so liquid.

There are ways to ensure even greater protection by investing in only those instruments that are evaluated and rated by independent credit services such as Standard & Poor's or Moody's. The federal government provides depositors' insurance for federally chartered savings and loans institutions as well as for banks.

Near-Money in Relation to Other Assets

Cash is unique because all other asset categories are valued in terms of the cash they can generate. In a diversified portfolio, cash provides a hedge against inflation because the rates on money market instruments will rise as inflation increases. Don't confuse this rise with profiting from inflation, though. Cash equivalents act to preserve your capital rather than produce profits.

In the initial phases of an inflationary spi-ral, the interest rates on short-term instruments tend to lag behind the rate of inflation. Once inflation becomes well established, short-term rates tend to rise quickly to reflect the current rise in prices. In recent years, short-term interest rates fell at a slower pace than inflation. Over a full inflation-deflation cycle the purchasing power of your cash (plus interest earned, of course) should remain fairly constant.

Although cash is generally considered to be a stable, nonspeculative preserve, the financial markets have developed products that enable you to speculate on short-term rates. The futures market offers the chance to buy certificates of deposit, Eurodollar deposits, three-month Treasury bills (T-bills), and other short-term instruments in a highly leveraged form. The major components of the broad category known as "cash and money market instruments" includes passbook savings accounts, credit union share deposit accounts, NOW and super-NOW accounts, certificates of deposit, commercial paper, banker's acceptances, repurchase agreements, and money market funds.

**Lasser's Recommended Allocation Range for the 1990s
Cash and Money Market Instruments**

Allocate as little as 10%.
Allocate as much as 40%.

Passbook Savings Accounts

Passbook savings accounts are short-term interest-bearing deposits with banks or thrift institutions. They were the staple of the savings industry until the 1970s. Banks and savings and loan institutions would acquire most of their funds for loans from low-yielding passbook savings accounts. They'd pay 5.25% for the deposits and then loan money out at a higher rate. Their profit came from the difference.

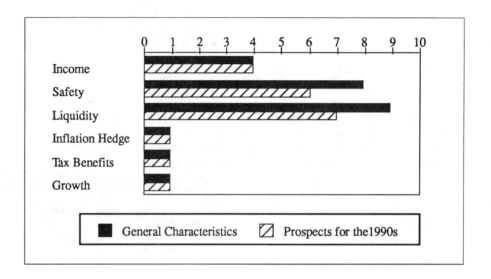

General Characteristics ▨ Prospects for the1990s

Type IV

C

Low Taxes
High Expenses

The passbook savings account has understandably withered in importance for many consumers. However, the deregulation of the financial industry has also presented many Americans with such a confusing array of alternatives, that the old passbook simplicity and convenience kept many customers. To this day, there are billions of dollars safely ensconced in passbook savings accounts.

The inflationary experience of the 1970s created a whole new savings and banking environment. Money market mutual funds available to most consumers began offering substantially higher yields than passbook accounts.

When inflation was raging at 10% to 15%, a passbook account paying 5.25% was a losing proposition.

Most savings institutions still offer passbook accounts. While the ceiling on passbook interest was eliminated in 1986, most savings institutions created numerous other products to compete with the money market funds. (See sections on NOW and super-NOW accounts, and certificates of deposit, later in this chapter.) As a result most passbook accounts still only pay about 5.25%.

You should investigate all the different types of savings accounts your bank offers. Other products may pay higher interest with no more fees than a passbook account and a reasonable amount of liquidity.

Usually no fees are assessed on a passbook account unless the activity is considered abusive.

Banks will advise you not to consider a passbook account a substitute for a checking account. Frequent withdrawals within a month (usually more than three) will trigger a fee. Accounts with *no* activity and minimal balances may be closed by the bank after a certain amount of time, usually six months.

Investment Potential

The days of the passbook savings account as your largest cash holding are long past. Its chief value now is for short-term savings while you are deciding where to place your funds. Such an account pays current income with no potential for capital gains.

A passbook savings account is the classic secure, nonvolatile, liquid investment. Under normal circumstances, you can obtain your money immediately by presenting your savings book (many institutions have replaced the "passbook" with computerized cards that resemble credit cards). However, you should be aware that all banks include a provision in the savings agreement that allows them to require as much as 30 days' advance notice for withdrawals. In practice, this provision is not invoked, but you never know what may happen in a financial crisis.

Federal deposit insurance covers most passbook savings accounts. The FDIC (banks) or Federal Savings and Loan Insurance Corporation, FSLIC (savings and loans) insurance covers account balances up to $100,000. You should be sure that accounts in your name do not exceed that amount in any one bank.

Passbook savings accounts offer no protection from inflation. They are not designed to offer variable interest rates that could offset higher inflation.

Strengths

 Passbook savings accounts are very liquid. They are insured by an agency of the federal government up to $100,000. They are convenient for short-term savings. You are not re-

quired to commit your money for any fixed period. Their concept is simple and widely understood in an increasingly complex financial world.

Weaknesses

 Passbook savings account typically pay much lower rates than money market funds or even other bank accounts. They offer little protection from inflation. Many institutions now require minimum monthly balances to receive interest.

Tax Considerations

Tax Consequences

Interest paid on passbook savings accounts is fully taxable at your ordinary income rates. The interest is also taxed by most states.

Summing Up

Many financial institutions are actually discouraging passbook savings accounts by assessing fees for small amounts. Formerly the backbone of the savings industry, passbook savings accounts are fading as realistic alternatives in a more sophisticated financial world.

Passbook savings offer a simple, safe, short-term "parking place" for your funds between other investments. However, the emphasis is on "short-term." There are equally safe alternatives that pay better yields.

Credit Unions

Credit unions are nonprofit cooperative savings organizations. This means that the members own the institution and have some common bond. Typically they are started by a company's employees, a church, a community, or even civic or fraternal organizations.

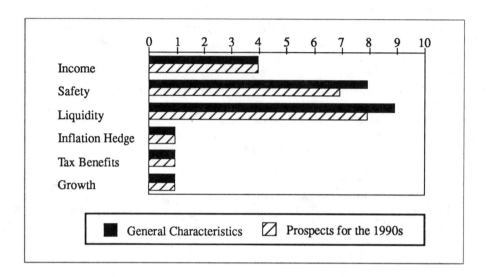

Type IV

C

Low Taxes
High Expenses

Credit unions offer services similar to other savings institutions, such as savings and checking accounts, time deposits such as certificates of deposit, and in recent years even credit cards, mortgage loans, and discount brokerage services. Generally smaller organizations, they offer more personal and informal contact and transactions.

Membership in many credit unions is offered as a fringe benefit for employees of a company. Often the employer provides free office space and other amenities. In addition, many credit unions use volunteer workers to accomplish some of their required tasks.

Many people find the informal, close-knit credit union environment more amenable for obtaining credit than large banking establishments. Loans are usually offered at lower rates than in profit-oriented enterprises because their costs are lower (credit union

profits are not usually subject to federal taxes).

There is usually no cost to join other than meeting the "common bond" requirement. Credit unions have become so widespread that most people qualify for at least one. Information on credit unions around the country is available from the Credit Union National Association, P.O. Box 431, Madison, WI 53701.

Federally chartered credit unions are covered by insurance issued by the National Credit Union Administration. Depositors (not accounts) are insured up to $100,000. Most state-chartered credit unions are also required to have equivalent insurance. However, not all are. You can write NCUA at 1776 G Street, NW, Washington, DC 20456 for details on those credit unions that are federally insured.

A credit union works much like any other savings institution, although the terminology is different. Your deposits are called *shares*. The interest earned on a credit union account is called *dividends,* though it is treated as interest for tax purposes. Checking accounts are called *share draft accounts*.

Investment Potential

For all intents and purposes, a credit union savings account is the same as a savings account at any banking or thrift institution. You should compare the returns with those offered by competitive organizations. As a part owner there is, of course, the intangible benefit of working with fellow employees or other organization members. Many credit unions offer their members a very real chance to participate in the business.

Credit unions offer interest for income on your savings. There are no capital gains (unless your credit union offers brokerage services). Employer credit unions offer a convenient way to save for retirement plans through payroll deductions. Loan payments can often also be structured this way.

The interest rates offered on credit union accounts are usually competitive with other savings institutions. However, keep in mind that savings accounts are not good protection from inflation.

Minimum accounts are small, and there are no (or very nominal) fees charged. If your account is less than $100,000, you should have no problem with liquidity.

Strengths

 Credit unions offer personalized attention no matter how small your account is. Accounts in federally chartered credit unions are insured to $100,000. Your money is liquid. Credit is readily available with minimal hassle. You can become personally involved. As a member of a cooperative, you may be entitled to receive an annual payout from the credit union if it meets certain performance criteria.

Weaknesses

 Higher returns are available through money market vehicles. Not all credit unions are insured. Interest (dividends) are taxable as ordinary income. After-tax returns may be higher in municipal securities. Credit lines are generally smaller than may be available at other institutions.

Tax Considerations

Tax Consequences

Although most credit unions call the money paid on deposits *dividends*, it is taxable as interest at ordinary income rates.

Summing Up

Credit unions offer a safe, liquid (if unexciting) haven for savings. The small, informal structure of most offer a chance for increased personal involvement. Deregulation of the savings industry has enabled many credit unions to expand their range of services.

They will never offer the highest return available but convenience may outweigh other considerations.

NOW and Super-NOW Accounts

The first effort to provide interest on checking accounts was the NOW account. NOW stands for "negotiable order of withdrawal." Basically it is the same as a checking account, but renamed to enhance its product value in the marketplace.

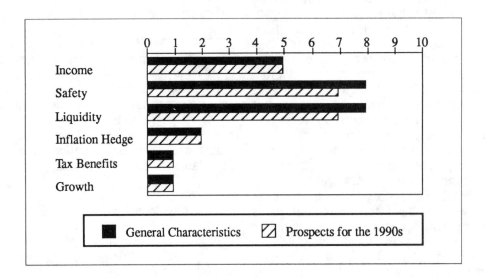

Income
Safety
Liquidity
Inflation Hedge
Tax Benefits
Growth

■ General Characteristics   ▨ Prospects for the 1990s

Type IV

C

Low Taxes
High Expenses

Many consumers don't realize or remember that interest-paying checking accounts haven't been around for very long. In the 1970s, the money market funds launched by the mutual fund industry threatened to "put a stake in the heart" of the banking industry. Banks and savings and loan institutions were limited to paying 5.25% interest on normal passbook savings accounts and nothing on checking accounts. The NOW account was born as a defensive measure.

The money market funds became instantly popular, and a huge amount of cash moved from savings institutions into the hands of the mutual fund industry. To combat this, the savings industry united to promote legislation freeing them from interest rate ceilings.

In the 1970s, NOW accounts were limited to paying only 5.25%. With the advent of bank-sponsored money market deposit ac-

counts that paid a fluctuating market interest rate, the super-NOW account was created. A super-NOW account is not bound by the 5.25% limitation imposed on NOW accounts. Initially, super-NOW accounts could pay market rates only on those accounts with a minimum balance of $2,500. This legal minimum was eliminated on January 1, 1986. However, banks continue to impose additional fees and restrictions on super-NOW accounts, making them unsuitable for small balances.

In fact, most banks no longer advertise or talk much about NOW accounts. Common sense has prevailed, and most banks merely term the accounts "interest-paying checking accounts." The fees vary widely. It would be wise to comparison-shop before plunking down your money. Most super-NOW accounts still require a minimum monthly balance, or additional fees are assessed.

NOW and super-NOW accounts are available only from banks and thrift (savings and loan) institutions. They will be glad to explain their programs to you. Be cautious though, fees vary widely. You should speak to several banks to find a program that most closely fits your financial needs. For example, some fees go up if you write more checks. Others allow you a set number of checks each month without triggering those extra charges. You may be surprised to find that some banks charge very high fees for certain very basic accounts. The bottom line is "Shop around!"

Investment Potential

NOW and super-NOW accounts pay interest. They do not offer the potential for capital gains. However, an account can obtain good returns through the effect of compound interest.

NOW and super-NOW accounts are very stable. They offer no leverage. There is no market volatility to worry about. Your principal is always secure. The only thing that fluctuates is the interest on your account. Most people regard their NOW accounts as long-term savings programs. In order to minimize fees, few checks are drawn and then only when the minimum balance required for receiving the best interest rate is maintained.

NOW and super-NOW accounts are very liquid. As mentioned earlier, most banks impose minimum account limitations on these accounts. If your balance falls below the minimums, you're assessed additional fees.

NOW and super-NOW accounts are covered by federal insurance up to $100,000. Since they pay a flexible interest rate, NOW and super-NOW accounts provide some measure of protection from inflation. The lack of growth potential limits the potential for outperforming the inflation rate.

Strengths

NOW and super-NOWs are very safe. They are insured for $100,000 by an agency of the federal government if your savings institution is federally chartered. They are very liq-uid accounts. The variable interest rates afford some inflation protection. They pay safe and secure current income.

Weaknesses

Interest paid is typically less than comparable uninsured vehicles such as money market funds. Fees are complex and can amount to a substantial portion of earnings. They offer no growth potential. There are no tax advantages. Taxes must be paid on interest as earned. There is no deferral.

Tax Considerations

Tax Consequences

The 1986 Tax Reform Act eliminated preferential treatment for any interest paid on bank accounts. You are taxed at ordinary income levels for any interest earned on NOW and super-NOW accounts.

Summing Up

NOW and super-NOW accounts are standard services offered by banks and savings institutions. You can generally obtain higher rates with lower fees through money market funds. However, money market funds are not insured by an agency of the federal government.

NOW and super-NOW accounts usually are not limited to writing checks over $100, as are most money market funds. If a secure, convenient, flexible checking account is what you want and you are willing to pay higher fees, check these out.

U.S. Savings Bonds

U.S. savings bonds are debt instruments backed by the full faith and credit of the U.S. government. In order to receive the highest allowable rate, you must hold the bond for a minimum of five years. The initial rate is 5.5% in the first year. It rises gradually after that until you've held it five years, when you're eligible to receive the maximum rate.

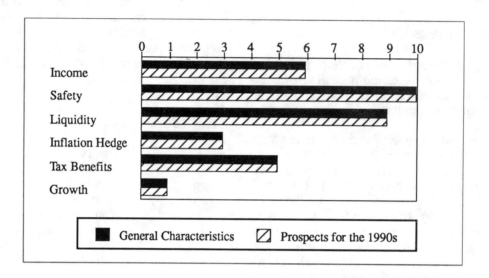

Income
Safety
Liquidity
Inflation Hedge
Tax Benefits
Growth

■ General Characteristics   ◨ Prospects for the 1990s

Type IV

A

High Taxes
High Expenses

For many years during and after World Wars I and II, U.S. savings bonds were a part of almost everyone's savings. Except during times of inflation, U.S. savings bonds offer competitive yields when the convenience of buying in small amounts, the absolute safety of principal and interest, and the long-term tax deferral features are considered.

However, the classic Series E savings bond, with its fixed low-interest rate, became a victim of the deregulation of the financial markets. When U.S. savers were able to obtain money market interest rates rather than being locked into the low fixed rates paid by bank savings accounts and Series E savings bonds, they moved quickly and decisively. The market for savings bonds dried up.

Congress recognized the problem and in 1982 authorized the new Series EE bonds. EE bonds pay a floating interest rate, which is 85% of the average rate paid by five-year U.S. Treasury bonds. The interest is paid on redemption, not as current income. There is a fixed minimum rate after the bonds have been held for five years at 6% (prior to 1986, the minimum rate was 7.5%).

In addition to the Series EE bonds, there are HH bonds, which pay current interest of 7.5%. HH bonds cannot be purchased for cash. You can acquire them only by exchanging your EE or E bonds. The idea is that EE bonds serve as a tax deferral device to enable you to accumulate a nest egg, which can be converted to HH bonds when you need to start receiving current income.

Information on savings bonds is available from any bank or savings and loan. You can buy savings bonds with no sales charge from these same institutions or from the Federal Reserve Bank. Series EE bonds are available in 10 denominations ranging from $50 to

$10,000 face value. They are sold on a discount basis. You pay 50% of the face value ($50 for a $100 bond). The bond value increases with time as interest accrues. Their stated maturity is 10 years, though historically the government has permitted virtually unlimited extensions beyond that.

Investment Potential

U.S. savings bonds earn interest income. There is no capital growth potential. They are long-term investments. Bonds must be held a minimum of five years to receive the maximum interest rate. Redemptions prior to a five-year holding period result in a lower effective yield.

Savings bonds are very safe, secure, non-volatile investments. Prices do not fluctuate with interest rates—though the interest paid on the bonds may. Your principal is very secure.

Savings bonds are very liquid. You can redeem them at any savings institution any time after an initial six-month holding period.

Savings bonds offer little protection from inflation. The Series EE bonds, with their floating interest rate feature, provide moderately more protection than the previous Series E. However, they are not a good inflation hedge.

Strengths

 Principal and interest is guaranteed by the full faith and credit (including taxing power) of the U.S. government. They are very liquid. Series EE bonds interest accumulates on a tax-deferred basis. They are available in a wide variety of denominations. There are no sales charges. Many companies offer payroll deduction plans for accumulating savings bonds.

Weaknesses

 There is no capital growth potential. Interest paid is low relative to competitive products. Minimum holding period is five years to receive the maximum rate.

Tax Considerations

Tax Consequences

Series EE bonds offer a number of tax benefits. Interest accumulates on a tax-deferred basis until redemption. Interest paid on redemption is exempt from state and local taxes. Series EE bonds can be exchanged for Series HH bonds without incurring taxes on the interest until the HH bonds are redeemed.

Series EE bonds issued after December 31, 1989 offer the additional tax benefit of tax-exempt interest if used to pay college tuition. However there are many requirements: the exemption is phased out if your income exceeds $40,000 (single) or $60,000 (joint). The buyer must be 24 years or older and must be the person who pays the tuition (not just a relative or friend).

Series EE bonds are not appropriate for most retirement plans since the interest earned is already tax deferred.

Summing Up

The changes made in 1982 and 1989 have substantially enhanced the investment attractiveness of savings bonds. However, the maximum interest rate paid is still only 85% of government-guaranteed five-year U.S. Treasury bonds.

The advantages of small minimum investments, high safety, good liquidity, and tax deferral of interest earnings make savings bonds a viable alternative for a portion of your long-term savings. Investors who have the time to devote to alternative investments can achieve higher yields, though.

Certificates of Deposit

A certificate of deposit is a loan from an investor to a bank or thrift institution for a specified time at a set interest rate. Certificates of deposit (commonly called CDs) are perhaps the most widely used money market instrument for individual investors.

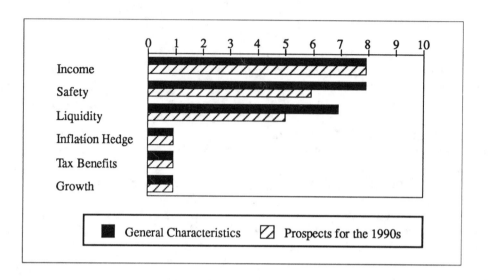

Type III

C

Low Taxes
High Expenses

Type IV

C

Low Taxes
High Expenses

CDs are bank deposits. They are covered by federal insurance up to $100,000 per account. "Jumbo" CDs are a minimum of $100,000 and therefore may subject the purchaser to the additional risk of no insurance on amounts over $100,000.

Banking deregulation has resulted in a wide variety of options for CD investors. Interest rates vary with the length of the CD.

Longer maturities and larger CDs generally pay higher rates. It is possible to find just about any combination to meet investors' needs. "Designer" CDs are offered by many savings institutions. These offer investors the opportunity to invest whatever sum they want in the form of a CD. For example, if investors have an odd sum, they can obtain a CD specifically built around their requirements.

The most common CDs include 31- and 91-day maturities in which the yield is tied to the 13-week Treasury bill rate. Six-month and 30-month CDs generally pay higher rates, usually through some formula tied to Treasury bills.

As in any interest-bearing investments, there are a number of ways to calculate interest. For example, the interest may be simple interest or it may be compounded. It is important to ascertain exactly how the interest is calculated to ensure accurate comparison with competitive products. The time period used in compounding may change the effective annual interest rate received. A 7% CD rate compounded daily will yield a 7.25% annual rate, compared to only 7% if compounded annually.

Although the most common method for investing in CDs is direct purchase from a savings institution, most brokerage firms also offer CDs from a variety of banks and S&Ls around the country. These CDs are generally from mid-sized institutions you may not know, which are trying to tap a wider source of deposits. Brokered CDs are usually offered for no commission. They are often more liquid than buying direct.

Investment Potential

You invest in CDs for income. Jumbo CDs and CD pools offer institutional investors some chance for capital gains that may result from interest rate fluctuations. Individual investors normally do not participate in this sophisticated, high-level process.

CDs range from as little as seven days to as much as seven years. Most CDs offer fixed interest rates for the specified maturities. In recent years, yet another option has been offered: variable interest rates based on a preset formula. Variable CDs offer slightly lower current interest rates in exchange for this flexibility.

As money market investors become more demanding, CDs have undergone a revolution themselves. There are now so many different types of CDs that you can pick and choose exactly the one that is right for you. The characteristics of some of the more widespread variations are as follows.

"Rising rate" CDs feature a guaranteed periodic increase in the interest rate being paid on your CD. Usually the rate is increased annually, but that feature varies from place to place. Some banks offer increases every six months or even every month. Don't be surprised, though, when you find out that that attractive-sounding rate advertised in the newspaper is the last and highest rate paid.

Find out the average rate over the full term of the CD *before* you invest. Also be sure to check into your right of withdrawal and what penalties may be assessed for early withdrawal.

"Bump-up" CDs have garnered considerable press in the past year. This innovation allows you the right (usually once or twice in the life of your CD), to increase the interest rate for the balance of the term. Obviously, this feature would only be interesting if the general level of interest rates has risen! Normally a cap is placed on how much your rate will be allowed to rise.

"Variable-rate" CDs are typically tied to the prime rate. Since the prime rate can change numerous times throughout the life of your CD, the rate paid on your CD will theoretically follow the market rates. The kicker here, of course, is that the initial rate is usually less than that paid on straight CDs.

"Pullout" CDs offer you the chance to withdraw a set percentage of your CD (usually 10–15%) without penalty if rates rise. Most stipulate, though, that the amount withdrawn must be reinvested with the same bank in a higher-paying certificate.

Some Texas banks have initiated a different type of CD, called the "bitter-end" CD. With these CDs, you get a bonus if you leave your money in the entire term of the CD. For example, First City National Bank of Houston pays an additional 2.25 percentage points if you stay with its five-year CD to the "bitter" end (hence the nickname).

CDs offer the average investor no capital gains potential. They offer little protection against inflation.

Strengths

CDs under $100,000, purchased from federally insured savings institutions, are covered by federal deposit insurance. The wide variety of maturities and interest rates offers you substantial flexibility. Typically no fees or commissions are assessed. CDs offer a secure fixed compounding of income over the selected maturity. CDs do not require large investments. They are available for sums as little as $100.

Weaknesses

Liquidity is limited for most non-brokered CDs. Early withdrawal typically entails substantial penalties. Banks usually have the option of denying early withdrawal. Long-term CDs at a fixed rate may suffer purchasing power loss in an inflationary environment.

Tax Considerations

Tax Consequences

All earned income is interest and is taxed as ordinary income in the year in which it is paid. Reinvestment of interest does not defer the tax due.

Summing Up

CDs are a widely used cash equivalent vehicle. The wide variety of available options means you can tailor a savings plan to suit your needs. Banking deregulation has already resulted in a wide variety of CD vehicles, and you can expect such innovation to continue (see next section). It is important to investigate the alternatives offered by more than one institution to ensure the best possible return on your investment.

The proliferation of CDs brokered through major investment houses has spawned advisory businesses dedicated to ferreting out high-yielding CDs. Three newsletters that track CDs in the United States are *Income & Saftey: The Consumer's Guide to High Yields*, 3471 N. Federal Highway, Fort Lauderdale, FL 33306; *100 Highest Yields* and *Bank Rate Monitor*, P.O. Box 088888, North Palm Beach, FL 33408; and *Tiered Rate Watch* or *Jumbo Rate News*, P.O. Box 145510, Coral Gables, FL 33114.

---

10 Largest U.S. Government Money Market Funds

1. Capital Preservation Fund
2. Carnegie Government Securities Money Markets
3. Dreyfus Money Market Instruments/Government Securities
4. Kemper Government Money Market Fund
5. Massachusetts Cash Management—government
6. Merrill Lynch Government Fund
7. UST Master Funds—government money
8. Vanguard Money Market Reserves—federal
9. UMB Money Market—federal
10. Kidder Peabody Government Money Market

Source: Forbes

Speculative Certificates of Deposit

The basic CD is simply a loan from the investor to a savings institution for a specified maturity at a set interest rate. Although that is still the dominant form of CD, innovations are rampant. A speculative CD offers variable returns based on a preset formula. The depositor trades a secure return for the potential of higher returns if certain conditions are met.

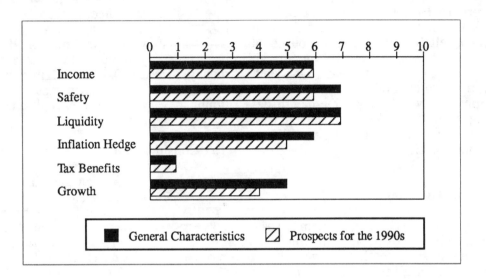

Type III

Rather than offering a fixed interest rate, an adjustable-rate CD's interest rate is tied to the rate or performance of another investment vehicle, usually a 91- or 180-day Treasury bill.

Chase Manhattan Bank was the first to offer a CD tied to the performance of the stock market in early 1987. This was in response to the most common complaint about CDs: the lack of growth potential. This is most evident in a low-interest-rate environment. The attraction of 20% annual growth, such as the stock market achieved from 1982 through August 1987, made marketing low-interest-rate CDs more difficult. Chase Manhattan Bank responded with its "market index" CD. Other banks including Northern Trust Co. in Chicago and Fleet Financial Group in Providence, R.I., now also offer "market index" CDs.

A market index CD is a hybrid between the safety of a CD and the potential for greater returns if the stock market appreciates. In exchange for a lower initial interest rate on the CD, the investor buys the chance to earn a higher return by tying it to the S&P (Standard & Poor) 500 stock market index.

Chase initially offered two choices for the CD purchaser: a 4% minimum annual interest rate or a zero-minimum return. At maturity, the investor receives the higher of the two possible outcomes: the minimum guaranteed rate or a percentage of the rise in the S&P 500. The amount of stock market participation depends on which option is taken and the maturity of the CD.

For example, if the 4% guarantee is selected, the investor's potential higher return alternative would be 25% of any rise in the S&P for a three-month deposit or 40% for a 12-month deposit. If the zero guarantee is selected, the S&P participation ranges from 40% to 75%.

In October 1987, Chase introduced the "decreasing index alternative" CD. This version of the market index CD is the "bear market" version of the originial CD. Buyers of the decreasing index alternative CD profit when the stock market goes down rather than up.

This alternative enables savers to earn interest ranging from nothing to a maximum of 105% of any percentage decline in the S&P 500 index over 12 months. Shorter-time period CDs earn a smaller percentage of market declines. For example, if the S&P 500 index fell 10% over a year, you could earn 10% interest on your 12-month decreasing index CD. If you held a six-month CD, you would earn 60% of the decline for the period. If you held a three-month decreasing index CD and the market fell 10% in the three months, you'd receive 45% of the decline—4.5%.

Investment Potential

A market index CD is a short-term investment. This characteristic puts a premium on market timing since the longest maturity is only one year. It gives you the opportunity to participate in stock market growth or decline without risking your principal. Although all income earned is considered interest, the return can be substantial.

A program of staggered buying in different CDs with different expiration dates would give your retirement plan a diversified exposure to the stock market over time. This approach would lessen your exposure to what happens on only a few particular dates.

Slight inflation is historically bullish (very favorable) for stocks initially. The market index CD would offer some protection from inflation.

Strengths

 Principal is guaranteed by federal insurance for amounts under $100,000. The market index CD gives you diversified exposure to stocks. You're betting on the market as a whole, not just one or a few stocks. Great flexibility is offered. You can choose the level of risk that is most suitable to your situation. Minimum investment is only $1,000.

Weaknesses

 There are substantial penalties for early withdrawal. Liquidity is limited, as there is no secondary market. If you guess wrong on market direction, you may earn nothing on your money. These CDs are ineligible for IRAs. The one-year maximum means that market timing, never an exact science, is crucial.

Tax Considerations

Tax Consequences

All gains are taxed as ordinary income. The initial offering by Chase made early *withdrawal penalties apply immediately*. This makes these CDs ineligible for IRAs. Check with your tax advisor *before* investing.

Summing Up

Market index CDs are only the latest in a long line of innovative developments in CDs. Improvements and variations on the theme can be expected as long as the deregulation environment exists. To make sure you obtain the best return for your situation, it is vital to carefully investigate the wide variety of products being offered. The market index CD is an important step in the development of risk-averse investment products.

Commercial Paper

Commercial paper is a money market instrument issued by corporations, financial companies, or state/local governments to cover short-term cash needs. Investors loan money to the issuing entity for a specified time period at a set interest rate. Normally the paper is issued on a discount basis. This means that the buyer pays less than the face amount and on maturity receives the full face amount. The difference is the interest earned.

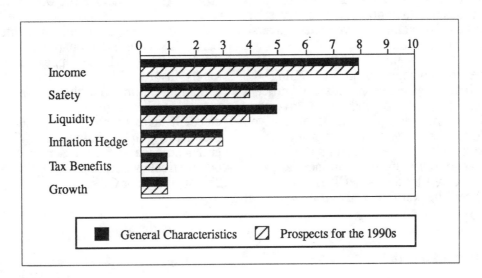

General Characteristics ▨ Prospects for the 1990s

Type I

C

Low Taxes
High Expenses

Commercial paper is available in a wide variety of maturities ranging from a few days to nine months. It is usually backed by a bank line of credit, but it is typically not secured by the assets of the issuer.

There are a few exceptions to this "nonsecured" status of commercial paper. Some manufacturers have turned to the commercial paper market to raise funds for their receivables. Instead of relying on the age-old practice of "factoring" (selling their receivables at a discount to obtain immediate cash), they back their commercial paper issues with their trade receivables. According to Merrill Lynch, approximately $10 billion of commercial paper outstanding is backed by trade receivables.

As of the end of 1987, every issue backed by trade receivables involved a 100% guarantee from insurers or banks, which ensured an AAA rating. That may be changing, though, as some issuers are pushing the rating companies to rank these offerings without insurance being required.

Although commercial paper is not required to be registered with the SEC (Securities and Exchange Commission), regulations do require that it be sold only to "sophisticated investors." A sophisticated investor is one who is experienced and meets capital requirements.

High income (over $100,000 per year) or substantial net worth (over $500,000 exclusive of home) are sufficient proof of "sophistication" for the SEC. Because of this requirement, you will not find commercial paper offered through advertisements in your local paper.

It can be purchased direct from the issuer or through banks or brokerage firms. Purchasing direct saves commissions and fees. Minimum denomination is usually $100,000, though some issuers do sell amounts as low as $25,000.

Independent credit rating services such as Standard & Poor's or Moody's rate some commercial paper. There is no federal insurance. Institutions issue commercial paper to borrow money at rates below what they could get from banks. It competes in the money market with Treasury bills, certificates of deposit, and banker's acceptances. Money market funds are heavy buyers of commercial paper. These funds offer substantial benefits to nonprofessional investors. These benefits include convenience, diversification, and liquidity.

Since there is no established secondary market for commercial paper, selling the paper before maturity presents a significant liquidity problem for individual investors. The issuer may take back the paper, but you should expect to pay a fee for that service.

There have been few defaults historically, but it bears repeating that commercial paper is not secured by the issuer's assets. Therefore, heed the warning—*caveat emptor*—let the buyer beware.

Investment Potential

Commercial paper is a short-term debt instrument. Individual investors have little chance of obtaining capital gains by selling the paper before maturity. Gains made at maturity are considered interest income.

Short-term interest rates are subject to wide volatility. Although the short-term nature of commercial paper is some protection from the ravages of inflation, a nine-month commitment may lock your funds up at a time of rising rates.

Strengths

 The yield on commercial paper is usually slightly higher than that of Treasury bills and certificates of deposit. Defaults are rare. The short-term nature of commercial paper limits the risk to your principal. If you have the time

and expertise, you can earn the higher returns that commercial paper offers without having to give up the fees that money market funds assess for buying it.

Weaknesses

 Liquidity is limited for individual investors. Initial investment amounts are substantial, usually $100,000, though denominations as low as $25,000 are available in limited numbers. Most commercial paper is not insured. Trade-receivable-backed paper often is privately insured. Therefore, diversification is even more important than with CDs. The money market is both volatile and complicated. It takes much time to understand all the maturity options available. With no federal insurance and no assets backing most commerical paper, it is a higher risk than Treasury bills or CDs.

Tax Considerations

Tax Consequences

Money earned from commercial paper held to maturity is deemed interest income. It is taxable at ordinary income rates. The lone exception is commercial paper issued by local or state governments. Interest earned on this commercial paper is usually free from federal taxes. Check with your tax advisor to be sure in each situation.

Summing Up

Commercial paper is one of a number of money market vehicles offering good returns when compared to bank savings accounts. However, there is a definite trade-off. Commercial paper involves higher risk. Unless you have the time to monitor and understand the money markets, most investors are well served to pay the management fees of money market funds.

Banker's Acceptances

Banker's acceptances are a type of letter of credit, developed to aid international trade. They facilitate imports and exports by providing a third-party guarantee of payment. For example, a manufacturer in a foreign country wants to sell a product in the United States. The company makes arrangements with a U.S. importer on price and shipping. Given the distances and problems of multiple jurisdictions involved, the exporter wants to get paid at once. The importer is faced with the same considerations and wants to ensure that he or she receives the product and can distribute them to outlets.

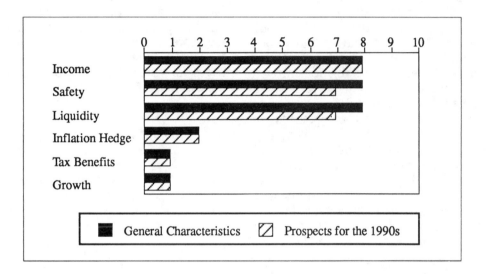

Type I

C

Low Taxes
High Expenses

The financial portion of the transaction is handled through banker's acceptances. A bank accepts a record of the financial particulars for a fee. The bank either holds the note (the banker's acceptance) to maturity or sells it to an outside investor. The exporter receives its funds from either the bank, if it holds the paper, or from the investor who buys the acceptance. On maturity (usually 30 to 180 days), the importer pays the bank, which directs the funds to the investor.

Obviously, neither a bank nor an investor will invest without earning fees for their participation. When the note is originally ac-cepted, it is "discounted from face value." This phrase means that the exporter receives less than the face value of the note; the purchaser of the acceptance pays less than the face value of the note. The difference between the discounted value paid and the face value on maturity is the interest earned on the transaction. Treasury bills are sold in the same discount manner. This discounting method means quoted yields are generally understated since you do not put up the full face mount.

Banker's acceptances are one of a number of money market instruments that have attracted more individual investor interest over the past few years.

Deregulation of the financial markets has resulted in wider availability of many sophisticated money market vehicles for individual investors. Banker's acceptances have historically been of interest primarily to institutional and professional investors. Many individual investors with substantial assets now include banker's acceptances in their short-term money market portfolios.

Investment Potential

Banker's acceptances are short-term, high-yielding, money market instruments although there is no central market auction. To buy a banker's acceptance, you need to approach individual banks and ask if they handle acceptances and whether they sell them to individual investors. You will also need to learn what denominations are available and what interest they pay.

Fees vary widely. Not all banks handle acceptances. Banks that do handle them on a regular basis can offer better fee structures. A good long-term business relationship with the bank should mean competitive fees and ready access to the market.

Returns from banker's acceptances are considered interest income. There is no capital gain potential. Interest rates are generally among the highest paid for short-term secured instruments. Since banker's acceptances are of short maturity, there is little exposure to inflation risk.

Banker's acceptances play an important role in the portfolios of money market mutual funds. Although the yield is slightly less due to management fees, these funds offer daily liquidity and diversification.

Strengths

 Banker's acceptances offer generally high yield compared to competitive money market instruments: T-bills and CDs. They are secured by both the bank and the importer(s). In addition, the short maturities makes for a relatively safe investment.

Weaknesses

 Limited liquidity for individual investors. Institutional investors have access to secondary market, but individual investors generally are limited to selling back to the issuing bank for an additional fee. Banker's acceptances are not considered bank deposits and therefore are not covered by federal insurance. The non-uniform nature and lack of accessible secondary market require greater educational effort on the part of investors.

Tax Considerations

 Income earned is taxed at ordinary income rates.

Tax Consequences

Summing Up

Banker's acceptances fluctuate with short-term interest rates. They provide an avenue for further diversification of a sophisticated investor's cash portfolio.

Repurchase Agreements

A repurchase agreement (popularly called a "repo") is an agreement between two parties (usually large institutions) in which one party that needs short-term cash sells a portfolio of securities to another party for a short period ranging from three days to as much as three months. The receiving party agrees to pay a set amount for the securities contingent on the selling party agreeing to buy them back at a higher price within the specified time period.

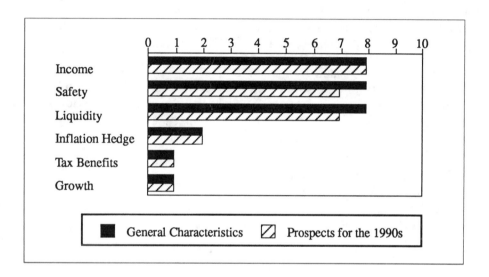

Income
Safety
Liquidity
Inflation Hedge
Tax Benefits
Growth

0 1 2 3 4 5 6 7 8 9 10

■ General Characteristics   ▨ Prospects for the 1990s

Type I

C

Low Taxes
High Expenses

Until recent years repurchase agreements have been solely the domain of very large institutions and of little interest to the average investor. The deregulation of financial markets has resulted in more interest in repurchase agreements (repos) by more and more investors.

Almost daily, the financial press reports on the latest transactions taken by the Federal Reserve (the Fed) to add or delete monetary reserves. The level of monetary reserves determines the relative liquidity of the economy. A major tool employed by the Fed in "fine-tuning" the national money supply is the use of repos.

Of more direct interest to many investors is the use of repos by most money market funds. Even funds that advertise that they invest solely in government securities for rea-

sons of safety often employ repos backed by government securities rather than direct investment in the securities.

In other words, the securities that are sold are like collateral for a short-term loan to the selling party. Why would anyone want to do that? Well, often an institution's portfolio will contain securities that the institution wants to hold long term rather than actualize a taxable gain. By selling the securities as a repo, the seller can obtain cash without having to actualize a gain or loss immediately.

Even though the seller agrees to buy back the securities at a higher price, the profit on the transaction is considered interest, not capital gains.

Professional
Advice

Repos are debt instruments. Numerous problems, involving just exactly who is the owner of the securities that back a repo have resulted from the failure of a few government securities dealers. Even now it is unclear exactly who owns the securities used to secure repos. This is one reason why professional management in a diversified portfolio such as that offered by money market funds is the most logical way for most people to invest in repos.

When researching money market funds, find out what part repos play in their portfolios. As already mentioned, some funds that actively trade in repos advertise that they invest solely in government securities. If safety is your primary concern and you are willing to give up some yield, consider sticking with those funds that only invest directly in government securities. All money market fund managers are compensated by a management fee deducted from the income generated by the funds assets.

Investment Potential

Repos pay high current income. For example, in July 1989, you could have purchased six-month repos yielding nearly 9%. Six-month CDs averaged 8.4%. There is no capital gains potential. Because of the way they are structured, the difference in the price paid by the original buyer (the one who loans money to the seller) and the higher buyback price does not constitute capital gains. The very short maturities of repos limits their price volatility. There is an active market for repos of all maturities among large financial institutions. The complexity and very high cash requirements (usually $100,000 minimums) make repos impractical for most individual investors.

Even though repos often are backed by government securities, they should not be confused with the safety associated with Treasury obligations. In a case resulting from the failure of one bank that had sold repos backed by government securities, it was held that the securities backing a repo actually belonged to the bank that initiated the repo transaction. In other words, the holders of the repos were left holding the bag, not holding the securities! But every case is different, as repos are structured in a variety of ways.

Repos offer you the chance to obtain higher yields on short-term money. For ex-

ample, in May 1988, you could have done better buying a six-month repo at Sovran Bank in Richmond, Virginia, than in most CDs offered around the country. On May 20, for example, the national average on six-month CDs was 6.63%. Six-month repos offered by Sovran yielded 7.4%

Repos of any sort are not backed by government depositors insurance. The greatest risk to repo traders is the stability of the firms with which they do business. There is no independent rating of repos.

Strengths

Repos pay high relative income. Very short maturities limit capital risk. Repos are very liquid among large institutions.

Weaknesses

The complexity and high sums required to trade repos make investment impractical for most individual investors. Uncertain legal status makes risk evaluation difficult. There is no capital gains potential.

Tax Considerations

Gains from repo transactions are considered interest income. They are taxed at ordinary income levels.

Tax Consequences

Summing Up

The popularity of money market funds makes the indirect investment in repos by individuals a near certainty. Deregulation of the financial markets limits the appeal of retail repo agreements since they are not covered by depositors' insurance.

If maximum safety is your chief priority, you should buy only in money market funds that invest directly in Treasury securities. However, professionally managed diversified funds are able to pay slightly higher yields if they invest in repos. The risk is moderately greater than direct investment in Treasury securities.

If you are a well capitalized investor willing to take the time to earn the higher returns available through repos, you should take some precautions to ensure maximum safety. When you buy a repo through a bank, make sure the collateral is really yours. The bank should deposit the collateral securities in an escrow account. Or even better, request that they deposit the securities in your own custodial account in another bank or institution. (You'd better be a very good customer of the bank!) Make sure you get the collateral securities identification numbers. Without these precautions, there may be confusion over who owns the collateral—you or the bank.

---

10 Largest Taxable Money Market Funds

1. CMA Money Fund (Merrill Lynch)
2. Merrill Lynch Ready Assets
3. Fidelity Cash Reserves
4. Dean Witter/Sears Liquid Asset
5. Pacific Horizon (Concord Financial)
6. Dreyfus Liquid Assets
7. Cash Equivalent Fund (Kemper)
8. Vanguard Money Market Reserves
9. Pru-Bache Moneymart Assets
10. Kemper Money Market

Source: Forbes

Taxable Money Market Funds

A money market fund gathers together a group of investors to pool their funds for investing in short-term money market vehicles. The fund managers buy large lots of various money market instruments such as jumbo CDs (certificates of deposit), banker's acceptances, commercial paper, or Treasury bills. Each investor buys a proportionate share of the fund.

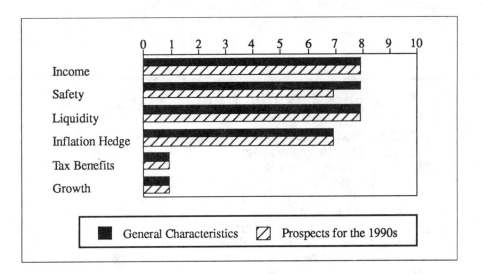

Income
Safety
Liquidity
Inflation Hedge
Tax Benefits
Growth

■ General Characteristics   ▨ Prospects for the 1990s

Type IV

C

Low Taxes
High Expenses

The advent of money market funds is a classic "chicken or egg" question. Did the rise of money market funds lead to deregulation of the financial markets, or did deregulation lead to the sharply increased interest in money market funds?

Either way, money market funds are here to stay as an important part of the financial markets. When inflation ran to double-digit levels in the early 1970s, savings accounts were paying 5 or 5.25%. So investors were actually losing purchasing power.

Large investors always had the option of investing directly in money market instruments such as commercial paper, Treasury bills, or banker's acceptances. The high minimum investments (often $25,000 or more) and extensive study needed to purchase the highest-yielding instruments safely prevented many investors from taking advantage of the higher yields.

Creative financial entrepreneurs recognized the need and demand for a way for average investors to participate in these markets. They developed the open-end money market fund.

Typically, each fund share is $1. So a $1,000 investment buys 1,000 shares. Interest is usually paid in whole and partial shares on either a monthly or quarterly basis. Since the interest is normally reinvested rather than withdrawn each time, your money appreciates on a compound basis. That is, you earn interest on previously earned interest left in your account.

Although minimum investments vary, most funds accept as little as $500 initially and as little as $100 for subsequent investments. You are buying short-term debt instruments. The shorter the term, the lower the risk if interest rates rise. For example, if the average maturity in your money market fund is 12 months (and no money market fund should ever have an average maturity any longer), a rise in interest rates would result in at least a temporary loss in principal because a full 12 months elapses before all the instruments in the fund mature.

On the other hand, if your fund's average maturity was 90 days, a rise in short-term interest rates would be more quickly reflected in a higher average yield, because the fund could roll its investments over to higher-yielding instruments sooner as the current portfolio matures.

Most money market funds offer virtually instant liquidity. Many also feature checking privileges (normally, the minimum amount of the check is $100).

All major full-service brokerage firms offer money market funds. All major mutual fund groups also offer the funds. They are sold on a no-load basis. The funds earn their money by taking a small fee out of the interest paid on the money market portfolios under their management.

The yields available to money market fund investors are competitive with those available in the marketplace. However, there is usually a slight difference due to the management fees paid by the funds.

Investment Potential

Money market funds pay current income. There is no capital gains potential. Money market funds by definition are short-term investments. This doesn't mean they can't be held for the long term, but rather that the average maturity in their portfolios is short. They are an attractive alternative to savings institutions' savings accounts.

Money market funds are very liquid. You can get your money out in 24 hours. The only potential exception would be in cases of poor or dishonest management of the fund. For example, if your money market fund manager extends the average maturity of the fund's holdings to one year, instead of the more normal 60–90 days, there may be a problem if interest rates rise. See Chapter 10 on fixed income for a full explanation of the potential loss that bond buyers may suffer if interest rates rise and you need to sell the bond before it matures.

In the early 1980s interest rates fell steadily. Many money market fund investors who had become accustomed to the high yields paid in the late 1970s became restless. In order to stem the outflow of money seeking higher returns, some fund managers bought longer-term debt securities. Instead of buying just short-term vehicles like three- or six-month vehicles, they bought two- or three-year notes.

Although this longer term gives the fund a higher yield, it also has greater risk. If interest rates went up, the notes would drop in value, diminishing the current asset value of the fund. If fund redemptions became heavy, the fund could theoretically be unable to pay each shareholder promptly.

Look At This:

We say "theoretically" because to date there has been no instance of a money market fund being unable to meet all redemption requests. However, you should be careful that your fund does not engage in such practices. One way to protect yourself is to purchase funds that are restricted by their charters to buying securities with maturities of six months or less. Another alternative is to carefully monitor the average maturity of your money market funds holdings. This information is available directly from the fund, and newsletters such as the Donoghue *Moneyletter* (800-445-5900), or in the *Wall Street Journal* listings.

Money market funds, like money market instruments themselves, have a wide range of risk. The safest funds are those which invest solely in 90-day Treasury bills. Since maturities are short and the investment is in direct obligations of the U.S. government, there is little chance of default. The only risk would be fraud. Higher yields and hence more risk are available from funds that invest in short-term corporate securities such as commercial paper. The guarantee of payment is dependent on the financial stability of the company issuing the paper.

The length of maturity is another risk factor. The shorter the average maturity, all other things being equal, the safer the investment. In 1990 the average maturity of money market funds tracked by Donoghue ranged from 1 to over 100 days. Money market funds, especially those with the shortest average maturities, provide some protection from inflation. Inflation will cause interest rates to move higher. Money market yields will move higher with interest rates.

The funds actually offer greater safety than direct investment in the money market instruments because you are buying a diversified portfolio. If a single issuer runs into financial difficulty, a well-managed fund with only a small percentage of assets in one company's paper will be only slightly affected.

The major risks in money market funds are the risk of failure on the part of an issuer of a money market vehicle or the risk of incompetent or dishonest management. All funds must provide prospective investors with a prospectus detailing what the fund invests in, its prior track record, and information on the manager. All money market funds must be registered with the SEC and comply with stringent financial requirements.

Strengths

Money market funds are very liquid. Yields fluctuate with interest rates and provide a measure of protection from inflation. The wide range of funds offers you great flexibility in choosing one that most closely fits your investment needs and risk tolerance. Fees are minor. Yields are typically higher than those of bank passbook savings accounts. Substantial diversification minimizes risk. Investment minimums are small for most funds. Funds are closely regulated by the SEC. Most funds offer checking privileges.

Weaknesses

There is no government insurance. Poorly managed funds may yield substantially less than the average money market instrument. The biggest factor in differing yields among funds is their expense ratios. That's the amount the management company charges for its services. A higher expense ratio means a lower effective yield.

Tax Considerations

Tax Consequences

Interest earned on money market funds is taxable at ordinary income rates. Interest earned on funds that invest solely in U.S. Treasuries is exempt from state and local taxes in most states (check with your tax advisor for your locale).

Summing Up

Money market funds are here to stay. In only a few short years they have become an established part of the financial world. For most investors, money market funds offer an attractive alternative to the yields paid by passbook savings accounts.

The great variety of funds ensures that investors large and small can tailor their savings to closely fit their own objectives and risk tolerances.

In times of rising interest rates, money will flow into those funds with the shortest average maturities invested in the safest vehicles. In times of declining rates, money will flow to those funds with longer average maturities.

Not all money market funds are the same, though. Watch expense ratios closely. For the past few years, the average ratio has been 0.75%. But there are over 30 funds with expense ratios exceeding 1%.

A number of newsletters track money market funds. William Donoghue publishes two widely followed newsletters: *Money Fund Report* and *Moneyletter*, P.O. Box 540, Holliston, MA 01746. The same company also publishes *Donoghue's Money Fund Directory* twice a year.

The Institute for Econometric Research publishes a series of excellent newsletters on investing. Their *Income and Safety* newsletter focuses specifically on safety ratings, yield forecasts, and recommendations.

Tax-Free Money Market Funds

Tax-free money market funds are no-load mutual funds that invest only in short-term municipal debt issues. You buy into the funds at $1 per share. Interest is paid in whole and fractional dollar shares on a monthly basis. Reinvestment of interest results in compounded earnings. Most funds compound interest daily and pay monthly. The interest payments are referred to as "dividends" because of the mutual fund structure.

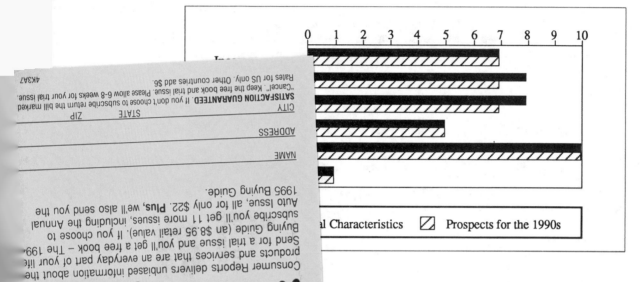

...al Characteristics   ▨ Prospects for the 1990s

effects of ...ket creep." ...re bumped ...ets without ...se in stan-...mers who ...they were ...ax-exempt ...market in-...hat on an ...yields on ...eant more

...s invest in ...nts. Nor-...x-exempt ...r taxable ...supply of ...et paper. ...funds generally fill out their portfolios with previously issued bonds that mature in the near future.

Residents of many states are able to buy "double-tax-free" money market funds. These funds invest solely in debt securities issued by the state and local governments within the state. Income from municipal bonds is exempt from federal taxation at present. Income paid by municipal debt securities issued by the state in which you are a resident is also exempt from state taxation.

Another way to avoid state income taxes on your money market funds is to buy funds that invest only in U.S. Treasury debt securities. Interest paid on federal government debt instruments is exempt from state and local taxes. Interest paid on most state and local debt securities is exempt from taxation at the federal level.

The 1986 Tax Reform Act changed many features of the law for investors. General-obligation municipal bonds are the only source of tax-free income to escape changes. However, the Supreme Court in 1988 held that the federal government could tax municipal interest if it chooses. Congress has limited the quantity of "private activity" bonds that may be issued by state and local governments. Changes were also made in exactly how these latter debt securities are to be taxed. For example, the type of municipal bond you buy may affect your alternative minimum tax calculations.

Tax-free money market funds are sold by major brokerage houses and most large mutual fund groups. No commission is charged when you are buying a tax-exempt money market fund. Fund managers take a small percentage of the income paid by the securities in the portfolio they are managing for their fees. You receive a slightly lower yield in exchange for flexibility, liquidity, and professional management.

Investment Potential

Tax-exempt money market funds are purchased for the current income they pay. There is no capital growth potential.

The short maturities of the securities in the portfolios limits any risk to principal that rising interest rates cause for long-term bond portfolios. The average maturities for tax-free money market funds is higher than for the average taxable fund because fewer "money market type" debt securities are offered by state and local governments.

If you are a resident of a large state, you can avoid state taxation as well as federal taxation by buying funds that invest solely in the debt securities of the state and political sub- divisions of your state. Risk is moderately higher than that for taxable funds because of the longer maturities. The market for municipal securities is less liquid than that for Treasury securities.

All money market funds are closely regulated by the federal government. They must be registered with the SEC, meet stringent financial requirements, and provide a detailed prospectus to all investors in the fund.

A number of financial newsletters rate the relative safety of money market funds. Two well known letters are *Income & Safety* and William Donaghue's *Moneyletter*. Most tax-free money market funds offer the same services provided by taxable funds. Checking privileges, 24-hour liquidity, and the ability to switch among a family of funds by telephone are typical services.

Tax-free money market funds are an at-tractive alternative to passbook savings accounts. Minimum investments are normally small. One major difference is the lack of federal insurance protection for the funds. Municipal securities are rated by major services such as Standard & Poor's or Moody's. They are less secure than Treasury obligations.

The short maturities limit market risk. Incompetent management can affect returns. Expense ratios for tax-free funds tend to be slightly higher than those for taxable funds. The funds offer some measure of protection against inflation. Their yields will increase as interest rates are pushed higher. The diversified portfolios limit the dangers of risk due to default by a single issuer.

Strengths

Tax-free funds are very liquid. Most offer checking account privileges. Professional management provides diversified portfolios that minimize the potential problems of default by a single issuer. Short-term maturities minimize market risk. Rolling over (reinvesting) constantly maturing securities enables money funds to continually offer competitive yields. Interest income earned from funds that invest solely in municipal debt securities is exempt from federal taxes.

Weaknesses

No government insurance covers investor funds. Yields will lag behind sharp interest rates rises. Poor management may result in lower returns. There is no capital gains potential.

Tax Considerations

Tax Consequences

Interest paid on municipal debt securities issued before August 7, 1986, is exempt from federal taxes. Certain limitations apply to "private activity" bonds issued after than date. Carefully read the prospectus and consult with your tax advisor prior to selecting a tax-free money market fund.

Summing Up

The 1986 Tax Reform Act lowered the value of tax-free income by lowering the tax rates. The 1988 Supreme Court decision on munis may result in changed tax status in coming years. In other words, you don't save as much as you used to! However, municipal securities are about the only safe investment for obtaining a tax-exempt cash flow. With more investors being pushed into higher tax brackets as their incomes increase, tax-free money market funds will attract more interest.

---

10 Largest Tax-Exempt Money Market Funds

1. CMA Tax-Exempt Fund (Merrill Lynch)
2. Fidelity Tax-Exempt
3. Federated Tax-Free Trust
4. Dreyfus Tax-Exempt
5. Vanguard Muni Bond
6. Nuveen Tax-Exempt
7. Tax-Exempt Money Market Fund (Kemper)
8. Municipal Cash Reserve (Shearson)
9. Tax-Free Instruments (Federated)
10. T. Rowe Price Tax-Exempt Money

Source: Forbes

Notes

CHAPTER 12

DOMESTIC EQUITIES

Personal
Financial Keys
for Domestic
Equities

Growth

Volatility

Ordinary Income
Capital Gain

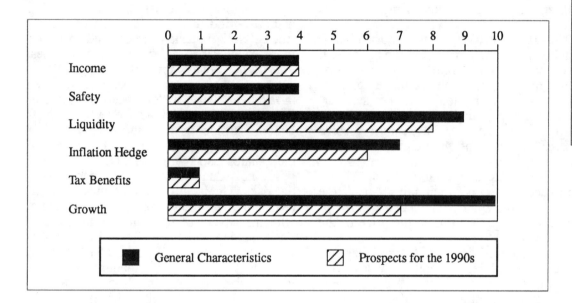

*Outlook for
the 1990s*

High Volatility

Probable sideways
  to down trend in
  first half of
  decade

Will rise if
• GNP growth
  picks up to 3% of
  rate
• Inflation stays
  low
• Interest rates do
  not rise

Will fall if
• DJIA breaks
  2400
• Long-term rates
  rise over 9.50%
• Inflation climbs
  over 8%
• Dollar fall
  continues

A GLANCE AHEAD

In this chapter, you'll discover the wide variety of U.S. equity (domestic stock) investments that are offered to the public. You'll learn

- *The role of stocks in the U.S. economy*
- *How stock ownership differs from bond ownership*
- *What an initial public offering (IPO) is*
- *The vital role stocks play in any diversified portfolio*
- *How listed and over-the-counter (OTC) stocks differ*
- *How the mutual fund industry has ex-*

panded its public offerings to suit the needs of most investors.

DOMESTIC STOCK

In January 1982, the United States was mired in a deep recession. Real interest rates (adjusted for inflation) were near an all-time high, the U.S. dollar was sliding ever lower, and U.S. prestige was waning internationally. As summer approached, the stock market's slide seemed irreversible. The June 14, 1982, issue of *Business Week* headlined its investment section "Running Scared from Stocks."

Few analysts recognized that that pervasive pessimism was setting the groundwork for one of the greatest bull markets in history. That summer the stock market, as measured by the Dow Jones Industrial Average (DJIA), started from below 800. By August 1987 the DJIA had run to over 2,700! Of course, that bull run ended in October 1987 when the DJIA collapsed over 500 points in a single day. By July 1990 the stock market had rallied back from the post-crash depths to challenge the 3000 level on the DJIA. That followed a strong performance in 1989 when the Dow posted a 32% gain. The S&P 500, another widely followed measure, was up 31.50%.

The stock market is the most closely watched investment market in the country. It plays an important role in the economy. Companies that need to raise money to start, expand, or diversify their business sell partial ownership in their corporation to interested buyers. The buyers in turn receive "shares" representing their equity interest in the corporation.

If the business is profitable, the shareholders expect to receive their fair share of the earnings. This share can take the form of dividends or appreciation in the price of the stock itself.

Stock market price cycles are closely related to underlying economic cycles. Perhaps the most widely watched cycle is the four-year presidential cycle. The stock market tends to move higher in the two years prior to a presidential election. In the years following the election, the market tends to be weaker.

There are two primary types of stock: common and preferred. Common stock is the purest form of part ownership in the company. Preferred stock holders trade some of the potential for future growth for the ·greater guarantee of steady dividend payments.

Stocks come in many forms. The stock of most well-known large companies are traded on the major stock exchanges: the New York Stock Exchange (for more established, seasoned issues) and the American Stock Exchange. But many companies have not been around long enough to qualify for listing on either exchange or they may not want to be traded on listed exchanges for their own reasons. They trade on the over-the-counter (OTC) market.

In times of rising prices (bull markets), many corporations see an opportunity to raise capital by selling partial interest in their company to the public. An initial public offering (IPO) is the first sale of a company's shares to the public. Many investors watch this market closely in the hope of finding the next IBM or Xerox.

RISKS

Price volatility—fluctuation in value during a short period of time—is a fact of life for stocks. New, untested issues tend to be far more volatile than older, mature companies. That is not always the case, though. When even seasoned companies become involved in takeovers (such as RJR/Nabisco, Time or .Pennwalt) or unanticipated events (such as Union Carbide in the Bhopal disaster, or Texaco in the Pennzoil lawsuit), the price of their shares also swings widely.

An individual stock issue has many potential risks. The health of the company's business will affect the share price. For example, with the advent of the automobile, the carriage making and buggy whip business began a long decline. When transistors were in-vented, vaccum tube manufacturers ran into trouble. New technology has always been the investor's biggest friend—and often a potential enemy—depending on which shares the investor owns.

Usually the most important factor in the price of an individual issue though, is the state of the stock market as a whole. Even during the Great Depression certain companies managed to show steadily increasing earnings. However, few stock issues were able to buck the falling trend of the overall market. It is vital to know the market's trend, even when selecting individual stocks.

Historically, stocks are considered good inflation hedges, yet the high inflation in the late 1970s demonstrated limits to this assumption. When inflation hit double-digit rates, it so distorted business pricing that the stock market actually fell sharply in nominal and real inflation-adjusted terms. Rising interest rates generally tend to hurt stock prices over the long term. Initially, rising rates are often a sign of increased economic activity, which is beneficial to stocks. As economic activity increases, company earnings turn higher. Eventually higher interest rates compete with the return on stocks, drawing money away from the market. As credit becomes tighter, marginal companies lose their access to the credit markets. As they cut back production or fail, their suppliers also become financially troubled. The whole process can snowball into a recession—the downward side of the business cycle.

A key advantage of most stock ownership is liquidity. For the most part, listed stocks are very liquid. Most OTC issues also have liquid markets, though it pays to find out *how* liquid before investing in an OTC issue.

The stock market crash of October 1987 raised one other point about the liquidity of the OTC market. Allegedly a number of "market makers" (companies that maintain an active bid-ask auction market for OTC issues) simply quit answering the telephone on October 19. Some investors who wanted to exit their stocks were not able to get out when they wanted to. In fact, many investors could not even get quotes on the issues they wanted to sell.

The National Association of Securities Dealers (NASD) has moved to prevent this type of "market lockout" from happening again. Specifically, it now requires that all market makers become part of an automated system of bid and ask quotes. This computerized system enables investors to buy and sell at the best possible prices because their brokers are able to execute the order right off the quote machines.

That, at least, is the theory. The Small Order Execution System (it handles trades up to 1000 shares) passed its first big test in October 1989 when the market plunged 190 points on Friday 13th.

A liquid market merely means there is a ready supply of buyers and sellers for each issue. More obscure, untried companies naturally have fewer buyers and therefore have lower liquidity.

All investments are subject to some degree of political risk. Wars, embargos, tax policies, and many other political events can and do affect the markets and even individual issues. It is important to guard against the adverse affects of unanticipated political developments by diversifying over several stocks in several industries. You should also diversify over several asset categories (stocks, bonds, real estate, cash equivalents, gold, etc.) for maximum protection.

RATINGS, INSURANCE, AND GOVERNMENT REGULATION

Stocks offered to the general public must be registered with the SEC (Securities and Exchange Commission). Registration consists of disclosure of pertinent facts regarding the business. The prospectus for the intitial stock offering contains these details. Most companies ($1 million or more in gross assets) are required to file annual financial reports (Form 10-K) with the SEC. This report details total sales, revenue, and pretax operating income. It also includes a breakdown of sales for various products for the past five years. The SEC does not pass judgment on the stability or worthiness of corporations that register their stock. However, various private companies examine public records and rate companies' financial condition. The largest rating companies are Standard & Poor's and Moody's Investor Services.

The Securities Investor Protection Corporation (SIPC) insures customer accounts of member firms in much the same manner as the FSLIC insures thrift institutions and the FDIC insures banks. All brokers and dealers registered with the SEC must join the SIPC. The SIPC guarantees securities and cash in customer accounts to $500,000 with a limit of $100,000 on the cash portion. Unfortunately, this only protects investors from fraud or brokerage business failure—not losses they experience in the market.

STOCKS COMPARED TO OTHER ASSETS

In the initial stages of inflation, stocks provide a good counterbalance to bonds. For example, as inflation picked up in April 1987, the bond market began a long, hard slide. The Consumer Price Index, the Producer Price Index, and the prices of gold and oil had all jumped higher in the first few months of the year. While bonds were falling, the stock market climbed higher. In balanced portfolios, the gains of the latter helped offset the losses of the former.

As inflation continues, however, stocks begin to get hurt, especially when compared to tangible commodities such as gold. In the late 1970s, stock market investors lost purchasing power as inflation was greater than the return that stocks produced. At that stage of the economic cycle, stocks ran "contracyclically" to gold. That is, gold appreciated while stocks declined in real terms.

The stock market is an important leading indicator of the economy. In fact, stock prices are a component of the U.S. Commerce Department's index leading economic indicators. Stock prices generally begin to rise before other areas of the economy show signs of improvement. An example was the strong stock market move that began in the recession summer of 1982. Most analysts at that time viewed the economy's prospects as bleak.

The market will also tend to turn downward well before the rest of the economy. The average lead time of the index of leading indicators is 10 months of downturn before the onset of a recession.

The popularity of stock trading has resulted in an abundance of investment vehicles. Chapter 16 gives details on trading the stock market and even individual stocks on the options and futures markets.

The major avenues for investing in U.S. domestic stocks include listed, IPO, and OTC issues or are through a wide variety of mutual funds.

Lasser's Recommended 1990s Common Stock Allocation

Allocate as little as 15%.
Allocate as much as 40%.

Listed Common Stock

Common stock represents shares of ownership in a public corporation. Common stock holders usually have the right to vote on the company's board of directors and on other important corporate decisions. Stock owners receive dividends as declared by the board of directors. Listed stock is stock traded on the New York Stock Exchange, the American Stock Exchange, and regional exchanges.

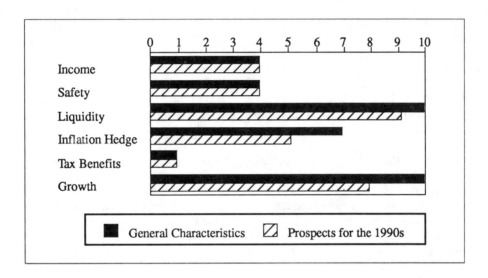

Income

Safety

Liquidity

Inflation Hedge

Tax Benefits

Growth

■ General Characteristics ◿ Prospects for the 1990s

Type I

C
Low Taxes
High Expenses

D
Low Taxes
Low Expenses

Common stocks receive more attention than any other investment class in the country. Local newspapers, radio, and television all carry regular reports on the latest fortunes of the stock market. The market is the single best proxy for the current and future state of the economy.

When corporations are formed, those people who invest either money or time receive proportionate ownership shares in the enterprise. These shares are stock in the company. In "closely held corporations," the outstanding stock is owned by only a few people, often family members or long-time business associates. These shares do not have an active market and are not easily bought or sold. Many companies, however, decide to broaden ownership in their companies. This is usually done to raise additional capital to pay for business

expansion, or to pay the founders for their efforts. To do so, they sell shares of stock to the public. This action is called "going public." These shares represent ownership interest in the company.

As a part owner of the company, the stock owner shares in the wealth of the company in two ways. First, he or she may receive dividends if the board of directors elects to pay them. Profits generated by the business tend to influence the price of its shares. If a company's earnings increase, it theoretically makes shares of the company's stock worth more to another investor, increasing the price you may get for your shares. And finally, a holder of common stock is entitled to his or her proportionate share of the company's assets in case of liquidation, after holders of the company's bond and preferred stock are paid.

The value of a share of common stock is based on a wide variety of considerations. Primarily, you invest in a company based on your perception of its prospects for future earnings and dividend growth. A company with a growing, profitable business will naturally be more valuable as the earnings accrue. This increased wealth may be reflected either in further expansion as a result of reinvestment of the earnings, or in increased dividends paid to shareholders.

No matter how well the company's business is doing, if the economic environment is depressed the price of your stock may actually go down even with record earnings. Other factors that may affect a stock's price include interest rates, inflation, general investor psychology, and investment fads (the company may not be an "in" industry group).

Once a company has established an earnings record, a sufficiently diverse shareholder base, and enough outstanding shares, it may qualify for "listing" on a stock exchange. As noted, the major exchanges are the New York Stock Exchange (NYSE) and the American Stock Exchange (ASE). There are also a number of regional exchanges such as the Pacific Stock Exchange (PSE). Listing requirements are most stringent for the NYSE. This is where older, more established, mature companies are found. Companies in mature industries are more inclined to pay out a larger percentage of earnings in dividends. They generally represent the cream of U.S. industry. Most major corporations whose names are household words such as IBM, Kodak, Xerox, and General Motors, are listed on the NYSE.

The American Stock Exchange also has requirements for companies to be listed. Since these ASE requirements are less stringent than the NYSE guidelines, companies listed on the ASE tend to be newer, more aggressive, more speculative ventures. Since earnings are reinvested to stimulate further rapid growth, dividends are low or nonexistent.

Investment Potential

Stocks are an excellent source of long-term total returns. The existence of well-established stock exchanges facilitates liquidity. Independent objective price information is readily available through newspapers, radio, and even television. Statistical information and professional investment advice are easily accessible. Publicly owned companies are required by law to thoroughly describe the financial details of their business in the annual 10-K reports that are filed with the SEC. Most companies also send shareholders an annual report detailing the most important elements of these 10-K reports. Computer databases such as those offered by Dow Jones or Media General make accessible literally thousands of pages of financial information to anybody who has a computer and the funds to pay for computer time.

Although the main attraction of stocks is their capital gains potential, many stocks offer competitive income through dividends. You should remember that dividends, unlike bond interest, are paid at the discretion of the directors of a company—they are not a guaranteed part of your ownership benefits.

A major attraction of stocks is the great variety of investment objectives that can be met through judicious stock selection. Growth stocks—those which are in developing and growing industries and that reinvest the major portion of their earnings rather than paying dividends—offer the chance for substantial long-term capital gains. Typical listed growth issues include Amoco Corporation, AMP, Bankers Trust, Consolidated Natural Gas, Capital Holdings, Equifax, General Cinema, Humana, Motorola, Scott Paper, Time, Warner-Lambert, and Zurn. Short-term traders can also find volatile stocks to suit their temperament. Conservative risk-averse investors can select "blue-chip" issues from the New York Stock Exchange with relative long-term safety. Blue chips are companies with long, proven earnings records, stable management, and nonvolatile stock prices. They are companies that are leaders in the business world. Blue-chip issues are large, well-established companies you are probably familiar with. A few representatives include American Express, Abbott Laboratories, IBM, Dow Chemical, Alcoa, Chevron, DuPont, Kodak, General Electric, General Motors, Ford, McDonald's, Merck, Sears, Smith Kline, Westinghouse, International Paper, and others.

A number of listed stocks meet other objectives, such as the need for current income with the potential for capital appreciation.

For example, utility stocks offer high yields. Income-oriented issues range from utilities to mature, established companies. Some representative examples include American Electric Power, Bell Atlantic, Columbia Gas Systems, Commonwealth, Edison, Exxon, GTE, Houston Industries, NYNEX, Niagara Mohawk Power, Pacific Enterprises, Pacific Gas & Electric, Hawaiian Electric, and others.

As noted earlier, a number of independent companies rate stocks for their financial stability. These include Standard & Poor's, Moody's, and Value Line. In addition, a wide range of stock advisory newsletters provide specific trading advice.

Strengths

Listed stocks are very liquid. The wide variety of listed stocks offers alternatives to meet most investment objectives. Stocks offer substantial growth potential. A vast amount of information on listed stocks is accessible. You can choose from a wide variety of brokerage services and fee structures. Stocks are not a zero-sum game. In a rising market, everyone can profit. One investor's profit is not another's loss. A number of professional management services are available for investors who do not have the time to devote to stock investing.

Weaknesses

Price fluctuations (volatility) affects all stocks regardless of the soundness of the issuing company or the stability of the current market. Special circumstances such as suspension of trading in a stock may limit liquidity. The general economy affects stock prices. Unforeseen political developments may negatively affect certain stocks. Dividend income is not as secure as bond interest, because directors may elect to cut or suspend payments. Adverse market trends may exist for years.

Tax Considerations

Tax Consequences

The 1986 Tax Reform Act eliminated preferential long-term capital gains treatment effective in 1988. That means all capital gains are taxed at your ordinary income tax rate. Dividends are also taxed as ordinary income. As we go to press in late 1990, the question of reinstating preferential tax treatment for capital gains is being hotly debated in Congress.

Interest on margin loans secured by stocks is tax deductible up to the amount of investment income earned. Losses from stock trading can be carried forward. It is important to consult your tax advisor for specifics that may concern you.

Summing Up

Listed stocks are the favored long-term investment for pension funds. The S&P 500 index is the most widely used criterion against which money managers measure their relative performance.

Listed stocks represent the best of U.S. industry. Both the New York Stock Exchange and the American Stock Exchange set minimum requirements for companies to list their stocks. These requirements consist of minimum length of time in business, size of financial assets, and spread of shareholders over the country.

U.S. domestic equities remain the single most widely used investment, other than simple savings accounts, for most Americans. The wide variety of companies offers investors the opportunity to select issues that fit their particular investment needs. Investors seeking some income will choose the less volatile stock of more mature companies that pay a steady dividend. Others, looking for short-term profits, will concentrate their portfolio on young, untested issues that generally pay little or no dividends but offer the potential of rapid share appreciation. These companies reinvest their earnings in the company in an attempt to maximize growth. Top-performing stocks on the NYSE during 1989 were the Spain Fund

(+198%), LA Gear (+184%), Claire's Stores (+179%), Asia Pacific Fund (+178%), Thai Fund (+174%), Mylan Labs (+173%), Holiday Corp. (+166%), Shaw Industries (+164%), Tyler Corp. (+164%), and Germany Fund (+157%).

Top performers on the ASE were Thermo Proc. (+299%), New World Entm. (+274%), Central Pacific (+258%), Graham Corp. (+244%), Turner Broadcasting B (+242%), Mission Resources (+240%), and Keane Inc. (+218%).

The mutual fund industry has been a major beneficiary of this latest and longest-running stock market boom. Mutual funds have become so specialized that it is possible for investors to tailor their own portfolios with a variety of mutual funds that specialize in certain market sectors. For example, certain funds invest only in gold shares and bullion, some funds invest solely in high technology shares. There is a wide variety of stock funds that specialize in industry sectors such as high technology, basic industry, capital goods, utilities, retail stores, energy, natural resources, and more. Of course, the older distinctions between mutual fund objectives—growth (even aggressive growth) versus income—still apply.

As you can see in the list of top performing NYSE issues, foreign country funds were very popular as world political and economic events moved center stage for American investors. For example, Spain's economy grew at a rapid 5% rate in 1989 with its currency also gaining. Many investors see Spain as a major beneficiary of the 1992 ending of trade barriers in Europe.

The reunification of Germany generated enthusiasm for Germany-based investments as many people see a reunited Germany as an economic superpower. With trade barriers among Common Market countries due to fall in 1992 and most Eastern European countries turning away from socialist economies, Europe presents outstanding prospects for dynamic and profitable change in the 1990s.

---

10 Top-Performing Balanced Funds
(ranked by 10-year total return)

* 1) United Income
− 2) Vanguard Windsor
+ 3) Washington Mutual Investors
* 4) Lindner Dividend
* 5) AMEV Capital
* 6) Mutual Shares
* 7) Dodge Cox Stock
* 8) Investment Company of America
* 9) Vanguard High Yield
* 10) Fundamental

o Unchanged from previous edition
* New appearance on list
+ Moved up from previous edition
− Moved down from previous edition

Source: Fund/Search, Information Edge, Inc. (800) 334-3669

Over-the-Counter (OTC) Common Stock

Over-the-counter stocks are securities that are not traded on a major stock exchange. Trade is conducted through a complex telephone and computer network that brings together a wide varitety of dealers throughout the country. Dealers choose to "make a market" in a particular stock by offering constant bid (to buy) and ask (to sell) prices for issues their clients have chosen to trade.

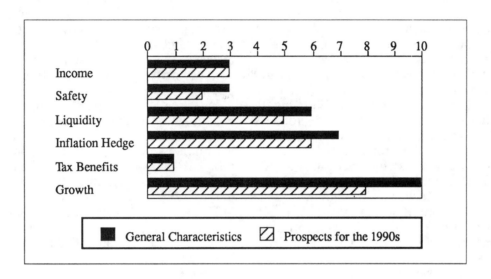

Income
Safety
Liquidity
Inflation Hedge
Tax Benefits
Growth

■ General Characteristics ▨ Prospects for the 1990s

Type I

D

Low Taxes
Low Expenses

As we remarked earlier, every investor dreams of finding a fledgling IBM or an infant Xerox in which a modest investment will yield huge profits. The nation's stock exchanges, however may not be the best place to find such start-up companies: stocks listed on the exchanges must meet certain requirements—minimum length of time in business, an established record of earnings, so many shares outstanding, and a diversity of shareholders. Instead, the over-the-counter (OTC) market offers companies in their formative years, those that may not qualify for listing on the exchanges, the opportunity to raise capital from the public. Many investors turn to the OTC market to invest in brand new, fast-growing companies.

When shareholders buy stock in a company, they look to profit from appreciation in

the value of the stock as well as from dividends paid out of business profits. Most newer companies in dynamic industries, however, strive to maximize growth by plowing earnings back into the company rather than pay dividends to shareholders. The OTC market provides an organized liquid market for newer growth stocks.

Over the last 20 years, the OTC market has significantly upgraded its efficiency and responsiveness to investor needs. Governed by the National Association of Securities Dealers (NASD), the OTC market offers a competitive and liquid investment opportunity. Historically, price information on OTC issues was spotty. Accurate timely price quotes are now available through NASD's Automated Quotation (NASDAQ) system. Member dealers are tied into the computerized NASDAQ system. The dealers offer to buy and sell selected stocks on a regular basis. Their bids and offers are carried on the NASDAQ system. This display of information gives investors a reliable picture of the market for various issues. An OTC stock can have as few as one or many dealers who make markets in the issue.

This "market maker" system differs from that for listed stocks where exchange member "specialists" have a monopoly for making a market (matching buyers and sellers) in assigned stocks. Although much debate rages over which system is more fair for investors, the very existence of readily accessible quotes greatly facilitates trading. NASDAQ prices are updated continually throughout the day on a ticker much like that used by stock exchanges.

Stocks must meet certain minimum requirements to qualify for inclusion on the NASDAQ system. Very small or highly speculative, risky issues that trade for less than $1 per share are called "penny stocks." In 1990 the NASD proposed tightening its listing requirements for inclusion on its NASDAQ automated trading system. The proposed revisions would eliminate hundreds of low priced stocks from NASDAQ. That would make it more difficult to follow and trade these issues. Even though no NASDAQ system exists to bring continuously available quotes to the public on these penny stock issues, market makers have a highly organized and sophisticated network through which they can buy or sell these issues. Prices are listed on "pink sheets" available in most brokerage offices. Initial steps to automate price quotes for even these penny stocks have been initiated by the NASD.

Investment Potential

Liquidity varies widely for OTC issues. Some stocks are heavily traded with many market makers and a substantial number of institutional investors. Other issues may only have one or two market makers and a limited following among investment analysts. Less liquid markets are called "thinly traded." It may be difficult to buy or sell large blocks of these issues in a short time period. Generally speaking, the OTC market is the home of less seasoned, more speculative, and more volatile stocks. The primary attraction of this market is the potential for substantial capital

gains. It is of course accompanied by higher risk. Since most OTC issues have shorter track records, it is more difficult to determine a stock's trading "character," such as its price volatility or sensitivity to economic news. Some of the companies traded in the OTC market may very well turn out to be tomorrow's IBM and Xerox corporations. But in a universe of over 50,000 stocks, picking the right one is a challenging task.

OTC stocks are mostly growth oriented and therefore pay little or no income. Some exceptions exist, such as insurance companies or regional banks that still trade over the counter. As a general rule, though, investors seeking current income are better served elsewhere.

Historically, the price of growth stocks benefits during the early stages of inflation. Specific industry groups such as gold or silver mining stocks are direct beneficiaries of inflation and provide an excellent hedge against inflation. Leading OTC performers during 1989 were American Travelers (+318%), Pacificare Health (+316%), Oceaneering (+300), Adaptec Inc. (+284%), Vivigen Inc. (+267%), and Offshore Logistics (+248%).

Keep in mind though that there were also large losers: 1st American Bank & Trust (–97%), Cityfed Financial (–96%), Pioneer Savings (–96%), Miniscribe (–95%), United Building (–95%), and Chartwell Groups (–95%).

Strengths

In the right economic environment, new, small, growth-oriented companies offer good capital gains potential. Many OTC stocks are very liquid. Investors can readily find out the number of shares outstanding and the number of market makers for these issues—two important factors in liquidity. Performance for NASDAQ system stocks is easily tracked. Substantial financial and investment information is available for actively traded OTC issues. Competing market makers ensure fair pricing.

Weaknesses

Volatility is a fact of life for OTC issues. Generally they have fewer institutional investors and are subject to sharp, unexpected price moves. Small, untested companies are vulnerable to competitive moves made by larger, better-capitalized competitors. Bankruptcies are more common in developing companies. OTC stocks are vulnerable to adverse economic events as well as adverse developments in their own industries. Transaction costs are harder to find out, because many OTC issues are bought and sold with dealer markups rather than clearly disclosed commissions. Developing companies are more vulnerable to investment fads that come and go. Low or no dividends means there is no protection on a downward trend.

The OTC market was rocked by the October 19, 1987, market crash. Allegedly some market makers refused to answer their phones during the crash. The NASD has moved to automate purchase and sales of OTC issues via a computerized system to eliminate such problems in the future. In 1988-89 "penny stock" scandals were widespread, cheating investors out of millions.

The SEC has proposed tough new regulations designed to eliminate the many abuses involving penny stocks. The largest penny stock broker, Blinder Robinson, has been under constant regulatory pressure for years.

Tax Considerations

Tax Consequences

The 1986 Tax Reform Act eliminated preferential capital gains treatment as of 1988. Dividends are taxable at ordinary income rates. Capital gains are now also taxed as ordinary income. The Bush Administration favors a cut in capital gains taxes, but by 1990 had been unsuccessful in getting Congress to agree. Interest from margin loans secured by OTC stocks is tax deductible up to the amount of investment income earned. Losses from stock trading can be deducted from other capital gains. Consult your tax advisor for details about your own situation.

Summing Up

The OTC market offers investors the chance to buy shares in new developing companies. Although some well-established corporations trade on the OTC market (for example, regional banks) this market is typically the domain of "up and coming" issues.

Traders of OTC issues need to know a number of things that do not affect listed stocks. For example, the liquidity of an OTC issue cannot be taken for granted. It is important to know how many "market makers" there are for each issue. The more market makers, the more liquid the stock.

Prices are less accessible for many OTC issues than for listed stocks. Stock prices of issues on the NASDAQ system are widely available. Lower-priced and less liquid issues are quoted on "pink sheets." The NASD targets automation for these quotes soon. The NASDAQ index is a widely followed measure of the performance of NASDAQ-quoted issues. This index complements the Dow Jones Industrial Average, which measures the performance of 30 of the leading well-established corporations on the New York Stock Exchange.

Initial Public Offerings (IPOs)
of Common Stock

Initial public offerings (IPOs) are the first public issue of a company's stock. When a company decides to go public, it contracts with an investment banker to underwrite its offering. Together, they decide such questions as the number of shares and price of each share for the offering. For example, XYZ Corporation may decide to try to raise $100 million through a public offering of 10 million shares at $10 per share.

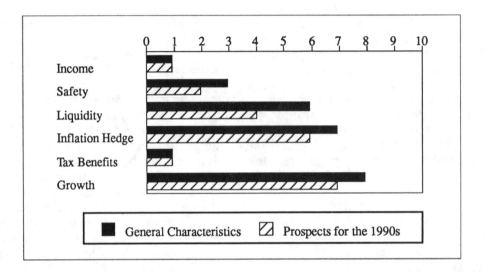

During bull markets (that is, rising markets) the demand for "hot new issues" outstrips supply as investors rush to buy the latest offerings of highly touted stocks in the hope of quick and large profits. It is not unusual to see "hot issues" rise as much as 25% to 50% within hours after their initial release to the public. The most important factor in this phenomenon is investor psychology rather than the actual financial and investment prospects of individual issues.

The underwriter puts together a "syndicate" made up of brokerage firms to distribute the offering to the public. An initial prospectus (called a "red herring") details the financial status of the company, its prospects, and risks. It is filed with the SEC. Once approved by the SEC, this prospectus is printed and made available to potential investors so they can evaluate the facts about the company and decide whether they want to invest.

The demand for IPOs varies directly with market conditions. In rising markets, investor euphoria results in overwhelming demand for issues underwritten by established quality firms. In fact, demand is often so great that only very good, sizable customers for participating brokerages can get stock in so-called "hot issues" before it trades in the secondary (previously purchased stock) market. In flat or falling markets, however, this condition reverses and some IPOs become difficult to sell regardless of the actual future prospects of the company.

IPOs are offered without a broker's commission to the public. The broker is paid by the issuer to market the new issue. Soon after release of the offering, the new issue be-

Type I

D

Low Taxes
Low Expenses

gins trading in the secondary market. Usually this market is the OTC market, since most IPOs are relatively new enterprises that do not meet the criteria for exchange listing. Exceptions arise when a long-established, privately held company decides to go public, such as Ford Motor company's first public offering in the 1950s.

The underwriting syndicate works to maintain a minimum offering price. Typically this effort ends about four weeks after the offering, and then market forces take over. This price "floor" provides some downside protection for initial investors.

Investment Potential

Since most IPOs are from relatively new companies, the chief attraction is their prospects for future growth. Rarely do IPOs offer any dividend income. Most IPOs are high-risk speculative investments because their operating track records are short. As noted, the "red herring" draft of the prospectus details the financial status of the company, gives facts about the management such as experience in the industry, and outlines business risks for the company.

An important part of the initial prospectus is a detailed breakdown of just how the money will be used. There are three major uses of the capital: expansion of the business, paying founders and officers, or paying off accumulated debt. Many professional advisors recommend that you avoid IPOs that intend to use more than 25% of the proceeds for things other than investment in the business itself. However, in euphoric markets this restriction is routinely ignored by investors who want to "get in on the ground floor." (It would be more accurate to say that the public is getting in on the mezzanine or second floor, since the company's founders own the "ground floor"—and potentially most valuable—stock!)

Good-quality, well-managed companies in growth industries offer good long-term capital gains potential. However, because of the euphoria that often surrounds these offerings in a bull market, it is not unusual to see large short-term gains. These "hot" issues are in short supply and are usually only obtainable by long-time proven clients of

syndicate members (brokerage firms).

Less fortunate investors who want to buy the stock must acquire it in the secondary market, where the stock often trades at a substantial premium to the offering price. The unrealistic euphoria surrounding these offerings is demonstrated by the fact that over 60% of all IPOs trade below the initial offering price within one year of issue. Nevertheless, the dream of large, quick profits motivates investors to buy on offering day.

These high-risk speculations do offer some inflation protection. Growth stocks normally keep ahead of moderate inflation.

Strengths

 Early participation in dynamic growth companies in expanding industries can yield substantial capital gains. Hot-issue IPOs are very liquid, initially. The demand for the stock far outstrips the supply. There are no commission costs for purchase. Quick, sizable profits are the norm in bull markets for issues sponsored by proven underwriters.

Weaknesses

 Once underwriting support is withdrawn, liquidity may dry up if there is not sufficient investor interest. It is impossible to know in advance which issues will draw substantial investor trade after the offering period. Lack of dividend income means there is no downside protection in adverse markets. A short management track record, heavy debt, or earnings volatility increase IPO price swings. The large fees paid to underwriters means that initial investors are paying a hidden premium for the company. For most individual investors, hot issues are virtually impossible to purchase at the initial offering price.

Tax Considerations

IPOs are subject to the same taxes as any

Tax Consequences

common stock. The 1986 Tax Reform Act eliminated preferential long-term capital gains treatment in 1988. Long-term capital gains are now taxed at your ordinary income rate. The Bush Administration has proposed substantial tax cuts for capital gains, but by 1990 Congress had not gone along. Dividends (if any) are taxed as ordinary income.

Interest on margin loans secured by stocks (most IPOs do not qualify for margin) is tax deductible up to the amount of investment income you earn. Losses from stock trading can offset other capital gains. Consult your tax advisor for specifics for your situation.

Because of the high-risk speculative nature of IPOs, they are not appropriate for retirement plans governed by ERISA.

Summing Up

IPOs are a highly speculative type of stock. During bull markets (such as the one from 1982 to August 1987), IPOs become the "hottest game in town." Many IPOs come to market and shoot up in price within minutes of the time actual trading begins. This quick and volatile activity attracts many investors willing to take substantial risks for large quick profits.

Statistics point out the dangers of IPO investing. Most IPOs trade below their offering price sometime within the first 12 months of issue. Since many IPOs trade significantly above their offering price within hours of release, only savvy, well-heeled, and well-informed investors should pursue this avenue regularly.

Initial public offerings generally do best during roaring bull markets. The IPO market slipped in size and performance following the October 1987 market crash. In 1988 there were 255 new issues, which raised $22.4 billion. Of the 15 largest IPOs that year only one, Burlington Resources, finished the year higher than the initial offering price.

In 1989 the IPO market slipped further with 245 new offerings raising only $13.8 billion. Compare the 1988 and '89 totals with 1987 when there were 533 issues raising $24 billion.

IPO price performance in 1989 also logged with only 3 of the 15 largest issues posting gains by year end. Popular offerings in 1989 included closed end funds which invested in specific countries such as Chile, Turkey and Austria.

---

10 Top-Performing No-Load Balanced Funds
(ranked by 10-year total return)

```
o   1)  Vanguard Windsor
*   2)  Lindner Dividend
*   3)  Mutual Shares
*   4)  Dodge Cox Stock
*   5)  Vanguard High Yield
*   6)  Elfun Trusts
*   7)  Financial Ind. Income
−   8)  Fidelity Fund
−   9)  Vanguard Index Trust
− 10)  Selected American
```

o Unchanged from previous edition
* New appearance on list
+ Moved up from previous edition
− Moved down from previous edition

Source: Fund/Search, Information Edge, Inc. (800) 334-3669

Preferred Stock

Preferred stock is a hybrid investment combining features of corporate bonds and stock. Preferred stock is primarily of interest to institutional investors such as pension funds and insurance companies because 80% of the dividends paid is tax exempt for them. Unfortunately, that exemption does not exist for individuals.

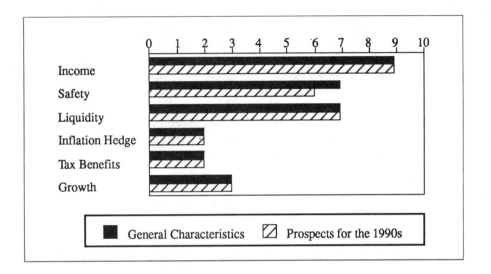

Income
Safety
Liquidity
Inflation Hedge
Tax Benefits
Growth

■ General Characteristics   ▨ Prospects for the 1990s

Type I

C

Low Taxes
High Expenses

Despite its unique characteristics, preferred stock is an equity investment—not a debt investment, as are bonds. However, because the dividend is typically a set percentage of par value, preferred stock trades similar to corporate bonds. When interest rates rise, preferred stock prices fall. Preferreds appreciate when interest rates decline.

Although it is an equity investment, preferred stock does not normally carry voting rights. The chief attraction for individual investors is the slightly higher yield compared to bonds that some preferreds offer. This is because the dividend paid to preferred holders is not a legal obligation, as is the interest on a corporate bond. Preferred dividends are paid at the discretion of the corporation. If the company's earnings fall, it can elect not to pay dividends in a given payment cycle.

However, when dividends are declared, preferred holders must be paid before dividends are paid to common stockholders. Most preferred stock dividends are cumulative, which means that if dividends are not authorized in a given year, they accrue until such time as the company is able to pay them again. A cumulative preferred shareholder would receive all arrears before any dividends are paid to common stock owners.

Preferred stock should usually be purchased through full-service brokerage firms. Since there is little short-term trading in preferreds, and there are many types of preferred stocks, including cumulative, preference, participating, or floating-rate, discount brokerage houses catering to individuals are not normally well equipped to deal with them. A commission is charged for both the sale and purchase of preferred stock.

The prices of preferred stocks are quoted daily in the *Wall Street Journal* and in larger dailies. There is generally less volume in preferred issues, because they are primarily purchased by corporations which hold them for the tax-exempt income.

Investment Potential

Although preferreds are technically an equity investment, their primary attraction is the current income they pay, which makes them competitive alternatives to bonds. Their dividends take precedence over dividends for common stock. In the case of liquidation, preferred shareholders have priority over common stockholders. Bondholders, though, take precedence over both preferred and common stock owners. Capital gains are also possible. Preferreds are normally long-term investments. Thin markets limit the appeal of short-term trading. Although primarily designed for institutional investors, preferreds can offer slightly higher yields for individual investors. They are considered "less safe" than bonds due to their lower-priority claim on a company's earnings and assets. Therefore, their yield is sometimes higher than bonds. Large, full-service brokerage firms have specialists in preferred stocks, who try to ferret out these undervalued situations for their clients.

Preferreds are generally less volatile than common stock. However, with interest rates becoming increasingly erratic, preferreds are prone to wider swings. Many preferreds are very thinly traded. This limits their liquidity.

Preferreds are rated by a number of independent services such as Standard & Poor's, Moody's Investor Services, and Value Line Investment Survey.

Strengths

Preferred stocks normally pay higher dividends than common stock. They have priority claim over common stock on a company's earnings and assets in the case of liquidation. Dividends paid on preferred stock are 80% tax free to corporations. Preferreds, like bonds, appreciate when interest rates fall.

Weaknesses

Preferred shareholders usually have no voting rights. Preferred dividends are paid at the discretion of the company's board of directors. They are not legal debt obligations. Preferred stocks offer no protection against inflation. Preferreds are subject to the market risk arising from interest rates rises. Preferred stocks also carry business risk. If the financial condition of the underlying company deteriorates and its rating is lowered, the preferred stock will decline in price even if interest rates do not move. Preferred stock usually does not appreciate with improving company prospects, as does common stock. The low volume and activity in many preferreds limits their liquidity.

Tax Considerations

Tax Consequences

No special tax benefits accrue for individual preferred stock buyers. Dividends and capital gains are taxed at your ordinary income rate. However, corporate buyers have substantial tax benefits: 80% of all dividends paid is exempt from federal taxes.

Summing Up

Preferred stocks escaped major damage from the draconian tax law changes of 1986. Their dividends are still 80% tax free to corporations, though that is down from 85%.

Preferred stocks have enjoyed a bull market since 1982, with the decline in interest rates. In the first nine months of 1987, the upsurge in rates drove preferred prices down. However, preferreds, like bonds, benefitted from the interest rate downturn that followed the October Crash that year.

The primary beneficiaries of preferred stock are institutional investors. Individual investors can find comparable after-tax yields and greater liquidity in corporate or municipal bonds.

Convertible Preferred Stock

Convertible preferred stock is a hybrid investment combining features of both common stocks and preferred stock. It is preferred stock with the right to convert to a fixed number of common shares at a set price. Usually the stock is in the issuing company, although occasionally, when the issuing company holds a large interest in another corporation, it may be convertible into the shares of that other company.

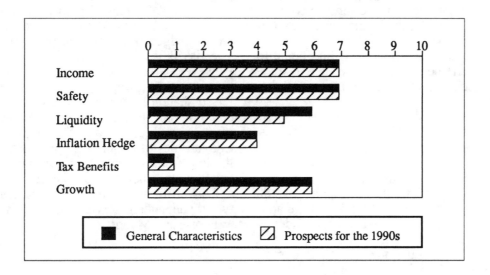

Type IV

C

Low Taxes
High Expenses

Convertible preferred stock provides a more secure, higher income than common stock. It offers a greater growth potential than straight preferred stock through the conversion to common stock feature. Although it may appear that convertible preferred stock is the best of both worlds, there are tradeoffs. The interest paid is lower than that offered by comparable nonconvertible preferreds. You must pay a higher price to get the conversion rights. In the same way, the potential growth is also less than that of outright purchase of the common stock. The conversion premium mitigates some of the gain.

Convertible preferred stock has a priority claim on the assets of the corporation over common stock in the case of bankruptcy or liquidation. However, bonds (both straight and convertible) have precedence over preferred stock in the same circumstances. Dividends from convertible preferred stock must be paid before any dividends are paid to common stock holders. However, unlike bond interest, which is a legal obligation of the company, dividends are paid at the discretion of the corporation.

The dual nature of convertible preferreds results in two different ways to assess their value: investment value and conversion value. The investment value is the price the preferred would have without the conversion privilege. For example, to determine the investment value of an XYZ Corporation convertible preferred, compare it to a straight preferred with similar dividend yield (e.g., 8%).

A company's convertible preferred will sell for a higher price than an equivalent straight preferred (meaning a lower current yield). The investment value of the convertible affords downside protection in adverse market conditions when the value of the common stock is below conversion value.

In normal markets, convertible preferreds

trade on their conversion value. Conversion value is the current price of the underlying common stock multiplied by the number of shares the preferred is convertible. For example, if XYZ Corporation's common stock is trading at $30 per share, and its preferred is convertible into five shares, the conversion value is $150 per preferred share.

When the convertible is trading for less than the conversion value (a bear market in stocks may be one instance), the convertible will trade like a bond fluctuating with interest rates rather than with the underlying stock. If the convertible is trading equal to or above the conversion value, it will trade like a stock, closely tracking the underlying common.

Investment Potential

Convertible preferreds provide you with higher income than the dividends of the common stock. A key attraction is the added potential for capital gains if the underlying common stock rises. To achieve this dual potential, you trade off lower current income than is paid by straight preferreds. In addition, you give up some potential capital gain that you would earn from purchase of the common stock.

Convertibles offer downside protection from a dropping stock market because they will never trade below their investment value. The tradeoff for the lower risk is lower returns than if you bought only the preferred or the common stock.

Convertibles are well suited for conservative investors willing to forgo top returns in exchange for less risk. They are most appropriate for long-term objectives. They lessen the need for precise timing of the stock market since they pay competitive income while you wait for the common stock to rise. As such, they are excellent vehicles for retirement plans.

The capital gains potential affords you inflation protection that straight bonds do not. The biggest risk is an environment in which the stock market declines and interest rates rise. When interest rates rise, preferred stocks fall. If the common stock does not rise to support the price when interest rates are climbing, the convertible will trade like

straight preferred stock.

Strengths

Convertible preferred stocks pay higher income than that paid by common stock. They are convertible into common stock. They offer the potential for capital gains. As a hybrid between preferred and common stocks, they are a "hedged bet" between the two types. The risk is lower than either type outright. However, you trade off greater potential gain for the lower risk. Convertible preferred shareholders have priority claim over common stockholders on company assets in case of bankruptcy or other liquidation. Convertibles of major corporations are quite liquid. You also have the right to convert to the common stock at your option.

Convertibles are rated for financial stability by independent services such as Standard & Poor's and Moody's.

Weaknesses

The income paid by convertible preferred stock is lower than equivalent straight preferred stock because of the greater potential for capital gains. On the other hand, capital gain potential is less than that of the underlying common stock.

Most convertibles have "call" provisions that allow the issuing company to redeem them after a specified time period. In addition to the market risk of falling prices, convertibles are subject to risk from adverse developments in the company's business.

Tax Considerations

Tax Consequences

Dividends are taxed as ordinary income. The 1986 Tax Reform Act eliminated preferential tax treatment for long-term capital gains. As of 1988, all capital gains regardless of holding period are taxed as ordinary income. However, the Bush Administration favors cutting taxes on capital gains. This political hot potato was hotly debated in 1989 and 1990. Congress had shown no inclination to go along with any capital gain tax cuts by late 1990.

One benefit is that gains resulting from conversion to common stock are not taxable unless the common stock is not that of the company that issued the convertible.

Summing Up

Convertible preferred stock is a viable alternative for risk-averse, long-term investors. Forgoing some profit potential for greater safety makes good sense to many investors. Price information is widely available Extensive information and professional advice on convertibles are available. Professional management can be obtained through closed-end funds and mutual funds.

Notes

Growth Mutual Funds

A mutual fund is a pool of individual investors' contributions that is professionally managed to invest in a variety of securities. Different funds are designed to meet different investor objectives. A growth fund invests in stocks of companies that are expected to appreciate due to increased earnings. Mutual funds have enjoyed a surge in popularity with the strong stock market since 1982. Record amounts of money have been invested in stock funds by investors seeking to participate in the market growth.

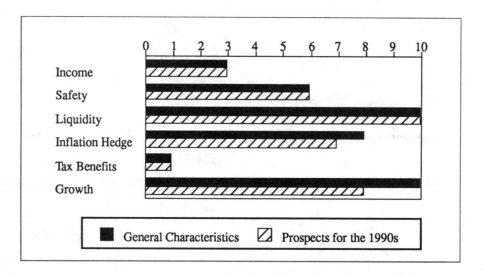

There are many different types of growth funds. For example, aggressive growth funds invest in small, developing companies with short track records. These stocks are often traded on the over-the-counter market (OTC). Other growth funds specialize in locating undervalued stocks of companies listed on the major exchanges.

Type II

D

Low Taxes
Low Expenses

You can usually find a fund that closely matches your investment objectives and risk tolerance. Funds that specialize in newer small companies will be higher risk investments than funds that concentrate on established firms.

Mutual funds can be purchased through brokerage firms. In fact, the major full-service brokerage firms usually have in-house funds managed by employees of the firms. Funds purchased through brokerage firms are called "load" funds. The load is the commission paid to the salesperson for handling the transaction. Loads run from as low as 2% to as high as 10%.

No-load funds are usually purchased direct from the investment company that manages the fund itself. A no-load fund does not assess a sales charge. Your full investment is put to work in stocks. There is little difference in performance between the two types. Some investors feel more comfortable with investments that their brokers follow and hence stay with load funds. Others are content to manage their investments without the "hand holding" that a full-service broker can provide.

Mutual fund prices are widely available. The *Wall Street Journal* regularly publishes fund prices. Most financial magazines, such as *Business Week*, *Money*, or *Changing Times*, devote substantial space to mutual fund coverage.

The boom in mutual fund investing has spawned an active newsletter advisory industry. Many newsletters provide detailed trading advice for mutual fund investors. Some of the larger-circulation newsletters that focus on mutual funds include *Growth Fund Guide*, Box 6600, Rapid City, SD 57709; *Fundline*, P.O. Box 663, Woodland Hills, CA 91365; *Margo's Market Monitor*, 175 Bedford St., #14, Lexington, MA 02173; *Moneyletter*, P.O. Box 540, Holliston, MA 01746; *Mutual Fund Investing*, 7811 Montrose Rd., Potomac, MD 20854; and *Telephone Switch Newsletter*, P.O. Box 2538, Huntington Beach, CA 92647.

Investment Potential

The main objective of growth-oriented mutual funds is capital gains. Although some growth companies may pay dividend income, it is usually negligible.

When you buy a mutual fund, you are buying a proportionate share of the net asset value of the holdings of the fund. The net asset value (NAV) is computed by subtracting the fund's liabilities from the value of the cash and securities it holds and dividing by the number of shares outstanding. If the stocks in the fund's portfolios appreciate, you make money as the net asset value goes up.

Mutual funds are very liquid. Federal law requires a fund to pay you for withdrawals within seven days of your sell order. Some funds offer ancillary services such as periodic payouts.

The volatility of a growth fund is directly related to the volatility of its stock portfolio. Because funds are invested in a diversified portfolio, their volatility is less than that for individual issues. All mutual funds are registered with the SEC. They must meet stringent financial and disclosure requirements. Before you invest, a fund must provide you with a prospectus that gives a detailed

Look At This:

report on the fund's investment approach, objectives, and track record. The fund is required to keep you apprised of developments on a regular basis. The hue and cry over the many and varied ways funds have come up with to exract fees from their shareholders has resulted in a proposal by the SEC to require uniform accounting and reporting of fees. At issue is the SEC's Rule 12b-1. This provision allows funds to dip into assets to pay for marketing and distribution costs.

This rule means that funds that theoretically are "no load" can still wind up taking shareholder money to pay for certain expenses. On June 10, 1988, the SEC proposed certain restrictions on 12b-1 plans. First, the proposal would bar funds with 12b-1 plans from calling themselves "no load." More significantly, the proposal would sharply restrict the use of 12b-1 money. Currently 12b-1 plans range from 0.25% to 1.25% of annual assets. The SEC proposals on restricting 12b-1 fees are a hot point of contention right now. After months of complaint by investors the NASD in December 1989 proposed rule changes that would require mutual funds to disclose to investors via confirmations that they are subject to "exit fees." Exit fees are load charges which are assessed when fund shares are sold rather than the more common practice of paying a load when purchasing shares. After approval by NASD members, the proposal goes to the SEC for its approval.

In June 1990 the SEC announced that it was undertaking a thorough review and overhaul of its 50-year-old regulations that govern the mutual fund industry.

Regardless of what ultimately develops it is clear that regulatory overview of the mutual fund industry will be changing in the direction of more regulations.

The safety of your investment is a function of the type of stocks in which the growth fund invests. A growth fund that concentrates on "blue chip" stocks is safer than one that seeks to uncover small, untested companies.

Growth funds are subject to market risk. If the price of the stocks purchased fall, so will the value of the fund.

Also, there is a business risk with all funds. If the fund's management proves inept at selecting stocks, your investment may suffer even if the stock market is moving higher. Just because someone manages a fund doesn't mean he or she will necessarily do it profitably. The performance of mutual funds varies much more than you'd suspect from the hype that inundates investors. However, there are funds you should avoid. Elsewhere, we've included lists of top-performing funds. The *poorest*-performing funds on a total return basis in 1989 were Strategic Gold/Minerals (–16%), Alliance Bond: High Yield (–14%), Dean Witter High Yield (–14%), American Investors Income (–13%), Pilgrim Preferred (–13%), Christos Fund (–12%), American Capital High Yield (–11%) and National Bond (–11%). The hard hit junk bond market was reflected in mutual fund performance.

Growth funds provide some protection from inflation. Stocks have historically been good inflation hedges in times of moderate inflation.

Strengths

Growth funds offer the potential for substantial capital gains. Growth funds enable small investors to achieve the safety of diversification. No-load funds assess no commission charges. An investor in individual issues does not enjoy that luxury. Well-managed growth funds have enabled investors to achieve above-average gains over the long term. Growth funds offer very high liquidity. The variety of growth funds offers investors great flexibility in matching their investment objectives and risk tolerance.

Weaknesses

Management fees may offset much of the gain in the funds portfolio. You must depend on the ability of the fund manager to select good stocks. A poor manager may significantly underperform the market averages. The commissions paid for load funds come off the top. If you invest $1,000 in a growth fund with an 8% sales charge, your actual investment in the portfolio of the fund will only be $920. Growth funds do not invest in companies that pay high dividends. High-dividend yields afford some protection against falling prices.

Tax Considerations

Tax Consequences

The 1986 Tax Reform Act eliminated the preferential tax treatment for capital gains. Capital losses can be used to offset capital gains, and these losses can be carried forward.

Summing Up

Growth mutual funds represent the backbone of the mutual fund industry. Growth funds are designed to provide above-average growth over the long term. Unfortunately, not many funds have actually outperformed the S&P (gained better returns than the index) for a 10-year stretch. Approximately 60% underperform the S&P 500 Index.

There are many sources of information on mutual fund performance. Before investing in a fund, it is prudent to research the fund's performance. Almost all mutual fund prospectuses contain the so-called "mountain chart" that shows in graphic form how much richer you'd be if you had invested 10 years ago. When you see such charts, remember that compounding interest in a savings account can be made to look like a similar "mountain" of growth—so study the other aspects of potential and past performance as well.

Long-term investors should evaluate a fund's performance over a complete (bull and bear) market cycle. Buying a fund that has done well in the past few years may show its performance only in a bullish market. Many aggressive funds shine during bull markets but then lose so badly when the market turns downward that their overall performance is mediocre. One such fund is 44 Wall Street. In strong up markets, it is often among the leaders. Yet over the last 10 years its total return is negative! Consistent performance over a 10-year span is far more important than occasional years of outstanding returns.

Equity Income Mutual Funds

Equity income funds are mutual funds that invest in stocks that pay competitive dividends. The primary objective of these funds is current income. However, the fund managers are happy to take capital gains if the opportunity presents itself. Many stock groups pay good current income in the form of dividends and still have the promise of capital appreciation.

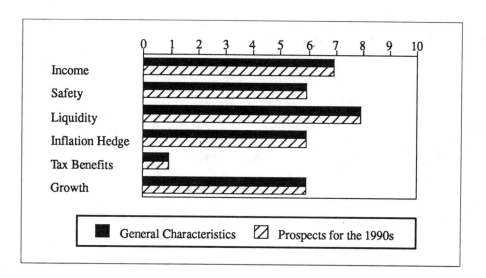

Income
Safety
Liquidity
Inflation Hedge
Tax Benefits
Growth

■ General Characteristics ▨ Prospects for the 1990s

Type II

C

Low Taxes
High Expenses

Equity income mutual funds are designed to ferret out stocks that pay high dividends. Just as with growth funds, a wide variety of equity income funds offer programs to meet differing investment objectives and risk tolerances.

For example, investors who are primarily interested in income and only secondarily concerned with growth will select funds that concentrate on certain types of stocks such as utilities or preferreds. On the other hand, investors who are willing to forgo the highest possible dividends in favor of some income plus a greater growth potential will focus on funds that buy shares in established companies in mature industries. These stocks generally pay good dividends—though less than those paid by utilities. However, a strong economic climate will benefit these companies more, and hence they have greater growth potential.

Mutual funds offering good income are generally less volatile than pure growth funds. If you decide to invest in this type of fund, you'll be trading off greater growth potential for more predictable current income.

Money
Management
Tip

Equity income mutual funds are available both as load funds (sold through brokers), and no-load funds, (sold directly by the fund itself). A no-load fund is usually purchased or sold through the mail. Many fund families offer telephone switch (interfund transfer) and selling privileges.

Load funds typically charge sales commissions of 2% to 8%, charged as soon as you invest. As noted for growth funds, a $1,000 investment in an 8% load fund would leave $920 invested in the fund after the commission had been taken.

In recent years there has been a trend to disguising load charges by assessing the fees when fund shares are sold rather than at purchase. These "exit fees" have engendered much controversy as investors claim they were never advised of the fees when being sold the fund shares. Both the NASD and SEC are investigating proposals to limit or more fully disclose these fees.

No-load funds charge no commission. They attract customers through the mail via advertising.

Both types of funds assess management fees and incur other operating expenses, which vary widely. They can amount to as little as 0.25% to as much as 2% of the funds assets on an annual basis. You should carefully check a fund's fee structure before investing.

The leading financial periodicals, such as *Business Week*, *Money*, *Changing Times*, and *Barron's*, frequently feature articles on different types of funds. The performance rankings in these articles can give you a good starting point in making your fund investment decisions.

Investment Potential

Some income-oriented funds invest in a combination of fixed-income instruments (bonds or shorter-term notes) and stocks that pay high dividends. Yet another alternative is balanced funds. Balanced funds offer a combination of good income with good capital gains potential. Typically they invest in stocks that pay reasonable dividends while also investing in select growth issues. The income-paying stocks add a measure of stability to the portfolio.

Equity income funds are very liquid—many shares can be sold with just a phone call. Federal law requires that payments be made within seven days of your sell order.

The diversification of a typical equity income fund provides a measure of safety. Problems with a single issue should not have a major effect on the portfolio's performance. The government does not insure mutual funds.

Income funds are best suited to long-term investments. Generally investors are seeking a reliable income for the future. They are appropriate vehicles for retirement plans.

Equity income funds are subject to market risk. Even though the dividend income provides some protection in a down trending market, a falling stock market will be reflected in income fund share prices. There is the added risk of poor management. Wrong stock selection or trading decisions by the funds investment advisor can adversely affect the performance of the fund.

Income funds do not provide good protection from inflation. Dividend growth rarely is sufficient to offset even moderate inflation. Rising interest rates may hurt equity income funds more than growth funds initially. This is because some income-oriented stocks, such as utilities, tend to trade like bonds, moving inversely to interest rates.

Strengths

 Equity income funds offer good safety for small investors through diversification. Equity income funds are very liquid. No-load equity income funds charge no commissions. There is a wide variety of funds, each with different objectives and philosophies. Investors have great flexibility in selecting funds to match their own objectives and risk tolerance. Equity income funds tend to be less volatile than growth funds. The high relative income offers downside protection.

Weaknesses

 Equity income funds offer less capital gains potential. Poor investment decisions by the fund's investment advisor will adversely affect the value of your fund. Some funds' high fees hurt their investors' return. Rising interest rates often hurt equity income funds more directly than they hurt growth funds. Equity income funds do not provide much protection from inflation.

Tax Considerations

Tax Consequences

The 1986 Tax Reform Act eliminated the dividend exclusion. Income and capital gains are taxed at ordinary income rates. Capital losses can be used to offset other capital gains. Excess losses can be carried forward.

Summing Up

Money
Management
Tip

Equity income funds are ideal alternatives for conservative investors willing to forgo maximum capital growth for greater stability and more current income. The low interest rates, low inflation, and moderate economic growth of the past five years have aided equity income funds growth.

As always, it is important to monitor the Federal Reserve's money supply policy. Rising interest rates will hurt income funds directly.

---

10 Top-Performing Long-Term Growth Funds
(ranked by 10-year total return)

```
*   1)   Capital Growth Mgt. Capital Development
+   2)   New England Growth
–   3)   Lindner Fund
*   4)   Phoenix Growth
–   5)   20th Century Select
o   6)   IDS New Dimensions
o   7)   Fidelity Destiny I
*   8)   Stein Roe Special
*   9)   Sequoia
* 10)    IAI Regional
```

o   Unchanged from previous edition
*   New appearance on list
+   Moved up from previous edition
–   Moved down from previous edition

Source: Fund/Search, Information Edge, Inc. (800) 334-3669

Sector Mutual Funds

Sector funds are mutual funds that are restricted to investing in a particular industry sector. Until recent years, this specialization was usually restricted to a few sectors such as utilities, gold, or high technology. Now, however, there are many offerings, including energy, natural resources, biotechnology, real estate, brokerage, property and casualty insurers, regional banks, health, chemicals, telecommunications, software, computers, electronics, leisure, paper and forest, capital goods, transportation, automotive, restaurant, and many more!

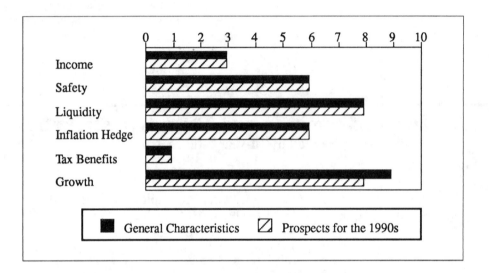

Type I

D

Low Taxes
Low Expenses

As indicated by the cover story of the May 1987 issue of *Changing Times,* "The Hottest Idea in Mutual Funds: Sector Funds" this area is drawing increasing interest. Sector funds are a method for getting "selective diversification." They concentrate on a specified industry but buy a diversified portfolio of stocks within that industry. Some analysts believe that by switching your portfolio among a number of industry groups as the economic cycle unfolds, you can significantly outperform the averages. The idea is that certain industry groups perform better at different times in an economic cycle.

An example of this industry group leadership can be seen when you compare the funds' performance for the first half of 1990

with their performance for the previous five years. In the first six months of 1990, Science & Technology Funds posted a strong 24.55% gain, placing second in performance. Over 5 years though the group posted an 88% gain, below the equity fund average of 92.55%.

Gold-oriented funds jumped 12.4% in the 4th quarter of 1989 to lead all industry groups in performance for the quarter. Yet only 6 months later, gold-oriented funds were down an average –10.3% to trail all industry groups. For the last quarter of 1989 science & technology funds were down –1.3%, lagging most other industry groups. As mentioned above, this group rallied by the 2nd quarter of 1990 to place 2nd in overall group performance. Growth funds were down –1.2% in the 4th quarter of 1989 compared to a 25.4% gain in the previous 12 months.

The average equity mutual fund was up 11.76% in the 12 months ending June 30, 1990. That compares to 20.92% for the average equity fund in 1989. Compare that with the S&P 500 (dividends reinvested), which posted a 16.46% gain in the 12 months ending June 30, 1990. The S&P (dividends reinvested) climbed 31.52% in 1989.

Sector funds, like most mutual funds, are available in two forms. Load funds assess a sales charge, no-load funds do not. The net asset value of each mutual fund is calculated at the close of every business day. When you buy a load fund, a sales charge of 2% to 8% is tacked on to the net asset value. A no-load fund sells at the net asset value. Load funds are purchased through brokers who provide ongoing service. No-load funds are purchased directly through the mail.

Sector fund prices are carried daily in the *Wall Street Journal.* and *Investor's Daily.* Major financial magazines devote substantial space to mutual funds. *Forbes* features a detailed rundown on fund performance every August. *Money*, *Business Week*, and *Changing Times* also feature periodic performance rankings.

Investment Potential

Sector funds are generally considered the most appropriate short-term mutual fund investments. That is part of their attraction. Most sector funds are part of a "family" of funds managed by the same sponsor. The sponsor offers the right to switch among the different funds by telephone. Even some load fund families allow you to switch funds within their own family for no or nominal fees after an initial investment in one of their funds. It is a losing proposition to trade load funds without this proviso on a short-term basis. Typically, you need to hold a load fund for five to seven years to amortize the commission charge before it makes sense to trade it, unless you can switch without paying the full load charge again.

Money Management Tip

Sector funds offer the greatest flexibility of all mutual funds because there are so many alternative ways to structure your portfolio. Some investors build a diversified portfolio filled with nothing but sector funds. Others switch among sectors, depending on their advisors' timing advice.

Sector funds, like all mutual funds, are very liquid. They have relatively short track records, so it is difficult to analyze their performance. Some sectors, like high technology or biotechnology, tend to be very volatile. Mutual funds specializing in those sectors are more volatile and hence more risky.

Sector funds generally provide capital gains, although there are exceptions. Utility funds pay high current income. Most sector funds, though, are growth oriented and pay little income. Sector funds are appropriate for actively managed retirement plans, especially in the early years.

Strengths

Sector funds offer great flexibility to design a diversified portfolio that fits your objectives and risk tolerance. Astute selection of sector funds can yield returns far above the average market return. Sector funds offer excellent liquidity. Properly chosen sector funds offer outstanding protection from inflation. No-load switch funds offer a low-cost method of short-term trading.

Weaknesses

Sector funds place a premium on good timing. If your investment is in the wrong sector at the wrong time, it can significantly underperform the market. Sector funds depend heavily on good research for their performance. The higher fees charged for some sector funds may offset portfolio gains. Most sector funds pay little or no income (unless of course their "sector" is income-oriented, like utilities). Track records for most sector funds are too short to see how they've performed throughout an entire bull/bear market cycle. The stock market has been in a sustained upward trend since 1982. There has been no good "bear market" experience for most sector funds. Until these relatively new funds go through a thorough stock market down cycle, it is difficult to assess how they will do.

Tax Considerations

Tax Consequences

No special tax advantages apply to sector funds. The dividends of some utilities are not taxable as return of capital. Your fund will tell you of such dividends but they will not be substantial. All capital gains and dividend income are taxed as ordinary income. Capital gains taxation is a political football between the Bush Administration, which wants to cut taxes on capital gains, and Congress, which opposes any cuts as of 1990.

Summing Up

Sector funds are here to stay. They have drawn an increasing share of investor money over the past five years. Every month more funds are announced specializing in heretofore unexploited areas. For example, the hottest new "sector" in 1990 were "environmentally conscious" funds. Schield Progressive Environment Fund was launched in February 1990. Its prospectus proclaims that it invests in "companies engaged in contributing to a cleaner and healthier environment." The fund lead all others in the second quarter of 1990, posting a 29.5% return in the quarter.

Investors who have expertise in a particular industry will also find these funds of value. If you are unable or unwilling to spend some time researching the matter, a diversified growth fund would be more appropriate for you.

Selecting a particular fund or funds requires a bit of research itself. The number of funds being offered to the public has grown sharply over the last 10 years. Personal computer owners may want to investigate programs that allow them to screen the universe of funds for those which meet predefined criteria.

Business Week Mutual Fund Scoreboard is designed for use with IBM PC or compatible computers. A database of over 700 equity funds and over 500 bond funds is available. Purchasers of the program can subscribe to quarterly updates of this database.

The analytical program enables investors to sort through various performance factors and data fields to find the funds that match their needs; for example, it is possible to tell the program to sort through all equity funds and print out those which meet specified criteria. The criteria may be chosen from over 25 different factors. You can screen for no-load funds which have: outperformed the S&P 500 for the last five years; a low volatility; have at least $100 million in assets under management; an expense ratio below 0.75%; and so on.

Business Week Mutual Scoreboard can be reached at P.O. Box 621, Elk Grove, IL 60009, (800) 553-3575.

Information Edge offers Fund/Search for IBM PC owners. This program features quarterly and monthly performance data for all no-load and load funds that are actively traded. Fund/Search features many unique graphs for comparing funds.

In addition, it includes a useful diversification tool. It can tell you what funds to put together to meet performance and risk parameters. For example, it will help you combine funds that outperform the market in both bull and bear cycles to reduce overall portfolio volatility.

You can compare a particular fund's performance over different time periods with an index such as the S&P 500 or with its own category of funds.

For more information on Fund/Search, write Information Edge, 96 Lake Drive West, Wayne, NJ 07470, (800) 334-3669.

Index Mutual Funds

Index funds are mutual funds that are designed to emulate the performance of one of the major stock indices such as the Standard & Poor's 500 or the Dow Jones Industrial Average.

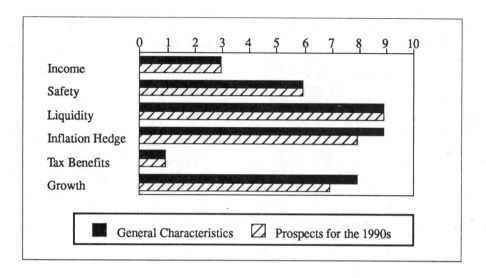

Type IV

D

Low Taxes
Low Expenses

Index funds developed as a result of the inability of most investment managers to beat the market averages consistently. Prices for index funds are carried daily in the *Wall Street Journal* and *Investor's Daily*. Other financial periodicals, such as *Money*, *Business Week*, and *Forbes,* regularly devote space to these funds. An active and diverse newsletter advisory field, specifically devoted to advising investors about mutual funds, has bloomed.

Investment Potential

Index funds are normally purchased for the long term. Their primary attraction is the potential for capital gains. They usually pay only small dividends.

The stock market has become increasingly volatile in recent years. This volatility is naturally reflected in the prices of index funds. A properly managed index fund will closely track the performance of the stock market on a daily basis. You would have a very good idea how your fund did on any particular day by just checking the performance of the stock indices.

Index funds are very liquid. Most will execute sell orders over the telephone. Your money will be sent to you within seven days after the sale has taken place. Index funds are designed to do one thing: replicate the performance of a particular stock market index, usually the S&P 500. Not much flexibility is offered in terms of investment approach.

Index funds are as safe as the stock market as a whole. Long-term bear markets, such as the one from 1966 to 1975, saw price losses as much as 50% to 80% in major companies' stocks. The most recent bull market, which began in 1982, was up over 350% by the summer of 1990. Many individual issues were up much more.

As you would expect, index funds fell sharply when the stock market crashed in October 1987. Most index funds are required by their own investment rules to be

100% invested at all times. Naturally this fully invested posture is a positive in bull markets. For example, during the 1980s, the largest index fund, Vanguard Index Trust-500 Portfolio, averaged 17% per year. That was better than 75% of all stock mutual funds. Don't expect an index fund manager to resort to timing. When the market crashes, so will the funds.

It is impossible to exactly duplicate the portfolio making up the index that an index fund is tied to. For example, of the 10 largest index funds, six are tied to the S&P 500. In 1989 the S&P posted a 31.5% gain. The Principal Preservation S&P 100 Plus Portfolio climbed only 24%. Vanguard Quantitative was up 31.9%. Colonial U.S. Equity Trust posted a 29% gain.

The Vanguard Index Trust 500 Portfolio which is also designed to replicate the S&P 500's performance, posted a 30.9% gain for 1989. Kidder Peabody Marketguard Appreciatin Fund lagged its S&P 500 target with an 18% gain in 1989.

There are a number of different market indices that are used by various funds in an attempt to provide "market related" performance. While the S&P 500 is the most widely used, the S&P 100 is also popular. The S&P 100 is used by Gateway Option Index Fund, Rushmore Stock Market Index Plus Portfolio, and Principal Preservation S&P 100 Plus Portfolio.

The top performing index funds in 1989 were those tied to large capitalization indices such as the Vanguard Index 500 and Quantitative, both tied to the S&P 500.

All mutual funds must register with the SEC. Securities law requires a fund to provide prospective investors with a prospectus detailing the fund's objectives, philosophy, management team, past track record, and all financial details. There is no federal insurance.

Look At This:

Many of the periodicals mentioned earlier publish performance rankings and relative safety ratings. Index mutual funds are suitable for most retirement plans.

Strengths

Index funds are liquid investments. Many in-

 dex funds offer flexible withdrawal options. For example, you may opt for periodic automatic payment. Index funds minimize the risk of a poor investment advisor underperforming the market. Index funds afford some protection from inflation. They offer good capital growth potential. The stock market is considered the best long-term growth investment in the United States.

Weaknesses

 Index funds offer little current income. They do not offer the chance to significantly outperform the stock market averages. They do not offer downside protection in bear markets.

Tax Considerations

Tax Consequences

The 1986 Tax Reform Act eliminated the preferential tax treatment of long-term capital gains. Capital gains and dividend income are taxed at your ordinary income rate. Capital losses offset other capital gains. Losses can be carried forward. Tax treatment of capital gains is a hot political subject and may change. Check with your tax advisor.

Summing Up

In 1982, the stock market was deeply undervalued by most commonly used fundamental valuation methods. A high number of stocks were trading below book value. Price-to-earnings ratios were very low. Dividend yields were 5% to 6%, an historically high rate. By August 1987, most stocks were overvalued by these same measures. After the October Crash, stocks have settled into a median range between these valuation extremes.

The potential for future gains is closely tied to the potential for increasing corporate profits. Many companies recently have restructured into much more efficient, cost-effective organizations.

Low inflation, low interest rates, and moderate economic growth are ideal for stock prices. Index funds thrive in such an environment. The danger signals of an impending recession seen in falling real estate prices, declining corporate profits, slow job growth, and slower consumer spending point to a more settled sideways, even down-trending market in the early 1990s. Many analysts project a maximum downside of 1500–1600 on the DJIA. Upside resistance is very heavy, between 2900–3100. Significant penetration of either level would signal substantial follow through. A drop below 1500 with heavy volume would signal severe economic problems. A sustained rise to new highs over 3000 will point to renewed economic vigor.

---

10 Top-Performing Aggressive Growth Funds
(ranked by 10-year total return)

```
*   1)  Fidelity Magellan
*   2)  Quest Value
*   3)  Janue Fund
*   4)  AIM Weingarten
–   5)  New York Venture
+   6)  Tudor Fund
–   7)  United Vanguard
*   8)  All Quasar Fund
*   9)  Penn Mutual
* 10)  Putnam Voyager
```

o Unchanged from previous edition
* New appearance on list
+ Moved up from previous edition
– Moved down from previous edition

Source: Fund/Search, Information Edge, Inc. (800) 334-3669

Closed-End Equity Funds

Closed-end Equity funds are companies organized for the specific purpose of investing their shareholders' funds in select portfolios. These portfolios range from diversified stocks, specialized stocks, bonds, or a combination. Typically, closed-end funds specialize in one area such as the stocks of an individual country (the Korea Fund) or a specific investment area (ASA: in gold or Bancroft Convertible Fund in convertible securities).

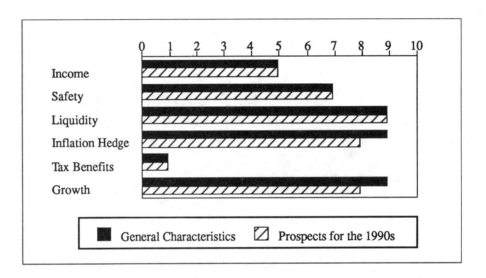

Type II

D

Low Taxes
Low Expenses

Closed-end funds differ from the more numerous open-end mutual funds, in that they do not continually sell new shares nor redeem outstanding shares for investors. Their shares are bought and sold on stock exchanges or over the counter, just like individual stocks. Thus their price is determined by supply and demand at any particular time. Because their price is determined by the marketplace, rather than by the net asset value of the portfolios they manage, that price can trade at a premium or discount to the asset value. This feature contrasts sharply with how prices are determined for open-end mutual funds. The price of open-end funds is determined by the net asset value of their portfolios.

Closed-end funds present an opportunity for investors to buy assets at a discount from their market value. Although a number of theories seek to explain why most closed-end funds trade at discounts to their net asset value, the most widely accepted explanation is that the fixed capitalization of a closed-end fund (i.e., the amount of money the fund has available to invest) restricts its ability to take advantage of opportunities that may arise—a limitation that is reflected in a lower price.

Yet a closed-end fund need not keep capital on hand to handle redemptions, which may actually give them an advantage by keeping more money fully employed. Even so, there is no clear evidence that the type of fund—open or closed-end—affects its performance.

Dual-purpose funds are a unique form of closed-end fund. Two classes of stock are issued: preferred and common. Preferred stock holders receive all income from dividends and interest. The common stock holders receive all the capital gains realized through stock sales in the portfolio. Dual-purpose funds have a finite life (typically 10 years). On expiration, the preferred shares are redeemed at a predetermined price and the common shareholders receive the balance left after sale of the assets.

Investment Potential

Closed-end funds are suitable for a variety of investment objectives. For example, if you seek capital gains, select a closed fund with the same objective, not one that concentrates on income-producing stocks. Since closed-end funds usually trade at discounts to net asset value, they offer the potential of capital gains through a rise in their stock price to reflect that discount quite apart from appreciation of the portfolio under management.

Closed-end funds specializing in utilities on preferred stock are appropriate when income is your goal.

Some closed-end funds that concentrate on gold or investments in foreign countries offer substantial protection from inflation. However, the market price may not reflect a rise in the value of the underlying portfolio. That is the key difference with open-end funds. On the other hand, closed-end funds may trade at a premium. ASA, the South African gold fund, traded at substantial premiums in the 1970s. In late 1989 a flurry of foreign buying in a number of single country closed-end funds pushed them to huge premiums. At one point in September, frenzied buying by Japanese investors pushed the Spain Fund to an unheard of premium of 78% over the value of its portfolio holdings. Interest in the freeing of markets in Europe resulted in large premiums in the Germany Fund and Italy Fund as well.

Strengths

 Closed-end funds trade like stocks and offer the same liquidity. Liquidation should only be a problem in unusual market conditions or for thinly traded issues. There are about 70 closed-end funds, offering a wide variety of portfolios to meet many investment objectives. You can borrow against your closed-end shares subject to current Federal Reserve margin requirements. The interest is tax deductible up to the amount of investment income. Closed-end funds offer substantial diversification, which lowers risk.

Weaknesses

 Market volatility can mean wide swings in price. Poor management of the portfolio can be costly in two ways: (1) lower asset value and (2) bigger discount to asset value. Liquidity depends on market conditions, not on the financial resources of the fund. Brokerage commissions and management fees will diminish your net return.

Tax Considerations

 Tax treatment is the same as that afforded common stock. Preferential capital gains treatment was phased out in 1987. Margin interest paid on loans secured by closed-end shares is tax deductible up to the amount of investment income earned. Check with your tax advisor for your specific situation.

Tax Consequences

Summing Up

Closed-end funds offer a good diversified approach for stock and bond investors. They are appropriate vehicles for retirement plans, especially when purchased at discounts. Investors seeking international diversification should certainly investigate these funds.

Closed-end funds underperformed the market in 1987 for the most part. However, the October Crash renewed investor interest in closed-end funds for some reason. In 1988 14 of the largest 15 initial public offerings were closed-end funds.

However, by 1989 the pace of closed-end mutual fund new offerings had slowed considerably. For the first time in three years, closed-end fund offerings did not dominate the IPO market. Funds raised only $7 billion. That was about 50% of the total IPO market.

Following the stock market crash in October 1987 many closed-end funds outperformed the market for the next six months. Many analysts attribute that superior performance to a narrowing of the historical discount. The average discount for the 20 funds tracked by the Herzfeld Average dropped from the after-crash level of 16.6% to 14% by April 1988.

As we mentioned above, frenzied buying in European single country funds resulted in unprecedented premiums. For example, the Spain Fund in September 1989 stood at a 165% premium over the value of its portfolio!

The fastest growth area for closed-end funds has been in bonds. This trend closely mirrors developments in the open-end mutual fund industry over the last few years. In 1989 most closed-end bond funds once again slipped to discounts.

THE OUTLOOK FOR DOMESTIC STOCKS IN THE 1990s

 The consensus economic forecast for the early 1990s is for a slowdown in growth from the robust pace experienced in 1989, slightly rising inflation, and higher interest rates. Stocks rallied to post-crash highs in early 1989, finishing the year strongly higher.

There are important warning signals in the market action of late 1989 and 1990. The great bull market that lasted from June 1982 until September 1987 was concentrated in upper-tier blue-chip issues. Secondary issues, represented by broader indexes such as the Value Line or NASDAQ, underperformed the Dow Jones stocks.

For the first six months of 1989, the board-based Wilshire 5000 Index was up 15.7%. The Amex was up 18%. NASDAQ posted a 15.3% gain. That compares to a 13.5% rise in the Dow Jones Industrials Average.

However, in the second half of 1989 and in 1990, the split between upper tier "quality" stocks and secondary issues once again turned in favor of the well known upper tier

issues. While the stock market as measured by the Dow Jones Industrial Average, surged to historic highs, broader based measures such as the Wilshire 5000, the Value Line Index, and the Advance/Decline Line (a measure of the total number of advancing issues compared to declining ones) diverged significantly. Historically this type of divergence does not bode well for the market as a whole.

Many of the top-tier stocks went to historical valuation extremes during the bull market. Even after the October 1987 crash, many of these stocks are still richly valued. Remember, the crash essentially took back the gains that had been made in 1987, but the previous four years' gains still made prices rich, on a fundamental basis. Stock prices in 1989 and early 1990 rose strongly, putting upper tier stocks even more overpriced by historical fundamental measures such as dividend yield and Price/Earnings ratio.

Mix this pattern with a much more cautious outlook by most investors, and you would expect the turn to secondary issues. Whereas most listed issues have been well picked over, many OTC issues were still selling for less than their book value in late 1990.

Values such as these have turned the institutions to checking out the secondary stocks. This "value" orientation will be the key factor in stock selection. If past market cycles hold true to form, the "cats and dogs" (i.e., low priced secondary and even tertiary level stocks) will have a run up. That will signal an end to the bull market. However, the bull market of the late 1960s ended without the secondary issues ever participating. Blue Chip issues were simply bid way out of line with any possible measure of value, then collapsed precipitously.

A major surprise during 1989 was the continuation of the high-powered takeover merger mania. In 1988 there were numerous billion dollar-plus deals. Leading the pack was the Phillip Morris buyout of Kraft for $13.4 billion, the Campeau/Macy fight over Federated Department Stores, BATUS's $5.2 billion takeover of Farmer's Group, Eastman Kodak's $5.1 billion buyout of Sterling Drug, and BFB Acquistion Group's $3.8 billion acquisition of Montgomery

Ward. Other well-known companies, including Fort Howard Corp., American Standard, Firestone, Media General, Koppers, and others, were swallowed up in megadeals.

The hostile and competitive takeover fervor led to a shareholder bonanza in many issues. When the bidding for American Standard started, bids were at $60 per share. The final deal closed at $78. Campeau's first offer for Federated was $37. After a bidding war with other potential buyers, Campeau finally paid $73.50 per share. The initial offer for Firestone was $45. When Bridgestone finally won the bidding war, they paid $80 per share. Kodak's final bid was $89.50 per share for Sterling. That bidding had started at $54.

In early 1989 this trend continued with the huge RJR Nabisco deal totalling over $30 billion. Other prominent buyouts or mergers included the Squibb-Bristol/Myers $12 billion deal, Time Inc.'s purchase of Warner Communications for $7 billion, Grand Metropolitan's purchase of Pillsbury for $5.75 billion, and Sony's buyout of Columbia Pictures for $4.79 billion.

But the most telling deal of all was one that was never completed: the failed management-union buyout of UAL. In fact, the failure of the deal led to the second largest one day drop in the DJIA: 190 points. In percentage terms it was the 12th largest one day decline.

For most analysts though, the significance of that October 13, 1989 drop was that it signaled an end to the takeover, LBO, merger mania of the 1980s. In retrospect it does look like that Friday the 13th will be known as an end to an era. Many stocks whose prices were inflated by takeover rumors prior to that day were very hard hit. Examples include Hilton which dropped $21.50 per share, a 20% loss; Campbell Soup off $5.50 down 11%; Paramount off $6.60 down 10.5%; and Woolworth down $6.75 to finish off 10% on the day.

Other failed deals in the wake of the UAL fiasco (called "the broken deal of the decade" in many corners) were Paramount's $12.7 billion bid for Time Inc., Donald Trump's $7.1 billion bid for American Airlines', Irwin Jacob's bid for Avon, and Shamrock Holding's bid for Polaroid.

Closely related to the collapse of the LBO market was the continued slide in the IPO market. In 1989 initial public offerings totalled 245, raising $13.82 billion compared to 1988's 255 new issues raising $22.4 billion. By late 1989 IPO performance lagged badly. The last 100 IPOs of 1989 rose a mere 7% by year's end. That compares to the S&P New Issues Index which rose 25% for the year.

For the 1990s, it will be doubly important to select stocks carefully. With an economic recession pending, defensive issues will offer your portfolio some downside protection. Seek stocks that have some dividend yield to cushion a downturn.

The best-perfoming mutual funds in the first half of 1990 were "theme" related funds like environmental funds, biotechnology/health funds, European funds, and science and technology funds. This trend toward socially conscious investing and especially investing with an eye to international political and economic developments such as the freeing of Eastern European economies and the unifying of Germany will continue strongly through the 1990s.

A common thread in leading funds through 1989 and 1990 was the tendency to invest in smaller companies that have strong growth potential. As the merger and acquisition activity among huge companies is dying out, investors will look to smaller companies. Institutional interest in small cap stocks should pick up as larger companies reach full valuation. Over 1989 and 1990, funds investing in smaller issues have been leading performers.

This is in sharp contrast with the record over the past five years. The average small-company growth fund appreciated 85.6% compared to the average stocks fund rise of 108.4%.

Leaders among the growth mutual funds for the 12 month period ending June 30, 1990 were Fidelity Select Biotechnology, Financial Portfolio: Health, Equity Strategies, RCS Emerging Growth, Fidelity Select Electronic, T. Rowe Price Int'l. Disc., Bull & Bear Special Equities, Financial Portfolio: Technology, DFA Group: Contl. Small Companies, and Fidelity Select Energy Services.

But don't be fooled into buying a fund based on six months, or even one year's performance.

Summing Up

Stock market leadership has rotated through industry groups. You can expect this to continue as the economic cycles unfold. The strongest mutual fund stock groups in the 12 months ending June 30, 1990 were health/biotechnology, science and technology, Pacific Region, European Region, International, Small Company Growth, Global, growth, Specialty/Miscellaneous, capital appreciation, world income, growth & income and balanced.

The key things to watch in the early 1990s will be Federal Reserve policy, interest rates, inflation, the status of the dollar, and the twin deficits: trade and budget.

The Federal Reserve is targeting the federal funds rate as its key for action. The federal funds rate is the interest rate charged by banks for overnight interbank loans. If the rate moves too high for the Fed, it injects money into the system. That "ease" drives down rates in the short term.

With the economy slowing its rate of growth to under 2% in 1990, the Fed has the leeway to ease up the tight reins on the money supply. If the fed funds rate moves out of its set range (for most of 1990 that range was 7.5% to 8.5%), that is a clue to Fed action. A rise in the fed funds rate indicates a worry about inflation on the part of the Fed.

If long-term interest rates—use 30-year Treasury bonds for a proxy—move into double-digit yields once again, look for a sideways to down stock market. Stick to defensive issues such as food, drugs, and tobacco.

If the trade deficit continues to improve, the chief beneficiaries will be export-oriented capital goods and basic industries.

If inflation turns higher (as evidenced by a rising CPI or PPI), buy tangibles such as gold-related stocks. Companies with large real estate holdings or natural resources should also provide good returns in an inflationary environment.

Inflation as always will play an important role in the 1990s. Rising inflation will trigger higher interest rates. That will hurt bonds, preferred stocks, and utilities, especially. Watch the following four indicators for clues on inflation.

First, the Consumer Price Index (CPI) and Producer Price Index (PPI) are the most widely watched inflation indicators. Three consecutive months of rising price trends over 6% per year will signal a dangerous resurgence of inflation.

Second, watch the price of gold closely. This is the single best proxy for inflation. A move over $400, then a strong close over $450 will signal an upward turn in inflation. Hedge your exposure in this case, with some precious metals stocks and/or real estate investments.

Third, bond traders watch the trend of the Commodity Research Bureau's commodity index for early clues on the trend of inflation. This index is heavily weighted toward agricultural commodities. The drought over much of the grain-growing states pushed it high in early 1988. The CRB Futures Index is reported daily in the *Wall Street Journal* where it is charted over 18 months. It climbed steadily in early 1990 but turned back as it neared the 250 level which was also the high in 1989. The trend is more important than absolute numbers. A rising CRB index will point to higher food prices down the road.

Fourth, and finally, oil prices are still an important factor in inflation. OPEC is struggling to get its act together once again. There is currently a worldwide glut in oil, which should moderate price. However, a renewed move by oil prices over $28 per barrel should be viewed as a critical indicator of rising inflation and rising interest rates.

A continuation of low inflation (under 5%), low interest rates (long-term rates under 10%), and moderate GNP growth (between 2%–4%) is bullish for stocks. Deviations from these trends should be carefully watched as they will affect stock prices. Move to a conservative position if things appear to be deteriorating.

The stock market fooled us and most other analysts by rallying strongly in the first half of 1990. However, the length of the economic recovery points to the high possibility of a recession beginning soon. A recession will knock stock prices much lower. It will be most important to stay well diversified within your stock portfolio. Do not exceed the upper limits we recommend for stocks in your portfolio.

CHAPTER 13

DOMESTIC FIXED-INCOME INSTRUMENTS

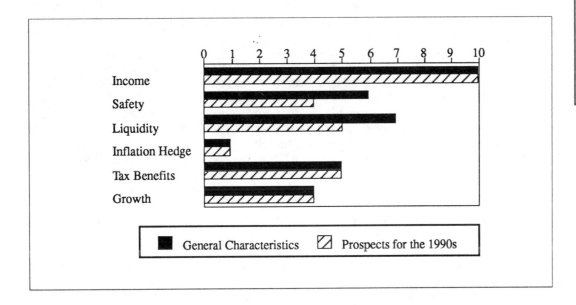

Income
Deflation

Interest rate
Inflation

Ordinary income
Tax exempt

Personal Financial Keys for Domestic Fixed Income

Outlook for the 1990s

Lower volatility

Rising market if
• GNP growth 2% or lower
• Inflation stays low
• Dollar stabilizes or strengthens
• Interest rates fall

Falling market if
• Rates rise
• Inflation moves above 6% per year
• GNP growth rate moves over 4%
• Dollar resumes slide

A GLANCE AHEAD

Stocks seem to get all the front-page press, yet the total dollar volume of the bond market dwarfs that of the stock market. Bonds play a critical role in business.

Through the issuance of debt, many corporations have been able to raise capital for expansion that would have been impossible through selling stock. Treasury bond sales literally finance the current federal budget deficit. The state of the bond market is crucial to the economy and other investment markets.

In April 1987, the bond market began one of the sharpest collapses in its history. Oil prices were climbing as Middle East tension mounted, and OPEC once again began to flex its muscles. The Consumer and Producer Price Indexes both jumped to annual rates above 5% from 1986's lowly 1.1% level. That price collapse was finally stemmed only with the stock market crash of October 1987. Bonds trade inversely with interest rates. Interest rates ultimately are a function of inflationary expectations. The course of the bond market in the 1990s will tell the tale for most other investment markets.

In this chapter, you'll learn about the wide variety of debt instruments available to the public. You'll learn

- *How bonds differ from stock*
- *How bonds and interest rates are related*
- *How to minimize risk to principal in a bond portfolio*
- *Why bonds are an integral part of a well-diversified portfolio.*

BONDS

The U.S. economy depends on debt. Many analysts warn that the current historically high debt levels for corporations, government, and individuals bode ill for the future.

When interest rates rise, bond prices fall and vice versa. Bond prices typically rise (interest rates fall) after the initial stages of the contraction or recession leg of the business cycle when demand for credit tails off. During the expansion phase, when credit demand climbs, interest rates rise and bond prices fall.

Historically, bonds have been considered conservative investments because the buyer was assured a set interest rate and the return of full face value at maturity. However, as interest rates have become more volatile, so have bond prices. During the late 1970s, inflation dominated the U.S. economic scene. Interest rates fluctuated more in a few months during that period than they did during the entire decade of the 1950s.

Mutual funds specializing in bonds were the fastest-growing segment of the fast-growing fund industry in the 1980s. This growth has contributed to increased volatility. When interest rates rise, bond fund values decline. Shareholders then move to sell their fund shares, forcing the funds to sell more bonds to raise capital to meet the redemptions. This additional selling forces bonds even lower, extending the vicious cycle.

Risks

Bonds are subject to a variety of risks. Only U.S. Treasury issues (guaranteed by the full faith and credit of the U.S. government) are immune from business risk. Corporate bonds will fluctuate with interest rates as will Treasury issues. But corporate issues are also affected by the fortunes of the issuing company. Many investors have learned to their chagrin that municipal bonds (issued by state and local governments) are not immune from business risk. New York City and Cleveland bondholders have both been hurt by financial difficulties experienced by those municipalities.

Higher inflation leads inevitably to higher interest rates, which means lower bond prices. As bond investors learned in the first nine months of 1987, inflationary expectations are far more important for bond prices than is the actual inflation rate. By August 1987, bond prices had collapsed in one of the sharpest falls in history based on *expectations* of higher inflation, even though inflation as measured by the Consumer Price Index was under 4%.

Liquidity varies widely for bonds. Treasury issues are by far the most liquid. Investment-grade corporate bonds have an active liquid market. However, the merger and acquisition mania of the 1980s has hurt liquidity in even the high grade corporate bond markets. Huge corporate LBOs such as the RJR Nabisco $30 billion reduced former investment grade bonds to "junk" class overnight. Bond buyers became very leery of buying even the best grade bonds unless issues included covenants to protect buyers from losses due to downgrades in quality due to taking on huge debts. The junk bond market in 1989 and 1990 was very illiquid at times as buyers began to seek quality rather than simply high yield. Municipal bonds are less liquid, though issues of many entities can be readily bought and sold.

The world economic environment affects the liquidity of bonds also. During the recent times of heightened international tensions, occasioned by debt problems of lesser developed countries in recent years, only Treasuries actually benefitted. Traders were willing to trade some yield for the greater safety of Treasury issues.

With a recession looking more likely as 1990 comes to an end, the market for low quality high-yield junk bonds looks ever more treacherous. As many investors discovered in early 1989 and again following the Friday, October 13, 190 point stock market crash, junk bonds become virtually unsaleable in times of panic. A recession would throw into question the profitability of marginal companies that issue junk bonds.

All asset categories are subject to political risk. The municipal bond market was changed by the 1986 Tax Reform Act. And on April 20, 1988, the Supreme Court dropped a bombshell when it ruled that the federal government could tax the interest paid by municipal bonds. Unanticipated political developments could wreak havoc in any debt market.

Ratings, Insurance, and Government Regulation

The largest single business for independent rating services is in rating bonds. There are a number of such services, including Fitch's, Moody's, and Standard & Poor's. You should match your bond purchases with your own risk tolerance level. A very conservative investor should not hold B-rated bonds regardless of their yield. A-rated issues will provide the necessary peace of mind, though at a lower yield.

Private insurance has become a major role player in the municipal market. Many state and local governments contract with an insurance company to insure the interest and principal of their issues. This enables them to get better ratings (usually AAA), so that they can pay lower rates. Insured munis are only as secure as the financial strength of the insurance company. They certainly do not qualify as risk free, as do Treasuries.

The corporate and municipal bond markets are regulated by the SEC. Investors' accounts at brokerage firms are protected by SIPC coverage the same as stocks.

Bonds Compared to Other Assets

Most investors watch the relationship between stocks and bonds very carefully. Typically the bond market will peak before the stock market. The lag time varies from 10 months to even longer.

Bonds trade contracyclically with gold. Inflation pushes gold higher while knocking bonds lower.

It is no longer necessary to confine your bond trading to physical bonds. You can speculate on bonds and hence interest rates through options and futures.

Fixed-income instruments include Treasury, corporate, and municipal issues. In addition, federal agency issues such as Ginnie Maes and Fannie Maes have become very popular. Wall Street is busily "securitizing" mortgages on both single-family homes and business buildings.

PROSPECTS FOR THE 1990s

The prices of fixed-income securities, more than most other asset classes, are directly tied to the current economic environment. Stocks perform a discounting function. They usually lead economic trend changes by 10 months or more. When the stock market crash occurred in October 1987, many analysts pointed out that stocks have a superior record as a leading indicator for the economy. The S&P 500 Index is one component of the U.S. Commerce Department's Leading Economic Indicators.

Bonds on the other hand are directly tied to interest rates. Investors tend to forget that other asset classes have their own unique response to interest rate changes. Most people think that rising interest rates drive down stocks, gold, real estate, or other assets. They will tell you that an increase in interest rates pulls money out of the other assets. If only it were so simple!

Unfortunately, history does not bear out that simplistic diagnosis. Stocks have risen for long periods in the face of rising interest rates. Many analysts said the precious metals market broke in 1980 because of high interest rates. They didn't explain what was now different then from the preceding three years when gold rose with rising interest rates.

The most common conundrum has to do with high rates and real estate. Every time rates go up in recent years, demand for housing falls off. Yet in the 1970s—a period of generally rising interest rates—real estate prices rose in one of the strongest bull markets of all time. It was not unusual for investors to earn 30%, 40%, or even 50% in a matter of a few months.

The difference, of course, is that inflation often boosts stocks, at least in the inflation's early stages. Gold and real estate are direct beneficiaries of inflation, even with rising interest rates. Bonds, though, never benefit from inflation.

In fact, the slightest hint of inflation in the 1980s has served to crash bonds, even when the stocks have screamed to ever higher levels. Look at the first nine months of 1987. In March, the Consumer Price Index jumped for the first time in many months. Combined with the falling dollar, inflation worries, despite little confirming evidence from factors such as wages or commodity prices, caused traders to bail out of bonds. From March until the October 19 stock market crash, bonds swooned in one of the worst bear markets in history.

Interest rates on 30-year Treasury bonds went from below 8% to over 10% in nine months. Bondholders' equity was devastated. Bond mutual funds were forced to raise cash for redemptions after experiencing dramatic growth in the previous three years.

What Lies Ahead

The bond market has never shaken its fear of inflation. After the October Crash, bond prices rallied sharply. Although much was made of the fact that almost $1 trillion was lost in stocks, the same amount was made in bonds. The lesson to be learned is simple: an impending recession will lower demand for money and lower interest rates will follow. A booming economy, on the other hand, will tend to push inflation and interest rates higher, knocking bonds lower.

The problem with the recession scenario is that usually an interest rate spike appears before the onset of the recession. The spike (or inverted yield curve) results from businesses borrowing in the mistaken belief that they are experiencing only a temporary slowdown.

An inverted yield curve simply means that short-term interest rates (e.g., the rate on 91-day T-bills or commercial paper), goes higher than long-term rates (e.g., the rate on 10-, 15- or 20-year bonds). The more inverted (i.e., the more the short-term rates exceed the longer-term rates), the tighter the credit squeeze.

Following the stock market crash, many analysts predicted a recession no later than 1989. However, the robust economy in 1988 fooled many. GNP growth in 1988, and 1989 did not slow as much as many economists expected.

However, by mid-1990 evidence of a pending recession was becoming more prominent. Corporate earnings had slumped for 12 months. Retail sales and consumer spending was trending down. Job growth, a major positive throughout the long economic expansion, was showing signs of turning down. The Commerce Department's index of leading economic indicators was flat in June after a turbulent two preceding months: a .7% rise in May after a .2% drop in April. Three consecutive down months for this index is the classic signal for a recession in the next 10-12 months.

Construction spending, a major component of the economy, apparently peaked in early 1990. The National Association of Purchasing Management announced that its index of manufacturing health plunged to 47.4% in July from 51% in June, reflecting a large fall off in factory orders. The report is significant for its reading of the manufacturing side of the economy.

There are only three possible alternatives. If 1991-92 continues in the same mold as 1989-90, bonds will trade in a sideways to up pattern. More robust growth will mean lower bond prices as interest rates are pushed higher by a combination of increasing business loan demand and higher inflation. If economic growth suddenly reversed, bond prices would drop before the onset of a recession. They then would rally strongly as interest rates came down, due to slackening business.

Four main areas should be watched for clues. The Federal Reserve is always a key player in interest rates. It is important to watch Fed actions (ignore Fed *pronouncements*!). The best short-term indicator of Fed policy is the federal funds rate. This is the rate at which banks loan reserves on an overnight basis.

Banks with excess funds loan money to banks in need of reserves, for regulatory purposes. The Fed targets this rate. It can influence the rate through its open market transactions. When the Fed injects money into the financial system through these transactions, it can effectively lower the fed funds rate. When it draws funds out of the system (i.e., tightens money), it can push the fed funds rate higher.

If the fed funds rate goes more than 1.5 to 2% over the discount rate—now at 7%—the Fed may be forced to raise the discount rate. A change in the discount rate is a more drastic stop by the Fed and indicates its seriousness in pursuing a tighter (or easier) policy.

Although most analysts look to the Fed as the initiator in financial affairs, it is, in fact, a reactor. By monitoring the economy, you can anticipate what the Fed will do. Watch industrial production. If it climbs too fast (at a double-digit annual rate for three or more consecutive months), the economy is overheating as more industrial plant and workers wil be used. Expect the Fed to tighten money raising interest rates.

Other useful lead indicators of inflation and higher interest rates include the factory capacity utilization rate. If the rate goes over 85%, it signals that the productive plant is being stretched to its limits. That can lead to higher prices as manufacturers compete for scarce resources.

The unemployment rate is a good indicator of labor market pressures. A sustained drop below 5% would signal a very tight labor market. Look for wages to move higher, again pressuring inflation and interest rates.

The state of the dollar is a major factor for the bond market. The dollar strengthened during the last half of 1988 and 1989 despite many dire predictions. However by 1990 the dollar resumed its downward spiral. In the summer of 1990 the dollar approached historic lows against the German Mark and Swiss Franc. The strength of European currencies was largely due to increasing interest rates in those countries and a perception by investors that political developments there were positive for continued growth in their economies. A stable sideways dollar will help to temper inflation. A slumping dollar may force the Fed to tighten money, pushing interest rates higher.

The last major factor overhanging the economy besides inflation and interest rates is the budget deficit. After improving for the past few years, all indications are that the budget deficit will once again start to increase. This will undoubtedly become a political football in the 1990s. In July 1990 President Bush announced that the budget deficit for 1989 and 1990 would significantly exceed previous estimates. It is unlikely though that anything constructive will come out of it. The deficit will eventually become a major problem for the economy as the government will need to borrow more money "crowding out" less creditworthy borrowers. This would push interest rates considerably higher. It will probably be a major factor by the mid-1990s.

As this book is being written, there are increasing signs of a major downturn in the economy. Slow, steady growth is ideal for bonds. With GNP growing at a slow 1.2% in the second quarter of 1990, the bond market has been strong.

We have kept our fixed-income allocation at the same level as last year. Reduce your fixed-income exposure if inflation shows signs of picking up. If GNP growth stays over 4% for two consecutive quarters or if the price of gold breaks out over $400 and stays there, cut your fixed-income allocation to the lower suggested range. Place the balance in money market funds.

**Lasser's Recommended Fixed Income
Allocation Range for the 1990s**

20% to 40%

U.S. Treasury Securities

Treasury securities are debt instruments that are issued with set maturities paying fixed interest rates. Treasury bills have maturities from 91 days to one year, Treasury notes run from one year to seven years, and Treasury bonds run from over seven years to 30 years.

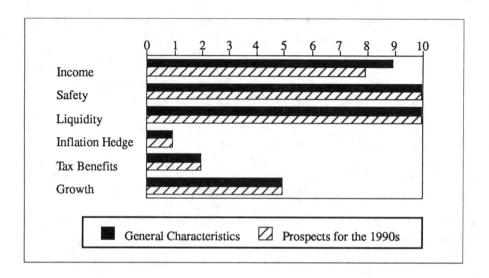

Chart showing ratings (0 to 10) for:

- Income
- Safety
- Liquidity
- Inflation Hedge
- Tax Benefits
- Growth

Legend: ■ General Characteristics ▨ Prospects for the 1990s

Type III

A

High Taxes
High Expenses

C

Low Taxes
High Expenses

Treasury securities—bonds, notes and bills—constitute the safest (if held to maturity) investment vehicle. Treasury securities trade as one of the most liquid investment markets in the world. When you buy a Treasury issue you are loaning money to the federal government with the full faith and credit (including the taxing power) of the U.S. government guaranteeing both interest and principal. There has never been a default on U.S. debt. Even debt issued during the Revolutionary War was redeemed after Alexander Hamilton pushed hard for the fledgling government to demonstrate its creditworthiness to the world.

The Treasury market has expanded greatly in recent years as the federal government continues to run up huge budget deficits. Like anybody who spends more than he or she takes in, the government must finance the gap by borrowing. U.S. Treasury debt is held by many foreign investors as well as U.S. citizens. In fact, Japanese purchases have accounted for as much as 30% of the debt issued in recent years.

T-bills are sold on a "discount basis." This means that you buy a $10,000 bill for less than the face value. When it matures, you receive the full face value of $10,000. The difference you receive is the interest paid for your loan.

T-notes and T-bonds are sold on the more common "coupon" basis. You receive interest twice a year at the fixed rate. If you buy a T-note or T-bond in the secondary market (i.e., after it has already been sold through a Treasury auction) the price you pay may be at a discount or premium to the par value. If interest rates rise after the note or bond was originally issued, the bond price will drop, to make the effective yield competitive with current interest rate. If rates fall in the interim, you'll pay a higher price than the price of the original issue.

Treasury notes can be purchased through full-service brokers, banks, specialty brokers, or even direct from the Federal Reserve. Fees are normally very low. The minimum investment for T-bills is $10,000, with multiples of $5,000 thereafter. T-notes and bonds trade in $5,000 face value lots.

Prices are regularly quoted in the major financial media. Many types of loans, such as adjustable rate mortgages, are tied to Treasury interest rates.

Investment Potential

Treasury securities are purchased primarily for income. They can be purchased for the short term (T-bills) or for as long as 30 years (T-bonds).

Like all bonds, Treasury issues fluctuate inversely with interest rates. Rising rates drive prices down, while falling rates push prices higher. This fluctuation offers investors the chance to earn capital gains.

As interest rates become more volatile, so too does the price of Treasury issues. The longer the maturity of the issue, the more volatile is the price action.

Because Treasury obligations are backed by the full faith and credit of the federal government, they are considered very safe investments. It is possible to borrow up to 90% of the market value of your Treasuries from most full service brokerage firms. This affords great capital gains potential if interest rates fall. However, fully leveraged positions are subject to large losses if interest rates rise.

The wide variety of maturities and the active affiliated markets such as futures and options offers great flexibility. Treasury issues are the safest debt instruments you can buy. Treasury obligations are appropriate for all retirement plans.

Strengths

Treasury obligations are very liquid, and offer the safest guarantee of both interest and principal of any debt instrument. They pay secure current income and offer a wide variety of maturities that can be used to closely match your individual needs. Treasuries are universally accepted as collateral to borrow against, transaction fees are nominal, and pricing information is widely available. They offer the chance to earn good capital gains on accurate interest rate speculations.

Weaknesses

Treasury yields are lower than other similar debt instruments, due to their greater safety. Also like all bonds, T-bonds will fall in price and result in losses if sold before maturity in rising interest rate environments. Highly leveraged positions can be costly if interest rates rise. Longer-term maturities offer no inflation protection.

Tax Considerations

Tax Consequences

All interest paid by Treasury obligations is exempt from state and local taxes. Interest is subject to taxation at the federal level at your ordinary income rates.

Summing Up

Treasury debt securities constitute the largest and safest single investment market in the world. Risk-averse investors should concentrate their debt investments in Treasury obligations. Keep in mind that you receive lower interest payout for the lower risk.

Even Treasury obligations are not risk free, though, if you sell before maturity. Treasury bonds are subject to the same market forces that affect all bonds. Rising interest rates will push down the principal of the underlying bond. Rising interest rates in the late 1970s resulted in substantial losses for bond buyers who chose to sell their bonds before maturity.

Other than the risk to principal that rising interest rates may cause for investors who may need to sell their Treasury bonds before maturity, the only real risk for average investors is the brokerage firm where they buy the bonds. In May 1990, the General Accounting Office, the watchdog agency for Congress, released a report that called for greater government regulation of the largely unregulated U.S. Treasury market.

Noting that many investors had lost money in supposedly super-safe Treasury bonds due to questionable dealer sales tactics, the GAO urged Congress to give the Treasury Department authority to write rules governing sales practices of brokers and dealers. Touching on a particular sore point among investors, the GAO recommended that Congress mandate fuller public access to bond price information that is currently closely held by only the largest brokers and dealers.

The report followed legislation passed in 1986 that imposed some regulations on banks and securities dealers which trade government securities. Several unregulated securities firms folded in 1984 and 1985 causing major problems throughout the financial markets.

Experienced investors who require the income that their investments generate know that it is imperative to stagger the maturities of the bonds in their portfolios. This technique, known as "laddering," provides a measure of protection from adverse interest rate movements. The longer the maturity, the greater the risk to principal.

Just as you should always maintain diversification throughout your investment portfolio, you should diversify within a selected investment area when possible. For example, you should keep a portion of your Treasury investments in the short term (91-day or 180-day Treasury bills). These short-term instruments provide a measure of inflation protection since their interest rates will rise as rates rise in the marketplace. Since they mature every three or six months, there is minimal risk to principal if you must sell before maturity. At maturity, you will be able to roll over to new bills paying the higher current market rate.

Keep a portion in Treasury notes and a portion in long-term bonds. More conservative investors should keep the average maturity of their Treasury portfolio shorter. This is especially important if you need to sell the securities before maturity.

---

10 Top-Performing U.S. Government Bond Funds
(ranked by 10-year total return)

o 1) Lord Abbot U.S. Government Securities
o 2) AMEV U.S. Government Securities
+ 3) Vanguard Fixed Income - GNMA
+ 4) FPA New Income
* 5) U.S. Government Securities
* 6) Fidelity Government Securities
* 7) Kemper U.S. Government
– 8) Mutual of Omaha America
– 9) Franklin U.S. Government Securities
– 10) Hancock Government

o Unchanged from previous edition
* New appearance on list
+ Moved up from previous edition
– Moved down from previous edition

Source: Fund/Search, Information Edge, Inc. (800) 334-3669

Mortgage-Backed Certificates— Pass-Throughs

A mortgage-backed certificate is a security backed by home mortgages. They are issued by government agencies. They have become an increasingly popular investment for investors seeking income with relative security. Three main government agencies package and sell mortgage-backed securities. They are the Federal Home Loan Bank (FHLB), the Federal National Mortgage Association (FNMA), and the Government National Mortgage Association (GNMA). The securities they issue are called Freddie Macs, Fannie Maes, and Ginnie Maes, respectively.

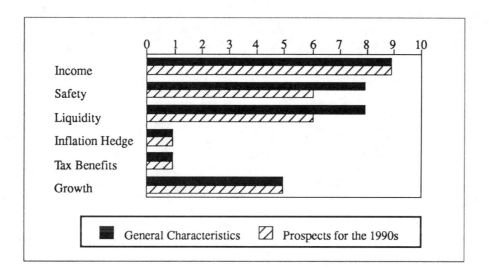

General Characteristics   Prospects for the 1990s

Type I

C

Low Taxes
High Expenses

These agencies act as middlemen. They acquire a large supply of mortgage loans from savings institutions. The volatile swings in interest rates that accompanied the inflationary 1970s has prompted many savings institutions to sell their mortgage loans immediately, rather than hold them to maturity.

The middlemen then sell pieces of the packaged loans to individual and institutional investors. Investors receive a proportionate share of the interest and principal paid by the "pool" of securities.

Most mortgage securities are "pass-throughs." In other words, interest and principal payments pass through directly to investors on a monthly basis. A variation called "collateralized mortgage obligations" are corporate bonds backed by mortgages that make interest payments semi-annually. Passthroughs are by far the most common form of mortgage-backed securities.

Mortgage-backed securities trade like bonds (they are debt instruments) with one major exception. Bonds have a fixed maturity date. Mortgage-backed securities are sold with "average" maturity dates (typically 12 years). This is because in an environment of falling interest rates, it is often in the interest of the mortgagee to refinance his or her mortgage ahead of schedule. The old mortgage is paid off, and a new mortgage with more favorable interest rates is taken. If you purchase a Ginnie Mae and substantial prepayments are made on the mortgages in the pool, you'd receive a return of principal as well as the expected interest on the balance of the mortgages in the pool.

Mortgage-backed securities have long been the domain of the professional and institutional investors. However, this market experienced sharp growth beginning in the early 1980s when interest rates began to fall. Money market fund yields started to drop off, and investors who had come to expect the higher-income payouts searched elsewhere.

There is a large and active secondary market for mortgage securities. They are purchased through brokerage firms. The sharp rise in trading interest in mortgage securities has led to the establishment of many firms that specialize solely in them. A commission is charged for handling the transaction.

Investment Potential

Ginnie Mae pass-throughs are the most widely traded mortgage security. They are backed by Federal Home Loan (FHA)-insured and Veterans Administration (VA)-guaranteed mortgages. In addition, they carry the guarantee of GNMA itself, a government agency. Even though Ginnie Maes are backed by the full faith and credit of the U.S. government, they typically yield 1% to 2% higher than Treasury bonds.

Freddie Maes are backed by FHA, VA and privately guaranteed mortgages. They carry the general guarantee of the Federal Home Loan Mortgage Corporation, a privately managed public institution.

Fannie Maes are backed by VHA, VA, and conventional mortgages. They are issued and guaranteed by the Federal National Mortgage Association, a government-sponsored, publicly held corporation. Fannie Maes and Freddie Maes generally yield up to 1/2% more than Ginnie Maes, because they are not directly backed by the U.S. government.

Mortgage securities are income-producing investments. Capital gains are possible if interest rates fall resulting in appreciation of the security. The primary risk of mortgage securities is early payoff of the mortgages. You would receive (1) principal payments

for those mortgages that are paid off early and (2) reduced income that is paid by the balance of the securities that have not been prepaid. You then have the problem of reinvesting your money to earn a comparable return. If interest rates have fallen, the only way you could get a comparable yield would be through investing in higher risk securities. This prepayment risk is an important factor to consider because it means you will not be able to lock in a specific higher yield in times of declining rates. If you anticipate falling rates, you would be better advised to buy Treasury bonds themselves, rather than pass-throughs.

The principal of mortgage-backs are secure since they are backed by not only the mortgage collateral but by guarantees of various government agencies.

Strengths

Mortgage-backed securities are very secure, backed by not only collateral of homes, but by guarantees of government agencies. They are also very liquid—there is a large and active secondary market. Mortgage security income is higher than that paid by Treasury bonds. Like bonds, mortgage securities offer capital gains potential in a declining interest rate environment. Interest on passthroughs is typically paid monthly.

Weaknesses

Mortgage-backed securities offer no inflation protection. Rising interest rates cause declining principal values. Monthly income may fluctuate since early payment of mortgages will lower the principal value of the mortgage pool. It is impossible to ascertain what the full maturity term of the security will be because of the potential for early payoffs.

Finally, as a mortgage pass-through pool matures, principal payments will be an ever larger part of the monthly payments.

Tax Considerations

Tax Consequences

There are no special tax preferences for mortgage securities. Interest income and capital gains (if any) are taxed at ordinary income levels. Since monthly payments are a mix of interest payments and principal repayments "passed through" to the security holder, taxes are assessed only on the interest portion of the monthly payments.

Summing Up

Mortgage-backed securities have enjoyed explosive growth in recent years. The low-inflation, low-interest rate environment has prompted increased interest in longer-term, secure, income-producing investments to replace ever-shrinking money market yields.

Investors who need an assured monthly income should concentrate on low-rate mortgage pools, because the risk of refinancing is much lower. Of course, these pools should only be purchased when their yield is competitive with those available in the marketplace through discounted prices. For example, look for Ginnie Maes issued in 1986 with coupon interest of 8.5% to 9%. Even if mortgage rates fall 1% or 2%, it would not be economically feasible for mortgage holders to refinance. Hence these Ginnies should be secure from that danger. You will be able to depend on locking in the yield for about 10–12 years without worrying about reinvestment. There have been many innovations in the mortgage-backed security markets in recent years. More private issuers have entered the market. After ignoring the mortgage security market for most of the 1980s, Japanese investors moved aggressively into the market in late 1989 and 1990. By some estimates as much as 10% of new U.S. mortgage securities issued by FNM and FHLB (Fannie Maes and Freddie Maes) were being absorbed by Japanese buyers in 1990. The widespread interest assures good liquidity for most mortgage securities. The ongoing savings and loan problems have hurt mortgage security prices. When an S&L folds its mortgage security portfolio is usually its most liquid saleable asset.

The 1986 Tax Reform Act created yet another entity, the real estate mortgage investment conduit (REMIC) for multiclass mortgage pools. The Federal National Mortgage Association's first REMIC offering in 1987 drew heavy investor participation. In a unique twist, FNM agreed to keep investors (mostly institutions) updated monthly on changes in both yield and maturity of the pools of mortgages.

Stable interest rates are the most favorable condition for mortgage securities. Dropping interest rates result in heavy prepayment ratios, which cause widely fluctuating monthly interest payments. Rising interest rates depress the principal value of the securities, since they must compete with other fixed-income instruments for available cash.

Government Agencies

Government agencies are debt obligations issued by agencies of the federal government. Although usually not specifically backed by the full faith and credit of the U.S. government, they are guaranteed by the issuing agencies with implied backing by Congress. It is highly unlikely that Congress would let any agency bond be defaulted, though that theoretical possibility has led the market to place a slight premium (usually about a 0.5%) on their yields over equivalent Treasury issues. Many federal government agencies issue their own securities to raise funds within guidelines set by Congress.

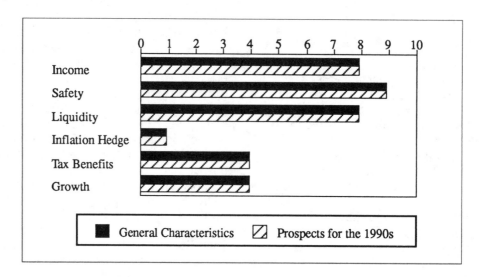

Unlike Treasury notes and bonds, which are initially marketed through auctions (usually quarterly), agencies are sold by the Federal Reserve Bank of New York through its network of dealers. They are sold on a "best yield possible" basis.

Type III

A

High Taxes
High Expenses

Government agencies that issue debt securities include the Asian Development Bank, Export-Import Bank of the United States, Farmers Home Administration, Federal Housing Administration, Federal National Mortgage Association (FNMA), Government National Mortgage Association (GNMA), Interamerican Development Bank, International Bank for Reconstruction and Development (commonly known as the World Bank), Small Business Administration, Student Loan Marketing Association (SLMA), Tennessee Valley Authority, United Postal Service, Federal Home Loan Banks, and others. A recent addition to agencies issuing bonds is the Resolution Funding Corp. which handles sales of assets from failed S&Ls.

Agencies can be purchased through major securities brokerage firms, from dealer commercial banks, or direct from the New York Federal Reserve on new issues. A commission or retail markup is charged for the transaction.

There is an active liquid secondary market for most agencies. The wide variety of agencies ranges from maturities of 30 days to 25 years. Minimum denominations range from as little as $1,000 to as much as $25,000.

Unusually structured agencies may result in a large spread between the bid and offer prices, due to poor liquidity. Agencies in general are liquid, though less so than Treasuries.

As debt instruments, agencies will fluctuate directly with swings in interest rates. The increasing volatility in interest rates is directly reflected in wider oscillations in the prices of agencies.

Investment Potential

Professional Advice

Agencies are bonds that provide good current income. Capital gain potential is possible if interest rates drop subsequent to purchase (bonds trade inversely to interest rates). The chief attraction for most investors is the secure, government-backed income.

Agencies generally are exempt from state and local taxes as are Treasuries. The most notable exceptions are the mortgage-backed securities issued by GNMA, FNMA, and the Federal Home Loan Mortgage Corporation (FHLMC). If this consideration is important for you, be sure to check with your broker and/or tax advisor prior to purchase. Agencies provide no protection from inflation. As is the case with Treasuries and corporate bonds, the shorter the maturity, the less inflation risk.

Because of their high relative safety, agencies are appropriate for long-term retirement programs that allow accumulation of interest on a tax-deferred basis. They offer excellent flexibility through the wide variety of denominations and maturities available.

Short-term speculators trading on interest rate expectations often leverage agencies. Lenders may lend up to 90% of their market value. This is not an appropriate strategy for long-term investors.

Strengths

Income and principal (if held to maturity) are very secure. Income is slightly higher than equivalent Treasury issues. Most agencies are exempt from state and local taxes. Agencies are generally very liquid with a large and active secondary market for most issues.

Weaknesses

Principal is subject to wide fluctuations due to changes in interest rates. Agencies provide no protection from inflation. Income, while higher than Treasuries, is less than for high-grade corporate issues.

Tax Considerations

IRS

Tax Consequences

Interest income paid by agencies is fully taxable on the federal level at ordinary income rates. Interest income from most agencies is exempt from state and local taxes.

Capital gains resulting from sales before maturity from interest rate drops is taxable as ordinary income. Capital losses can be used to offset other capital gains. Unused loses can be carried forward. Tax treatment of capital gains is a hot political topic and things may change. Check with your tax advisor.

Summing Up

Government agencies are secure, fixed-income instruments offering slightly higher yields than straight Treasury obligations. Trade is quite active, and most are liquid. They should be investigated by serious, fixed-income investors who require very safe investments.

Municipal Bonds

Municipal bonds are debt securities issued by state or local governments. All municipal bonds issued before August 7, 1986, pay interest that is exempt from federal taxation. Municipal securities issued by states or their political subdivisions pay "double tax-exempt" interest to residents of their own states.

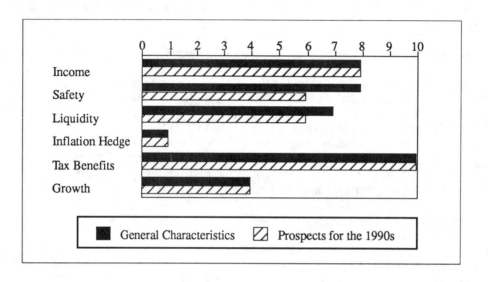

Type III

A

High Taxes
High Expenses

The 1986 Tax Reform Act muddied the clear distinction between tax-free municipals and other bonds. Municipal obligations are now divided into two groups: public purpose bonds and private purpose bonds. Public purpose bonds are those securities issued by state and local government to raise funds for direct "governmental purposes."

As if that were not enough complexity, on April 20, 1988, the U.S. Supreme Court clouded the whole future of the tax-exempt status of *all* municipal bonds. By a 7–1 vote, the Court ruled that Congress has virtually unlimited authority to tax and/or restrict the issuance of tax-exempt bonds. The Court upheld the restrictions that Congress had been using to chip away at the states' right to issue tax-exempt bonds.

The muni market reacted immediately, falling sharply. However, the fall was over

in a matter of hours as investors analyzed the full meaning of the decision. Few analysts expect Congress to eliminate the tax-advantaged status of all municipal issues. The sharp restrictions put in place by tax law changes in the 1980s had already sharply reduced the volume of new muni issues.

Many advisors expect that the Supreme Court decision will make munis even scarcer in the future. Although no one is sure what will happen in the near future, this treasured tax shelter will unquestionably be under attack from many quarters in the years ahead. One probable early change is to make even the interest paid by public purpose munis subject to the alternative minimum tax.

Private purpose bonds are those bonds issued by state and local governments in which more than 10% of the revenues go to benefit private parties. For example, bonds issued to help finance construction of an industrial plant would be a private purpose bond. Many private purpose bonds are fully taxable. For example, bonds issued to finance sports, convention, trade show, parking, or pollution control are no longer tax exempt. There are some exceptions.

As the 1986 Tax Reform Act's provisions wend their way throughout the economy, a few areas are drawing increasing investor interest. Although the Tax Reform Act changed the status of many muni bonds, it also opened up another previously unavailable area. An active market developed in AMT (alternative minimum tax) bonds. AMT bonds are bonds that fall into the "exception" class listed above. The interest is tax exempt for those investors who are not subject to the AMT.

The interest paid by AMT bonds is considered a "preference item" that must be included in calculating alternative minimum tax. According to IRS statistics, only 388,000 out of 107 million personal tax returns will be subject to the AMT. That means for the large majority of people, the interest paid by AMT bonds is fully tax exempt.

AMT bonds typically yield one-quarter to one-half of a percentage point more than comparable fully tax-exempt municipals. As more and more investors clarify their status in regard to the AMT, experts expect the volume and interest in AMT bonds to pick up.

AMT bonds are issued by municipalities to finance "nonessential" government activities such as student aid, housing construction, airports, and the like. In fact, in February 1988 Chicago's O'Hare International Airport sold a $100 million AMT issue. Rated A-1 by Moody's and A by Standard & Poor's, the 30-year maturity bond yielded 8.19% That AMT bond's yield compared favorably with similarly rated tax-exempt bonds from the Municipal Electric Authority of Georgia that yielded 7.92%.

Other AMT bond issues include an issue by California to fund the state's veteran's organization. Other issuers announced AMT bond offerings to finance such things as airports and housing.

Professional Advice

However, it is beyond the scope of this book to detail the many intricate distinctions imposed by the new tax law. Your broker can advise you on the tax status of the interest paid by municipal bonds you are interested in purchasing.

Municipals pay lower rates than taxable securities. It is important to calculate your after- tax returns by comparing the yields of comparable taxable and tax-free bonds.

All municipal bonds issued before August 7, 1986, qualify for full tax exemption. Tax-exempt private purpose bonds issued since then (those that meet certain criteria) are limited in the amount each state can issue.

Municipal bonds, like all bonds, are subject to fluctuations in principal value as interest rates change. Rising interest rates depress principal, while declining rates can yield capital gains as well as tax-free income.

The major bond-rating services cover municipals. Ratings reflect the relative financial stability of the issuing governments. Some municipal bonds are insured by private companies. Their yields are lower because the insurance gives them a higher rating.

Look At This:

Municipal bonds are sold by full-service brokerage firms and a number of firms that specialize in tax-exempts. Commissions or "dealer markups" are assessed by the firms. Commissions are normally low relative to equivalent investments in stocks. However, high markups are often not fully disclosed. Make sure you know what fees you are paying before investing.

Investment Potential

The primary attraction of municipal bonds is the tax-free income they pay. Declining interest rates may result in some capital gains.

Money Management Tip

The municipal bond market is quite liquid for large well known issuers. However the volume of new issues is shrinking due to tax law changes. There were $121 billion new municipals sold in 1989 (a 3.5% increase). Volume in 1986 and 1987 actually fell 30% each year. The shrinking volume means that liquidity in some issues is going to be limited. If liquidity is a major concern to you, you should invest only in issues that are at least $50 million from a well known municipality or state issuer. Even then it is not as liquid as the Treasuries market, though. Obscure or unpopular issues (e.g., New York City's securities for a period in the 1970s) can be very difficult to sell. If you stick with investment-grade bonds rated A or better, there should be no liquidity problem.

Historically, bonds have been considered safe, nonvolatile investments. The volatile interest rates of the past 10 years has changed that perception. Bonds are directly influenced by interest rates. While a number of factors may influence stock prices, bonds are primarily moved by interest rates. Next in importance is the quality of the issuer. Bonds trade inversely with interest rates. Higher rates mean lower bond prices and vice versa.

Municipal bonds are secured in one of two ways. General-obligation bonds are backed by the full faith and credit (i.e., the taxing power) of the issuing government. Revenue bonds are used to finance specific public projects. They are repaid by the revenues generated by the facilities they finance. For example, revenue bonds may be issued to build a hospital or bridge. The security of the bonds depends on the economic viability of the project.

Municipal bonds, like all bonds, are hurt by inflation. Inflation brings higher interest rates, which result in lower prices.

There is the additional risk that the financial condition of the issuing government body may deteriorate after you've purchased the bond. If a rating is lowered on a bond, it will drop in price. The lower price produces a higher yield to compensate for the perceived additional risk.

Minimum investment in municipals is typically $5,000 or higher. Professionally managed bond mutual funds or unit investment trusts offer the average investor the chance to diversify.

Recent years have seen a wide variety of features tacked onto municipals. These include floating-rate bonds and notes, bonds with put options, and enhanced security issues. The drive to obtain sufficient financing at the lowest possible cost will no doubt result in even more innovations. Following the stock market crash in October 1987, caution became the watchword for most investors,

and muni investors were no exception. Muni investors turned to insured bonds. During the first quarter of 1989, 27% of muni issues were insured. That was up from 21% in 1988 and 18% in 1987. Keep in mind though that municipal insurance is largely untested.

Although some people doubt how valuable such privately issued insurance would be in the case of major problems in the muni market, investors generally were willing to give up some yield for the added protection. The most famous and largest muni default in history, the 1983 default of the Washington Public Power Supply System on $2.25 billion of its bonds, produced proof of the value of that insurance for some bondholders. Only a small portion was insured by AMBAC (one of the four major muni bond insurers), but those bondholders escaped disaster.

Bonds backed by insurance from one of the four major insurers—AMBAC, MBIA, FGIC, and BIG—are rated AAA. As of May 1988, these insurers had more than $1.6 billion in capital. No insured muni has ever defaulted.

It is important to note the disturbing trend of rising defaults in the muni market. Since 1983 (after the WPPSS default) there have been more than 500 defaults totaling over $3.5 billion. In the first quarter of 1989 municipal defaults totaled $175.8 million, up from $109.9 million in the same period one year earlier. Since 1988 in Florida alone there have been over 10 defaulted issues totaling $140 million. Illinois was next in line with 18 failures for $80.6 million. Following closely behind are Minnesota, Pennsylvania, and Tennessee.

Many municipal bonds are issued with "call" provisions. A call provision enables the issuer to redeem outstanding bonds before maturity, at the issuer's discretion. Usually there is a minimum time period of five to 10 years after issue when the bonds are "safe" from being called.

Call provisions should be carefully watched by investors who require a secure income for living expenses. A bond would be called only during declining interest rates when the issuing body could refinance the bond

Look At This:

at lower interest rates. If you had planned on the income from a bond that was called, you could not replace the income with an equivalently rated bond. Just when you were planning on a tax-free 8% yield for the next 10 years, the bond gets called and the market yield on the same type of bond is only 6%.

Strengths

Public purpose municipal bonds pay tax-exempt income. Investment-grade municipals (those rated A or better) are quite safe from default. They are also more liquid than lower- rated bonds. Municipals can generate capital gains if interest rates decline. Finally many munis carry privately issued insurance on both interest and principal.

Weaknesses

Rising interest rates depress bond prices. Call provisions may limit how long you can lock in high relative yields. Inflation is devastating to municipals. Revenue bonds are not backed by the taxing power of the issuing entity. Adverse business developments in the project could affect both interest payments and principal value. And liquidity is limited in some issues.

Tax Considerations

Tax Consequences

The interest paid by public purpose and previously issued municipal bonds is exempt from federal taxes. The 1986 Tax Reform Act eliminated the tax-free feature of municipal private activity bonds in many cases. And to confuse the issue even more, the interest paid on certain qualified private activity bonds is subject to

Professional Advice

the alternative minimum tax even though totally exempt for regular tax calculations!

The complexity of the tax law changes ushered in with the 1986 Tax Reform Act make it prudent to check with

your tax advisor. Each individual's situation is unique.

Summing Up

Public purpose municipal bonds are the most widely used vehicle for obtaining tax-free cash flow. Although the 1986 Tax Reform Act tightened things somewhat, carefully selected munis remain the single best option for tax-free income.

Historically, the municipal bond market has been the domain of institutional investors. However, this pattern began to change in the 1980s. The presence of many individual investors with shorter time horizons resulted in a highly volatile market. Individual investors tend to have a much shorter time horizon (and lower loss threshold!). As a result, they buy and sell much more actively than do institutional investors.

When the bond market broke in April 1987, the municipal market fell more sharply than the Treasury market. The larger drop by munis was attributed to the big influence of the mutual fund market. As bond values dropped, mutual fund investors sold their shares, forcing many of the funds to sell more muni bonds to meet redemptions. This forced the market lower than would have otherwise been the case. In October 1989 the stock market suffered a stunning crash, falling 190 points in a single day. Junk bonds also suffered a sharp decline. Treasury bonds and municipals held up well. In fact, by year end, returns on municipal bonds had gained relative to Treasury issues. This contrasted with the performance of municipals in 1987.

The April 20, 1988, Supreme Court decision broadening the power of the federal government to tax interest paid by municipal bonds has thrown another variable into the market. Expect greater volatility in some issues, especially private-purpose bonds, which are still tax advantaged. Political rumors will make the muni market skittish. The increasing volatility means greater risk to your principal. As a result, municipal bond investments should be made with money you are able to commit for long periods of time. Remember, if you hold a bond to maturity price, fluctuations resulting from interest rate moves will not affect you.

Municipal Bonds—Discounted

Municipal bonds are debt instruments issued by state or local governments. When interest rates move higher, the price of bonds with lower coupons (the set interest rate paid by the issuer) falls, or is discounted, to bring their yield into line with the market.

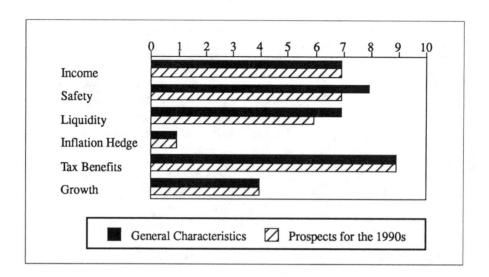

Income
Safety
Liquidity
Inflation Hedge
Tax Benefits
Growth

■ General Characteristics ▨ Prospects for the 1990s

Type III

A

High Taxes
High Expenses

Discounted municipal bonds (munis) are popular with investors who want to lock in yields for the long term. Since many munis have call provisions that could result in early redemptions, savvy investors who want to lock in a yield without danger of being called prematurely will buy discounted munis that carry low coupons. The yield will be comparable to the market, but because the bonds carry a low coupon they are less likely to be called before maturity.

Bonds are called early when the coupon yield is higher than the going market rate. Issuers are able to save money in interest payments by redeeming their high coupon issues and selling new lower coupon bonds. Since discounted bonds by definition carry lower coupons, they are less susceptible to being called before they mature.

Money Management Tip

You wouldn't buy a bond with a 5% coupon at full face value when you could get a bond yielding 8% for the same price. For example, assume that a 20-year muni bond issued in 1972 carries a coupon of 5%. The face value would be $5,000 per bond. A buyer would receive $250 per year. If market rates move to 8% for the same class of muni in 1988, the price of the 5% bond would fall to $625. At that price, the 5% bond would yield a competitive 8%.

Bonds trade inversely with interest rates. When rates move higher, bond prices move lower. When rates move lower, bonds will move up in price.

Look At This:

Discounted munis can be purchased through major full-service brokerage firms or through smaller firms that specialize in munis. The fee for buying the bond is assessed either as a commission or as a "dealer markup" from the price the dealer obtained the bond. The latter practice may hide the actual costs of transaction. You should find out in advance what the fees will be.

Prices of actively traded muni bonds are reported in the *Wall Street Journal* and *Investor's Daily*. There are a number of other sources for price information, including your broker, for munis that are not carried in these two newspapers.

Professional management of muni portfolios is available for individuals who maintain large (usually over $1 million) portfolios. Smaller investors can obtain professional management through mutual funds specializing in muni bonds. Funds offer the additional advantage of diversification.

Investment Potential

Munis are primarily purchased for income. The interest paid on most munis is exempt from federal taxes. There is also potential for capital gains if interest rates fall. Capital gains are taxed at ordinary income rates (see section on tax considerations).

Bonds have historically been considered a relatively safe nonvolatile investment. However, the widely fluctuating interest rates of recent years have resulted in much more volatility in the bond markets.

Many muni bonds are insured by private companies for both income and principal. General-obligation munis are backed by the full faith and credit (including the taxing power) of the issuing government body.

Revenue muni bonds are issued to finance specific projects. Interest and principal on maturity are paid out of revenues generated by the project. Revenue bonds carry slightly higher yields due to this increased risk.

Municipal bonds are rated by independent services. Two of the most prominent services are Standard & Poor's and Moody's Investor Services. Bonds rated A or higher are considered "investment grade." Lower-rated bonds are higher risk and carry higher yields as a result.

There is an active secondary market for most muni issues. This ensures good liquidity for investment-grade munis and those of major issuers. Obscure munis from less well-known issuers are less liquid. You may have to accept steep discounts from market prices to sell these bonds quickly.

Muni bonds are generally long-term investments. Speculators trading on interest rate expectations trade them for short-term profits.

Muni bonds are subject to market price risk if interest rates rise. They are also subject to price falls if the financial condition of the issuer deteriorates. If a rating is downgraded due to this deterioration, the bond price will fall. The yields on higher-rated bonds are lower due to the greater safety they offer.

Municipals are not good inflation hedges. Higher inflation brings higher interest rates, which will depress prices.

Strengths

Discount munis offer competive tax-free income. Discount munis are less susceptible to being called early. Discount munis will appreciate if interest rates decline. Investment grade discount munis have good liquidity. Highly rated munis offer security of principal and interest payments.

Weaknesses

Discount munis will fall in price if interest rates go up. Many discount munis are not liquid. Deterioration in the financial condition of the issuing entity may result in falling prices even if other munis are appreciating. A properly diversified portfolio of discount munis requires substantial capital. Discount munis that are "revenue issues" are subject to price risk if the underlying project fails to generate sufficient money to pay interest and principal when due.

Tax Considerations

Tax Consequences
Prior to the 1986 Tax Reform Act, all interest paid by munis was exempt from federal taxes. All munis issued before August

7, 1986, are still exempt from federal taxes.

However, municipal bonds issued to finance "private activities" after that date are fully taxable on the federal level. There are some exceptions depending on exactly what the money is used for and on how many such private-purpose bonds have been sold by the issuing body.

Interest paid by munis is usually exempt from state and local taxes for residents of the issuing body.

The 1986 tax law eliminated preferential treatment for capital gains. Capital gains are taxed at ordinary income rates.

Summing Up

Municipal bonds appreciated substantially in the environment of falling interest rates and

Money Management Tip

low inflation that has existed since 1980. Fears of inflation in the first half of 1987 knocked prices down but they rallied back in 1989 and 1990.

Bonds are direct plays on interest rates. For clues on interest rate trends, you should monitor the Federal Reserve's discount rate. Consecutive increases in the discount rate will signal higher interest rates. An early indicator for interest rate trends is the direction of the overnight fed funds rate. This rate is closely monitored by the Federal Reserve.

A pickup in inflation will also depress munis, discounted or not, because higher interest rates inevitably follow increased inflation.

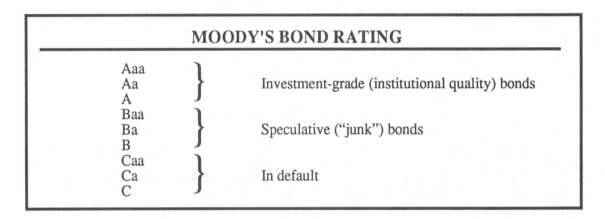

MOODY'S BOND RATING

Aaa Aa A	Investment-grade (institutional quality) bonds
Baa Ba B	Speculative ("junk") bonds
Caa Ca C	In default

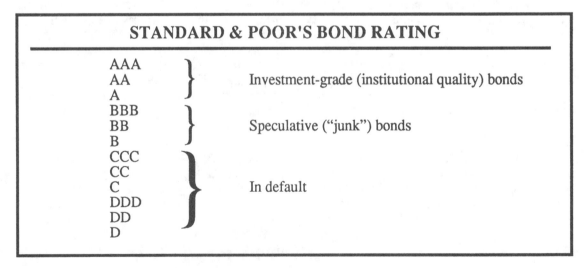

STANDARD & POOR'S BOND RATING

AAA AA A	Investment-grade (institutional quality) bonds
BBB BB B	Speculative ("junk") bonds
CCC CC C DDD DD D	In default

Corporate Bonds

Corporate bonds are debt securities issued by companies for a set amount (the "par value") and maturity. Most corporate bonds specify a fixed interest rate to be paid at specified time intervals (usually semi-annually). During the late 1970s, when inflation was a dominant concern for investors, "variable-rate" bonds were marketed. These bonds feature a flexible interest rate according to a preset formula (e.g., tied to the Federal Reserve's discount rate). Variable-rate bonds generally sell for a lower current yield because they provide some measure of protection against loss of purchasing power due to inflation.

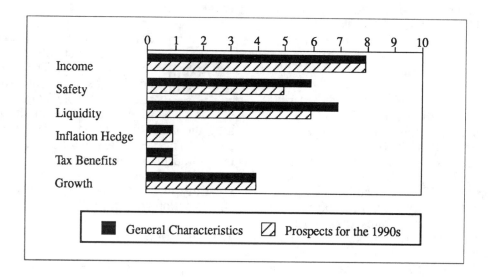

Type I

C

Low Taxes
High Expenses

Type II

C

Low Taxes
High Expenses

There are two types of corporate bonds: mortgage and debenture. A mortgage bond is secured by specific assets. A debenture is an unsecured loan backed only by the corporation's credit. A debenture has a higher claim on a company's assets than stock investments in the company. This means that if a company goes bankrupt, bondholders are paid out of liquidated assets before stockholders are paid.

Bonds are rated for their creditworthiness by independent services. These services evaluate the financial condition of the issuing company and assign letter ratings. For example, Standard & Poor's ratings for investment-grade bonds run from a top grade of AAA, AA, or A. Moody's Investor Services equivalent ratings are Aaa, Aa, and A. Lower quality issues carry BBB or lower ratings by Standard & Poor's, and Baa for Moody's. Investment-grade bonds are the most secure since they are backed by companies deemed to be in good financial condition. BBB or Baa bonds and lower are considered "junk bonds" (see section on junk bonds for more details).

Look At This:

You should also be aware of a bond's "call" provisions. The call date is the first date when the bond issuer may redeem the bond before maturity. Call provisions are spelled out in the bond's prospectus. Routinely, the issuer must pay a premium to the bondholder to call a bond. It is in the interest of a company to "call" a bond early (i.e., before maturity) if interest rates dropped significantly from the time of issue. The company could then call in bonds requiring high interest payments and reissue lower-yielding bonds. This is similar to refinancing your home mortgage to lower your monthly payments.

Bonds of major corporations are traded on exchanges much like stocks. They are also traded over the counter. They are generally purchased through brokers who assess a commission for the transaction. The commission rates are normally lower than equivalent amounts invested in stock.

Investment Potential

Par (or face) value of most bonds is $1,000. They are normally sold in "5-lots" (i.e., five bonds or $5,000 par value). "Baby" bonds have a par value of $500 or less.

Bond prices vary inversely with interest rates. For example, if the current interest rate for AAA 20-year bonds is 10%, you'd receive interest payments of $100 per bond each year. If interest rates rise to 12% for this class of bond, the market value of your bond would drop to about $833 ($100/833 = 12%). This is because a buyer could obtain $120 for a $1,000 par value bond in an environment of higher interest rates.

No one would pay you $1,000 to receive $100 per year, when he or she could pay the same amount for the same quality bond and get $120 per year in interest. Since bonds are purchased primarily for the income they pay, the underlying principal will fluctuate. Of course, it works in your favor if interest rates drop. For example, if market rates dropped to 8%, your bond would appreciate to about $1,225 ($100/$1,225 = 8%).

Bonds are primarily purchased for the income they pay. Capital appreciation is possible, though, if interest rates fall. Yields are lower on higher-rated bonds of the same maturity, due to their greater safety. They should generally be considered long-term vehicles because if you hold to maturity (and the issuer does not go under!) the company pays you the full par value.

Bonds are suitable for retirement plans

such as IRAs where interest accrues on a tax-deferred basis.

Strengths

 Bonds pay high current income. Investment-grade bonds have little principal risk if held to maturity, and bonds issued by major corporations are liquid. Bonds appreciate when interest rates fall.

Weaknesses

 Security of bond income depends on the stability of underlying company. The value of bonds falls when interest rates rise. A callable bond may be redeemed before maturity, limiting the time you receive your expected income. The secondary market for bonds is less liquid than that for stocks. Finally, high volatility in interest rates translates into high volatility in bond prices, and bonds provide no protection from inflation.

Tax Considerations

Tax Consequences

Bond interest is taxed as ordinary income. Capital appreciation is also taxed as ordinary income since the 1986 Tax Reform Act eliminated capital gains preference.

Summing Up

Corporate bonds pay higher interest than other fixed-income instruments such as Treasuries and municipal bonds. But that higher return comes in exchange for higher risk. While we believe that the takeover mania of the 1980s has peaked, you should be aware of the fact that investment grade bonds can lose that quality rating if the company is loaded up with debt as part of a leveraged buyout. Before buying, ask your broker what protection you have against this happening to your bonds.

Corporate Bonds — "Junk"

Junk bonds are debt securities issued by companies for a set amount (the "par value") and maturity. Most junk bonds specify a fixed interest rate to be paid at specified time intervals (usually semiannually).

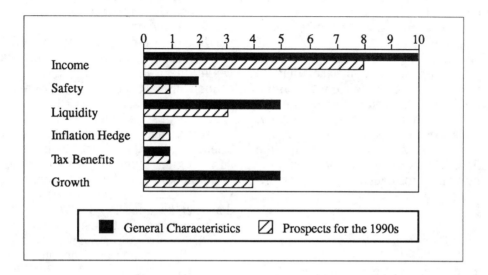

Bar chart showing ratings from 0 to 10 for: Income, Safety, Liquidity, Inflation Hedge, Tax Benefits, Growth. Legend: ■ General Characteristics, ▨ Prospects for the 1990s

Type I

C

Low Taxes
High Expenses

Junk bonds are unsecured debt instruments called *debentures*. A debenture is an unsecured loan backed only by the corporation's credit. A debenture does have a higher claim on a company's assets than stock (equity) investments. If a company goes bankrupt, bondholders are paid out of liquidated assets before stockholders. Although even junk bonds are backed by the assets of a company, payment of interest requires ready liquid assets. Capital assets such as buildings, land, and machines may not be easy to sell (or only at steep discounts) to meet corporate obligations to bondholders.

Junk bonds have been widely used to finance corporate takeovers in the 1980s. These takeovers are usually highly leveraged transactions: credit rather than cash is used to finance the deal. As a result, corporate assets are stretched to the breaking point and corporate liquidity is impaired. Junk bonds, and the massive corporate restructurings that they played such a large part in

generating were the main story of the financial markets of the 1980s. Junk bonds truly rewrote the face of corporate America.

Junk bonds are rated for their creditworthiness by independent services. These services evaluate the financial condition of the issuing company and assign letter ratings. For example, Standard & Poor's ratings for junk bonds are BBB, BB, B, CCC, or lower. Moody's Investor Services equivalent ratings are Baa, Ba, B, Caa, or lower. This compares to investment-grade ratings of AAA, AA, and A for Standard & Poor's, or Aaa, Aa, or A for Moody's.

A market exists for even lower-rated junk bonds. Low-C ratings indicate a bond which is not paying current interest. D ratings are reserved for bonds that are in arrears on interest and/or principal payments. These bonds have value solely as speculations, since they pay no current income.

Junk bonds occasionally have "call provisions." As noted earlier, a call provison specifies the conditions under which an issuer can redeem a bond prior to its maturity. Call provisions are spelled out in the bond's prospectus. Routinely, the issuer must pay a

Look At This:

premium to the bondholder to call a bond. It would be in the interest of a company to "call" a bond early if interest rates dropped significantly from the time of issue. The company could then call in bonds requiring high interest payments and reissue lower-yielding bonds. This is similar to refinancing your home mortgage to lower your monthly payments.

The high relative yield paid by junk bonds in the 1980s attracted a significant market. The junk bond market grew from $2 billion to $200 billion by the end of the decade. Liquidity of individual issues varies widely. Junk bonds are usually purchased through brokers who assess a commission for the transaction. The commission rates are normally lower than for equivalent amounts invested in stock.

Investment Potential

The par (or face) value of most bonds is $1,000. They are normally sold in "5-lots" (five bonds or $5,000 par value). "Baby" bonds have a par value of $500 or less. Junk bonds are normally issued at par value. The current price of any individual issue will vary in the secondary market depending on the general level of interest rates, the company's prospects, the industry's prospects, and even the political environment.

Junk bond prices (like all bond prices) vary inversely with interest rates. For example, if current interest rates for BBB 20-year bonds is 10%, you'd receive interest payments of $100 per bond each year. If interest rates rise to 12% for this class of bond, the market value of your bond would drop to about $833 ($100/833 = 12%). This is because a buyer could obtain $120 for a $1,000 par value bond in an environment of higher interest rates.

No one would pay you $1,000 to receive $100 per year, when they could pay the same amount for the same quality bond and get $120 per year in interest. Since bonds are purchased primarily for the income they pay, the underlying principal will fluctuate. Of course, it works in your favor if interest rates drop. For example, if market rates

dropped to 8%, your bond would appreciate to about $1,225 ($100/$1,225 = 8%).

Junk bonds are speculative vehicles offering relatively high current yields and capital gains potential. The capital gains potential is tied to the general level of interest rates, the business prospects and financial condition of the issuer. If an issuer of junk bonds is able to reduce its outstanding liabilities sufficiently, it may improve its rating. A higher-rated bond of the same maturity will sell for a lower yield. In such a case, the junk bond would go up in value. Yield is equal to the coupon interest rate divided by the current price of the bond.

Junk bonds are speculations on both interest rates and the underlying company. Therefore, they should not be considered secure long-term investments like investment-grade bonds. However, like other bonds, if you hold them to maturity (and the company does not go under!), you will get back the full par value from the company.

Junk bonds are suitable for retirement plans only as a small percentage of the overall assets of the plan. They should only be considered for inclusion in a portfolio able to undertake substantial risk.

Strengths

Junk bonds pay very high current income. They appreciate when interest rates fall and/or if the financial condition of the underlying company improves.

Weaknesses

Junk bonds are highly speculative. Both interest and principal are at risk if the issuer's financial condition deteriorates further. Prices will fall if interest rates rise. Junk bonds are volatile. The secondary market depends on widespread confidence in business and the economy. The value of junk bonds is subject to interest rate, political, economic, and market risk. Finally, junk bonds offer no protection from inflation.

Tax Considerations

Tax Consequences

Junk bond interest is taxed as ordinary income. Capital appreciation is also taxed as ordinary income since the 1986 Tax Reform Act eliminated capital gains preference.

Summing Up

Junk bonds have played a major role in the merger and acquisition mania of the 1980s. The insider trading scandal has cast a pall over the takeover market, but junk bonds continue to be big business for Wall Street.

After the October 19, 1987, stock market crash, the junk bond market suffered a furious drubbing. Prices of some B-rated bonds dropped so sharply that yields on 10-year maturity bonds jumped as high as 14.5% from the 11% to 12% level. Some issues that were involved in leveraged buyouts fell even more, dropping to yields of as much as 16%. Fear of impending recession and the problems that could cause for highly leveraged junk bond issuers combined to shrivel new issue volume.

In late 1988 the junk bond market was pounded again when the record-breaking RJR-Nabisco leveraged buyout was announced. RJR's outstanding bonds dropped 15% virtually overnight!

Each time the junk bond market has rattled, it has bounced back. However, as the economy slips closer to recession investors are approaching junk bonds much more carefully. After the October 1989 190 point single day drop in the stock market, junk bonds were hammered. On Friday 13, the day of the big market break, trading in virtually every junk bond issue ground to a halt. The following Monday the junk bond market rallied, led by better quality issues such as RJR Nabisco.

With the 1990 collapse of the creator of the junk bond market, Drexel Burnham Lambert, many of the borderline issues have virtually no liquidity at all. During 1989 and 1990 large institutional investors in junk bonds such as Prudential ($6 billion) did most of their trading with an eye to upgrading the quality of their portfolios.

As uncertainty over the economy's prospects and a high level of defaults by junk bond issuers (38% according to a study released in 1990 by the Bond Investor's Association, Miami Lakes, FL) bond buyers turned to quality. For 1989, total return for long-term Treasury bonds was 18.88%. That compares to 4.22% for corporate junk bonds. The difference is the decline in price of junk bonds as investors required ever higher yields to compensate for the risk of owning "junk." Total return is a combination of both the interest paid and the change in the price of the bond itself.

This pattern clearly indicates the price you pay for safety in today's market. Even though interest rates declined, other factors hurt junk bonds. As long as there is a fear of impending recession, you can plan on the spread between junk and investment grade widening.

A study by Harvard Professor Paul Asquith claims that the real default rate on junk bonds is 34% rather than the widely quoted 2.5%. That means that even with a spread of 4% to 5%, there may be substantially more risk in junk bonds than had previously been thought. Here more than anywhere else, it is critical to maintain a diversified portfolio. Be very cautious about buying junk bonds if the spread with Treasuries narrows to less than 5%.

If this market interests you, most analysts recommend that you stick with established companies with stable cash flows that have already gone through a buyout or that have restructured to prevent a takeover. A few examples include Owens-Illinois 12 1/4% bonds of 1996, National Gypsum 11 3/8% bonds of 1997, Best Products 12 5/8% bonds of 1996, or Wickes 11 3/8% bonds of 1997.

Junk bonds should be viewed as specula-

Money Management Tip

tive vehicles. Many investors have turned to junk bonds to get higher yields as interest rates dropped from 1982 through 1986. However, don't be lulled into complacency. In times of economic growth, defaults on bonds are minimal. However, a turn in the tide to recession or a pickup in inflation could devastate the junk bond market quickly. Most investors should restrict their junk bond exposure to less than 15% of their total bond portfolio.

Convertible Bonds

Convertible bonds are a hybrid investment combining features of both common stocks and bonds. They are initially sold as debentures (unsecured bonds) with the right to convert to a fixed number of common shares at a set price. Usually, though not always, the stock is that of the underlying company. In cases where the issuing company holds a large interest in another company, the bonds may be convertible into shares of the other company.

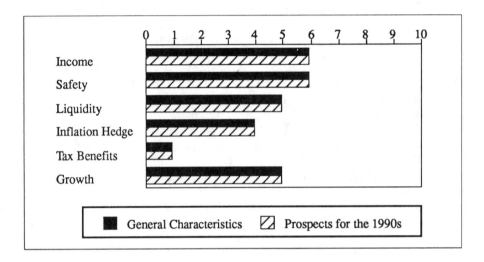

Type I

C
Low Taxes
High Expenses

D
Low Taxes
Low Expenses

Convertibles offer you a higher, more secure income, with the opportunity to participate in the growth of the underlying company. At first glance, it would appear that convertibles are the best of both worlds, but the perfect investment has still not been invented! The interest paid is lower than that offered by comparable instruments. The conversion feature obviously adds value, which is paid for through the lower interest paid.

On the other hand, the potential growth is also less than that offered by outright purchase of the common stock. The premium paid for the conversion privilege diminishes the gain.

Convertible bonds have a priority claim on the assets of the corporation over both its preferred and common stock in liquidation.

However, convertibles' claim on assets follows that of straight bonds. Income from bonds is more secure than dividends because bond interest is a legal obligation of the company. Dividends are paid at the discretion of the directors of the corporation.

Because of their dual nature, convertible bonds have two aspects of value that must be considered: investment value and conversion value. The investment value is the price the bond would have without the conversion privilege. For example, to determine the investment value of an XYZ Corporation convertible bond, compare it to a straight bond with the same coupon yield (e.g., 8%), same maturity, and same rating. Convertibles are usually lower-rated "junk" bond class.

An 8% convertible bond due in 20 years will sell for a higher price (meaning a lower yield) than a straight bond because of the conversion privilege. In adverse market conditions when the value of the common stock is negligible, the investment value of the convertible offers downside protection.

In normal markets, convertible bonds trade primarily on their conversion value. Conversion value is the current price of the underlying common stock multiplied by the number of shares into which the bond is convertible. For example, if XYZ Corporation's common stock is trading at 30 per share, and its 8% bond is convertible into 30 shares, the conversion value is $900 per bond.

When the convertible bond is trading for less than the conversion value (a bear market in stocks may be one instance) the convertible will trade like a bond rather than fluctuating with moves in the underlying stock. If the convertible is trading equal to or above the conversion value, it will trade like a stock, closely tracking the underlying common.

Investment Potential

Convertible bonds provide higher income than the dividends of the underlying stock. There is also capital gains potential if the underlying common stock rises. The tradeoff is that you receive a lower current income than is paid by an straight bond. Also, the potential capital gain is less than you would earn from purchase of the common stock.

Convertible bonds offer downside protection from a dropping stock market because the interest they pay will attract income-oriented investors when their price drops. The tradeoff for the lower risk is lower returns than if you bought only a straight bond or common stock.

Convertible bonds are well suited for conservative investors willing to forgo top returns in exchange for less risk. They are most appropriate for long-term objectives. They lessen the need for precise timing of the stock market since they pay good income while you wait for the common stock to rise. As such, they are excellent vehicles for retirement plans.

The capital gains potential affords you inflation protection that straight bonds do not. The biggest risk is an environment in which the stock market declines and interest rates rise. When interest rates rise, bonds fall.

Without the underlying common stock rising to support the price, a convertible will trade like a bond.

Convertibles are suitable for most retirement plans including IRAs.

Strengths

 Convertibles offer higher income than is provided by common stock, potential for capital gains, and lower risk than outright bonds or common stock. They have a priority claim over stock on company assets in case of bankruptcy or other liquidation. Convertible bonds of major corporations are quite liquid. You also have the right to convert to the common stock at your option. Convertibles are rated by independent services such as Standard & Poor's and Moody's.

Weaknesses

 Income is lower than for equivalent straight bonds. Capital gains are lower than would be realized by the underlying common stock. Most convertibles have "call" provisions that allow the company to redeem them after a specified time period. In addition to the market risk of falling prices, convertible bonds are subject to risk from adverse developments in the issuing company's business.

Tax Considerations

Tax Consequences

Interest and dividends are taxed as ordinary income. The 1986 Tax Reform Act eliminates preferential tax treatment for long-term capital gains. All capital gains regardless of holding period are taxed as ordinary income.

One benefit is that gains resulting from conversion to common stock are not taxable unless the common stock is not that of the company that issued the convertible.

Summing Up

Convertible bonds were one of the hardest-hit investment vehicles in the October 1987 stock crash. Already rated "speculative" (why else would the issuer have to include an equity "kicker" to borrow money in the bond market?), suddenly safety-cautious investors dumped convertibles full force.

Goldman, Sachs & Co.'s widely followed index of convertibles dropped 18.3% in October 1987. That was slightly better than the 21.4% drop in the S&P 500 stock index, but considerably worse than the Shearson Lehman Brothers corporate bond index, which rose 3.3%.

However, convertibles bounced back in 1988, 1989 and 1990 largely due to the strong stock market. By 1990 declining interest rates also helped. Convertible security mutual funds posted a 13.27% gain for 1988 and followed that with another 4.58% in the first quarter of 1989.

The fear and unsettled economic environment following the October Crash drove down new convertible issues to a dribble. In 1988 there were less than 50 new convertible issues compared to over 150 in 1987.

It is important to keep close track of the market's valuation of convertibles relative to the underlying stock. The bullish stock market led to aggressive buying of convertibles in early 1987. When the market crash came, the most overpriced securities naturally fell the most.

A relatively new entrant in the convertibles market is zero coupon convertibles. In 1989 companies such as MCI Communications, Turner Broadcasting System, Blockbuster Entertainment and others, raised more than $2.5 billion selling zero-coupon convertible bonds. The face value of these issues was more than $7 billion. That was the largest supply of zero-convertibles since they were first introduced by Merrill Lynch in 1984 under the trademark name Liquid Yield Option Notes.

You can expect to see this trend continue if the stock market stays buoyant. Corporate treasurers are attracted to the issues because they can raise cash at interest rates lower than on other debt securities. Also the issuer does not need to make periodic interest payments.

As a rule of thumb, convertibles give you about 80% of the upside of stocks and 50% of the downside. In 1987 that ratio reversed, giving about 50% of the upside and 80% of the downside. That was a loud and clear warning signal that the market had become overpriced. By 1990 the ratio was back in line.

Be very careful of the premiums you pay for convertibles over the underlying common stock. Aggressive investor buying pushed those premiums too high in the first quarter of 1987. The good performance in 1988 ignited renewed interest in this market. Select issues carefully. Do not pay more than 40% premiums.

Convertible securities offer a viable alternative for conservative risk-averse long-term investors. Forgoing some profit potential for greater safety makes good sense to many investors. Price information is widely available. There is extensive information and professional advice on convertibles. Professional management can be obtained through closed-end funds and mutual funds.

Convertible bonds have been the beneficiaries of the best of worlds: declining interest rates and rising stock prices. A decline in interest rates pushes up bond prices. A bull market in stock, raises the value of the underlying common stock.

With the continuation of low inflation, and low interest rates, a moderate growth environment will be very favorable to convertible bonds. It will be important to watch inflation indexes such as the Consumer Price Index. An annualized rate of over 7% would be very negative. Federal Reserve policy is critical. The "easy money" environment is beneficial. Watch for increases in the discount rate as a negative.

Mutual Funds—Bonds

Bond investing has historically been the domain of institutional investors. Proper bond investing is more difficult for the average investor than stocks. Considerably less coverage of the intricacies of bond investing is provided in the mass media. Even financial publications such as Forbes, Business Week, *or* Money *devote more space to stocks than to bonds. Perhaps most importantly, though, it takes more money to purchase a well-diversified portfolio of individual bonds. Most professionals recommend a minimum of $200,000 to build a properly diversified bond portfolio.*

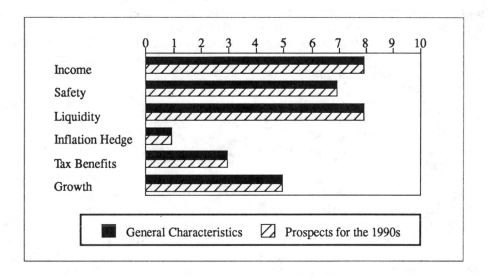

Type II

A

High Taxes
High Expenses

C

Low Taxes
High Expenses

Bond funds are professionally managed pools of bonds that sell proportionate shares to the public. Net asset value is calculated at the end of each business day by totaling the market value of all bonds owned plus all other assets such as cash, and subtracting all liabilities. This figure is then divided by the total number of shares outstanding.

The high interest rates paid by bonds in the late 1970s and early 1980s generated increased interest in bonds by individual investors. Bond funds have enjoyed rapid growth in the rush to meet investor needs.

You buy a no-load bond mutual fund (or any other type of no-load fund) at net asset value (NAV). A load fund is purchased at net asset value plus the sales charge, which may range from 2% to 8%. Some funds that call themselves "no load" assess a fee when you sell the fund (or even part of your holdings). Before you invest in any fund, be sure to clarify what fees are charged.

The largest bond mutual fund prices are carried in the *Wall Street Journal.* A number of computer databases carry up to date prices for most bond prices. These can be accessed with a personal computer. There is usually a charge for the time you are connected to the database.

The popularity of bond investing has led to the publication of investment advisory newsletters devoted exclusively to bonds and bond mutual funds. Both *Fortune* and *Money* magazine publish annual volumes listing the names and addresses of investment advisory newsletters.

Investment Potential

Bond funds are usually purchased for income. They are generally considered long-term investments. However, there is an increasing interest in trading no-load bond funds as speculations on short-term changes in interest rate. Bond funds, like bonds, trade inversely to interest rates. When rates move higher, bond fund prices go down. When rates move lower, fund prices rise. The high front-end charges of load funds make short-term trading impracticable for them.

Bond prices have become more volatile in recent years as interest rates tend to fluctuate more. The diversification offered by bond funds adds a measure of stability compared to single issues, but they won't move contrary to interest rates.

Bond funds are available in a wide variety. There are funds that concentrate on long-, intermediate-, or short-term corporate, municipal, or Treasury bonds and notes. For example, the largest bond fund is Franklin U.S. Government, with over $12 billion under management.

Putnam's U.S. Government High Income Fund, on the other hand, invests primarily in long-term Treasury bonds.

Putnam also offers the Putnam GNMA Plus, which invests primarily in mortgage-backed shorter-term bonds.

Benham Capital offers a series of zero-coupon goverment funds: the Benham Target series. Maturities include 2000, 2015, 2005, and 2010. These highly volatile funds (see section on zero-coupon bonds) were down over 40% for the first nine months of 1987, then rallied sharply following the market crash in October. Benham 2010, for example, posted a 20% gain in the *week* following the crash! This volatile performance is an excellent illustration of the risk that zero-coupon bonds represent over the short term. The lack of current income to cushion price falls when interest rates rise, means zeros are the most volatile type of bonds.

Some funds specialize in long-term municipal issues also. Value Line's Tax-exempt Fund–High Yield buys a diverse selection of municipals and trades its portfolio actively. Other municipal bond funds are available, with different lengths of maturities. Van-guard Municipal Short-Term and Rochester Municipals are two that have shorter average maturities.

Funds that concentrate on junk bonds include Oppenheimer Management Corporation's High-Yield Fund, Fidelity High-Income, Financial Bond–High Yield, and Investment Portfolio–High Yield.

Because bond funds vary greatly in their trading activity it is important to find out what the fund's current average maturity is. The shorter the maturity, the lower the risk. But that, of course, also means lower potential return if interest rates drop. It is a good idea to try to buy a selection of funds—a U.S. government fund, a corporate high-grade, a junk bond fund—and mix the maturities.

Some funds specialize in bonds that are rated investment grade, while others buy high-yielding or "junk" bonds. You have great flexibility in selecting funds that meet your investment objectives and risk tolerance.

Bond funds offer greater safety than any single issue because of the diversification offered. However, there is no government insurance on them. All bond funds are registered with the SEC. They must meet strict financial and reporting requirements. All funds must provide prospective investors with a prospectus that details information about the fund and its management.

Bond funds are appropriate investments for most retirement plans.

Strengths

 Bond funds offer professionally managed, diversified portfolios to small investors. Many large investors also take advantage of this professional management. The variety of bond funds enables you to tailor your investment to meet your unique objectives and risk tolerance. Bond funds offer competitive current income and the potential for capital gains if interest rates fall. No-load funds can be traded for short-term capital gains on your expectations for the direction of interest rates. Bond funds are liquid investments.

Weaknesses

 Bond funds are subject to market risk. If interest rates rise, fund prices will fall. Bond funds are also subject to the risk of poor performance by the funds investment advisor. Inflation will hurt bond fund prices. High fees may affect your return.

Tax Considerations

Tax Consequences

The tax consequences of investing in bond funds varies with the type of fund selected. The income paid by most municipal bond funds is exempt from federal taxes.

The income paid by Treasury bond funds is exempt from state and local taxes for most localities. The income paid by corporate bond funds is subject to taxation at your ordinary income rate.

Capital gains from any type of bond fund is taxed at ordinary income rates. Capital losses offset capital gains. Excess capital losses can be carried forward.

Summing Up

Bond funds invested in long-term issues are more vulnerable to interest rate rises than funds concentrating on shorter maturities.

When bond prices fall, the asset values of bond funds fall concomitantly. Investors move to liquidate their bond funds. Many funds may be forced to sell some of the bonds in their portfolios to raise sufficient cash to redeem their shares.

Mutual bond investors actually hurt their own cause by selling too quickly. The additional selling by the funds themselves will push bonds lower faster than they might have otherwise have gone.

You should view mutual fund bond investing as a long-term proposition. Short-term trading is a self-defeating proposition. Full-time professionals are not able to forecast short-term interest rate fluctuation with a great degree of accuracy. Part-time investors certainly will fare no better.

---

10 Top-Performing Low-Risk
Tax-Exempt Bond Funds
(ranked by 10-year total return)

* 1) ELFund Tax Exempt
* 2) Colonial Tax Exempt
* 3) Mass Municipal Bond
* 4) Oppenheimer Tax Free
* 5) IDS High Yield Tax Exempt
* 6) Kemper Municipal
+ 7) Merrill Lynch Muni Ins. A
− 8) Fidelity High Yield Muni
* 9) Tax-Exempt American
* 10) Evergreen Muni Bond

o Unchanged from previous edition
* New appearance on list
+ Moved up from previous edition
− Moved down from previous edition

Source: Fund/Search, Information Edge, Inc., (800) 334-3669

Zero-coupon Securities

Zero-coupon securities are fixed-income debt securities that sell at steep discount from face value and pay no interest at fixed intervals, like most bonds. They pay full face value at maturity. You receive your return from the gradual appreciation of the security as it approaches maturity.

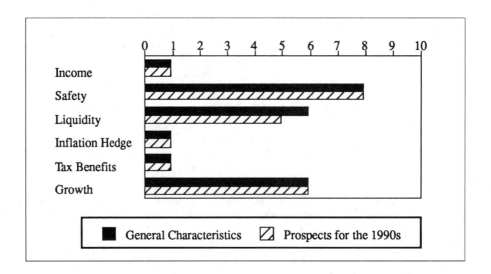

The market for zero-coupon bonds began in 1983, when Merrill Lynch introduced TIGRs (Treasury Investment Growth Certificates). Merrill stripped the interest coupons from the principal portion of the underlying Treasury bonds and sold each piece separately. Since then other brokerage firms have introduced competing products with such acronyms as CAT or LION. Despite the various names, they are all essentially the same product.

In February 1985, the U.S. government stepped into the market with its own STRIPS (Separate Trading of Registered Interest and Principal of Securities). STRIPS are the safest zero-coupon security because they are backed directly by the U.S. government.

Zero-coupon securities issued by brokerage firms are also safe, but there is some risk. Typically the issuing brokerage firm places the underlying bonds in an escrow ac-

Type I

D

Low Taxes
Low Expenses

count with a major bank—Manufacturer's Hanover and Morgan Guaranty are big players in this market. It then sells certificates of varying maturities to investors. When the underlying bonds pay their interest, the brokers use those funds to pay off the certificates that are maturing. Those certificates issued with the longest maturities are paid off when the underlying bond matures.

There are many types of zero-coupon issues:

- Corporate zeros are bonds backed solely by the full faith and credit of the underlying corporate issuer.
- Municipal zeros are based on underlying municipal bonds. Unlike other zeros, the interest is not taxable each year.
- Certificate of deposit zeros are issued by banks and savings and loans.
- Convertible zeros come in a number of varieties. The most common are those issued with a put option that enables the buyer to convert the zero into common

stock. Some convertible zeros are based on municipal bonds and are convertible into interest-paying bonds.

- Mortgage-backed zeros are secured by Fannie Maes, Ginnie Maes and Freddie Maes. Just as straight mortgage-backed pass-throughs have the unique risk of early prepayments, so do these zeros. Therefore they tend to carry higher returns to compensate for the potential risk of early redemption.
- "Derivative zeros" (TIBR's; LIONs, etc.) are secured by Treasury bonds but are issued by brokers who place the bonds in escrow.
- STRIPS are issued directly by the U.S. Treasury Department and are the safest of all zeros. They therefore pay the lowest returns.

Zero-coupon issues are sold by leading full-service brokerage firms. Many banks and savings institutions now sell them also. Fees vary widely. In fact, the high fees associated with zeros when they were first introduced were the source of widespread complaints. As the market has grown and competition intensified, fees have dropped from as high as 5% to around 2% or less.

The fees are typically assessed as either dealer markup (the difference between what the dealer pays and what he or she sells to you for) or commissions. Usually the trading cost is in the form of markup or spread. With zeros it can be as much as four times greater than the spread for regular bonds. The spread is often wider when you sell.

Prices are quoted in major business dailies such as the *Wall Street Journal* or *Investor's Daily*. The popularity of this device has resulted in coverage by large-circulation financial publications such as *Money* and *Changing Times*.

Investment Potential

The chief attraction of zero-coupon issues is the ability to lock in a fixed compounding rate of return for a specific period of time. When you buy an interest-paying bond, you're never sure what return you will be able to earn when you reinvest the interest. Interest rates fluctuate widely and may be lower or higher than the rates when you bought the bond itself.

The low initial investment and known return make zeros popular vehicles for people who need a specific sum of money at some point in the future. For example, an 11% zero would return 10 times its initial investment in 20 years.

Zeros enable investors to lock in the power of compounding for their savings. For example, an investment of $31 in a 12% 30-year zero-coupon bond will return $1,000 at maturity.

Although the gains on zeros appear to be from growth, they are considered interest income for tax purposes. In fact, the IRS requires you to pay taxes on the "imputed interest" earned each year on a zero-coupon bond, *even though you don't receive interest from the bond itself!*

Zero coupons should be viewed primarily as long-term investments. They are highly volatile because they pay no current interest. Every change in interest rates greatly affects the future value of a zero due to the compounding effect. They offer potential capital gains when traded on the secondary market. Zeros are gaining popularity as trading vehicles for capital gains. If interest rates fall after purchase, the zeros will appreciate.

This inherent volatility can be increased by buying zeros on margin. This would be a viable strategy only for someone seeking to trade the bonds for capital gains. Better trading vehicles are available.

Since most buyers of zeros plan to hold to maturity, there is not a large active liquid secondary market. Treasury-based zeros are somewhat more liquid than corporates and municipals. In fact, the two largest managers of zero-coupon bond funds, Benham Capital and Scudder, carry only Treasury issues.

Zeros vary widely in degree of safety. STRIPS are the safest, of course, because they are issued and backed by the Treasury department directly. Other zeros secured by Treasuries are structured to be held in escrow accounts. The small additional risk of problems developing with the issuer or the escrow bank results in slightly higher yields.

Corporate zeros carry a substantially higher yield since the buyer is subject to risk of total loss in the case of default by the issuer. A buyer of a 20-year interest-paying bond will at least have received interest for 10 years if the issuer defaults then. However, holders of a zero issued by the same company will lose their entire investment.

Look At This:

Municipal zeros that have "call" features (see section on municipal bonds) present the peculiar case of defeating the whole purpose of zero investing. If you need a specific amount of money at a set date in the future, you would not want to buy a zero that can be "called" earlier.

Municipal and corporate zeros are rated by independent services such as Standard & Poor's or Moody's. Since the risk of total loss is possible through zero investing, credit ratings are particularly important.

Inflation represents a substantial risk for zeros. Once you've purchased a zero, its potential return for you will not change regardless of the underlying inflation rate. Inflation will diminish the purchasing power of the money you receive on maturity.

Zero-coupon securities are very popular with retirement programs that enable you to defer taxes on income. Buying zeros in this manner enables you to avoid paying taxes on "phantom income" until you elect to withdraw the funds.

Another advantage of buying zero-coupon bonds in tax-deferred accounts is that you are taking a long-term position and shouldn't be affected by the very wild swings in this market. For example, in 1986 zero-coupon bonds were the single best-performing asset among financial assets. Yet by September 1987, zeros were the worst-performing asset by far. Zeros react so closely with interest rate swings that their volatility can be terrifying for conservative investors who take too short a perspective.

As a general rule, a 1% move in interest rates will move a zero-coupon bond approximately 1% for each year left to maturity. For example, if you hold a zero with a year 2000 maturity date in 1990, and interest rates increase 2%, your bond will fall approximately 20%. If rates fall by 2%, your bond will appreciate by about 20%.

You can monitor zero-coupon bond funds yourself to see how volatile they are. In 1986, the Benham Target 2010 zero-coupon fund posted a 54.4% gain for the year. That was the top performance by any bond fund that year. Yet that same fund fell 12.3% in the first six months of 1987, winding up near the bottom of bond fund performance for that span!

The two largest managers of zero-coupon bond funds are Benham and Scudder. Both groups invest only in Treasury zeros. Neither group assesses a sales load.

The post-October Crash environment of lower interest rates buoyed trader interest in zeros. Paine Webber put together zero-coupon bonds and gold in a new fund called U.S. Treasury Gold Series 1. Half the fund is invested in zero-coupon bonds, and half in gold. When the trust matures in eight years, investors will receive their principal back from the zeros and any gain the gold may have added to their investment.

Strengths

Low initial investment is required. A $1,000 20-year bond paying 12% would only cost about $100. Yield to maturity is locked in. This takes the guesswork out of the potential return from reinvestment of interest. The investor knows the exact cashout value of investment on maturity date. Zeros offer convenient automatic compounding of interest.

Weaknesses

Taxes are due annually on interest as it accrues even though interest is not paid out to the zero bond holder. Zeros are more volatile than interest-paying bonds because you don't receive any current income to cushion price swings when interest rates change. The purchasing power of the zero-coupon bond may be impaired by inflation during holding years. Corporate zeros carry greater risk than interest-paying bonds because you never receive any money until maturity. If the company goes bankrupt the day before your bond matures, you stand to lose your initial investment plus all accumulated interest. Finally, there is a less liquid secondary market for zeros than for regular bonds.

Tax Considerations

Tax Consequences

As we've detailed above, zero-coupon securities present a unique tax situation. You are required to pay tax annually on the interest that has accrued to your bond even though you have not actually received payment. This "imputed" interest payment is a major drawback to zeros.

Interest from municipal zeros is exempt from federal taxes. Interest on U.S. Treasury zeros is exempt from state and local taxes.

Interest is taxed at ordinary income rates. The 1986 Tax Reform Act eliminated the preferential capital gains treatment. Capital gains are taxed at ordinary income rates.

Summing Up

The market for zero-coupon securities has grown rapidly since their recent introduction. Issuers have developed a number of innovative products and even more will be introduced in the future.

Zeros are bonds that are not appropriate for investors who need current income. They are ideal vehicles for setting aside money to grow at a compounded rate for some purpose in the future. Many financial planners include zeros in programs designed to cover future college costs or other substantial fixed costs in the future.

Because the interest is taxable as accrued, zeros are ideally suited for retirement accounts where taxes are deferred.

---

10 Top-Performing Corporate Bond Funds
(ranked by 10-year total return)

* 1) General Electric Long-term
− 2) Kemper High Yield
+ 3) Bond Fund America
* 4) Aetna Income
* 5) CIGNA High Yield Fund
* 6) United Bond
− 7) Fidelity High Income
* 8) Mutual of Omaha Intermediate
− 9) Fidelity Intermed. Term Bond
* 10) IDS Selective

o Unchanged from previous edition
* New appearance on list
+ Moved up from previous edition
− Moved down from previous edition

Source: Fund/Search, Information Edge, Inc., (800) 334-3669

Commercial Mortgage Securities

Commercial mortgage securities are debt instruments secured by commercial real estate. Commercial mortgage securities are very similar to the more common residential mortgage securities. Syndicators pool a group of commercial mortgages to back securities sold to the public. For example, in April 1987 the brokerage firm Salomon Brothers sold $250 million worth of 12-year notes backed by the Chrysler Building in New York City.

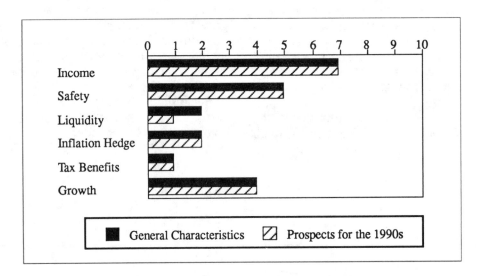

Over 30% of the $1.7 billion in outstanding residential mortgages have been converted into securities for sale to the public. Most fixed-income investors are well aware of the alternatives to bonds offered by mortgage-backed securities such as Ginnie Maes or Fannie Maes. Only recently has Wall Street turned to the commercial real estate market in an attempt to create another product of interest to individual investors.

Type I

C

Low Taxes
High Expenses

The residential mortgage market has experienced rapid growth over the past 10 years. "Securitizing" (i.e., packaging a pool of mortgages to back securities sold directly to the public) is much easier with residential mortgages because they are generally fairly standard and often guaranteed by an agency of the federal government. Commercial mortgages are much more individualized and lack federal guarantees.

As a result, it is more difficult to put together a marketable product. Many of the commercial mortgage securities sold to date have been offered to private investors who meet stringent financial requirements. More public offerings can be expected in the future as the market becomes more established. The market for residential mortgages has been one of the fastest-growing financial markets in history. Although financial experts do not foresee the same explosive growth for commercial mortgages, they do look for substantial growth from this sector over the next five years.

Professional
Advice

You buy a CMS through a licensed broker. The current market is small (only about 4% of the $800 billion of commercial mortgages outstanding are securitized). Given the thin market, CMSs should be viewed as long-term investments. Major independent financial services such as Standard & Poor's and Moody's have started rating CMSs.

Investment Potential

CMSs offer good current income. They are mortgage-backed securities that trade like bonds. This means that the principal value of the underlying security will fluctuate inversely with interest rates. When interest rates rise, CMSs fall in value. Capital growth is derived from principal fluctuations resulting from interest rate swings.

High volatility in interest rates translates into wide price swings for fixed-income securities such as CMSs. This relatively new market is quite thin. The illiquidity increases risk.

Conventional mortgage-backed securities are considered relatively safe investments. Most CMSs have been issued with a third party guaranteeing payment of principal and interest. For example, the Chrysler Building offering mentioned earlier was guaranteed by Fuji Bank.

In addition, any offering to the general public will carry a rating by one of the independent services such as Standard and Poor's or Moody's. These organizations evaluate the financial strength of the issuers. You can determine the risk profile of your portfolio by buying only those issues that meet your rating requirements. Investment-grade CMSs will pay lower current income in exchange for greater safety. CMSs offered to the general public must be registered with the SEC and meet government regulations.

In addition to the risk engendered by interest rate fluctuations, CMSs are subject to other risk factors. For example, business problems of major tenants of commercial rental property may drive down the principal value. Political and economic factors germane to the property backing a CMS may adversely affect its price. CMSs provide no protection against inflation.

Strengths

 Commercial mortgage securities offer a higher yield than equivalent residential mortgages or bonds with similar maturities. Most CMSs are secured by third-party guarantees of principal and interest. CMSs are collateralized by the underlying property, and CMSs yield capital gains when interest rates fall.

Weaknesses

 Commercial mortgage securities offer no inflation protection. There is no government insurance or guarantees for CMSs. CMSs are relatively new securities, and the market is illiquid. Some mortgages in the pool may mature before others because of refinancing. As a result, you may receive a return of principal earlier than expected, lowering your monthly interest payments.

Tax Considerations

Tax Consequences

There are no special tax preferences for commercial mortgage securities. Interest and capital gains are taxed at your ordinary income levels. Since regular payments may represent a mix of interest and "return of principal," taxes are assessed only on that portion representing the interest payment.

Summing Up

Wall Street is enthusiastic about the potential for Commercial Mortgage Securities, but that enthusiasm has not been shared by the investing public to date. Major problems still need to be resolved before CMSs take their place alongside residential "pass-through" mortgage securities or collaterialized mortgage obligations.

However, that very "newness" offers you the chance to obtain excellent yields with moderate risk. Yields relative to competitive products will come down as CMSs become more widely accepted as good-quality alternatives to bonds.

Commercial mortgage securities are a good income-paying investment. They offer capital gains potential when interest rates decline.

Unit Investment Trusts

Unit investment trusts (UITs) are professionally selected pools of securities. Like mutual funds, unit investment trusts sell proportionate ownership in the pool to investors. Usually UITs are pools of income-producting securities, typically bonds both taxable and tax-exempt. Unlike mutual funds, once selected the pool of securities is not actively managed. The trusts expire when the securities in them mature.

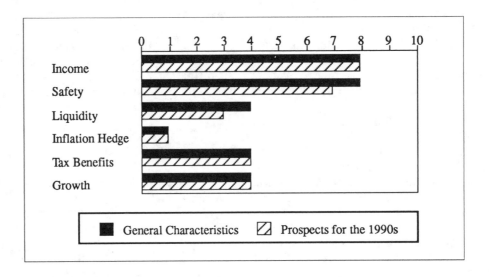

Type IV

C

Low Taxes
High Expenses

A

High Taxes
High Expenses

Although the vast majority of UITs are in bonds, some trusts in recent years have been formed to emulate stock indexes such as the S&P 500. Other types of UITs include money market securities, corporate bonds of different quality and maturities, Treasury securities, mortgage-backed securities, preferred stocks, and foreign bonds. This investment is in a constant state of flux, with new varieties being introduced regularly.

Despite the wide variety of securities currently being used in UITs, most are designed to provide income-seeking investors with dependable diversified portfolios. Although trust covenants vary, typically the trust is restricted in what can be done. If a bond deteriorates, the trust normally may sell the bond and pay out the proceeds to unit holders.

They are not usually allowed to buy new issues.

UITs came into their own in the early 1980s when individual investors started to buy municipal bonds. In the 1970s, only about 15% of all munis were purchased by individual investors. By 1983, that had begun to change. In 1983 and 1984, individual investors bought almost 80% of the new muni debt issues, largely through unit investment trusts.

Brokerage firms created the UITs to enable more individual investors to take advantage of the benefits of tax-free income. Since a well-diversified portfolio of individual municipal issues would require $150,000 to $200,000, UITs filled the niche. For minimum investments of as little as $1,000, investors could buy a proportionate share of a diversified muni portfolio.

Since that time, tax laws have changed dramatically. Now many investors who previously benefitted from the tax-free status of their municipal investments, earn more on an after-tax basis from taxable bonds. There are as many new issues of Treasury and corporate UITs as there are municipals.

Most issuers of UITs— full-service or bond brokers— agree to maintain a secondary market for UITs. However, the pricing mechanism of these markets leaves much to be desired. If you need to sell your UIT before maturity, expect to take a discount from what the broker would sell that same unit for. Also, there is no guarantee that the broker will take your units back. You should carefully check your rights in this regard if there is a chance you may need to sell before maturity.

As with all fixed-income investments, the price of UITs varies inversely with interest rates. If rates move up, your UIT investment trust will drop in value. On the other hand, if interest rates decline, your trust will appreciate.

Most major brokerage firms maintain active ongoing unit investment trust series. You should be able to find a UIT that matches your maturity requirements. The commission charges to buy UITs vary from 1 to 5%. Usually 4%, the fee is negotiable depending on volume.

Typical minimum purchase is $1,000 (the size of a single unit). There is also a small sponsor's and trustee's fee factored into the yield. This fee runs from 0.15% to 0.2%. That compares to an average management fee for mutual funds of about 0.8%. The difference is due to the fact that a unit is not actively managed.

UITs have fixed lives. They pay out proceeds to unit holders as securities mature or are sold. Typically, UITs have long lives— 25 to 30 years. However, shorter-term units are available.

Details of each trust are set forth in the offering prospectus that must be provided to buyers. Fees, buyback arrangements, reinvestment options, exchange rights, etc. are spelled out in the prospectus.

Investment Potential

Unit investment trusts should be viewed as long-term investments. If held to maturity, there is little risk that you will not receive your principal back (unless of course, some bonds in the trust defaulted). In the shorter term, unit prices are subject to wide swings resulting from interest rate changes.

Most UITs are sold to income-seeking investors. The potential for capital gains stems from interest rate swings. UIT prices trade inversely with interest rates. As interest rates become more volatile, so have the prices of UITs.

Liquidity varies greatly among UITs. It depends on a number of factors. The size of the issuing broker, its willingness to support past unit buyers, and the demand for the particular units available. Some UITs allow unit holders to exchange their units for other unit trusts for a small fee. There is usually a fairly wide spread between the bid and ask prices for UITs in the secondary market.

Some UITs that invest in municipals are insured. In fact, in the months following the October market in 1987, insured municipal bond unit trust outsold uninsured products for the first time.

Money Management Tip

As a rule of thumb, it is normally more economic to buy a no-load bond mutual fund than a unit investment trust if you are going to hold the investment less than eight years. If you will be holding the UIT for more than eight years, you will have been able to amortize the front-end load charge and the lower annual fee over a long enough period to make it the wiser choice.

UIT investors run a number of risks. First, there is the ever present risk of interest rate volatility. A prolonged rise in interest rates will depress the price of your UITs. Second, there is the issuer of your UIT who may go out of business or suspend its redemption of previously issued UITs. Drexel Burnham Lambert did exactly that in 1989 when it closed its retail business (Drexel subsequently folded in 1990). From 1984 through 1987 Drexel brokers sold more than $300 million in junk bond UITs called HITS (High Income Trust Securities). Drexel liquidated the HITS over a short period of time, severely depressing the market for some of the bonds in their portfolios.

That may make selling it before maturity virtually impossible. And third, as the April

1988 Supreme Court decision shows, there is always the risk that what you thought was going to be tax-free income could change. The court held that Congress has virtually unlimited authority to tax bonds issued by state and local governments. Now it is up to Congress to define the rules.

Strengths

With UITs you can buy into a diversified portfolio for a minimal investment. Annual fees are negligible. There are no redemption or marketing and distribution fees (12B-1) as with mutual funds. UIT holders do not have to worry about poor management decisions. Once the bonds have been purchased, they cannot be traded. Transaction costs are therefore minimized. Most trusts offer a wide range of unit holder services including monthly payouts, reinvestment of income, etc.

Weaknesses

There is no active independent secondary market. You depend on the issuer to either buy your unit back or find a buyer. Upfront sales fees mean you must hold the UIT for eight years, to make economic sense. The UIT has virtually no flexibility to react to changing market conditions like a mutual fund. UITs are very vulnerable to inflation. A poorly selected initial portfolio may significantly underperform the market for an extended period.

Tax Considerations

Tax Consequences

There are no special tax benefits for UITs. However, because of their structure, a portion of the proceeds in a municipal unit trust may be tax exempt, depending on your place of residence. For example, if you live in California, and California bonds constitute 10% of the trust portfolio, that portion directly attributable to California bonds is doubly tax-exempt for you.

Summing Up

Unit investment trusts represent a good way for long-term passive investors to buy into diversified bond portfolios.

The prospects for the 1990s are dependent on the direction of interest rates. Watch especially the Federal Reserve's control of the fed funds rate for early indications on the direction of rates.

If you do not plan to hold your bond investment for at least eight years, UITs are not the vehicle for you. Stay with no-load mutual funds.

Most major media carry occasional updates on unit investment trusts. The *Wall Street Journal* and *Investor's Daily* both feature stories on the latest UIT innovations; *Money* and *Changing Times* feature UIT updates for their readers.

Collateralized Mortgage Obligations

Collateralized mortgage obligations (CMOs) are repackaged mortgage-backed pass-through certificates such as Ginnie Maes or Fannie Maes. The packager (typically a brokerage firm) puts the pass-throughs in a trust. The trust then issues the CMO securities—bonds with short-, medium-, and long-term maturities.

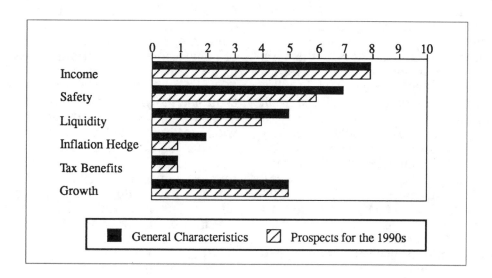

CMOs arose as a direct result of problems investors had with straight pass-through bonds. In 1986, when interest rates were declining, Ginnie Mae investors learned to their chagrin the problem with pass-throughs. When home mortgage rates dropped from 13–14% to 9% or 10%, homeowners moved to refinance. That meant they paid off their old loans and took out new mortgages at the lower rates.

As a result, Ginnie Mae investors, who thought they had locked in high yields for 12 years (the average most often quoted for the average life of a Ginnie Mae bond), got their principal back in only two or three years. They then had to reinvest it at the lower interest rates prevailing then.

The Ginnie Mae and other passthrough markets lagged behind the sterling performance of most bonds in 1986 (remember, bonds appreciate when interest rates decline, and vice versa). Even Ginnie Mae- and Fannie Mae-oriented mutual funds were no protection. They will tend to underperform other types of bond funds in declining interest rate environments.

The CMO is a direct response to the problem caused by early payoffs. CMOs split up the pools into four maturity classes. Each class has a different coupon rate and maturity date. When principal payments are received on the underlying passthroughs, the cash flow is first used to pay off the short-term bonds. Once those are paid off, the next class is paid off and so on.

By dividing the cash flow from repayments into different maturities, investors are able to get a better idea of the average life of their investment. If you are interested in shorter maturities, you'd buy the lower short-term classes. If you want to improve your odds of holding the bond and its stated interest rate as long as possible, you'd buy

Type III

C

Low Taxes
High Expenses

the long-term maturity class.

CMOs enable mortgage investors to get some "call protection." Refinancing of a home mortgage has the same effect on a mortgage investor as call provisions on conventional bonds. A corporate bond's call provision allows the issuer to "call in" or buy back the bond at the issuer's discretion. But in the case of a call provision, the investor usually has a good idea of when it will be called because the bond covenants limit the time period and usually require a premium to be paid.

Mortgage investors have no such luxury. As conventional pass-through investors found to their chagrin, a 2% drop in mortgage rates over a short time period can result in heavy prepayments.

Until 1986 CMOs were sold exclusively to institutional investors. These were primarily savings institutions. In 1986 some major Wall Street brokers, including Merrill Lynch, Prudential-Bache, and Shearson Lehman, started offering CMOs in $1,000 denominations. That was a substantial drop from the $25,000 previous minimum size. Although most firms that sold CMOs at first sold individual investors only the long-term classes, Shearson has offered them with maturities as low as five years.

When you buy a CMO in the secondary market, your broker will tack on a commission. When you buy a new issue, the sales fee is factored into the selling price. The brokerage firm is making money on the spread between its buy and sell price for the bonds.

Investment Potential

CMOs offer the same benefits of pass-through certificates. They pay high yields (about 2% over comparable Treasury issues) with high safety. The pass-throughs that form the basis for most CMOs are backed by a government agency such as the Government National Mortgage Association or the Federal National Mortgage Association.

Virtually all CMOs are rated AAA. However, keep in mind that you do not own the underlying pass-throughs directly. They are owned by the subsidiary company that the CMO packager set up to buy the pass-

throughs. That additional layer is one of the reasons the yield is higher than Treasury issues.

Look At This:

Be sure to check out the details of any CMO offering. Although most are backed by government agencies, Citicorp made a CMO offering of home mortgages without the government agency conduit. The offering carried a limited guarantee from Citicorp. It was rated AA rather then the AAA rating that most CMOs carry. The Citicorp offering featured two maturity classes. The long-term class had an average estimated life of 5.8 years. That short maturity also contributes to greater safety.

It is possible to borrow against CMOs with most brokerage firms. Because they are rated so highly, they can be highly leveraged. That is not a practical or safe strategy for most individual investors.

CMOs have not eliminated the problem of reinvestment risk. Unlike corporate bonds, which offer precise maturities or call dates, the life span of CMOs still ultimately depends on the actions of the individual mortgagees. You should clarify with your broker the stated maturity date—i.e., when your bond will be redeemed if there are no prepayments. Secondly, find out the estimated life of the CMO if morgages are paid off early.

The typical CMO prospectus will refer to the "average weighted life" of the portfolio of mortgage issues. If the average weighted life is 16.5 years, it means that at some time between 14 and 17 years you will start to receive a return of your principal. Unfortunately, even then you cannot count on specific amounts. And remember, the "average weighted life" is just an estimate. There is no guarantee. If interest drops precipitously you should expect to get heavier prepayments sooner.

CMOs offer income- and safety-oriented investors a better vehicle for obtaining higher returns than paid by Treasury issues with only moderately higher risk to principal. Although CMOs offer some protection against reinvestment risk (having to reinvest money at lower interest rates than you had anticipated) there are no guarantees.

At present, few mutual funds invest in

CMOs. However, as this attractive market expands in the near future, there will be more.

Some issues that received good response when first sold include Merrill Lynch's ML Trust XI, Shearson's Ryan Series 19-A CMO, and Pru-Bache's Oxford CMO Trust I. Ask your broker for details on upcoming new issues and performance data on older issues.

CMO's investors face two main risks: market risk from rising interest rates and reinvestment risk. Rising interest rates will depress the value of the CMO.

Falling interest rates will encourage mortgage holders to refinance their mortgages at lower rates. CMO's investors have an additional level of protection over straight passthrough buyers here. Whereas Ginnie Mae investors are never sure where they stand in regard to payoff of mortgages in their pool, a CMO investor knows from the class of CMO purchased the likelihood of early payoff.

An additional risk from falling interest rates is similar to what happened to the passthrough market in 1986. The pass-throughs underperformed other bond types because of the fear of prepayments. However, that overhanging fear is liable to affect the CMO market less than the pass-through market. What this means is that if you are speculating on interest rates rather than looking for income, you should stick with Treasury or corporate issues. CMOs are best suited for income-oriented investors rather than for traders.

Like all fixed-income securities, CMOs offer little inflation protection. Some advisors argue that since inflation will enhance the value of the homes collateralizing the mortgages they will be more secure. However, the price of CMOs themselves will fall as inflation rises because interest rates will also climb.

Strengths

CMOs offer high yields, often as much as 2% higher than comparable Treasury issues. They are very secure, typically backed by passthroughs issued by government agencies. They offer some protection from early prepayments. They offer a variety of maturities.

Weaknesses

CMOs do not offer precise maturity dates. Hence investors may be saddled with a reinvestment problem at the worst possible time—when interest rates are falling. They are subject to price declines if interest rates rise. CMOs are still very new, and liquidity may be a problem for a few years. CMOs do not have an established track record, so it is difficult to tell how they may react in different economic environments. Like other fixed-income instruments, CMOs are subject to the increased volatility as interest rate volatility increases.

Tax Considerations

Tax Consequences

There are no special tax advantages to CMOs. Interest and capital gains are taxed at ordinary income rates. Capital losses may be used to offset capital gains.

Summing Up

CMOs have already cut into the corporate bond market. Many analysts see them as a growing threat to corporate bonds because of their high yields and high safety.

They are appropriate vehicles for income- and safety-oriented investors. Like other bonds, the best strategy with CMOs is to buy a diversified portfolio—diversified both in issuers and in maturities.

CMOs are destined to become a major player in the fixed-income world. Their relative newness and complexity mean that yields offered by CMOs in the early 1990s will probably be higher relative to Treasury issues than in later years when investors are more familiar with them.

The market for CMOs is growing rapidly. Since their initial offering in 1983 they have grown to more than $110 billion.

Notes

CHAPTER 14

REAL ESTATE

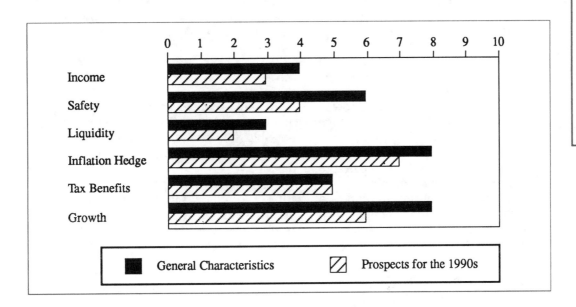

Legend:
- ■ General Characteristics
- ▨ Prospects for the 1990s

Categories rated 0–10: Income, Safety, Liquidity, Inflation Hedge, Tax Benefits, Growth

Outlook for the 1990s

- Tempered growth for metropolitan residential property

- Office space still a glut in many areas

- Fewer tax benefits

- Rising inflation a plus

- Recession would hurt prices

A GLANCE AHEAD

Real estate represents a secure, solid, conservative investment for most Americans. Although its fortunes have fluctuated over the years, the long-term trend in prices has been up. And unlike the stock, bond, or gold markets, periods of price weakness in real estate are not cause for concern, because there are always some geographical areas that seem to buck the trend.

This perception of real estate as a bastion of value is at least partially due to the fact that there is no central auction market where prices are set daily. Each piece of real estate is unique. When you want to sell a share of IBM, you know what price you can get today. When you go to sell your house or another piece of real estate, the selling *price is not so sure. Even after getting a professional appraisal, there may be no one who wants to buy at the adjudged "fair price."*

In this chapter, you'll discover the many types of real estate and the many ways you can invest in them. You'll learn

- *How the 1986 Tax Reform Act has changed real estate limited partnerships*
- *What a real estate investment trust (REIT) is*
- *Why you should treat your home as an investment*
- *The pros and cons of owning rental property*
- *The varying degrees of liquidity offered by different types of real estate investments.*

REAL ESTATE IS
A LONG-TERM INVESTMENT

The advertising slogan "Buy land—they're not making any more of it" sums up the "can't lose" attitude that many real estate investors had in the 1970s. But as happens with all "perfect" investments at some point, the early 1980s proved that even real estate is subject to sharp downdrafts.

Analysts have identified a number of cycles in real estate. The most widely accepted one is the 18-year cycle. That cycle peaked in 1979; the ideal trough would be in 1988. Unfortunately there were few concrete signs that real estate was bottoming by late 1990. Major banks in the Northeast, formerly a real estate "hotbed," were busily writing down massive losses in their real estate loan portfolios. Even California, the last holdout to a slumping real estate market, showed signs of price fatigue by 1990. Orange County, home of the seemingly perpetual price increase, saw new home sales plummet 18% in the 2nd quarter of 1990 compared to the same period 12 months earlier. At the same time the inventory of unsold homes in the county rose to an 18 month high. Keep in mind, these developments occurred in the strongest market in the country.

Real estate affords investors the luxury of not having to face reality when prices are down. Individuals and even institutional investors are able to delude themselves far after prices have begun to fall. The S&L fiasco is a good case in point. Many S&Ls were allowed to plunge ahead losing millions of what ultimately was taxpayers money because their balance sheets carried real estate at grossly inflated values.

The high vacancy rates in metropolitan areas around the country have been dismissed by many analysts in recent years simply because they've been that way for 4 or 5 years. Yet if you take the time to look at the historical record, Texas exhibited high vacancy rates as early as 1983 but banks did not actually mark properties down to their real value until 1985-6. Of course, massive bank and S&L failures followed shortly thereafter.

Consumers typically read about real estate prices published by the National Association of Realtors. Not surprisingly their data is strongly biased toward rising prices. For example, NAR data showed that median home prices jumped 8.9% in 1981-82 at a time when many builders were forced to auction off homes in projects at discounts of 30% or more. That NAR reported that median home prices in Dallas from 1985 to 1986 was $90,000, but increased to $94,500 by 1987. Yet the oil and real estate depression that struck Dallas and Texas at that time drove home prices down as much as 20% to 30%! Because managers in real estate don't have to compare their performance to an easily watched barometer (such as the S&P to which stock managers are held accountable), it has been far too easy to ignore blithely what was really happening to prices.

Risks

Most real estate investments suffer from liquidity problems. While certainly not impossible, it is rare to be able to sell a piece of real estate and get your cash out in only a day or two.

Also, real estate investments are more subject to regional influences than are many other types of investment. For example, from 1984 through 1986 oil prices collapsed, devastating many heretofore rapid growth metropolitan areas such as Dallas and Houston. The situation got so bad in Houston that thousands of apartment units were actually plowed under! Oil companies in the area were also hurt, but many had already diversified into other businesses, which helped stem stock price falls.

Real estate is very sensitive to "real" interest rates. The real rate is the nominal rate (the published or announced rate minus the rate of inflation). Higher real rates depress real estate prices. It is important to note the significance of the distinction between real and nominal rates. In the late 1970s, nominal rates went well into double digits. Real estate continued to boom right along, however, because the inflation rate was rising faster than the nominal rate. Only when the real rate moved higher did real estate finally peak.

Whether you own residential, commercial, or industrial real estate, you're subject to the whims of the political process. The U.S. Supreme Court moved to protect private landowners' rights in a number of landmark decisions in 1987, but you still run considerable risk of loss through arbitrary rezoning. In some parts of the country, anti-development groups have forced building moratoriums that devastated property values for years.

Independent Ratings

Any real estate purchased by mortgage loans is appraised by an independent source before the bank will make the loan. The bank wants to ensure that it has sufficient collateral in the property. It is a good idea to have any property appraised before entering any binding purchase agreement. You may lose your deposit if you haven't protected yourself in advance.

Compared to Other Assets

Money magazine published the results of a study showing that stocks and bonds are top-performing assets when inflation is 4% or less. Not surprisingly, gold is the best performer in double-digit inflation. Real estate also outperforms financial assets during very high inflation, but really shines during moderate inflation of 7% to 9%.

THE OUTLOOK FOR REAL ESTATE IN THE 1990s

The fortunes of real estate, unlike other asset classes, varies greatly depending on a number of factors unique to each type. For example, shopping malls have been the top performers for commercial real estate investors for the last five years. However, if you invested in shopping malls in areas such as Houston or Dallas, the depressed local economy hurt even this type of property.

But just as some stock investors do better in down than up markets, some real estate speculators are able to profit in almost any environment. A case in point is Weingarten Realty, a REIT with 67% of its portfolio invested in the Houston area. This would have been a disaster for most companies but Weingarten's conservative non-leveraged

approach proves that even in the worst of markets there are opportunities. Their strip centers have a 94% occupancy rate, compared with 70% for most Houston strip shopping centers.

The safest property investment in recent years has been single-family homes. In almost all areas of the country (again with the exception of the "oil patch" states), single-family home values have climbed steadily. Some areas have experienced dramatic growth. For example, the East Coast metropolitan areas, particularly Boston and New York, experienced above-average increases until the stock market crash of October 1987. Since then the financial services industry has cut back employment hurting the booming Boston-New York real estate corridor. Over 22,000 jobs have been lost in Boston with an additional 40,000 financial services positions being eliminated in New York. New York city's high taxes and other urban problems has also driven major employers such as J. C. Penney, Mobil Oil, and Exxon out of the city. Even in California real estate prices have begun to moderate. With the average home in the San Francisco and Los Angeles areas selling for six times the median family income in those areas, prices still have a way to go to bring prices in line with the national average of 3 times.

Once you move beyond the single-family home, though, there is an even wider disparity in fortunes. Office buildings have been overbuilt in almost every part of the country. The national office vacancy rate by 1990 hovered near 16% increasing slightly from 1986 levels. This compares to a 9% rate for midtown office buildings for the early 1980s. As long as supply exceeds demand, rents will be under pressure. It is not impossible to find commercial deals that offer a fair return, but that is the exception, not the rule.

Many analysts point to the slowing building rate for new office space as evidence of a bottoming of the commercial real estate market. Supply of new office space in 1988 only grew 90 million square feet. That compares to 120 million square feet in 1987 and 150 million square feet in 1986. However the shrinking job market in key areas such as New York city has left many large office buildings virtually empty by late 1990. For example, a new 50-story building at 712 Fifth Ave. owned by Salomon, Inc. and Taubman Co. had filled only 10% of the space by late 1990. Carnegie Tower next to Carnegie Hall had similar problems leasing space.

The slowdown in new construction is most evident in suburban markets where vacancy rates are still over 20% in many locales. Many downtown building projects have been delayed or canceled, due to poor demand.

However, investing here will require careful selection of areas. Manhattan has traditionally been one of the strongest commercial real estate markets in the world. However, the stock market crash is still reverberating throughout the financial services industry. In 1988 through 1990, rents showed signs of weakness. Vacancy rates actually went over 15% for the first time in years.

Other major metropolitan areas may also be hurt by the retrenchment in the financial services industry. Boston has also experienced rising vacancy rates and even residential prices rises are slowing. In late 1989 Bank of New England announced that it would increase reserves to more than $1 billion as a result of potential losses on New England real estate. In 1990 other Northeastern banks joined Bank of New England in setting aside large reserves for potential loan losses. Midlantic Corp. upped loan loss reserves $75 million. Dime Savings of New York and Citytrust Bankcorp also announced substantial increases in loan loss reserves.

In the West, Los Angeles holds itself out as the major financial center of the West and Pacific Rim. If the economies in these countries falter, problems could arise for office building as demand falls off. The key for many markets is Japanese investors. They have been very active in the San Francisco and Honolulu markets.

By late 1989 the U.S. dollar slumped badly. The weak dollar (by July 1990 it was nearing historic lows against the D-Mark) was largely due to rising interest rates in foreign countries. While foreign investors continued to be aggressive buyers, real estate prices softened in most parts of the country.

Surging exports, though, bode well for industrial property. Formerly depressed land in the "Steel Belt" (or "Rust Belt," as pessimists sneer), bounded back from the depths reached in 1984-5. However by 1990 prices here also quit rising.

Another beneficiary of the export boom will be warehouse and distribution space. Major international trade- and domestic distribution-oriented markets include Miami, Jacksonville (Florida), New York, Chicago, Dallas (and it needs the help!), Memphis, Los Angeles, and Portland.

Raw land (or "predevelopment property," as syndicators prefer to call it) will prosper in those areas of the country experiencing good population growth. These markets include New Jersey, Florida, Atlanta, Seattle, as well as traditional growth areas in California, Arizona, and Florida.

What to Expect

The key variable in real estate's prospects will be the state of the economy. The stock market crash actually boosted real estate's fortunes by illustrating the need for diversification. Many institutional investors began to nibble at real estate projects as a hedge against the volatile financial markets.

A recession would be catastrophic for real estate in general. A slowdown in industrial production would knock the supports from under the strongest commercial sector of the market—industrial space. A slowdown in job growth would crush the already shaky office market.

As this is being written in mid-1990, the economy is slowing, with GNP growing at under a 2% annual rate. Unemployment has started to rise above 5%. Industrial production has slumped despite export growth. Consumer spending also turned down as employment prospects slumped and consumer confidence turned down following the market crash.

The economy appears headed for either a "soft landing" (slow GNP growth of 1%-2%) or a recession (actual negative growth). If inflation does not pick up, and it doesn't look likely at this juncture, real estate price increases will moderate. Real estate is a prime beneficiary of inflation.

Barring an economic collapse, real estate should continue to be a steady, if not sterling, perfomer during the 1990s. However, it is more important than ever to be selective about what you buy. Be conservative with your financing. Highly leveraged deals can look very appealing when everything is working perfectly. But if problems arise, the leveraged house of cards can collapse quickly.

For most real estate investments, it is critical that you take a long-term perspective. The hottest real estate region is California where the median price of homes is over $170,000! In some areas that median has broken the $200,000 barrier. Be very cautious in such "hot markets." For years the Northeast was very hot but now prices are weaker. After peaking in 1988 median home prices dropped 10-15% in New York by late 1990. Real estate will be under pressure for much of the 1990s. More than at any time in recent history, it will be critical to buy selectively. Areas of the country which have experienced sharp price runups represent the greatest risk

For those investors with patience and sufficient capital to be able to hold out through tough times, the depressed real estate prices in the oil patch states represent excellent long-term value. But as always, you should spread your risk over different types of real estate as well as different geographical areas.

Lasser's Recommended Allocation Range for 1990s Real Estate

Allocate as much as 25%.

Allocate as little as 10%.

Notes

_____

_____

_____

_____

_____

_____

_____

_____

_____

_____

_____

_____

Rental Real Estate

The most common type of real estate investment, other than your private residence, is the purchase of developed property to generate income through rentals. Such rentals can be either single- or multiple-family residences, office buildings, or even industrial property.

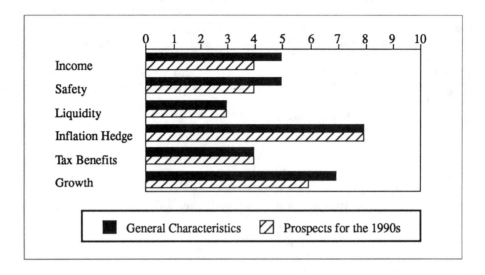

Historically, real estate has been valued for the cash flow returns that can be achieved. The fundamental value of any given real estate project was considered a function of the cash flow that could be earned from rentals. This conservative valuation approach was lost in the high-flying inflation of the 1970s. Rather than carefully assess the future value of cash flows, investors bid prices steadily higher, betting that prices would continue to rise. By the late 1970s, most real estate deals offered negative cash flows for years into the future. The idea was that appreciation of the property combined with preferential tax treatment featuring substantial writeoffs against your ordinary income would yield above-average returns. To their chagrin, many smaller investors discovered

that nothing, not even real estate, goes straight up in price.

When land prices began to flatten out and even fall after 1980, mortgage defaults rose to record highs. No longer did it seem like such a great idea to buy a rental property in which the rents did not even cover the costs of the mortgage.

This mania to buy at any price was largely "tax driven." The limited partnership industry before 1986 was based on passing through the great tax benefits to individual investors. You could write off unlimited interest expenses and negative cash flows, and accelerate depreciation to offset other income. Far too many investors focused on the tax benefits rather than on the economic value of the properties.

Tax law changes, beginning in 1984 and culminating in the major 1986 reform, curtailed these tax advantages while encouraging income and growth investing through lower tax rates. Real estate is once again being marketed to investors for solid funda-

A
High Taxes
High Expenses

B
High Taxes
Low Expenses

Type I

A
High Taxes
High Expenses

B
High Taxes
Low Expenses

Type II

mental economic reasons.

The massive overbuilding that accompanied the real estate mania of the late 1970s has left some types of real estate, such as office buildings, severely depressed. However, some undervalued, conservatively financed projects are now being marketed. In fact, the limited partnership industry has turned from tax shelter selling to emphasizing positive cash flows and conservative financing. Income-producing real estate is widely marketed by the industry. Your real estate agent or full-service broker can provide plenty of information on current deals. A commission is charged for handling the transaction. This fee can be substantial. If you are a regular customer or large investor, the fee is usually negotiable.

Investment Potential

Investing in income-producing real estate is a long-term project. Capitalization rates comparable to the yields offered by competitive income-producing investments are available if you are patient and willing to search out undervalued situations.

Real estate prices tend to be less volatile than more liquid markets such as bonds or stocks. You can use leverage in buying real estate to just about any level that is comfortable for you. Keep in mind, though, that the new tax law limits the amount of interest that can be deducted. The more highly leveraged the deal, the greater the risk.

Income-producing real estate is illiquid. Occasionally you'll be able to find a buyer in a matter of days, but it is not unusual for properties to remain on the market for months before a buyer is found.

Many different types of income-producing properties are available. Most individual investors concentrate on rental housing, but commercial properties such as shopping centers, or industrial sites can also offer good income.

Capital growth in real estate has been much less dynamic in the 1980s than the 1970s. Over the long term, however, real estate has historically proven an excellent vehicle for growth. It is an excellent inflation hedge.

Strengths

Rental real estate can provide good current income. It offers good capital growth potential. Prices tend to be less volatile than in auction markets such as bonds or stocks. In addition, the wide variety of rental projects offers great flexibility in finding one that fits your financial needs and risk tolerance. Finally, you can leverage your real estate investment. Real estate is an excellent inflation hedge.

Weaknesses

Rental real estate does have weaknesses. It is illiquid. Rental real estate investors are subject to political risks such as the imposition of rent controls, zoning changes, or tax increases. Finally, being a landlord can be costly and time consuming.

Tax Considerations

Tax Consequences

A major goal of the 1986 Tax Reform Act was to return real estate investment decisions to considerations of economic value rather than tax avoidance. If you actively manage your property (as opposed to buying it through limited partnerships or other arrangements), there are still some tax advantages. For example, an active participant in the his or her real estate rental properties can deduct up to

Professional Advice

$25,000 in losses from other income. This amount diminishes, however, if your annual income is above $100,000. The tax law is complex in this area. You should consult with your tax advisor for full details for your particular situation.

Summing Up

Over the long term, the return to value-driven real estate investing will provide a safer, less risky market for investors. The declining interest rates of the last six years have helped boost real estate prices. However, the heady days of buying virtually anything and making huge profits in a matter of months are gone. Tax law changes, strong financial markets, and the still very depressed state of many real estate syndicators have put a cap on the unrealistic real estate speculative euphoria of the 1970s.

Carefully researched, conservatively financed, positive cash flow projects should appreciate in value as well as pay competitive current income.

Notes

Raw Land Real Estate

Investing in raw, undeveloped land received a boost from the 1986 Tax Reform Act. Now national syndicators are putting together partnerships to buy undervalued land that may be ripe for commercial development in the near future. The very fact that raw land is often the least expensive way to buy real estate has triggered increased interest among individual investors.

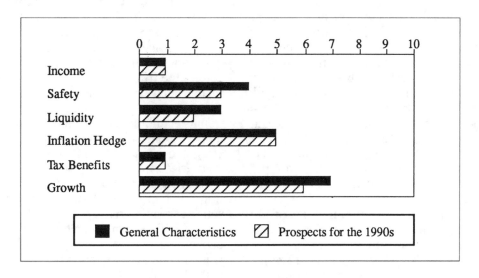

General Characteristics ■   Prospects for the 1990s ▨

B
High Taxes
Low Expenses

D
Low Taxes
Low Expenses

Type II

B
High Taxes
Low Expenses

D
Low Taxes
Low Expenses

Type I

Look At This:

For many years real estate appeared to many investors to be the perfect investment, no downside risk. Then the boom of the 1970s gave way to the reality of the 1980s. Real estate values, which had climbed steadily for years, suddenly plummeted across the country. High interest rates, disinflation, and illiquidity combined to take the bloom off. After the passage of the 1986 Tax Reform Act, many pundits predicted further weakness.

Few areas came in for more pessimistic assessment than raw land. In the high-flying 1970s, everything seemed a good investment. Investors bought land in Hawaii sight unseen. Only later did they learn that large patches of barren lava were not very good investments. Thousands of investors still own acres of California desert or Florida swampland that had been marketed as future vacation spots.

Raw land has typically been the domain of developers. They bought prospective land sites and set them aside ("bank them") until they could move ahead with their projects. The high interest rates of the 1970s made this approach very expensive.

Developers then approached syndicators to package raw land and sell it to individual investors, as a method for "banking it" for later use. However, before 1986 no improvements could be made on the land after it was purchased or investors would lose the favorable capital gains tax treatment. They could only wait for the price to move up through inflation or until demand from expanding communities pushed the price higher.

Paradoxically, the elimination of preferential tax treatment for capital gains has generated renewed interest in raw land investing. Now syndicators buy raw land and sell it to investors with the prospect that improvements will be made to increase its value more quickly. Rather than waiting for the market to come to them, syndicators work to increase the land value through subdividing it, bringing in utilities, building access roads, and arranging building permits with local governments. The raw land is thus converted into made-to-order residential, industrial, or commercial sites.

Syndication deals are typically local arrangements financed and developed by companies and individuals with contacts and knowledge in the area. Recently, though, some large syndicators have begun putting together deals that are marketed nationally through real estate brokers and investment advisors. These national arrangements generally require smaller investments, from as little as $1,000 to $10,000 to participate. Some full-service brokerage houses are preparing to launch their own programs in the near future.

There is a relatively small number of limited partnership programs available to the general public. Only three years ago, there were none. Most syndicators emphasize that their programs are for "predevelopment," not raw land. Most properties in these offerings are located near highways, close to other developments, and near growing cities. Three favored geographical areas are Florida, Arizona, and the Chapel Hill, North Carolina, area.

Most raw or predevelopment land programs are designed to achieve good returns in short time spans, sometimes as short as two or three years. Most advisors suggest that raw land investors seek out deals that expect to liquidate within five years. Unlike income-generating limited partnerships, raw land deals have no cash flow to support them over downturns.

Check with your local real estate agent or your broker to find out about specific deals in your area. Commissions are normally assessed to pay the salespeople. Local real estate agents are the best source of price information on respective properties.

Investment Potential

Raw land is a long-term investment. Even the new syndication deals suggest you plan on a minimum holding period of five to seven years. If the economy slows down or local regulations change, that wait could be much longer.

Raw land offers the opportunity for capital gains. Normally it pays no income. In fact, because you usually put down only a fraction of the purchase price, there is a cash outflow for interest payments until the property is sold. This leverage adds to the potential return and to the potential risk.

Land prices are not quoted in an active daily auction market so it is difficult to ascertain the true price in the short term. Many factors can affect the desirability of the property in any one area. The general national economy, local economic developments, political events (zoning changes, etc.), and pending tax law changes all affect land prices.

Real estate, and especially raw land, is an illiquid investment. It may take months to sell even attractive parcels. Raw land is more flexible than other types of real estate because it can be put to a variety of uses, from residential to industrial and commercial, depending on demand and legal environment.

You can obtain an independent appraisal of the value of any property by hiring a professional real estate appraiser. However, getting an appraised value does not necessarily ensure finding a buyer at that price.

Most syndications must be registered either with the state in which the project is being sold, or with the SEC for interstate projects. A prospectus is usually available for review prior to investing.

Be sure to read the prospectus carefully. The fees for partnership programs can be quite high. For example, on the eight public programs available in June 1988, syndication fees and other expenses total almost 18% of your investment. That means only 82% of your funds were going into the actual purchase of the land.

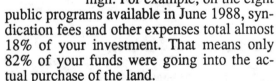
Look At This:

You should also check your liability for future payments. If the partnership is unable to sell its property over the short term, it may make additional assessments from the partners to pay such things as interest payments, property taxes, and insurance.

One danger of private placement offerings is that you may not even know what property is going to be purchased with your money. These "blind pool" arrangements are particulary risky if you are not familiar with the general partner.

Strengths

Raw land offers substantial capital growth potential. You can leverage your investment. Mortgage interest rates are usually lower than other types of loans.

Weaknesses

Raw land has some weaknesses. First, it is illiquid. It is also subject to political vagaries. For example, the land could be rezoned to much less lucrative uses after your purchase. Moreover, investment in syndications risks poor judgment by the syndicator. And it may take years for the project to become economically viable.

Tax Considerations

Tax Consequences

No special tax benefits apply to raw land investments. Capital gains are taxed at your ordinary income rates. Limited partnership raw land invest-ments generate passive income or losses that offset other passive income or losses.

Summing Up

Many people are boosting the investment potential of raw land. But many of the same people were behind the "vacation home in a resort area" boomlet that cost many investors thousands. Keep in mind that developers and salespeople put the best face on the potential for their projects. And even the best-sounding project may get entangled in legal proceedings (permits, etc.) for years before getting off the ground.

Raw land is the riskiest type of real estate investment. There is little downside protection if anticipated growth does not develop in the region of the project. Liquidity is always a problem.

Now that preferential tax treatment for capital gains have been eliminated, raw land is attracting more interest. You're no longer stuck with the dilemma of having to give up preferential tax treatment if improvements are made. Sometimes even minor improvements can significantly enhance a property's value.

Residential Real Estate

The largest and most important purchase in the lives of most people is their home. In years past, such purchases were not thought of as an investment as much as just a secure place to live. However, times are changing. High inflation and the resultant explosion in real estate prices propelled many people's homes into becoming the major asset of their personal wealth.

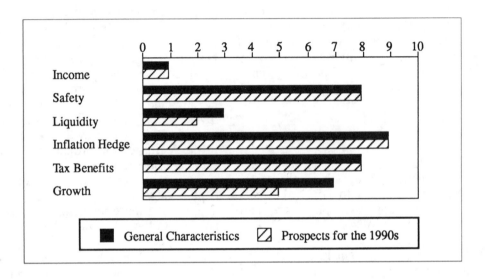

A
High Taxes
High Expenses

B
High Taxes
Low Expenses

Because consumer interest is no longer deductible, home equity loans are becoming a major force in consumer spending habits.

If you own your home and have sufficient equity in it, you can borrow at far lower interest rates than you pay for credit card and personal loans. You can then use that money to pay off those loans. The interest on your equity loan is also tax deductible, giving you a double benefit as a homeowner.

Home equity loans are growing faster than other types of consumer debt. As of the end of 1987, homeowners owed $80 billion on their home equity loans. That seems small compared to the $619.6 billion in other types of consumer debt. However, the figures show that equity loans are the fastest-growing area of new credit. Home equity debt grew $45 billion in 1987 compared to a $34 billion increase in other forms of consu-

mer credit and continues to grow rapidly.

Most surprising is that this debt expansion represents only 5% of homeowners. Those who have opened home equity lines of credit were using only about 35% of their credit lines by the end of the 1987.

Many investment "gurus" got their start with purchases of their own homes. As the price of their house rose, they were able to parlay the additional equity into other investments. Unfortunately, some of the gurus proved better at selling advice than investing. A number of the "no money down, buy highly leveraged real estate" advisors were pushed into bankruptcy, including Albert Lowry, author of the best-selling book *How You Can Become Financially Independent by Investing in Real Estate.*

Most financial advisors quantify all investment returns in terms of capital gains and yields. But home ownership affords an emotional profit to many people that is more important than all the economic benefits!

Home ownership affords a sense of security, a fixed known monthly payment (unless your mortgage has an adjustable interest rate), and an opportunity to increase its value and your potential profit through your efforts.

Home ownership gives you a way to begin to accumulate wealth at an early stage in your life. The demand for housing is increasing as the "baby boomers" become adults and start their own families.

The supply of housing is not growing as fast, because government red tape and other factors are slowing growth.

The pace of housing starts was so slow by June 1990 that starts were at the lowest level since the bottom of the last recession in 1982. Only 1.17 million units were contracted in 1982, with projections pointing to a meager 1.21 million units for 1990.

Some doomsayers think that the overheated real estate markets in California and the Northeast are due for a sharp fall due to demographic changes taking place in the 1990s. The number of people aged 25-34 (most likely to form new households) will fall over seven million in the 1990s.

On the plus side, at least for those who already own a home, is that rising prices are considered only one of the main culprits in the slowdown in starts. The median price for a new single-family home in the United States in May 1989 was $91,600. That's up up 3.4% in the first three months of 1989. There has been little appreciation since then.

The housing market is very flexible. There are numerous financing options; different types of housing, from single-family homes to condominiums to cooperatives; and a wide range of prices, depending on location. Although you have no guarantee that residential real estate prices will continue to move higher, ownership itself conveys certain advantages that don't show up on your financial balance sheet.

For example, many banks consider home ownership a sign of stability and are more

Professional Advice

likely to make consumer loans or approve credit card applications.

Although you can buy a home yourself, the complex laws of different localities make it far more prudent to go through a licensed real estate agent. There will be a commission charge. The fee is often negotiable. Using an agent will prevent unpleasant, time-consuming, and costly problems that may crop up later over incorrectly completed paperwork.

Investment Potential

Home ownership is a long-term proposition. Your first objective should be securing comfortable, convenient living quarters. That goal does not conflict with the chance for long-term capital growth. Buying a home in a growing, dynamic community affords a good opportunity for future growth.

Every community is different. Some areas are declining for various reasons. Others, which may be just as convenient, may be attracting people.

Your real estate agent should be able to tell you about growth patterns in the locales that are of interest.

Residential home prices are not usually volatile. The expenses involved in buying a home make short-term investing impractical. Also, residential real estate suffers the same liquidity problems that investment real estate has. You simply cannot be assured of a quick sale at market prices.

In virtually all economic environments, homes have been a very good store of value. They have become one of the very best inflation hedges.

Strengths

Residential real estate offers secure long-term capital growth potential, and fulfills one of the basic requirements of life: shelter. Moreover, the interest on home equity loans is still tax deductible. Your ability to borrow against your home equity affords great flexibility for undertaking other investments. And residential real estate is an excellent inflation hedge.

Chapter 20, "Your Home as an Investment," gives more information about buying, selling, and maintaining the value of your home.

Weaknesses

Residential real estate is illiquid. In addition, you are subject to substantial economic risk if your area is rezoned. Other uncontrollable events such as a declining local economy may also hurt prices. If a major employer, for example, moves out, property values may be hurt.

Tax Considerations

Tax Consequences

The 1986 Tax Reform Act confirmed the importance of home ownership in the United States. Although many deductions were eliminated, home ownership maintained the deductibility of mortgage interest and property taxes. You can avoid taxes on capital gains by reinvesting in a home of equal or greater worth. If you are over age 55, you are eligible for a one-time exemption for the profits realized on the sale of your principal residence. Home ownership itself is a valuable retirement vehicle. You cannot buy a home through retirement plans, however.

Summing Up

There is little likelihood that the American dream of home ownership will fade. Although there are no guarantees of future performance, home ownership should continue to provide an excellent store of value for most people.

There is a surprisingly wide disparity in real estate appreciation around the country. Prices in New England suffered weakness in 1989-90. Prices in Boston for single family residences declined almost 3%. The average time it takes to sell a house lengthened from 46 days to 84 days. New York and Philadelphia experienced similar price weakness. In the Midwest prices remained stable. In Chicago the average time to sell a home lengthened from a few weeks to a couple of months. In the South, most metropolitan areas are buyers markets as 1990 comes to a close. In the West, Arizona real estate prices continue to weaken due to massive overbuilding. Even the hot California market showed signs of cooling off as the average time to sell lengthened considerably.

Real Estate Investment Trusts (REITs)

The beneficial tax treatment of home ownership will enhance the attractiveness of real estate investment trusts (REITs). REITs are companies that pool investor money to invest in real estate properties or loans. They are required to pay out 95% of their income received to shareholders as dividends. REITs resemble mutual funds as they invest in a diversified portfolio and distribute income to shareholders as dividends. Their structure is similar to closed-end funds because they do not stand ready to redeem shares at net asset value.

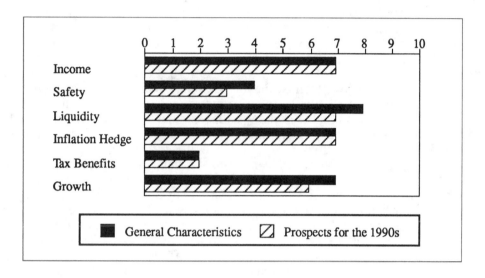

Investing in real estate presents two main problems for the average investor: illiquidity and the need for substantial capital for most multifamily or commercial properties. Wall Street's answer to these problems is the real estate investment trust (REIT).

Prices of REITs fluctuate like common stocks. They are determined by the free play of supply and demand, not by the trust's net asset value. Many investors consider this a key favorable attribute, because it is possible to buy REITs at a discount to the value of the underlying portfolio of properties.

C Low Taxes High Expenses

D Low Taxes Low Expenses

Type II

C Low Taxes High Expenses

D Low Taxes Low Expenses

Type I

REITs were very popular in the late 1960s and early 1970s as real estate rose in price. Many REITs were bid up in price to multiples that were unrealistic, in retrospect. REITs were viewed as a hedge against inflation. However, in the recession of 1973–1974, REITs joined many other stocks as prices dropped sharply. Some REITs were unable to weather the storm and went into bankruptcy. The severe shakeout in REITs has taken years to overcome, though they are once again being included in the portfolios of major institutions.

Although most REITs operate indefinitely, reinvesting proceeds from one liquidated project into another, "self-liquidating" REITs have a finite life. Typically they are structured to liquidate all properties in seven to 10 years (or earlier, at the discretion of the management) and to distribute the proceeds to shareholders.

REITs are purchased through licensed stock brokerage firms. Many full-service firms have analysts who specialize in the field and provide regular research updates. A commission is charged for handling the transaction.

Investment Potential

REITs invest either directly in real estate properties (equity) or in mortgages. Some specialize in one or the other, while others divide their portfolios between the two types. REITs that invest solely in loans pay higher dividend yields. Those invested primarily in real estate equity offer greater capital growth potential.

Since REITs are liquid investments, they can be long- or short-term. Keep in mind that short-term trading incurs higher transaction costs, which will affect your return. Also, the underlying asset, real estate, typically takes time to realize its full investment potential.

REITs have had a very volatile history. During periods of inflation, they tend to outperform the market as a whole, providing a good hedge. However, volatile interest rates and the economy can cause wide price swings. The high dividend yields offer some downside protection. Those yields, though, depend on the stability of the underlying portfolio. Defaults in the portfolio can deal you a double whammy, because the income drops as well as the price of the REIT.

REITs offer you good flexibility in choosing the type of real estate to invest in. For example, different REITs tend to specialize in different types of real estate. If you are interested in commercial real estate, look to those REITs that concentrate in that area. Others specialize in industrial properties, multifamily rental dwellings, or even geographical areas.

Among mortgage REITs, there are a number of well-known company sponsors. Some of the more actively traded issues include L&N Mortgage, MONY Real Estate, and Wells Fargo Mortgage.

The ratio of mortgage to equity REITs was once 60 to 40. That ratio has reversed. More equity REITs are available now. And some of the previous mortgage REITs are now converting to equity. Rockefeller Center Properties has targeted the year 2000 to convert to equity REITs.

Equity REITs specialize in many different types of real estate. For example, Meditrust and Healthvest are two successful REITs that concentrate on nursing homes, retirement centers, and other health care facilities. Healthvest also invests in the mortgages of health care properties.

Federal Realty Investment Corporation concentrates on rehabilitating shopping centers in the Mid-Atlantic states. First Union Real Estate Investments has an enviable record for anticipating trends. It began selling out of office buildings in the late 1970s, when vacancy rates were bottoming. Now about 70% of its properties are in enclosed shopping malls. That has been real estate's hottest area over the last five years. Beverly Investment Properties is sponsored by Beverly Enterprises, the largest nursing home operator in the country. It owns over a hundred nursing home properties.

Weingarten Realty concentrates on large shopping centers anchored by big tenants in depressed Texas and Louisiana markets. This strategy depends on an oil patch economic recovery. Washington REIT uses very little leverage in buying its properties. It owns residential, office, and commercial space in the Washington, D.C. area. Such space has been one of the strongest real estate markets for the past few years.

These are just a few examples of the diversity available in REITs. Your stockbroker can give you additional information on any of these or other REITs.

Some mutual funds invest in REITs such as Fidelity Real Estate Investment Portfolio (800) 544-6666 and National Real Estate Stock Fund (800) 223-7757. Fidelity has a 2% load, and National assesses a 7.5% load fee.

All REITs must register with the SEC and provide annual financial reports. Most full-service brokerage firms provide research opinions on the prospects for individual REITs, but no widely accepted service rates their financial condition.

It is important to remember that when you buy an REIT you are not making a direct investment in real estate. You are buying real estate investment expertise, in the form of the company's management. Therefore, even if real estate in general is appreciating, poor management could limit your profits. However, good management can provide protection when the market is falling.

Strengths

REITs provide a liquid method for investing in real estate. The minimum required investment is small, and dividend income is high. REITs give you a diversified real estate portfolio that minimizes the risk from any one property. And REITs are not required to pay corporate taxes. Therefore, you avoid double taxation of dividends. Finally, REITs provide a good hedge against inflation.

Weaknesses

The management of REITs may be poor or inefficient, hurting your profit potential. A poor real estate market will knock down REIT prices even if the stock market in general is moving higher. Also, the underlying portfolio is illiquid. It may take months to sell troubled properties. In addition, the dividend yield varies, and in a negative environment a REIT may sell at a sharp discount to the value of the underlying assets.

Tax Considerations

Tax Consequences
Dividends and capital gains are taxed at your ordinary income rates. However, part of the dividend may be considered return of capital and therefore not taxable. REITs are appropriate investments for most retirement plans.

Summing Up

After living under the dark cloud of poor and volatile performance for many years, REITs are gaining wider acceptance once again. The 1986 Tax Reform Act eliminated the benefits of most tax shelter limited partnerships that had competed with REITs in bidding for properties.

The October 1987 stock market crash dragged virtually every issue down. However, there was a wide disparity between different groups' performances in the days and weeks following the crash. For the week after the crash, REITs fell 17%. That compares with a drop by the DJIA of 24.9% and the S&P 500 Index of 22.9%.

Concern over real estate prospects resulted in only an average of 1% gain in 1989 for equity REITs. While dividend income was over 8%, price declines resulted in the meager gain. Over the long term though, REITs are much more competitive. In the 1980s REITs posted a 12.6% annual compounded return. That compares to return on common stock as reflected by the S&P 500 stock index of 17.4% over the same period of time. However in times of high inflation, such as the 1975-1986 period, REITs outperformed common stock by a 16% to 20% annual margin.

It is important to understand the type of REIT you are considering. Brokers too often sell all REITs as plays on real estate itself. Yet some REITs specialize in making loans. Others buy properties directly. The latter type, called equity REITs, are more direct investments in the direction of real estate prices.

Since inflation often boosts real estate prices but also pushes up interest rates, a mortgage REIT will tend to drop in price even though land prices are rising. The loans they make are just like bonds. When interest rates rise, the value of the loan goes down.

Real Estate Limited Partnerships (RELPs)

Before the 1986 Tax Reform Act, the business form known as the limited partnership *was widely used for tax shelter investments. Although there are many types of tax shelters, the most common was organized around real estate investment.*

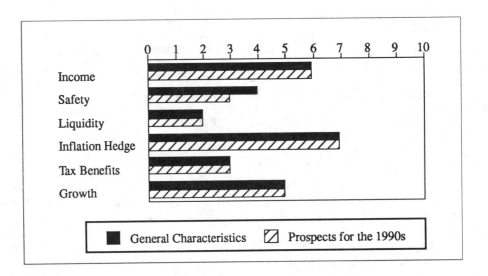

There are two major ways to organize joint business projects. Corporations are legal entities, registered with state governments. They have their own legal identity, pay taxes, and assume a wide range of legal and financial responsibilities.

The other major form is the partnership. In a partnership, many legal obligations pass through to the individual owners of the enterprise. The most important difference is that losses that exceed the financial means of the partnership become the liability of the individual owners. This liability exposure deters most investors from participating in various ventures in which they do not have direct expertise or involvement. The form of business organization called the *limited partnership* arose as an answer to this problem.

Many ventures require capital far beyond the resources of a single investor. For example, many apartment buildings, office build-

ings, and industrial projects are too expensive or risky for an entrepreneur to fund. A general partner will organize a partnership to fund a project. To convince outside investors to contribute capital, the general partner exempts the limited partners from some of the risks and liabilities involved in the business. In return, the limited partners entrust the day-to-day operations to the general partner.

Before the 1986 Tax Reform Act, the most popular limited partnerships were those which invested in real estate. Previously, real estate investment had many tax advantages that were not available to other investments, such as accelerated depreciation, investment tax credits, and interest deductibility over and above the amount of investment. Multiple writeoffs were common features of real estate partnerships. The deductions generated by these tax shelters could be used to offset earned or investment income. This has changed with the new tax law. Now real estate limited partnerships (RELPs) are geared to producing "passive" income that can be offset with the passive

Type II

C
Low Taxes
High Expenses

D
Low Taxes
Low Expenses

losses produced by previous tax shelter investments! Passive income-generating real estate partnerships are called PIGs. They've become big business.

In 1989, sales of limited partnerships dropped 28% from 1988. RELPs were by far the largest segment of the limited partnership business with sales of slightly over $3 billion in 1989. Sales were hurt by high interest rates available on low risk money market investment.

Given the volatile nature of the investment markets in recent years, RELP syndicators are finding it difficult to attract investors willing to lock up their money for 7 or 8 years. Troubles by some leading partnership syndicators such as VMS, Southmark, and Integrated Resources cast a pall over the whole RELP market. Shearson Lehman Hutton, once Wall Street's leading seller of limited partnership investments cut back so sharply from the business in 1989 that some brokers fear it is a prelude to a total pullout. After selling more than $1 billion in limited partnerships in 1988, its volume for 1990 is estimated at only $100 million. The poor performance by many of the partnerships sold by Shearson, including RELPs syndicated by Balcor Co., a subsidiary, has resulted in mounting legal problems for the firm.

Brokerage industry officials concede that as much as $10 to $20 billion (and probably much more) of the $100 billion of partnership investments sold in the 1980s are in trouble.

Real estate limited partnerships are either private or public offerings. Private offerings are not registered with the Securities and Exchange Commission (SEC). They are restricted in the number of investors who may participate. For example, most private offerings limit the number of nonmillionaire participants to 35. In addition, strict income and wealth requirements must be met.

Public limited partnerships are registered with the SEC. They are subject to stringent financial and disclosure rules. A prospectus that has been filed with the SEC must be provided to all prospective investors. Private offerings also use a prospectus but the information disclosed is usually less complete than in SEC-registered documents.

Limited partnerships are sold by major full-service brokerage firms as well as by smaller specialty firms. Normally the salespeople are compensated by the general partner out of revenues generated by the sales. You are still paying a sales fee, it is just paid indirectly. After all, the assets of the partnership are yours on a proportionate basis. These fees can be quite high.

A book by former broker Mary Calhoun, *The Guide to Investor Protection*, lists the commission charged for limited partnerships as among the highest for any financial transactions. Typical commissions run from $600–$1,000 or more on a $10,000 investment. That compares to $200–$250 for buying NYSE stocks, or $100–$600 for buying corporate or municipal bonds. Be sure you know all fees in advance.

Investment Potential

Real estate limited partnerships offer the average investor a chance to participate in very large real estate projects that he or she might not otherwise be able to afford. The objectives are twofold: (1) generation of current passive income and (2) potential capital gains stemming from property appreciation.

Many conservatively financed deals (less than 50% of the partnership's assets are financed with borrowed money) offer good income that can be offset by other limited partnership income (such as previous tax shelter-oriented real estate partnerships). They also offer good protection from inflation. Real estate has historically been a good hedge against the ravages of inflation.

More highly leveraged deals promise income with at least some portion sheltered from taxation. The new tax law eliminated the multiple writeoff deals of years past. In those investments, the chief attraction was the tax benefits rather than the economic prospects of the property.

There are a wide variety of real estate limited partnerships. You can invest in apartment buildings, industrial property, farm land, or commercial real estate. Some partnerships specialize in a single type of real estate or even a single project, while others diversify over different types.

Partnerships can also be used to invest in disparate geographical areas. Some general partners restrict their investments to particular areas, states, or even cities. Others search out what they consider to be good values anywhere.

Limited partnerships are notoriously illiquid. Following the 1986 Tax Reform Act, which severely restricted the tax benefits of limited partnerships, many investors sought ways to sell their holdings. A number of dealers have sprung up to provide a secondary market service for limited partnerships. Volume for one of these auction houses—National Partnership Exchange in Tampa, Florida—has increased steadily over the past two years. Of the some 3000 public partnerships in existence, NAPEX trades about 900. About 30% of those trade "actively" (at least once very 3 months).

Those partnerships that were highly leveraged and packaged as tax shelters are in deep trouble. Many such partnerships have dropped over 50% in price. A recent survey indicated that about one third of all public RELPs haven't paid any cash to investors for at least two quarters.

On the other hand, partnerships that paid cash or used very little leverage in buying properties have held up much better. Because they generally produce passive income, which can be tax-sheltered at least in part by losses from older tax shelter partnerships, they are still attractive to new buyers.

The bulk of partnerships, though, fall in between these extremes. Typically they leveraged their properties with about 40% cash. They still have some good cash flow, but obviously not as much or as securely as the lower leveraged deals.

Those "middle of the road" partnerships tended to concentrate in healthy geographical areas such as California, or stong East Coast markets such as Boston or New York. But, because of those markets, these partnerships are very hard to evaluate accurately.

For example, the Equitec 81 Real Estate Investor partnership was valued by an outside appraiser at $1,260 per $1,000 investment in 1987. Since that appraisal, though, prices crashed. In May 1988, Equitec Financial Group advised the limited partners that those same units were worthless! Proceeds from selling the properties owned will only cover the partnership's debt.

The secondary market for limited partnerships should not be confused with an open outcry auction market such as the NYSE or the future exchanges. There are no continuous quotes and no independent valuations for most units. Those dealers who make the markets typically base their bid price (the price they are willing to pay for your units) on a formula that includes a discount from the partnership's liquidation value.

Resale markups also vary widely from 7% to as much as 20%. There is also usually a $200 to $250 transfer fee. Some of the major market makers include Liquidity Fund Investment Corporations, 1900 Powell St., Ste. 730, Emeryville, CA 94608; Equity Resources Group, 1280 Massachusetts Ave., Cambridge, MA 02138; MacKennzie Securities, 650 California St., 19th Flr., San Francisco, CA 94108; Partnership Securities Exchange, 1814 Franklin St., Ste. 820, Oakland, CA 94612; and Oppenheimer & Bigelow Management, 489 Fifth Ave., New York, NY 10017.

Limited partnerships should be considered long-term investments. Although it is possible to sell partnership shares, usually such sales are only at steep discounts from net asset values. Many partnership agreements include restrictive clauses on selling shares.

Typically real estate partnerships are structured to liquidate their assets in seven to 10 years. The proceeds are distributed to shareholders.

Strengths

 Limited partnerships offer the chance to invest in large real estate projects by spreading the risk with other investors. They offer the chance to take advantage of a good general manager's expertise in finding undervalued real estate. You can get good diversification and hence run less risk in real estate investing through partnerships. Moreover, income generated through real estate partnerships is passive income. You may use passive losses from previous investments to shelter gains. Well-managed, properly structured deals still offer good current income, which may be partially tax sheltered. And, of course, real estate provides a good hedge against inflation.

Weaknesses

Lack of liquidity is a major drawback. In addition, partnership investors run not only market risk but also the risk of poor management. Transaction fees are often high.

Independent verification of asset values is difficult. Usually you must obtain that information from the general partner, who has a vested interest in making things look as good as possible. Furthermore, there is no widely accepted rating service. There is no government or substantial private insurance in case of defaults.

Tax Considerations

Tax Consequences

The 1986 Tax Reform Act made fundamental changes in how real estate partnerships are taxed. Any losses that are generated are passive losses and can only offset other passive gains.

A number of changes have taken place in tax treatment of gains and losses from limited partnerships. When combined with substantial tightening of the alternative minimum tax, these changes make it crucial for you to check with your tax advisor before investing in any limited partnership.

Summing Up

For much of the 1980s, real estate fell on hard times in many areas. The elimination of favored tax treatment for leveraged real estate transactions will result in more sensible real estate investing. The days of buying purely for tax reasons are gone.

The severely depressed real estate market in many areas of the country offers the chance to buy truly undervalued real estate for the first time in years.

Changing demographics—there is a smaller pool of people in the typical home buying age group, political changes (Congress is actively debating applying limits to the deductions that mortgage interest currently provides), and the huge (over $300 billion) inventory of properties that the Resolution Trust Corp. (RTC) acquired from failed S&Ls and which it must sell, all point to a more subdued real estate market in the coming years in virtually all sections of the country.

Although the emphasis has changed from selling tax benefits to selling income, the real estate limited partnership industry continues to be a viable alternative for investing in land.

However, be aware that partnership investing is a long term proposition. Over $15 billion in public RELPs sold by major brokerage firms are estimated to be in financial trouble!

Notes

Notes

CHAPTER 15

INTERNATIONAL SECURITIES

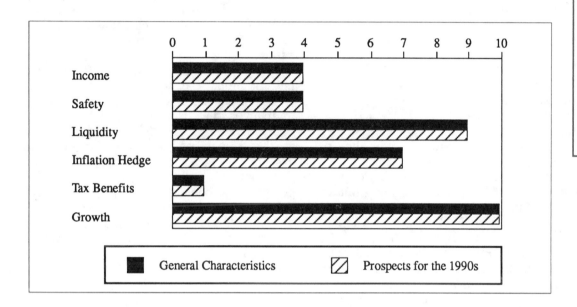

Income
Safety
Liquidity
Inflation Hedge
Tax Benefits
Growth

0 1 2 3 4 5 6 7 8 9 10

■ General Characteristics   ▨ Prospects for the 1990s

Personal Financial Keys for International Securities

Growth

Volatility
Business failure

Ordinary income
Capital gain

Outlook for the 1990s

Widespread disparity among markets

Volatile dollar will make it difficult to profit in most foreign markets.

Expect high volatility.

Positives:

Declining U.S. interest rates

Vibrant international trade

Growing foreign economies

European economic integration

Negatives:

Volatile dollar

Falling U.S. inflation

Passage of trade protectionist legislation

Mideast turmoil

A GLANCE AHEAD

The times are certainly changing. In the 1960s and 1970s, the international trend was toward greater government involvement in all aspects of the economy. The idea was the government was needed to direct economic affairs away from individual greed to enhance the "public good." The failure of government intervention to improve economic conditions became widely recognized by the early 1980s.

Now countries that were in the forefront of the campaign to nationalize industries have backpedaled sharply. Britain, Japan, and even France have either sold or are planning to sell major state-owned indus-

tries to the private sector. Such important companies as British Airways, Nippon Telegraph & Telephone, and Banque Paribas of France have been put on the public auction block.

The leveraged buyout mania that has dominated the U.S. investment markets in recent years is now affecting even European markets. The European Common Market will lower the remaining trade barriers by 1992, creating a more unified financial community. On June 27, 1988, a new "merger policy" was proposed to the Common Market countries to replace the maze of often contradictory national laws on takeovers.

In this chapter you'll discover the in-

creasing importance of foreign investment markets to the world's economy. You'll learn

- *Different ways you can invest in foreign economies*
- *How international investing offers your portfolio important inflation protection.*
- *The many ways you can invest in foreign securities*
- *Which foreign markets are viable alternatives to the U.S. market*
- *The important differences between foreign markets and the U.S. markets*
- *Why international securities should play an important part in any well-managed, diversified portfolio.*

INTERNATIONAL SECURITIES

The declining U.S. dollar contributed about 20% of the gains in 1985, 1986, and 1987 and contributed to making foreign stock markets and bond markets lucrative havens for U.S. investors.

According to Lipper Analytical Services, as of June 1990, the top performing mutual fund over the past five years was an international fund: Japan Fund. In fact, the top 10 funds in this survey were international funds. The others were Fidelity Overseas, Oppenheimer Global Fund, GT Global Fund, Kleinwort Benson: International Equity, Trustees Commingled International, T. Rowe Price International Stock, Vanguard World: International Growth, GAM: International, and International Fund for Institutions.

Many foreign markets posted excellent returns for the 12 months ending May 31, 1990 (in dollar terms):

Austria	+115%
Denmark	+50%
Germany	+62%
France	+44%
Switzerland	+49%

Only once in the last 10 years has the United States been the top-performing market! Even 1986's outstanding 27.1% gain was only good enough for fifteenth place worldwide.

Many Americans do not realize the sub-stantial inroads that foreign securities markets have made over the last 10 years. In 1970, the United States accounted for 47% of the world's GNP. At that time U.S. markets capitalized 66% of the world's equity markets.

By May 1989 the U.S. economy accounted for only 39% of the world's GNP. At the same time, the U.S. equity market's share of world capitalization had dropped to 31%!

The international bond market is larger than the equity markets. Total capitalization of the world's major bond markets in 1985 was $5,850 billion. That compares to equity market capitalization of $5,642 billion. As of 1985, the U.S. bond market accounted for 52% of the total world bond market capitalization.

Many bond markets were devastated by the inflationary experience of the 1970s. Once confidence is lost, it takes a long time to recover. The U.S. market still actively trades bonds that have 20- and 30-year maturities. The average long-term foreign bond has an eight- to 12-year maturity.

Over the last ten years, total returns for government bonds of Japan, West Germany, Britain, and Canada have been comparable to that of U.S. bonds. Total returns for each country (including the effect of currency changes) were

Japan	14.0%
West Germany	9.0%
Britain	13.0%
Canada	11.0%

Total return for U.S. Treasury bonds was 10.3%.

Risks

International securities markets present substantial risks. Just as the U.S. market has become more volatile in recent years, so have foreign markets. When markets trade at unprecedentedly high levels, it is only natural for volatility and risk to increase. And an investor in international securities faces unique risks in addition to price volatility. Each country has different regulations for the disclosure of financial information. The whole industry of stock and bond research is relatively new in Europe. Historical records for comparison purposes are certainly not as complete as in the United States.

Money Management Tip

Political risks play a large part in foreign stocks. It would be unwise to concentrate all your money in any one country, especially if that country has a history of nationalizing industries. As mentioned earlier, a number of countries are now selling state-owned companies to the private sector—at public auction, but that trend can always change with the next election.

Although worldwide developments affect all markets, the effects may be different for each one. For example, when the Iran-Iraq war broke out, the U.S. market rallied in the belief that the United States would have the strongest, most stable economy in times of international turmoil. Yet when Iraq invaded Kuwait in the summer of 1990, all major stock markets around the world declined. While the U.S. dollar rallied moderately, many analysts noted that the dollar seemed to have lost its historic edge as the "safe haven" currency.

The frequent oil crises affect markets differently. Japan depends more heavily on imported oil than do most other industrialized countries. When oil prices go up, or The Organization of Petroleum-Exporting Countries (OPEC) discusses an embargo, Japan's markets usually suffer more than most others.

The worldwide inflationary experience of the 1970s has resulted in much more careful monetary policies for many countries. For example, the United States tried to push West Germany into expansionist economic policies in 1987. West Germans resisted these pressures, fearing that expansive monetary policies would re-ignite the inflationary fires. They believed that inflation would be far worse than sluggish economic growth. 1989 and 1990 were years of the bond bear markets internationally. Interest rates rose in West Germany, Japan, and Britain. Bond markets fell sharply. Although the equity markets were able to resist the downward momentum in 1989, the decline is a major concern for the future.

Liquidity varies widely in foreign markets. Listed issues in major markets such as Japan, Britain, and West Germany are quite liquid.

Look At This:

One problem with investing in foreign securities is that there is no SEC regulation to give you uniform information. Each country has its own regulatory body. Some practices, such as insider trading, are considered more reprehensible in the United States than in other jurisdictions. However, things may be changing here, too. Both British and French authorities announced programs to "clean up" insider trading problems. On March 14, 1988, French Finance Minister Edouard Balladur announced strict new disclosure laws directed at curbing insider trading abuses. Yet, most countries do have regulations against fraud and similar abuses.

Your securities are insured to $100,000 of their value in the case of failure by the brokerage firm. This coverage applies whether they are U.S. securities or foreign ones.

Compared to Other Assets

International securities can play a vital role in reducing overall portfolio risk, while enhancing total return potential. This benefit is perhaps best seen in a comparison of returns over the past ten years. According to a study by Morgan Stanley Capital International (published in the August 6, 1987 *Investor's Daily*) the U.S. market over the past 10 years has risen 194%. This falls far short of returns achieved by the following major markets:

Hong Kong	+2435%
Japan	+1084%
Britain	+591%
Canada	+352%
Australia	+288%

When you want to ascertain whether diversification into another asset category will provide any net benefit, it is important to establish the level of correlation between markets. For example, if foreign equity markets are to reduce risk, their performance must not be closely correlated with U.S. market performance. In other words, when the U.S. market goes up, the other markets should not usually rise proportionately. When the U.S. market falls, the other markets should offer some downside protection for the equity portion of your portfolio.

That pattern is exactly what international equity markets show. The average correlation between the U.S. market and the markets of other leading countries—including West Germany, the United Kingdom, Hong Kong, Japan, and Indonesia—is less than 40% over the last ten years.

Money Management Tip

Diversification to include international markets offers you a prudent method for reducing overall portfolio risk. As you can see by the average returns just noted, such diversification has enhanced returns over the last 10 years.

Low correlation also appears among international bond markets and the U.S. bond market. International bonds offer excellent risk reduction diversification for the fixed-income portion of your portfolio.

PROSPECTS FOR THE INTERNATIONAL MARKETS IN THE 1990s

Many international stock markets outperformed the U.S. market over the last 10 years. Even the great bull market from 1982 to August 1987 in the United States did not move the U.S. market into number one. In fact, according to Lipper Analytical Services, the majority of top 10 equity mutual funds over the last five years have been international funds.

1. Japan Fund
2. Fidelity Overseas
3. Oppenheimer Global Fund
4. GT Global Fund
5. Kleinwort Benson: Int'l Equity
6. Trustees Commingled: Int'l
7. TRome Price International
8. Vanguard World: Int'l Growth
9. GAM: International
10. International Fund for Institutions

For the 12 months ending May 31,1989, international equity funds were strong due to the strong U.S. dollar. As of April 30, 1989, the average return of 39 World income funds dropped to a negative 1.72% for the year. Over the last 12 months that was a plus 1.1%.

After writing our forecast last year, the U.S. dollar resumed its sharp downtrend. Increasing fears of a stagnating U.S. economy which would lead to declining interest rates, combined with evidence that the Federal Reserve was adopting an "easy money" policy in the face of political pressure from the White House and Congress pushed the dollar sharply lower in 1990. On July 31, 1990 the dollar fell to its lowest level against the D-Mark in 31 months. Rising interest rates abroad when U.S. rates were softening contributed to the trend.

On July 30, 1990 the dollar traded midday at 1.6023 marks, the lowest level since January 4, 1988 when the dollar hit 1.5615 marks, the lowest level since the modern exchange rate system began after WWII.

The key variable for you to watch is still the status of the dollar. If it stays weak, you should shift assets to the upper range of our recommended allocation range for international securities.

A number of factors will determine the

fate of the U.S. dollar. Monitor the inflation rates for our major trading partners: Japan, West Germany, Switzerland, Canada, and Britain. A rise in U.S. inflation that is not matched in other countries will eventually translate into a weaker dollar once again.

Domestic problems still must be closely watched. Although the trade deficit has shown improvement over the last 12 months, a wider measure, the current account deficit, is getting worse. The current account deficit is the balance of payments in goods, services, and investment earnings. The quarterly GNP reports provide details on the trends of trade. If export sales are in a steady up trend that is positive for the dollar.

Slow but steady growth in the economy would be ideal for the dollar. If the economy grows too fast—a GNP rate of over 4.5%— the dollar may actually be hurt. This is because of the inflation phobia that still grips the investment markets almost 10 years after the double-digit inflation of the 1970s.

If investors think the economy is going too fast, they look to the potential for increasing inflation. If the factory utilization rate goes over 85%, capacity will be strained. Companies will bid prices higher to obtain what they need. If unemployment goes under 5%, look for wages to turn higher, another inflationary danger.

One measure of the currency's value is its "purchasing power parity." Purchasing power parity is an attempt to measure what $1 will buy in the United States versus what it will buy in other countries when converted to that country's currency. For example, if an item costs $1 in the United States when the exchange rate is 135 yen to the dollar, then 135 yen should buy the same item in Japan. If it takes 125 yen, then the dollar is fundamentally undervalued.

On this basis, the dollar is still undervalued in yen, D-mark, and Swiss franc terms. Unfortunately, it is not unusual for currencies to be out of line with their purchasing power parity for years before adjusting.

A weak dollar has important implications for U.S. investment markets as well. For example, in the first quarter of 1990 foreign investors dumped a net $3.3 billion of U.S. stocks and $900 million of U.S. bonds. Foreign buying is critical to the health of the U.S. bond market as it provides necessary funds to help finance our huge budget deficit. Japanese investors have been key players in this area. Evidence in early 1990 that the Japanese were backing away from U.S. bond markets is cause for concern and should be monitored carefully.

According to the Security Industry Association, the Japanese sold a net of $700 million of U.S. stocks and $3.9 billion of U.S. Treasury bonds in the first quarter of 1990. That trend continued in the second quarter.

Looking at the Markets

You will need to be careful and selective in the 1990s. The performance of international markets varies greatly. However, many markets still offer substantially better performance than you can get in the U.S. market. For example, in 12 months ended May 31, 1990 the S&P 500 was up about 16.9%. In dollar terms that was exceeded by Austria (+115%), Belgium (+19%), Denmark (+50%), France (+44%), Germany (+62%), Italy (+40%), Netherlands (+29%), Norway (+40%), Singapore (+22%), Sweden (+27%), Switzerland (+49%) and Britain (+21%).

Smaller exchanges around the world offer even greater profit potential. However, concomitant with that greater profit potential is greater risk. For example, in 1989 market values soared in Thailand, Singapore, Indonesia and Taiwan. Other smaller markets though were beset by political troubles and experienced lackluster performance. These included Hong Kong, the Philippines, South Korea, Australia, and New Zealand.

The Pacific Rim continues to be a growth area. 1990 should be no exception. Japan has moved to the forefront of the world's economies. It is now taking a leading role in the financial problems of the less developed countries.

Although the Japanese market is grossly overpriced by most fundamental U.S. measures, it bounced back from the early 1990 crash of over 30%. Japan appears to be successfully building domestic demand to take up the slack from their slowing export sales.

Despite the strong yen, the Japanese economy surged ahead in 1990. The Japanese markets are still pulling in investors from around the world. Although we recommend that Japanese issues should only be a part of your international portfolio, you should have some position there.

Other Pacific Rim markets with excellent potential for the 1990s include Singapore, Taiwan, South Korea, and Hong Kong. These countries are referred to as the "Four Tigers." All are on a fast-track growth for their economies. Inexpensive and diligent labor and high savings rate ensure a good mean-term furture for these markets. However, political problems will continue to plague these markets, especially the latter two.

You can select and invest in most of those markets that interest you through closed-end mutual funds. In the last few years, many single-country closed-end funds have been launched, including the Korea Fund, the Taiwan Fund, the Malaysia Fund, the Italy Fund, the Brazil Fund, the Spain Fund, and the First Iberian Fund (invests in Spanish and Portuguese stocks). Diversify, with no more than 5% of your international portfolio in any one of these smaller countries' markets.

International Bonds

Inflation appears to be under control in most parts of the world. Obviously, you do not want to buy bonds denominated in any currency when inflation is increasing. The buoyant Japanese economy and weak Yen point to increased danger of a pickup in inflation.

The following table lists total returns over the last 10 years for government bonds in major world markets (in dollar terms):

Britain	+243.1%
Germany	+137.1%
Canada	+184%
Japan	+269%
United States	+167%

With inflation rates well under control in these markets, a diversified portfolio of international bonds should be an integral part of your portfolio in the 1990s.

International bonds are most attractive on a total return basis for U.S. investors if the dollar is weak, international interest rates are falling, and the issuing countries are politically stable. If the U.S. dollar stabilizes the high double-digit returns of recent years may be out of reach. Good, solid returns are reasonable, however, if international inflation is held under control.

---

10 Top-Performing International Funds
(ranked by 10-year total return)

o	1)	Merrill Lynch Pacific A
*	2)	GT Pacific Growth
–	3)	Oppenheimer Global
o	4)	United International Growth
–	5)	Sogen International Fund
–	6)	Putnam International Equity
+	7)	New Perspective
–	8)	Scudder International
–	9)	Templeton World
*	10)	Templeton Growth

o Unchanged from previous edition
* New appearance on list
+ Moved up from previous edition
– Moved down from previous edition

Source: Fund/Search, Information Edge, Inc., (800) 334-3669

Foreign Currencies

Foreign currencies are legal tender issued by foreign governments. In today's highly interdependent world, the value of currency in the country that manufactures the product you want is a key variable in its price. For example, during 1985 and 1986 the Japanese yen climbed to over 60% against the U.S. dollar. This meant that Japanese products became more expensive for Americans (reflected in higher prices for Japanese-made cars, for example). At the same time, U.S. products became less expensive for the Japanese. Japanese investors' investment in U.S. real estate more than doubled in 1986 and climbed steadily in 1987, 1988 and 1989.

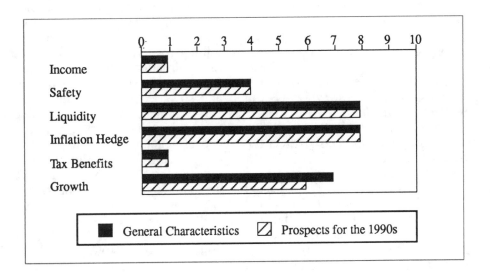

Although all currencies fluctuate, the primary market for foreign currencies in the United States has been concentrated in the Japanese yen, the Swiss franc, the West German mark (Deutschmark), the British pound, and the Canadian dollar. To a lesser extent, the Mexican peso, the French franc, the Italian lira, and Dutch guilder are traded. The high inflation of the 1970s increased interest in foreign currencies as investments, as people scrambled to find ways to protect their assets from the ravages of inflation.

Following World War II, the world's currencies were fixed in relation to each other and the dollar by the Bretton Woods agreement, whereby the United States agreed to convert foreign dollar claims into gold on demand. However, as inflation depressed the value of the dollar, the United States was forced to close the "gold window" in 1971. Thereafter, currencies began to "float." Basically, the open marketplace (free flow of supply and demand) replaced government fiat in determining the value of respective currencies.

Foreign currencies can be bought and sold in a variety of ways. Physical possession can be taken by exchanging dollars for the desired currency at a currency broker's or at most major banks. In addition, travelers' checks can be purchased in denominations of the major currencies. Savings or checking accounts can be opened in foreign countries.

The three most popular countries for foreign currency checking and savings accounts are Switzerland, Austria, and Holland. The long popularity of Swiss banks has led to an increase in minimum initial account sizes to $10,000 for most banks. There is also a 35% Swiss withholding tax on interest-bearing accounts. Austria is attracting new business with its low minimum policy for most banks. In Holland, the AMRO (Amsterdam-Rotterdam) Bank offers interest-bearing checking acconts in a wide variety of currencies. AMRO's savings accounts are denominated only in Dutch guilders, though.

In addition to interest-bearing checking accounts and savings acconts, most banks in these three countries also offer international certificates of deposit denominated in your choice of one of the world's major currencies. As with checking accounts, Swiss banks assess higher CD fees than do Austrian institutions. These fees typically run about 1% over a 12-month period.

Foreign currencies are actively traded in the futures and options markets both in the United States and elsewhere.

The fees for exchanging currencies with dealers can be steep. Normally, dealers maintain a current bid–ask spread. The bid is the price they are willing to pay for the currency. The ask (or offer) is the price for which they are willing to sell the currency. The spread can vary from less than 1% to 5% or more, depending on the currency, on the market's current interest in the currency, and on the dealer's normal profit margin.

Once you have purchased the currency at the offered price, it must appreciate enough to cover the spread before you can make money. Some dealers also assess a "transaction fee" or commission.

Foreign bank account fees vary widely. Swiss banks and their affiliates in areas such as the Bahamas or the Cayman Islands generally charge higher fees than other banks. Typical Swiss fees include such things as a $6 fee every time you make a deposit to your checking account. On CDs, Swiss banks assess a commission fee (usually 0.125% per quarter) and a safe-custody fee (usually about 0.15% per annum). In addition to the 35% Swiss withholding tax on interest payments, there is also a stamp tax on CDs (0.115% on three-month CDs and 0.165% on longer-term CDs).

Be sure to establish exactly what fees are charged when you are dealing with a foreign bank or domestic currency dealer. Although the fractional percentages do not seem like much, they do add up. Remember, these fees do vary widely. Take the time to shop around.

Investment Potential

Investing in currencies is highly speculative. Income is not guaranteed, nor are capital gains assured. Many nonquantifiable factors may influence the day-to-day price fluctuation of any currency. For example, some factors that are considered important in determining relative currency values are interest rates, inflation rates, political environment (government stability, upcoming elections, and so on), trade and budget deficits, war and weather, monetary and fiscal policy, purchasing power parity, and investor confidence—to name only a few!

Currencies can be highly volatile. Several times in the first quarter of 1987, the yen appreciated over 5% in one day against the U.S. dollar. From 1981 to 1985, the U.S. dollar enjoyed a rise against other currencies. However, from 1985 through 1987 the dollar fell over 40% against the D-mark, yen, and Swiss franc.

The primary motivation for currency speculation is capital gains. In the 1970s, the U.S. dollar was losing value both domestically and relative to foreign currencies due to high inflation. Americans bought foreign currencies to protect themselves from inflation.

Foreign currency speculation is highly flexible. A broad variety of currencies exist, and a plethora of methods for investing in them. In addition to the methods already listed, professional money managers will trade currencies for you individually. Also, some mutual funds specialize in currency speculation. Foreign currency mutual funds are gaining in popularity as the world becomes increasingly interdependent. Three major sponsors include Huntington Advisors' International Cash Portfolios, Shearson Lehmen Hutton's Global Currencies Portfolios, and Fidelity Investments' three single-currency funds (mark, pound, and yen).

Currency speculation is a short-term business. The vagaries and ever changing conditions make long-term positions treacherous at best.

Strengths

The many different currencies and methods of investing offer maximum flexibility. Major currencies have active, highly liquid markets. The capital gains potential is substantial for both short and long terms. Foreign currencies offer considerable protection from inflation.

Weaknesses

Currency markets are very volatile. Transaction costs are high for cash buyers. Risk is not limited to market considerations. Political uncertainties play a major role. Accurate timing is vital, because of high volatility. No current income is available to protect against wrong timing.

Tax Considerations

Tax Consequences

The 1986 Tax Reform Act eliminated the favorable treatment of long-term capital gains. All gains from currency speculation are taxed at ordinary income rates. Foreign currency speculation is not suitable for most retirement plans.

Summing Up

The volatility of the U.S. dollar has become a fact of life since the 1970s. The rapid fall of the U.S. dollar in early 1987 resulted in significant inflation fears and even rising interest rates. By mid-1989, the dollar rallied strongly, raising concerns about a deteriorating trade deficit again. By 1990 though the dollar resumed its swoon!

Yet only a few short years ago, the U.S. dollar was criticized as being too high! Since the end of the Bretton Woods fixed-exchange agreement for currencies, volatility has increased substantially. The erratic behavior of the U.S. dollar in relation to the currencies of our major trading partners is regular front-page news. For most of 1987 and 1988, the gyrations of the U.S. dollar were the single most important events in the fate of the U.S. bond market. By 1990 relative interest rates had replaced the dollar's value as the key factor in bond pricing.

Foreign currency trading has grown explosively in the past 10 years. Approximately $500 billion in foreign currencies change hands every day. That's double the rate of only three years ago. You can now hedge your bets in many ways. But make no mistake—it is important to know what the U.S. dollar is doing and why.

In a later chapter, we discuss some of the most common methods for investing in currencies other than simple cash purchase. The options and futures markets offer highly liquid—and very risky—ways to profit (or lose) from dollar volatility. Another important variable will occur in 1991 when U.S. banks are allowed to accept foreign currency deposit accounts. They have been forbidden to accept same to date. That will put them on a competitive basis with many foreign banks such as Swiss, Austrian, and Dutch entities.

International Stocks

International stocks are equities issued by foreign companies denominated in foreign currencies. You acquire an equity interest in the foreign company, much the same as you would when buying U.S. stocks.

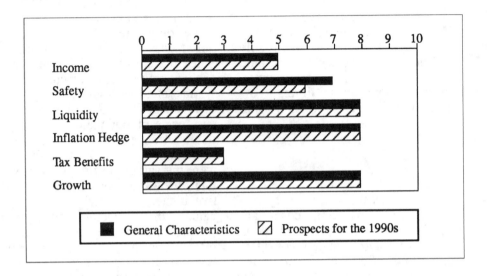

General Characteristics ▬ Prospects for the 1990s ▨

Type I

D

Low Taxes
Low Expenses

International stock markets have experienced substantial growth over the past 20 years. In 1970, the U.S. stock market constituted 66% of the world's stock market capitalization. That share dropped to 31% in 1989. In fact, the Japanese market, with a capitalization of $2.7 trillion, surpassed the U.S. market as the single largest equity market in the world. The increasing interest in stocks of foreign companies is yet another indication of the internationalization of the world's economy. The economic growth of all countries is closely tied to trade flows. Even Peking launched its own stock market in 1986!

The attraction of international stocks is not hard to understand. The ready liquid access to many different companies in different countries offers investors even more opportunity to seek out fast-growing businesses that are not matched in the United States. The floating currency exchange rates afford investors the chance to profit not only from internal growth of a disparate selection of companies but also from currency exchange fluctuations. For example, a stock purchased in Japan may appreciate only 10% in a year. But if the U.S. dollar falls an additional 10%–15% or more, a U.S. stockholder earns that extra increased purchasing power.

International stocks are purchased in a number of ways. Larger multinational brokerage firms are only one source. International banks, especially banks in countries such as Switzerland or Luxembourg, buy and sell stocks around the world for their clients. Substantial risks are involved in purchasing international stocks. These risks include differing regulatory requirements for each country, high transaction costs, widely varying tax treatment, and substantial political risk in addition to market risk. Substantial investors, willing and able to take greater risks, can purchase foreign equities directly through their brokers or foreign-based banks.

One alternative to direct purchase on foreign exchanges is the American Depository

Receipt (ADR). These negotiable receipts, issued by U.S. banks, represent actual shares held by the bank's foreign branches. ADRs are actively traded on major U.S. exchanges and on the over-the-counter (OTC) market. For example, Sony is traded on U.S. exchanges as an ADR. Other actively traded, well-known ADRs include British Airways, British Petroleum, Glaxo Holdings, Japan Air Lines, Nissan Motor, Telefonos de Mexico, and Honda. Dividends, stock splits, and other changes are handled by the bank. Dividends are converted into U.S. dollars. This arrangement eliminates many of the problems associated with holding foreign stock directly.

Another alternative that you should seriously consider is the purchase of stock in mutual funds that specialize in international stocks (see the section on international mutual funds). This approach assures you good diversification.

Investment Potential

Foreign stocks offer capital gains potential. Dividend income is also paid by many foreign issues.

Levels of regulation of stocks among foreign nations vary widely. This variance is a major problem for investors used to the strict U.S. regulations. Moreover, financial information is usually not as widely disseminated as for U.S. stocks. Only in the past 10 years have independent investment analysis firms become established for many markets such as those in West Germany, Denmark, Sweden, and Spain.

Volatility is also a problem in some of the newer markets. It is important to have access to a specialist for the market where you intend to invest. The specialist can advise you on matters such as liquidity, potential political risks, and other factors that may be different for U.S. investors. Although liquidity can be assured for most exchange-listed U.S. stocks, that is not necessarily the case with foreign exchange-listed issues.

Professional Advice

Minimum purchase requirements may also be quite high. Given the maze of transaction costs, including commissions, transfer fees, transfer taxes, custodial fees, and currency conversion fees, direct investment in foreign stocks is usually appropriate only for wealthy investors.

Leverage through purchase on margin is available for foreign stocks traded on U.S. exchanges and some ADRs. The Federal Reserve Bank decides which stocks are marginable. Regulations elsewhere vary widely. Check with a broker with international branches or with banks in foreign contries for details on specific issues.

Foreign stocks of well-known concerns in politically stable countries are appropriate for long-term investment. However, you should carefully monitor changes in political conditions as well as economic prospects. Remember, foreign issues are not subject to SEC regulations even when purchased by U.S. citizens.

Strengths

Foreign stocks offer (1) greater selection of potential growth prospects and (2) protection from the inflation in the United States. Purchasing power is enhanced in times of U.S. dollar weakness, too. International diversification lowers portfolio risk. Some international stocks offer above-average growth potential.

Weaknesses

Currency fluctuations can hurt potential returns if the U.S. dollar appreciates against the currency in which the stock is denominated. Foreign stocks are not subject to SEC financial reporting requirements, and reliable financial information is difficult to obtain. Different accounting procedures are used in many countries. These problems make direct comparison with U.S. data more difficult. Price information is not as widely available as that for U.S. stocks.

Many foreign stocks are less liquid than equivalent U.S. exchange-listed issues due to large holdings by foreign governments, which are rarely traded.

Tax Considerations

Tax Consequences

Gains and losses on foreign stocks are treated the same as domestic stocks for U.S. tax purposes. Capital gains and dividend income are taxed at ordinary income rates. Capital losses can be used to offset other capital gains. Unused losses can be carried forward.

However, it is important to learn the tax policies of respective foreign countries. Many countries assess withholding taxes of

Look At This:

20 to 30% on interest paid to foreign investors. Numerous tax treaties have been made between the United States and other countries. You should investigate the many possible tax consequences before you invest in foreign securities of any type. Some taxes may be so heavy as to negate the value of the investment for U.S. citizens.

Summing Up

Some foreign stock markets have outperformed the U.S. market for years. Combined with gains resulting from U.S. dollar weakness, many investors in foreign stocks have reaped returns as high as 30%–50% per year from 1984 through 1990.

As with U. S. stocks, some issues always experience explosive growth far beyond the norms. Top-performing issues in 1989 included Allgemeine Bauges Vorzug in Austria up 552%. In Singapore the top performing issue was UMW Holdings up 411%. In Italy, Mondadori Risp. Non Convert. posted a 239% gain. Top gainer in Japan was Kata-

kura Industries up 215%. In Australia, Homestake Gold Australia posted a 212% gain while Strabag-Bau in Germany was up 166%. Compare those returns to the leading U.S. performer, Holiday Corp., up 166%.

Of course, not all issues go up. Big losers in 1989 included Chase Corp. in New Zealand, down 99%. Bond Corp. of Australia fell 93%. Campeau of Canada was down 77%. Amstrad of the United Kingdom dropped 74%. The largest fall in the U.S. market was Imperial Corp. which declined 90%.

Given the increasing interdependence of industrialized economies around the world, diversification with foreign investment markets adds value to your portfolio. In the 1950s, the U.S. dollar did not fluctuate widely in value. Investors had little need for protection from the complex vagaries of international markets.

Most professional managers now consider it prudent to diversify internationally. In addition to the potential for excellent returns in many foreign markets, such diversification also helps to minimize risk. When bouts of dollar weakness depress U.S. equities, holding nondollar-denominated assets affords you protection from losing purchasing power. Although inflation has not been a problem here since 1982, the threat of a resurgence is always present. For example, Iraq's invasion of Kuwait in the summer of 1990 poses the very real danger of another "oil price shock" such as that of the early 1970s that ignited massive inflation then. As this is being written, many analysts project a move by Iraq against Saudi Arabia which would be a major blow to Western energy needs. Many analysts warn that such events could trigger a new wave of inflation. Also, inflation fears push interest rates higher, which often hurts stocks. International diversification minimizes the effects of adverse political and/or economic developments in a single country.

International Bonds

International bonds are debt instruments issued by foreign governments and companies denominated in their own currencies. Just like U.S. Treasuries and corporate bonds, they have set maturities and "coupon" yields. For example, 10-year Japanese government bonds in February 1990 yielded 6.77% compared to 8.25% on equivalent U.S. bonds. Both the principal at maturity and the interest are paid in yen. These bonds would be attractive to U.S. investors if the U.S. dollar dropped enough relative to the yen to make up the difference.

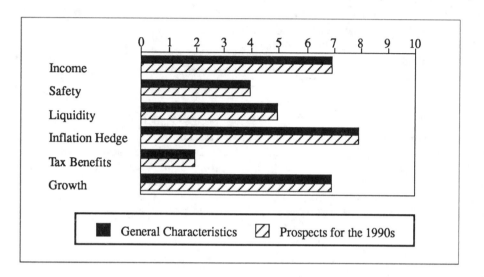

The large gyrations in both interest rates and currency values have stimulated substantial interest in international bonds.

The interest rates paid by Japanese, Swiss, and West German bonds, however, have generally been lower than the rates paid by equivalent U.S. bonds. However, rising foreign interest rates in 1990 due to growing economies narrowed the gap between foreign bonds yields and U.S. bonds yields to historic levels. Their returns, plus the appreciation of their respective currencies, paid off handsomely over the past 10 years.

For 1989 the total return (interest payments plus or minus changes in the price of the security) for U.S. Treasury bonds was 18.9%. Over the last ten years performance of U.S. bonds trailed that of most of our major trading partners. For example, Japan's

Type I

bonds posted a 270% gain, Britain's were up 244% and Canada's climbed 184%. Only Germany, up 137% trailed U.S. bonds total return of 167%.

Like international stocks, international bonds must be evaluated for many different factors. Fluctuations in the interest rates in the issuing country and the United States may affect relative value. Fluctuations in currency values among countries also influence relative value.

Because of the myriad price factors, investing in international bonds is a difficult undertaking for the average investor. Although an investor may be able to get a fairly accurate picture of the earnings prospects of a foreign concern for purchasing its stock, evaluating the many factors that affect interest rates is certainly no easier in a foreign country than it is in the United States.

Few analysts have been able to forecast

U.S. interest rates with any accuracy for the short term (three to 18 months). Many factors must be evaluated. For example, monetary and fiscal policies, trade balances, economic growth, and relative inflation are only a few necessary considerations. Of course, this tangle is even more complicated for foreign countries. International bonds are bought and sold through international brokerage firms and banks that have branches in various countries. Many foreign banks, such as Swiss banks that have U.S. branches, are specifically set up to handle such transactions. Transaction fees typically are higher than fees for equivalent bond purchases in the United States. Foreign banks that handle security transactions generally assess steeper fees than United States-based brokers.

Investment Potential

International bonds offer a variety of investment returns. They are primarily income producers. The income is paid in the currency in which the bond is denominated. This means you can earn additional profit through currency appreciation. For example, in 1987 if you held a West German government bond you would have earned a total return in D-marks of 5.8%. However, because of the steep drop in the dollar, that same return in dollar terms would have been 29% because of the gain you would have received in the change in the relative values of the currencies. Finally, capital gains are earned when interest rates fall (see the section on corporate bonds).

The volatility of bonds depends on the political and economic environment of the issuing country. The interest rates of stable low-inflation countries such as Switzerland fluctuate much less than in the United States. However, government regulations and registration requirements vary widely. Do not make the mistake of assuming that foreign-issued bonds have met requirements similar to those imposed by the SEC in the United States. Evaluating foreign bonds through independent rating services is considerably more difficult than for U.S. bonds.

Although foreign banks often will make loans for purchases of foreign bonds, the costs tend to be quite high. Swiss banks, for example, tend to charge for many services that Americans take for granted. Custodial fees can be high. However, full-service bank customers can generally negotiate fees.

Both domestic or international bonds should be viewed as long-term investments. Interest rate fluctuations can create short-term opportunities.

Strengths

 International bonds offer investors the opportunity to play currency exchange rate swings, with downside protection provided by the income paid by the bonds. High-risk investors can earn higher-than-average returns on bonds issued by countries that have high-risk economies.

International bonds offer good diversification for income-oriented portfolios and international bonds provide a hedge against U.S. inflation because foreign currency exchange fluctuations key off relative inflation rates.

Weaknesses

 Liquidity may present a problem for many international bonds. Timely pricing information is not as uniformly available abroad as in the United States and different foreign accounting practices make direct comparison to U.S. bonds difficult.

International bonds are sensitive to adverse political developments. A country's abrupt decision to devalue its currency can devastate its bonds. Worldwide inflation drives bond prices down.

Tax Considerations

Tax Consequences

Tax treatment of foreign bonds is complex. Not only U.S. tax authorities, but many countries assess withholding taxes on foreign investors. Generally,

Look At This:

tax treatment on capital gains and interest income is the same as for equivalent U.S. securities. The United States makes tax treaties with many foreign countries, and you should check the details before investing. Adverse tax decisions made after you invest may substantially erode your returns.

Although foreign bonds *can* be used for retirement plans, the complexities rule them out for all but the very largest investors. To get proper diversification and professional management, consider mutual funds that invest in foreign securities.

Summing Up

Investors in international bonds profited handsomely in 1985, 1986, and 1987. For the first quarter of 1989, the total returns on government bonds in leading financial centers (expressed in dollar terms) were

Britain	-3.50%
Japan	-6.78%
Switzerland	-13.00%
Netherlands	-6.64%
West Germany	-5.87%
Australia	-4.61%
Canada	4.50%

That compares to a total return of 3.08% for U.S. Treasury bonds in the same period. The rise in the U.S. dollar offset the interest income paid by each country's bonds, producing poor returns. In addition, rising interest rates produced substantial capital losses as extra burden for income-oriented investors.

Investing in international bonds is a complex undertaking. When you purchase U.S. bonds, you can get a pretty good understanding of the financial strength of the underlying company through the ratings of independent agencies. Then the primary consideration is the direction of interest rates. If rates go up, bonds will fall in price. If rates go down, bond prices rise.

International bonds offer sophisticated investors a good method for diversifying the risk in their fixed-income portfolio. For example, a weak U.S. dollar usually has a negative effect on U.S. bonds. However, if you own foreign bonds, depreciation in the dollar yields a currency exchange profit to U.S. citizens who hold bonds denominated in foreign currency. These bonds become more valuable in dollar terms.

Investing in international bonds is very complex. As we've seen, over the past 10 years it has been virtually impossible to forecast U.S. interest rates with any real degree of accuracy. Imagine the additional problems of forecasting rates in a foreign country! Moreover, different countries' currencies move at different rates relative to the U.S. dollar. By mid-1987 the U.S. dollar had declined over 40% since 1985 against the yen and the mark. Yet the trade deficit showed little real improvement, because the currencies of other important trading partners—including Taiwan and South Korea—showed little appreciation.

International Mutual Funds

Sophisticated investors can appreciably improve the returns on their fixed-income and equity portfolios through diversification with international bonds and stocks. However, the complexities make it difficult for the average investor to participate directly. Over the last 10 years, an increasing number of mutual funds have provided professional management in this area. The internationalization of security markets is accelerating markedly in the 1980s. International bonds will play an increasingly important role in the future. International mutual funds allow you to invest in foreign stocks and bonds with less trouble. A mutual fund is a pool of professionally managed securities. You buy into a fund and receive a proportionate share of the fund's assets. International mutual funds trade like domestic open-end funds, with fluctuating prices determining your profit or loss. Most international funds invest only in foreign stocks, but some funds also buy foreign bonds. An even smaller number invests in both.

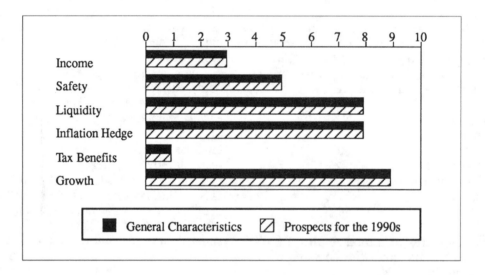

Type II

D

Low Taxes
Low Expenses

The world's economies are steadily becoming more interdependent. The prosperity of the U.S., Japanese, and other economies is no longer only a factor of each country's own domestic demand. The profitability of major companies in the industrialized world is closely tied to their export business.

This "internationalization" of the world's economies is reflected in the rise of stock markets around the world. Investing in foreign markets is a difficult procedure. Different regulations apply to each country's markets. This red tape is further complicated by the differing currencies of each country.

There are two primary types of international mutual funds. A no-load fund assesses no sales fees. Such funds are usually purchased directly from the fund itself through the mail. When you purchase a no-load fund, you buy it at its current net asset value on the day of your purchase. Net asset value (the fund's assets minus its liabilities divided by the number of outstanding shares) is calculated at the end of every business day.

A load fund charges a sales fee. The fee ranges from 2% to 8% of your investment. This fee is added to the net asset value when you purchase a load fund. Some funds call themselves "no-load," yet assess a fee when you sell all or part of your shares. Investigate a fund's fee structure before you invest. Fees may significantly affect your total return.

Most large mutual fund groups have at least one international fund. Some fund issuers, such as T. Rowe Price, Dreyfus, Merrill, and Paine Webber, offer both international stock and bond funds. You can follow prices of the larger funds in the *Wall Street Journal* or *Investor's Daily*. Financial magazines such as *Money* and *Changing Times* periodically feature detailed reports on the performance of most international stock and bond funds.

Investment Potential

The primary attraction of international stock funds is the capital gains potential. The primary attraction of international bond funds is twofold: (1) a hedge against a depreciating dollar and (2) income. The potential and risks, though, are unique. International stock and bond funds offer capital gains and losses resulting from the price action of the selected stocks and bonds. However, your "bottom-line" return, though, is often just as heavily influenced by the relative value of the U.S. dollar. Foreign securities are denominated in the currency of the country in which they trade.

A number of international stock funds achieved returns of over 50% per year for 1985 and 1986. In 1987 those returns dropped to more conventional levels of 8%–10%. For the 12 months ending June 30, 1990, the average international equity fund was up 20%. This performance was largely due to the weakness of the U.S. dollar. When you invest in a stock on the Tokyo exchange, you profit in yen if the stock price rises. If the yen is also appreciating against the U.S. dollar (as it did in 1985, 1986, 1987, and 1990), you gain more profit from the currency move! In 1989, international bond funds rose 4.9%.

For example, if the yen is trading at 200 per U.S. dollar when you buy a stock, and it rises to 150 per dollar when you sell the stock at the same price you bought it, you've earned 33% despite the flat stock price!

The volatility of foreign markets varies. An international fund's diversification tempers this factor somewhat. But a fund invested in only one foreign market that goes through a cycle of wide swinging prices will reflect that volatility in its own prices.

International mutual funds, like most funds, are liquid investments. However, political changes in foreign countries can cause some liquidity problems. For example, in the 1970s Mexico suspended market trade temporarily after it announced its first devaluation in many years. Following the October 1987 market crash in New York, the Hong Kong market was closed for a few days.

Look At This:

All United States-based mutual funds must register with the SEC. They are required to meet stringent financial and disclosure regulations. A prospectus must be provided to prospective buyers before they buy the fund. Some international funds are based off the United States' shore, in places such as the Cayman Islands, the Bahamas, and the Antilles. These funds do not always register with the SEC. They do not always follow the strict disclosure requirements that govern domestic funds. There have been many scandals involving offshore funds over the years. Although many are legitimate, offshore funds cannot be considered as safe as domestic registered funds.

Mutual fund investing, especially in load funds, is generally a long-term proposition. Short-term trading of no-load funds is becoming more popular. Accurately timing fund investing is no easier than timing individual stock selection. That ability has proven elusive even for many professionals.

Strengths

The wide variety of international funds offers great flexibility. You can buy funds that invest in only one country (such as Japan), or in a single geographical area (such as Europe), or in many different countries. International funds are normally very liquid, offer a viable method for speculating on the U.S. dollar, offer capital gains potential, simplify investing in foreign markets, and offer good protection from inflation.

Weaknesses

Foreign stock markets operate under very different regulations. Abuses may occur that U.S. markets guard against.

Currency speculation works both ways. If the U.S. dollar strengthens while your investment is denominated in a foreign currency because it is invested in foreign markets, you may lose money even if the stock goes up! Note that foreign currency markets have been very volatile over the past 10 years. And foreign political developments may result in liquidity problems.

Tax Considerations

Tax Consequences

There are no special tax advantages to investing in international funds. The 1986 Tax Reform Act eliminated preferential treatment of capital gains. Capital gains and gains from currency changes are taxed at your ordinary income rate. Capital losses offset capital gains. Excess losses are carried forward.

Some foreign countries assess withholding taxes on foreign purchases of their securities. Your fund takes care of those matters. If you are entitled to a credit for such transactions, the fund will advise you on an annual basis.

Summing Up

International investing is here to stay. International funds will attract ever larger amounts of U.S. investors' funds. Investors are recognizing interdependencies among the industrial countries.

The complexities of directly investing in foreign markets rule it out for most investors. International funds, however, give you the global diversification that many professional investment advisors recommend.

A weak U.S. dollar enhances the attraction of foreign markets. It can bail out investors who do poorly in selecting stocks, yet who are buying in the correct currency. A strong dollar requires greater care in selecting foreign issues. The stocks then have to rise enough to offset gains in the dollar as well as to yield capital gains in their own currency.

Notes

CHAPTER 16

PRECIOUS METALS AND TANGIBLES

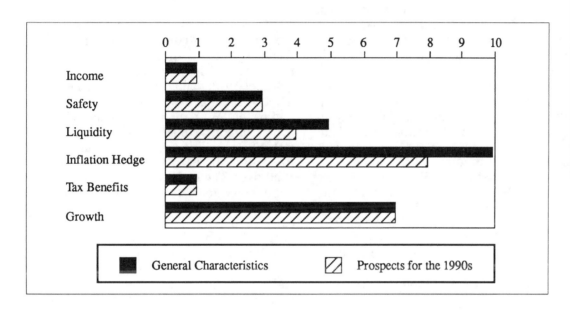

| | General Characteristics | | Prospects for the 1990s |

Inflation
Liquidity

Volatility
Business failure

Ordinary income

*Outlook for
the 1990s*

Platinum often
leads precious
metals complex
market

Chief value as
inflation hedge

Positives:
• Rising inflation
• Weak dollar
• International
  unrest
• Strong GNP
  growth
• Rising oil prices
• Rising wages

Negatives:
• Recession
• Falling oil prices
  or strong stable
  dollar
• Declining
  inflation

A GLANCE AHEAD

Wall Street gurus generally do a better job coming up with catchy phrases to describe market developments than they do explaining those events. By 1983 and 1984, it had become obvious to even the most convinced "gold bug" that momentum had switched from "tangibles" (commodities) to "financial assets." In this game of words, the term commodity is often confused with futures. Smart investors, however, refer to commodities as interchangeable with tangibles but as distinct from futures. Precious metals are the most prominent class of tangibles.

In this chapter, you'll learn
• *How many different ways there are to*
own gold
• *What role gold plays in even the most conservative investor's portfolio*
• *How "tangibles" differ from "financial assets"*
• *How gold, oil, and inflation are connected.*

PROSPECTS FOR PRECIOUS METALS AND COMMODITIES IN THE 1990s

The October 1987 stock market crash illustrated clearly the difficulty of precious metals investing. Tradition holds that gold is the single best "chaos hedge." Yet gold proved to be a poor hedge during the October massacre.

On the day of the crash, October 19, gold rallied $10. However, the next day gold fell $18. For the month, it finished up at a meager 2.7%.

Gold shares did even worse. The 24 gold funds monitored by Lipper Analytical Services fell over 30% for the two weeks that ended October 30. Funds that had invested in North American and Australian shares were the hardest hit. For example, Financial Strategic Gold Portfolio, which was 65% invested in Canadian and Australian shares, fell 24.3% the week of October 19 and 23.7% the next week. That compares to a drop of 15% and 17% in the two weeks for International Investors and Fidelity Select Precious Metals, which also buy South African shares.

The non-South African funds had been the strongest segment of the gold fund group in the nine months leading up to the crash. Heavy positions in Australian, Canadian, and U.S. gold mines helped the Van Eck Gold/Resources fund soar 122% for the 12 months ended September 30, 1987.

Through September 1987, gold was the strongest fund category. Gold funds were up 81.6% to that point, However, in the chaotic fourth quarter, when investors were presumably scrambling for safety, gold funds slipped badly. Gold funds fell an average of 21%, from the strongest group to sixteenth out of 20.

Even then, the strong performance in the early part of the year left gold funds as the strongest group for 1987, up 35.7%. In 1988 though, gold funds dropped 14.9%. In comparison, the average for all equity funds was 12.3%. The metal itself dropped 15.24% in 1988 compared to a 21% gain in 1987. Silver fell 10.15% in 1988 after climbing 23% in 1987.

In fact the performance of gold funds throughout the '80s lagged significantly behind that of general stock funds. That is in sharp contrast to the '70s when inflation dominated the economic picture and gold and silver were the investment winners of the decade. For the ten years ended in 1989, gold funds posted a 146% gain. That contrasts with general stock fund performance over the same period of 324%.

The Outlook

Gold's role as inflation hedge has not changed. It is now obvious that gold's reaction to "chaos" situations will depend on more than just uncertainty. The reason gold fared so badly in late 1987 and in the first half of 1988 was the overhanging fear that the stock market crash signaled recession rather than inflation. Yet following the 190 point stock market crash of October 13, 1989 gold and gold shares rallied strongly for weeks. After being up only 1.2% for the first half of 1989, gold mutual funds rallied the second half to finish up 22.5% for the year.

We have increased the allocations for precious metals this edition due to a number of factors (i.e., the Iraqi invasion of Kuwait and the myriad of problems that presents for the world economy and oil prices in general). In addition there is the growing domestic problem of the S&L bailout. What started out as a $60 billion rescue has already escalated into a $500 billion fiasco with many experts forecasting the need for $1 trillion before it is all over. The Federal Reserve indicated its willingness to bend to political pressure when it eased its money supply policy in early 1990. An eminent recession will cause further problems for banks as well as S&Ls. The money to pay these bills will not be gotten solely from taxes as that is simply politically untenable. The key will be to watch how determined the Fed is to fight any inflationary bursts.

The Iraqi invasion of Kuwait in the summer of 1990 led quickly to sharp increases in oil prices despite huge extant inventories throughout the world. In recent years, oil has proven to be an even better lead indicator of inflation than the price of gold. Keep a close eye on the Commodity Research Bureau's Spot Price Index of raw material prices. If it exceeds the highs hit in the drought scare of June 1988, expect inflation to pick up again. Precious metals should lead the way.

Some areas of the economy should be used as early warning indicators, as follows.

Increase your allocation to precious metals if unemployment falls below 5%. That will signal a very tight labor market. Wages will move higher, ultimately pushing prices up.

Another early indicator is the capacity utilization rate. In 1989, that rate was 83%. If the rate moves over 85%, it historically signals the need to expand productive plant capacity. Prices will be bid higher as companies move to increase market share.

When watching the Consumer Price Index (CPI), you should watch the figure minus the oil and food components. These two are very volatile. Without these two elements, the CPI has risen at about an annual 4% pace for 1985 through 1990. A rise over 7% for 3 straight months would trigger inflation hedge investing.

The single most important thing to watch is the price of gold itself. After surging near $500, it settled back below $400 in 1989. Two consecutive higher closes over $450 will signal resurgent inflation. Increase your allocation to precious metals investments in that case.

Oil prices have been a key to inflation for the past 20 years. OPEC is still in disarray as this book is being written. However, if oil prices moves over $22 a barrel, and stays there, it will ignite another round of inflation. Within days of the Iraqi aggression, oil prices jumped from $18 a barrel on July 16, to $28 on August 6. The key will be what happens to prices over the next few months. If prices stay high look to increasing inflation and an economic shock similar to the severe recession of 1974-75.

Conclusion

Last edition we concluded, "We do not expect inflation to be a major problem in 1990. Although inflation levels as seen in the CPI or PPI may be slightly higher, we expect continued low inflation." We cannot be so certain for the 1990s. There are a number of factors militating for a higher inflation rate as we move into a new decade. We believe that there is considerably greater risk that inflation *could* flare up if the economy continues to grow at an annual rate of over 4% or if the political situation in the Middle East remains tense due to military activity. A full blown war will be very inflationary. However, do not become overly complacent. Watch the indicators we have just noted. At any rate, you should keep a small investment in gold funds or coins at all times.

THE ROLE OF TANGIBLES AS A BASIC ASSET CATEGORY

Investing in commodities is motivated by a desire to protect the purchasing power of your assets. In the 1970s it was common wisdom to "Buy now—it will only get more expensive later." Financial assets, however, are certificates representing ownership or a loan relationship. Gold bugs sneeringly refer to financial assets as "paper" claims. A true investor in tangibles expects to take delivery of an actual commodity such as gold. You would turn to tangibles in times of great uncertainty. Rather than "trust" in the fortunes of a company, of which you may be partial owner through stock shares, or even in the banking system, extreme advocates of tangible investing much prefer physical possession of gold: you don't have to trust anyone then. Tangibles do not default. Although "gold fever" has cooled off in recent years, you'll discover in this chapter a wide variety of products that are still tied to gold.

Gold has served as a final, inviolable refuge of value for all history. The Pharaohs of ancient Egypt were adorned with gold. The Aztecs offered gold as tribute to their sacred ruler, Montezuma. More recently, gold has surfaced as the only sure medium for the purchase of personal freedom from authoritarian regimes such as in Vietnam and the People's Republic of China.

The 1960s and 1970s were difficult years. The Vietnam War tore the country apart. U.S. inflation ran to levels unprecedented in modern times. Interest rates on short-term money market instruments such as Treasury bills went to double digits.

Many accepted academic economic theories were being disproven in the most important laboratory of all—reality. The so-called Phillips curve had postulated a connection between employment and inflation. The idea was that increasing inflation would raise employment by boosting the economy. Its limitations became evident when the marketplace began to factor increasing inflation into decisions about the future.

Now the country was burdened with increasing unemployment *and* rising inflation. The Keynesian economists (disciples of John Maynard Keynes) had long held that proper government stimulation could level out the sharp rises and falls of the business cycle. Yet increased fiscal stimulation through heavy spending by the federal government did little to alleviate the economic crisis.

People began to turn to the historic "chaos hedges": gold, silver, and physical commodities. When you purchase a stock, you are far removed from actual possession and control over what you own. Trust in management and the marketplace plays a strong role in your investment decisions. When this confidence is shaken, investors turn to those investments that are much less removed from actual possession and control. The price of an ounce of gold is pretty clear-cut. It has very little variance worldwide. The same could be said for most physical commodities.

The price of a financial asset such as stocks or even bonds, however, depends on a whole panorama of subjective factors. How good is the management of the company? How good and competitive are its products? Does the marketplace recognize its true value? Many considerations make up the price of a financial asset, and they vary daily.

Characteristics

Europeans have been inflation conscious for centuries, as the result of many bouts with runaway inflation. Americans have become more conscious of the dangers of inflation over the last 20 years. Purchasing power was lost by savers earning 5.25% on their passbook accounts when inflation ran 10% and much more in the 1970s. Investor and consumer resistance to such confiscation resulted in the rise of a major new financial industry: money market funds.

Most Americans were not able to participate in the sophisticated high-priced money market instruments used by the rich. But they did know they were losing money by saving the old way. When first one, and then many entrepreneurs offered the average saver the chance to at least "stay even," there was a rush of money to money market funds.

As Americans became more used to active money management, many investment vehicles became more volatile. Gold and sil-

ver prices rose to unprecedented levels, and then (in early 1980) fell even more sharply. Commodity prices in the late 1970s ran to all-time highs, boosted by raging inflation and investor rejection of traditional "paper" investments.

Make no mistake: investing in tangibles—whether gold, silver, wheat, oil, diamonds, or whatever—is a very risky game. Heavy participation in the stock and bond markets by long-term institutional investors gives these markets some stability over the long haul. But there is no such institutional support in precious metals and straight commodity investing. Also, tangibles do not pay any current income. High dividend paying stocks or bonds with high coupon yields afford some downside protection since owners do receive some regular payout. As a result, these markets are more volatile.

Risks

Commodities are highly vulnerable to political risk. For example, in the 1980s President Carter, without warning, declared an embargo on U.S. grain shipments to the Soviet Union. Since the Soviet Union was one of the largest buyers of our grain, that announcement devastated the grain markets overnight. Wheat, corn, and soybean prices fell so sharply in the futures markets that few buyers could be found for days. In 1933, President Roosevelt decreed that ownership of gold was illegal for American citizens. That ban lasted until 1975! True, gold held during that time had value as determined by demand in other countries. But its value for Americans was diminished by the criminal penalties attached to its ownership.

A prominent risk for holders of financial assets is business risk. What if a company is mismanaged or simply overlooked by the market? Investors in precious metals and commodities do not have to worry about that risk if they own the actual commodity. Owners of gold stocks, though, may not benefit from a rise in the gold price because of business problems. A mine may be poorly managed. Or, as has often been the case, individual mines may have suffered disasters such as floods or cave-ins that rendered the mine less valuable.

A sidelight to the business and political

risk consideration is the political situation in the Union of South Africa. Further political upheavals there would be "bullish for gold." Since South Africa accounts for the majority of new supply, an upheaval would shrink the supply, boosting prices. However, owners of South African gold *stocks* would lose substantially. Most gold mutual funds have some investments in South African mines.

Contrary to conventional wisdom, rising interest rates are not usually a negative for gold prices. Since rising rates are often caused by increased inflation, gold and commodity prices will also be lifted by the same concerns. Only at the top of the inflation cycle, when inflation begins to turn down, would rising rates hurt gold prices. When interest rates go above the inflation rate by more than 2 to 3%, it will cause a turndown in inflation hedges because it no longer makes sense to borrow to buy today.

Keep in mind that the last inflation cycle peaked in 1980, but interest rates continued to rise for two more years. They lagged behind the rise in inflation, and significantly lagged behind the turn.

The worldwide inflation of the 1980s spawned a vibrant "inflation hedge" industry. Gold and silver in their many forms are quite liquid. However, some forms, such as coins or futures, are considerably more liquid than others.

Compared to Other Assets

Gold and physical commodities play an important part in any well-designed portfolio. They tend to trade contracyclically with the stock market gains. Precious metals typically rise when the stock market is falling.

This is not to say that gold and the stock market always trade opposite one another. For example, the last stages of a bull market are often the most exciting and rewarding for investors who have the capital, knowledge, and fortitude to hold on to their positions.

During those last stages, gold usually reverses its downward slide, or awakens from a long sideways trading range. Thus they may both go up together for a while.

As the experience of the 1970s showed, prolonged inflation distorts market processes. These distortions result in wrong business decisions, which eventually cause stock prices to decline. In these times, precious metals and other raw commodities offer the best returns.

How to Invest

You can purchase gold, silver, and platinum in bullion or coin form and store them yourself. However, such direct possession is not practical for most commodities or even for sizable amounts of the precious metals.

Stocks are available for companies that produce most raw commodities. We've mentioned gold mining stocks, but many companies exist whose primary business is the production of natural resources. Ask your broker for a list of companies in the industry groups that interest you. Or investigate mutual funds that specialize in precious metals, natural resources, or energy stocks.

Highly leveraged futures trading is the most liquid method for direct investment in a wide range of raw commodities and precious metals. This market is really only suitable for investors willing and able to risk substantial sums for substantial earning potential. It is very high risk!

The five largest gold funds are International Investors, Fidelity Select Precious Metals, United Services Gold Shares, Franklin Gold, and Fidelity Select—American Gold. The only silver fund is Strategic Silver.

Lasser's Recommended Portfolio Allocation
in Gold and Other Precious Metals for the 1990s

Allocate as little as 5%.

Allocate as much as 20%.

Precious Metals

The label "precious metals" is the most widely used label for metals valued for their monetary role as hedges against inflation. Precious metals are primarily gold and silver. In recent years, platinum and even palladium have been included. Although the latter two are now usually included, neither really has any monetary role.

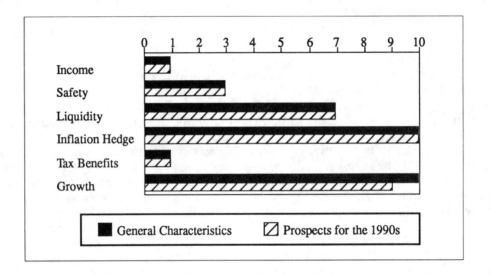

Type I

D

Low Taxes
Low Expenses

Before January 1, 1975 (as already noted), it was illegal for Americans to own gold in any form other than numismatic coins. Gold ownership had been declared illegal during the Great Depression. For many years, the huge U.S. gold bullion reserves were used to "fix" gold at prices from $32 to $35 per ounce, the final exchange rate prior to gold legalization. The Bretton Woods agreement between the major political powers after World War II set the U.S. dollar as the world's reserve currency. The United States stood ready to redeem dollars for gold.

In the early 1970s, inflation began to pick up around the world. Some countries, most notably France, began to exchange large quantities of U.S. dollars for gold. Rather than allow this continued outflow of gold ("the great gold drain"), President Nixon

closed the gold window in August 1971.

Gold has been the classic inflation hedge throughout history. Although countries (including the United States) have virtually always tried to "demonetize" gold, individuals have ultimately turned to it rather than to government-issued currency. Before 1975, Americans either bought gold coins that were recognized as numismatic (having collector's value) or silver coins (the "poor man's gold") to hedge against inflation.

There are now many ways to buy precious metals. Gold and silver stocks are freely and actively traded. Gold and silver are traded on futures and even option exchanges. You can buy gold and silver coins, numismatic or bullion (having no value other than their gold or silver content). You can buy "warehouse receipts" for gold held by a third party. The third party may be a Swiss bank or a domestic storage facility. Some mutual funds even offer "shares" in gold bullion stockpiles.

You can buy gold in any one of many different forms from full-service brokerage firms, many banks, and independent metal dealers. Some forms of gold investing are closely regulated by the federal government, such as stocks, mutual funds, options, or futures. Coin and bullion dealers are not always subject to government regulation. There have been many scandals involving nonregulated and regulated precious metals dealers who have not bought and stored the gold or silver for which they sold warehouse receipts. Fraudulent coin dealers are always a threat to the naive investor.

Fees can vary widely. Commissions are assessed for stocks, options, and futures. Coins are usually sold with an undisclosed dealer markup. Bullion, such as bars, must be assayed before resale.

The precious metals industry has generated many independent investment advisory newsletters covering everything from penny stocks to futures, and to coin and bullion. Gold prices are quoted daily in the *Wall Street Journal* and *Investor's Daily*.

Investment Potential

Gold, silver, and platinum are the three most commonly traded precious metals. The purchase and sale of precious metals produce capital gains (or losses). The chief drawback to precious metals investing is the lack of income (except for dividend-paying gold stocks). Also, with precious metal coin or bullion you cannot take advantage of compounding. Inflation-wary investors hold gold as long-term protection from the ravages of inflation. Investors in gold and silver options and futures are oriented toward short-term trading.

The most popular bullion gold coin is the American Eagle. These coins can be purchased in a variety of sizes from 1 ounce to 1/10 of an ounce. There is usually a 5% to 10% premium. Other popular bullion gold coins include the Canadian Maple Leaf, the South African Krugerrand (while an active market still exists for the Krugerrand, it is illegal to import new coins into the U.S.), the Mexican 50 Peso, and the Austrian Corona.

Money Management Tip

Numismatic gold coins share the appreciation potential of gold bullion, with the added factor of "collector value." Popular numismatic gold coins include the U.S. $20, $10, and $5 gold pieces and the British sovereign. This highly specialized market is crucially dependent on "grading." A numismatic coin is graded for its condition. A change in grade can mean a substantial change in the value of a coin. For example, if you buy a coin graded BU ("brilliant uncirculated") from one dealer, and another grades the same coin AU ("almost uncirculated") you can lose as much as 50% or more of your investment, with no change in the price of gold!

Silver coins also have an active market. Silver dollars were once traded primarily for their silver content. However, now most silver dollars trade for significant premiums over their silver content. Even bags (usually $1,000 face value) of "junk" silver coins (worn, well-circulated) often trade at premiums over their silver content.

Precious metals prices are quite volatile. Since they do not pay any income, there is little protection from sharp drops in price. Do not overlook this volatile nature when buying gold. If you stick with popular bullion coins or have a good working relationship with a gold bullion dealer, your investment should be quite liquid.

Fees vary widely. Some dealers assess a commission in addition to a price markup. Even if you buy bullion or coins at a small premium of 3 to 8% over gold value, when you sell you will lose that premium. Most gold and silver coins and bullion are quoted with a bid (the price the dealer is willing to pay) and an ask (the price they are willing to sell). This spread is your cost for the transaction.

No federal insurance protects bullion or coin purchases. Nor is there a widely recognized rating service for precious metals dealers.

Strengths

Precious metals provide an excellent hedge against inflation. Carefully selected precious metals investments are liquid. Numismatic gold and silver coins provide downside protection from price weakness in the metals themselves. Some banks will loan money against gold or silver collateral. South African gold-mining stocks pay high income, on average.

Weaknesses

There is no government regulation of precious metal coin and bullion dealers. Also, numismatic coins are subject to wide variances in "grading," which can significantly affect the resale value of the coins. Bullion must be assayed before resale. Precious metals (except for dividend-paying stocks in precious metals) pay no income, and fees may be very high, limiting profit potential. High fees are particularly prominent in "leveraged" or "bank financing" programs, where investors are conned into leveraging their investments and paying commissions of as much as 10-15% plus other fees. It is not unusual for fees to be so high in these programs (though rarely disclosed as such) that it would take a 30% to 40% price rise just to break even! Furthermore, precious metals prices are volatile. Finally, numismatic coin investors run a business risk of unscrupulous dealers as well as market price risk.

Tax Considerations

Tax Consequences

No special tax benefits apply to precious metals investments. All gains are capital gains, which are taxed at your ordinary income rates. Until 1987, gold coins and bullion were not legal for IRAs. Some coins such as the American Gold Eagle are now legal for IRAs. Check with your tax advisor.

Summing Up

Precious metals serve a twofold economic purpose. First, they have some value through their industrial uses. For example, silver is very important in photography. Gold is critical in high-technology uses. Both are valued for their beauty in jewelry.

Gold (primarily) and silver (to a smaller extent) also serve an important monetary role. Throughout history, people have opted for gold (or silver) rather than for government-issued money if they have reason to suspect fraud in the issuance of a government's legal tender.

This protective role as a hedge against financial instability survives to this day. When U.S. inflation moved to double digits in the late 1970s, it was obvious to most consumers that the traditional havens for savings—stocks, bonds, and bank savings plans—were losers. Many investors turned to gold, silver, and platinum as the last resort for protecting their purchasing power.

Despite the long bull market in stocks that started in 1982, savvy investors continue to monitor the gold markets for early signs of resurgent inflation. Just as the stock market tends to "discount" (predict) the economic future (the market will typically peak before the economy does), so does gold discount the future of inflation.

Strategic Metals

Strategic metals are rare metals such as titanium, chromium, and cobalt that have crucial high-technology uses. Usually these metals are mined as by-products of gold and silver. The major supplies of these metals are in Zimbabwe, the Union of South Africa, and the Soviet Union. Advocates of strategic metals investing argue that the metals are crucial for U.S. defense and that the unstable political situation in countries that supply most of the metals could create shortages.

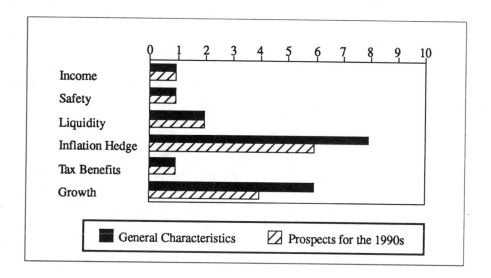

Many of the same investment advisors who correctly identified the fundamental factors that led to the great precious metals bull market of the late 1970s, began to tout strategic metals as the next great growth market in the late 1970s and early 1980s. Initial interest and activity was high, fueled by inflation and political fears.

Type I

D

Low Taxes
Low Expenses

Prices boomed initially as inflation-wary investors sought to diversify their portfolios. When the precious metals bull market peaked in early 1980, the strategic metals market also was hurt. After an enthusiastic beginning—including the launching of a mutual fund, numerous warehouse certificate programs, and even the minting of bars for physical possession—interest fell off dramatically.

Strategic metals now have a very thin, hard-to-follow market with only a few sources of reliable information for the average investor. Prices are very difficult to follow, because no real, active auction market exists for many of the metals.

Most major precious metals dealers can provide information on investing in strategic metals. Fees vary widely and are a major problem with investing in this esoteric market. The best alternative for most investors is a mutual fund that offers some liquidity.

Investment Potential

Like precious metals, strategic metals offer capital gains potential. No income is paid. This market is a long-term investment. Given the erratic pricing caused by the thin, closely controlled market, bid–ask ranges are very wide. Substantial appreciation is needed just to cover such a spread.

Prices are very volatile. The lack of easily accessible prices and market information limits the potential for leveraging your investment.

Strategic metals are very illiquid. Gaining access is a problem even for an average investor. The paucity of investment vehicles limits flexibility. A few investment advisory newsletters are on the market, but they are usually produced by interested parties who want to sell their particular investment vehicle.

The government does not regulate strategic metals trading. A mutual fund or limited partnership offering of any size must register with the SEC and provide detailed financial information.

Only one mutual fund currently specializes in strategic metals investing: Strategic Investments, run by Strategic Management (214) 484-1326.

Strengths

Strategic metals provide a good inflation hedge and are one of the few markets that offer investors the chance to hedge geo-political events. The very small supply of some metals can result in large capital gains.

Weaknesses

Strategic metals are very illiquid. Moreover, they are not an accepted asset class in the investment community, so accurate information is difficult to obtain. Flexibility is limited by the fact that very few markets are available.

They pay no income and the very thin markets can result in large losses overnight. You have no way to hedge your exposure with other markets. Finally, the trading history is too short to make reliable forecasts of future price action.

Tax Considerations

Tax Consequences

No special tax benefits for strategic metals investing. All gains are capital gains and are taxed at your ordinary income rates. Capital losses can be used to offset other capital gains. Losses are carried forward.

Summing Up

After a promising beginning, strategic metals have not fulfilled their potential as a real investment alternative. Intensified political problems in the Union of South Africa could reignite this market. Until more independent pricing information is available, however, you are placing too much trust in the firm that handles your strategic metals investments. As in diamond investing, you have to get price information from the people who sell you the product. They tend to interpret all developments in the very best light. Also, the problem of buying retail and selling wholesale works against you. This market is best left to adventurous, risk-oriented souls willing and able to risk and lose their entire investments in exchange for the potential of large profits.

Gold and Silver Mutual Funds

Precious metals funds invest in a diversified pool of gold- and silver-related stocks. Some funds also invest directly in the bullion. Gold stocks provide substantial leverage for precious metals investors.

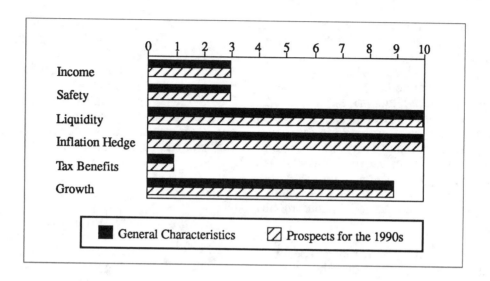

Gold and silver are classic inflation hedge investments. They tend to be very volatile, though. The major gold-producing mines are in South Africa, and the tenuous political situation there inflames price volatility. The stocks tend to outperform the bullion because costs of production are relatively fixed. Historically, the price of gold stocks climbs about 1.5 to 2 times as fast as the gain in bullion prices. It costs $200 to $300 per ounce to mine gold, so price increases above that amount dramatically enhance a mine's profitability. For example, from September 29, 1989 through February 8, 1990, gold rose 14%. Many individual gold stocks rose more than 30% in the same time period. The *average* gold mutual fund appreciated 30% in that same time period! The universe of gold stocks is small compared to common stock issues. Only about 15 mutual funds are oriented toward gold, compared to hundreds

Type II

D

Low Taxes
Low Expenses

of stock funds. Only one fund invests strictly in silver stocks and bullion. You have considerably less flexibility in finding funds that closely match your investment objectives and risk tolerance. The bull gold market in the 1970s led to an explosion in the investment advisory newsletter field. Many advisory letters still specialize in precious metals. Most major financial periodicals cover the precious metals markets. Most gold fund prices are listed in the *Wall Street Journal* and *Investor's Daily*.

Both load and no-load gold mutual funds are available. Load funds assess an up-front charge of 2% to 8%. No-load funds have no sales fees. No difference in performance is discernible between the two types of funds.

Investment Potential

The chief attraction of gold funds is large potential capital gains. However, many funds also offer attractive income. Many South African gold stocks pay relatively high dividends. Since gold is a depleting asset (once the reserves are mined, more gold cannot be created), high-dividend payouts should be considered, at least in part, return of capital.

Some gold funds invest a small portion of their assets in "penny stocks." Penny stocks are issues that trade for less than $1 per share. They are new, untried companies that trade more on future promises than on actual present-day results. Penny stocks are very high risk. They have a high bankruptcy rate. They also offer substantial leverage if their properties actually do become viable as a result of high gold or silver prices.

The diversified portfolios of gold funds enable them to invest in these highly speculative ventures without worry that their failure will greatly affect the fund's assets. Yet they are so highly leveraged that one successful penny stock venture out of a hundred can be sufficient to actually make money overall.

The underlying high volatility of gold prices is reflected by gold funds. The funds are liquid and diversified, and thus provide greater safety than investing in a single gold stock. Gold funds are usually rated "high risk" by catalogers such as *Money, Forbes*, or *Business Week*.

Gold funds are subject to market price risk. Funds that invest in South African stocks are subject to substantial political risk. Both gold and silver funds provide excellent protection from inflation.

Gold funds are suitable investments for well-diversified retirement plans. They would not be appropriate as the only asset in such plans.

Strengths

 Gold and silver funds are liquid investments. The funds provide greater safety through diversification than investing in single stocks. Gold funds offer potential for excellent capital gains, excellent protection from inflation, and professinal management in a high-risk area.

Gold share investments usually outperform bullion. This is because the cost of mining an ounce of gold remains the same for a gold mine whether the price of gold is $200 or $400 an ounce. Every dollar gold rises above the cost of production is high profit money for a gold mine.

Weaknesses

 Gold fund prices are volatile. Gold funds substantially underperform the stock market in noninflationary times. Also, funds that invest in South African shares are subject to the political uncertainty surrounding that country. Poor management may result in high fees and bad performance.

Tax Considerations

Tax Consequences

The 1986 Tax Reform Act eliminated preferential treatment for capital gains. Capital gains and dividend income are taxed at your ordinary income bracket.

Summing Up

Gold has been in a long-term downtrend in the 1980s. It is highly unlikely that gold will now experience a superbull market like that of the 1970s anytime soon. However it is always possible that international political developments could ignite just such a market. In the 1970s the OPEC oil embargo and U.S. involvement in Vietnam triggered the worst inflation in U.S. history. As this is being written, the Iraqis have invaded Kuwait and are threatening Saudi Arabia. Oil prices have shot up over $10 a barrel in only a couple of weeks. The media is talking about deployment of U.S. forces into the Middle East. It is impossible to forecast how this will all develop but it does pose the possibility of yet another inflationary spiral in the 1990s similar to the 1970s.

Gold funds will benefit from a surge in inflation. Gold usually goes up when the U.S. dollar goes down. Monitor inflation indexes and dollar performance as key factors for the future of gold.

Many investment advisors believe that gold and gold funds should be a small part, 5% to 10%, of a diversified investment portfolio. The variety of gold funds offer you good flexibility in selecting a fund that meets your objectives and risk tolerance. Funds investing solely in South African shares would run higher risk than funds investing in North American and Australian gold shares. Funds that invest a portion of their assets in bullion will be less volatile than share-only funds.

Most gold-oriented mutual funds invest in South African gold shares. However, because of the political uncertainty and moral repugnance many people feel for South Africa, a number of funds in recent years have been launched that do not invest in South African shares. They include USAA Gold Fund, United Services New Prospector Fund, Midas Gold Shares & Bullion, Colonial Advanced Strategies Gold Trust, and Fidelity Select—American Gold. The last three are allowed to invest in South African shares but have elected not to do so. To be sure, check with the fund before investing.

These funds that do not invest in South Africa outperformed South African funds during most of 1987. However, performance reversed following the October market crash. For example, United Services Gold Shares, which invests solely in South Africa, fell 9.5% in the week after the crash. Meanwhile, United Services New Prospector Fund, which has no South African investments, fell 19.8%.

One of the problems was that non-South African funds typically invest heavily in Australian mines. The Australian market is quite thin. When the market panic swept the world's markets, Australian mining shares were hard hit. Another reason for the poorer performance by the non-South African investing funds was that they had risen more in price in the months leading up to the crash.

In addition to buying the shares of gold-mining companies, some funds invest in bullion. These include Midas Gold Shares & Bullion, Lexington Goldfund, and Golconda Investors Ltd. These funds outperformed other gold funds following the October 1987 market crash. Gold stocks funds fell an average of 15%. The bullion-based investing funds did not fall as sharply as the all-share funds.

Collectibles

The term "collectibles" encompasses a wide variety of items. The most popular markets include stamps, antiques, art, and photography (see also the section on rare coins). Collectibles are nonfinancial physical assets found in limited supply that provide esthetic, psychological, or practical value to the owner. They are expected to appreciate as a result of inflation or through increased recognition of their rarity.

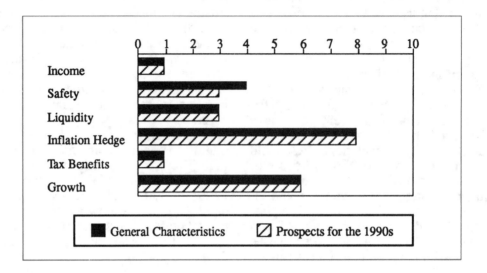

Type I

D

Low Taxes
Low Expenses

Collectibles attracted much attention from investors in the inflation-torn 1970s. Although experts and neophytes alike profited in those years, 1982 marked a reversal for inflation and resulted in a severe shake-out in these markets.

Unlike financial assets, collectibles are not traded in a central auction arena. Rather, thay are bought and sold through loose networks of dealers, collectors, and even flea markets. Prices fluctuate widely from transaction to transaction. Experts recommend that investing in collectibles should only be undertaken by those with an abiding interest in the particular item.

The collectible market is susceptible to fraud and to well-intentioned, but mistaken valuations.

Because no uniform method is used for valuing collectible assets, there is a wide range for legitimate differences of opinion.

This variability makes the market particularly treacherous for amateur investors.

Costs are a two-edged sword: Not only is a price paid for an item, there is also the cost of lost opportunity for the money invested. *Opportunity cost* is merely the return that is given up in order to hold the collectible. For example, to figure opportunity cost calculate how much interest would have been paid by an equivalent investment in Treasury bills over the same time period. That is the cost of holding an investment such as a collectible that pays no income.

The profit acquired when the item is sold is the return *over and above* what could have been earned in the safest financial vehicle.

Investment Potential

Investing in collectibles is a long-term project because rarely can short-term profits be made. Often nonprofessional investors wind up paying retail prices, but can sell only at wholesale levels. For many investors, the psychic benefit is well worth the aggravation. This is a decision only you can make.

Collectibles provide capital gains when buying at one price and selling at a higher price. There is no income.

Strengths

Collectibles have an outstanding record in protecting your assets from the ravages of inflation. They have esthetic value to their owners.

Weaknesses

Liquidity varies greatly. Some collectibles can only be sold through auction houses, via consignment or with dealers.

The two major auction houses for collectibles are both British: Sotheby's Holdings, Inc., and Christie's International PLC. Both are headquartered in London, but have offices in major cities around the world. You can get a good feel for the trend of collectible prices by watching auctions by either or both of these houses.

Even "fairly" priced assets may take a long time to sell in depressed economic environments. Prices for collectibles are not established through the free flow of supply and demand in an open auction market as in stocks and bonds. Obtaining an accurate valuation of your collectibles is difficult. As many investors have learned to their chagrin, even if an independent expert values a particular collectible—whether it is a painting, a classic car, or an antique—there is no guarantee that a buyer can be found willing to pay that price.

Price information on some collectibles is more accessible than on others. For example, the annual *Lyle Antiques Review* price guide has been issued for 25 years. In 1988, Putnam Publishing added the *Lyle Price Guide To Collectibles and Memorabilia.*

Many factors go into determining the value of collectibles, including such subjective details as their condition. There is no current

income, and costs vary greatly. Also, collectibles are not eligible for IRAs. And, finally, each collectible carries its own unique risks, including potential loss of value due to deterioration, widespread fraud (widespread fraud can depress prices of a whole category of collectibles, even if the one you own is legitimate!), changing interest in "fads," or even a large increase in supply, such as the discovery of additional units of a previously rare commodity (e.g. an unknown stash of coins).

Tax Considerations

Tax Consequences

No tax advantages apply to collectibles. In fact, because the IRS may determine that your collectible investing is a "hobby" rather than a business, associated costs may not be deductible.

However, tax on gains is due regardless of whether your collectible investing is deemed a hobby or an investment.

Summing Up

The popularity of collectible investing has decreased considerably in recent years due to widespread fraud in major markets such as coins or art. As art prices climbed, forgeries became more common. Overgrading of coins is commonplace. If you have a real interest in a specific area and have the time to pursue detailed study, it can certainly be very profitable. However, for most investors the prime consideration should be whether the enjoyment derived from the activity is sufficient to offset the potential financial drawbacks.

Even in the absence of surging inflation, there have been some sterling performers among collectibles. Sotheby's "Art Index" prepared by the auction firm shows that art appreciated at a 20.9% annual rate from 1984 through 1988. That compares to an annual rate of 17% over the same period for the S & P 500 stock index. According to a study prepared by the large international brokerage firm, Salomon Brothers, paintings by "impressionist artists" grew 771% in the

1980s, placing second only to Japanese stock (in U.S. dollars) for overall gains in the decade. Other collectibles that ranked high on its list included American Paintings (pre-WWII) up 335%, Chinese ceramics up 317%, and diamonds plus 76%. Those gains compare to U.S. stocks as represented by the S&P 500 Index up 375%, international stocks (in U.S. dollars) 449%, growth stock funds on average up 301%, long-term Treasury bonds up 232%, gold bullion down 21%, and oil (Saudi light) down 34%.

In 1988 the art world was shaken by the publication of A. S. Huffington's book *Picasso: Creator and Destroyer,* which argues that Picasso was a cruel, mean-spirited man, whose later works were inferior. Despite concern that it may have an adverse affect on prices for Picasso's works, no harm was evident by July 1990.

The hottest segment of the art market has been work of the Impressionists. Some experts estimate that collectors spent over $500 million buying Impressionist art in 1988 alone.

Other collectibles have enjoyed renewed investor interest. Hollywood memorabilia also drew sharply higher prices. In June 1988, a pair of sequin-covered shoes worn by Judy Garland in *The Wizard of Oz* was sold for $165,000. That compares to the sale of a similar pair in 1981 for $13,200.

Business in Hollywood memorabilia is so good that a number of companies hold monthly auctions. Collectors Bookstore in Hollywood (1708 N. Vine St., Hollywood, CA 90028) pioneered these affairs. It has even sold a number of Oscar statuettes in recent years.

Serious collectors should investigate publications such as *Movie Collectors World* (Box 309, Fraser, MI 48026) or *The Big Reel* (Route 3, Box 3, Madison, NC 27025).

And finally, classic car collectors have reaped big profits in recent years. Collectible cars, especially 1930s and 1940s autos, rose 30%–40% in price in 1988 from the previous year.

But the rise in prices for cars has brought problems with conterfeits as it has with art and coins.

Collectibles represent potentially profitable investments. However, the ones who make money consistently are the professionals, not the seat-of-the-pants investors. If you have a real interest in some type of collectible for nonmonetary reasons, it may turn out to be an area for investment also. However, despite all the glamorous stories about high profits, remember, there are many more examples of big losses resulting from ignorance, fraud, or simple mistakes.

---

10 Popular "Exotic" Investments

1. Rare coins
2. Art
3. Stamps
4. Classic cars
5. Hollywood memorabilia
6. Guns
7. Wines
8. Scotch whiskey
9. Antiques
10. Baseball cards

Rare Coins

Rare coins are coins, issued by governments as legal tender, that have collector's value over and above the face value of the coin.

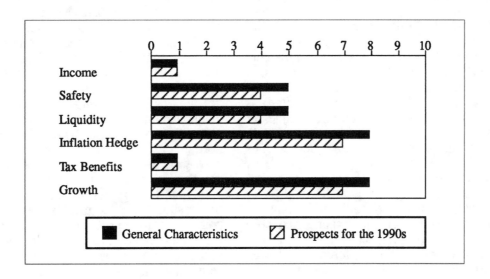

General Characteristics   Prospects for the 1990s

Type I

D

Low Taxes
Low Expenses

According to Salomon Brothers, the major investment banking firm, rare (numismatic) coins have been one of the best investments for the past 20 years. The Salomon Brothers numismatic coin index has outperformed the stock market, bonds, and gold. For example, a $1,000 investment in rare coins in 1968 would have grown to $16,650 by 1988, according to Salomon Brothers. That compares to stocks growing to $3,727, and bonds going to $4,748. Of course, that assumes you bought the same 20 coins used by Salomon in its index! The Salomon Rare Coin Index is based on the performance of a 20-coin portfolio.

The numismatic value of coins was recognized by the U.S. government in the 1933 Gold Reserve Act. That law made it illegal for U.S. citizens to own gold but it specifically exempted gold coins of "recognized special value to collectors." Numismatic coins are not limited to gold and silver. Coins minted in other metals, such as copper, are also actively sought by rare coin investors.

The rare coin market is loosely organized. Sales are made through coin dealers in shops and through the mail. The most common method for the sale of highly valued coins is through auctions. Often investors bid for coins through "mail auctions." Another popular marketplace is coin shows that convene in major cities around the country.

The rare coin investment community is well served by many periodicals, including weekly newspapers such as *Coin World* and *Numismatic News*. One national teletype service provides up-to-date price information for dealers. Most dealers subscribe to the *Coin Dealers Gray Sheet* newsletter, a weekly update of price information and market trends. Also, many investment advisory newsletters ferret out good values in rare coins for their subscribers.

The loosely knit organization provides fair liquidity for more actively traded coins, including most U.S.-issued gold coins. U.S. silver dollars also offer a very popular market. More obscure coins are less actively traded and hence provide substantially less liquidity. Fees vary widely. Most pricing is done on a "markup" basis whereby the dealer purchases a coin with its resources and then resells that coin at a higher price. This markup is usually not disclosed to the buyer. The best way to tell if you are being charged excessive fees is to comparison-shop with a number of dealers before buying. Competition serves to limit abuses for actively involved investors.

The most troublesome area for rare coin buyers is the grading of individual coins. A coin's grade is a rating of its condition. A coin sold as BU (brilliant uncirculated) is supposed to be in mint condition. A lesser grade is AU (almost uncirculated). A widely accepted numerical rating now accompanies these letter designations.

Regardless of the numerous enhancements that grading has gone through over the years, evaluation of individual coins remains largely subjective. Experienced coin investors and dealers detect the subtle nuances that make the difference between grades. Neophyte investors must rely on the dealer's integrity. Brown and Dunn's *Guide to Grading of United States Coins* is the classic book on grading and evaluating coins.

There have been a number of attempts to make the grading of coins more reliable. In 1979 the American Numismatic Association launched a certificate program called American Numismatic Association Certification Service (ANACS), which provided a certificate with a picture of the coin, identification information, and a grade on the coin's condition. After enthusiastic initial response, the program was racked by dissension following the sharp break in price in 1980. A trend to stricter grading left the ANACS program with decreasing support.

Recently, the Professional Coin Grading Service has attracted much support from savvy coin dealers around the country. PCGS uses experienced, proven professional numismatists to grade and certify coins. And, in a unique departure, the PCGS guarantees its grades with cash.

In August 1987, yet another competitor entered the market. The Numismatic Guarantee Corporation of America approaches the market with the same professionalism exhibited by PCGS. Only time will tell which service will prevail in the marketplace.

Investment Potential

Rare coin investing is a long-term proposition for most investors. Most investors buy coins at retail prices but can only sell them wholesale. It takes time for the appreciation to cover transaction costs. Coin experts suggest that an investor should expect to hold coins for at least five to seven years.

Rare coin investing generates capital gains. No income is paid. Coin prices are generally not volatile. The coin market in normal circumstances unfolds in a stable, slow-growth manner. However, times of great volatility do occur. The high inflation in the late 1970s and the subsequent disinflation resulted in wide price swings for many coins, especially gold and silver issues.

As mentioned earlier, liquidity is a factor in the decision of which coins to buy. Some coins have quite liquid markets and can be sold quickly. However, even widely traded gold coins can suffer large overnight price movements. A buyer can always be found, but the investor may be forced to take steep discounts if the coins must be sold quickly.

Rare coin investing is straightforward. Coins are bought, held, and sold. Only a limited number of strategies are available. Some dealers offer leveraged investments where a fraction of the cost of a portfolio of coins is paid. The dealer holds the coins for the investor who makes periodic interest and/or principal payments. Rare coins are also accepted by some banks as collateral for loans.

In an effort to boost credibility, the rare coin industry has stepped up its own self-policing mechanism. One trade group, the Industry Council for Tangible Assets, began recruiting dealers for its accreditation program in October 1987. The program features background checks of dealers and their businesses. Members are provided with advertising guidelines. Also members are required to provide customers with risk disclosure statements outlining the risks of rare coin investing.

Also, the Professional Numismatists Guild is expanding its accreditation program. Full membership requires $100,000 in assets and five years' experience. In addition, all applicants undergo a review by a member panel. However, the federal government does not regulate the rare coin industry. This freedom may change in the near future as a result of scandals involving overgrading of coins by large national dealers.

Strengths

Rare coins offer good potential for long-term capital growth, and they are an excellent inflation hedge. Most rare coin investors are motivated by the esthetic satisfaction of putting together beautiful collections as well as by the potential profit. Most U.S. gold and silver coins are quite liquid.

Weaknesses

A coin's condition is the most important factor in determining that coin's price. Grading is a subjective art with valid disparities of opinion. A change in grade of only one level may mean the reduction of a coin's value by as much as 50% or more. There is no central auction market that generates accurate fair prices for all coins. And high value coins are often conterfeited. Some counterfeits are so good they can be detected only with expensive, high-tech procedures.

Fees are not usually disclosed. They can be very high and consequently hurt your potential return. In addition, rare coins pay no current income.

Finally, rare coins can be stolen or misplaced.

Tax Considerations

Tax Consequences

No special tax benefits apply to rare coin investments. The 1986 Tax Reform Act eliminated the preferential treatment of long-term capital gains. All gains are taxed at your ordinary income rates.

Summing Up

Rare coin investing is a rapidly growing industry. As more investors participate, disparities in pricing will even out. Market information will increase. Rare coins are excellent inflation hedges.

Supply and demand ultimately determine all prices. The supply of rare coins is fixed. As the interest in them increases, their prices should continue to rise.

It is vital to do business with reputable, established coin dealers. The potential for fraud is high, and the investor must be careful. Never rush to buy a coin. Verify the price with independent sources to ensure you are not paying more than the market price. A coin that is a good value today will still be a good value in the two or three days it takes to evaluate its worth.

Notes

Income

Volatility

Ordinary income

CHAPTER 17

OPTIONS, FUTURES, SPECIAL INVESTING TECHNIQUES

A GLANCE AHEAD

Many analysts believe that the margins, high leverage, and general speculative fervor were responsible for the severity of the Great Depression. In 1929 you could buy stock from full-service brokerage firms for only 10% of the total price of the stocks being purchased. When prices started to fall, the heavily margined public couldn't come up with the money necessary to prevent liquidation.

Since those heady days, the Federal Reserve Board has controlled margin requirements. Today you must put up a minimum of 50% of the value of the stock you want to buy. Certainly that's far more conservative than 60 years ago.

But some advisors worry that the market has moved ahead of the regulators and ahead of the desire for control over speculation. At the peak of the last inflationary surge, President Carter went so far as to blame inflation on commodity speculators who were bidding prices to what he felt were unconscionable levels.

Most recently these leveraged investment vehicles—options, futures, and options on futures—have come under fire for the role they played in the October 1987 stock market crash. The opinions range from those who feel that these instruments were a pri-mary cause of that debacle, to others who feel their impact was negligible. There is certainly no conclusive evidence one way or another. However, this area has been targeted for closer scrutiny by Congress and government regulators. In addition, the various exchanges have worked out agreements to minimize any further market shock from special trading techniques. So-called "circuit breakers" that were put into place after the October 1987 crash are:

1) If S&P futures fall 5 points at opening, S&P futures trading pauses for 10 minutes.

2) If Dow Industrial Average drops 25 points, small orders get priority on Big Board computers ahead of programs.

3) If S&P futures fall 12 points (equivalent to about 100 points on the DJIA), trading is halted for 30 minutes. Program trades on the NYSE are diverted to a separate computer file to determine buy and sell orders.

4) If S&P futures fall 30 points, trading is restricted for an hour to that price or higher.

5) If Dow Industrials fall 250 points, trading on the Big Board halts for an hour. S&P and MMI futures trading also halts.

6) If DJIA drops 400 points, NYSE trading stops for 2 hours. Trading in MMI and S&P futures also stops.

A Glance Ahead   **321**

In this chapter, you'll learn

- *How put-and-call options can help you cash in on short-term market changes, but at considerable risk to your principal*
- *How futures help investors share business risks—and profits—with commodity producers and other investment companies*
- *How special trading techniques such as short selling and leveraged contracts can help to hedge your market bets.*

THE HOW AND WHY OF ADVANCED TRADING TECHNIQUES

In the 1920s, the futures markets were called the *commodity markets*. Agricultural commodities dominated the trade. Now agricultural commodities play a smaller role in futures.

The rise of the listed stock options market has made highly leveraged speculation easily accessible to anyone with a few thousand dollars. Most option premiums cost less than 10% of the value of the underlying stock.

There is one significant difference between options and futures. Option buyers don't have to come up with additional money if their stocks fall. Your loss is limited to the amount you paid for the option. And you can't buy options on margin!

Although there will always be "doom-and-gloomers" decrying every innovation, every change of any sort, no real evidence supports the notion that the rise of stock options and financial futures has resulted in widespread speculative excesses. In fact, one reason for the huge volumes in both these vehicles has been their widespread acceptance by institutions, from mutual funds to banks to international corporations.

Many mutual funds hedge downside risk with stock index futures. Savings institutions use financial futures to hedge their portfolios. This hedge helps them even out the wide swings in earnings that plagued the industry during the 1970s.

Risks

Concomitant with the higher returns possible with options and futures is the higher risk. The fact is that the vast majority of option and future traders lose money. You have to decide whether or not you are smarter and more disciplined than most other speculators.

Don't confuse option buying with investing in stock. You have no ownership interest in the underlying company. A well-managed company should show appreciation over time. But time is one thing an option buyer does not have. Stock buyers earn money from the growth of a company's assets even if it is not reflected immediately in the price. They may also receive dividends. Option buyers earn money only when the price of the stock appreciates more than the time value of the option depreciates! It does option buyers no good to have an option on an undervalued company if the market doesn't recognize it immediately!

In the past, much attention was directed to ferreting out undervalued stocks on the assumption that "you can't buy the market." That is no longer true. Stock index futures and options afford individuals the chance to "buy the market."

Some advisors would have you believe that timing the whole market is easier than selecting individual stocks, but the evidence certainly doesn't support that contention. Accurate timing has proven as elusive in today's high-tech environment as it was 50 years ago.

Futures trading is very high risk. The money you are required to deposit represents only about 5–10% of your total exposure.

Time Sensitive

Futures trading is dominated by short-term trading. Holding a position for more than two months is the exception for most traders. It requires close daily contact with your broker. Because of the leverage involved, you must track prices every day or risk substantial losses. This kind of trading is for risk takers, willing and able to sustain intense activity and sizable losses.

Options are hyped as a "safe" alternative to futures. But beware of the glossy language. Do you *really* feel all that much safer knowing that your total investment becomes worthless on a set day in the near future? It is said that "time heals all." Obviously, whoever thought up that proverb didn't trade options! It cannot be emphasized too strongly that *of all investments, option buying requires the best timing*.

Conclusions

We don't mean to discourage all interest in option or futures trading. We do mean to emphasize that both endeavors are not suitable for most investors. Most readers of this book have full-time jobs that occupy their primary attention. The speculative tactics we are about to discuss in this chapter are not to be engaged in part-time, casually. The stakes are too high.

If you are willing to take the greater risk but still do not have the time to devote, consider professional management. However, just as you shouldn't believe everything a securities salesperson tells you, neither should you take a manager's claims at face value. Get a manager whose philosophy most closely fits

Professional Advice

your own outlook. An intense, short-term, big risk taker may perform well over time. But are you willing to sit through the bad spells? If not, select a manager with more consistent, if less spectacular, results.

Keep in mind that the power of compounding ensures that a steady performance of 10% to 15% per year will yield huge returns over 10 or 15 years. There are many advisors who show spectacular performance for a short time; but no one makes 50%–100% a year consistently over the long term.

The odds are that if a manager manages to achieve spectacular returns such as 50% to 100%, that manager will suffer huge drawdowns (losses) at some point. Do you want to put yourself at risk choosing just such a manager just before he/she has a large turndown?

Notes

_____

_____

_____

_____

_____

_____

_____

_____

_____

_____

Buying Stock Options

The two types of listed stock options are: calls and puts. A call option gives the buyer the right to buy 100 shares of a specified stock at a specified price within a specified time period. A put option is the reverse. A put option gives the buyer the right to sell 100 shares of a specified stock at a specified price within a specified time period.

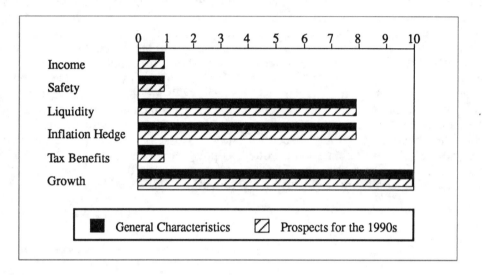

Type I

D

Low Taxes
- Low Expenses

Options offer investors an opportunity to leverage their investments. For example, an investor who buys an IBM July 150 call has purchased the *right* to buy 100 shares of IBM from the seller of the option at $150 per share up to the third week in July (see the section on stock options income). Assume that in March, the July 150 call was $8 when the price of IBM on the New York Stock Exchange (NYSE) was $150. Since each option is for 100 shares, multiply 100 by $8 to get the day's price of $800 for the option.

Puts are the exact opposite. For example, on the same day in March, the IBM July 150 put sold for $7 per share, or $700 for the option. Its expiration is the same day as the call.

A combined example can help sort out these complexities. Assume that on the day of our transaction, IBM sold for $150 per share on the NYSE. If you felt that IBM had a good chance to rise to $160 or more by the end of July, you could have profited in two ways:

- You could buy 100 shares of IBM stock for $15,000 (plus commission)
- Or you could buy a July 150 call option for $800 (plus commission).

If you believed that the price of IBM will go *down* by the end of July, you again would have had two alternatives:

- Sell short 100 shares of IBM for $15,000 (plus commission)
- Buy a July 150 put option for $700 (plus commission).

Investment Potential

The difference between stock and option investing is *leverage*. Options enable investors to control stock with an investment of only 5% to 10% of the value of the underlying stock. However, an options buyer has one important consideration that a stock buyer doesn't: time. Time works against the options buyer because the option loses value every day up to expiration.

On the transaction day in March, the May 150 call option was worth only $550 compared to $800 for the July contract because only eight weeks were left before the call expired. The July option had an *additional* eight weeks for IBM to make its anticipated move, and therefore commanded a higher price.

Options buying offers capital gains potential only. Purchased options pay no income (see later section on stock options income).

Options trading is very high risk, highly volatile. Most options trading is now done via the major exchanges. The uniform contract specifications and active markets make them very liquid.

As mentioned earlier, options run the unique risk of time. An option buyer always has time working against him or her. Therefore timing expertise is at a premium. In addition, of course, options are subject to the same business, political, and economic risks as are the underlying stocks.

Strengths

Exchange-listed options are very liquid. Options offer significant leverage. Option investing requires less capital than does stock trading. Losses are limited to the amount of the premium.

Weaknesses

Options are very high risk. On expiration date, the option value drops to zero! If your timing is off by even a few weeks, you can lose your whole investment. Options pay no income. (Most optionable stocks pay at least some dividends.) Option trading requires close attention to market action. Options have finite lives. Option traders must meet stringent financial suitability requirements.

Our example (see p. 329) of the call option assumes that IBM appreciated from $150 to $160 per share between March and July, when the option expired. If the stock rises to $160 *before* the third week of July, the option usually trades with some premium for the time left before expiration as well as "intrinsic value." Intrinsic value of a call option is determined by subtracting the strike price of the option from the current price of the stock. For example, when IBM is trading at $155, the intrinsic value of the 150 call options (any expiration month) is $5. In other words, the minimum value of the option would be $5.

The put option example (see p. 329) assumes that IBM falls from $150 to $140 per share between March and July when the option expired. As with the call option, the more time left before expiration, the more valuable the option will be. Calculate the intrinsic value of a put by subtracting the price of the underlying stock from the strike price. For example, if IBM is selling at $145, the intrinsic value of the 150 put options will be $5. A study by Investment Research Institute in 1989 shows just how risky option buying is. The study concluded that an option buying strategy using the S&P 100, OEX option, would have yielded a return of just 4.6% between December 31, 1986 to July 21, 1989. That compares to a rise in the cash S&P 100 stock index of 35.6% in the same time period.

Option buyers bet on making money through extraordinary events. Unfortunately such events are rare. The above mentioned study showed option buyers making more money than stock investors only in 1987, when large moves both up and down defined stock market price action.

Summing Up

The bull market in stocks that commenced in the summer of 1982 has resulted in increased interest in options trading. Put options offer traders a method for profiting from drops in the stock market. The wide swings in stock prices in recent years has drawn increased investor interest. Astute call buyers can profit handsomely in bull markets. And, of course, the opposite is also true: Put buyers profit handsomely in falling

Look At This:

markets. The profits made by many put buyers prior to the October 1987 market crash made up in a single day for many months of losses! This is not, however, an area for neophyte traders. Experienced traders who can devote considerable time to the market have a distinct edge.

Option buying is highly speculative. You should use only funds you can afford to lose. Never invest more than 10% of your liquid assets in option-buying strategies. Remember, a call will profit *only* when the underlying stock rises quickly. A put is profitable *only* when the underlying stock drops quickly. "Trading range" (flat) markets and contrary markets (that is, contrary to the anticipated direction) will result in losses!

Notes

_____

_____

_____

_____

_____

_____

_____

_____

Selling Stock Options

As noted, there are two types of listed stock options: calls and puts. A call option is a contract between a seller and buyer that gives the buyer the right to buy 100 shares of a specified stock at a specified price within a specified time period. A put option gives the buyer the right to sell 100 shares of a specified stock at a specified price within a specified time period.

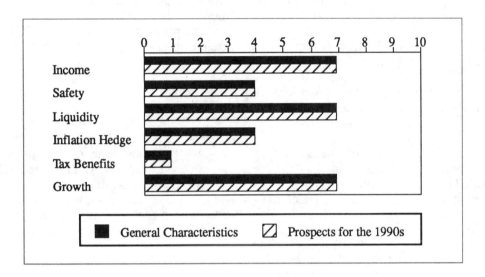

Income
Safety
Liquidity
Inflation Hedge
Tax Benefits
Growth

■ General Characteristics   ▨ Prospects for the 1990s

Type I

C

Low Taxes
High Expenses

Options are most commonly thought of as a leveraged short-term approach to stock investing. Many professionals find, however, that over the long haul it is more profitable to be on the selling side of an options contract. When you are the seller, you receive the option premium (minus commission) paid by the option buyer.

To better understand how this works, look at an example. Let's say that in March, IBM sold for $150 per share on the NYSE. If at the time you felt the stock might rise, you could

- Buy 100 shares of IBM stock for $15,000 (plus commission).
- Buy a July 150 call option for $800 (plus commission).

Or you could

- Sell a July 150 put option for $700 (you needed to post margin funds, a portion of which could be Treasury bills).

If you bought the stock or the call option, you'd make money only if the stock rose (not counting the dividend paid by the stock). However, if you elected to sell the put option, you'd pocket the premium if the stock (1) rose, or (2) stayed flat. This is because the "time value" of the premium deteriorates with every passing day. If the stock price was still $150 in June, only a few weeks are left before expiration. The put option would be much less valuable to an investor than if he or she had bought it in March.

This "selling" or "writing" of options works both ways. To profit from flat markets, you can sell either puts or calls or both!

Investment Potential

If you believed that the price of IBM would go *down* by the end of July, you could

- Sell short 100 shares of IBM for $15,000 (plus commission).
- Buy a July 150 put option for $700 (plus commission).

Or you could

- Sell a July 150 IBM call option for $800 (minus commission).

If you sold the stock short or bought an option, you'd only make money if the stock actually falls. If you sold the call option, you'd make money (1) if the stock price fell, or (2) if the stock price stayed flat. The time value of the option deteriorates every day the price does not go up!

Contrary to popular belief, the stock market spends most of the time in flat "trading ranges." The option-selling strategy is an ideal method for capitalizing on flat markets.

Unlike the situation when you are buying options, when you write (sell) options time works for you because the option loses value every day up to expiration. In March, the May 150 call option was worth only $550 compared to $800 for the July contract, because only eight weeks were left before the call expired. The July option had an *additional* eight weeks for IBM stock to make its anticipated move and therefore commanded a higher price.

There are two ways to approach writing options. If you already own 100 shares (or multiples) of the underlying stock, you can sell a call option without having to post additional margin funds. This is called "covered writing." For example, if you had bought IBM at $130 per share, you could have sold the July 150 call options as in the preceding example, for no additional money. You'd have received the premium income immediately.

If the stock moved above 150 by the third week in July, you could buy the option back and keep your stock. You might decide to let your stock be "called" away at the $150-per-share price. Your profit on the transaction would be the $20-per-share profit you made

on the stock, plus the $800 premium you received for the option.

A more aggressive approach is to sell call options on stock you do not own. This is another method of selling short. It is called "naked writing." If the underlying stock shoots much higher in price, you could lose far more than your original investment. To sell naked options, most firms require that you have a minimum of $10,000 in your account. Margin money must be posted and is adjusted daily depending on the price movement of the stock. If you sell a call option and the price of the stock moves higher, you are required to deposit additional capital.

Strengths

Exchange-listed options are very liquid. An option writer has time on his or her side. Option writing generally requires less capital than equivalent stock transactions. An option writer receives income up front. That income can earn interest immediately.

Weaknesses

Options are very high risk. Because they are leveraged plays on the underlying stock, their price movements are even more volatile than the stock's movements. Option writing requires close attention to market action, because options are time related. Option traders must meet stringent suitability requirements. Option writing, particularly naked writing, requires substantial money. An options writer is liable for losses that could exceed his or her investment.

Tax Considerations

Income earned from options writing is taxed as ordinary income. No special tax advantages apply to options writing.

Tax Consequences

Option writing is highly speculative. You should use only funds you can afford to lose. Never risk more than 10% of your liquid assets in option-writing positions. Unlike option buying, option writing offers the potential to profit in "trading range" (flat) markets. However, unlike the situation in option buying, your loss is not limited to your initial investment if the market moves contrary to your expectations.

The record for making money writing options is slightly better than for buying because the market tends to trade in narrow ranges for extended periods. Generally, option buyers tend to be individual investors, while option sellers tend to be professionals, typically floor traders and institutional investors.

Option writing can significantly increase your income on a portfolio of stocks but must be closely monitored. If you cannot devote full time to watching your investments, consider retaining a professional manager or investigate option-writing mutual funds.

Comparisons Between Stocks and Options

Stock Purchase

1. 100 IBM at $150 = $15,000
2. Sell IBM at $160 = $16,000
3. Profit = $1,000 (before commissions)
4. Return = 6.66% (profit ÷ purchase price)

Call Option Purchase

1. 1 IBM July 150 at $8 = $800
2. Sell July 160 at $10 = (minimum value with IBM at $160)
3. Profit = $200 (less commissions)
4. Return = 25% (profit ÷ purchase price)

Stock Short Sale

1. Sell 100 IBM at $150 = $15,000
2. Buy back IBM at $140 = $14,000
3. Profit = $1,000 (less commissions)
4. Percent return = 6.66% (profit ÷ sale price)

Put Option Purchase

1. Buy IBM July 150 put at $7 = $700
2. Sell 150 put at $150 = $1,000 (minimum value when IBM is at $140)
3. Profit = $300 (less commissions)
4. Percent return = 43% (profit ÷ purchase price)

Stock Index Options

Index options are contracts between buyers and sellers just like stock puts and calls. However, instead of trading on an individual stock's rise or fall, index options are tied to broadbased indexes such as the S&P 500, the Major Market Index (which closely follows the Dow Jones Industrial Average), the NYSE Composite, and others. Unlike options on individual stocks, buyers of index options settle for cash because it would be impossible to deliver stocks that exactly fit the indexes. Many new index options are being added all the time. The latest group has been for industry sector indexes such as technology.

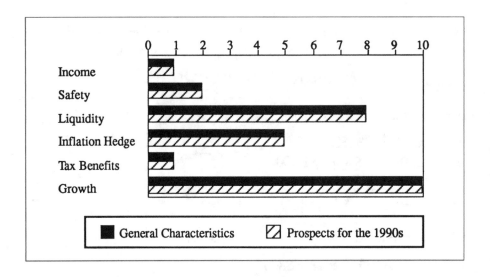

Type I

D

Low Taxes
Low Expenses

Most investors have had the frustrating experience of being right on stock market direction but wrong in the individual stocks they bought. On Wall Street, there used to be a saying that "It's not a stock market, but a market of stocks." In other words, the stocks you select are more important than the direction of the market. But that's no longer true.

There are now a number of ways to bet on the direction of the market as a whole without having to select individual stocks. There are stock index futures, options on stock index futures, and stock options on market indexes. The most heavily traded option in history is the S&P 100 option traded on the Chicago Board of Trade. The market is so well known that it is often merely referred to by its ticker symbol—OEX.

As with all stock options, stock index options are either calls or puts. Stock index options have one major difference from options on individual stocks: they settle for cash. It is impossible to deliver "the S&P 100 Index." Instead, you figure the prices—and your profit and loss—by multiplying the quoted price of the option by $100.

For example, assume that in May the S&P 100 Index closed at 284.96. The July 285 OEX call option closed that day at 9. To buy the July 285, you'd pay $900 ($100 x 9) plus the commission. If the market rallied before the third Friday in July, and your option went to 12, you would make $300 minus commissions if you sold.

Time
Sensitive

Like other stock options, there is a nonquantifiable "time value" in each option. This merely means that the more time left in the option before expiration, the more valuable it is. For example, on the day in May the S&P 100 closed at 284.96, the July 285 OEX call option was selling for only 51/4 ($525).

Put options are also available for stock index options. Just like their counterpart for individual stocks, a put option appreciates if the market goes down. The value is calculated the same way. Multiply the price times $100 to get the value. You'd buy a put if you felt the stock market was going to go down.

Index options have become so popular as trading vehicles that the *Wall Street Journal* and *Investor's Daily* carry their prices in a separate section daily. In addition to the S&P 100, there are index options for the Value Line Index, the NASDAQ Index (for the OTC market), the S&P 500, the Financial News Composite Index (FNCI), the Major Market Index (MMI), and the New York Stock Exchange (NYSE) Index. A number of subgroup indexes have recently been started. These include the gold/silver index, the technology index, the oil index, the institutional index, and even the NYSE Beta index (for speculating on volatility).

All the major option exchanges trade at least one of the indexes just listed. You can buy a stock index option through a licensed broker. A commission is charged for both buying and selling index options.

Investment Potential

Index options have been called "the ultimate speculation." You are not buying the right to real entity such as stock ownership in a company. You are speculating purely and simply on the direction of the stock market as a whole.

Stock index options are short-term (remember that there is an expiration date) capital gains speculations. They produce no income.

Stock index options are highly leveraged investments. In our preceding example, a

$900 investment actually controls almost $28,500! As a result, minor changes in the underlying indexes can mean great profits or losses. However, unlike futures indexes, your loss is limited to the amount of money you have invested.

Index options are very volatile investments. They are very high risk. It is possible to lose your entire investment in a short time. S&P 100 options are very liquid. Most other index options are liquid in varying degrees. It is important to check the average daily volume of the index option you wish to trade to ensure that there is an active liquid market.

Professional
Advice

Investment professionals have developed a number of sophisticated strategies for trading options. These include spreads, straddles, and numerous other concoctions. Neophyte traders should beware of the high costs many of these strategies impose. They are usually best left to professionals with the expertise and time to carefully monitor these wide-swinging markets.

Options are not appropriate investments for most retirement plans.

Strengths

Stock index options allow you to "trade the market" without having to select from among over 50,000 individual issues. The required initial investment is small. Your loss is limited to the amount of money invested. They offer tremendous leverage and consequently the potential for large capital gains. Most stock index options, especially the S&P 100, are very liquid. You have great flexibility to profit in both up and down markets.

Weaknesses

Stock index options are very volatile. You can lose 100% of your investment on expiration day. You are subject to both market and timing risk.

Commission costs are high relative to the amount of invested capital. They pay no income.

Tax Considerations

Tax Consequences

Stock index options generate capital gains and losses. Gains are taxed at your ordinary income rates. Losses offset other capital gains. Excess losses are carried forward.

Summing Up

Stock index options are one of the fastest-growing markets in the financial arena. However, following the great October 1987 market crash, volume in stock index options—even puts—dropped off sharply. After five years of fairly steady profits, traders learned quickly that options trading is a two-way street. Many investors who had pyramided their profits into buying ever more options saw years of profits lost in a single day.

The shock of the crash has tempered the overzealous enthusiasm that stock index options had engendered. Although volume started to increase again by mid-1988, option traders were once again victimized in October 1989 when the stock market fell 190 points in a single day. Experts estimate that option traders lost millions of dollars in that debacle.

The volatile nature and timing element limit the market to those investors with the expertise necessary to carefully monitor them. They should only be traded with risk capital that you could lose entirely without affecting your lifestyle.

No more than 10% of your investment funds should ever be devoted to buying stock index options. Selling (or writing) index options is a very high risk venture that should be tried only by experienced investors.

Agriculture Futures

A futures contract is a binding contract between a buyer and a seller that specifies the commodity, the amount of the commodity, and the delivery date when the seller must deliver the commodity. Futures originally arose as a method to enable producers, principally farmers, the ability to shift some of their business risk to speculators.

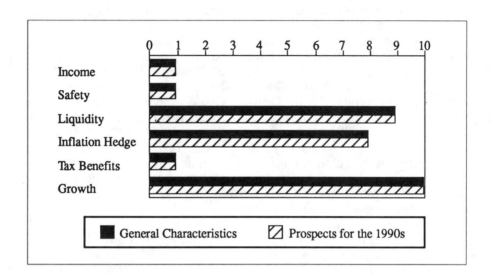

It seems only fitting that the most dramatic changes in the financial markets over the past 10 years have occurred in the most dramatic marketplace—futures. Originally called *commodities*, the futures markets have evolved so much that the agricultural commodities that once formed the foundation for industry now play a much smaller role. However, two events in 1988 combined to boost trading volume in agricultural futures at the expense of financial futures. The first, and probably most lasting was the October 1987 stock market crash. The reverberations of that event will affect most investment markets for years to come.

Second, the drought in the summer of 1988 pushed grain prices sharply higher for the first time in five years. For example, volume in soybeans and sugar jumped over 70% from May 1987 to May 1988. In that same time period, volume in the S&P 500

Type I

D

Low Taxes
Low Expenses

Index, the most heavily traded futures contract, dropped 47%. Volume in the D-mark, a popular currency contract, fell 39%.

This pattern reverses the trend to financial futures that dominated the scene for most of the 1980s. In 1987, trading in only three financial futures—the S&P 500 Index, T-bonds, and Eurodollars—accounted for 46.4% of the volume on all U.S. futures exchanges. It is certainly too early to draw any conclusions about long-term trends but the revival of interest in agricultural futures is a boon for traders, since it increases liquidity. By 1989 trading volume had slipped 17% in the grains, while volume in the financial instruments once again surged ahead.

Over the last 20 years, futures markets have expanded to include bonds, T-bills, Eurodollars, crude oil, and even the stock market.

Farmers' decisions to "hedge" their risk is made at planting time. They know how much corn they will have at harvest. They have two choices. They can wait until they harvest their corn and sell it at the price available at that time. Or they can sell the future, yet-to-be-harvested crop at planting time, for physical delivery after harvest. The decision depends on the prevailing price and the expectations for the future.

For example, assume that when farmers plant corn in the spring they know that their costs will be $2 per bushel if all goes well by harvest. If corn for December delivery is selling at $2.50 per bushel, farmers may elect to lock in the $0.50 profit by selling the in-the-ground crop in the spring. One contract of corn on the Chicago Board of Trade is for 5,000 bushels. A single contract at $2.50 per bushel would be worth $12,500.

In order to sell one contract of corn, farmers would have to post a margin "good-faith" deposit of about $600 or less if intended as a hedge. Someone would buy the contract, expecting the price to go higher than $2.50 per bushel. Since each contract is 5,000 bushels, a $0.01 move is worth $50. If December corn's price goes up $0.05, buyers would make $250 (5 cents x $50) per contract. Farmers would lose $250 in potential profit they would have received if they had waited to sell. If the price goes down $0.05, speculators would lose $250 per contract. The farmers would gain because they locked in the higher price.

The speculator is motivated by profit. The farmers' motivations are more complex, since they must choose whether to take a set profit margin and to forgo additional potential profit by selling futures on their crops. If they guess wrong and sell early to lock in a fixed profit, if they meet no other surprises such as a drought, the worst that will happen is that they will not make as much money as they could have. They have shifted the price risk to the speculator.

On delivery day—which is always specified for each commodity—the seller must deliver the specified amount to the buyer. The buyer is obligated to pay the full value of the contracted price to the seller. In the preceding example, the buyer would pay the seller $12,500 per contract.

In actual practice, less than 2% of all futures contracts are settled by delivery. What actually happens is that the buyers and sellers "offset" their positions before delivery date. If you *sell* the December corn contract,

you'd merely *buy* a December corn contract to offset your obligation to deliver 5,000 bushels. If you are a buyer, you sell an equivalent contract to offset your obligation to pay the full $12,500 value of the contract.

Agricultural futures contracts are actively sold on exchanges around the world. The most popular agricultural commodities include wheat, corn, soybeans, soybean oil and meal, cotton, sugar, coffee, cocoa, and the meats—live cattle, hogs, and pork bellies (bacon). The largest exchanges trading agricultural commodities are the Chicago Board of Trade (CBT), the Chicago Mercantile Exchange (CME), the New York Cotton Exchange, and the Coffee, Sugar & Cocoa Exchange. Buyers and sellers do not actually know who is on the other side of their contracts. Just remember that for every seller there is a buyer, and the reverse. Someone is always on the other side of the contract, hoping it moves against you and for him or her.

Investment Potential

Futures offer great capital gains potential. They pay no income. Futures trading is a "zero-sum" business. That means for every winner there is a loser. This situation differs markedly from stocks, where everyone can win in a rising market. Even more than in stock trading, you are competing with other traders for available profits.

The greatest attraction, and greatest danger, to futures is the leverage. As we detailed in the preceding example, a deposit of $600 can control a $12,500 contract. That's putting up only 5% of your total liability. A futures investor is liable for the full value of the contract, not just the deposit.

Leverage works both ways. A 6% rise in price from $2.50 per bushel to $2.65 means a profit of $750 (before commissions) for a $600 investment. That's a 125% return!

But remember, the seller loses $750. He or she would get a "margin call" once the corn rose $0.06 ($300) against him or her. The initial deposit is merely a good-faith deposit required by the exchanges to ensure that the contracts are fulfilled. If price movement causes a "paper loss" of 50% of the initial margin, the broker will require additional money to ensure the seller can still meet his or her obligations. If you posted the minimum of $600 and the price of corn went against you $0.06, the "equity" in your account would drop to $300 ($600 minus the $300 loss from adverse price action). You would be required to either post an additional $300 to bring your equity back to initial levels, or you'd be forced to liquidate your position if you refused to commit further money.

In other words, leverage—which looks so attractive if you are correct on the direction of the market—can be devastating if you are wrong. In the case of corn at $2.50 per bushel, if you guess wrong a price move of only 2.4% ($.06) will wipe out 50% of your initial $600 deposit!

Futures are not appropriate for most retirement plans.

Strengths

Leverage offers the chance for tremendous profits. Actively traded futures contracts are usually very liquid. You do not pay interest on the balance between your margin deposit and the full value of the contract. Commodities offer excellent protection from inflation. There are no "insider" (merger, acquisition, or takeover) rumors to distort the market price. Much flexibility can be achieved through various strategies such as spreads. Traders have equal capability to sell short (profit from price drops) or to buy long (profit from price rises).

Weaknesses

Leverage can be devastating if you are wrong on price direction. The short-term nature of futures puts a premium on accurate timing. News events may cause adverse price reactions, which reach exchange-specified "lim-

its" that make it impossible to get out of a position. Futures are characterized by high volatility. Futures trading is high-risk investing by any definition.

Tax Considerations

Tax Consequences

The previous preferential capital gains treatment accorded futures was eliminated in the 1986 Tax Reform Act. All capital gains are taxed as ordinary income for speculators.

Summing Up

The futures market is a highly leveraged, very risky investment arena. This market is not for casual investors. Over 80% of futures traders lose money.

Agricultural futures do offer you a direct play on tangible assets. During the inflationary blowoff in the 1970s, agricultural futures were big gainers. The 1988 summer drought pushed grain prices sharply higher. For example, in January 1988 soybeans were trading slightly over $6 a bushel. By mid-June, the price climbed over $10. For the preceding five years, the average monthly range for soybean prices was only about 30 cents. In the first half of 1988, that average was over $1!

In 1989 the futures markets came under a dark cloud as FBI investigations resulted in the indictment of a number of traders on various exchanges. While the media and numerous pundits were quick to condemn the futures industry, the first trial of traders from the currency pits acquitted the traders on all but very minor charges. The government's case appears to be a case of grandstanding with little evidence of real wrong doing. Further trials are expected though.

The futures market offers good liquidity for most commodities. Many professional advisors will manage your funds for a fee. There are also mutual funds which trade futures only.

Stock Index Futures

Most futures contracts are binding contracts between a buyer and a seller that specify the commodity, the amount of the commodity, and the delivery date when the seller must deliver the commodity at the price at which the contract was entered. However, stock index futures are unique in the futures world. Rather than settling in terms of a specific quantity of a specific commodity, stock index futures are settled in cash on delivery day.

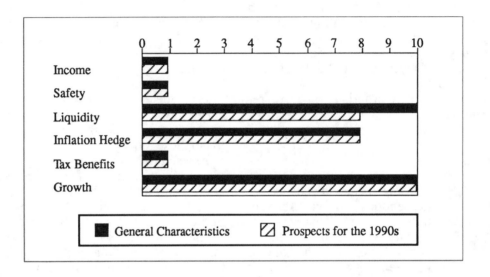

Type I

D

Low Taxes
Low Expenses

The newest development in the ever changing world of futures has been the start of stock trading. Shortly after S&P Index futures first began trading on the Chicago Mercantile Exchange, it quickly became the most popular futures market of all time. It displaced U.S. Treasury bond trading in terms of volume and open interest. T-bonds trading had replaced gold and silver as number one. They superseded the traditional agricultural commodities. During the 1988 summer drought, though, volume increased in agricultural futures rapidly. Volume in the S&P 500 Index slid sharply. However volume picked up steadily as memories of the Great Crash of 1987 faded.

The S&P Index trades on the Chicago Mercantile Exchange (CME), the New York Composite Index is on the New York

Financial Exchange (NYFE), and the Value Line Index trades on the Kansas City Board of Trade. They all are priced by multiplying $500 times the index. For example, if the June S&P contract was selling at 260, the value of the contract would be $130,000. The Major Market Index (MMI) is designed to emulate the Dow Jones Industrial Average and is traded on the Chicago Board of Trade. Its value is calculated by multiplying $250 times the index.

Stock index futures have been blamed for much of the volatility of the stock market in recent years. Numerous government and private studies of the crash could not agree on the exact role that stock index futures played in its development. Despite much talk about the need for new government regulations, no new proposals were adopted by 1990. However, the Bush Administration introduced legislation that would transfer jurisdiction over stock index futures from the Commodity Futures Trading Commission (CFTC) to the Securities Exchange Commission (SEC). The most likely result, as of the summer of 1990, is the passage of compromise legislation by which the CFTC would retain jurisdiction but the Federal Reserve would set margin requirements for all stock index futures contracts. If such legislation passes, look for the volume and open interest in stock index futures to shrink considerably.

Large institutional traders use index futures to hedge their stock positions. For example, if the S&P 500 cash index in May was selling at a significant discount to the June S&P futures index, institutional investors (especially arbitragers, who seek to profit from price differentials) would buy a basket of stocks closely related to the makeup of the cash index and sell the futures index. On settlement day, the futures index will come down to the cash index, or the cash index (and the basket of stocks) will move up to what the futures index sold for. Either way, the institutional investor makes money.

Also the concept of "portfolio insurance" is closely related to the use of futures indexes to hedge money managers' stock portfolios. Once managers have a profit in their portfolios, they may elect to sell futures contracts in anticipation of a market drop rather than sell out their stocks. This saves commissions and stresses timing accuracy.

Stock index futures contracts offer the individual investor the chance to trade "the market" literally rather than individual stocks. Many investors have experienced the frustration of correctly anticipating the direction of the stock market, only to have the stocks they purchased do nothing!

Stock index futures are purchased through licensed brokerage firms. Commissions are charged only when a transaction (both the buy and sell) is completed (position closed).

Investment Potential

Stock index futures trading is a zero-sum game. For every winner, there is a loser. When you purchase an index contract in anticipation of a market rise, the other half of the contract is filled by someone who believes the market is going down!

Like other futures contracts, index futures are highly leveraged. Initial margin deposit requirements run approximately 10% of the value of the contract. In addition to the initial deposit requirements, most brokerage firms require that futures traders have substantial incomes and net worth.

Stock index futures are very high risk investments. The markets are very volatile. The high leverage results in even greater volatility for your account's equity.

The very high interest in index trading provides very good liquidity. Stock index futures do not have exchange-established limits like other futures contracts. You cannot get "locked" into a position with no escape, as in other futures markets. However, large price movements can and do occur frequently.

In addition to market risk, index futures are very sensitive to economic and political news. Unforeseen developments can result in rapid price changes.

The availability of cash stocks and varying delivery months has resulted in numerous investment strategies. This enhanced flexibility enables astute investors to devise strategies to fit their investment objectives and risk tolerance.

Index trading generates capital gains. There is no income.

Stocks historically provide some measure of protection from inflation. Index futures can be sold short (can profit from price drops) as easily as being bought for price rises. This flexibility differs from stock trading, which has various rules that limit short selling.

Many professional managers trade stock indexes exclusively. Other managers use index futures in combination with cash stock transactions. Fees vary widely, and you should thoroughly understand them before signing any contracts. Active trading in index futures can result in large commission charges.

Strengths

 Index futures offer very high leverage and consequently the potential for large profits. Index futures give investors the chance to trade the market without having to select from over 50,000 individual stocks. Index futures offer large investors the opportunity to hedge their cash stock portfolios. As the most heavily traded of all futures contracts, index futures are very liquid. Cash settlements are paid 24 hours after the close of a transaction. Exchanges set no "limits" on daily price movements, further enhancing their liquidity.

Weaknesses

 High leverage means high risk. Index futures are very volatile, making for substantial risk. Index futures tend to exaggerate stock market movement caused by unanticipated news. Index futures may diverge from cash index movements. The large dollar value of daily price moves places a premium on accurate short-term timing. Losses may significantly exceed your initial investment.

Tax Considerations

Tax Consequences

Index profits are taxed as ordinary income. Net paper profits as of December 31 each year are taxed as though the gain was realized in that taxable year.

Net profits are determined by calculating all paper (unrealized) profits and losses on open futures positions that day. Losses can be used to offset other capital gains. Losses not used in one year may be carried forward.

Summing Up

Stock index futures have found a permanent place in the investment world. Not only are they widely used by individuals who are willing to undertake high risks for high profit potential, they are also being increasingly employed by large institutions to hedge their portfolio's performance.

Daily volume in the S&P futures alone far exceeds that of traditional commodity markets such as wheat, corn, or soybeans.

This is a very high-risk market. Only investors well schooled in the risks and rewards should venture here. The high leverage is a very attractive feature when you are right about market direction. However, that leverage works both ways. You are at risk for the entire value of the contract, not just the amount of your margin deposit, if you are wrong about market direction.

Interest Rate Futures

A futures contract is a binding contract between a buyer and a seller that specifies the commodity, the amount of the commodity, and the delivery date when the seller must deliver the commodity. Futures originally arose as a method to enable producers, principally farmers, to shift some of their business risk to speculators.

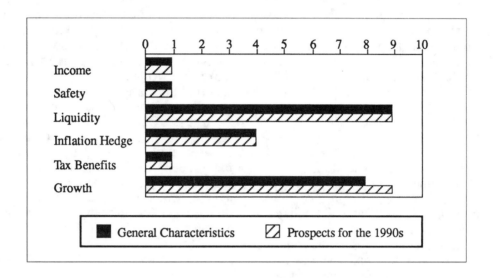

Type I

D

Low Taxes
Low Expenses

Commodity futures markets changed forever with the introduction of interest rate futures in the early 1970s. Trading volume in Treasury bond futures quickly became the largest of all futures markets. The subsequent introduction of S&P Index futures supplanted T-bonds as the most widely traded futures contract up until the October 1987 crash. Now both the Eurodollar and T-bond contract have greater open interest (number of outstanding contracts) than the S&P.

Interest rate futures were introduced during the high-inflation 1970s when interest rates were nearing all-time highs. Many banks and thrift institutions were in deep trouble for having committed the grave error of borrowing short term while lending long term. Typically a savings institution would secure deposits for three months, six months, or one, two, or three years through its certificates of deposit. Its liabilities, however, were often for much longer time periods. Thrifts at that time were pretty much limited to mortgage loans with 20- to 30-year maturities.

What happened was that their long-term obligations, such as mortgage loans, were lent out at a fixed rate, say 8%. This was fine when they only had to pay depositors 5% or 6%. But when inflation turned higher, many depositors shopped around for better yields. The money market mutual fund industry played a very large part in making consumers aware of alternatives to the low interest rates paid by banks.

Just as grain, metals, stock index, and foreign currency futures are used by commercial interests to hedge their risks, savings institutions can make use of interest rate futures to lock in a profitable spread between their assets (deposits) and liabilities (loans). The risk is shifted to speculators in the futures market.

There are a number of interest rate futures

contracts; the four most actively traded are Treasury bills (91 days), Eurodollars (91 days), Treasury notes (seven years), and Treasury bonds (20 years). T-bills and Eurodollars trade on the International Monetary Market (IMM) in Chicago. T-notes and T-bonds trade on the Chicago Board of Trade.

Interest rates futures are bought and sold through licensed futures brokers. All brokers must be members of the National Futures Association, a self-regulating body. A commission of $25 to $100 is charged when closing out a transaction. The fee varies based on factors including type of service, size of account and how actively the account is traded.

Investment Potential

Interest rate futures are very highly leveraged. Margin deposits of $3,000–$5,000 control $1 million face value in both T-bills and Eurodollars. T-note and T-bond contracts are $100,000.

Trading in interest rates puts you into very volatile markets. Small changes in interest rates mean large dollar-amount fluctuations in futures contracts. For example, T-bonds and T-notes minimum price movement is $1/32$ of a point. A $1/32$-point move is worth $31.25. The minimum 1-point fluctuation for T-bills and Eurodollars is $10.

Interest rate futures trade inversely to interest rates. This feature often confuses neophyte traders. When interest rates move higher, the futures move lower. If a newspaper headline reads "T-bond Futures Rally," you know that long-term interest rates have dropped.

Investing in interest rate futures offers tremendous flexibility. The different maturities from 91 days to 20 years makes it possible to take advantage of the yield curve with a variety of sophisticated strategies. The complexity of interest rates and the various strategies used makes it a difficult area for inexperienced traders.

There are a number of professional management programs available. Fees vary widely, and you should fully understand them before you enter into any contract with a manager.

Interest rate futures are not appropriate for

most retirement programs.

Strengths

Tremendous leverage (often the initial required margin is less than 5% of the value of the contract) offers great capital gains profit potential. Most interest rate futures contracts are very liquid. Even though exchange-specified limits exist, the market for Treasury bonds is so huge that there is little risk of being locked in by the limits for more than one or two trading sessions. Traders expecting rising interest rates can sell short as easily as buying. No special provisions limit short selling. No interest is charged on the balance between the value of the contract and the margin deposit. By short-selling interest rate futures, you gain protection against the ravages of inflation because you'd gain from the falling price of bonds due to rising interest rates induced by inflation.

Weaknesses

Great leverage means that small adverse moves in interest rates can mean large losses. Markets are very sensitive to news and therefore are very volatile. A premium attaches to short-term timing since expiration dates normally run only one or two years. Interest rate futures are a very high risk investment.

Tax Considerations

Tax Consequences

Profits or losses from interest rate futures are capital gains or losses. The 1986 Tax Reform Act eliminated preferential capital gains treatment. All gains are taxed at ordinary income levels. Losses can be used to offset other capital gains. Losses can be carried forward. As with all futures contracts, prices on open positions are "marked to the market" on December 31 each year. You must pay taxes on any net profits on these open positions, even if you have not closed the positions.

Summing Up

Interest rate futures have become one of the most heavily traded of all futures markets. For example, T-bonds, S&P 500 Index, and Eurodollar futures alone constituted 46.4% of all U.S. futures volume in 1987, and 45% in 1986. T-bonds were not hurt nearly as much as the S&P 500 Index after the October Crash.

Volume in T-bonds dropped about 8% in May 1988 from a year earlier. But open in-

Professional Advice

terest actually climbed 50%. That's an indication that the market was attracting more institutional hedging-type investing while losing some of the short-term-oriented speculative trading. Financial institutions now play an active role in this market. They use futures as one way of hedging their interest rate risks.

The high leverage inherent in interest rate futures makes this field very dangerous for part-time investors. If you do not have the time or expertise to devote to careful detailed monitoring of these treacherous markets, consider professional management.

Notes

_____

_____

_____

_____

_____

_____

_____

_____

_____

_____

_____

_____

Metals Futures

A futures contract is a binding contract between a buyer and a seller that specifies the commodity, the amount of the commodity, and the delivery date when the seller must deliver the commodity to the buyer for the set price. For example, the most widely traded gold contract is for 100 ounces of gold for delivery in February, April, June, August, October, and December. Although you can buy and sell gold contracts for as much as a two-year delivery "future," most trading involves contracts for delivery within 12 months.

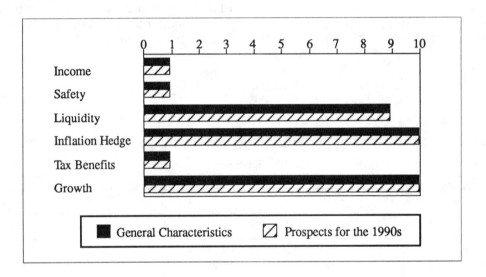

The first futures product to gain widespread trader interest after the agricultural commodities was the metals markets. Specifically, the inflationary 1970s saw the rise of interest in the precious metals—gold and silver. Gold bullion was illegal for Americans to own from 1933 until 1975. Silver—"poor man's gold"—served as a proxy for inflation-conscious investors until 1975. By the late 1970s, gold and silver became the most actively traded futures markets, far outstripping the traditional agricultural commodities.

Type I

D

Low Taxes
Low Expenses

Futures developed as a method for producers or consumers to hedge their risk by shifting it to speculators. Mine owners know what it costs to produce one ounce of gold. They have customers such as jewelry manu-facturers who require certain amounts of gold for their products. Once a mine owner knows how much gold will be needed by customers, he or she works out an agreement for delivery of the gold. Since jewelry makers will need their biggest supply for the December holiday season, the mine owner can hedge the risk by "preselling" in the futures market the determined amount of gold for December delivery.

For example, the mine owner may sell 10 contracts (1,000 ounces) of gold at $400 for December delivery in March. He or she knows the cost (say it's $350 per ounce). By selling the gold when the deal with the jewelry maker is completed, the mine owner locks in the profit. Of course, there is a tradeoff for this security. If gold goes to $450 in the interim, the mine owner has given up the potential additional profit of $50 per ounce in exchange for protection from a drop in price.

The buyer of the contract may be a speculator who believes that the gold price will go higher. Since each contract is for 100 ounces, each $1 move in gold will mean a $100 profit (if the price goes up) or loss (if the price drops). The speculator's motivation is purely one of profit. The hedger also wants to make a profit of course, but is willing to forgo some profit potential to ensure a profit in the business of gold production. The price the mine pays for this "insurance" is the loss it takes on the transaction. It's merely a cost of business, like insurance for other industries.

Gold, silver (5,000-ounce contracts), and copper are traded on the New York Commodity Exchange (called the Comex). Platinum and palladium are traded on the New York Mercantile Exchange. Silver (1,000-ounce contracts) is traded on the Chicago Board of Trade. The Chicago Mercantile Exchange has tried to launch a gold contract in recent years but has had little success in attracting traders. You buy or sell futures contracts through licensed brokerage firms. A commission is charged for the transaction. Unlike stocks, commissions for futures are charged when the transaction is closed out. (Stock and bond commissions are charged on each purchase and sale.)

The futures business is closely regulated by the Commodity Futures Trading Commission (CFTC), a government agency. The National Futures Association (NFA) is a self-regulating entity that handles most of the regulatory procedures such as registration. All futures brokers must be members of the NFA and registered with the CFTC.

Investment Potential

The greatest attraction of futures for speculators is the leverage. For example, a contract of gold at $400 per ounce is worth $40,000. To buy or sell one contract, though, the trader must post a deposit called *margin*. The amount of the margin is set by the respective exchanges. The margin for gold is typically about $3,500.

In other words, you can control $40,000 with less than 10% of the full value of the contract. If you buy a contract of gold for December delivery at $400 per ounce, you'll need to post the $3,500 margin. If gold goes to $450 in the interim, you can sell the contract and pocket $5,000 profit ($50 x 100 ounces) before commissions. That's 43% profit on a price move of only a 12.5%!

Keep in mind, though, that you are legally bound for the full value of the future contract. Even though only $3,500 is required as initial deposit, a drop in price would mean that you would have to post more money to hang onto the contract. Typically, if the price drops so that 50% of the initial deposit is lost ($17.50 in this case), the brokerage firm will issue a "margin call" requiring you to post an additional $1,750 to bring your account back up to the initial level. If you do not post the additional margin within 24 hours, the brokerage firm will close your position. Because of this leverage, futures markets are highly volatile. They are very high risk. Any number of economic or political developments can dramatically affect prices overnight.

Futures investing generates capital gains. There is no current income. Historically, precious metals offer an excellent inflation hedge.

A wide variety of trading techniques is available to precious metals futures traders. For example, spread trading involves the simultaneous buying of one delivery month and the selling of another in the same metals. Sophisticated traders even do spread trading between related commodities such as gold and silver. This flexibility means there are many different ways to trade precious metals futures, with varying degrees of risk. However, even the "safest" approach carries substantial risk exposure.

Look At This:

The late 1970s precious metals futures markets revealed a risk unique to futures trading. Each exchange specifies "limit" ranges within which the price of a specific commodity is allowed to trade each day. For example, if the limit for gold is $10, the price can only go $10 higher or lower than the previous day's closing price. Once it reaches that limit, no further trade can take place unless additional buyers or sellers decide to enter the market at the limit price or lower, in the case of a price rise, or higher, in the case of a decline.

In January 1980 the long bull market rises in gold and silver were reversed. Many traders who had bought contracts were unable to get out of their positions because the price dropped the daily limit very quickly each day. There were many more sellers willing to sell at any price than buyers. Large profits turned into huge losses with no chance for escape. The billionaire Hunt brothers suffered losses totaling hundred of millions of dollars in their silver positions over a few short weeks.

Strengths

Under normal circumstances, futures contracts are very liquid. Settlement is made in 24 hours. Gold bullion and coins are subject to fraudulent valuations. Uniform futures markets avoid these subjective valuations. High leverage can yield excellent profit potential. No interest is charged on the difference between the value of the contract and your margin deposit. Precious metals futures can be sold short (that is, profit is earned from price drops) as easily as they can be bought. Commissions are low, relative to the value of each contract.

Weaknesses

High leverage and high volatility make for very high-risk investments. Exchange-set "limits" may hamper liquidity. The short-term nature of trading puts a premium on accurate timing. Precious metals are very sensitive to political news (such as developments in South Africa). Potential loss substantially exceeds required minimum investment.

Tax Considerations

All futures profits are taxed as ordinary income. Open positions are "marked to the

Tax Consequences

market" as of December 31 each year. In other words, open, unrealized profits are taxed as though the position were closed on that day. Losses are capital losses and can offset other capital gains or can be carried forward.

Summing Up

Precious metals dropped very sharply from January 1980 to 1986. After a brief rally in prices, the downtrend continued into 1990. The Iraqi invasion of Kuwait in the summer of 1990 triggered a strong rally in gold. The economic implications of the move: higher oil prices, heightened political tension, may finally be the factors needed for a resurgent bull market in gold. A surge in inflation is usually reflected in rising gold and silver prices. A return to the runaway inflation of the 1970s is not likely at this time.

Despite inflation fears engendered by rising grain prices and a robust economy, precious metals prices were subdued in the first half of 1990.

Increasing global supply at a rate of 7% per year pressured prices. Slow economic growth, generally relaxed international political environment (until Iraq's moves), and heavy selling by Saudi Arabia and the Soviet Union kept precious metals prices depressed.

Some precious metals investors sought relief in the highly volatile platinum market. The political fortunes of South Africa, which supplies 80% of the Western world's platinum, play an even bigger role here than in gold.

The futures markets gives well-capitalized, sophisticated investors the chance for high returns. If you do not have the time or experience to follow these markets closely on a daily basis, consider retaining a professional manager. This area is high risk. You should limit your exposure to no more than 10%–15% of your investment funds.

Foreign Currencies Futures

A currency futures contract is a binding contract between a buyer and a seller that specifies the currency, the quantity of the currency, and the delivery date when the seller must deliver the currency for the transaction price.

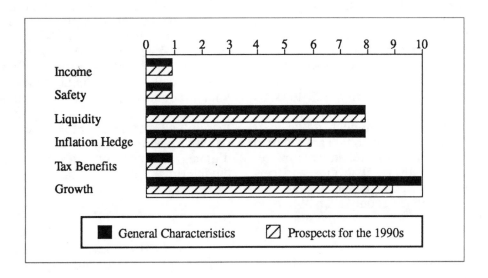

Income

Safety

Liquidity

Inflation Hedge

Tax Benefits

Growth

■ General Characteristics   ▨ Prospects for the 1990s

Type I

D

Low Taxes
Low Expenses

Following the abrogation in 1971 of the Bretton Woods agreement, which had fixed currency exchange rates, foreign currencies have been a volatile market. Futures in foreign currencies arose to give businesses a method for hedging the risks inherent in international trade.

When a U.S. business concludes a business agreement with a foreign company or government to supply a particular product or service in the future, both sides to the transaction have a substantial risk of loss if the currencies of their respective countries vary relative to each other.

For example, assume a U.S. business agrees to sell a set supply of equipment to a West German manufacturer for delivery in six months for Deutsch marks (DM) 3 million. At the time of the transaction, the exchange rate is 2 Deutschmarks to the dollar.

If the dollar goes up to 3 DM in the interim (a "strong" dollar) the U.S. supplier will receive only $1 million instead of the expected $1.5 million, even though nothing has changed in the contract. If the exchange rate drops to 1 DM per dollar, (a "weak" dollar) however, the U.S. firm stands to receive $3 million, and at no extra cost to its German partner.

Obviously the opposite is true if the deal is struck in U.S. dollars. When the dollar goes up, the Germans will have to fork over more marks. When the dollar goes down, they will have to pay fewer marks even though the U.S. supplier will receive the same $1.5 million in either case.

This shows that not only exchange rate fluctuations but also the currency in which a transaction is denominated may influence the amount of money that is ultimately paid or received.

This risk can be hedged in the futures market. Futures offers a liquid active market for shifting the exchange risk to speculators.

Foreign currencies are traded on the International Monetary Market (IMM) in Chicago. The most active markets are in West German Deutschmarks (D-marks), Japanese yen, Swiss francs, British pounds, and the Canadian dollar. Other currencies, such as the Mexican peso and the French franc, have much less active markets.

Foreign currency futures are bought or sold through government-licensed brokers. As mentioned earlier, all futures brokers must be members of the National Futures Association, a self-regulatory body of the futures industry. The NFA is charged with ensuring compliance with federal regulations.

Commissions ranging from $25 to $125 per contract are typically charged for handling the transaction. Although initial margin deposits of $3,000 to $6,000 are required for each contract, most brokerage firms require proof of substantial income and personal assets prior to opening an account. The initial margin deposit is only a small portion of the potential liability of the investor.

Investment Potential

Foreign currency futures are highly leveraged investments. The initial margin deposit is typically only about 5% to 10% of the full value of the contract. For example, both the Swiss franc (S-franc) and German D-mark contracts are for 125,000 francs or D-marks respectively. If each S-franc is worth $0.50, a single contract would be worth $62,500.

The yen, S-franc, and D-mark are quoted in dollar terms. Currencies are quoted to four decimal places. A quote of 0.5000 would mean $1 can buy two of the quoted currency. To give you a better perspective, a 0.0001- point move is worth $12.50 per contract.

Foreign currency futures are short-term investments—liquid contracts usually only run about six months. They are not appropriate for most retirement plans. The high volatility of the markets requires close attention by investors.

Foreign currency futures offer capital gains (and loss) potential. There is no income.

Foreign currency futures offer great flexibility. Many different strategies can be used, involving buying and selling of related currencies (such as the S-franc and D-mark). "Spread" trading (the simultaneous buying and selling of different contract months of the same currency or different currencies) is a common tactic.

Your initial margin deposit is only a small portion of your total liability. In the preceding example, a S-franc trader is liable for the full $62,500 value of the contract even though the margin deposit may have only been $6,000. If you buy a S-franc contract and the franc drops 0.0250 (a loss of $3,125), your brokerage firm will issue a "margin call" for additional money to bring your account equity back to the initial deposit level. You have 24 hours to meet a margin call, before the brokerage firm sells out your position. You are liable for any additional loss that may have been incurred in the interim.

Strengths

 High leverage offers above-average capital gains potential. A small amount of money can control much larger sums. Foreign currencies provide substantial protection against inflation in the United States. The Swiss franc is considered a inflation hedge second only to precious metals. Currency futures of major U.S. trading partners are liquid. It is possible to ascertain the relative liquidity of a futures contract by looking at the "open interest" figures. Open interest is a total of all outstanding contracts for that currency and delivery month. Liquid contracts have an open interest of 10,000 contracts or more. No interest is charged on the balance between the amount of a contract and the margin deposit.

Weaknesses

 Leverage works both ways. A small adverse move can wipe out your equity very quickly. Potential risk is substantially greater than your required initial margin deposit. Foreign currency futures are characterized by very high volatility. Foreign currencies are very sensitive to news developments. A multitude of factors influence currency values. Sometimes relative interest rates are the most important factor.

At other times, each country's relative trade balances prove crucial. There are many other potential determinants of relative value, which change all the time. Direct government intervention is a much greater factor in currency trading than in other markets.

Tax Considerations

Tax Consequences

Gains and losses from foreign currency futures are capital gains and losses. They are taxed at ordinary income levels. Losses can be used to offset other capital gains. Losses can be carried forward.

Summing Up

The flexibility of either buying or selling short with equal facility makes foreign currency futures a viable alternative in any market environment. After four years of dollar strength, 1986 witnessed a reversal. In 1986 and 1987, the U.S. dollar fell sharply. In the 12 months ending June 1989, the dollar rallied strongly, gaining on the D-mark, Swiss franc, and J-Yen.

However by late 1989 and into the summer of 1990 the dollar once again swooned on international markets. In June 1990 the dollar approached 3 year lows against the D-Mark. The Iraqi invasion of Kuwait in the summer of 1990 threw an undetermined variable into the pot. Typically the U.S. dollar is seen as a "safe reserve" currency and in times of international tension money flows to the dollar. However, with the worldwide political picture changing so dramatically, especially in Europe with a reunified Germany, the dollar did not rally as strongly as in the past.

Professional Advice

This market is highly volatile, very risky. It takes considerable time and expertise to trade with any degree of success. If you can't devote substantial time to learning the intricacies of foreign currencies, consider hiring professional management.

Options on Futures

A futures call option is a contract giving the buyer the right to buy the underlying futures contract for a specified price within a specified time period. A put option is the opposite. It gives the buyer the right to sell the underlying futures contract at a specified price within a specified time period.

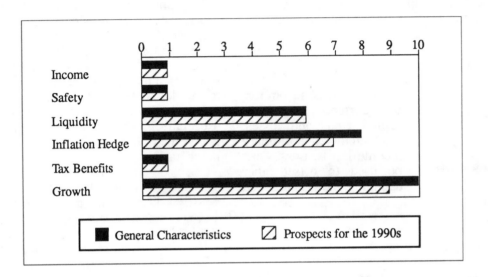

Type I

D

Low Taxes
Low Expenses

The futures market, with its promise of large profits with relatively small investments, has attracted many investors. Yet this promise has turned into nightmares for inexperienced traders who learned too late that small investments all too often turn into large losses! When you make an initial margin deposit on a futures contract, you are legally obligated for the full value of the contract, regardless of the amount of money invested. The initial deposit is usually only 5% to 10% of the value of the contract.

An option has the advantage of limiting the potential loss to the amount of your investment. If you pay $1,000 to buy a call option on a futures contract of gold, the most you can lose, even if gold falls to zero, is $1,000. In contrast, if you put up $1,000 to buy a gold futures contract, you are liable for the full value of the contract. If you buy a gold contract at $500 per ounce, you're liable for up to $50,000!

Future options are relatively new. The most heavily traded futures options at the moment are the S&P 500 index, T-bonds, Eurodollars, the D-mark, the yen, gold, silver, crude oil, and soybeans. Interest is picking up in copper, sugar, corn, live cattle, the British pound, the Swiss franc, T-notes, and the NYSE Composite. The summer 1988 drought triggered more interest in corn and wheat. The summer 1990 Iraq invasion triggered interest in oil options.

Futures options can be purchased through specially licensed futures brokers. Not all futures brokers are licensed to sell futures options. A commission is typically assessed when the transaction is closed. A number of independent advisory newsletters serve this market. Prices are quoted daily in the *Wall Street Journal* and *Investor's Daily*.

Investment Potential

Futures options are short-term, highly volatile investments. They generate capital gains (and losses!). They pay no income. Because their underlying instrument—futures contracts—are highly leveraged investments, the options reflect their volatility.

Professional traders have developed a number of highly sophisticated trading strategies combining different expirations, commodities, and both puts and calls in spread and straddles. These complex tactics are beyond the reach of most part-time investors.

The increased popularity of many different markets, as listed earlier, make futures options very flexible investments. Most are also very liquid. However, it is crucial to check the average daily volume and the open interest (the number of outstanding contracts) in those futures options you are interested in trading. Low average volume, or an open interest of less than 8,000 contracts, may mean problems with liquidity.

Futures trading is very high risk. Futures options are also very high risk. The primary difference is that a futures option investor cannot lose more than his or her initial investment. However, he or she also has to contend with the potential for completely losing the premium on expiration day.

Strengths

Losses are limited to the amount of investment. Futures options are highly leveraged investments offering the potential for large capital gains. Most options are liquid. Futures options, especially on gold and silver, offer good inflation protection. Futures options offer the opportunity for substantial short-term gains.

Weaknesses

Futures options are very volatile. You can lose 100% of your investment on expiration day. Time works against you, since the option loses value every day that the underlying futures contract does not move in the antici-

pated direction. Futures option premiums are high relative to stock options. The trading history of futures options is too short to provide accurate precedents for calculating over- and undervaluations of their premiums.

Tax Considerations

Tax Consequences

The 1986 Tax Reform Act eliminated preferential tax treatment for capital gains. All gains from futures options are taxed at your ordinary income rates. No special tax benefits apply.

Summing Up

Futures options have quickly established themselves as a viable market for speculators and hedgers. Many financial institutions and large stock managers use futures options to hedge interest rate and portfolio risks. Futures options are also the source of some of the worst "boiler room" abuses. High pressure telephone salespeople used futures options to sucker many people into no-win investments due to the very high commissions being charged. In some cases, firms assess commissions as much as 40% of the value of the option. Typical commissions run 5% or less of the premium.

In 1989 the CFTC filed suits against 2 options-brokerage firms, International Trading Group (ITG) and Siegel Trading Company, alleging that the firms misrepresented the potential for realizing profits, the firms' track records, and the expertise of staff members. According to the suit ITG customers sustained loses of $428 million between January 1984 and May 1989, while ITG pocketed $283 million in commissions. During the same period, Siegel made about $40 million in commissions, while customers were losing $33.6 million.

You should only speculate in futures options with risk capital you can afford to lose. Never risk more than 10% of your investment capital in buying futures options (or options in general).

Investors who do not have the time to devote to careful research of these markets should consider professional management.

Short Selling

Everyone knows that the secret to successful investing is to buy low and sell higher. But it does not always have to go in that order! To profit from down moves in prices, you can sell high and then buy lower. This technique is called short selling.

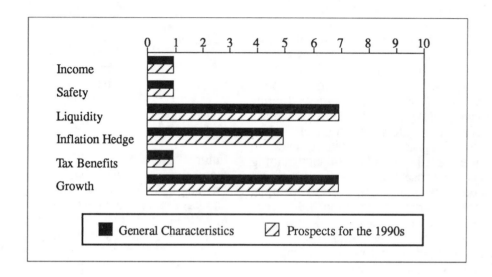

Income
Safety
Liquidity
Inflation Hedge
Tax Benefits
Growth

■ General Characteristics   ▨ Prospects for the 1990s

Type I

D

Low Taxes
Low Expenses

Although everyone is encouraged to "buy a piece of America" and profit from stock market rises, most investors are discouraged from short selling. Government regulations make it more difficult to do than simply buying stock. For example, in order to sell a stock short it has to have an increase in price first. In other words, before you can sell short, the stock has to move contrary to your expectations! Brokerage firms usually require more stringent financial requirements for short sellers.

It is not hard to understand corporate America's negative attitude toward short selling. No company wants to see the price of its stock go lower. Yet the very same people who discourage for the average investor from selling short—major brokerage firms and exchange members—sell short as a regular practice.

Short selling is riskier than buying stock for the simple reason that a stock can move infinitely higher, but can only fall to zero. However, intelligent professional investors know ways to protect against unlimited losses (for example, using stop loss orders). And at least so far, no stock has risen to infinity, while many stocks have gone to zero.

When you sell a stock short, you enter an order with your broker that he or she has to specify clearly on the order ticket. Your brokerage firm takes the stock from its inventory of stock held in "street name" (in the broker's account on behalf of its clients) and sells it. Since the stock held in street name belongs to someone, it must be replaced on demand. In practice, however, you won't be forced to replace the stock by the owner. However, you may be forced to buy the stock back by adverse price action.

To sell stock short, you must open a margin account. A minimum of 50% of the value of the stock to be sold must be deposited as initial margin. If the stock rises after you've sold it, the value of your account drops. If the equity (the value) in your account drops to 30%, a margin call will be issued requiring you to deposit additional money if you want to keep your short position. If you do not deposit the additional funds within 24 hours, your brokerage firm can buy the stock back to close your position. You are liable for any loss that has been incurred.

On the brighter side, if the stock drops your account equity increases. You buy the stock back and it is returned to your broker's pool of stock held in street name. When most investors buy stock, they leave it with their stockbroker. The brokerage firm holds the stock in street name. Therefore, every brokerage firm has a pool of stock in street name. When one of its customers wants to sell a stock short, the firm merely borrows some of its street name stock. It would be highly unusual for all customers to want to take delivery of their stock certificates or to sell their stock all at once, so some stock is almost always available for borrowing.

Some investors take delivery of their stock certificates rather than let their broker hold it in street name for just this reason. They don't want their firm to loan out their stock to someone who will sell it to knock the price down.

If the stock price is lower when you buy than when you sold, you've made a profit.

For example, if XYZ Corporation stock is selling for $60 per share, you can sell short 100 shares for a $3,000 margin deposit. If you later buy it back at $40 per share, you will have made a profit of $2,000 before commissions. The math looks like this: when you sell 100 shares at $60 per share, you receive $6,000. Now, since you have sold borrowed stock, your brokerage firm will not let you take out that $6,000 until you return the stock.

When you buy the stock back at $40 per share, it will cost a total of $4,000 (plus commission). Since you received $6,000 when you sold it, and paid $4,000 when you bought it back, you made a $2,000 profit before commissions. That is how you can make money by selling something you do not own. There is an old Wall Street saw that covers the situation: "He who sells what isn't his'n, must replace it or go to prison."

Fees are an important consideration for short selling. You must pay a brokerage commission for each buy and sell, just as when you are buying stock. Also, an interest charge must be paid on your margin account. And finally, if the stock you sold short pays a dividend during the time you are short the stock, you must pay the dividend amount to the stockholder from whom you borrowed the stock.

Stocks can only be sold short through licensed stock brokers. A monthly report is issued on the extent of short selling in individual stocks for the New York Stock Exchange, the American Stock Exchange, and the NASDAQ over-the-counter market. The list is published in both the *Wall Street Journal* and *Investor's Daily*. The extent of short selling is called "short interest." If the short interest is high for the market as a whole, that is a negative for a short seller (positive for the market), because that stock has to be bought back at some time.

Investment Potential

Price falls tend to occur quicker and more dramatically than price rises. Short selling is a short-term business. Time works against a short seller because he or she must pay interest and dividends in the interim.

Short selling is a high-risk venture. The increasing price volatility in stock prices offers opportunity and danger for short sellers. It is also a short-term venture. The long-term trend of stock prices is up, so short sellers are bucking history.

Short selling is a leveraged transaction because you borrow to effect the trade. Short selling offers the potential for capital gains. There is no income from short selling.

Alternatives to direct short selling now offer the chance to profit from price drops while limiting your risk. The purchase of put options limits the risk to your initial investment while enabling you to profit from price falls. Other option strategies are employed by professionals to achieve the same goals.

Strengths

 Short selling offers the potential for capital gains. Short selling enables you to profit from price declines. In combination with options, short selling offers wide flexibility in structuring trades to meet your objectives. Short selling is quite liquid if confined to large-volume, actively traded stocks.

Weaknesses

Short selling offers no income. Fees are high and require substantial price moves to cover. Potential losses are unlimited. Time works against you in flat trading range markets.

Tax Considerations

Tax Consequences

Even before the 1986 Tax Reform Act, short selling was denied preferential long-term capital gains treatment. All gains are taxed at your ordinary income rates.

Summing Up

Short selling is generally discouraged by most brokerage firms. They prefer that you buy a piece of America rather than sell it before you own it!

The regulations themselves discourage shorts because a stock must tick up before a short sale can be executed. And finally, history shows that the market has a definite upward bias over time.

Nevertheless, short selling plays an inte-gral part in the investment strategies of many professionals. The 1982–1987 bull market gave way to a dramatic collapse in September and October 1987.

Even after a 25% gain from the October lows to June 1988 highs, the market was still far below the 2700 DJIA high of August 1987. It wasn't until 1989 that the 2700 point DJIA August 1987 highs were ex-ceeded. Short sellers were obviously big winners in the crash.

Short selling is a high-risk tactic. It is not appropriate for most investors. However, if you are willing and able to undertake sub-stantial financial risks, short selling can yield good profits in the inevitable down cy-cles that will occur.

There are always many big winners on the short side. Big losers (profit makers for short sellers) on the NYSE in 1989 included Inte-grated Resources (–99%), Western S&L (–95%), Lomas Financial (–92%), Bay Fi-nancial (–91%), Commonwealth Manufac-turing Co. of America (–91%), Imperial America (–90%), Home Owners Savings Bank (–87%), and Thortec International (–85%).

On the American Stock Exchange big los-ers included Seamens A (–99%), Residential Resources (–95%), Manufactured Homes (–91%), Geothermal Resources (–91%), Centrust Bank (–90%) and Punta Gorda Island (–86%).

The OTC Market also had its share of bombs: 1st American Bank and Trust (–97%), Cityfed Financial (–96%), Pioneer Savings (–96%), Miniscribe (–95%), United Bldg. (–95%) and Chartwell Group (–95%).

These are only a few of the big losers that lined short sellers' pockets with profits.

Leveraged Contracts

A leveraged contract is a form of forward investment in which the buyer makes an initial margin deposit on an amount of the underlying precious metal. Monthly interest charges are assessed on the balance between the initial margin and the full value of the contract.

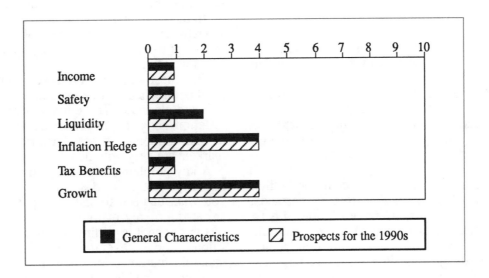

Income
Safety
Liquidity
Inflation Hedge
Tax Benefits
Growth

■ General Characteristics   ▨ Prospects for the 1990s

Type I

D

Low Taxes
Low Expenses

Leveraged contracts (also called collateralized loan programs) are a hybrid investment that gained a wide market in the precious metals boom in the 1970s. Subsequent widespread fraud and business failures among many "leveraged contract" dealers resulted in the imposition of stringent federal registration requirements in the early 1980s. Replacing many of the leveraged contract dealers are "bank financing" dealers who operate in much the same manner. Very large upfront fees, high pressure sales tactics, and very little chance to make a profit for anyone but the broker characterize the business, regardless of what it is called. *Business Week* estimates that leveraged sales of precious metals amounts to $1 billion annually.

Leveraged contracts developed as an alternative to futures contracts. Typically firms selling leveraged contract investments set less stringent requirements for investors than firms dealing in futures. Initial deposits of as little as 10% are used to control substantial amounts of precious metals.

For example, a $1,000 deposit may control $10,000 worth of gold at the price prevailing on the transaction day. A major difference with futures is that in a leveraged or bank financial deal, the difference between the deposit and the value of the underlying commodity is financed and the investor must pay interest on that balance. If gold is trading at $500 on the transaction day, 20 ounces of gold would be controlled by the $1,000 deposit. Theoretically, the issuing firm would buy the gold and store it for the purchaser. Once the contract is paid off, the buyer can either take delivery of the gold or let the issuing firm "warehouse" it for a custodial fee until the buyer elects to sell.

Many shady firms entered the business in the heyday of the inflationary bull markets of the 1970s. These firms often failed to purchase the gold to back the full value of the leveraged contracts they had sold. When the precious metals bull market reversed, many investors were left holding worthless paper when the firms went under. Some of the failed firms went under owing investors millions of dollars. Only a handful of legally registered leverage contract merchants are active today.

Investment Potential

Leveraged contracts or bank financing programs offer capital gains potential. No income is paid. Leveraged contracts are attractive to many investors because of the high degree of flexibility offered. Unlike futures contracts, which have uniform sizes and maturities, leveraged contracts are often tailored to meet the specific needs of their investors.

Leveraged contracts are sold for bullion and various coins ranging from Krugerrands, American Eagles, Candian Maple Leafs, Australian Nuggets, and Mexican Peso gold coins to bags of "junk" (no numismatic value) silver coins. Purchases can be made for a wide variety of contract sizes, not just the 100-ounce contracts available in the futures markets.

Typically, no maturity date is set for a leveraged contract. Interest is assessed monthly at rates established by the issuing firms. Investors are required to keep prespecified equity levels in their accounts.

For example, if accumulated interest charges reduce your equity below the specified minimum requirements, a "margin call" will be issued requiring additional deposits. If you fail to meet the margin calls (different firms have different time requirements for meeting the calls), your position will be sold at the prevailing market price of the underlying commodity. That "prevailing market price" is usually set by the dealer. All too often it bears little resemblance to the cash price of the commodity outside the dealer. You are liable for any losses that exceed your equity at the time.

In this way, leveraged contracts are similar to futures contracts. You are liable for the full value of the contract. Your potential loss is not limited to your initial investment.

Leveraged contracts are very high risk in-vestments. High interest charges may not be offset by appreciation of the underlying commodity. This factor alone can result in losses in flat markets. Interest rate charges are typically tied to some independent market interest rate. If interest rates rise and the underlying commodity stays flat or rises more slowly, your equity again can be lost.

With passage of the 1986 Tax Reform Act, investment interest is deductible only up to the amount of investment income. Previously the interest charges of leveraged contracts were fully deductible against your gross income.

The most prominent markets for leveraged contracts are precious metals: gold, silver, and platinum. These markets are classic inflation hedges. They provide little return in noninflationary times. Historically, these markets are very volatile.

A key problem with leveraged contracts is liquidity. There is no secondary market. If you want or need to sell your position, you are at the mercy of the issuing firm, which sets the price it is willing to pay for your position. Some leveraged contract dealers maintain market prices with a large spread between their bids (what they will pay) and their offers (what price they will sell for). In times of falling prices, the bids for leveraged contracts or bank financing contracts may drop substantially more than the market price for the commodity.

Leveraged contracts are not appropriate for retirement plans.

Strengths

 Investor requirements to trade leveraged contracts are usually less stringent than those for futures traders. Leverage contracts are typically offered in a wide variety of sizes. Leveraged contracts are one of the few ways an investor can purchase gold or silver coins with leverage other than futures, options, or stocks.

Weaknesses

Liquidity for leveraged contracts depends on the good will of the issuing firm. There is no secondary market. Interest charges are generally high. Precious metals markets are volatile. No government or well-established private insurance exists for leveraged contract accounts. Prices of leveraged contracts are set by the issuing firm and may vary widely from market prices for the underlying commodity. Transaction costs typically are very high relative to costs for competitive products. Investors are subject to the business risk that the issuing firm may fail as well as to market risk. The high built-in costs may mean that even if you are right on market direction, you may lose money by the time you close out your position. Your potential loss is not necessarily limited to your initial investment.

Tax Considerations

Tax Consequences

Gains and losses from leveraged contracts are capital gains and losses. Gains are taxed as ordinary income. Losses may be used to offset other capital gains. Unused capital losses may be carried forward. Interest charges are deductible up to the amount of investment income, and may also be carried forward.

Summing Up

Leveraged contract dealers have shrunk from hundreds to only a few federally registered firms. The largest and most active firm is Monex, located in California. If inflation turns higher, you can expect to see increased advertising and public exposure on the part of the remaining firms. Leveraged contract dealers have been largely replaced by collaterized loan program vendors (also called bank financing programs). However, the many drawbacks inherent to leveraged contracts are equally present with these alternatives.

Investors interested in leveraged investments in precious metals should investigate the futures and futures options markets. The transaction fees are considerably lower, and the market is more liquid and less subject to manipulation. If you do not qualify for futures trading, you probably should restrict your investments to precious metals mutual funds or cash coin purchases. We do not recommend leveraged contracts or collateralized loan programs for anyone. If you have a desire to throw your money away, we suggest you find a charity that can make good use of the funds rather than wasting your time and effort with these so-called investments.

Option-Buying Mutual Funds

The mutual fund industry was slow to capitalize on the popularity of the options market for a number of reasons. Mutual funds invest large sums. The fledgling options market simply couldn't handle the volume. Without sufficient track records, it was difficult even for professional traders to develop consistent usable trading systems. And finally, few investors will place money with an untried trading advisor. Once actual track records began to develop, the mutual fund industry began to offer aggressive investors the chance to have professional management in the high-flying options market.

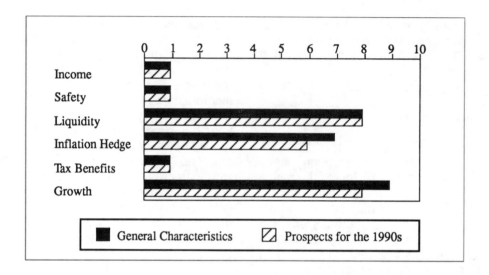

General Characteristics   Prospects for the 1990s

Type II

D

Low Taxes
Low Expenses

Options have developed into a very large, very liquid, and very popular market since the inception of exchange-listed options in 1974. At first only a few stocks had options, and for years only call options were traded. Now there are five major options exchanges: the Chicago Board Options Exchange (CBOE), the PBW, the Pacific, and the American and New York option exchanges. Most listed and many OTC stocks now have listed options, both put and call.

A call option gives the buyer the right to buy 100 shares of a specified stock at a specified price for a specified time period. For example, assume that XYZ stock is selling at 50 in January. The March 50 XYZ call

option is selling for $5 ($5 x 100 shares + option = a total premium of $500).

For an investment of $500, you have the right to buy 100 shares of XYZ from the seller (or writer) of the option at $50 per share until the third Friday in March. If the stock goes to $60 per share before the end of March, your option would go to at least $10 ($1,000 total value per option). In other words, a 20% move in the stock price translates into a 100% move in the price of the option!

A put option is just the opposite. A put option is a contract that gives the buyer the right to sell 100 shares of a specified stock at a specified price for a specified time period. You'd buy a put if you thought the price of a stock were going to go down. For example, assume that XYZ stock in January was selling for $50 per share. The XYZ

March 50 put option sells for $4 ($4 per share x 100 shares = total value of option $400). Put options generally trade for a smaller premium than do call options. If XYZ fell to $40 per share, your put gives you the right to sell 100 shares at $50 per share to the seller of the put option. You've profited from a fall in price.

Mutual funds that concentrate in option buying are usually structured so that 80 to 90% of the funds on hand are used to buy Treasury bills. Because options expire worthless, it would not be prudent to invest everything in vehicles that may expire! The balance of funds are used to speculate in calls and puts. The tremendous leverage that options provide make this strategy viable. Small percentage price moves in the underlying stocks can translate into large profits by the options.

Option mutual funds are either load or no-load. A load fund assesses a sales charge that is added to the fund's net asset value (NAV) when you purchase the fund. A no-load fund sells at its NAV without any sales charges. A load fund is usually purchased through a broker. A no-load fund is purchased direct from the fund.

Investment Potential

Option funds generate capital gains. Generally they pay no income since interest earned from Treasury bills is reinvested in the option-buying portfolio.

Aggressive option funds trade as very short-term vehicles. There is much activity in the funds' portfolio because options are short-term investments. An advantage of using a mutual fund rather than trading options yourself is that a fund can be viewed as a long-term investment. If you buy a load fund, it is impractical to trade the fund in the short term because of the large up-front fees you paid.

The stock market has become increasingly volatile in recent years. As leveraged plays on stocks, options are even more volatile. A mutual fund that is structured to buy options is a high-risk investment. Investors run market risk, timing risk, high fees from high portfolio turnover, and management risk.

Option mutual funds are very liquid. They keep a large portion of their assets in Treasury bills to ensure that liquidity. However, no federal insurance is available on mutual funds. Mutual funds that specialize in option buying are more appropriate for retirement plans than direct purchase of options because of the professional management and diversification. Even then, only a very small portion of your money should be invested in this type of fund.

Strengths

Option-buying mutual funds offer the potential for very large capital gains. They trade broadly diversified portfolios that minimizes the damage that any one position could wreak. Professional management fees of mutual funds are generally less than the fees you'd pay for a manager to trade your account. Option funds are very liquid. Option funds offer inflation protection.

Weaknesses

Options are very volatile and high risk. Mutual funds investing in them are less risky than outright positions but still high risk. The high management and commission fees that accompany active trading may hurt your bottom-line return. No income cushions adverse market moves. Option-buying funds have generally underperformed other growth-oriented mutual funds.

Tax Considerations

Tax Consequences

The 1986 Tax Reform Act eliminated preferential tax treatment for capital gains. All gains from option mutual funds are capital gains. Capital losses offset other capital gains. Excess losses are carried forward. Capital gains are taxed at your ordinary income tax bracket.

Summing Up

Surprisingly, option funds were not sterling performers in the bull market from 1982 to the August 1987. Many explanations are possible, but the bottom line is that the funds have not done the job commensurate with the higher risk inherent in options trading. Option-buying funds are classified as option growth funds in annual performance rankings by Lipper Analytical Services. 1988 was a poor year for option growth funds. As a group, they finished up a meager 0.95%, to finish as one of the weakest groups for the year. Option growth funds again trailed most other fund groups in performance in 1989 and the first half of 1990. This is certainly in line with our expectations that option buying is a losing proposition in most cases. The relatively short track records of these funds may be misleading. For the present, though, aggressive growth stock funds appear to offer better performance.

Notes

Option Income Mutual Funds

A mutual fund pools the money of a number of individual investors to invest in securities through professional management. An option income fund sells put and call options in accord with some plan in order to generate current income from the premiums received.

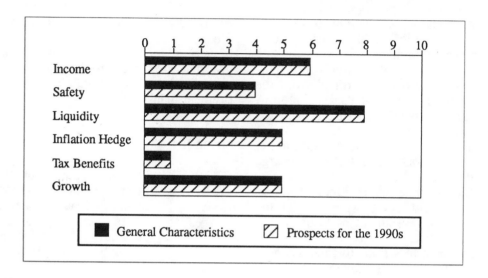

General Characteristics ■   Prospects for the 1990s ▨

Type II

C

Low Taxes
High Expenses

The stock option market began to receive widespread investor interest in 1974 and 1975 after the Chicago Board Options Exchange (CBOE) was launched. For the first time, option contracts were standardized and listed on a central exchange. Previously, stock options had traded on the over-the-counter (OTC) market but a lack of uniformity in contract specifications limited their use primarily to professionals. Now stock options are traded on the CBOE, the PBW Options Exchange, the Pacific Options Exchange, and the American and New York options exchanges.

A call option gives the buyer the right to buy 100 shares of a specified stock at a specified price for a specified time period. A put option gives the buyer the right to sell 100 shares of the specified stock at the specified price within a specified time. Every option contract has both a buyer and a seller.

A buyer is motivated by the potential for growth. A seller earns income because he or she receives the premium minus commission. For example, a three-month call option with a strike price of $50 on XYZ stock is selling for $400. A buyer who thinks XYZ will move significantly above $50 would pay the $400 for obtaining the right to buy 100 shares for the next three months at $50 per share regardless of what the market price is. The seller of the option, receives the $400 immediately. This is payment for undertaking the risk of guaranteeing that the seller will deliver the stock if "called" by the buyer.

The seller is called the "writer" of the option. Investors "write" options in two ways. A covered option means that the seller owns the stock he or she may be forced to deliver. A "naked" option means that the seller of the option does not own the underlying stock. Naked writing is very high risk. If the stock price jumps sharply higher, the seller may be forced to buy it at a much higher price than he or she has agreed (via the option contract) to sell it to the call buyer.

Professional options traders use many sophisticated option strategies. A mutual fund that specializes in generating income from its option trading, undertakes writing strategies. An income program would not be involved in the outright buying of options, although it may buy options as one part of a spread. A spread is the simultaneous buying and selling of options with different strike prices or expiration dates.

Option income mutual funds are purchased through brokers or direct from the fund. A load fund assesses a sales charge. A no-load fund is purchased direct from the fund without a sales fee.

A no-load fund is bought and sold at net asset value. A load fund tacks its charge onto the net asset value.

All option income mutual funds must register with the SEC. A prospectus detailing the fund's fees, investment philosophy, objectives, and strategies must be provided to prospective investors prior to sale. There is no federal insurance. The diversification offered by income option funds offers greater safety than writing single options would.

Investment Potential

Option income mutual funds are designed to generate good current income. They should be thought of as long-term investments, though options themselves are short-term vehicles. A fund that engages in "covered writing" may also earn some capital gains on its stock.

The stock market has become increasingly volatile in recent years. Options, which are leveraged stock market investments, are even more volatile and risky. In addition to the market risk of adverse price movement, there is a timing risk. Options expire totally worthless on specified days. An option buyer can lose 100% of his or her investment through deterioration of the time value in the option, if the underlying stock price stays flat.

This withering of the time premium plays a crucial favorable part in the option writer's strategy. However, the option writer can also be badly hurt by bad timing. If a stock price explodes upward before expiration, the writer will lose money. Option trading, both writing and buying is a high-risk proposition.

Option income mutual funds are liquid investments. Most funds allow you to redeem shares over the telephone. Most funds also offer a variety of payout options for shareholders. You can elect to have a fixed amount paid out periodically, or have interest or dividends paid out. Read a fund's prospectus for full details.

Option income mutual funds are appropriate for retirement plans. However, they should not be the only investment in retirement plans.

Strengths

Option income mutual funds offer a professionally managed diversified portfolio that generates current income. They are liquid. They offer a variety of withdrawal options for investors in need of income. An option income fund offers some downside protection in bear markets.

Weaknesses

Option income funds do not offer significant capital gains potential. Trading options is a very high risk, highly leveraged investment, and includes the unique risk of time deterioration. Since options expire at set times, their value shrinks as the expiration date gets closer. Option income funds have generally underperformed the market since their inception. According to Lipper Analytical Services, option income funds from 1982 through 1987 gained approximately half the compounded return on the S&P 500 Index. However, you should note that although the performance is only half, so is the volatility. The premium income offers downside protection in down markets. Funds trade off unlimited gains in bull markets by selling options on stock, which limits their upside potential.

Tax Considerations

Tax Consequences

Income generated in options trading is taxed as ordinary income. Capital gains are also taxed at your ordinary income levels. Capital losses offset other capital gains. Losses are carried forward.

Summing Up

Option income mutual funds do best in flat sideways markets when the deterioration of the option's time value becomes an important factor. In the strong bull market from 1982 to August 1987, these funds underperformed most equity funds. Even though performance has been only about 50% of the S&P 500 Index, option income funds have enjoyed dramatic growth in recent years. By early 1988, option income funds had almost $7 billion under management. In 1988 they gained 14.74% and in 1989 10.28% For the 12 months ending June 30, 1990 option income funds returned 4.35%, well under the average for all equity funds of 12.56% .

A bull market limits the appeal of option income mutual funds. To a lesser extent, so too would a bear market. A flat market is ideal for them. They should be considered as a good alternative or diversification with bond funds for current income.

Warrants

A warrant is a security, usually issued with either a corporation's bonds or preferred stock which gives the holder the right to buy a specified number of shares of the company's common stock at a specified price within a specified time period. There are some warrants which are issued in perpetuity, i.e. with no expiration date.

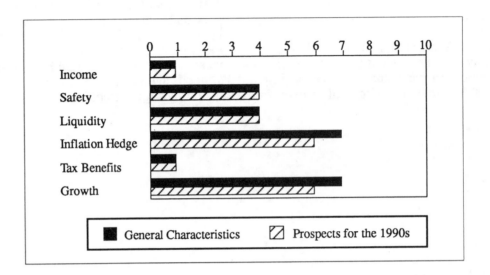

The exercise price is normally higher than the common stock's price at the time the warrant is issued. Most warrants are initially offered as "sweeteners" to help a company raise capital. Often they are issued in units with bonds or preferred stock by small or new companies needing additional operating capital.

Type I

D

Low Taxes
Low Expenses

Warrants are similar to call options in many respects. Holders have the right to buy a set number of shares of a specified stock within a set time (unless the warrant is perpetual). However, there are some clear differences. Listed call options are for 100 shares. Warrants are not uniform. Sellers of call options are motivated by the desire to see the option expire so they will profit from the premium they receive. Warrants are issued by corporations that do not want to see their warrants expire worthless. After all, an exercised warrant will mean they can sell more stock. Also there is a negative connotation to a warrant that expires without value. Companies often extend the life of their warrants to avoid the stigma. Another key difference is the universe of available call options versus that of warrants. There are only about 100–150 actively traded liquid warrants. Call options are available on most NYSE listed stocks and many Amex and OTC issues.

Warrants are traded separately, usually shortly after an initial offering when they are sold as "units" with a bond. They are traded on the stock exchanges and the OTC market. Their price is set by supply and demand in the auction market.

You buy warrants through licensed stock brokers, the same as you would stocks. A commission is assessed when you buy and sell. Prices are quoted regularly in the *Wall Street Journal* and *Investor's Daily*.

Investment Potential

Warrants offer the potential for growth. They pay no income. Much like call options, their price is dependent on the price of their underlying stocks.

There are two components to price. First is the time premium. The more time to expiration, the more valuable the warrant will be. For example, if two stocks are selling at the same price, and the exercise price of their warrant is for the same price, the longer-term warrant will usually be more valuable.

The second element in the price is the relation of the exercise price of the warrant to the underlying stocks. If a stock is selling at $10 per share, and its warrant is for exercise at $50 per share, there will not be much value. The closer the warrant strike price is to the price of the underlying stock, the more valuable the warrant.

Warrants tend to be quite volatile because their market is generally thinner than stocks. Also, warrant prices tend to be lower, therefor a small change represents a larger percentage move.

Many arbitrage professionals use warrants in sophisticated strategies to achieve income or capital appreciation goals. Such strategies are beyond the scope of this book.

Warrants are registered with the SEC when initially registered. A few newsletters report on the warrant market. Perhaps the best known is Value Line's *Options & Convertibles* (711 3rd Ave., New York, NY 10017) .

Warrants present a number of risks. There is, of course, the risk that the market price of the warrant and/or stocks will decline due to the onset of a bear market. There is business risk that the underlying company will be poorly managed or find itself in an out-of-favor industry. And there is also the time value risk. If the underlying stock price does not move up, the time value of a dated warrant will deteriorate.

Strengths

 Investing in warrants requires relatively small amounts of money compared to buying stock. With warrants, you have good leverage because you only have to post a small percentage of the value of the underlying stock. A small price move yield a high percentage profit. Warrants offer good capital growth potential. Many warrants of well-known issuers are liquid.

Weaknesses

 Warrants offer no income. This lack of income means they afford investors no downside protection in the case of declining markets. Dated warrants can expire worthless if the price of the underlying stock does not appreciate enough to make exercising them worthwhile. Time works against a dated warrant investor. In rising markets, the premiums on warrants may become steeply overvalued. Warrant holders have no claim on the underlying company's assets in the case of business failure.

Tax Considerations

Tax Consequences

Before the 1986 Tax Reform Act, warrants had one distinct advantage over call options: they could be held over six months to gain favorable long-term capital gains treatment. However, the 1986 law eliminated the distinction between long- and short-term capital gains. All gains from warrants are taxed at your ordinary income rates.

Summing Up

Warrants offer investors a long-term method of speculating on stocks prices without having to post the full amount of the underlying stock. The rise of the listed option market has dampened enthusiasm and interest in warrants.

However, the active liquid market in about 100–150 issues presents reasonable investment prospects for some investors. You should not invest more than 10% of your liquid assets in warrants, though.

Notes

Personal
Financial Keys
for Exotics and
Special
Situation
Investments

CHAPTER 18

EXOTICS AND SPECIAL SITUATION INVESTMENTS

Growth
Income
Inflation

Business failure
Illiquidity
Volatility
Deflation

Tax shelter
Ordinary income
Capital gain

A GLANCE AHEAD

Many investors like to venture beyond the basics into the realms of the so-called exotics, the limited partnerships and tangible assets that can add zest and personality to a well-balanced portfolio. In this chapter you'll learn about

- *How the limited partnership business structure makes it possible to invest in a wide variety of ventures with relatively small amounts of money and limited risk*
- *Investments that combine the pleasures of hobbies with the potential for profit*
- *How to decide when an "exotic" investment may be appropriate for you.*

SPECIAL INVESTMENTS AND SPECIAL INVESTORS

Colin (Ben) Coombs, a well-known financial planner from Woodland Hills, California, likes to say, "If it eats, grows, or glitters, I don't touch it." That attitude reflects the way a number of respected planning professionals think. However, a growing number are coming to recognize the investment value of the so-called exotics: the special limited partnerships and other investments that offer great potential and varying degrees of

risk. Coombs and those who agree with him remember all too well various jojoba-bean-growing programs, diamond deals, or other "tulip bulb" investing schemes that either failed to produce or were pure fraud from the outset. But not all unusual investments are losers or fraudulent. Today's exotics include many programs that have produced profits for careful investors.

It is important that you approach your financial planning in a consistent, logical manner. Be sure to build a firm foundation in any asset category of tried and true investments. With the wide range of no-load mutual funds making professional management available to all types of investors—regardless of how conservative or speculative they are—there is no excuse for not having a liquid "nest egg" to provide for emergencies and retirement.

We all have read or heard about someone who succeeded in making money "off the beaten path." While the *Wall Street Journal* chronicles the fortunes and misfortunes of the stock, bond, real estate, and futures set, few articles appear on those who make a living (or even get rich!) pursuing a hobby or interest in investments that are far removed from those markets.

We've classified these investments as "exotics." Perhaps you know someone who "dabbles" in oil and gas limited partnerships, or boasts about the money he or she's made through clever equipment-leasing deals. These are both unusual investments for people in special tax, growth, and money-management situations.

If you are interested in the history of the region where you live, you may know of projects to rehabilitate historical buildings. You probably never thought of these as investments. But for many people, usually those who are strongly drawn to these endeavors for personal esthetic reasons rather than for financial gain, their "hobbies" have turned into good investments.

Exotics are the limited partnerships and tangibles categories generally considered too risky for pension planning and core portfolio building. Many of them are as old as investing itself. Others, like leveraged buyout (LBO) limited partnerships and cable TV partnerships, are newer concepts that may hold appeal for sophisticated well-heeled investors. For many products, the term *exotic* implies far too harsh a judgment on their stability—they are "plain vanilla" safe. For others, the term fits just right. Clearly, the word *exotic,* although widely accepted, can be misleading: a better choice is "special situation investments," which more accurately describes the opportunities of nontraditional investing. Special situation investments are for seasoned investors who have made their cash equivalent investments, who are well positioned in cash and mutual funds, who have done their defensive planning, who own their homes and have structured retirement plans. Such people have protected their long-term security and have balanced portfolios. Special-situation investments may be for you if you can afford to experiment with nonessential investment dollars and want to do so. Keep in mind, though, that these investments carry greater risk than the body of your portfolio. And importantly, these investments are for people who don't require good liquidity for their investment funds.

You may be attracted to some exotic investments because you have a personal interest in that area. Such investments have the potential to earn higher returns than more traditional products. At the same time, they have the equal potential to produce bigger losses. Exotics often are imaginative and have some sizzle—some "sex appeal."

Unfortunately, that "sizzle" all too often turns into fizzle.

The lack of an ongoing auction market is a problem with all exotics. Don't be fooled by high-pressure salespeople anxious to earn top-dollar commissions selling products for which no easy comparison shopping can be done. Some people have a feel for certain industries, and others get pleasure out of owning objects they enjoy tangibly. Many people own collections of cars or art or china that are as valuable for their esthetic appeal as for the investment they represent. Often, tangible assets are favored by people who need to have investments that they can get their hands on.

Exotics can be good inflationary hedges, too, but they are more speculative than core investments and can be highly illiquid.

LIMITED PARTNERSHIPS

A limited partnership is a form of business organization that enables small investors to pool their funds and participate in programs otherwise available only to investors with much larger sums. Normally, the partnership diversifies its investments within an industry such as real estate, oil and gas, agriculture, or equipment leasing. Limited partnerships are set up to be self-liquidating, usually within five to 12 years.

A limited partnership consists of (1) a general partner (or partners), who organizes and manages the ongoing affairs of the partnership, and (2) a number of limited partners, who contribute capital but have no role in the day-to-day management of the partnership. Limited partners are usually liable for nothing beyond their original investment. Some partnership agreements include stipulations that limited partners can be called for additional money. However they are protected from legal liability for the partnership if all legal steps are carefully followed. The general partner—who should be a professional in the targeted field—receives a management fee for organizing and running the business.

Originally, some limited partnerships were structured as tax shelters to create paper losses. Such losses were used by the limited partners to offset income at tax time.

However, the tax laws were dramatically altered in the 1980s. Beginning in 1984 and culminating with the 1986 Tax Reform Act, most tax advantages of these limited partnership "tax shelters" were eliminated. The new law divided income into three different and distinct classes.

- *Active income* is defined as that from wages, salaries, and other businesses in which the taxpayer owns a minimum of 10% interest and for which he or she actively participates in management decisions.
- *Passive income* comes from ventures in which the taxpayer does not "materially participate"—is passive, in other words. This includes income from rents.
- *Portfolio income* is derived from interest, dividends, royalties, and capital gains and losses from security transactions.

The three types of income are kept separate for most purposes. This means that losses created in "passive activities" cannot be used to offset active or portfolio income. Hence, the 1986 Tax Act sounded the death knell for most leveraged tax shelters. People wanted the tax shelters to offset active income.

But the concepts that underly limited partnerships are still sound. Now limited partnerships are usually structured as income-producing vehicles. In many cases, the income produced by a contemporary limited partnership can be sheltered by passive losses of the type incurred by the old loss-generating partnerships. In addition, some of the older, loss-oriented partnerships still have value to some—mainly wealthy—investors who need to generate passive losses to offset passive income.

Unlike the corporate structure, profits and losses in a limited partnership flow through directly to the limited partners. This path eliminates the double taxation of dividends that occurs when the corporation is taxed on its profits and then shareholders are taxed on their dividend income.

Historically, limited partnerships were structured as highly leveraged operations to take full advantage of tax provisions. In many cases, more than 50% of a leveraged partnership's assets were financed with borrowed money. Unleveraged partnerships are more conservative. They borrow lightly, usually relying almost entirely on invested cash. This approach presents significantly less risk for the partnership. The new limitations on deductibility of interest and depreciation from passive investments make many of the unleveraged partnerships increasingly attractive.

Limited partnerships are sold in a variety of ways, chiefly through major full-service brokerage firms and small, specialized broker/dealers. Sales fees are normally paid by the general partner out of capital generated through the sales. As the source of the capital, the limited partners pay the fees indirectly. Sales fees can vary considerably and should be considered when evaluating a limited partnership offering.

Look At This:

Various surveys show that the fees charged for limited partnerships typically are among the most expensive of all investments. A $10,000 investment may be charged as little as $600 or more than $1,000. These fees are rarely spelled out clearly to investors. Investors are even told they pay no commissions because the general partner pays the marketing fees. Don't forget where the general partner gets the capital—from the limited partners!

The reputation and track record of the sponsor or general partner also should be a major consideration for the investor. Major brokerage firms and most broker/dealers maintain "due diligence" departments that carefully evaluate limited partnership offerings, determine risk levels, and establish criteria to help protect investors from getting into partnerships that are too risky for their means.

The two types of limited partnership offerings are private and public. Public offerings are registered with the SEC and must meet strict disclosure requirements; prospective buyers must be provided with a prospectus. Private offerings are not registered with the SEC. They may sell only to (1) "accredited" investors with annual incomes of $200,000 or a net worth of $1 million and (2) to a limited number (usually 35) of "unaccredited" investors with smaller incomes and net worth. The minimum investment usually is much higher in private offerings, so smaller investors should avoid private offerings in favor of less risky public partnerships. The specific requirements vary from state to state.

Investment Potential

Most current limited partnerships are now sold as income-producing instruments. These new products are called PIGs—passive income generators. They are being marketed to owners of old tax shelter partnerships as a source of income that can still be sheltered. However, the IRS issued 47 pages of PIG regulations in February 1988, which eliminated this feature for all but the most carefully structured PIG.

Basically, the regulations say that most partnerships marketed as PIGs generate both passive losses and active income! Although many advisors thought that rental properties would be about as passive as possible, the IRS specifically ruled against a number of rental programs, including parking garages and furniture leasing. Income from publicly traded master limited partnerships was also ruled active income (see below).

The key to passing muster with the IRS appears to be syndications which produce income with big losses from depreciation. One area that most experts expect will pass includes a series of partnerships in auto dealerships, offered by Smith Barney. Another is cable television partnerships. Both have good cash flow, little depreciation, and slight or no leverage.

Professional Advice

If you do not want a surprise from the IRS, make an extra effort to have your tax advisor clear any limited partnership investment in advance. Do not rely on the opinion of salespeople. They have a vested interest in interpreting the law as liberally as possible. And their opinion carries little weight with the IRS.

There may be capital gains potential, but typically such gains are realized when the partnership is closed out. The capital gains are dictated by the amount of money raised when the assets are liquidated. Most partnerships are structured to sell or refinance their assets in five to 12 years. The proceeds are then distributed to the limited partners.

There isn't a significant secondary market for limited partnerships yet, so a partner who needs to get out early may take a loss. Limited partnerships must be considered an illiquid investment. Considerable demand is developing, however, for successful partnerships in their third or fourth year of maturity.

Although limited partnerships must be classified as illiquid at this time, there are some encouraging developments. A secondary market is developing around the country.

Some dealers "make markets" in select partnership programs. These dealers typically keep lists of partnerships they are willing to buy.

They maintain bid prices (prices they are willing to pay) and ask prices (at which they are willing to sell). If you want to sell your limited partnership units, you call them and get their quotes.

The Liquidity Fund Investment Corporation (1900 Powell St., Suite 730, Emeryville, CA 94608) pioneered in the field. It is now the largest "market maker," buying units in more than 300 real estate limited partnerships. Liquidity fund is unique in that it creates new limited partnerships with the units it buys.

Other market makers in real estate partnerships include Equity Resources (1280 Massachusetts Ave., Cambridge, MA 02138), MacKenzie Securities (650 California St., 19th Floor, San Francisco, CA 94108), Partnership Securities Exchange (1814 Franklin St., Suite 820, Oakland, CA 94612), and Oppenheimer & Bigelow Management (489 Fifth Ave., New York, NY 10017).

Be forewarned, each of these dealers buys units at steep discounts from appraised value. The discounts run from as little as 20% to over 50%. That is why limited partnerships must be considered illiquid! But even with the rise of partnership market makers, the vast majority of limited partnerships simply have no secondary market. That means you should be prepared to hold a limited partnership investment for the average of 8 to 12 years it takes for liquidation of LP assets and distribution to investors.

It's difficult to judge the volatility of limited partnerships because no central marketplace exists with current prices for outstanding shares. Also, there are no widely recognized rating systems for limited partnerships. The Robert Stanger organization has begun a ratings system for subscribers to the Stanger Register (1129 Broad St., Shrewsbury, NJ 07701).

Limited partnerships are subject to a variety of risks. One risk is that the investments may simply turn out poorly, owing to sagging markets or poor management. Do not invest in a limited partnership unless you are entirely confident in the management abilities of the general partners. Limited partnerships in general have had terrible track records. By the late 1980s large LP dealers and syndicators faced rising complaints about dismal performance. Some analysts project that as much as 30-40% of the $100 billion LP market are in financial trouble or could wind up in trouble even without a recession.

Strengths

Most limited partnerships offer passive income that can be offset by the passive losses of leveraged tax shelter credits. Limited partnerships offer investors the chance to invest relatively small amounts without assuming full financial risk for the success or failure of the enterprise. And limited partnerships allow for diversification with the chosen area of investment. For relatively small investments, investors can increase diversity by sampling a variety of partnerships in different asset areas. Some limited partnerships offer the potential of capital gains. And finally, some limited partnerships may provide a good hedge against inflation.

Weaknesses

Limited partnerships offer poor liquidity. No insurance is available for them. It is difficult to independently ascertain the value of a partnership share. The ability and integrity of the general partner is a key factor in success. If market or political conditions (such as the tax laws) change, a limited partnership that began well may start to fail and offer little chance for escape. Limited partnerships are long-term investments. Performance in general since 1983 has lagged that of very secure government bonds.

Tax Considerations

Tax Consequences

The 1986 Tax Reform Act dramatically changed the tax treatment of partnership income and losses. Passive losses can be used only to offset passive gains—not active or investment income. In effect, the TRA traps portfolio income, such as dividends and interest from investments, and makes it wholly taxable.

In a partnership, income may build up as a cash fund that can be sheltered and the gains may be·offset by other passive losses. This passive-income, passive-loss provision becomes increasingly attractive with higher incomes and bigger net worths. Many limited partnership investors have learned to their chagrin that the IRS assesses penalties and interest on partnership deductions that are subsequently disallowed. In at least some cases, whole partnerships have been termed frauds and investors who were hoodwinked themselves, have been assessed huge penalties and interest.

Summing Up

Limited partnerships sales were down sharply in 1989. They've been sluggish since 1986 when the TRA undermined the value of the old loss-oriented partnerships. But the fundamental concept survived, although they are now usually structured to generate passive income rather than tax deduction. The basic concepts of the limited partnership are sound and can be applied to almost any investment category. Most experts expect to see partnerships proliferate, if the slowly developing system of market makers begins to attract more investors in older, seasoned partnerships. However the very poor average performance and large fees have soured the public on partnership investing to the extent that Shearson Lehmen Hutton, the largest dealer in LPs has cut back their sales dramatically. Reports in the financial media indicate that Shearson got negative feedback from its own sales force for the many underperforming partnerships it has sold.

MASTER LIMITED PARTNERSHIPS (MLPs)

In the late 1970s and 1980s, a new type of organization came into being that combined the benefits of a limited partnership with the liquidity of corporate stocks. These *master limited partnerships* (MLPs), as they are called, were originated by a realty and construction company that spun off its real estate division by issuing partnership "shares." The firm assumed the responsibility of a general partner, which limited the liability of the limited partners, just as in a standard limited partnership. This structure qualified the limited partners for passive income tax advantages before the 1987 law changes.

For MLPs in existence on December 17, 1987, the Revenue Act of 1987 retains partnership status until 1998, unless a substantial new line of business is added. However, for purposes of the passive activity rules, income from MLPs is treated as "portfolio" income. That means that the income cannot be used to offset passive losses, and MLP losses cannot be used to offset passive income. MLPs not in existence on December 17, 1987, are taxed as corporations unless 90% or more of their income is from real estate rents, interest, dividends, gains from property sales, and other passive-type income. However, MLPs had grown to many other areas in recent years. These included hotel chains, equipment leasing, and even the Boston Celtics basketball team. These "operating company" MLPs are now taxed the same as corporations if they were not publicly traded on December 17, 1987. That eliminates one of their chief advantages over corporations. Their investors are hit with double taxation—first at the company level and then on the income paid to them. The high payouts that MLPs were able to make were in part due to the fact they were paying

their investors money that now goes to the IRS.

Until 1985, almost all MLPs were in the energy field, but since then the opportunities have proliferated. In 1986, the owners of the Boston Celtics raised $48 million through the sale of partnership interests.

Other tradable limited partnerships are formed by "rolling up" several standard limited partnerships into a single MLP. They offer greater diversity and the liquidity of public trading. MLPs do limit the liability of the limited partners to their original investment, although they've lost their tax advantages.

MLPs are bought and sold through licensed securities brokers just like stocks and are registered as securities by the SEC. They may be disguised as "no-load" products, but in fact the commission and management fee structure is essentially the same as that of an untraded limited partnership. However, fees may be more difficult to detect, due to the way shares are marketed. Because they are buried in complex acquisition costs, unnecessarily high management fees may be made invisible. MLP prices are listed in the financial pages of major newspapers and the financial press.

Because MLPs are publicly traded, they are more liquid than untraded partnerships. The investor who must sell during the first few years is not as likely to take a substantial loss. However, the value of MLP shares will vary according to a variety of market influences, so investors must determine the "right time to sell."

Two significant warnings should be stated. First, since the major marketing benefit of an MLP is liquidity, general partners may employ a number of techniques to maintain artificially high yields and thus ensure a healthy secondary market. Before investing in an MLP, investors should familiarize themselves with the yield on equity as well as the advertised yield. Some MLPs resort to returning investors' own money (i.e., a return of capital in the guise of a return on investment) to make their yields seem higher than they actually are. A 10% return from an MLP that includes some return of principal is not comparable to a 10% return from a bond. In the first case you are actually receiving some of your own money back.

Investment Potential

MLPs meet a number of investment objectives. Some are specifically designed to provide current income, while others are primarily oriented to the growth of capital. MLPs should be considered long-term investments.

MLPs are available in a wide variety of industries and price volatility closely reflects the volatility of the underlying business.

Some MLPs qualify for margin and can be leveraged. The investor posts a maximum of 50% of the value of the desired MLP and is loaned the balance by the brokerage firm. Margin purchases are inherently a more speculative investment: the investor pays interest on the loan balance, and adverse price moves may result in "margin calls" that require an immediate deposit of capital.

Exchange-listed MLPs may be sold short to profit from price declines.

The safety of MLPs depend on good business management and economic conditions, not on their organizational structure. Some are much safer than others. MLPs must be registered with the SEC and provide annual audited financial information.

Strengths

MLPs offer better liquidity than limited partnerships. Some offer good income while others provide capital gains potential. The income paid by some MLPs is nontaxable as a return of capital or may be partly sheltered from taxation. MLPs in such industries as real estate and energy are good hedges against inflation.

Weaknesses

Management fees for MLPs vary widely. High fees adversely affect performance. Moreover, since partnerships typically pay out cash flow, reinvestment options at the same yield may be limited. In addition to the market risk of price fluctuations, poor managment also poses a risk. Finally, uncertainty about future tax treatment creates political risk.

Tax Considerations

Tax Consequences

Some MLPs are designed to pay tax-exempt income as a return of capital. However, this design means that the assets of the MLP are being diminished. Other income and capital gains are taxed at ordinary income rates.

MLPs are appropriate for most retirement plans, provided they meet the specific investment objective being sought.

Summing Up

The 1986 Tax Reform Act was thought to be the death knell for master limited partnerships, but that didn't happen. Since the tax law changes in 1987 changed the way MLPs are taxed, fewer MLPs have come to market. The very depressed MLP market meant that some very high yields were available. MLP sales soared once again in 1989 raising $613 million, a 52% increase over 1988. Two large MLPs for the year were a $102 million oil and gas pipeline syndication by Kaneb Services of Richardson, Texas and a $57 million real estate offering by UDC Corp. of Phoenix, Arizona.

SOME TYPES OF LIMITED PARTNERSHIPS

The variety of limited partnerships is as wide as the economic activities they are designed to support.

Oil and Gas

The 1970s oil embargo by the Organization of Petroleum-Exporting Countries (OPEC) shook U.S. complacency as no other economic event since World War II. "Energy independence" became the accepted political slogan of the decade. Predictably, investors began to seek out energy investment plays. Domestic oil companies with substantial reserves were the darlings of Wall Street. Oil and gas investments—mostly structured as tax shelters—had been around for many years, but suddenly the demand for further exploration and development expanded the market.

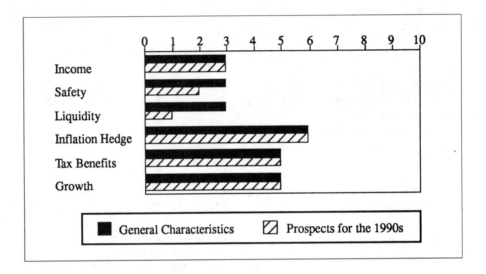

Limited partnerships quickly formed to get in on the potential profits. Huge tax credits were allowed for investments in energy. Oil and gas limited partnerships programs commonly offered writeoffs of 90% to over 100% of the initial investments. Rising prices meant good potential for large capital gains. They became the hottest limited partnerships on the market. The 1986 TRA eliminated the investment tax credits previously enjoyed by the energy industry, but left intact the depletion, intangible drilling costs, and equipment depreciation allowances.

Type I

A

High Taxes
High Expenses

B

High Taxes
Low Expenses

Investment Potential

Oil and gas partnerships offer both income and the potential for capital gain. They are long-term investments, usually scheduled for liquidation within 7 to 10 years. Income is paid when the project begins earning money, and capital gains are normally achieved when the partnership is liquidated.

Partnership investors are subject to market and business risk. The price of oil is quite volatile, and fluctuations of oil prices directly affect the value of partnership shares. There are two types of oil and gas drilling partnerships: *exploratory* and *development*.

Development projects bring known reserves to the market. They normally begin to pay income relatively quickly. They generate fewer losses to offset income payouts. Since the reserves are already known, the risk is lower and capital gain potential is less.

Exploratory projects are devoted to locating new reserves. You may have heard of "wildcatting," or trying to locate new oil supplies. Initial expenses are great and risk is high, because no guarantee exists that oil or gas will be found. The odds of success are minimal for any given well; most partnerships expect to drill a number of wells to increase the odds for success. The potential for capital gains is substantially higher than for a development project.

Some oil and gas partnerships are combinations of the two types, and many partnerships of this sort opt to direct some earnings back into development to maintain or boost the partnership income stream. This approach offers greater capital gains potential than straight development projects and less than exploratory projects.

This flexibility is enhanced by the wide range of leverage possible. Investors can search out those projects that most closely fit their own investment profiles.

Strengths

Oil and gas partnerships are good hedges against inflation. A successful exploration project offers capital gains potential. They may also offer income potential depending on how the program is structured. Development projects pay current income that usually is sheltered to some degree.

Weaknesses

Exploration projects are very high risk. Oil prices are volatile and directly affect the value of a partnership share. Initial costs tend to be very high. Transaction fees are among the highest for all investment vehicles.

Tax Considerations

The 1986 Tax Reform Act changed much of

Tax Consequences

the treatment for limited partnerships—the chief form of direct investing in oil and gas for most individuals. However, the beleaguered oil and gas industry did manage to keep favored treatment for some things. Unlike virtually all other limited partnerships, losses generated through intangible drilling costs can still be used to offset ordinary income. As discussed earlier, most other limited partnerships losses are considered "passive" and can be used only to offset passive income. There are, of course, some changes in details. Check with your tax advisor before investing.

Summing Up

In 1974, people widely believed that oil prices would never go down again, because of OPEC's obvious muscle. History and the marketplace proved that forecast to be short-sighted.

After moving as high as $40 per barrel in the early 1980s, oil prices entered a long downward slide that finally ended late in 1986, when oil briefly sold for around $9 per barrel. OPEC agreed to cut production, and the price per barrel had risen to $28 by summer 1990. For most of 1987, 1988 and 1989, it hovered around the $18 to $20 level.

With the Iraqi invasion of Kuwait in the summer of 1990, oil prices jumped sharply higher. As this is being written, the U.S. is committing U.S. armed forces to Saudi Arabia. It is far too early to know what the final outcome of this matter will be. However, there is no doubt that the heightened political tension and unsettled situation in the Middle East will mean higher prices for at least the next few years. If inflation rises, oil and gas prices will benefit.

Americans can now more easily monitor oil prices by watching the crude oil futures contracts traded on the New York Mercantile Exchange. There is much talk of imposing a high tax on imported oil; such a measure would have a short-term negative impact on oil prices. However, the Iraqi aggression probably put an end to talk of an oil import tax.

Agriculture

Agriculture is the world's largest industry. Food consumption naturally increases as more children are born and life expectancies increase. Worldwide, the agricultural industry is so vast that its scope defies casual discussion. It is enough simply to observe that in every country in the world, food and related issues—food production, processing and distribution—have become key concerns. Keeping up with food demand is changing the way the world looks at a variety of economic, political, and technological issues. As usual, where a need exists an economic solution is in the making. Some solutions are old, and some are new, and almost all hold out potential for wise investors.

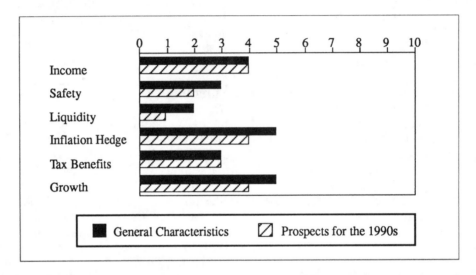

Income
Safety
Liquidity
Inflation Hedge
Tax Benefits
Growth

■ General Characteristics   ▨ Prospects for the 1990s

Type II

A
High Taxes
High Expenses

B
High Taxes
Low Expenses

Land use is one consideration. As farmers in the agricultural states of the U.S. West and Midwest have discovered, financing the farm through mortgage payments can be a dead end. Fixed mortgage payments and other costs continue despite erratic production and uncontrollable prices and demand. One solution is the recent development of limited partnerships that take over land in default and create joint ventures with the farmer to produce crops. The farmer is paid a management fee, shares in the profits, and has the option of buying back the land on a lease-back basis. This strategy is being called "the new sharecropping."

But the truly important developments are in food production, processing, and distribution. Limited partnerships developed by Granada Corporation (Houston, Texas) are structuring their operations to control the entire process. The "green revolution" of the 1960s and 1970s turned many "third world" countries into agricultural producers, crowding markets for traditional products. Companies such as Granada are responding by developing important new technologies to increase yields in traditional product areas and to create breakthroughs in new areas. Genetic engineering, for example, is creating new products such as the Lite Beef (trademark) breed, which is lower in fat and carcinogens than are standard beef cattle. However, the success of Granada in some areas has not helped the 20,000 investors who poured $228 million into LPs of Granada: Integrated Cattle Systems U and Granada 1 through 5. In September 1989 Granada announced that it was repackaging these six cattle-feeding limited partnerships into two publicly-traded corporations. Angry investors learned that they would be getting only $700 of stock for every $10,000 they had invested (not including tax benefits they had received).

U.S. Department of Agriculture experiments with jojoba beans hold exciting promise, as does USDA's work with a new plant called *knauf*, which produces both long and short fibers for paper products. Progressive partnerships also are working to establish vertical market penetration. Limited partnerships have the resources to produce, process, and market the product. Partnerships have created important marketing breakthroughs that create demand and help stabilize prices. Examples are turkey hams from the dark meat of the turkey, which retail for $2.29 a pound (not $0.29 a pound, as for the unprocessed meat); gourmet food products; and convenient restaurant packaging. These offerings are known as "niche" products. The profits increase as value is added through processing and specialized marketing.

Some current agricultural limited partnerships include livestock and poultry breeding, processing, and distribution; timber; aquaculture; basic food crops; orchards, including citrus, walnuts, pistachio nuts, avocados; and row crops such as beans, corn, and peas.

Investment Potential

Like all limited partnerships, agricultural opportunities are long-term investments. Some partnerships offer exceptional cash returns: held for at least 10 to 12 years, some jojoba bean operations are projecting returns as high as 80% per year. Then again, they may generate loses. And after three years of operation, Imperial's aquaculture farms estimate cash flow at 13% to 20%. Agriculture partnerships are structured primarily for capital gains.

Strengths

 Agriculture provides an excellent inflation hedge, and benefited from the weak dollar of 1985–1986. The drought conditions of the summer of 1988 were a mixed blessing. Some farms were totally devastated, while others reaped additional profits as grain prices rose to five- and six-year highs.

Weaknesses

 Agriculture limited partnerships are subject to worldwide price volatility. Technological advances have enabled many previous grain importers to become exporters. Government price support and policies are uncertain. In disinflationary times, leverage is dangerous. Farmers risk loss of property if debt can't be serviced. Rising interest rates will squeeze profit margins. Weather extremes cannot always be anticipated. These partnerships are notoriously illiquid.

Tax Considerations

Tax Consequences

The tax treatment of agriculture-related partnerships is complex. A number of changes made by the Tax Reform Act tightened the rules for obtaining writeoffs. It is particularly important to check with your tax advisor in this area.

Summing Up

Many factors combine to make modern agriculture an exciting investment arena for limited partnerships. The earth's ever-increasing population, the ongoing concern over the cost of financing a family farm, the potential inherent in creating a vertical marketing structure that takes into account all aspects of production, process, and distribution—all contribute to a healthy picture.

Of course, food production is closely linked to uncontrollable factors such as the weather, political and social upheaval, and the availability of resources. But careful and creative partnerships are uncovering new ways to make agricultural production and marketing profitable.

Equipment Leasing

Equipment leasing is one of the great success stories of limited partnerships. Properly administered, leasing programs are profitable both for the lessor (the owner of the property) and the lessee (the user of the property). The lessor—in this case, a limited partnership—buys equipment from the manufacturer and leases it for a substantial portion of its useful life span. At the end of the lease, the lessee may purchase the equipment or return it to the lessor, which in turn sells it as used equipment.

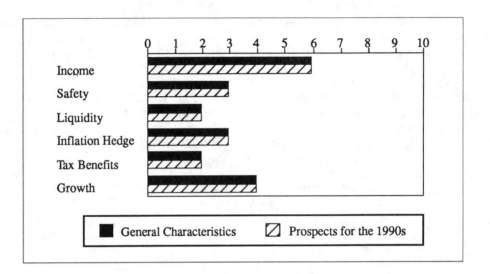

Type II

A
High Taxes
High Expenses

B
High Taxes
Low Expenses

Commonly leased equipment includes steel shipping containers, airplanes, truck fleets, copy equipment, and vending machines. The demand for leased equipment has grown since the 1986 TRA introduced the alternative corporate minimum tax, which in many cases penalizes businesses that buy large amounts of equipment. Leasing allows companies to conserve capital for use in more profitable areas than equipment. Northwest Airlines leases its DC-10s and uses capital in customer services. Corporations no longer consider off-balance-sheet financing a liability; from a net worth standpoint, leasing improves the balance sheet.

In 1984, U.S. businesses spent $84 billion to lease equipment; in 1985, they spent $93 billion; in 1986, $100 billion; and in 1987,

$120 billion. That kind of activity has made equipment leasing one of the most attractive investments of the decade. Leasing continues to show steady growth with many analysts projecting 10-20% annual growth into the 1990s.

The two types of leases are (1) full payout leases and (2) operating leases. Full payout leases require the lessee to pay off the full value of the equipment over the duration of the lease. Full payout leases are a "do-or-die" proposition backed by the credit of the lessee. Operating leases are short-term leases in which the equipment is leased more than once during its useful life span—clearly, a riskier position than the one assumed in a full payout lease.

Investment Potential

Leasing partnerships generate revenues in two ways: through the lease payments and through the subsequent sale of the equipment. In some cases, the lessor's original purchase is highly leveraged, so during the early years of the partnership the lease payments may be used to amortize the purchase costs. Of course, the returns paid to the partners are passive income and may be used to offset the passive losses of tax shelters purchased before the 1986 TRA.

The major U.S. leasing companies lease only to highly rated corporations. In addition, equipment leases hold a position senior to that of corporate bonds, so the holdings of the partnership are secured by the value of the equipment. Depending on the credit-worthiness of the lessees and assuming equipment with a long useful life span, leasing partnerships are among the most stable and conservative partnerships available.

Leasing partnerships provide excellent current income and growth of capital when the equipment is liquidated.

In inflationary scenarios, the value of the equipment increases for higher residual worth at the lease's end. Residual values also are sustained in recessionary markets since corporations are likely either to re-lease or buy used equipment. However, the danger exists that in a recession the value of the equipment will be seriously compromised. There is also the danger of technological obsolescence, which can hurt equipment values.

Strengths

Leasing partnerships provide good current income, generally 12-15% (though some yield may be return of capital). They also offer the potential for capital growth. They generally are regarded as a conservative investment if the lessee is a high-quality company and the equipment is long-lived. The holding is collateralized by the equipment; a lease has a senior position to that of corporate bonds.

Weaknesses

In a deflationary scenario, the residual value of a leasing partnership may not be profitable. Leasing partnerships are also vulnerable to the failure of the lessee's business. And high-tech equipment may become obsolete by the end of the lease period, destroying residual value. Leasing partnerships are illiquid.

Tax Considerations

Tax Consequences

Highly leveraged leasing deals were formerly the darlings of the tax shelter industry. Losses can only be used to offset passive income, not ordinary income. The death blow to the tax shelter aspect of these programs, though, was the elimination of the investment tax credit. There are no particular tax advantages for leasing deals now.

Summing Up

Every indication suggests that equipment leasing will continue to be popular for limited partnerships. Barring further tax law changes, the desire of major corporations to lease so that capital is freed for other uses should result in an increase in leasing activity.

Potential profits depend on (1) the value of the equipment on the resale market at the end of the lease and (2) the ability of the lessee to maintain lease payments. High-tech equipment—including computers—is especially vulnerable to obsolescence. In 1989 leasing limited partnerships was the only type of limited partnership to show any growth. While real estate LP sales dropped 43%, and oil and gas sales fell 7%, leasing LP sales climbed 12.5%.

Leveraged Buyouts

Everyone knows the story of Victor Kiam, "the man who liked the razor so much he bought the company." Buy you may not know that Kiam didn't buy the company with his own money—not much of it, anyway. When Kiam bought Remington, he used a financing mechanism known as a leveraged buyout (LBO), *which enabled him to buy a multimillion-dollar company with less than $1 million down. A lending institution provided the balance.*

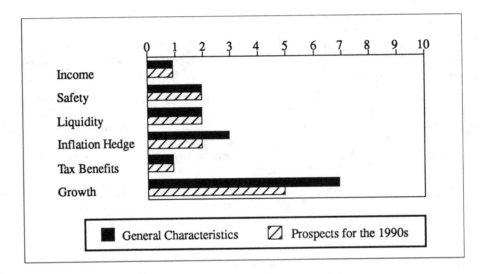

How can so little buy so much? It's quite simple: in a leveraged buyout, the assets and anticipated future cash flow of the acquired business are used as collateral. Of course, the acquisition target must be profitable and relatively debt-free, to be attractive to the lender.

In the last few years, the financial press has been full of tales of leveraged buyouts, and great amounts of wealth have been generated by the strategy.

Many analysts had predicted a sharp drop-off in LBOs following the stock market crash in October 1987. At that time, the worst-hit stocks were those involved in some way in the LBO game. But 1988

Type II

D

Low Taxes
Low Expenses

proved to be a fertile breeding ground for a whole new round of billion-dollar deals. Among the largest takeovers were RJR-Nabisco at $25 billion, Kraft at $13.44 billion, Farmer's Group at $5.20 billion, Sterling Drug at $5.1 billion, American Standard at $2.3 billion, and Media General at $1.6 billion. LBO volume has dropped significantly since late 1989 when the UAL deal fell through, triggering the October 13, 1989 190 point drop in the DJIA.

But until recently the game was open only to the big players—investors with between $10 million and $25 million to invest at one time. Companies such as Kohlberg Kravis Roberts and Forstmann Little generate revenues as high as $5 billion a month with their LBO acquisitions.

Now, however, the LBO game can be

played even by average investors with stable portfolios who want to add some sizzle to the mix. Pioneered by Equus Capital Corporation (Houston, Texas), limited partnerships are now getting into the LBO hunt.

Equus specializes in the friendly acquisition of healthy, middle-sized companies in fragmented industries. These may be niche businesses: operations that have learned to use a specialized technique or product to succeed in a competitive environment. However, be sure to read each prospectus carefully. Just because Equus is structured for friendly takeovers, that doesn't mean that all subsequent programs will be the same. The hostile takeover business can be very lucrative but there are no guarantees. There have been a number of costly takeover attempts too. If you had invested in a partnership involved in a takeover during the October Crash, it could have been very costly. The failure of the UAL buyout is estimated to have cost professional arbitragers as much as $500 million!

Once a business has been located and identified as an potential target for acquisition, it is carefully analyzed by both the partnership and prospective lending institutions for fundamental soundness. This double-check gives the program stability.

If a business qualifies for acquisition, a financing package is structured in which assets and future cash flow are used to support borrowing; the partnership may put up only from 10% to 25% of the total purchase price. To assure that the business is managed properly, existing management is maintained and brought into an ownership position. The tactic is especially valuable for businesses in which the owner wishes to retire or restructure the organization. In some cases, owner and/or management wants to take a public company private or go public with a private company—in which case the partnership will sell the business back after the financing package has been consolidated by the partnership. The goals of a leveraged buyout are to restructure the business for increased profitability, quickly reduce the debt, and ultimately dispose of the assets or refinance.

Investment Potential

Because they are highly leveraged, LBO partnerships aren't structured for immediate income. They may begin to produce some income within three or four years, but the real goal is capital gains. They are long-term investments.

Strengths

LBOs target a higher-than-average profit. Moreover, LBO partnerships invest in a diversified portfolio of companies. Equity buildup is expected through debt reduction from both sales of a company's assets and its continuing operation's cash flow. Participation by present management creates added incentive for increased productivity and performance.

Weaknesses

The LBO could falter if cash flow expectations don't materialize or if general economic conditions deteriorate. Rising interest rates make these highly leveraged deals very risky. Political intervention in the form of restrictive laws on LBOs and tax law changes make LBOs susceptible to uncontrollable risk.

Tax Considerations

Tax Consequences

Income from an LBO limited partnershp is passive income. Losses are deductible only against other passive income. Tax laws have tightened up the amount of interest that an LBO can write off thus limiting the tax advantages. Congress continues to view the LBO business quite skeptically. Be sure to get the latest tax interpretation from your tax advisor on any LBO investment.

Summing Up

The limited partnership LBO is a seemingly attractive way for average investors to participate in the high stakes merger and acquisition business that dominates the front pages of the financial press. It has even reached Hollywood with the successful movie *Wall Street*, featuring an aggressive corporate raider.

However, the LBO business is not a one-way street. There have been many losers, though you don't read about the failures as often as the successes. For example, in 1986 an investor group led by Donaldson, Lufkin,

Jenrette bought Republic Health. In 1987 Republic lost $283 million on $537 million in sales. That led to a default. Even later, losses were still piling up. Efforts to renegotiate the huge debt load were being made, and the company was re-structured.

In 1986 the prestigious brokerage firm Salomon Brothers led a buyout of Revco. Sales for the fiscal year ended May 31, 1988, were $1 billion below forecasts! Operating profit only covered half the $140 million interest charges. The huge debt load shaved earnings from a $141.4 billion profit in fiscal year 1986 to $70 million for 1988.

These are two examples of the less glamorous side of the business. LBOs are a very difficult and high-risk business. Managment ability is crucial for success. Approach any such investment with caution.

Notes

_____

_____

_____

_____

_____

_____

_____

_____

_____

_____

_____

Cable Television

Cable television has surprised everyone. In 1976, the Arthur D. Little Company predicted that by 1980, 3.4 million Americans would subscribe to a pay television service, and that by 1985 the number would be up to 5.7 million. In fact, those numbers fell far short of the mark, and the industry continues to grow.

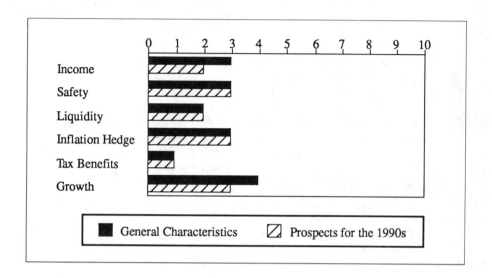

Type II

C

Low Taxes
High Expenses

D

Low Taxes
Low Expenses

Cable originally was attractive primarily in remote areas where normal television signals were weak or unavailable. But now cable franchisers can offer their subscribers a wide variety of programming unavailable on standard UHF and VHF frequencies, and cable penetration in urban areas has grown substantially.

Cable systems are franchised by the communities where they market their services. The cable company receives TV signals via satellite and distributes the signal throughout its service area via coaxial cable. After the initial costs of installing a service grid are paid, maintenance costs are generally very low. Because the system is franchised to service an area, it can operate much like a utility, with stable revenues and predictable expenses. Cable TV is sometimes called the "unregulated monopoly."

Although the costs of establishing cable are high, the stability of the industry has encouraged lending institutions to provide financing that is leveraged against the assets of the future company. Cable television has proved sensitive to inflation, so investors can position their cable investments as inflationary hedges.

The 1986 Tax Reform Act was a boon to cable TV partnerships. Most cable equipment is depreciable over five years, compared with 27.5 to 31.5 for real estate and income is fully or almost fully sheltered during the early years of the partnership.

Investment Potential

Originally, cable partnerships were growth oriented, but income partnerships have come on strong recently. Growth partnerships are heavily leveraged—usually from 50% to 75%—and thus produce very little cash flow, if any. Revenue left over after debt service usually is plowed back into the system for maintenance and expansion.

Income-oriented cable TV partnerships use leverage ranging from 25% to 35% to buy profitable existing systems. Aside from maintenance of the service (which can be expensive if the system is outdated), overhead is minimal. Revenues can pass directly through to partners.

Strengths

Cable TV systems are an "unregulated monopoly"; existing systems are virtually immune from competitive pressures. Cable systems traditionally produce high operating margins. Cable partnerships are "recession-proof," since cheap entertainment is a priority in hard times. New technologies keep cable fresh, ensuring long-range viability. And most cable TV equipment is depreciable over five years, so income is fully or almost fully sheltered during the partnership's early years.

Weaknesses

As in any equipment-heavy partnership, management qualification is a crucial issue. An increasing demand exists for a limited number of cable franchises in good locations. Man-

agement might be tempted to pay too much for a system. Finally, in a rapidly changing industry, partnerships need to be wary of the costs of necessary equipment upgrades. More than most investments, cable is subject to political vagaries and legal challenges. Many systems have gone bankrupt as a result of poor management and/or political intervention. Moves are afoot in Congress and state and local legislatures to impose significant regulatory changes on the industry.

Tax Considerations

Tax Consequences

Cable television partnerships are no longer being marketed for their tax benefits. Losses can only be used to offset passive income.

Summing Up

After some industry-wide shakeups, cable TV partnerships are offering a combination of growth and/or income. Investors seeking growth who don't mind the Damocles' sword of increased government intervention should look to a number of reputable established syndicators who are now expanding their existing systems and buying new ones.

More than a dozen bills were introduced in Congress in 1990 to reregulate the cable TV industry.

Historic Rehabs

Perhaps no other investment product meets with more universal favor than "historical rehab" (rehabilitation), a subcategory of the real estate market. Virtually every community in the country boasts an important, yet fragile, architectural tradition that gives the community character and provides a link with the past. But time takes a toll on old buildings, and historical properties can be kept alive only with the infusion of new capital.

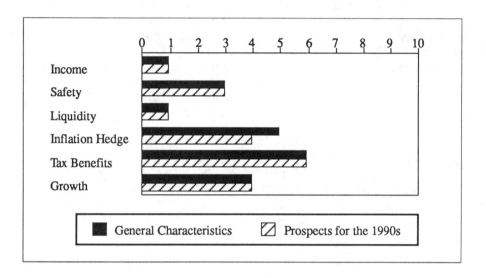

Type II

C

Low Taxes
High Expenses

These realities were recognized by Congress when it passed the 1986 Tax Reform Act. Although Congress eliminated investment tax credits in almost every other investment area, it maintained a 20% investment tax credit for certified historical rehabilitation. Now some very successful limited partnerships are taking advantage of the opportunity by structuring historic rehab programs in accordance with the standards of the U.S. Department of the Interior.

The rehab market got off the ground in 1982, following the 1981 Economic Recovery Tax Act (ERTA), which first allowed tax credits for rehab investments. Under the provisions of the 1981 law, most rehab programs were structured as private placement partnerships. They were highly tax oriented and were sold only to accredited investors with annual incomes of at least $200,000

and net worths in excess of $1 million.

The 1986 TRA eliminated the tax credits for individuals with adjusted gross incomes of over $200,000. So the rehab programs were restructured as niche products to satisfy the needs of investors with incomes of less than $200,000. Unit sizes are as low as $3,000. The 20% investment tax credit is more favorable to taxpayers in lower brackets. Historical rehab is an exception to the passive loss rules of the 1986 TRA; investors can shelter writeoffs against other income up to $25,000 per year regardless of passive loss limitations.

Strengths

Outstanding demand exists for historical buildings, yet there is a finite supply of qualified buildings. Historical rehabs are an excellent inflation hedge.

Excellent tax favors exist even after the 1986 Tax Reform Act.

Weaknesses

 Historic rehab is subject to the same economic and market influences that affect real estate in general. The success of a historic rehab program largely depends on the capabilities of the management. Moreover, certification must be granted by the government. And Historic rehabs are highly illiquid. There is a five-year recapture rule for tax purposes.

Tax Considerations

Tax Consequences

The 1986 Tax Reform Act did provide continued tax-favored treatment for investment in rehab projects. Investors get 20% credit for "qualified" expenditures incurred in the rehabilitation of certified historic structures. A 10% credit is given for nonresidential buildings that are *not* certified historic structures. Definitions that have been changed include that of "qualified rehabilitation housing." As always in these more complex matters, be sure to check with your tax advisor.

Summing Up

The tax advantaged status of rehabs should attract continued investor interest, and a diminishing stock of old buildings are certain to increase the demand for qualified partnerships. Also, investors can know that their money has contributed to the well-being of a community.

Self-Storage

A number of national trends have given rise to self-storage, one of the most important new subcategories of the real estate industry. The most obvious trend is the reduced size of the U.S. home: many more Americans are living in apartments and condominiums than ever before, and the size of the average home continues to shrink. There's less storage space in these new dwellings, at a time when people are buying more possessions. Factor in the increasing cost of commercial space, and you have fertile ground for self-storage. Over 12,000 self-storage facilities are now scattered across the country. Self-storage began in Texas and spread throughout the South and the West; it is not yet well established in the Northeast.

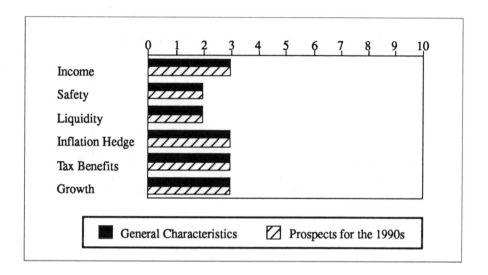

Self-storage units are owned primarily by individuals, by joint ventures of a few people, or by limited partnerships. An industry-wide analysis shows the importance of small ownership in the self-storage industry:

Type II

C
Low Taxes
High Expenses

D
Low Taxes
Low Expenses

Facilities

Public Storage (limited partnership)	700
U-Haul (private ownership)	200
Shurgard, Inc. (limited partnership)	125
Balcor Colonial (limited partnership)	100
Others: (includes individual ownership, corporation and small partnerships)	10,875

Strengths

Self-storage offers the potential of increasing income. Operating expenses are low. Properly selected sites yield high demand. Unleveraged, self-storage partnerships provide a hedge against inflation.

Weaknesses

Self-storage units are illiquid. Highly leveraged properties are subject to interest rate risks. Poorly placed units may not generate sufficient business. Competition is fierce in many areas of the country. Larger syndicators can hurt small operators through price wars and national marketing efforts. Low occupancy affects cash flow and market value. And, in deflationary times, people will cut back on expenses such as self-storage.

Tax Considerations

Tax Consequences

There are no special tax benefits for self-storage investments. Sole proprietors may be able to structure financing to take advantage of the writeoff allowed for business interest. However, limited partnership participation limits the use of any losses to offsetting passive income. See your tax advisor.

Summing Up

The huge number of small operators in this field create a healthy takeover market for limited partnerships. The junk bond market debacle hurt the largest "mini warehouse" LP syndicator, Public Storage in 1990. After years of success raising money for its partnerships, Public Storage saw the average return on its LPs drop from 40% on its early deals to less than 10% on programs launched in the late 1980s and 1990. As a result, investor resistance has made it difficult for this large successful syndicator to raise funds.

Many areas of the country are now saturated with mini warehouses. The high fees associated with LPs make these investments less appealing than in their earlier high growth days.

There also appears to be considerable potential for new ideas in self-storage. The newest idea is record retrieval centers, which store records for downtown offices and provide pickup and delivery services. Companies such as Shurgard are moving into city centers with high-rise storage facilities. Freeway storage facilities are being tagged for later sale and potential development for higher and better use. Self-storage firms are augmenting their business with auxiliary sales in areas such as shelf sales, support materials, and other related services.

CHAPTER 19

ANNUITIES AND INSURANCE

A GLANCE AHEAD

Although the 1986 Tax Reform Act dealt a death blow to many tax shelter schemes featuring limited partnerships and multiple writeoffs, the life insurance industry managed to come out virtually unscathed. You can still earn money on a tax-deferred basis on cash value insurance. You can still borrow on your cash value insurance policies tax free. The latter loophole is already coming under close scrutiny in Congress but the insurance company lobby has proven formidable to date.

It's increasingly likely that your stock broker will approach you about your life insurance needs. Many insurance products now appeal more to investment needs than your protection needs. The proliferation of complex products makes the arcane world of life insurance even more difficult to understand.

This chapter introduces the most important of these new insurance/investment products. You'll learn

- *The difference between term and cash value insurance*
- *Why life insurance may be the right product for deferring taxes on part of your investment portfolio*
- *How life insurance can increase your protection with wise investment decisions*

- *Why life insurance products are not appropriate for short-term investing*
- *Two important indexes you should use in evaluating policies.*

THE WORLD OF LIFE INSURANCE

The 1986 Tax Reform Act did not so much bestow new benefits on the life insurance industry as preserve elements that have existed since 1913. The 1986 act decimated the competition by virtually eliminating multiple (greater than one to one) real estate-based writeoffs and most other shelter techniques.

Life insurance products have maintained their favored status, because they are seen as providing private alternatives to public finance. Three main tax-favored benefits have been with us since income tax began in 1913:

1. Earnings on the cash value of a policy accrue tax free.
2. Loans taken against the cash value of a policy are tax free.
3. The death benefit proceeds are tax free to your beneficiaries.

Recent years have seen a veritable flood of new products. No longer is life insurance merely a contract providing your dependents with financial protection in the case of your death. In fact, that is one of the real dangers that the complex new products present. The heavy emphasis on them as investment products (stockbrokers are becoming an increasingly important segment of the market) tends to obscure the real reason for having life insurance in the first place: protection for your dependents.

The insurance market has undergone dramatic changes in recent years. In 1982, term insurance accounted for 60% of all life insurance policies. Today that figure has dropped below 40%. Insurance companies (with a few exceptions) have put their advertising money in programs emphasizing tax shelter investing and high-yield returns—with protection almost as an afterthought!

Risks

Those products that enable you to tie part of your return to stocks or bonds subject you to the same risks as outright investing in those markets. Rest assured, the one time you need to borrow will be the time when your selected investment option is performing at its worst!

Historically the insurance industry has been conservatively managed and quite safe. However, in the early 1980s a major issuer of annuities, Baldwin-United, went bankrupt. Their products had been heavily marketed by leading brokerage firms, including Merrill Lynch and E. F. Hutton. It is obviously vital to do business with only the most financially secure companies.

Remember, insurance-related investment products are very long term. Typically, you must hold a cash value product for a minimum of 10 years before you can expect to achieve a competitive return. It takes that long for the policy's investment income and tax advantages to cover the higher commissions and fees that insurance products charge.

Professional Advice

It is now possible to protect yourself to at least some extent from inflation through selection of products that fluctuate with market prices. A policy tied to money market interest rates will rise in times of infla-tion, offering at least nominal inflation protection. Because of the long-term nature of the investment, you should discuss this factor with your agent, broker, or financial planner.

You can always cash in your cash value policy for something. However, you'll take a substantial loss for redemptions in the early years of the policy. You are able to borrow tax free from most policies though not from single premium annuities and whole life policies. You take a big risk, though, if you borrow too much against your policy's value. If you do not repay the loan, your policy could lapse (be canceled). If that happens, the IRS will assess a massive tax bill on the basis that the unpaid loans are investment income.

Although the life insurance industry has enjoyed a favored tax status, there are now risks of significant political changes. Members of Congress are already directing their attention to the tax-free status of policy loans. This large loophole (no other investment lets you withdraw funds from tax-deferred plans at any time without penalty) has been closed for single-premium whole life policies. Loans are taxed at ordinary income rates and are subject to a 10% penalty before age 59½, just like IRA withdrawals. No penalty is assessed against outstanding loans.

Purchasers of insurance products do run risks that are unique to the product. Fitting the right coverage to each individual's singular circumstances leaves much room for abuse. Regardless of how the various products are touted to the public, the main reason for buying life insurance is protection, not investment. Many families are underinsured; but many others are overinsured, with the wrong type of coverages.

For example, a common sales pitch against term insurance is that the premiums are "wasted" money because no cash value accrues (insurance agents receive much higher commissions for selling cash value insurance than for term insurance). However, since term premiums may amount to as little as 10% of a comparable whole-life policy, the money saved may yield a far greater return if wisely invested. Insurance companies gladly offer to manage your money for you but they inevitably charge you for the service. Many life insurance products, especially single-premium items, are being sold by investment specialists rather than by life insurance agents. Although such specialists are often well versed in the *investment* aspects of the products, they are not usually conversant with the best information about the necessary *protection* aspects for you.

Independent Ratings

All life insurance companies are rated by A. M. Best & Company annually. Best's Insurance Reports are available from most libraries. The National Insurance Consumer Organization (121 North Payne Street, Alexandria, VA 22314) offers numerous publications to help consumers sort through the complexities and hype of insurance sales. For example, their booklet "Taking the Bite Out of Insurance" ($8.25) features a list of the maximum rates they recommend paying for renewable term policies.

Money
Management
Tip

The National Association of Insurance Commissioners is an organization of state insurance regulators. They've developed two indexes to give you a method for comparing policies. Although the indexes won't tell you whether a term policy is better than a whole-life policy, they are good guides for comparing two policies of the same type.

The interest-adjusted net payment cost index measures the present value of the premiums you pay for the next 10 years. This index takes into consideration the fact that you could earn interest on the premium money. The index number represents the cost of insurance per each $1,000 of death benefit. The lower the number, the cheaper the policy.

The other index is called the surrender cost index. It measures the present cost of cash value policies if you cancel them to take your cash in 10 years.

Most states' regulations require insurance agents to provide you with these numbers on request. Since insurance policies are increasingly complex, with fees varying widely even for the same type of coverage, it is important that you do your own comparison shopping.

PROSPECTS FOR INSURANCE PRODUCTS IN THE 1990s

Much growth of the many new insurance/investment products now being widely touted depends on continued favored tax treatment. There is little likelihood that U.S. Congress will further trim the tax-deferred advantages of cash value life insurance. The tax-free status of policy loans on single premium life policies has been eliminated. There are no penalties or changes for loans already taken out. Future loans may come in for different tax treatment in the near future. If this consideration is important for you, watch tax law changes very closely. Your agent or broker should be able to provide up-to-date information on this aspect of the business.

The targeted insurance product was single-premium life insurance. However, don't let that lull you into thinking that all other aspects are safe. The tax change legislation was introduced by representatives Fortney Stark (Democrat, California) and Willis Gradison (Republican, Ohio).

The bill, retroactive to October 7, 1987, left single-premium and other types of life insurance products the tax-advantage of accruing earnings on a tax-deferred basis. However, the bill penalizes any withdrawals as loans or otherwise.

Remember, the cash value of a policy is part premium money paid by the policyholder and part earnings on that money paid by the insurance company. The Stark-Gradison legislation regards any borrowing from a policy as withdrawing the earnings portion of the cash value. Policy loans would be taxed as income. In addition, the bill includes a provision to assess additional penalties for withdrawals made before the policyholder reaches age 59½.

If you think the industry seems confusing now, just wait! Over the next few years there will be an even greater proliferation of products from the insurance industry. Presently less than 50% of the hundred largest insurance companies offer some type of variable policy. That will change rapidly as more and more companies move to selling investment-related products. Many experts predict that within the next ten years 50% of all life insurance products will be variable.

Uncertainty over the changes ultimately made in the tax treatment of single-premium life insurance policies affected that market. Single-premium policies accounted for about $1 billion in 1984. That figure jumped to $9.5 billion in 1987. However, sales volume dropped significantly after passage of the Stark-Gaddison bill, eliminating some tax advantages for single premium whole life policies. Sales for 1988 plunged nearly 50% to $4.8 billion.

A number of companies responded to the uncertainty at the time by offering escape clauses to buyers. Essentially the escape clauses stated that the company waived its cancellation fees (usually 6% to 9% of the initial premium) for buyers who are affected by future tax law changes.

These refund offers typically give policyholders 30 to 90 days to act following passage of tax law changes. For variable policies, the refund offer is for the current account value. For interest-earning policies, the companies will usually return the initial premium plus interest.

If you decide to buy a single-premium policy, be sure to check out the details on escape clauses. The interest paid varies from company to company.

Some of the companies, that are including escape clauses in their single-premium policies include Fidelity Bankers Life, Kemper Investors Life Insurance Company, Life Insurance Company of Virginia, and Monarch Capital.

A number of other changes are also underway. We have mentioned the increasing presence of stockbrokers in the business. Mutual funds are gearing up for a major push into the business. Charter National Life and Security National Life have both retained mutual fund managers for their portfolios. The well-known fund manager Value Line now manages portfolios for Guardian Life.

The largest fund group in the country, Fidelity Investments, has launched a fund for a single-premium variable life policy. The policy is issued by Monarch Resources, but will be marketed by Fidelity.

All too often the consumer's real reason for buying life insurance is lost in the shuffle. The great flexibility offered by the range

Look At This:

of products currently available is certainly a boon to many people. However, overselling the investment aspects tends to overshadow the real reason for buying life insurance. Don't be fooled into buying a speculative investment vehicle when what you want is protection. The tax benefit of life insurance is the most widely touted feature since passage of the 1986 Tax Reform Act. However, the high fees are not quite so prominently mentioned. Don't hesitate to investigate alternatives.

The insurance industry is changing. Now more than ever it is crucial to your financial health to know your financial status: what you have, what you need, and what you want. Careful planning is necessary to prepare you with the facts you need to make intelligent long-term decisions. The many new insurance products offer great variety and flexibility for tailoring a program to your specific needs. But rest assured, insurance products are not a substitute for a well-managed investment portfolio. Fees are high. Even the best insurance investment-type products require long-term commitment to make them worthwhile.

FIXED DEFERRED ANNUITIES

A fixed deferred annuity is a contract between an insurance company and the purchaser of the annuity (called the *annuitant*) that specifies the premium and the payout options. In exchange for a premium paid by the annuitant (the premium can be either a single lump sum or can be paid over time in installments), the insurance company guarantees a minimum rate of return. Usually, a return substantially higher than the contract minimum is guaranteed for one year. The interest rate is then adjusted according to a specified formula annually, but can never be set below the contract minimum.

Although you can buy an annuity with a single premium that begins monthly payments immediately, the more common form is a "deferred" annuity. With a deferred annuity, the buyer pays either a single or installment premium, which earns income until the buyer (the annuitant) elects to start taking payments, at age 59½ or later. The amount of monthly payments will be determined by the size of the cash value that has built up in the interim "accumulation" period.

Annuities have gained new life with the 1986 Tax Reform Act. They are now being aggressively marketed as an alternative to the recently changed IRAs (see Chapter 8 for further information), for many investors who want to defer taxes on income and capital appreciation investing above the $2,000 IRA limit.

Interest income is accumulated while taxes are deferred until "payout" begins at age 59½ or higher. The amount of the payout is determined by the amount of money invested, the length of time invested, and of course, the rate of return. The payout schedule is specified in the annuity contract.

A basic annuity is structured to pay income for the balance of an annuitant's life. However, like many other financial products in recent years, annuities have undergone a number of changes. Many options are now available. For example, the standard annuity expires with the death of the annuitant. Some companies now offer a provision to transfer the payments to a specified beneficiary such as a spouse. Such added benefits do cost more, though. There are a wide variety of options available, but investigate each carefully. It is important to balance the potential gain with the added cost. Remember, there may be other ways to accomplish the same goals for less money.

Investment Potential

Fixed annuities are long-term investments. Although early withdrawals can be made, substantial penalties are usually levied. Penalties include assessment of a charge by the insurance company (typically 7% the first year, declining 1% per year thereafter) and tax penalties.

Investment characteristics of fixed annuities include

- No capital appreciation (see section on variable deferred annuities)
- Interest income accumulated on a tax-deferred basis
- No current income
- Payout provisions specified in the con-

tract (typical options: payout of fixed monthly amount for the life of the annuitant, for a set time period, or for a set total amount).

Strengths

Insurance companies are strictly regulated and must maintain reserves. Annuities of established companies are very low risk, although no federal insurance is available at this time. Moreover, you can borrow against your annuity's cash value, and interest accumulates on a tax-deferred basis until withdrawal. Finally, annuities provide a secure retirement income.

Weaknesses

You run a small risk that the issuer may go bankrupt. In the early 1980s, Baldwin-United Corporation, one of the largest issues of deferred annuities, filed for bankruptcy. Although arrangements were made to minimize losses, it is a risk that should be noted. There is no secondary market that limits liquidity. Early withdrawals are subject to substantial penalties. In addition, fixed annuities offer no protection from the ravages of inflation, and fees may be high for the benefit received.

Tax Considerations

Tax Consequences

Deferred annuities are being aggressively marketed due to their favored tax status. Interest paid accrues on a tax-deferred basis. Taxes are paid only when payout begins. Presumably, your tax bracket on retirement will be lower than during your peak earning years.

A portion of the payments to annuitants are considered "return of principal" and are not taxable. This feature differs from IRA payouts, which are taxed as ordinary income.

Early withdrawal (before age 59½ or within five years of purchase) is subject to a

10% tax penalty. There are exceptions, so check with your tax advisor *before* investing.

Summing Up

Annuities should be viewed as part investment and part insurance. The security of a fixed income for life should be balanced against the lower guaranteed returns you can earn. A wide variety of options are available. These include payment options, payout options, and insurance options (naming a beneficiary).

VARIABLE DEFERRED ANNUITIES

A deferred annuity is a contract between an insurance company and the purchaser (the annuitant) that specifies a premium to be paid by the annuitant in exchange for a specified payout schedule, which begins at some future date. The payout depends on how much money is invested, the length of the "accumulation" period, and the rate of return earned during the accumulation period. Historically, the rate of return was a specified interest rate (a fixed annuity).

Variable annuities allow the annuitant to select from a variety of investment vehicles during the accumulation phase. For example, you may elect to invest your premium money in a stock fund, a bond fund, or a money market fund. A relatively recent innovation in this area is "real estate" annuities which are similar to stock or bond annuities but which are invested in real estate in some form (e.g., real property or REITs). All are managed by the insurance companies issuing them. Most variable annuities allow you to switch among the different types of funds at your option. Limits are usually set on how often you can switch without being assessed additional fees. This arrangement is similar to switching between different types of funds in a mutual fund group except that the gains earned in an annuity are sheltered until payout begins.

Rather than being locked into a fixed interest rate, in a variable annuity you can earn a return tied to the stock market, gold or some other investment. However, unlike a fixed annuity, variable annuities do not feature a guaranteed minimum return. If the investment you select goes down, you may actually lose some of your principal. The variable annuity offers the opportunity to trade a guaranteed minimum return and a set maximum return (the set interest rate) for unlimited upside potential with equivalent downside risk.

Interest in annuities has rebounded following the 1986 Tax Reform Act. The inflationary 1970s and the bankruptcy of the major deferred annuity issuer, Baldwin-United Corporation, in the early 1980s severely depressed this investment category. New life was breathed into annuities by the 1986 Tax Reform Act, which sharply restricted competitive products for accumulating tax-deferred income. The inflationary 1970s served to limit the appeal of fixed annuities, as the purchasing power of the earnings was devastated over time. Annuitants found that payout levels that seemed adequate when the program was started, later proved inadequate due to inflation during the payout phase. The variable deferred annuity was specifically developed to meet inflation concerns.

Investment Potential

Variable annuities are long-term investments. Although substantial penalties are levied for early withdrawals, you can remove without charge up to 10% of the principal that has been in your account for over a year. If you exceed the 10% annual limit, a 5% redemption charge is made—although withdrawal of earnings is never penalized. After seven years, any amount of principal can be withdrawn without charge. A typical penalty fee is 7% the first year, declining 1% per year thereafter. In addition, tax penalties may be assessed.

Investment characteristics of variable deferred annuities include

- Potential for capital appreciation
- Flexibility to choose from a variety of investment options
- Fluctuating returns based on your selection of investment vehicle and the management of that vehicle by the insurance company
- All gains tax sheltered until withdrawal begins
- Ability to hedge against inflation.

Strengths

Security is a major strength. Insurance companies are closely regulated and required to maintain minimum cash reserves. Default is a minor risk. You can borrow against your annuity's cash value, and all earnings (capital gains and interest) compound on a tax-deferred basis. You can switch between different investments in differing economic environments, and participate in capital growth as well as just interest income. Finally, a flexible, probate-free death benefit ensures that your beneficiary will receive the greater of two amounts: either your total contributions (less withdrawals), or the current account value.

Weaknesses

There is always the slight risk that the issuer could go bankrupt. In the early 1980s, a major issuer of deferred annuities filed for bankruptcy. Although most investors were able to recover the majority of their investment, the event clearly demonstrated that annuities are not as secure as U.S government obligations. No secondary market limits liquidity. Annuities must be liquidated directly with the issuer who sets redemption fees. Also, there is no guarantee of principal. If the investment you select goes down, your principal is at risk. Finally, you are dependent on the management ability of the insurance company issuing the annuity. For example, if you select a stock fund, the stock market may appreciate more than the value of your fund due to poor management. Your selection of funds is restricted to those offered by and managed by the issuer.

Tax Considerations

Deferred annuities are being aggressively marketed as tax-sheltered investments. All earnings (whether through capital appreciation or interest payments) accrue tax deferred.

Tax Consequences

Taxes are assessed only when payout begins. A portion of your receipts are considered a return of principal and are not taxable. This differs from the tax treatment accorded IRA payouts, which are fully taxed as ordinary income at the time of withdrawal unless nondeductible contributions were made. This feature is obviously of most value if your tax bracket is lower on retirement than during your peak earning years. Therefore you would pay less tax on the earnings than you would have if taxed when earned. This is not always the case, and you should check with your tax advisor *before* investing.

Early withdrawal also triggers tax penalties. If you withdraw before age $59\frac{1}{2}$ or within five years of purchase, a 10% tax penalty is levied. There are exceptions depending on the exact type of annuity.

Summing Up

Annuities are a hybrid investment. They should be viewed as part insurance and part investment. Consider a variable deferred annuity as a tax-deferred retirement savings plan. Carefully evaluate your insurance needs and status before you buy an annuity.

It is impossible to delineate all the many options that modern annuity plans offer. However, it is crucial to understand in detail the annuity's withdrawal policies. Fees vary greatly and can make a significant difference in the policy's yield to you.

VARIABLE LIFE INSURANCE

Variable life insurance is a cash value policy that provides set minimum death benefits with the potential for increased benefits and cash value if your selected investments perform well. It gives you the option of selecting different types of investments for the cash value portion of your premiums. The choices are among mutual fund-type portfolios of stocks, bonds, or money market instruments. The insurance company manages the portfolios. Usually you can switch among these options by notifying the insurance company.

Long-term fixed-return investments fell into disfavor in the 1970s as inflation ravaged the purchasing power of historically secure vehicles. Cash value insurance was one of the hardest hit areas as policyholders learned that the investment portion of their policies was lagging behind the returns that could be obtained from the safest of all investments, the 91-day Treasury bill.

The insurance industry responded by creating more flexible products to meet the needs of conservative investors. Variable life is one form of cash value life insurance that has gained widespread acceptance.

Features include the following:

- A minimum death benefit is established when you purchase the policy. It can increase depending on how your investments do.
- The premium is a fixed amount paid monthly, quarterly, or annually.
- You can take out loans against the cash value for rates that usually run between 6% and 8%.
- There is no minimum rate of return on your cash value. It fluctuates with your chosen investment.

Life insurance companies are rated by Best's Insurance Reports. Companies rated A and A+ are financially secure. There is little risk of default.

Variable life policies are sold by licensed insurance agents and brokers. Many full-service investment brokerage firms have in-house insurance specialists. Substantial fees are charged. The fees are "front loaded," which means that they are higher in the early years of the policy.

Variable life offers greater flexibility than other cash value life insurance because you can choose among three different investment categories.

Like all cash value insurance decisions, you must take two considerations into account before buying variable life. Does it provide the necessary insurance protection for your family's needs? When buying life insurance, that is the most important question. The investment potential is important but secondary to the primary purpose of life insurance: protecting the insured's beneficiaries.

Investment Potential

The attraction of variable life insurance is enhanced by the tax-deferred status of accumulated earnings. Variable life is a long-term investment. Fees are very high in the first few years of the policy. It must be held for a long time (10 years) in order to amortize the front load so that the returns are competitive.

The portfolio alternatives are managed accounts, much like life mutual funds, that are managed by the issuing insurance company. The track records of variable life's portfolios are short. Some of the investment portfolios are tracked by Lipper Analytical Services, which monitors leading mutual funds.

You should evaluate insurance company investment portfolios as you would mutual funds. Insurance company portfolios generally charge much higher fees than do competitive mutual funds. For example, one major investment portfolio assesses commissions and other expenses of up to 35% for $1,000 premium payment by a typical investor the first year. This load drops to 18% for the next three years, after which the load drops to 15%. Such fees are very high compared to fees charged by most mutual funds. Of course, mutual funds do not provide insurance protection as part of their fees.

The stock and bond portfolios offer capital gains potential. The money market portfolio offers a lower income potential than the bonds but with less risk to principal.

A well-managed stock portfolio may offer some protection against inflation. The short maturities of a money market portfolio also offer some measure of inflation protection since yields would rise with increasing inflation.

A variable life policyholder faces a variety of risks. These include the financial condition of the issuing company, market risk for both the stock and/or bond portfolios, and the political risk that the tax benefits of life insurance may be phased out.

Strengths

There is very little risk of default for companies rated A and A+. Minimum death benefits are provided regardless of the performance of the investment portfolios. Variable life policyholders have great flexibility to switch among the various portfolios to take advantage of current economic conditions. Earnings, both income and capital gains, accumulate on a tax-deferred basis. Both death benefits and cash value can be increased through good performance by selected investment portfolios. Lastly, loans against cash value are readily accessible.

Weaknesses

Investment performance will lag behind that of straight mutual funds, due to very high fees. Your cash value principal is at risk if the investment portfolio drops. The track records of most investment portfolios are very short. Because three years constitutes a long track record in the industry, it is impossible to know how the portfolios will react through a full investment cycle. Also, front-end fees require long-term commitment to make competitive investment returns. No minimum return on your investment is guaranteed. Substantial penalties are levied for cash withdrawals in the first few years of the policy.

Tax Considerations

Tax Consequences

All earnings—whether capital gains, dividends or interest—are accumulated on a tax-deferred basis. Interest charged on policy loans is only 10% deductible for 1990, and not deductible at all after 1990.

Summing Up

Variable life insurance has enjoyed increasing popularity over the past few years. A bullish stock market enhances its appeal. However, the short track records of most of the portfolio managers give little clue to what performance may be over a complete market cycle (both bull and bear markets).

You should purchase any life insurance policy only if you need the insurance protection. Don't be misled by the hype over their investment value. The high fees, low short-term liquidity, and moderate investment potential rules them out for serious investors looking for maximum investment returns.

Variable life offers savvy investors who need insurance protection the best alternative among cash value policies. It is important to check the track records of the investment portfolios before buying. Performance varies widely.

WHOLE-LIFE INSURANCE

Many years ago, before the proliferation of life insurance products now available, there were two main types: term and whole life. Term insurance has no direct investment value other than freeing up additional money through its much lower premiums. That "freed" money can of course then be invested. But the term policy itself provides protection only. There is no cash value buildup during the life of the policy. Typically, term premiums increase as the insured grows older. The only payment that a term policy makes is the death benefit paid to the beneficiary.

Whole-life insurance is the classic alternative to term insurance. When the yields paid on whole life were actually less than those paid on bank savings accounts, buyers began to turn to other products. Sales volume dropped sharply during the late 1970s when the yields on very safe money market funds climbed to record levels.

However, in recent years whole-life insurance has staged a comeback as the rates paid on cash value buildup have become more competitive. Typically premiums are invested in secure long-term government or high-grade corporate bonds, mortgages, and blue-chip stocks.

Whole-life insurance features include:
- A fixed death benefit selected when the policy is purchased
- A fixed premium for the life of the policy, paid annually, quarterly, or monthly

- Policy loans at rates generally ranging from 6% to 9%.

Premiums for whole-life insurance are substantially higher than for term premiums because whole life provides for guaranteed cash value buildup, fixed premiums, and ready access to loans against the cash value.

Whole-life insurance is purchased from licensed insurance agents or brokers. The sales charge is substantial. Typically, sales commissions are 50% to 100% of the first year's premium. As a result, it takes 8-10 years for the policy to build up a positive competitive return.

Investment Potential

A whole-life policy is a long-term investment. More favorable returns are paid the longer the policy is held. As a rule of thumb, a policy must be held about 15 years to be earning at the maximum rates. This is because it takes about 10 years for the investment income to cover the commissions and fees assessed by the insurer.

Most whole-life policies pay annual dividends. These are called *participating policies* and charge higher premiums. Over the long term, however, these policies are actually less expensive, because of consistent dividend payments. Dividends can be taken in cash, or, as an offset to premiums, or as additional cash value in the policy.

Whole-life insurance is essentially a method for enforcing savings discipline while providing death benefits protection for your family. There is limited liquidity, especially in the early years of a policy. Withdrawals are typically assessed a penalty that declines annually over a seven- to nine- year period.

The security of your investment rests with the financial stability of the insurance company. Best's Insurance Reports rate all major insurance companies. For safety and peace of mind, you should stick with companies rated A or A+.

One drawback to whole life is that you have no choice as to how your cash value is invested. In fact, insurers do not spell out what rate of return your cash value is earning. The policy specifies a guaranteed cash value, which accumulates each year to a new level. However, the insurer never specifies how much of your premium pays for insurance.

Look At This:

A key factor to be checked prior to purchasing a participating policy is the length, consistency, and amount of the insurer's annual dividend payouts.

Whole-life insurance does not provide any protection from inflation. Investments are typically made in long-term bonds, which suffer in inflationary times.

Strengths

Whole-life policies issued by A or A+ companies are very safe. Risk of default is negligible. Earnings accumulate on a tax-deferred basis. Irregular withdrawals are tax free. No volatility affects the base insurance value, which guarantees a set increase in cash value annually. Death benefits are federal tax free to the beneficiary.

Weaknesses

Initial fees are high. Policies must be held for 10 years or longer to achieve competitive returns. Return on investment is not clearly disclosed. Early withdrawals (usually before nine years) are subject to penalties. You have no choice about how your cash value is invested.

Tax Considerations

Tax Consequences

Earnings paid on cash value insurance policies accumulate on a tax-deferred basis. You can borrow earnings from your policy tax free if the policy satisfies tax law tests. The policy's beneficiary receives the proceeds federal tax free on the death of the insured.

Summing Up

The returns paid on whole-life policies have increased substantially in recent years. However, you should view whole life as a viable investment only if you need the insurance feature. High fees and the long-term commitment necessary to achieve a competitive return make other investment products better values in the absence of death benefits.

Single-premium whole-life insurance is heavily marketed as a tax shelter. However, investors who need current tax-sheltered income should consider municipal bonds or municipal bond funds as lower-cost alternatives.

UNIVERSAL LIFE INSURANCE

Universal life is a widely accepted form of cash value life insurance featuring a flexible premium and death benefit program that keeps the premium lower than other whole-life policies. Universal life clearly separates the cash value and the death benefits elements of the policy. The cash value is typically invested in a tax-deferred savings program tied to a specified money market rate.

Although life insurance is not usually thought of as an investment in the popular sense of "earning profits," the 1986 Tax Reform Act provides substantial tax-preferred treatment of insurance products. As a result, many insurance companies are aggressively marketing a wide variety of products. Regardless of the investment potential of tax-deferred accumulation of earnings offered by many life insurance products, the primary consideration should still be whether and how much *insurance* coverage you need. Wage earners whose families depend on their income should seriously investigate various forms of life insurance.

Term life insurance offers you pure protection (no investment "frills") for a specific amount of time. You pay only for death benefits: usually premiums are low at first, then they move higher as you get older. Although term insurance is (at least initially) the most economical insurance of all, it can become the most expensive if your age is quite advanced; and some policies even exclude renewals past age 65 or 70. Younger people often favor term insurance because of the low initial premiums, sometimes calling it "mortgage insurance" because the untimely death of the insured would not result in loss of the family's often highly leveraged home.

Term insurance can be renewed in a variety of ways. At the end of the term, you may elect to extend the coverage period at a specific additional premium. If the policy is guaranteed renewable, it will specify an age at which you may receive the policy's face value. "Level" term policies are good for a specific number of years. The premiums are averaged into equal installments—even if the term is for 20 to 30 years. "Declining balance" term insurance features constant premiums too, but the amount of coverage decreases each year. For people who want to use term insurance as a bridge to permanent insurance, a "modified" term policy might be best. This plan converts a term to a whole life policy after a specified period of time.

The alternative to term life insurance is variously called *cash value, whole life, straight,* or *ordinary life.* The key difference is that cash value life insurance offers the death benefits of term with the added feature of building up a cash value over the life of the policy. Some advisors refer to this feature as "forced savings."

There are many different varieties of cash value insurance. More are being added every

Professional Advice

year as the life insurance industry develops products to meet the diverse demands of a diverse population. We can only touch on the distinguishing aspects of the more popular policies here. We strongly advise that you check with an independent financial planner or insurance agent to evaluate the myriad of available options.

A very new development is variable universal life. First sold in 1985, variable universal offers the opportunity to invest in stocks, bonds, or money market portfolios rather than just a savings program for the cash value portion of your policy.

One key feature of universal life is that the death benefit amount is chosen at the time of purchase. However, it can be changed annually. A second key feature is that the premium varies depending on what the cash value portion is earning. The cost of the insurance depends on a number of variables, including your age, sex, and health. Some policies offer a slightly higher guaranteed yield on the cash value portion of your policy if you agree to pay a fixed premium monthly, quarterly, semiannually, or annually.

This flexibility—to vary not only the death benefits, but the premium (and in the case of variable universal life, your investments)— is a major attraction of universal life insurance. The premiums tend to be lower than that for straight whole life with equivalent death benefits.

Investment Potential

The investment appeal of universal life insurance rests on the tax deferral of earnings on the cash value. Universal life policies typically guarantee a relatively low minimum rate of return, about 4%. Rates above the minimum are variable and fluctuate day to day. It pays to comparison-shop, as rates may differ widely among companies.

Variable universal life policies are so new that it is difficult to evaluate track records at present. However, well-managed stock or bond portfolios may significantly outperform the normal "savings" program route.

Policyholders can borrow against the cash value. Typically there is a $25 fee for partial withdrawals. Policy loans (as opposed to direct withdrawals) are usually also offered. Interest charges are competitive, ranging from 6% to 8%.

Universal life should be viewed as protection for your loved ones. An added benefit is the long-term savings program, which offers tax-deferred earnings. Universal policies offered by companies earning an A or higher rating by the independent rating service (Best's Insurance Reports) are very secure.

Variable universal life policies may experience some volatility due to fluctuations in the stock or bond portfolios. Straight universal life will not experience volatility in the savings program.

Fees vary widely. "No-load" universal life policies charge no agents' commissions. Otherwise fees can run from 1% to more than 10%. No-load policies are sold through the mail without direct face-to-face agent contact.

Strengths

Universal life policies offer ready access to your cash value whether for withdrawal or for loans. Income and cash value of A-rated companies is very secure, and there is little volatility associated with the cash value. Universal life offers substantial flexibility in policy options.

Weaknesses

Universal life is first and foremost life insurance. Investment returns are lower than are possible in straight investments. If you select variable universal life, you are limited to management by the insurance company's portfolio managers. Their performance may not be up to par. No federal insurance covers company failures. Also, fees vary widely and can be very high.

Tax Considerations

Tax Consequences

The 1986 Tax Reform Act retained the tax-deferral feature of earnings on whole-life insurance policies. Earnings are taxed at your tax bracket at the time of withdrawal. Life insurance proceeds to beneficiaries are normally not subject to federal income taxes.

Summing Up

Cash value life insurance was a major beneficiary of the 1986 Tax Reform Act. The proliferation of insurance products will undoubtedly continue offering consumers an even wider variety of options. The relatively new variable universal life policies offer significant flexibility and the chance to profit from stock and bond market moves. Universal life can play an important part in the financial plans of many families.

CHAPTER 20

YOUR HOME AS AN INVESTMENT

A GLANCE AHEAD

Thanks to their homes, millions of Americans with few additional assets are substantial investors. For most of them, a home is the biggest investment they will make and the single most valuable asset they will own. A home is a great hedge against inflation and offers good tax benefits, but—like any investment—it has as much potential to deplete your resources as add to them. Skillfully choosing a home, financing it carefully, and managing your home equity wisely can make your home investment a cornerstone of your personal estate.

THE PSYCHOLOGY OF "HOME ECONOMICS"

Home ownership is the foundation of the American Dream. In fact, in the United States 64% of Americans own their own homes. For waves of immigrants, having a piece of that dream meant owning a home of their own, and that attitude has come down to us through the generations. Many of us feel unsettled and unfulfilled until we're among the hallowed ranks of homeowners—it's an impulse and a tradition as old as the nation itself.

Some people, on the other hand, simply believe in real estate as an investment. They see a personal residence as just another opportunity to make money, avoid taxes, and preserve their assets.

If you owned a home in the roaring '70s, for example, you rode a veritable tidal wave of asset growth: the average home appreciated by about 10% a year, well above the rate of inflation, and far better than many investments of comparable risk. In some residential markets, that tidal wave was a flood that raised many people's net worth into the millions.

Then times changed. In the more economically restrained '80s a home was not necessarily a free ride on the inflation train—largely because inflation wasn't nearly what it was a decade before.

All the same, the art of home buying—the hows, wheres, and whens of home purchase and disposition—may be more important to your long-term financial success than any quirk in the business cycle.

TO RENT OR NOT TO RENT: THAT IS THE QUESTION

Contrary to what much of the world believes, the decision to buy a home is not an automatic one. Home ownership is an active investment that requires an ongoing commitment of your time and resources, and is a considerably illiquid investment.

Despite the emotional tug to put yourself in the owner's chair by the fire, some people are simply better off renting.

When to Rent

If you do not own a home but are considering a purchase, you should weigh several important factors.

Market Conditions. The housing market varies throughout the country. In some cities, houses are in great demand; in other places, the buyer practically gets to name the price, and homesellers are grateful for what they can get.

The market is always fickle. While prices were escalating 10% to 32% in New England and New York City a few years ago, they were plummeting by 4% to 9% in Texas and Oklahoma. People were walking away from their homes in Alaska because they couldn't be sold. On a national scale, many of the overextended home buyers of the 1980s unloaded their heavy debt burden, causing home values to fall sharply in some markets.

It's a mixed bag. Recently California homes have appreciated so much that ordinary people find themselves living in very expensive houses valued between $500,000 to $750,000. $250,000 in Los Angeles doesn't purchase much of a house. You could expect one bath, single car garage, two bedrooms, and no amenities.

Is your community growing? Is the neighborhood stable? How long have other houses in the vicinity been on the market? These will be your first clues as to the economic viability of home ownership in your area.

Interest Rates. Because much of your home's purchase price will be financed with borrowed money, the current rates of interest on home mortgages is usually a key consideration. In our discussion of mortgages later in this chapter, you will see the amazing difference a percentage or two can make when the payment is due each month. A good house prospect in a bad lending market is seldom the bargain it appears to be.

Special Needs. If you and your family are in

STATE	MARKET	1988 PRICE	% CHANGE '87 VS '88	EST. ANNUAL TAXES	EST. MONTHLY RENT
ALABAMA	Birmingham	$111,415	3.5%	$ 354	$ 825
	Mobile	93,333	.7%	390	733
	Montgomery	103,628	− .1%	357	750
ALASKA	Anchorage	123,500	− 21.2%	1,797	1,150
	Fairbanks	94,213	− 17.3%	1,317	878
ARIZONA	Mesa	101,833	− 11.1%	577	800
	Phoenix	96,700	− 7.3%	702	833
	Scottsdale	142,667	2.7%	865	1,183
	Tucson	90,500	.8%	829	725
ARKANSAS	Little Rock	96,633	1.8%	945	750
CALIFORNIA	Fresno	115,500	11.2%	1,260	883
	Modesto	145,817	8.9%	1,818	900
	Monterey Peninsula	296,333	10.8%	2,963	1,450
	Sacramento	159,167	17.8%	1,910	1,067
	San Francisco Bay Area				
Northern California	Fremont	266,317	20.0%	3,337	1,300
	Los Altos	509,000	27.1%	6,363	2,733
	Menlo Park	509,667	25.6%	6,370	2,067
	Oakland/Montclair	304,667	12.2%	3,817	1,400
	San Francisco	556,667	24.4%	6,179	2,500
	San Jose	310,667	22.2%	3,912	1,608
	San Mateo	411,667	27.4%	5,159	1,833
	San Rafael	304,667	22.8%	3,809	1,517
	Walnut Creek	251,667	16.0%	3,102	1,400
	Los Angeles County				
	Beverly Hills	841,667	10.1%	10,520	4,500
	Covina	183,333	25.0%	2,292	1,367
	Encino	453,333	26.9%	5,667	2,000
	Glendale	396,667	21.8%	5,950	1,867
	Long Beach	382,667	34.6%	3,925	2,117
	San Marino	441,667	55.4%	4,640	1,967
Southern California	Torrance	326,633	14.0%	4,083	1,767
	Woodland Hills	320,500	12.3%	4,006	2,767
	Orange County				
	Fullerton	339,667	25.0%	4,245	1,567
	Newport Beach	445,833	30.0%	5,573	2,067
	Riverside County				
	Riverside	183,000	3.5%	1,872	1,217
	San Diego County				
	Chula Vista	190,500	27.0%	2,381	1,250
	Encinitas	292,333	5.9%	3,654	2,067
	La Jolla	517,375	15.3%	5,596	2,200
	Poway	178,667	18.4%	2,233	1,100
COLORADO	Colorado Springs	77,667	3.4%	725	525
	Denver	94,500	− 6.2%	1,229	750
CONNECTICUT	Danbury	234,250	3.0%	2,217	1,167
	Greenwich	671,667	3.4%	3,013	2,733
	Hartford	232,833	4.3%	2,557	1,233
	Stamford	343,333	3.7%	3,274	1,750
DELAWARE	Wilmington	184,167	5.8%	931	967
D.C. *Washington*	Inside Beltway	207,400	11.8%	1,783	1,433
	Outside Beltway	169,450	13.4%	1,926	1,217
FLORIDA	Clearwater	151,000	1.9%	1,679	1,017
	Ft. Lauderdale	140,900	1.9%	1,338	1,200
	Jacksonville	92,167	.3%	1,010	733
	Miami	134,500	1.9%	1,877	1,117
	Naples	186,333	14.2%	1,723	1,433
	Orlando	127,833	2.7%	1,574	967
	Tallahassee	110,333	3.0%	870	1,000
	Tampa	127,800	− .5%	1,798	1,183
	West Palm Beach	125,833	2.1%	1,081	992

*These figures are based on existing market conditions in December 1988, compiled in January 1989. Different subject homes are used each year, therefore data should not be compared from year to year. Percent change in price represents total market rather than just subject homes.

STATE		MARKET	1988 PRICE	% CHANGE '87 VS '88	EST. ANNUAL TAXES	EST. MONTHLY RENT
GEORGIA		Atlanta	$110,333	4.4%	$1,133	$ 842
		Columbus	92,980	5.2%	796	733
		Savannah	101,100	0.0%	1,229	833
HAWAII		Honolulu	252,667	11.2%	1,068	1,533
IDAHO		Boise	96,888	.1%	1,192	783
ILLINOIS		Bloomington	89,333	4.4%	1,616	828
		Chicago Suburbs	180,000	18.9%	1,993	1,450
		Springfield	102,967	5.8%	1,647	733
INDIANA		Fort Wayne	111,300	18.0%	870	650
		Indianapolis	102,400	7.8%	1,189	833
		South Bend	91,600	2.8%	1,070	767
IOWA		Des Moines	112,633	2.3%	2,047	900
KANSAS	Kansas City	Johnson County	97,167	5.0%	1,157	933
		Wyandotte County	82,333	0.0%	1,072	633
		Topeka	103,333	7.1%	1,515	800
		Wichita	101,000	−4.0%	2,615	900
KENTUCKY		Louisville	102,000	6.6%	1,095	842
LOUISIANA		Baton Rouge	83,027	−4.8%	259	712
		Shreveport	88,667	.3%	367	618
MAINE		Brunswick	129,300	4.8%	1,431	750
		Portland	153,000	10.9%	2,157	763
MARYLAND		Baltimore	191,667	11.6%	2,433	1,433
MASSACHUSETTS		Andover	223,300	3.6%	1,833	1,500
		Braintree	219,967	11.7%	1,883	1,467
		Framingham	214,333	2.7%	1,849	1,500
	Boston Area	Newton	319,167	7.1%	2,312	1,750
		Westboro	191,667	−3.2%	1,792	1,233
		Weymouth	219,387	2.4%	1,914	1,400
		Springfield	182,833	13.0%	1,833	967
MICHIGAN		Ann Arbor	155,667	9.4%	3,613	1,133
	Detroit Area	Macomb County	107,967	9.9%	2,200	1,167
		Oakland County	129,167	4.2%	2,433	883
		Wayne County	196,800	5.6%	3,968	2,067
		East Lansing	107,267	6.2%	3,526	1,067
		Grand Rapids	139,833	3.9%	3,267	1,400
		Traverse City	92,233	2.9%	1,902	683
MINNESOTA		Minneapolis	150,667	5.0%	2,586	1,150
		St. Paul	131,667	1.9%	1,676	1,050
MISSISSIPPI		Jackson	85,833	.6%	500	767
MISSOURI		Kansas City	95,917	1.6%	867	783
		St. Louis	94,633	4.6%	950	717
MONTANA		Billings	84,140	8.2%	2,311	750
		Great Falls	108,333	5.6%	1,637	700
NEBRASKA		Omaha	85,984	5.7%	2,298	800
NEVADA		Las Vegas	122,333	2.4%	960	1,167
		Reno	126,500	6.0%	788	933
NEW HAMPSHIRE		Manchester	191,633	1.2%	2,867	1,167
		Nashua	133,500	6.5%	1,685	850
NEW JERSEY		Bergen County NW	353,333	4.7%	4,670	1,733
		Essex County	223,667	−6.8%	3,667	1,283
		Hunterdon	238,500	9.7%	3,606	1,367
		Morris County	244,833	1.8%	4,123	1,167
		Somerset County	228,917	−4.4%	3,133	1,200
NEW MEXICO		Albuquerque	106,167	3.6%	943	779
NEW YORK		Buffalo	131,000	8.4%	3,342	1,100
	New York City Area	Nassau County				
		Long Island, North	387,833	3.1%	4,457	1,767
		Long Island, South	216,667	2.7%	3,900	1,300
		Putnam County	173,800	−3.8%	3,000	1,033

STATE		MARKET	1988 PRICE	% CHANGE '87 VS '88	EST. ANNUAL TAXES	EST. MONTHLY RENT
(cont.)		Rockland County	$225,300	5.0%	$4,074	$1,400
	New York City Area	Staten Island	201,667	−3.9%	1,200	950
		Suffolk County				
		Long Island, North	266,333	11.2%	3,960	1,483
		Long Island, South	211,667	2.4%	3,900	1,067
		Westchester County	392,000	−14.3%	5,725	2,200
		Rochester	146,667	5.6%	3,231	1,050
NORTH CAROLINA		Charlotte	123,000	5.8%	1,228	1,000
		Greensboro	127,800	4.0%	1,407	1,000
		Raleigh	130,000	1.8%	774	867
		Winston-Salem	93,167	3.3%	688	932
NORTH DAKOTA		Fargo	117,967	1.9%	1,510	833
OHIO		Akron	111,300	6.6%	1,339	900
		Canton	88,567	2.5%	914	783
		Cincinnati	128,333	5.4%	1,462	1,000
		Cleveland	118,667	4.8%	1,264	917
		Columbus	122,833	2.8%	1,620	733
		Dayton	100,300	14.8%	1,105	833
		Toledo	101,333	7.2%	1,308	942
OKLAHOMA		Oklahoma City	75,098	−.8%	817	608
		Tulsa	75,500	−1.7%	907	633
OREGON		Eugene	84,667	8.0%	2,674	900
		Portland	87,333	5.2%	1,962	767
PENNSYLVANIA		Allentown	155,600	24.1%	1,984	917
		Harrisburg	137,633	7.4%	1,399	817
		Phil. Mainline/W.Subs	167,667	2.9%	1,394	1,000
		Pittsburgh	114,917	2.8%	2,180	833
		York	113,100	11.1%	1,039	867
RHODE ISLAND		Providence	213,333	−.1%	2,812	1,250
SOUTH CAROLINA		Charleston	106,500	1.6%	809	683
		Columbia	129,167	5.1%	870	850
SOUTH DAKOTA		Rapid City	85,633	−2.2%	2,635	708
		Sioux Falls	120,633	.9%	2,695	1,150
TENNESSEE		Memphis	117,967	.2%	1,093	733
		Nashville	124,167	6.4%	1,130	900
TEXAS		Austin	98,083	−10.8%	1,234	650
		Corpus Christi	78,000	3.6%	1,724	800
	Dallas/ Fort Worth Area	Arlington	89,333	−5.2%	1,374	767
		Dallas	125,100	−7.0%	1,754	1,000
		Ft. Worth	101,667	−7.0%	2,334	750
		Plano	108,500	1.9%	1,628	750
		Richardson	127,917	1.5%	1,952	1,267
		El Paso	87,633	3.0%	1,569	683
		Houston	88,133	2.0%	2,190	625
		San Antonio	77,300	−7.9%	1,392	633
UTAH		Salt Lake City	112,800	−1.2%	1,323	700
VERMONT		Burlington	141,500	16.9%	2,015	875
VIRGINIA		Norfolk	136,067	5.0%	1,094	842
		Richmond	110,100	5.9%	982	775
WASHINGTON		Bellevue	147,967	18.0%	1,612	1,017
		Seattle	124,333	8.8%	1,281	1,017
		Spokane	82,167	−2.7%	1,092	608
		Tacoma	106,083	1.6%	1,250	750
WEST VIRGINIA		Charleston	127,083	1.9%	659	733
WISCONSIN		Green Bay	96,967	.3%	2,471	767
		Madison	91,822	5.2%	2,272	608
		Milwaukee	121,300	7.2%	3,127	1,000
WYOMING		Cheyenne	112,179	6.2%	685	683

Figure 20-1   Comparable Home Prices for a Variety of National Markets*

a situation that demands mobility, renting is probably your best bet. You can always negotiate a lease to coincide with a short-term period of employment, and you can break a lease and suffer consequences far less severe than those that result from defaulting on a mortgage or selling a home in a down market.

Investment Goals. In some cases, home ownership may conflict with your overall investment strategy. Home ownership costs money long before it pays you back. It costs to buy a home, to furnish it, and maintain it—and many investors can do better investing elsewhere the funds they would otherwise put into a home.

Tax Advantages. Although buying a home offers a great tax writeoff through the deductibility of mortgage interest payments, other forms of real estate may provide even greater tax advantages. Investment real estate may be depreciable, and in many cases expenses such as insurance and maintenance may be deducted—whereas they are not deductible on a personal residence. Under the current tax law, actively-managed rentals work best for incomes under $100,000 as losses of up to $25,000 are allowed despite the passive loss restrictions. After $100,000 the tax deductibility from ordinary income gradually phases out.

WHEN TO BUY

Although the decision to buy a home is often driven more by emotional factors than by the principles of sound investing, those non-financial factors should not be ignored. Home ownership creates a feeling of stability as you and your family establish roots in a community and it delivers other intangible rewards as well.

Personal Expression. Home ownership has definite esthetic benefits. You are free to paint and decorate and move walls and otherwise change your environment in ways that you simply can't do when you rent. And where homes are occupied by their owners, yards and structures tend to be better maintained than in neighborhoods where rentals prevail. Resident owners have a greater commitment to developing a community's image and retaining the value of its property.

Personal Stability. If you plan to be in your community indefinitely, home ownership allows you to sink roots in the community. It gives you a sense of permanence and commitment to civic issues you might otherwise ignore.

Increased Net Worth. Any increase in the value of your home can be regarded as investment growth. Because real estate markets tend to hold their value against inflationary forces, a home is usually an effective hedge against an ever-increasing cost of living.

Tax Benefits. Ownership allows you to claim as deductions major expenses, such as mortgage interest and the cost of property taxes. Early in the life of a mortgage, payments consist primarily of amortized interest, so your first year's payments are essentially tax-deductible "rents." Later, as you begin to reduce the principal, you increase the buildup of equity and your home becomes a true investment, as well as a tax shelter.

Unlike most other investments, home ownership represents a system of values as much as an investment philososphy. There is no effective rule of thumb or "one-size-fits-all" investment fashion that tells you when to buy a home. If you have a strong desire to buy, pay attention to your feeling, but temper that impulse with solid knowledge about the economics and responsiblities of home ownership, as well as the mechanics of the purchase itself. In most markets, a house needs to be held at least five years to recover both buying, selling, and other costs.

HOW TO BUY A HOME

First-time buyers, especially, may find it difficult to work their way through the complex maze of home-buying rules, regulations, rituals, and negotiations. In most cases, you will deal with a seller, the seller's realtor, your realtor, a lender, an escrow agent, and possibly one or more attorneys. True, if you use a realtor, he or she will serve as your contact with many of these parties—but rest assured that you must accommodate everyone's desires and will end up writing a check to the entire crew on the day of closing.

Finding and financing a home is as demanding as any corporate capital investment decision and many people say it's among the most stressful personal experiences of their lives. Consequently, it's worthwhile knowing just what to expect and how to cope with it.

Finding the Right Home

Buying the right property is as important as your home's suitability as an investment. The wrong home in the wrong place at the wrong price—or any combination thereof—can yield disaster, even in an otherwise booming local market.

To a large extent, determining the appropriateness of a prospective home as an investment begins with understanding the local market. If you don't have faith that the local market, or even the local *micro* market—the neighborhood in which the house is located—is going to prosper, you shouldn't buy. If the home is significantly larger or smaller than the other homes in the neighborhood, you should also think twice before buying. Why? Because neighboring homes tend to set the values and even a Taj Mahal among squatters' tents may not be worth the price. Similarly, a cottage set among mansions may be so overpriced you'll never find a buyer when it's your turn to move up. If it's an ultramodern in a conservative area, you'd better be willing to wait for another avant garde buyer when you sell. If the home is not near schools, churches, shopping, or local employers, evaluate your decision carefully before you make a commitment; you'll be limiting your future market to retired couples or singles.

For many people, finding the right home is often a matter of finding the right realtor. Realtors make it their job to understand the market and its dynamics. They can provide up-to-date descriptions of almost all the houses for sale in a specific area and have a good idea of what they'll sell for. They see a lot of houses in the course of a day's work,

and know what you can expect for the price you want to pay. And they know the ins and outs of negotiating, finance, and the myriad inspections and approvals necessary to close the deal.

Most buyers prefer working with a full-time, experienced realtor who is employed in local offices or branch of a national chain, although some prefer the attention smaller or freelance brokers give them. In crowded or complex markets, it's sometimes a good idea to work with more than one realtor, too, although one or the other will eventually ask to be your exclusive agent.

Look At This: A realtor is paid a commission on the houses he or she sells. A realtor may represent the buyer, but the commission is always paid out of the proceeds of the sale and is based on the price of the house. Thus a realtor actually represents the seller and makes more when the house sells for more. If you're depending on your agent to drive the hardest bargain possible, it's probably a good idea to entrust negotiations to your attorney or an agent hired to perform that function for a fee.

Realtors, also, make more on properties listed by their firms, so they may be inclined to push in the direction of a home they list and sometimes a seller may offer the realtor a bonus or a larger commission for completing a particular transaction. In the great majority of cases, however, realtors are interested in making fair and timely transactions. After all, they earn *nothing* if a deal falls through!

Negotiating the Price

When you have found a home you like, you will usually make an offer that is somewhat less than the asking price (10% lower is typical) and may also propose modifications to the terms of sale. The realtor takes the offer to the seller who may accept it, reject it, or more likely, make a counteroffer. A sincere counteroffer will address all the points you raise and often splits the difference between your offer and the original asking price—although the actual amount will vary according to the strength of the local market and your perceived credibility as a buyer.

The buyer normally includes "earnest money" (a small fraction of the offered price) with his or her bid to indicate that the offer is serious. Upon acceptance of the offer, the earnest money is deposited in an escrow account and becomes part of the down payment. Neither the buyer nor seller has access to the funds while they are in escrow; they are in the control of the escrow company, a third party to the transaction.

The Purchase Contract

Your purchase contract, usually prepared and submitted with your offer, will specify (1) the purchase price, (2) down payment requirements, (3) a closing date, (4) preliminary financing arrangements, (5) special requirement restrictions (such as specific repairs to be made by the seller), (6) a complete list of movable property within the house that is part of the sale, and (7) special duties of the buyer or seller.

If you fail to comply with the purchase agreement in any way, the seller may be able to cancel the contract and keep the earnest money. If the seller fails to comply, you may sue for specific performance and enforce the elements of the contract at issue.

In many cases, arrangements are made in the purchase agreement that the contract may be canceled and the earnest money returned if certain conditions exist. For example, a buyer has no real control over his or her ability to get a loan, so you may specify that the contract becomes void if interest rates rise significantly or if mortgage approval is not granted before the closing date.

Time Sensitive

The closing date is the date on which the transaction is expected to be completed, cash changes hands, and the house becomes yours. Usually, it is 45 to 90 days from the time that the offer was accepted. During this time, you arrange the financing and all the data collection, inspections, and approvals that involves.

FINANCING YOUR PURCHASE

Your realtor or financial planner can help you through this sometimes tricky house-

Professional Advice

buying maze. If you're not using a realtor, sit down with a loan officer at your local bank or savings and loan, or mortgage company. Above all, shop around—the monthly dollar difference and "liveability" among types of loans is truly amazing. Some people, therefore, go directly to a mortgage broker who shops for loans on their behalf.

Mortgage Points and Prepayment Penalties. You will probably pay a one-time fee when the loan begins; it effectively increases the interest rate on the loan. The fee is expressed in percentage "points": 1 point being equivalent to 1 percent of interest. The payment of points is treated as interest, and if you pay cash at closing and the loan is not a "refinance," you may deduct the interest in the points. Otherwise, if the points are added to your mortgage, they are not deductible up front. The points are really a fee charged for the privilege of doing business with a particular institution. If you're assertive, you can negotiate points with your lender. Some institutions will adjust the fees. Shop for institutions and mortgages that have the best possible interest rate and underwriting costs.

Types of Financing

Money borrowed to finance the purchase of your house is generally available from one of three sources: (1) a conventional loan through a commercial bank or savings and loan assocation; (2) a loan insured by the Federal Housing Administration (FHA); or (3) a loan guaranteed by the Veterans Administration (VA).

Fixed-Rate Mortgages. With a fixed-rate mortgage, the interest rate is established at the time the loan is made, and never changes. This is the time-honored mortgage arrangement, and the vast majority of today's homes have been purchased using fixed-rate mortgages. But as interest rates soared during the inflationary 1970s, banks found themselves losing money on previous fixed-rate mortgages, forcing them to develop a new generation of mortgages that are tied to prevailing interest rates. Fixed rate commercial mortgages are seldom assumable.

INTEREST RATE						
Mortgage	9%	10%	11%	12%	13%	14%
$ 50,000	$ 402	$ 439	$ 476	$ 514	$ 553	$ 592
70,000	563	614	667	720	774	829
100,000	805	878	952	1,029	1,106	1,185
120,000	966	1,053	1,143	1,234	1,327	1,422
150,000	1,207	1,316	1,429	1,543	1,659	1,777
180,000	1,448	1,580	1,714	1,852	1,991	2,133
200,000	1,609	1,755	1,905	2,057	2,212	2,370
220,000	1,770	1,931	2,095	2,263	2,434	2,607
250,000	2,012	2,194	2,381	2,572	2,766	2,962
300,000	2,412	2,634	2,861	3,082	3,316	3,552

Figure 20-2 Monthly Payments on a 30-year Mortgage

Adjustable-Rate Mortgages. Adjustable-rate mortgages (ARMs) have a variable interest rate that fluctuates over the term of the loan. The rate is usually tied to an index like the Federal Home Loan Bank Board's national average mortgage rate for existing homes. The rate is adjusted at pre-established times, rising or falling according to movement of the index. Some buyers qualify under these loans more easily than fixed since the beginning interest rate is usually discounted (lower than) the fixed rates.

Interest Rate Caps. A rate-capped mortgage limits the frequency of adjustments and/or the amount of the adjustments. The ceiling may be imposed on the rate of change for each adjustment period, or over the life of the mortgage, or both. At each adjustment date, the monthly payment schedule is recomputed so the mortgage will be paid off on time.

Payment Caps. Under the terms of a payment-cap mortgage, the interest rate may change frequently, but the monthly payments do not change. Instead, when the rate changes, the allocation of the monthly payment between principal and interest also changes. When interest rates rise, more of the payment goes toward interest; when rates come down, more of the payment is applied to the principal.

A real danger of a payment-capped loan lurks in the mathematics: as the rate goes up, the monthly payment might not be enough to to cover the increased interest charge. That leftover interest would be added to the remaining principal. Your next payment would then have to cover the original principal and the accruing interest, a condition known as "negative amortization." This has the effect of compounding your obligation in exactly the same way that your earnings are compounded in a savings account, and it's a situation you want to avoid.

Balloon Payments. A balloon payment obligates you to pay off the balance of a loan at a predetermined point in time, such as three or five years. At the beginning of the loan, payments are set up just as they would be with a conventional, fixed-rate 30-year-mortgage, but when the loan comes due, you must come up with the balloon payment or refinance the loan. Balloon payments may be suitable for real estate speculators or those with other guaranteed sources of cash—but historically, they spell trouble for the small investor.

Graduated-Payment Mortgages. Graduated-payment mortgages are designed for homeowners who expect their incomes to grow. Basically, you pay less at the beginning, and your payments increase each year for a predetermined period—usually five or

10 years. In the conventional form of the concept, payments are fixed at that point for the duration of the loan; a newer version uses an adjustable rate schedule.

During the early years, the payments don't cover the interest so unpaid interest is added to the principal, creating negative amortization. But after the graduation period, the payment is set at a high-enough level to pay the loan in full by the end of the term.

Shared-Appreciation Mortgages. Under this special arrangement, also known as an "equity participation mortgage," the lender loans you money at lower-than-market rates, and expects a share of the appreciated value of the house when you sell it.

Growing Equity Mortgages. Also known as a rapid pay-off mortgage, it combines a fixed interest rate with a changing monthly payment. The interest rate is a few percentage points below market. The mortgage term may run the normal 30 years, but the loan is generally paid off in less than 15 years because the payment increases are applied entirely to principal.

Seller-Arranged Financing Arrangements

In many cases, the seller is willing to finance the sale of the house. This financing may take one of several forms.

Mortgage Assumption. In the most common form, the buyer pays the seller a sum equal to the seller's equity and takes over the mortgage payments, usually at a rate far less than what is currently available. Institutions, including the Federal National Mortgage Association (FNMA, or Fannie Mae), are trying to curtail this activity by exercising a "due on sale" clause that forces the seller to cash out the mortgage when the home is sold. Consequently, in some situations you may be unable to assume a mortgage.

Resale Finance Mortgages. If the seller's mortgage is financed by Fannie Mae, you may be eligible for a resale finance mortgage. The Fannie Mae-approved lender quotes a special rate for each buyer based on the outstanding balance of the old loan and on the payment amount and period requested by the buyer. The old loan is paid off with the proceeds of the new loan, and often the rate of the new loan is less than the prevailing market rate.

Purchase Money Mortgages. In this case, the seller makes a loan directly to the buyer, less any down payment. The buyer assumes the title and the loan is secured by a mortgage or deed of trust that can be enforced in court if the buyer defaults.

Wraparound Financing. With a wraparound, the seller gives the buyer a new loan for the purchase price, less any down payment, and continues to make payments on the old mortgage.

Lease with Option to Buy. The seller allows you to move into the home and accumulate the down payment over a period of time as part of the lease payments. The buyer pays "option money" up front, which may be applied to the down payment and which may not be refundable.

Land Contract. An installment land contract allows the seller to keep his or her original mortgage while "selling" the home on an installment basis. Installment payments must be limited to short-term and can be applied to interest only; at the end of the term, the balance must be paid.

Because the seller holds on to the title until the final installment is made, the original lending institution is not able to exercise the "due on sale" option.

Buy-Down. In a buy-down, the seller, usually a developer, subsidizes the mortgage interest rate for the first few years of the mortgage.

Quick-Pay Mortgages

Money Management Tip

There's been much talk about quick-pay mortgages and how you can save thousands of dollars by taking a 15-year mortgage, a biweekly mortgage, or paying off your 30-year mortgage in 15 years.

The concept is essentially the same in each case: by paying off the principal more quickly than with a conventional 30-year mortgage, you cut interest payments by tens of thousands of dollars and shorten your mortgage term by half or even more. That means building equity at a much faster clip than with a conventional mortgage—and it really works. It works because the purchase of your home will probably be so highly leveraged (that is, the ratio of borrowed money to down payment will be so big) that paying even small amounts of principal ahead of schedule will cut your interest expense enormously.

Here's how it works when you apply the strategy to a 30-year, $50,000 conventional mortgage at 13%. (See Figure 20-2.) Each month, you pay $553.10 to interest and principal. But in the first month of the loan, $541.67 of your $553.10 payment goes to pay off the interest; just $11.43 goes toward the principal. In the second month, $541 is interest and $11.56 is applied to the principal.

After the first month, your unpaid mortgage balance is $49,988.57; in the second, it's dropped to $49,977.01. It doesn't feel—and isn't—much headway. And over the life of the loan, you will have paid $149,115.82 in interest.

Now suppose you had paid the second month's principal payment along with the first month's payment of interest and principal. You would have eliminated one month's loan payment and the interest that goes with it —$541.54.

The loan's balance has dropped to $49,977.01 in a single month, instead of two. Now you're in the second month of your loan, and the third month's principal and interest payment has just become your second payment. If you add to it the principal payment for the fourth month, you shorten the term by yet another month.

In six months, you would have reduced the mortgage to the same balance that you would have achieved after 12 months of regular payments. You would end up slicing 15 years from your mortgage and erasing tens of thousands of dollars of interest payments.

Of course, as your mortgage matures the amount of principal you pay each month increases, and it will become increasingly hard

to stay ahead of the payments. But the beauty of prepaying a 30-year mortgage is that you can quit anytime you want, or slow your prepayment schedule.

Some mortgages include penalties for prepayment, and in some cases the lending institution has guidelines for you to use when making early payments. Otherwise, simply add the extra amount to your monthly payment and indicate that the money should be applied to the principal.

Is prepaying the mortgage worth the bother? Maybe and maybe not—depending on how you approach home ownership as an investment.

Proponents of the strategy point to these advantages:

(1) by prepaying, a young couple can build substantial equity quickly, allowing them to finance their children's educations with a home equity loan or second mortgage;

(2) the quick equity buildup allows you to trade up more easily to a more expensive home;

(3) a middle-aged couple that chooses to prepay can own their home free and clear by retirement; and

(4) prepayment—especially a 15-year mortgage—is a kind of tax-deferred forced savings program where your savings dollars are allowed to build.

The arguments against prepayment include:

(1) you won't lower your monthly payments by prepaying, and since most people move within five to eight years, they'll never enjoy the benefits of an early payoff;

(2) you can't deduct the extra principal payments you make, so you don't increase your tax advantage—in fact, when you prepay your mortgage you give up the biggest tax advantage of home ownership;

(3) the extra dollars you apply to the mortgage each month might be better invested elsewhere, where they might be more liquid or pay a higher return; and

(4) most people stretch themselves to the limit with their mortgage payment anyway, so why make things worse with a quick-pay plan?

In the end, it often comes down to a question about feelings: Will you feel better saving interest and accelerating that day when your mortgage is paid off, or do you consider the long-term extra interest cost a justifiable lifestyle expense? The way you answer may really determine whether a prepay plan is best for you.

Money Management Tip

One other piece of advice: If you like the idea of a 15-year mortgage but aren't sure you can afford the monthly increase in payments, settle for a 30-year mortgage with no prepayment penalties. You can prepay as you are able, but you're not locked into a commitment you may not be able to maintain.

COMPLETING THE TRANSACTION

After you have come to terms with the seller, and finalized your financing package, you are expected to pay the balance of your down payment. At closing, the title is transferred and all costs are paid by the buyer—including attorney fees, escrow fees, taxes, insurance, and any other applicable fees. At this time, any previous mortgages that are not assumed or retained, as well as any other claims against the property, are cleared, and you receive clear title.

Congratulations—you are a homeowner. Now, can you make your investment pay off?

WHAT ABOUT WARRANTIES?

Look At This:

You can protect your investment by purchasing a warranty on a home, just as you would on an appliance or your car—although there are significant limitations.

The Home Owners Warranty (HOW) program provides you with insurance protection during the first 10 years of a new home's life. HOW is an organization of builders; they pay for membership, and you get the coverage. (Beware of warranties offered by individual contractors. They are only as good as the word and financial resources of the builder.)

The plan offers greatest protection during the first few years, when big defects (including labor, material, and any significant structural problems) are likely to show up. In the second year, coverage of labor and material are deleted, and for the remaining eight years the policy covers only major structural defects, which are defined as actual damage to a load-bearing component of the house.

There are two types of warranties for used homes. An inspection warranty covers items checked and found satisfactory by a warranty inspector. A noninspected warranty offers significantly limited coverage because there is no inspection. It may be bought by either the buyer or the seller.

Investment Potential

A home can be an important investment—home ownership is the most significant component in personal net worth for most people. But a home is also a functional investment— its value as an investment is often far less important than whether or not it's a good place to live. And a home also requires "care and feeding." Without constant (and often expensive) maintenance, the value of a home diminishes.

A home is a good hedge against inflation, and the equity that you build up over the years can be used to finance children's educations and may even help fund retirement. From this perspective, a home is a little like an involuntary savings plan, with growth and tax advantages built in.

Many factors—location, price, market stability, interest rates, to name only a few—affect the value of individual homes. Interest rates play the most direct role when it comes to resale financing, and an otherwise desirable home may be tough to sell if prospective buyers are locked out of the market by excessively high rates—as occurred in the early 1980s. Suffice it to say that over the years, interest rates and the price of houses have increased steadily. Will we soon again see the dramatic spiraling of interest rates in the 1980s or the escalating housing values of the 1970s? However, the increasing value of houses in general has been one of the constants in the U.S. economy.

The value of a home as an investment must also be weighed against the opportunity costs of renting, as rents also increase with the general economy, and the liquidity renting gives you may suit your objectives better. In general, though, if rents and mortgage payments are comparable in your area, and you are in a tax-sensitive financial situation with adequate cash to maintain your property, home ownership is usually advantageous.

Strengths

A home is a very good hedge against inflation—as the cost of living increases, so does the value of the home, all other things being equal. In addition, the equity you build in your home can become an important part of your overall fiscal strategy, as it can be leveraged to provide you with funds for other needs.

Weaknesses

The value of a home as an investment is only as good as the market conditions that support housing prices in your area. In deflationary periods, or when recession teams up with high interest rates, housing prices may actually drop. A home also requires constant reinvestment if it is to maintain its value. Finally, a home is an illiquid investment, particularly in sluggish markets where there may be more sellers than buyers.

Tax Considerations

Tax Consequences

By giving you the right to deduct interest payments from your tax bill, Uncle Sam helps subsidize the purchase of your home. That single consideration alone encourages the purchase of hundreds of thousands of homes each year. Of course, the amount that you are able to write off decreases each year as your mortgage payments shift to pay more principal than interest.

Before the 1986 Tax Reform Act, you could deduct the interest payments on all houses that you owned, including investment property. But TRA limited interest deductions to two homes, and both must be regularly used by their owners.

The home interest deduction may not be a sacred cow. Already there's a $1,000,000 mortgage limit placed on it. And experts point to Canada, where home ownership is 62% and they've never had a home interest deduction. Japan has none either, and its ownership is that of the U.S., 64%. By 1990 the subject of limiting mortgage interest deductions was being actively discussed in Congress. We expect that limits of some sort will almost certainly be enacted within 2-3 years of 1990.

How to Use Your Equity

The equity in a home is one of its hidden assets and, thanks to the 1986 Tax Reform Act, more homeowners than ever are tapping into this rich source of funds. TRA began a process of eliminating the interest on consumer loans; by 1991 the only consumer interest that will be deductible is the interest you pay on a loan secured by a first or second home. There is a limit: you can't deduct the interest on loan balances greater than the amount you paid for your house, plus improvements. You can deduct without limit the interest you pay on mortgage loans used for education or medical bills.

You may tap your equity in three ways: you can take a second mortgage, refinance the original mortgage, or take out a home equity line of credit.

Second Mortgages. If you need a lot of money and plenty of time to pay it back, a second mortgage may be the way to go. You can borrow up to 80% of the market value of your home, minus the unpaid balance on your first mortgage, from a bank, savings and loan, or lending company. You'll pay closing costs and a percent or two more than for a first mortgage, but you can get repayment terms ranging from 12 to 30 years. In many cases, you can borrow from $100,000 to $200,000 and there's usually no minimum, although closing costs may make it prohibitive to borrow less than $5,000.

On the downside, you should protect yourself against adverse caps on periodic or life-of-the-loan interest rate increases, including increases beyond the initial discounted rates some lenders advertise to market their loans. Shop for the lowest front-end fees available and avoid interest-only loans that require a balloon payment when the principle is due.

Refinancing the First Mortgage. In some cases, it pays to refinance the balance of your mortgage: you don't get any cash out of the deal, but under the right circumstances you can reduce your monthly payments. Refinancing usually pays off only when interest rates have fallen and you can get a new mortgage for substantially less than the original— most housing experts say you need a spread of a 1.5 to 3 points (1.5% to 3% difference between old and new interest rates) to compensate for the costs of closing. In addition, you need to plan on staying in your home at least 5 to 7 years longer to make refinancing pay off for you. The IRS also has imposed new regulations that prohibit you from deducting in the first year the points you pay for refinancing your home. Points paid to buy or improve a home, however, can be paid all at once. According to the IRS, the points paid at refinancing must be prorated over the life of the loan.

Home Equity Lines of Credit. The newest and most controversial method of plugging into the power of your equity is the home equity line of credit. Essentially, you can borrow up to 70 or 80% of the market value of your home, less the unpaid balance. You can borrow more than a second mortgage allows—up to $2 million—and they're less expensive than second mortgages because of lower closing costs. Rates fluctuate and are adjusted monthly, but they are about the

Look At This:

same as a second mortgage: they float about 1% to 3% above the prime rate. If interest rates go sky high, so will your cost of credit. The real attraction—and the real danger— of a home equity credit line is its accessibility. Just like a revolving credit account at a department store, you borrow as much as you want whenever you want, and you can pay it back over a period of 5 to 10 years. You are usually required to pay back only the interest in monthly installments and are allowed to pay back the principal as you are able. That makes the monthly commitment smaller than that of a second mortgage, but you will, at some point, have to come up with the principal. If you can't, the lender can foreclose and you lose your house.

It's clear that you should only take out a home equity line of credit if you are a disciplined money manager. In a standard bankruptcy, you are allowed to keep your home, but if you can't make your line of credit payments, you even lose that. Ironically, disciplined money managers, like "cash-and-carry" consumers, are among those least likely to need or use an equity-based credit line.

Does Remodeling Pay?

Your home is a working investment; unless you are willing to spend money on improvements, its value will diminish or at least not appreciate as fast as other, well-maintained properties. Even so, some improvements have no apparent market value. So when does it make sense to remodel an otherwise functional home?

There are two rules of thumb: (1) the more conventional the project, the more likely it is to pay back its cost when the house is resold, and (2) don't do anything major unless you plan to delay reselling your home for at least five years.

The projects that tend to be sure-fire winners are improvements to the master bedroom and kitchen renovations. Fireplaces are a big plus too, and will usually fetch at least what they cost.

You'll probably lose money on a room addition, however, because the high cost of construction usually exceeds the marginal value of the additional room in comparable homes on the housing market. If you have to add a room, be sure it can be used in a variety of ways—the next owners may want an office, or family room, not another bedroom.

Porches, decks, patios, pools and hot tubs usually fail to deliver the cost of construction as well, except in neighborhoods where such features are standard, or add dramatically to the exterior appearance.

Unless you're building your dream home and never plan to leave, limit improvements to about 10% of the market value of your home. Don't put yourself in the position of pricing your house out of the market because of unusual or quirky modifications—buyers are reluctant to pay more for a home than comparable neighborhood costs, and, as the saying goes, there's no accounting for taste.

Summing Up

Until the American Dream ceases to include home ownership, residential housing will continue to be a significant and advantageous investment for anyone who can muster the down payment and handle the sometimes hefty cash flow of mortgage and maintenance expenses. Aggressive (Type I or Type II) investors who wish to quickly "trade up" on their home investment, however, are probably better off in other forms of real estate. Remember, even as an investment, your home is still your castle!

PLANNERS TIP

Sacramento, California, Certified Financial Planner, Paul Pennington, states that the operating cost of a California home will break down as follows: Taxes, 1%; Insurance, 0.5%; Maintenance 1.5%; and Utilities 1%, totaling 4% of market value of the home. Using this example, a $200,000 house's annual operating costs are about $8,000. Although maintenance is variable cost, Pennington claims the 1.5% will average out. Since some homes have appreciated greatly and a retiree has the maintenance cost continuing, a sale using the $125,000 capital gains exclusion may free up idle dollars. On a free and clear $200,000 home the operating costs represent income foregone. Equity is tied up and nonproductive as well. You could give yourself a raise by selling your $200,000 house using the $125,000 tax exemption for people over age 55, and buying down to a $100,000 home. The freed up $100,000 can be used for income investments to produce $833 per month payment to you. Still you have no house payment, but there is a cost to idle equity. In this case the income lost is $10,000 per year.

Notes

SIZING UP THE HOUSE

Potential home buyers can hunt for hidden home defects and get a surprising amount of information about a house just by asking the right questions. Here's a list you can take with you when you visit the houses you're interested in.

1) Has the basement leaked within the past two years?
   What basement waterproofing repairs have been made within the past two years?
2) What type of roof do you have?
   How old is it?
   Has the roof leaked within the past two years?
   What roof repairs have been made within the past two years?
3) Has the plumbing system backed up within the past two years?
   What repairs or servicing has been done within the past two years?
4) How old is the heating system?
   Is heat provided to all finished rooms?
   Is it: Gas   Electric   Oil   Other?   When was it last repaired or serviced?
5) Is there a central-air-conditioning system?
   If yes, is it provided to all finished rooms?
   Comments:
   How old is it?   Is it: Gas   Electric?
   When was the last time it was repaired or serviced?
6) How much is the average monthly bill for: Electricity $___ Gas $___ Oil $___
7) Other than the central heating and air-conditioning systems, are any appliances, fans, motors, pumps, light fixtures, or electrical outlets in need of repair?
8) Is the fireplace in working condition?
   When was it last repaired, serviced, or cleaned?
   Comments:
9) Are there any storm windows or screens on the premises that are not installed?
   Specifics:
10) What type of floor is under areas covered by wall-to-wall carpeting?
       Finished hardwood   Plywood   Other
    Is flooring material the same for all covered areas?
    Specifics:
11) Do gutters and downspouts need any repairs other than routine maintenance?
    Specifics:
12) How old is the hot-water heater?   What is its capacity in gallons?
    When was it last serviced or repaired?
13) Does the property ever have standing water in front, rear, or side yards more than 48 hours after a heavy rain?
    Location:
14) Do fuses blow or circuit breakers trip when two or more appliances are used at the same time?
    Specifics:
15) Are all outer door locks in working condition?
    Will keys be provided for each lock?
16) Is there insulation in the ceiling or attic?
    The walls?
    Other places?
    Notes:

Source: Montgomery County (Md.) Office of Consumer Affairs

PART IV

ESTABLISHING AND EXECUTING A FINANCIAL PLAN

Your knowledge of yourself, money mechanics, and investment vehicles must come together in a coherent way if you are to maximize your net worth. In this final section, you'll earn how to gather and evaluate data about investment opportunities, allocate your resources over multiple assest categories, and implement an effective financial plan.

CHAPTER 21

EVALUATING POTENTIAL INVESTMENTS

A GLANCE AHEAD

The deregulation of financial markets has led to the rapid development of many new and complex investment vehicles. This diversity gives you greater opportunity for finding the "perfect" investments for your investor type and financial situation. However, it also means there is a greater chance of error in selecting the right investment vehicle.

In this chapter, you will learn

- *How to spot many types of investment frauds*
- *How to evaluate investment proposals*
- *How to select a stockbroker*
- *What to look for in a mutual fund prospectus*
- *What to look for in a limited partnership prospectus*
- *Where to find reliable newsletter advisors and investment computer software.*

"SURE-FIRE" PROFITS—BUT NOT FOR THE INVESTOR!

The rise of new and different investment vehicles has been accompanied by a boom in investment swindles. The new scams are often surprisingly sophisticated. Recently, the Council of Better Business Bureaus and the North American Securities Administrators Association (NASAA) issued a statement calling the rising tide of investment frauds an epidemic. By some estimates, over $1 billion a year is lost to con artists pitching legitimate-sounding investments in art, oil and gas, precious metals, currencies, rare coins, and others.

For the most part, "boiler rooms" are still the source of most of these scandals. The term "boiler room" comes from the basement locations of stock market swindlers in the 1920s. They offered small investors the chance to speculate on stock price gyrations without going through stock exchange brokers. Typically, the boiler room or "bucket shop" operator took the other side of the investor's bet without ever really buying or selling the stock in question.

Surprisingly, even the investor who is "too smart" to be hornswoggled by investment scams in stocks or bonds can suddenly become gullible when approached by a slick salesperson to invest in precious metals, art, or sophisticated-sounding investments in stock options or future options.

J. David Dominelli put together an impressive operation based in the wealthy San Diego suburb of La Jolla. The company, J. David & Company, recruited the sons and daughters of wealthy families to hawk his "phenomenal currency trading program."

Dominelli raised over $200 million from supposedly sophisticated—and most certainly wealthy—investors.

When the house of cards finally fell, millions of dollars were lost with no chance of recovery because much of the money had been spent on Dominelli's lavish lifestyle. His plush headquarters, garishly displayed personal wealth, and good connections (Dominelli gave generously to local charities) gave credibility to what was really a fraudulent operation.

How could millionaires—financial "experts"—be conned so completely? It wasn't anything new. In fact, Dominelli used the oldest investment scheme in the book: a "Ponzi" scheme. A Ponzi scheme is when early investors are paid off with funds from later investors. When the early investors see they really do earn some outrageous return (J. David & Company talked about earning 40% per year with little risk), they often reinvest and tell all their friends. The Ponzi operator never invests the funds in any legitimate vehicle. Once investors are convinced of the great returns, they leave their money in and let the paper profits roll up.

Eventually, of course, people begin to take money out for various purposes. When withdrawal requests outnumber new incoming cash, the pyramid collapses. Only those investors who got out early manage to win. And in the J. David & Company case, many investors who smelled a rat early were forced to return the money they did manage to withdraw. A bankruptcy court then split the proceeds among all claimants.

It is little satisfaction to J. David & Company investors that Dominelli now resides at Pleasanton Prison in California. His punishment does not return a dime to the many investors who put everything they had into financing his lavish lifestyle.

The Offshore Gambit

Another con artist, Alex Herbage, set up a supposed mutual fund to invest in currencies. Herbage established a whole range of intermediary companies in an attempt to shield himself from investigation. His lead company, Caprimex Group, was variously headquartered in England, Holland, and the Cayman Islands, as well as other distant lands.

He raised over $50 million in the early 1980s from investors before his scam was uncovered. And as many investors subsequently learned to their chagrin, this was not Herbage's first foray into investment fraud. He had previously scammed millions from investors in another commodity-related pool.

Yet he was able to create a façade of credibility by surrounding himself with expensive accoutrements such as an English manor, luxury cars, and art. He mingled with England's elite, even attracting a relative of the queen to one of his soirees.

In the United States, Herbage targeted his appeal to conservative older investors who were suspicious of government policy. Speaking in "hard money" terms, he hinted that investments in his fund would be sheltered from the prying eyes of the IRS. His themes were "protect yourself from the ravages of inflation" and "diversify your assets overseas to protect them from confiscation by the government in case of a crisis."

Herbage solicited investments for his "Currency Hedge Fund" via a weekly investment advisory newsletter and through brochures. Unfortunately for the investors, Herbage proved reluctant to pay out client monies on request. The very secrecy that many of his investors desired for tax avoidance led them directly to a much worse fate: the total loss of their money.

Boiler Room Bandits

By far the most common form of investment scam is the boiler room. Banks of phones are set up to call potential "customers" all over the country. Typically, boiler room operations concentrate on calling investors out of state—a tactic that avoids attracting the attention of local authorities. Cheating people from other states also raises the cost of prosecution. Witnesses must be located and flown in for trials. It also raises jurisdictional issues. Which is the proper authority to prosecute the matter? Many fraudulent operations have thrived for years because no one regulatory agency took charge to stop them.

Popular boiler room scams in recent years

include precious metals investing. In 1983, International Gold Bullion Exchange (IGBE) in Fort Lauderdale, Florida, was finally closed down after four years in business. Salespeople for the company hawked the purchase of gold bullion by putting down only a fraction of the cost of the metal. Investors were told that if they invested 15% of the value of the metal, the company would buy the bullion and store it for them. That way investors could "lock in the price" of the gold for a small amount. Investors only had to pay interest and a "nominal" storage fee until they took delivery. At that time, the balance was due.

Of course, they were assured that they wouldn't have to come up with a large sum for the balance because the price of gold would go much higher. The profits from the rise in the price would more than cover their expenses.

Unfortunately, IGBE never bought the gold bullion it was supposed to be holding for its clients. When the storage facility was checked in 1983, inspectors discovered pieces of wood painted to look like gold bars!

As long as gold prices were flat or falling, there was little danger of clients wanting to cash in their gold for dollars. But when prices rose, investors moved to take their profits. When IGBE was finally shut down, over $75 million had been lost.

Another popular scam in the early 1980s was the sale of oil and gas leases. The Federal Bureau of Land Management periodically holds lotteries, wherein the people who are selected win the right to buy land leases for $1 an acre. When oil prices were rising and energy concerns were on the front page of your daily newspaper, boiler room operations bought up these leases and resold them to investors for $300 or more an acre.

The problem was that the leases had very little value. Oil development is a complicated and expensive task and oil companies did not want the leases because they had little prospect of finding oil. The boiler room salespeople portrayed the game as one of chance—where you, the investor, have as much chance as the next guy. Unfortunately, the real rules of the oil game just don't work that way.

Few areas are immune to investment scams. Art is frequently hawked over the phone to unsuspecting investors. Much of the art is a total fraud. Other art pieces are grossly overvalued. Some experts estimate that over $500 million has been invested in forged Dali prints.

Typical scams include issuing more prints than authorized for an edition, forging artists' signatures, or forging new art imitating a known artist's style. Some of these virtually worthless works are marked up to $3,000 or $4,000 by unscrupulous art galleries.

A common scam for boiler room art sales is the inclusion of a "certificate of authenticity." Often a "money-back guarantee" is also offered. These fast-moving boiler rooms, though, tend to be gone by the time you may want to get your money back. The certificate of authenticity is only as good as the company that issues it. All too often, it's not worth the paper it's printed on!

The Financial Planning Scam

Over the past ten years, there has been a rapid rise in the number of financial advisors who call themselves "financial planners." For the most part, there are no regulations or registration requirements to become a financial planner. Currently steps are being taken in many states to start a registration process.

According to a study released by the North American Securities Administrators Association in 1988, more than 22,000 investors lost over $400 million in 1986 and 1987 alone through fraud and abuse in the financial planning industry. That compares to losses shown in a 1985 study of $91 million. To make matters worse, there has been a sharp rise in "big ticket" cases in recent years as new investment products receive even more media attention.

According to the Consumer Federation of America, over 400,000 people call themselves financial planners in the United States. The NASAA has developed model laws and regulations to fight fraud in the financial planning community. So far four states—Virginia, Georgia, South Dakota, and North Carolina—have adopted the model.

One of the most significant convictions under the new law came in Virginia in 1987 where a financial planner who had embezzled $1.3 million from 40 investors in eight states was sentenced to 222 years in prison.

Even the SEC has taken a more aggressive tack against unethical practices by some financial planners. In May 1988 the SEC censured and suspended for 120 days Nida Rae Ellis, a New Mexico investment advisor and president of the New Mexico chapter of a national organization of financial planners, for failing to tell clients she was earning money on the sale of securities she recommended. She failed to tell clients that she would receive a commission and that they did not have to go through her to purchase the real estate limited partnerships she recommended.

KNOWLEDGE IS POWER— AND PROTECTION

It is impossible to catalog all the possible schemes, swindles, scams, and frauds that devious minds can come up with. However, you can certainly lessen the risk of being taken for a ride by investigating a potential investment thoroughly.

Most boiler room operations depend on aggressive telephone "cold calling." Don't ever let yourself be pressured into buying something on the first phone call from a stranger. Perhaps the most common thread running through all fraudulent deals is the promise of high returns for little or no risk. Remember: if it sounds too good to be true, it probably is!

To get a good idea of the return you can reasonably expect from a very low risk investment, look up the yield of 90-day Treasury bills or the yield on your bank's short-term CDs. If you are offered "low-risk" investments with promises of returns that are significantly higher than these yields, look out! Salespeople who tell you that very high returns are possible without high risk are either mistaken or are really talking about the return *they* will earn for selling *you* a bogus investment!

Do business with local or well-established firms. Most boiler room operations zero in on out-of-state investors to avoid attracting the attention of local authorities. The fact that a firm advertises in major or local media is no guarantee of its credibility. For exam-

ple, the International Gold Bullion Exchange was advertising in the *Wall Street Journal* right up to the day it was closed down by law enforcement agents!

Obviously there are advantages in many cases in dealing with a national firm. See if the firm has an office in your area. Go and check out the office. Of course, there are some exceptions. Many reputable no-load mutual funds conduct all their business through the mails and by phone. Some national discount brokerage firms also conduct their interstate business by phone. You can check these companies out with the various regulatory bodies such as the SEC, the NASD, or your state's securities department.

Look At This:

Professional Advice

Before investing with someone over the phone, request details on the proposal in writing. If it is a complex investment, don't hesitate to have it checked by your accountant or lawyer. Don't be fooled by expensive glossy brochures. Check out the credentials of the party making the investment proposal.

When you choose an advisor, the financial planning industry has a number of different certifications. Perhaps the most widely recognized and respected is the Certified Financial Planner (CFP) designation. There are others such as Chartered Financial Consultant or Registered Financial Planner. Your financial planner should be willing to explain their credentials. To receive these designations, planners have to meet financial requirements and pass various levels of tests.

A firm that sells securities to the public must belong to the National Association of Securities Dealers (NASD). The NASD announced in 1988 that it will increase the amount of information it will disclose to investors regarding disciplinary actions taken against member firms and their employees. The previous NASD policy was not to disclose disciplinary actions unless they led to fines of over $10,000, the suspension of the firm or individual, or the expulsion of the firm or individual from the NASD.

The new policy significantly broadens the information that the NASD will release on written request. You can find out the past and current affiliations of individual employees, the criminal convictions and final disciplinary actions taken by federal and state agencies and the NASD relating to securities or commodity transactions.

If you have questions about stockbrokers or mutual funds, direct your inquiries to the Securities and Exchange Commission (SEC), 400 Fifth St., NW, Washington, DC 20549.

For checking out a real estate proposal, you should know that firms advertising land sales by mail or phone across state lines must register their projects with the Office of Interstate Land Sales, of the Department of Housing and Urban Development. The address is 451 Seventh St., SW, Rm. 6266, Washington, DC 20410.

Commodity brokers and advisors must be registered with the Commodity Futures Trading Commission (CFTC), 2033 K St., NW, Washington, DC 20581. Futures brokers, advisors, and pool operators must be members of the National Futures Association, 200 W. Madison St., Chicago, IL 60606.

Money Management Tip

When venturing into new investment areas, keep your initial investments small. A sure sign of a scam is pressure to make a large investment in a short time. There are two things to remember here: (1) if an investment is good, it will be good tomorrow, next week, and next month; (2) it never makes sense to make a large investment in an area with which you are unfamiliar.

Some investments seem more susceptible to scams than others. Complex oil and gas projects are often beyond the expertise of many professional investors. If you do not understand the details (and they can be very complex), stay away.

Commodity futures and options on futures have spawned many high-pressure sales programs that have resulted in millions of dollars being lost by investors. In 1986, the Commodity Futures Trading Commission closed down First Commodity Corporation of Boston for allegedly making false and misleading statements to investors in order to get them to invest.

In the 1970s, inflation-wary investors were the target of high-pressure sales tactics for diamond and gemstone investments. These areas truly require professional expertise in grading and evaluating potential investments. Many investors lost large amounts of money buying overgraded and overpriced stones from dealers who closed shop shortly after the boom faded.

As we mention in our discussion of collectibles, unless you have an abiding interest in rare coins, stamps, or art these are difficult products to trade as an amateur. Differences in the grades of coins are not readily apparent to the average person and can mean a difference of thousands of dollars in price. And the art world is filled with forgeries and frauds that even the top experts have difficulty in spotting.

DEALING WITH FINANCIAL PLANNERS

Complaints against financial planners have been rising steadily over the past few years. Typical complaints include misrepresenting the tax benefits and investment potential of limited partnership investments, failure to disclose the fee received by the financial planner from securities being sold, failure to diversify investments, and selling investments such as rare coins or stamps at inflated prices.

It is important to keep good records when dealing with your investment advisors. At the beginning of your relationship with a specific financial planner, provide that person with a written summary outlining your income, assets, ability to sustain risk, and tolerance for risk.

Money Management Tip

Request that your planner put specific recommendations in writing. A "low-risk" investment should be specifically identified as such. And finally, review and keep copies of all correspondence. It will be useful should you ever have to establish exactly what sort of advice you were given—and when.

By taking these measures, you can at least

minimize the chance of misunderstanding between you and your advisor.

SELECTING A BROKER WISELY

One of the most important decisions you will make in putting together your own investment program is your selection of a broker. Yet many people tend to take the first broker to whom they are introduced when they walk into a brokerage firm's office. Making the effort to sort through the candidates and select the broker who will work best with you can pay dividends for many years in terms of lower anxiety, less stress, and better investments.

Most brokerage firms use a rotating "broker of the day" system for assigning walk-in customers. You never know just what experience, background, or ability the broker of the day may have. It is important to talk to several brokers before deciding. Ask friends to recommend brokers they know. Then call and arrange appointments to meet with those that sound most appropriate. It's a good idea to interview brokers with different firms, too, to get a feel for how other firms operate as well.

It is a sad fact that brokers, like most salespeople, will tell you (1) what will make the most money for them, and (2) what you want to hear. So it is best to let the broker do the talking first about how he or she approaches the investment business—then ask a lot of questions. What is the broker's background, experience, and types of investments the broker works with best? If you are primarily interested in long-term growth, a futures or options specialist is not going to suit your needs. Above all, make sure the broker is interested in, and understands, your financial goals.

Ask how the broker comes up with recommendations. Are they developed on his or her own, or does the firm's research department develop the ideas? Ask if you can call some of the broker's clients for references, then choose from a list—don't accept the first name you're offered. Only after you have found out something about the broker should you provide more details about your own objectives.

You can verify background and experi-

Look At This:

ence information through your state's securities regulation department. Each state has access to the brokerage industry's Central Registration Depository. By requesting a broker's CRD file, you can determine employment history and whether there have been any disciplinary proceedings against the broker by the state regulators or the brokerage industry.

Specifically ask what fees are assessed for the broker's services. Does he or she handle mutual funds? How many? What are the load fees? Are commission rates negotiable? What are the criteria for lower commissions?

Once you have settled on a broker, it is important to provide written details of your income and investment objectives. Many problems develop when a broker makes unsuitable recommendations, even with good intentions. Make sure your broker is fully aware of exactly what you want.

Last, but certainly not least, never give discretionary authority over your account to your broker. There is a conflict of interest when brokers earn their income from the commissions charged to client accounts and can make trading decisions without that client's approval.

Money Management Tip

"Churning" is when a broker trades an account to generate commissions rather than to meet the client's investment objectives. If your account generates over 30% of its value in commissions each year, there may be a churning problem.

You should expect your broker to provide you with good understandable recommendations that fit your investment objectives, accurate timely execution of your orders, easily understood statements of transactions and account changes, and prompt service. If you are not satisfied after working with a broker for a while, don't hesitate to switch. It is your money and your future.

Reading a Mutual Fund Prospectus

When you inquire about a mutual fund (and

certainly before you buy a fund), you will be provided with a prospectus. All investment advisors will tell you that you should carefully read the prospectus in its entirety before investing, but they don't give you any idea how to stay awake while perusing these dense and often obscure financial documents!

A prospectus is the legal document that describes the history of an investment, the background of its managers, the fund objectives, its financial condition, and other essential data such as pending litigation or other material facts that may affect the fund and its ability to attain its goals. The idea behind the prospectus is to provide prospective buyers with full disclosure of all relevant information that may affect their investment.

Historically, most prospectuses have been drawn up by lawyers in almost impenetrable legalese. Fortunately, many funds now are having their prospectuses written by their marketing departments and checked by their attorneys. This has resulted in clearer, more readable documents that still provide their legal function. Also, the SEC has stepped in to require changes in the format to make information more accessible.

Specifically, as of May 1, 1988, mutual funds are required to move all fee information onto one page near the front of the prospectus. Previously, some funds spread discussions of their various fees throughout the whole prospectus, making it difficult to understand the full charges.

The new fee tables must be broken into three parts. First, the fund's management must disclose the total amount of shareholder transaction fees. These fees can be either sales commissions (load charge), commissions on reinvestment of dividends (if any), redemption fees (charges when the fund is sold), and fees to exchange shares (e.g., switch to another fund within the same fund family).

Second, the fee table must include a separate section detailing the fund's annual operating expenses. The largest item in this section is "Investment Advisory Fees" (typically 0.6 to 0.8%). The 12b-1 fee is a charge taken by funds for marketing and distribution costs. This most controversial fee can be as high as 1.25%.

Finally third, this section must include an expense ratio: a measure of the fund's costs as a percentage of assets. An expense ratio of 1% is average. Some types of funds such as international and gold funds, typically have higher expense ratios. Other funds, such as money market funds, are usually lower. Money market fund average expense ratio is 0.75%.

Although it is important to know a fund's expense ratio, don't be penny wise and pound foolish. The most important figure is what the fund does for you. Many advisors warn that you should avoid funds with high expense ratios, but a study by Financial Planning Information, Inc. (a Cambridge, Massachusetts think tank) shows that for 1987 the top-performing fund groups—international and gold—had the highest expense ratios of all fund categories. In addition, the top-performing fund for 1987, Oppenheimer Ninety-Ten Fund had one of the highest expense ratios of the 900 funds that were included in the study.

However, high expense ratios can be costly for investors over the long haul. If all other things are equal, a 1% difference in expenses on a $10,000 investment earning an average of 9% per annum will cost over $9,000 over 20 years. The ideal course of action is to find a top-performing fund with low expense ratios.

High-cost fund families in the study included load funds sold by Dean Witter Reynolds, Drexel Burnham Lambert, and Thomson McKinnon Securities. Other fund families without front-end loads but with high expenses included Keystone Corporation and Kemper Financial Services Investment Portfolio Funds.

Low-cost fund families included IDS Financial Corporation, Dreyfus Corporation, Merrill Lynch & Company, and the Vanguard Group.

The last item that the new SEC regulations require is disclosure of how the fund's costs would affect the performance of a hypothetical investment over 1, 3, 5, and 10 years.

Investment Objectives. Once you've had a chance to check out the fees in the new format, it is important to review other important sections of the prospectus before making any investment decision. Turn first to the

"Investment Policies and Objectives" section. This section describes the fund's objectives in detail. It also spells out differences in the way funds may pursue similar objectives. For example, two different funds may have growth as an objective but one may invest in seasoned blue-chip companies while another seeks out unknown smaller capitalization issues. Knowing your own investor profile will help you make the decision between these two funds.

Bond funds all typically have the same objective: to target "the highest level of current income consistent with preservation of capital." But by reading further into the fund's investment strategies, you will find information on whether the fund is appropriate for your risk tolerance. For example, a fund may specify that it will maintain an average maturity of five years or less for its portfolio. This means the price of fund shares will be less volatile than a fund which allows longer average maturities.

Typically, stock funds will spell out their first and second priorities: e.g., capital growth, dividend income, or some combination of the two. Some funds, especially the popular "sector" funds, will spell out in even more detail specific strategies such as buying special situation stocks or only small capitalization issues.

This section will also detail what business practices the fund may use. For example, some funds will use leverage (borrowed money) to achieve their goals. It will also spell out if a fund can sell short—an aggressive investment strategy. In recent years, more and more funds have turned to using futures and options to enhance their earnings. Although these techniques are often referred to as "portfolio insurance," the use of these various strategies has a direct effect on the riskiness of the fund.

Specialty funds generally have many restrictions, such as limiting investments to a particular industry. Other restrictions such as buying foreign securities, stocks options and futures, are spelled out here. A fund oriented to long-term conservative investments will usually spell out restrictions against short-term trading, short selling, and buying options.

Performance. Funds that have been around for at least five years include results in a table of "per share income and capital changes." This short financial statement details such important items as the turnover rate. The turnover rate is a measure of how actively the manager trades the fund's portfolio. A rate of 100% means that the manager trades every stock in the portfolio every year. A high turnover rate means higher costs and also implies an aggressive investment posture.

If the fund has been around 10 years or more, you will find performance data for the latest 10-year period. These data will give you a better perspective of how the fund has done through a complete business cycle. Often a shorter-term perspective can be misleading, because a fund may do very well in certain types of markets but lose it all when the market changes.

Newer funds (and the past three years have seen a record number of new funds launched) obviously will not have a performance record you can check. However, they will usually have an experienced fund manager whose past record can be verified. Find out as much information about the manager and his or her track record as possible—although it is certainly no guarantee of future success. Just because a fund is new doesn't mean that it won't be a good investment.

Many funds include a comparison of their performance with the S&P 500 Index. If the fund prospectus you are looking at does not include this information, you can easily compare it yourself. Bond funds represent a greater problem, because there is no single widely recognized measure of performance. Many advisors recommend that you compare the performance of a bond fund with the Shearson Lehman U.S. Government and Corporate Bond Index.

Management. There is a wide variance in how funds handle the management section. Some funds, such as IDS, emphasize the individual managers even to the point of including pictures. Other funds do not name individual managers for a variety of reasons. Sometimes the managers change frequently. Many experts believe that continuity in management is an important sign of stability for the fund, including those with aggressive objectives.

If the manager is not identified in the prospectus, you can usually get the name and background information from the fund's annual report. The annual report usually includes more information on the fund's outside directors. Outside directors are supposed to monitor the fund's activities without the potential conflict of interest that may occur for other directors.

Special Services. Normally, more mundane details such as the various types of services the fund offers are buried in the back of the prospectus. These items include exchange privileges between funds in the family, systematic withdrawal plans, dividend reinvestment privileges, share accumulation plan (adding to your investment at regular intervals), Keogh and IRA details, and telephone transaction privileges.

Some large fund families allow switches between various funds within that family

Type I

without assessing sales fees—a handy feature if you are following an active asset allocation philosophy. Usually you are limited to three "free" switches per year, although this is not always the case. This section of the prospectus will also detail rules for making switches or redemptions. Most funds now make some provision for telephone transactions. However, if your account doesn't already have this feature, you need to complete separate paperwork before you can perform redemptions or switches by phone.

Lower minimums for initial investments, lower fees for additions, voluntary accumulation plans, etc., are ways to encourage initial and regular investing. Funds typically offer discounts on fees for those investors who sign up for these regular addition plans or invest in larger dollar amounts, such as units above $10,000.

Notes

_____

_____

_____

_____

_____

_____

_____

_____

_____

_____

_____

_____

_____

Checklist for Evaluating Mutual Funds

In order to choose the fund that is right for you, you will need to compare various funds. The following checklist is a good starting point for organizing your thoughts:

1. What are the fees assessed by the fund? Is it load or no load? What is its operating expense ratio? Are there 12b-1 charges assessed?

2. How often does the fund advise its investors about its holdings and investment strategy? Does it supply monthly or quarterly updates in addition to the required annual report?

3. How long has the current manager been with the fund? If the fund is new, what is the manager's track record with other funds? Is the manager an inhouse employee or an outside contractor? If the latter, what are the terms of the contract?

4. How consistent has the fund's performance been? Does the performance vary widely from year to year?

5. How has the fund performed over the past 10 years (or whatever the life of the fund if shorter) compared to other funds and to the S&P 500? The average annual return for the top 25% of stock funds has been 18.2%. The average annualized total return for the S&P 500 has been 16.3%.

6. How does the fund's performance compare with the risk-free return of T-bills over the past 10 years? T-bills averaged 9.1% over that time.

7. How does the fund's operating expense ratio compare to the average? Average equity fund expense ratio is about 1%. Money market funds run about 0.75%.

8. How has the fund performed in up markets? How has the fund performed in down markets? Every August, *Forbes* magazine publishes a special mutual fund issue that shows fund performance in both up and down cycles.

READING MUTUAL FUND ADVERTISEMENTS

Over 1,500 mutual funds are currently being offered to the public. But not many people want to read 1,500 prospectuses before making investment decisions. One device that we all use as consumers every day to narrow our spending choices is advertising. Most mutual funds, especially no load funds, advertise in the major financial media and you can quickly isolate those that seem to meet your objectives.

Unfortunately, it was very difficult to make comparisons between various funds until July 1988 because funds often advertised yield and total returns for different time periods. The result is often a comparison of apples and oranges.

Effective July 1, 1988, however, the SEC required funds to report performance in ads in a standardized manner. Before the new rules, income funds would advertise the highest possible yield by quoting only the time period during which the fund did best. For example, a fund would sometimes report on the most recent 7-day period or the most recent 30-day period, depending on which figure would look better. With the new rules, income funds must advertise their most recent annualized 30-day yield. That enables investors to better compare the same factor in every fund.

Some funds, especially Ginnie Mae funds, will be forced to show lower average yields than they have been advertising because the new rules require them to factor in losses that result from homeowners' prepayments of mortgages.

Total return is the return that an investor receives by combining both dividend (or interest) yield plus (or minus) any capital gain. For example, if you bought a bond with a 10% coupon rate of return and interest rates were flat for the year, your total return would be 10%. However, if interest rates went down during that year, your total return would be higher because the underlying bond value would appreciate. If interest rates went up during the year, your total return would be less than 10%. You would receive the 10% payments in interest, but interest rates went higher, so the value of your underlying bond would fall.

Previously income funds would select the best time period for figuring total return and then advertise those figures. Now however, ads that mention "total return" must disclose the average annual total return for the past one, five, and 10 years (or for the life of the fund, if it hasn't been around that long).

Ads must now also disclose whether a sales charge is assessed. In cases where there is a load charge, the ad must disclose the amount.

The new rules also require that all print be a minimum size, eliminating the classic "small print" problem. With strict enforcement of these new rules, you can expect to see fewer performance-related ads, but at least you will know that those which do appear can be compared with others on a more reliable basis.

LIMITED PARTNERSHIP PROSPECTUSES

Although the SEC has moved to make mutual fund prospectuses easier to understand for the average investor, no such rules have been adopted for limited partnership prospectuses. Experts warn novice investors that prospectuses are designed to provide enough information to entice investors while keeping regulators happy.

You need to answer a number of questions when reviewing a prospectus for a limited partnership investment. First, you should know whether you are looking at a private placement program, which is not required to be registered with the SEC. These programs are generally designed for wealthy financially sophisticated investors who meet stringent income and asset requirements.

Public offerings are registered with the SEC, which reviews the documents to ensure that they meet the format required. However, the SEC does not pass judgment on the accuracy or adequacy of a prospectus. In other words, federal and state regulators mandate the form that these documents must take, but they never take responsibility for the substance in each.

When reviewing a prospectus for a limited partnership offering, whether it is for real estate, oil and gas, leasing, cable television, or whatever, there are a number of questions you should make sure are answered—and the answers should be found in the prospectus, not after calls to other sources. Typically a prospectus will carry the legend that the information contained herein is the complete information that is to be released to the public. If you have to get your answers from the salesperson or independent literature, the offering should be avoided. You want the details to be in writing. If something goes awry, you then have the complete evidence on which you made your investment decision.

The first item you should evaluate is the risk level of the proposition. Does the partnership depend on borrowed funds to effect its program? The more money borrowed (the more "leveraged" a program is), the higher its risk. Before the 1986 Tax Reform Act, many real estate programs were heavily leveraged to yield multiple tax writeoffs. Many of these programs were forced into bankruptcy when the tax law changed and real estate values were stagnant or even fell in many parts of the country.

The safest programs are designed to provide steady income. They borrow little or nothing to finance their purchases. In oil and gas programs, the safest programs are those which invest in producing wells rather than "wildcatting" unproven land for new wells.

A problem with public offerings is that they are often "blind pools." The limited partners are asked to invest money in a particular type of investment (e.g., income-producing real estate, and oil and gas drilling) without being told exactly what is being purchased. In a blind pool arrangement you are trusting the judgment of the general partner in acquiring the property at a good price. This arrangement, unfortunately, is subject to abuse. It is far better and safer to stay away from blind pools and invest only in those partnerships in which the properties are specified. That way you can independently verify that the prices paid are fair market value.

In evaluating an oil and gas project, ascertain how much is going to be invested in exploratory versus developmental wells. Exploratory wells only hit success an average of one in nine times! Developmental wells, on the other hand, are successful two out of three times. Of course, the potential for capital growth is much less for developmental wells. Fortunes are made in energy when "gushers" are hit in exploratory projects. However, it takes a lot of money to finance the dry spells until such a gusher is found!

A major concern when you review a prospectus for a limited partnership is determining exactly what fees you will be paying. Fees to your broker and the sponsor of a real estate partnership can amount to as much as 35%—money that will never be employed in your investment. In even the best deals, only about 85% of your money is used to buy property.

To find out what the fees are, check under the section titled "Management Compensation." Typical sales commissions are 8%. Organization expenses should not be more than 3%. Acquisition fees are the profits the general partner earns. These can vary widely. Be sure you know how much these fees are before you invest. For unleveraged real estate deals, experts suggest a maximum of 4%.

Once properties are purchased, the general partner typically keeps a portion of the income as a property management fee. That fee should not be more than 5% until your rate of return reaches 6% or more.

An important consideration is the past track record of the general partners. Keep in mind that partnership sponsors will portray their track records in the best possible light. When reviewing returns, see if the figures are adjusted for fees. Given the high fees assessed by these partnerships, a 30% annual return before fees can really be more like 10–15% actual in-the-pocket return to the limited partners.

When dealing with mutual funds, there is little real danger of bankruptcy and loss of your funds. With limited partnerships, however, it is vital to check out the financial condition of the general partners. You want your general partner to be able to survive during adverse times. In real estate, rising interest rates will put pressure on group investment vehicles. The collapse in oil prices in the early 1980s devastated many sponsors and pushed many more into bankruptcy. Because outside developments like these can never be entirely foreseen, your general partner must be strong enough to weather unexpected economic storms.

In general, see how much money the general partner has typically raised in past offerings. Is the partner trying to raise much more with the opportunity you are investigating? If so, that can be a warning sign that the program may be overextended.

You will want to get an idea how long it will take to get your money back. Check out the record of the general partner's previous programs. What is the average holding period for its properties. The average should be 7 to 10 years. For oil and gas programs, the average period before payback begins should not exceed three to four years.

RESOURCES

There is no shortage of opinions available on most investments. In addition to fee-based professional money managers who will handle all transactions on a discretionary basis, there are numerous public sources of independent opinions on a wide variety of investments.

Standard & Poor's and Moody's Investor Services are the two largest rating services for bonds. They look at a bond issuer's finances and issue ratings for the bonds sold by the company.

Overview

A number of periodicals cover the whole gamut of investments in varying degrees of depth. The *Wall Street Journal* summarizes the opinions of leading gurus in the financial markets as well as raw statistical data. A regular feature in the *Journal*'s second section, called "Money Matters," details background information for personal investing on a wide variety of subjects from limited partnerships and mutual funds to insurance products, and much more.

Type I

In 1982 the first real competitor to the *Wall Street Journal* was launched: *Investor's Daily*, also published every morning. It contains even more extensive statistical data that are of interest to stocks and bond investors. For example, the stock quotes feature bold markings for issues that make particularly noteworthy price moves or on which trade is especially heavy. If you are inclined to technical analysis, you should definitely investigate *Investor's Daily*, P.O. Box 25970, Los Angeles, CA 90025.

Business Week now features a quarterly update on mutual fund performance. In addition, each issue now features a page entitled "Investment Figures for the Week." This includes commentary on the previous week's price action for stocks, bonds, and the dollar. In addition, it lists the performance of the London, Tokyo, and Toronto markets. Particularly useful to investors who adopt our multiple-asset allocation approach, each week this page summarizes the results of a theoretical $10,000 investment in five different asset classes: foreign stocks, cash equivalents, Treasury bonds, gold and U.S. stocks.

Forbes has always been a leading magazine for serious investors. Its annual mutual fund issue is considered indispensable for mutual fund investors. In addition to the usual listings of top-performing funds, *Forbes* goes one step further by evaluating the performance of funds in both up and down markets. If you only select a fund that does well in one or the other environment, you may wind up giving all your gains back when the trend changes. If you invest in mutual funds, you should definitely read this issue, even if you don't have the time to read the magazine regularly.

Money magazine is one of the most successful publications of all time. By far the largest-circulation financial magazine, it covers a broad gamut of investment products. Its monthly coverage of mutual funds is extensive. In addition, the magazine features educational articles on a wide variety of investment vehicles. Even if you do not have the time to read the magazine every month, it pays to check the contents at the newsstand to see if there is something in that month's issue relevant to your financial plan.

Changing Times is published monthly by the Kiplinger organization. Perhaps the oldest personal finance magazine, it focuses on how to achieve good low-risk investment returns. The articles are well researched. Topics covered include mutual funds and how to select the right one for you, taxes, insurance and how to avoid getting ripped off, basic lessons in investing, real estate (especially how to buy a home), how to handle your financial affairs, and much more. It even includes things like how to buy cars and large appliances intelligently.

Sylvia Porter's Personal Finance magazine has grown steadily in circulation in recent years. Focusing on the whole personal finance picture rather than just investing, it provides information on everything from organizing your family's finances to specific tax-saving ideas to understanding how to invest to making career decisions to mutual fund updates.

All these publications and more are available at your local library and newsstand. Take the time to read a few issues and see which ones suit your individual needs.

Newsletters

Even when you've avoided all the con artists and fraudulent schemes on the financial scene, there still exists the very real problem of making money on honest investments. It is surprising how many successful people do not adopt the same work ethic investing their hard-earned money as they do in earning that money to begin with.

Entrepreneurs running their own businesses know that they have to work hard indeed to earn returns on the order of 10–15% every year—many survive on much less. But when it comes to the investment arena, there is a tendency to expect too much for too little work. Get-rich-quick schemes are widely advertised for this reason—but most are just that: schemes, not solid opportunities. The only ones getting rich are those selling the grand ideas—the "sizzle" and not the steak.

Some people, on the other hand, actually manage to do quite well with their part-time investing doing everything on their own. However, it is illogical to expect these people to compete with full-time professionals whose very livelihood depends on years of experience and successful investing.

One of the biggest growth industries in the past few decades has been the information business. In the investment field, newsletter advisories have experienced booming growth. In fact, the growth of newsletters closely parallels the fortunes of the stock market. When the market is bullish (going higher), more investment advisories are launched. When the market turns bearish, the number of advisories shrinks—even though the need for good advice is just as great, and maybe even greater.

You can receive the advice from these investment gurus in a number of different forms. Although most still publish regular newsletters, many now also maintain telephone "hotlines" for up-to-date advice. Others make use of telegrams, faxes, or even Federal Express-mailed letters to signal important, time-sensitive advice.

In recent years, some advisories have even started sending out their advice via telephone lines to their subscribers' computers. Typically, these services provide their subscribers with a phone number and a password for use with their personal computers. Subscribers call into the "host" computer maintained by the advisory service to get the very latest advice. This way they are able to get written instructions, rather than just a telephone voice, without the delay that occurs in the mail.

The Quality of Newsletter Advice. If you believe the advertising claims of the newsletters, you'd probably conclude that all subscribers everywhere are rich. Unfortunately, there tends to be a rather wide disparity between consistent long-term performance and the wild-eyed advertising claims made by many newsletters.

If you believe that all you need to do to make money in the investment markets is to subscribe to an investment advisory newsletter with a good track record, you are bound to be disappointed. Although the prices of newsletters vary from as little as $50 per year to over $1,000 per year, there is little correlation between price and performance. The fact is some very expensive newsletters provide some very poor investment advice.

How, then, are you to choose a good newsletter? A number of independent newsletters evaluate the performance of the specific investment advice rendered by newsletters. The best-known rating service for stock advisories is the *Hulbert Financial Digest* or *HFD* (643 S. Carolina Ave., SE, Washington, DC 20003, $135 per year, $37.50 for a five-issue trial).

Each month *HFD* publishes performance rankings for the leading stock market advisories. *HFD* also periodically publishes rankings for longer-term performance and its own special "risk-adjusted" performance rankings. In addition to stock market timing and stock selection expertise information, *HFD* regularly rates the newsletters' records for timing the gold and bond markets. Each monthly issue also includes lists of stock and mutual funds that have been recommended by three or more newsletters.

Commodity Traders Consumer Reports (1731 Howe Ave., Ste. 149, PO Box 254480, Sacramento, CA 95825, $195 per year) ranks 26 leading futures advisories in such categories as total profit, percentage return, best trade, worst trade, percent of profitable trades, percent of losing trades, and average profit per trade.

Selecting a Newsletter. One unchanging truth about the investment advisory business is that what works for one investor will not necessarily work for another. The primary reason for this is that we are all unique individuals. What makes sense to one person will not make sense to another. If you are uncomfortable with a particular investment method, you will not be successful using it over the long term.

Regardless of how mechanical you think the markets are, there is an indefinable subjectivity to many aspects of the business. You can get bad order executions, you can have misunderstandings with your advisor or with your broker, only part of an order may be filled, you may be yanked from the market on your "stop loss" order at prices that are far different from other investors with the same order!

A good example of this disparity is the performance of nationally known stock market guru Martin Zweig. His newsletter *The Zweig Forecast* (the top-performing stock advisory over the eight years that HFD has been publishing) features a sample portfolio. For 1987 that portfolio was up 52%, even after the October Crash. However, Zweig also manages a mutual fund—which was up a mere 8.5% for the same period.

If a top investment professional cannot show equal returns, how can part-time amateurs hope to duplicate the exact advice from a third party? Obtaining third-party advice is not a useless exercise, but you must be willing to check out a number of different newsletters until you find the one(s) that work best for you.

We have listed below a number of the leading advisories you may want to contact. However, new ones are always being launched. If you see an advertisement or receive a solicitation in the mail that looks interesting, send for a short trial subscription. You can always convert to a long-term subscription if you like the publication. *No matter how good the newsletter sounds, though, do not take a long-term subscription until you have had time to review a few issues.*

Stock Market Advisories. The following newsletters are devoted to the stock market. They range from educational services and market timing advice, to analyses of individual stocks. They serve as a good starting point for investigating stock related advisories. (Note: "biweekly" refers to newsletters issued twice every month.)

AAII Journal (American Association of Individual Investors, 625 N. Michigan Ave., Chicago, IL 60611, monthly, $48 per year)

The Astute Investor (edited by former *Wall Street Week* panelist, Bob Nurock: P.O. Box 988, Paoh, PA 19301, 17 issues per year at $197; four-issue trial, $57).

The Chartist (P.O. Box 3160, Long Beach, CA 90803, weekly, $65 per year, six issues for $15).

Dow Theory Letters (P.O. Box 1759, La Jolla, CA 92038, biweekly, $225 per year).

Dowbeaters (450 Springfield Ave., Ste. 301, Summit, NJ 07901, monthly, $100 per year).

The Elliott Wave Theorist (edited by Robert Prechter, Box 1618, Gainesville, GA 30503, monthly, $233 per year, three issues for $55).

The Granville Market Letter (edited by Joe Granville, P.O. Drawer 413006, Kansas City, MO 64141, 46 issues per year, $250; four issues, $25).

Growth Stock Outlook (P.O. Box 15381, Chevy Chase, MD 20815, 24 issues per year, $175).

Indicator Digest (451 Grand Avenue, Palisades, NJ 07650, biweekly, $175 per year).

Investment Quality Trends (7440 Girard Ave., Ste. #4, La Jolla, CA 92037, biweekly, $195 per year, four issues for $20).

Investor's Intelligence (2 East Ave., Larchmont, NY 10538, biweekly, $108 per year, six issues for $24).

Market Logic (3471 North Federal Hwy., Fort Lauderdale, FL 33306, biweekly, $200 per year).

Merrill Lynch Market Letter (165 Broadway, New York, NY 10080, twice monthly, $49 per year).

Money Forecasts (5656 Corporate Way, West Palm Beach, FL 33407, biweekly, $225 per year, four issues for $49.50).

Moody's Handbook of Widely-held Common Stocks (99 Church St., New York, NY 10007, quarterly, $135 per year).

Newsletter Digest (2335 Pansy St., Huntsville, AL 35801, semimonthly, $75 per year).

The Nicholson Report (7550 Red Rd., Coral Gables, FL 33143, twice monthly, $200 per year, four issues for $29).

The Outlook (Standard & Poor's, 25 Broadway, New York, NY 10004, weekly, $207 per year, 12 issues for $29.95).

Personal Finance (1300 N. 17th St., Suite 1660, Arlington, VA 22209, biweekly, $118 per year, 10 issues for $20).

The Professional Investor (2593 SW 9th St., P.O. Box 2144, Pompano Beach, FL 33061, twice monthly, $75 per year, six issues for $34.95).

The Professional Tape Reader (P.O. Box 2407, Hollywood, FL 33022, bimonthly,

$250 per year, three issues for $30).

The Prudent Speculator (P.O. Box 1767, Santa Monica, CA 90406, triweekly, $175 per year, three issues for $35).

Smart Money (6 Deer Trail, Old Tappan, NJ 07675, monthly, $98 per year).

Stockmarket Cycles (2260 Cahuenga Blvd., Suite 305, Los Angeles, CA 90068, 18 issues per year, $198).

Systems and Forecasts (150 Great Neck Rd., Great Neck, NY 11021, biweekly, $160 per year, three issues for $25).

Technical Analysis of Stocks & Commodities (9131 California Ave., SW, P.O. Box 46518, Seattle, WA 98146, nine issues annually, $54 per year).

Technical Trends (P.O. Box 792, Wilton, CT 06897, weekly, $147 per year, six issues for $25).

Value Line Investment Survey (711 Third Ave., New York, NY 10017, weekly, $330 per year, 10 issues for $33).

Wall Street Mircro Investor (P.O. Box 6, Riverdale, NY 10471, monthly, $60 per year).

Zweig Forecast (P.O. Box 5345, New York, NY 10150, every three weeks, $245 per year, three months for $50).

General Economic and Investment Market Forecasting Letters.

The Bank Credit Analyst (3463 Peel St., Montreal, Quebec, Canada H3A 1W7, monthly, $475 per year).

Blue Chip Economic Indicators (P.O. Box 1569, Sedona, AZ 86336, monthly, $322 per year).

Deliberations (144 Spruce St., Toronto, Ontario, Canada M5A 2J5, twice monthly, $164 per year, six issues for $40).

Desssauer's Journal of Financial Markets (P.O. Box 1718, Orleans, MA 02653, twice monthly, $150 per year, six issues for $45).

Forecasts & Strategies (7811 Montrose Rd., Potomac, MD 20854, monthly, $135 per year).

Free Market Perspectives (P.O. Box 471, Barrington, IL 60011, monthly, $95 per year).

Investment Strategist (37 Van Reipen Ave., Jersey City, NJ 07306, bimonthly, $225 per year).

The Kiplinger Washington Letter (1729 H. Street, NW, Washington, DC 20006,

weekly, $48 per year, 26 issues for $16).

The Kondratieff Wave Analyst (Box 977, Crystal Lake, IL 60014, monthly, $125 per year).

The Wall Street Digest (101 Carnegie Center, Princeton, NJ 08540, $150 per year).

Newsletters Devoted to Precious Metals and Commodities.

The Bullish Consensus (P.O. Box 90490, Pasadena, CA 91109, weekly, $345 per year).

Commodity Closeup (219 Parkade, Cedar Falls, IA 50613, weekly, $180 per year).

Dunn & Hargitt Commodity Service (22 N. Second St., P.O. Box 620, Lafayette, IN 47902, weekly, $195 per year).

The Elliott Wave Commodity Letter (Box 1618, Gainesville, GA 30503, monthly, $199 per year).

Futures Hotline (P.O. Box 5345, New York, NY 10150, twice monthly, $400 per year).

Futures (219 Parkade, Cedar Falls, IA 50613, monthly, $34 per year).

Futures Factors (P.O. Box 849, Cedar Falls, IA 50613, weekly, $400 per year).

Gold Newsletter (4425 W. Napoleon Ave., Metairie, LA 70001, monthly, $95 per year).

MBH Commodity Trading Letter (P.O. Box 353, Winnetka, IL 60093, weekly, $695 per year, six weeks for $20).

McKeever Strategy Letter (Box 4130, Medford, OR 97501, monthly, $195 per year).

Managed Accounts Reports (5513 Twin Knolls Rd., Ste. 213, Columbia, MD 21045, twice monthly, $225 per year).

The Reaper (P.O. Box 39027, Phoenix, AZ 85069, 40 issues per year, $195).

Silver & Gold Report (Box 40, Bethel, CT 06801, bimonthly, $144 per year).

Taurus (P.O. Box 767, Winchester, VA 22601, weekly, $700 per year).

Timing (3320 East Shea Blvd., Ste. 135, Phoenix, AZ 85028, weekly, $195 per year).

Money Market Newsletters.

Fedwatch (275 Shoreline Dr., Redwood City, CA 94065, weekly, $240 per year, eight issues for $25).

Income & Safety (3471 N. Federal Hwy., Fort Lauderdale, FL 33306, monthly, $100 per year).

Moneyletter (publisher William Donoghue, P.O. Box 540, Holliston, MA 01746, twice monthly, $125 per year).

Savers Rate News (P.O. Drawer 145510, Coral Gables, FL 33114, monthly, $69 per year).

Fixed-Income Services.

The Junk Bond Advisor (6349 Langdon Ave., Van Nuys, CA 91405, monthly, $120 per year).

Moody's Bond Survey (99 Church St., New York, NY 10007, weekly, $895 per year).

Mortgage-backed Security Letter (150 Broadway, New York, NY 10038, weekly, $780 per year).

R.H.M. Convertible Survey (172 Forest Ave., Glen Cove, NY 11542, weekly, $195 per year).

Reporting on Governments (1545 New York Ave., NE, Washington, DC 20002, weekly, $325 per year).

Standard & Poor's Bond Guide (25 Broadway, New York, NY 10004, monthly, $138 per year).

The Weekly Bond Buyer (1 State Street Plaza, New York, NY 10004, weekly, $200 per year).

Real Estate-Related Newsletters.

Crittenden Report (Box 1150, Novato, CA 94948, weekly, $237 per year).

The Land Advisor (378 Euclid Ave., Upland, CA 91786, monthly, $49 per year).

The Other Income Letter (P.O. Box 888, Woodstock, NY 12498, monthly, $97 per year).

Real Estate Insider (2315 Broadway, New York, NY 10024, weekly, $88 per year).

Real Estate Intelligence Report (7811 Montrose Rd., Potomac, MD 20854, monthly, $135 per year).

Real Estate Investing Letter (155 East 56 Street, New York, NY 10022, monthly, $79 per year).

Realty Stock Review (136 Summit Ave., Ste. 200, Montvale, NJ 07645, twice monthly, $264 per year).

Sound Advice (edited by Wes English, 2120 Omega Rd., San Ramon, CA 94583,

quarterly, $78 per year).

Mutual Fund Newsletters.

Fundline (P.O. Box 663, Woodland Hills, CA 91365, twice monthly, $97 per year).

Growth Fund Guide (Box 6600, Rapid City, SD 57709, monthly, $85 per year).

Margo's Market Monitor (175 Bedford St., #14, Lexington, MA 01273, twice monthly, $125 per year).

Mutual Fund Forecaster (3471 North Federal Hwy., Fort Lauderdale, FL 33306, monthly, $100 per year).

Mutual Fund Investing (7811 Montrose Rd., Potomac, MD 20854, monthly, $145 per year).

Mutual Fund Letter (205 West Wacker Dr., Chicago, IL 60606, monthly, $75 per year).

The No-load Mutual Fund Investor (P.O. Box 283, Hastings-on-Hudson, NY 10706, monthly, $79 per year).

Switch Fund Advisory (8943 Shady Grove Crt., Gaithersburg, MD 20877, monthly, $140 per year).

Telephone Switch Newsletter (P.O. Box 2538, Huntington Beach, CA 92647, monthly, $117 per year, eight issues for $87).

Investment-Related Computer Software

If you already own a personal computer or are considering buying one, you should be aware of the vast amount of software that is available to you. You can use your computer with a modem to tap into huge databases over telephone lines.

Perhaps the best-known database is the Dow Jones News/Retrieval Service (P.O. Box 300, Princeton, NJ 08540). Once you have signed up, you are able to access the Dow Jones databases covering not only stock market quotes, but also data on the economy, interest rates, articles in a number of business periodicals, and even up-to-date fundamental data on individual companies. You are charged hourly fees that vary according to the time of day you call and the type of information you want.

Competitors include CompuServe (800)-848-8199 and Genie (800) 638-9636. Their services and fees vary widely. Call and request more information from each before making decisions on which will be most appropriate for you.

Investment Analysis Software. The popularity of personal computers for individual investors has led to the creation of a large variety of programs to help investors sort through the mounds of information that are available. *Wall Street Computer Review* (5615 West Cermak Rd., Cicero, IL 60650) is a glossy monthly magazine devoted to reviewing the latest developments in computer-assisted investing.

There is even a newsletter dedicated to teaching its readers how to make the best use of computer software. *The Wall Street Micro Investor* or *WSMI* (P.O. Box 6, Riverdale, NY 10471) illustrates every month a number of different computer-generated analyses of individual stocks as well as timing tools for the market as a whole. *WSMI* has developed a number of low-priced yet sophisticated computer programs that forms the basis for its work. Subscribers are able to buy these programs at steep discounts.

The Software. Although most programs are designed to run on IBM or IBM-compatible systems, many programs are written for the Apple II and the Macintosh. New programs are being marketed constantly. It is impossible to do a comprehensive listing of programs in this book. SCIX Corporation (2010 Lacomic St., P.O. Box 3244, Williamsport, PA 17701) specializes in investment software. It carries a complete line of programs, many at discount prices.

Most programs have a demo disk that shows you their features. The following list includes a small number of the currently available programs. When writing to vendors, ask if they have a demo program and what their return policy is.

Popular fundamental stock-screening programs include the Dow Jones *Market Microscope* (P.O. Box 300, Princeton, NJ 08640, $349), Standard & Poor's *Stockpak II* (25 Broadway, New York, NY 10004, $245), *The Fundamental Investor* (Savant Corporation, 11211 Katy Freeway, Ste. 250, Houston, TX 7079, 800-231-9900, $395), and Value Line's *Value Screen Plus* (Value Line, 711 3rd Ave., New York, NY 10017,

$440 with 12 monthly data disks).

There are many more technical analysis programs than we can cover here. The "Rolls Royce" of technical analysis programs is CompuTrac (1017 Pleasant St., New Orleans, LA 70115). One of the pioneers in using personal computers for investment analysis, CompuTrac is designed to do everything a technically oriented investor needs.

It can be set up to collect data from any of a number of databases for either stocks, bonds, currencies, or futures. You can design exactly the type of analysis you want and CompuTrac will perform all the calculations automatically. It does everything from charting to drawing trendlines to plotting any of a number of different momentum indicators. This "Rolls Royce" also sells for a Rolls Royce price: $1,900.

Other popular technical analysis programs include MetaStock and The Technician by Computer Asset Management (P.O. Box 26743, Salt Lake City, UT 84126; $195 and $395 respectively). MetaStock is designed for analysis of individual securities while The Technician is for general market analysis. Dow Jones also offers a technical program called The Market Analyzer for $449. Savant Corp offers a sophisticated technical analysis program, THE TECHNICAL INVESTOR ($395) in addition to its fundamental program. They also offer an excellent portfolio management system, THE INVESTOR'S PORTFOLIO ($495). Call (800) 231-9900 for details on the programs and how all three work together.

Wall Street Micro Investor sells a comprehensive line of technical analysis software that is primarily designed for stock investors but can also be used for futures analysis. The basic program is called the "Ultra II SCTA" (Stocks Charting and Technical Analysis). It features a wide range of charting and technical indicators. Subscribers to *WSMI* ($60 per year) can get the SCTA program for only $30. Other programs available from WSMI include a Portfolio Management Progra ($15), a moving average Crossover Optimization Program ($30), various "expert" systems designed for specific securities such as IBM stock or the OEX options, and a series of tutorial programs on technical analysis and options.

Computer Programs for Mutual Funds.

As more and more investors turn to mutual funds to solve their investment problems, it is only logical that computer programs are being developed to specifically address these investors. *Business Week* offers its Mutual Fund Scoreboard program, which features a database of over 700 of the largest equity mutual funds and over 500 bond funds.

The program enables even novice computer users to specify criteria to screen through the databases. You can set parameters for such things as minimum annual return, size of the fund, volatility, and objective (e.g., growth, aggressive growth, and income). Your computer will then sort through the databases and single out only those funds that meet your predefined criteria.

You can get a good idea of the types of performance factors that the Scoreboard uses by reviewing one of Business Weeks's quarterly mutual fund issues. Because the database includes both load and no-load funds, you can specify only the type you want. You can also sort the performance data by 1-year, 5-year, and 10-year records. You can use over 25 different factors in this screening process.

For more information on the program write, Business Week Mutual Fund Scoreboard, P.O. Box 621, Elk Grove, IL 60009.

Another program, which offers more graphic features, is Fund/Search by Information Edge, our preferred mutual fund program.

Fund/Search's database consists of no-load and load funds that have a track record of at least 18 months. In addition to the screening functions that Scoreboard offers, Fund/Search has a numer of unique touches that will be of interest to multiple-asset investors.

For example, it offers a diversification feature based on the highly sophisticated algorithms of modern portfolio theory. Once you have found funds that meet your other criteria, you enter them into a theoretical portfolio. You then specify what return you expect and note your tolerance for risk (volatility). Fund/Search will calculate the optimum allocations for dividing your money among the funds.

In addition to presenting data in tabular form, Fund/Search features graphs that enable you to chart the performance of up to five selected funds (all compared to the S&P 500 Index), so you can tell at a glance their relative performance over the selected time period. The program also generates a pie chart of the recommended portfolio diversification discussed above. For more information on this MS DOS (IBM- or IBM PC-compatible) program, write Information Edge, 96 Lake Drive West, Wayne, NJ 07470, (800) 334-3669.

Look At This:

Literally hundreds of other programs are available, specializing in everything from options to bonds to economic forecasting to portfolio management. Most are advertised and reviewed in leading financial periodicals. Given the expense involved in buying most of these programs, you should have a very clear idea of what you need first. This focus will help you narrow the field. Reputable vendors should be able to provide copies or at least references to independent reviews of their products.

Summing Up

Investors have never had such a wide-ranging choice of investment vehicles. Although it's now possible to match your investor type and financial situation to tailor-made investments, it's easier than ever to be taken in by fast-buck artists that promise far more than they or their programs can ever deliver. If "eternal vigilance is the price of liberty," it is also the price of a more secure portfolio. Learning how to make those decisions wisely and confidently is the subject of the remaining chapters in this book.

Notes

_____

_____

_____

_____

_____

_____

_____

_____

_____

_____

CHAPTER 22

IMPLEMENTING YOUR FINANCIAL PLAN

A GLANCE AHEAD

In this chapter, you'll learn

- *Alternative steps to getting your financial plan off the ground*
- *How to choose and use financial advisors*
- *How to put financial needs in priority*
- *How to keep your financial plan on track.*

HARNESSING THOSE GOOD INTENTIONS

The years had been good to Nancy. She was a 45-year-old marketing executive with a major corporation, in good health, with a husband, two grown children, and a six-figure annual income. They were comfortable, and knew it. But Nancy and her husband Bob began to get the nagging feeling that things just might be too good to be true. They decided to make that long-put-off visit to a financial planner to discuss how and when they could begin putting their detailed but unimplemented financial plan to work.

It was a sobering discussion. The planner pointed out that Nancy and Bob were wasting, or using nonproductively, most of the money they made. After all, their kids still needed occasional loans, help with co-signing for major purchases, and countless emergencies experienced by young families. When a little extra cash was accumulated, it seemed there was always a pressing need for it—burst pipes, a roof leak, retiling the pool, car repairs, a therapeutic weekend out of town—and similar contingencies that are part of our hectic, modern, affluent society.

How could they "pay themselves first"—that all-important 10% of every dollar that came in the door—as their financial planner had so strongly advised them to do, when everything else took priority? Did net worth building mean a substantial reduction in their quality of life—the very thing they were working for?

By the end of the meeting, Nancy and Bob had learned that balance sheets, budgets, retirement goals, and all the rest were only so much paper unless *the plan* they represented was implemented with the same resolve and enthusiasm with which Bob and Nancy made and spent their money.

WHO NEEDS FINANCIAL PLANNING?

Like Nancy and Bob, millions of Americans would benefit from the application of financial planning concepts—but many never consider it.

You should consider the value of financial planning

- If you can't seem to put any money aside every month
- If you are unsure of how much money you will need to sustain a comfortable lifestyle when you retire
- If you want to make certain that your investment portfolio matches your investor type and financial situation
- If you want a portfolio that is truly diversified and balanced
- If you're concerned that your estate is going to vanish when you're gone
- If you don't know how much and what kinds of insurance you should carry
- If you don't know whether an individual retirement account (IRA) is still a good idea.

In other words, the concepts of financial planning can be valuable to virtually every person with an income and a desire to use it for a more secure and fulfilling life. As you read in Chapter 5, the discretionary income you set aside to do this doesn't have to be a large amount, just as long as it is consistent.

IMPLEMENTATION MEANS TAKING ACTION!

When you settle on a financial plan or strategy that requires implementation, the time has come to *act*! It does not matter if the action required is simple or complex—the important point is to *do it*!

Almost everyone struggles with procrastination. We have limited time and infinite choices for spending it. However, putting off the implementation of sound financial planning is an expensive form of procrastination. A financial plan is more than a household budget, a pension plan, an investment portfolio, or an estate plan—it's all those and more. A plan is a road map to financial comfort and security—but you've got to put the vehicle in motion if you're ever going to get there.

Household budgets, for example, don't just monitor and control expenses—they generate money that can be used to develop assets.

Pension planning doesn't just create an asset base that compounds over time. It also helps you save taxes on the money you earn today so that even more can be put to work for tomorrow.

Insurance programs can help preserve your assets—and they give you or your heirs an important financial floor in the case of your death or disability. But policies must be reviewed and updated regularly if they're to do their job.

In short, an implemented financial plan delivers peace of mind. A *working* plan frees you to do more constructive things with your time and money than simply worry about the future; *it makes that future happen*.

Time Sensitive

Start implementing your plan by reviewing Chapter 3. If you haven't yet set some goals for yourself, it's time to get off the dime. You have lots of new, useful knowledge and a wealth of good intentions that won't do a thing for you if you fail to act. This is a good time to assess your current situation and to get a handle on where you would like to go: Do the things you hope for in life seem far beyond your grasp? Are you doubtful about your ability to make complete, rational sense of where you are and where you want to be in 5, 10, or 30 years? Do you have a hard time thinking about these issues? Is it hard to discuss them with your mate?

The emotional factors discussed in Chapter 2 make it very difficult to answer these money-related questions. Built-in biases and fears can keep us from really *doing* something about the things that matter most. Couples may find it especially difficult to come to agreement about financial goals: effective communication within a relationship is always a challenge. When the subject is money, the difficulty multiplies.

Record This Information

Add a date and time to each of your implementation steps. Write down the specific things you have agreed to do in order to improve your financial life. Place specific target dates for completion immediately after each entry. Then pick a specific date each month to review your progress. Also specify the precise time of day for your review. Make an appointment with yourself (to include your spouse or other appropriate person). You will be amazed at how a monthly review will help you continue forward toward your personal financial goals.

The key points should be clear:

1. Do *something* each and every month, even if only a review.
2. Consult with *everyone* who is appropriate. Include your children.
3. If you notice a roadblock, write it down and give the *roadblock* its own date and time for resolution.
4. Year-end review should include updated financial statement.
5. Each month, ask yourself "What can I improve?"
6. Each month, ask yourself "Did I pay myself first and enough?"
7. Be organized. If you need help, hire it.

Sometimes—perhaps most of the time—the intervention of a third party is necessary. A good financial advisor can be your collaborator, validator, and motivator. Planners are futurists, they work in the gray area of the unknown. They rely on training and experience as their guideposts to help you implement your plan. Financial planners are trained to look at the whole picture.

ABOUT FINANCIAL PLANNERS

In reading this book, you've learned the principles of financial planning. They have not developed in a vacuum or some academic ivory tower; they have come about in response to the real needs of real people. The people who develop and implement them are professionals known as financial planners.

Good financial planners have a combination of education, experience, and wisdom that makes the cost of their services pay. They are able to coordinate most of your financial affairs the way a good health counselor takes care of your body's total needs.

Financial planners do more than manage investments. Good financial planners will help you find the money you need for your put and keep account. They can help with insurance, estate planning, and retirement planning. With the proper coordination, they can achieve benefits (including product dis-

counts, economies of scale, and better-tailored product choices) that may not be available if each financial discipline were handled separately.

Most important, they can create a realistic financial plan suited specifically to your needs.

Who Can Be a Financial Planner?

Almost anyone can call him- or herself a financial planner, and many have, but only those who have met certain educational standards and have demonstrated skill and experience may use one of the planning industry's professional designations. A designation is not a guarantee of competence, but planners who have worked hard to earn their designations are careful to protect them. A planner with credentials that can be revoked by a governing board is likely to be more thoughtful than a planner with no professional affiliations to risk.

In your search for a financial planner, you will encounter a slew of alphabetical designations that are less confusing than they seem at first.

Registry of Financial Planning Practitioners. Only professionals who have made financial planning their primary vocation can earn the designation, Financial Planning Practitioner, which is conferred only after a planner has satisfied certain educational standards, passed a four-hour written exam, and demonstrated essential skills. An important note: as with other serious designations, the registry has a continuing education requirement, so you know that the planner is keeping up on current developments.

Certified Financial Planner (CFP). To earn the Certified Financial Planner (CFP) designation, which is awarded by the College for Financial Planning, a financial planner must pass six three-hour exams covering all the elements of comprehensive financial planning. A rigorous continuing education program assures that CFPs keep their knowledge up to date. A CFP must belong to the International Board of Standards and Practices for Certified Financial Planners Inc. (IBCFP), which enforces a strict code of ethics and requires extensive continuing education to maintain the CFP designation.

Chartered Financial Consultant (ChFC).
The ChFC (Chartered Financial Consultant) is awarded by American College in Bryn Mawr, Pennsylvania, after the planner has passed 13 two-hour exams. This designation is often held in conjunction with the CLU.

Chartered Life Underwriter (CLU). The Chartered Life Underwriter program is the life insurance arm of American College in Bryn Mawr. Applicants must pass a 10-course program, each with an exam.

Chartered Financial Analyst (CFA). The Institute of Chartered Financial Analysts awards this highly respected securities designation only after the applicant has passed three six-hour exams. One must also have three years' experience as a financial analyst to earn the CFA designation.

Chartered Property and Casualty Underwriter (CPCU). The CPCU is primarily an insurance industry designation and has little bearing on one's abilities as a financial planner.

Registered Investment Advisor. In reality, this designation indicates only that the planner has paid a $150 fee and disclosed a significant amount of information about him- or herself to the Securities and Exchange Commission. It provides you with certain protections—i.e., that the prospective planner is not a convicted swindler—but it doesn't indicate any knowledge or skills. This device is primarily a policing mechanism used by the SEC to keep undersirable people out of the occupation.

Registered Representative (Reg. Rep.) A planner must pass the Association of Securities Dealers Series 7 exam to earn the Registered Representative designation. It tests knowledge of securities laws, but not planning expertise and allows the representative to broker securities products.

Who Needs a Financial Planner?

When Jim was nearly 55, his father died, leaving Jim's mother alone on their farm in Kansas. Death happens in every family, and every family suffers.

Like most people who lose a parent, Jim was devastated. His feelings were a mixture of grief and fear. The loss of his father was bad enough, but what about his mother? What would happen to her?

The funeral was held in the small hillside chapel Jim's family had attended throughout his childhood. He was comforted in the familiar surroundings. Sitting in the old pews where he had jostled and giggled with his boyhood friends and drawn the stern gaze of the pastor, he still sensed the underlying continuity and stability of life.

That evening, when friends and relatives had finally left the family farmhouse and his mother had retired, Jim and his wife, Anne, discussed his mother's future. She was still capable of getting by on her own, but the years had taken their toll and with her husband gone, there was no one to keep her company or care for her when she was sick.

Her most reasonable option seemed to be selling the farm and moving to the West Coast with Jim and Anne. Their children were grown and gone, and they had plenty of room for her. But she had always made it clear that she would never leave the property her grandfather had homesteaded, and where all her family had been raised. This was her home, where she would live and die.

That evening, for the first time, Jim talked to Anne about another option.

"You know," he said, drawing closer to her, "until today, I didn't realize how much I missed this place. It still feels like home to me. I sat in the church, and it just felt like I belonged. I'm not sure that moving Mom to the West Coast is the best way to solve the problem."

Over the next few days, a different plan evolved. Anne was reluctant at first, but as the details began to fall into place, she became more comfortable with Jim's growing desire to return to Kansas. They would sell their home, in which they had about $35,000 equity, quit their jobs (taking nearly $100,000 in pension benefits with them), and move to Kansas. Once there, they figured they would buy a piece of land, put a mobile home on it, and live for next to nothing. They could keep an eye on Jim's mother, and he would be close to his childhood home and all that seemed to mean.

In what turned out to be a stroke of good fortune, Anne got second thoughts. She felt they were moving precipitously. They had not been unhappy with the way they lived before the death of Jim's father, and now they were throwing everything away and heading into the unknown at a time when others were consolidating the gains of a lifetime. Perhaps, she thought, they should talk to someone else before they made such a dramatic change in their lives.

But who would be able to advise them about such an important move? Clearly, it wasn't a job for a therapist or a cleric, neither one of which could help with the practical financial problems involved. A CPA might be able to help them with some of the tax considerations they faced, but that didn't assuage Anne's fears. They needed someone with a bigger perspective.

Finally, a close friend suggested that they see a veteran financial planner, a person with whom that friend had worked for years. "I felt the planner understood what I really needed," the friend said. "Not just the financial part, but how the money related to my personal goals. When I got right down to it, I found that I needed someone who could hear me out and help me do something with all my good ideas." Without much further discussion, Anne and Jim made an appointment to see the planner.

"It's okay," the planner told them after hearing their story. "I've seen lots of people who are in the midst of a crucial change. One of the things that brings many people to see a planner in the first place is a death in the family or a large inheritance or a big change in a career. These things set off a chain reaction of events and circumstances that on the surface may not seem related, but that usually form pieces of one big puzzle.

"One of the things we commonly see when a parent dies, for example, is a son or daughter's desire to return home—it's a natural instinct to go back to the place where one grew up, where things are familiar and comfortable—and that's especially true when the deceased parent lived in the family home. To the family left behind, the home represents a place to reconnect to your roots and to gain a sense of emotional security.

"I'm no psychologist, Jim," the planner concluded, "but I've seen this situation often enough to suspect what you may be feeling."

The planner went on to recommend a cooling-off period for Jim and Anne, a time to recover from the grief and return to the routine of daily life before making any big changes.

"Your mother is in good health, and there's no need to rush back now. If, after everything settles down, you still want to move, you can go ahead—maybe with some careful intermediate steps. For example, you could take a leave of absence and rent a place near your mother's, keeping your old house and renting it while you're gone. Don't buy anything new until you know you'll really enjoy the new lifestyle. If you want to use the proceeds of one pension plan to try out a new way of living, fine, but don't use all your cash to buy a new home too soon. A year's wait might be more prudent."

Later, Jim admitted great relief when they left the planner's office. He agreed with Anne that, in retrospect, things had been moving too fast. Perhaps the planner was right; maybe a cooling off period would be the best bet.

As it turned out, they leased their West Coast house, and they moved to Kansas for a year. They enjoyed the change and revitalized their relationship, but soon found themselves longing for new challenges. At the end of the year, Jim's mother was doing fine, they missed their children and grandchildren, and they realized their life wasn't in Kansas after all.

Sometimes, when we are emotionally engaged by a problem, we can see only one solution, where an outsider can see many more. Financial planners aren't therapists, psychiatrists, or spiritual guides, but they can help address the financial side of a wide range of human issues. From this perspective, a good financial advisor is more an "enabler" than a planner.

Professional
Advice

You and Your Financial Planner

In Part I of this book, you identified your J. K. Lasser Financial Index—your investor style and current financial situation. Each style and each situation may involve different planning needs, but all may potentially benefit from the assistance of a skilled financial planner.

One of the first things a planner will do is help you assess your risk tolerance; virtually every financial decision made from that point on will take your feelings about risk into consideration.

Hand in glove with risk assessment comes an objective look at your current financial situation and whether it dictates a tax-sensitive or tax-insensitive investment strategy and whether you should be looking for growth or income, or balance and diversification from your investments. As you know by now, every financial decision and every investment strategy involves tradeoffs— between risk and return, between the desire for long-term growth and the need for current income, between tax-tolerant strategies and those in which tax guidance is more important.

And, finally, a good financial planner will be sensitive to the level of participation you desire. If you have a strong desire to manage your own portfolio, a planner will serve as an advisor and consultant. If your money management style is less engaged, your planner can handle many of these details for you, designing strategies and suggesting specific products to achieve them.

Ultimately, of course, every decision rests with you. Planning is an ongoing process; it must anticipate and accommodate swings in the markets and always be responsive to your changing needs and desires. Whatever your investor type, and however stable your financial situation seems to be, you should review your financial plan quarterly and revise it as conditions demand.

Interviewing Your Financial Planner

Once you've narrowed the field of candidates, you should interview your financial planner in depth. Most financial planners will give you a thirty minute to one hour's consultation without obligation. Of course, each professional has his or her own practice policies and fee schedule, so you should determine this up front.

When meeting with a financial advisor, here are some areas to inquire about.

Background. How long have the planners been in business? What special educational preparation do they have? To what professional organizations do they belong, what licenses and certifications do they hold? (Remember that planners with professional licenses to maintain may hold to a higher standard of performance.) What did they do before becoming financial planners?

Look At This:

Client Interest and Specialization. To earn the CFP designation, planners must have a broad-based financial knowledge, although many planners specialize. Some financial planners focus on pension and estate planning, others specialize in corporate planning, tax work, or particular investments.

To a large extent, a planner's specialty reflects the kind of clientele with which he or she is most comfortable. Some planners work primarily with people just getting started; others prefer to work with established investors or those on the threshold of retirement. Others work mainly with certain professionals, such as doctors, lawyers, or senior executives. Select an advisor who recognizes and appreciates your own special needs and whose clientele reflects your profile. Be sure your advisor's view is broad enough to oversee all your needs.

References. Don't be shy about asking for professional references. They may be testimonial letters of praise from former or current clients, or sample financial plans set up for other clients, with a track record of results. By asking for references, you may get some idea of the clientele with whom the planner works and a sense of how he or she works. If you want verbal assurance, ask for several clients to contact. Don't be satisfied with the first or only name you're given.

Professional Help. Most financial advisors work at the hub of a wheel, the spokes of which include bankers, attorneys, accountants, and specialists in different kinds of investments. The true value of your financial planner may depend on the quality of the other professionals he or she can bring to service your account.

Costs. Good financial advice is not free. The financial planner is a businessperson who works to make a profit. However, if the advisor makes money for you, then you won't resent paying the bill. The real question therefore, is how much value can and should the advisor add?

Financial planners generally charge in three different ways:

1. *Fee only*. Some financial planners work for a set fee. Such a planner may create a financial plan, suggest investments, create an estate plan or do whatever else you may need. A planner need not be licensed, but in that case he or she would not be able to implement the portions of the plan that require the services of a licensed professional, such as stockbrokers or insurance agents.

   The fee is usually based on time spent and the complexity of the work. It can be a flat amount, an hourly amount, or a percentage of your net worth or income. Fees may range anywhere from a few hundred dollars to several thousand dollars, and may be based on an hourly rate only with a minimum or maximum charge, depending on the assignment.

2. *Commission only*. Since many people balk at paying fees, many planners charge on a commission-only basis. Commission-only financial planners are licensed to sell specific investment products that may include securities, insurance, or even real estate. They collect commissions on the individual transactions that take place in implementing and administering your plan.

   Some investors believe there is a built-in conflict of interest when financial planners collect a commission on the investments they suggest. As a result, a third type of financial planner receives both a fee and a commission.

3. *Fee and commission combination*. Many planners set a fee for the services they provide, then receive commissions on products they sell to you. This arrangement tends to protect the client from the possibility that a planner will favor one product over another, since his or her income is not wholly dependent on commissions. Because some of the financial planner's income is coming from commissions, however, the planner is able to charge a much lower fee than a financial planner who operates on a fee-only basis. While this form is probably the most common, keep in mind that there is still a conflict of interest when your advisor receives compensation from specific investments recommended to you. You should take an active role in the decision making process.

Whatever arrangement you select, make certain the financial planner fully discloses all sources of compensation. Full disclosure is one of the tenets of trust on which financial planners—and any reliable professional—must operate.

The financial planner may be one of the most important people you can meet in your lifetime. He or she may become a counselor, researcher, educator, and family friend. Your financial planner could put you on the road to financial wealth and protect you from life-wrenching, costly mistakes.

BEGIN AT THE BEGINNING

When people begin to implement their financial plans, they sometimes expect things to happen fast, but structuring and implementing a financial plan in a hurry is like trying to "build Rome in a day." Dream castles won't rise overnight. It is helpful to compartmentalize your thinking by breaking tasks down into manageable steps.

The steps in establishing a financial plan follow a necessary and logical process. The first is to give some tangible shape to your dreams. In Chapter 3 you established your short-term, intermediate, and long-term goals—a procedure that translated your hopes and expectations into dollars and dates: the education fund for your children, the trips you want to make, or the future requirements for your retirement fund. You imagined where you really wanted to be in five, 10, 20 years, and more. You took control, in short, over your financial future and began to give it shape.

Many Investors Meet with Frustration in

Last September, Gerald M. Kirschner started feeling that his investments were getting too big for him to handle.

So the Birmingham, Michigan accountant gathered up his portfolio of roughly $250,000 and began searching for a money manager. It took him nearly a year to find one.

"I thought I had plenty of money to give someone," Mr. Kirschner says. "But the managers who have the right history and the right track record all want more money."

Mr. Kirschner is one of many investors with portfolios of under $500,000 who thought their search for a money manager would be simple—but who have been increasingly frustrated trying to find one who is trustworthy, experienced, and willing to take on relatively small accounts.

Limited Backgrounds

"You can find guys who haven't been in business for five years and who don't have a good client list," says James P. Owen, managing director of NWQ Investment Management Co., a Los Angeles-based money-management firm. "But it's very, very difficult today for investors who are demanding in their criteria."

The bull market of the past five years has swelled the ranks of investors looking for private portfolio management. Moreover, the wave of corporate restructurings and takeovers has resulted in lump-sum payments to droves of upper and middle executives unaccustomed to managing their own retirement money. As a result, established investment firms can set high minimum amounts for clients and still get all the customers they can handle.

And while the number of investment advisors registered with the Securities and Exchange Commission has nearly tripled in the past five years to 120,000, the best of the newer advisors usually aren't available to smaller investors for long. Money managers typically start out with smaller accounts, finding portfolio money where they can. But as their businesses grow, the accounts increase in both size and number, and the managers raise their minimums.

Balestra Capital, a New York money manager with about $45 million under managment from 25 clients, recently doubled its minimum portfolio to $500,000. "We just can't go on taking small accounts," says James Melcher, a principal in the firm. "It takes as much manpower, time effort, computer power, etc. to handle a small account as a larger account. If I'm spending time on the phone with the guy who has $250,000, I'm not spending time with the guy with five million."

Most money managers base their fees on a percentage of assets in an account—generally 1% to 2% of a client's total portfolio, annually. (Transaction costs for trades are extra.) For a client with a $250,000 portfolio, a money manager charging a 2% fee would earn $5,000 a year; for a $1 million client, a manager might charge 1.5% and earn $15,000.

The manager's workload, however, would be roughly the same in both cases. In fact, many managers argue that the $250,000 client needs more handholding, which takes valuable time.

Unlike certified financial planners, who advise clients on overall financial strategy, money managers specialize in specific investment decisions for a client's portfolio. For example, a client might hand over $500,000 to a manager, who will then buy and sell stocks, options, bonds and other investments in line with a specific investment goal. Those actions often are taken without the client's preapproval because the overall

Kevin G. Salwen, *Wall Street Journal*, August 13, 1987. Reprinted with permission.

Search for Established Money Manager

investment goal has been established. Investors, in turn, receive periodic statements of the account's status.

But the search for a manager can be frustrating. Andrea Wilcox Case, a La Jolla, California, housewife, began looking for a money manager about nine months ago, after inheriting $350,000.

Mrs. Case, 37 years old, contacted Thomas J. Hummer, a San Diego money management consultant, who arranged meetings with several advisors who shared Mrs. Case's investment concept: long-term growth that could provide some money for her three children.

After several weeks of studying her options, Mrs. Case selected a manager. The firm had a "fairly good record, and I liked the gentleman I was dealing with," she says. But a few days later, the president of the money managment firm, which Mrs. Case declines to identify, informed her that the firm had a $1 million minimum, and that her portfolio was too small.

"I was very disappointed," Mrs. Case recalls. After several weeks, she went back to the consultant and renewed her search; she has since found a manager.

Jack C. Collins of Rockville, Maryland, ran into similar problems when he left a small computer company in January and received a retirement fund payout of about $200,000. Since he needed to roll the money over into an individual retirement account and didn't feel he could manage the funds himself, he sought out a portfolio manager.

For six months, Mr. Collins, 53, researched and interviewed prospective managers, while his money languished in a money market account. He grew increasingly frustrated as manager after manager who would accept his account failed to meet his standards.

Finally, Mr. Collins found an E. F. Hutton & Co. program to which he was willing to entrust $130,000; he invested the rest of his funds in real estate.

Many banks and brokerages, though, offer only limited or costly assistance. Some banks set huge minimums. U.S. Trust Co., for example, requires $2 million for new accounts. Manufacturers Hanover Trust Co. doesn't set a minimum portfolio size but requires a minimum annual fee of $5,000.

New Options

In some sectors, though, intriguing options are springing up. Investment consultants, many of whom work for major brokerages, screen money managers for potential clients. Several have created limited partnerships that pool the money of investors with similar investment goals. Those partnerships are then managed by individual portfolio managers. Annual fees for such accounts, however, often run as high as $3,000 including transaction costs.

E. F. Hutton, the New York-based brokerage, has created a unit, Hutton Select Managment, that handles many administrative chores for money managers. Those managers, in turn, agree to accept investors with at least $100,000. Mr. Collins put his $130,000 in this program.

B. Hauptman & Associates, a Fairfield, Iowa-based investment consultant, will soonbegin a program for investors with as little as $50,000. Each client will have a separate account, but the money will be pooled and then sent to a money manager who none of the clients could have hired individually. The firm says the program should begin next Monday.

Of course, an investor can try to beat the odds in shopping for an advisor from among the newer, less established firms. "If the investor with $250,000 does his homework, it's possible to come up with the one firm in 20 that is both hungry and very successful," says NWQ's Mr. Owen. "But it's a window that doesn't stay open very long."

Now, to produce results, you must put that plan into action.

REVIEWING ACTIONS AND ALTERNATIVES

What are your choices for financial plan implementation? They are many—and, once your goals are set, most begin with selecting financial products and services.

The following *seven easily understood action steps can help make your plan happen:*

1. Review a category of financial products or investments yourself.
2. Review the products you favor with a financial advisor.
3. Make a rough draft of your will, trusts, and any estate transfer entities your plan requires.
4. Review the items listed in Step 3 with the appropriate advisors.
5. Complete a personal balance sheet annually. Ask yourself, "Has my net worth increased?"
6. If the answer to the preceding question is no, identify the area of your plan that is costing you wealth.
7. Go back to Step 1 and work through the action steps.

UPDATE YOUR WILL

Eight action steps apply to that most important of all wealth-preserving tools—your will:

1. Review your current will, if you have one.
2. Discuss your plans with family members, as appropriate.
3. Call your attorney, tax advisor, and/or financial planner as needed.
4. Instruct your attorney to draft and arrange for witness to your will.
5. Go into your attorney's office and sign the will(s).
6. Determine location of original (signed) and copies (unsigned) and place them.
7. Inform affected family members of the location of original and copies as well as content, as appropriate.

8. Check "Update will" off your list of plan implementation goals.

COVER ALL THE BASES OF YOUR FINANCIAL LIFE

Whether you work with an advisor or on your own, the steps to implementing a financial plan will remain the same. In one form or another, you will need to accomplish the following:

Establish a household budget, such as a 10/20/70 budget, to

1. Stabilize monthly cash flow
2. Create more cash for current expenditures
3. Build and maintain an adequate emergency reserve
4. Reduce debt
5. Free money for savings and investing.

Select investments that

1. Allocate funds over a wide variety of asset categories
2. Control risk while meeting your growth and income needs
3. Anticipate future risk
4. Are sufficiently liquid to take advantage of new investment opportunities.

Pay and shelter tax dollars in such a way that

1. Current taxes are reduced
2. Year-end tax liability is accurately deter- mined
3. Leftover tax issues from past years are disposed of.

Purchase insurance benefits that

1. Provide adequate cash payout in case of death
2. Cover medical and disability contingencies
3. Protect you against property and liability losses that could erode or eliminate net worth
4. Provide income in case of permanent disability.

Create an estate transfer structure that

1. Includes a will
2. Transfers assets to others now, if necessary
3. Reduces potential estate settlement costs
4. Provides for others after your death
5. Takes into consideration your charitable or philanthropic concerns.

Administer the mechanics of a financial plan that:

1. Keeps financial records
2. Simplifies your financial transactions
3. Keeps your advisors informed
4. Coordinates the efforts of planner, accountant, attorney, and other financial advisors
5. Establishes a review process to periodically assess your progress and replan and reimplement when necessary.

In the beginning, your financial plan may be little more than a financial first-aid program. If you are struggling, you must first concern yourself with making each paycheck work responsibly. You will need to compartmentalize your thoughts about money and direct the first 10% of your income to your "put and keep" account. Soon these skills will be like second nature as you regularly set aside money to replenish an emergency fund or contribute to retirement accounts. In the beginning stages, your new portfolio will probably consist of growth-oriented mutual funds. At first, it may seem that the money you are putting away is negligible, but don't forget the magic of compounding and dollar-cost averaging. In time, even the smallest deposits can produce significant wealth.

Some people choose to begin the planning process where the most obvious needs exist. If your wills and insurance are in order, but you regularly leave large chunks of cash in a checking or savings account, you should begin to direct some of that money to a retirement program or investment portfolio. Perhaps you have a great long-term strategy, but lack sufficient liquid assets to manage an emergency. Many self-employed people overlook disability income, one of the most important safeguards available, and some

Money Management Tip

people are simply unaware of the value of an IRA or Keogh.

By and large, you should buy products and services that address defensive needs first. Although there are exceptions, tax and pension planning and insurance strategies should be developed before sophisticated investment strategies can take shape. You may not yet have a large estate to protect, but you should have a will to transfer what you *do* have in an orderly, efficient way regardless of your circumstances.

Obviously, it may take weeks, months, or even longer to put your entire plan in place; once it's implemented, though, a well-orchestrated plan is a thing of beauty.

As you implement your plan, you should become good friends with either your local librarian or your local computer database club (or subscription service) because you will need a great deal of information to evaluate available financial products and services. Assuming you have a reliable advisor, think of that person as the "star quarterback" on your personal financial planning team as well as a resource for much of the information you may need.

GETTING THE MOST FROM YOUR PERSONAL FINANCIAL PLANNING TEAM

There are three key ingredients to implementing a successful financial plan:

1. Knowing *what* to do
2. Knowing *when* to do it
3. Knowing *who* will do it with you—or for you.

Building a personal financial planning team is like building a major league sports organization. You must have enough interpersonal skills to hire the best players you can afford and be adept at directing their subsequent contributions.

For example, when you invest in a product or vehicle directly (by yourself), you should certainly know the following:

THE NEW YORK TIMES, March 15, 1987

INVESTING/ John C. Boland

Why Brokers May Not Give Good Tips

They often must choose stocks only from approved lists. Customers may be getting stale advice.

When a stockbroker offers a client an investment idea the selection may have little to do with the broker's own judgment. At many large firms, brokers are severly restricted in picking their own stocks. They must toe the "party line"—if the firm's research department has not approved a stock, the shares most likely will be off-limits to the retail broker.

These restraints, which vary from firm to firm, are aimed at avoiding liability for a broker's ill-considered ideas. "The whole purpose is to give comfort that the broker does indeed have a reasonable basis for recommending the stock," said O. Ray Vass, head of compliance at Merrill Lynch, whose 12,000 "financial consultants" are kept on a short research tether.

But the price to investors, according to a number of long-time brokers, may be exposure to shopworn ideas, while better opportunities—perhaps local companies not followed by New York-based analysts—slip away. They argue that a good local broker who takes the time to do his or her own research may find some stock gems whose sparkle does not reach the home office.

One broker said research departments had become too powerful. "They would like nothing better than to control all the sales," he stated.

A Dean Witter broker, who, like others, spoke on this sensitive subject on the condition he not be identified, said that he must provide his firm's compliance department with detailed explanations whenever he seeks to accumulate shares of obscure companies. To buy stocks under $2, he said, his clients must sign a form acknowledging that the firm disavows its broker's selection. Typically, stocks that sell so cheaply lack the capitalization of more established issues. Moreover, such "penny" stocks usually cannot be bought on margin.

"We can't solicit orders for stocks under $2," confirmed a Dean Witter broker in another East Coast city. He said that last year one of the firm's oil analysts got in hot water by recommending "a nice company at F (7,8)." The broker went on: "The firm flipped out. They pulled the recommendation, and there was a systemwide memo."

The recommended issue, Weatherford International, was trading last week at 1 F (5,8) on Amex.

While both employees praised Dean Witter's intentions—"our compliance department is stronger than marketing," one said—such restrictions may not always serve customers' interests.

"There are brokers who make a lot of money for their clients not sticking to the recommended list," said a broker at A. G. Edwards Inc.

The "recommended list" draws scorn both from stock-picking brokers and from clients who complain about old familiar faces. "Why buy Raytheon or Texas Instruments?" asked a Bostonian who has worked at a number of firms.

The "list," which can contain hundreds of better known stocks, is particularly unhelpful to a contrarian-type investor, noted a West Coast money manager. "Since brokerage houses are sales firms, not investment firms, a research idea has to be something that will be bought," he said. "It must be benign, and as the market goes higher, good values usually aren't benign."

Stocks that are not on the list, of course, tend to be riskier. "Some brokers feel that using only research-recommended stocks gets the monkey off their back," said a Dean Witter executive. "I can't say that that's a stupid argument."

The constraints on offering personal research are complex enough at some firms to discourage any but the most determined stock picker. Merrill Lynch has one of the most "cumbersome" systems, according to a broker there who has worked at a number of other houses.

At Drexel Burnham Lambert, a broker needs only "a reasonable basis" for recommending a stock, he recalled, which in practice meant that "if you're asked about it you must have a file" on the company. He said he preferred that system and "felt it was in my client's best interest; but it's easier to do a 'no brainer' and just regurgitate the recommended list." Indeed, he has completed the lengthy justification requirement by Merrill Lynch for stocks not favored by the research department "only once or twice, years ago."

Mr. Vass, Merrill's compliance chief, defended his firm's system. He said that getting approval of independent research ideas generally takes only "three to four days." But he added, "if somebody comes in with an obscure company or a small company, they might take a longer time." And compliance people in general argue that such delays are a small price to pay to protect customers from risky stock plays.

According to some of those interviewed, the defensive research approach reflects a shift in emphasis among the large brokerage houses in recent years away from old-fashioned stock sales to so-called asset accumulation.

"All they want you to do is get out and sell the packaged product, the tax shelters and funds," said a broker with a major firm. "The brokers are strictly salesmen, that's what they are taught. New guys come back from training and they don't even know how to write a stock ticket. That is no exaggeration." The in-house mutual funds, in particular, offer brokers higher initial payouts than stock commissions and bring in what the firms view as captive money, which will pay management fees for years. For brokers trained in that school, stock selection may indeed be foreign ground. "Knowing what I know about brokers in general," said a Merrill executive, "if I were taught management at a brokerage firm I would want to have restrictions."

1. What is the investment's asset category and general characteristics?
2. What is the legal name of the investment?
3. What is the minimum required amount of investment?
4. What is the projected yield?
5. What is the projected term?
6. How liquid is this investment?
7. What are the potential risks?
8. Have I received at least one other opinion recommending this investment?

Your Investment Policy

It's not enough to know your net worth and design some goals and objectives, you must also determine what your investment policy should be. You would not begin a long trip without giving thought to such necessities as a vehicle, emergency equipment and adequate money. Many individuals invest by "winging" it with no consideration given to a planned approach, a "destination" or an ultimate purpose. Different investment choices affect the entire portfolio, as well.

Your Investment Policy is a set of "rules for the road" that you have established for your investing to keep you on track and out of trouble while managing your investments toward a predetermined target. The establishment of your Investment Policy is not difficult, but it does demand a little time and must be put in writing.

Below are some of the specific benefits of this process:

1. Clearly stated goals let you know where you are going with your investment portfolio; they give it purpose and direction. You will have defined and quantified information so you know when you have achieved your goals.
2. No more risk should be taken than is necessary to reach your goals.
3. Your investment process will begin with a clear idea of what types of investments are appropriate to your personality and financial situation.
4. A particular percentage allocation for each type of investment will guide the entire management process.
5. The risk reduction benefits of diversifi-

cation can be enjoyed, but the diversification is guided rather than haphazard as with most investment portfolios.
6. If you use professional management for a major portion of your portfolio, energies and attention can be focused on keeping the overall Investment Policy current, rather than spending all of your time selecting individual securities.
7. Your particular Investment Allocation Model (a key part of your Investment Policy) automatically determines whether or not a particular investment product is appropriate for you, and if it is, how much of it you should own.
8. The same model helps you "weed" out an existing portfolio and keep it properly allocated year after year.
9. The written investment policy creates an accountability to yourself, your spouse, and your advisor, who might be involved. "Spontaneous" investments or "hot tips" are far less likely to happen.
10. Investment decisions are made before hand in a dispassionate, obejctive frame of mind, away from enticing looking investment vehicles and the urgency of the markets.
11. Fear and greed are the investment related emotions which take large tolls on portfolios and people's peace of mind. Both are held in check using your Investment Policy, as it is rational and deliberate.
12. Progress is readily measurable and there is enormous peace of mind and a feeling of control when using this approach to investing.

(Investment Policy concept is with the courtesy and collaboration of Al Jeanfreau, CFP, Portland, Oregon.)

Sample Investment Policy

Establishment of an Investment Policy:

SITUATION:

Retirement targeted for age 58 (12 years)
Rollover of retirement capital chosen to allow for possible estate for children
Funds subsequently invested in 15 marketable securities
Lifestyle is not financially demanding

Widowed three years ago

Marital and residual trusts established with significant assets

Dependent children in college

STATED OBJECTIVES:

Financial independence at retirement

Move to a small residence

Extensive travel

Further involvement in community and social activities

Freedom from investment management.

Invest retirement capital for safety and income to supplement current lifestyle. Do not want to deplete capital, but wish for continued growth.

CONCERNS:

Currently investing without clearly stated policy

Portfolio has over emphasis in interest sensitive securities

Interest rate changes will have dramatic affect on portfolio value

(This value has decreased over the past three years due to interest rate changes.)

Retirement capital not invested according to investment objectives of safety and income

Portfolio is not actively managed

Suggested Investment Policy:

Invest for preservation of capital and income while maintaining adequate growth.

Maintain enough liquidity for emergencies and major purchases.

Include investment vehicles with some inflation hedge to maintain purchasing power.

Diversify among serveral investment areas to enhance safety of portfolio.

Engage full time, professional management in each investment area and use a financial advisor to help supervise investments.

Review investment policy and investment performance at least twice a year.

Place long term economic considerations before immediate tax advantages with regard to any investment vehicle.

Investing Through Brokerage Firms

Several different types of brokerage firms are available to the consumer. Most traditional stock and bond houses emphasize the stock market and current investment decisions. Most avoid comprehensive and long-term financial planning. However, a few do make a serious attempt, or at least retain a few competent planning practitioners—although the best service usually goes to the clients with the largest accounts. There is no substitute for a face-to-face (or at least voice-to-voice) interview to determine if there is basic compatibility with the planner or broker who will be relied on to implement any portion of your financial plan.

Money Management Tip

Other brokerage firms emphasize financial planning as well as traditional brokerage (security trading) services. These firms tend to be newer and smaller, and as a result, they may have more emphasis on the analytical and planning aspects of the process, with less emphasis on current research for specific securities. There is no reason not to use more than one firm when you feel it is appropriate. There is no law against using a full-service house one day, and a smaller, boutique-type specialty firm the next, and a discount broker the day after that. It makes sense, especially starting out, to keep an open mind and check out the competition.

Dealing with Attorneys

We have all heard jokes about greedy or contentious, litigation-oriented attorneys—but when your life's assets are at stake, a good lawyer is indispensable.

The first thing to find out from an attorney is whether or not he or she will be comfortable working with you as a part of a "team." That means the attorney you use should be willing to work closely with your financial planner, insurance agent, accountant, and/or whoever else you decide to hire for your personal financial planning team. If the attorney seems negative about the idea, then look up someone else. Once attitude has been cleared as a hurdle, discuss the attorney's expertise. If your biggest concern is taxation, don't pick an attorney who specializes in divorce. However, most legal general practitioners should be competent to care for a beginning estate plan: simple wills, trusts, or a review of the legal ramifications of special investment opportunities—such as closely held businesses or limited partnerships.

Finally, as with all of your "team" members, be clear and forward in asking about compensation at the beginning of the interview. There is no point going further if the money is going to present an insoluble problem from the outset.

Dealing with Accountants

If you need bookkeeping services, you may not necessarily need a certified public accountant (CPA). However, if you are a businessperson with several different accounting entities and requirements for tax and business planning during the year (and several tax returns to file), then by all means find yourself a good CPA. Again, you should focus on the *compatibility* and the *money*. If you leap over both hurdles easily, then you have found yourself another team member.

Dealing with Insurance Agents

With insurance, the caveat is (again) to use the specialists you need. Perhaps you have one agent who is great for property and casualty policies (home, auto, and so on), but doesn't know much about or deal much with life and disability products. If so, you will need two agents or brokers to obtain the protection you need. Just be certain that your agent reflects your own attitudes about money and understands your goals. Independent agents may be the best place to get a "sense of the market," but certain one-company agents may actually come up with either the best rates or best service in certain or specialized areas. Therefore, the best idea is to keep and open mind and shop for benefits instead of "one size fits all" off-the-rack insurance products.

How to Use Management Consultants

If you are an entrepreneur or executive for a large corporation, don't forget to check into the many management consulting firms that have existed for many years or may be servicing your firm in other fields. While their services may not all be appropriate, many offer personal financial advice to senior executives of client firms. These resources can be especially valuable in optimizing the links between your money-earning (salary and profitsharing plans and your personal wealth-building goals).

Using Financial Underwriters

If you have a business interest that involves the potential for public or private offerings either now or in the future, check with one or more underwriters (typically broker dealers or investment bankers) who are active in your field or industry. They may be helpful in the financial planning process if a strategy of "taking your company public" is a possibility, or in gaining access to the initial public offerings (IPOs) of other firms.

The Role of the Planner

Your financial planner is responsible for overseeing and coordinating the efforts of your financial team; he or she is the one person who is both equipped and inclined to address the big picture, from budgeting to tax, insurance, and estate planning. Other advisors seek specific solutions for specific needs, but the planner weaves these threads into a complete financial fabric.

For the addresses of the Certified Financial Planners in your area, write:

The Institute of Certified Financial Planners
10065 East Harvard Ave., Suite 320
Denver, CO 80231-5942
(303) 751-7600

or check your yellow pages for CFP's under Financial Planning.

DON'T FORGET TO REVIEW AND REVISE YOUR PLAN

Change is the one constant in the financial world. Every investment decision you make today may be invalidated by economic development tomorrow. Keeping your mind open to new ideas and new economic realities is a modern survival skill. Computers and their software are advancing at an ever faster pace and can be powerful financial planning tools. Information on all financial products is becoming more complete, more time-sensitive, and more complex to understand, so the skills of self-education are as important to your plan's success as your initial implementation steps. Take financial management and investment courses, read financial periodicals, check your statements from investment sponsors and read their annual reports. In short, learn more every year about your own money and supervise actively the wealth-building team you've created.

The planning process is ongoing. There is no end to it—simply transitions between successes and setbacks—all leading to steadily increasing financial muscle.

Notes

CHAPTER 23

PUTTING IT ALL TOGETHER: ASSET ALLOCATION STRATEGIES

A GLANCE AHEAD

Investment markets have undergone dramatic changes over the past decade. Investors now have to deal with unprecedented high volatility in traditional markets such as stocks and bonds. At the same time, they are bombarded with sales pitches for numerous new, supposedly "better," and certainly more complex investment vehicles.

In this chapter, you'll explore the multiple-asset methodology that many professional investment advisors and money managers have used to achieve above-average returns in a wide variety of economic environments. You'll learn

- *Why risk considerations are just as important as profit potential*
- *The power of diversification in delivering higher, more consistent total returns*
- *The difference between adding value with diversification and merely holding different assets*
- *How to design a portfolio that fits your investor type*
- *The strengths and weaknesses of market timing*
- *Why asset category selection is far more important than individual security selection.*

A CHANGING INVESTMENT ENVIRONMENT

The 1970s and 1980s will be remembered in years to come as an important turning point in investment history. Although stock and bond markets have gone through phases of high volatility earlier in the twentieth century (notably 1929 through 1933 and the late 1960s), it is now an accepted fact of investment life. In the long run, all markets are volatile.

The stock market throughout the 1980s was subject to huge daily swings despite a background of generally slow but steady economic growth. This fluctuation would be easier to understand if the markets were continuously being jolted by surprises. But the major surprise has been the accuracy of the consensus economic forecasts of slow but steady growth for the last 5 years of the 1980s. Historically, consensus forecasts have been notoriously wrong. For example, the October 1987 stock market crash was of historic proportions, yet the economy, as measured by GNP, continued its slow steady growth.

Just when high inflation and high interest rates seemed to be facts of economic life, the tide turned. Throughout the 1980s, disinflation and generally declining interest rates defined the economic environment. This resulted in a booming stock market dating from the dramatic bottom in the summer of 1982. Adjusting for real inflation, the stock market had made little progress for the previous 16 years, dating from the major peak in 1966.

Even real estate, the best investment for many Americans in the tumultuous 1970s, fell on hard times in the 1980s. Office space was grossly overbuilt. Office vacancy rates went over 20% nationwide, with some areas suffering over 50% vacancy rates! Even housing fell on hard times as rents actually declined in many parts of the country. Some areas were devastated. In Houston, over 14,000 apartment units were bulldozed!

Tax law changes have steadily stripped away many of the comparative advantages of owning real estate in recent years. Many tax shelter-oriented limited partnerships that were organized around highly leveraged real estate projects went bankrupt. In 1987, Equity Programs Investment Corporation alone was forced into placing 356 real estate limited partnerships into bankruptcy! In 1990 experts estimated that as much as $10-$25 billion in real estate limited partnerships were in dire financial straits.

The United States' role as world economic leader is being challenged. The 10 largest banks in the world are now Japanese. Foreign companies have made major inroads in industries formerly dominated by U.S. companies. The two largest food companies in the world are Unilever of the United Kingdom and Nestle of Switzerland. U.S. Steel has lagged behind IRI, S.A. of Italy as the largest metal manufacturing corporation in the world. Only two of the largest four oil companies are U.S. companies.

Even more perplexing has been the demise of tried and true economic relationships. The current economic expansion has already set a peacetime longevity record. By July 1990, the economic upturn was in its 90th month—almost four times longer than the average. Yet despite this favorable background, business failures are near historical peaks. Bank and thrift institution failures are at levels not seen since the Great Depression.

Individual consumers have not been spared. Consumer installment loan and mortgage delinquencies are near all-time highs despite the lowest unemployment rate in eight years! Consumers are heavily burdened with debt. Debt service requirements constitute a record proportion of income.

Other accepted economic relationships have changed. In the 1970s, high money supply growth was blamed for the high inflation rates. In the 1980s, we've seen growth rates as high or even higher while inflation declined!

The 1986 Tax Reform Act has thrown yet another wrench into the works. It has literally changed not only many long-held investment practices, but also how you should manage your business and your personal financial affairs.

Meanwhile, investment alternatives have exploded. The first step in the deregulation of the banking industry began in the 1970s with the rise of money market funds. Things have developed rapidly since then. Now you can speculate on interest rates or the stock market itself with futures, options, or options on futures. You can even speculate on stock market rises and falls through CDs!

Today is indeed the "age of information." High technology has ushered in a flood of information. As a result, it's easy to "drown" under the onslaught of available material. The problem is no longer one of obtaining information, but rather of winnowing out useful data. Today, anyone can readily access a mountain of details. Understanding and making practical use of the data are the real challenges.

There has never been more or greater profit opportunities. Unfortunately, the rapid growth in the variety of investment alternatives carries with it grave risks for the unprepared. Later in this chapter, we outline an investment approach that will help you minimize risk while still yielding above-average returns.

BUILDING YOUR PORTFOLIO: THE BEGINNING STEPS

As we've discussed in previous chapters, it is important to know where you are before you can plan where you want to go. You'll need to know how much you are worth now. Calculate your net worth by adding up what you own (your assets) and subtracting what you owe (your liabilities). Far from being a tedious exercise in number crunching, it is an important and recurring step in building and keeping a higher net worth.

After you've accomplished the preliminary financial planning described in Part II of this book, you'll know how much you'll be able to invest on a regular basis to achieve your goals. Remember, even a savings account is an investment. How much are you able to save, and how will that money be best deployed?

ALLOCATING MULTIPLE ASSETS TO ACHIEVE YOUR GOALS

We'd all like to get rich (or richer, anyway!) with our investments. If you read the junk mail investment solicitations or just the ads in many investment publications, you know that many people are out there offering systems or advice to make you rich. Well, if it were that easy to get rich, we'd all be millionaires.

Robert Nurock, a former panelist on *Wall Street Week*, advertises his investment advisory newsletter with the slogan "Get rich slowly!" Sound advice. Sure, getting rich quick certainly sounds more fun. But one indisputable fact of investment life is that no one *knows* the future with certainty. Your investment approach must be designed to minimize losses from the inevitable surprises that will occur.

In this chapter we emphasize the necessity of keeping your losses small, as the single most important factor in long-term investment success. Consider: if you lose 50% of your capital on a single investment fling, you need a 100% gain to get back to even! If you are able to limit your losses to 5%, it only takes a a 5.3% gain to get back on keel.

In defining your investment strategy, you must deal with the element of risk. No matter how smart you or your advisor may be, mistakes will be made. A typical strategy in pursuit of personal financial goals would include:

1. Preserving your capital; never taking a risk so large that it would devastate your

base capital
2. Achieving positive net returns after inflation and taxes
3. Earning returns competitive with an objective measuring stick, such as the S&P 500 index.

Your personal strategy may be more or less agressive. It is most important to focus on the risk you're willing, financially able, and psychologically prepared to take.

The third element is not just a restatement of the first. Many people think they are grand speculators. Often, though, these same people get very tense or worried over minor adverse price movements. An old Wall Street saw says, "Sell down to the sleeping point"—the price that allows you to sleep at night. If your investment positions keep you in a continual state of stress, you have not designed the correct system for *you*.

Professional investors are usually calm because they know their complete trading plan in advance. They know how much they are willing to risk on each investment. More importantly, they are able to follow the discipline necessary to ensure that a manageable loss does not turn into a disaster.

The Multiple-Asset Allocation Concept

There are two basic ways to approach your investments. You can concentrate on one particular asset category, or you can assemble a portfolio of different asset types. Some advisors advocate the first approach, saying, "Put all your eggs in the basket you know, and watch that basket closely!" The problem with that approach is that sometimes things may upset that basket so quickly you don't have time to react. "Watching closely" does not give you any better insight into future surprises.

Every investment cycle has its outstanding performers. During the late 1970s, tangible assets, particularly gold and silver, were the best-performing investments. Bonds were the place to be from 1982 through 1984. From 1985 to the summer 1987, the stock market drew most of the attention. Following the October stock market crash, there has been an increase in interest for tangibles such as real estate, agricultural commodities, art, and other collectibles.

Since you always want to earn the highest returns, there is a natural tendency to buy what is doing the best. Unfortunately, risk increases with every advance in price. Gold at $500 was riskier than when it was $200. The stock market at 2,700 on the Dow is a far riskier investment than when it was a lowly 800.

For single-asset investments, greater risk inevitably accompanies higher potential returns. In the late 1970s, many people felt that the U.S. economic system was on the verge of collapse and that gold and silver offered the only salvation. Many people contiued to buy the precious metals at steadily higher levels even though risk became much greater as prices soared. That was fine as long as their paper profits built up. But then most speculators saw it all turn to dust in a matter of weeks. The fall came so unexpectedly, so swiftly, that even billionaires were caught holding a rather sizable—and empty—bag!

Unfortunately, that incident is not so isolated. The stock market is just as liable to speculative excesses as precious metals or real estate. By August 1987, the stock market had posted a 40% gain for the year. Many investors and advisors didn't recognize the added risk inherent in the much higher prices. They had become so complacent that they greeted a record 91-point drop on October 6 with yawns. The market continued its plunge that week to finish down a record 158 points. It then plunged an additional 235 points the following week, including two more record single-day drops of 95 and 108 points—only to climax in the disastrous Black Monday collapse of over 500 points. Analysts and investors were stunned by the magnitude of the reverse. A market that had not set back more than 10% for three years suddenly was down over 20% in a single day.

The moral of the story is simple: prepare for the unexpected. When everyone is confident about the prospects for a particular investment, look out! This is known as "contrary opinion" among investment analysts.

The multiple-asset allocation concept is designed to minimize risk in any one asset class, while still enabling you to earn good returns through a wider range of opportuni-

Money Management Tip

ties. This concept is quite different, however, from merely diversifying over a number of different stocks or bonds.

Jeremy Black of InterFinancial Corporation in Denver notes that there are three main determinants of pension fund portfolio returns: timing, asset policy, and individual selection.

He notes that numerous academic studies show that over 90% of the net return comes from asset policy decisions. This pattern was illustrated very well by the performance of university endowment funds, as detailed in *Fortune* magazine, October 26, 1987. The seven largest funds returned an average of over 16% for the preceding three years. This performance contrasted with that of the New York University endowment fund. In 1981 the NYU trustees decided to abandon multiple assets and to buy bonds. Despite having highly qualified trustees, including CBS chief executive Laurence Tisch and the chairman of Bear Stearns, Alan C. Greenberg, the NYU performance ranked near the bottom for the 10-year period ending June 1986. The single-asset class, bonds, proved to be the wrong choice at the time.

No one knows for sure how the future will develop. By adopting a diversified portfolio incorporating slightly correlated assets, you can reduce risk without harming return. Different asset categories perform better in certain environments.

Bailard, Biehl, & Kaiser, a money management firm located in San Mateo, California, has done in-depth research on the multiple-asset approach. Using five major asset classes—domestic stock, domestic bonds, real estate, cash and equivalents, and foreign securities—they put together the BB&K Diversified Portfolio Index. This index assumes that a portfolio is divided evenly among the five major asset classes. Every quarter year, the portfolio is realigned to 20% for each category.

Over the 20-year period from 1966 through 1985, the BB&K Index showed an annual return of 10.2%. The S&P 500 earned a 9.4% annual return in the comparable period. Most significantly, though, the BB&K Index clearly demonstrates the chief value of multiple-asset diversification: lower risk. Risk, as measured by the standard deviation of annual returns in that time period, was only 50% that of the S&P.

Many investors make the mistake of thinking they have diversified their portfolio when they've simply purchased a variety of individual stocks. Yet study after study shows that the most important factor in stock price movement is the overall market's direction. That's where the concept of correlation comes into play. If all the asset classes in your portfolio are closely correlated—that is, if they move in the same general direction under the same conditions—you haven't really diversified. You need to include different assets that react differently in changing economic environments. For example, in an inflationary environment, gold and real estate will be performance leaders. Stocks provide a hedge in the early stages of an inflation. Bonds, however, would be hurt as higher interest rates accompany inflation. Cash and equivalents will provide some measure of purchasing power protection as interest rates rise, but little appreciation potential.

In a disinflationary environment such as the period since 1982, bonds and stocks will be leading performers. Gold and real estate will lag. International securities were sterling performers until the dollar turned higher in late 1988. This merry-go-round effect cushions your portfolio from adverse price movements.

STRUCTURING YOUR PORTFOLIO

You can take two different approaches to the multiple-asset portfolio: you can construct a permanent portfolio or a dynamic portfolio.

Permanent Portfolios

Type IV

A permanent or fixed-mix approach is most suitable for those investors who do not have the time or inclination to devote to close tracking of their investments. In this approach, you merely divide your investment monies equally among the asset categories you have selected. For example, if you have decided on domestic stocks, bonds, foreign securities, gold, cash and its equivalents, and real estate, divide your investment funds into six equal parcels.

At regular intervals, you will need to readjust your portfolio to bring all asset categories back to an equal percentage. Some investors review their portfolios annually, while others prefer to do so quarterly.

The permanent portfolio approach has a number of advantages:

- Minimum time is required
- By distancing yourself from daily market "noise," you can avoid emotional decision making
- Maximizes the return of long-term reliable trends, because you are always investing on an average down basis when you readjust your portfolio
- Transaction fees are kept to a minimum.

Of course, there are some disadvantages, too:

- Involvement and sense of satisfaction are minimal
- You settle for "median" returns
- The potential for greater profits is sacrificed to achieving greater safety
- You can't take advantage of short-term profit opportunities
- Flexibility is limited.

Dynamic Portfolios

Type I

Markets go through cycles. According to a study done by Salomon Brothers, gold, oil, and real estate posted double-digit annual returns during the inflationary 1970s. Yet during the first five years of the 1980s, both oil and gold showed negative annual returns! Meanwhile, T-bills, bonds, and stocks, which had lagged behind in the 1970s, all posted healthy double-digit annual returns.

The very fact of uncertainty about the future ensures there will always be business cycles. If we all had perfect knowledge of the future, such as what amount of what product would be demanded at what time and for what price, business cycles would disappear. Socialist "planned economies" have proven poor at filling consumer needs, to say nothing of eliminating business cycles. Individual human beings, not committees, still make the millions of daily economic decisions necessary to keep modern markets on the move.

Precise timing is impossible, despite the many claims you may hear. However, it is possible to identify long-term trends. By studying how various assets perform under different economic environments, you can weight your portfolio toward assets that have the greatest likelihood of performing well in the future.

For example, Bailard, Biehl, & Kaiser's staff have developed a number of valuation models they use for each asset class. Their asset allocation approach involves a detailed look at possible economic scenarios. They then calculate the potential returns for each asset under each potential environment. They calculate the probabilities of each scenario and then weight the potential returns.

When the BB&K staff identify an undervalued asset, they increase their portfolio's allocation in that asset class. When assets they hold appreciate and move to overvalued status in comparison to their models, they sell into strength and take their profits. For example, in the early 1980s their models identified stocks as being undervalued. They increased their allocation levels for stocks and decreased it for real estate. In March 1987, they began to lighten stock positions (even though they felt the market had further to go to the upside), because the risk was increased and other assets began to look undervalued. The key to their success has been the ability to trade on long-term trends and not get bogged down with short-term trading.

Jeremy Black of InterFinancial Corporation takes a different approach. His firm's staff have compiled a detailed performance record for the various asset categories they follow. They calculate the returns that each asset has earned over time. They also figure in risk (as measured by standard deviation). They then look at how each asset correlates to the others.

Their program, called RAMCAP (Risk Adjusted Multiple Capital Asset Program) is then used to evaluate portfolios or to design portfolios to meet specific return and risk parameters.

Rather than doing any economic projection, the program is based on the average reward and risk based on historical performance. By using the correlation coefficients of the various assets, they can design portfolios to stay within specified risk parameters.

For example, their work has shown that managed futures accounts have a *negative* correlation to stocks and bonds. That means that inclusion of managed futures as one asset category can significantly reduce your portfolio's overall variability. If stocks and bonds fall, managed futures should appreciate. Before this work was done, it was thought that gold provided the best counter-cyclical hedge for stocks. But both stocks and gold benefit in the early stages of inflation. Managed futures appear to be an even better pure hedge.

Black believes that the value of the multiple-asset approach rests in its distance from "timing." He cites studies showing that timing may actually have a negative effect on portfolio returns. He does concede, however, that it is not wise to plunge into all your positions at once, even in a diversified portfolio. For example, if RAMCAP calls for a particular client to have 40% invested position in stocks, the firm does not go out and buy the full allotment immediately.

Dynamic multiple-asset allocation offers some distinct advantages:

- Good timing can yield above-average results
- Diversification still reduces overall risk
- The client gains "hands on" involvement and sense of accomplishment
- Greater flexibility allows investors to take advantage of short-term developments.

But we've yet to find the perfect approach for all investors. Some problems with the dynamic approach are that:

- It is time consuming
- Transaction costs are higher
- Poor timing may result in poorer returns.

Considerations in Implementing Dynamic Multiple-Asset Allocations

Dynamic portfolio asset allocation should be done only with consistent objective guidelines. "Gut feel" is simply not good enough. You can develop your own guidelines or follow the advice of a professional manager. Whichever you decide, do it consistently!

Professional Advice

You may want to put together a "panel of experts" of your own. Take a stock market advisor who has a good record. When his or her position is "buy," increase your allocation. Sell down (though not out!) when he or she signals "sell." Use the same tactic for each asset class you've selected. Quantify the percentages you intend to use with each signal before embarking on the program. Remember, the whole process will be useless if you don't have an objective way to implement the signals.

When you select an advisor, it is important to find one who makes sense to you. There are many successful approaches (and many losing ways, too). You will find it difficult to follow the necessary discipline if you're not in tune with your advisor. Investment advisory letters advertise widely. Try a number of sample subscriptions.

If you prefer to meet with an advisor or planner in person, be prepared with a list of questions that are important to you. You would be mighty lucky if you found the ideal person the first time. Be prepared to spend time and effort in locating the right people to work with you. A good effort at the beginning will save much aggravation later.

Some people (including many high-priced analysts) use simple moving averages to signal purchases and sales. When the S&P 500 rises above its rising 30-week moving average, you could increase your position. When the 30-week average turns down, sell a portion. When the S&P penetrates the average, sell to your minimum position. The same method could be used with similar indexes for most asset categories.

Remember what we said earlier: 90% of successful investing is portfolio allocation. Only 10% of your return over time will be the result of timing and investment selection. Yet 95% of the information and advice that is so aggressively marketed is directed to market timing or stock selection. Don't be misled by extravagant claims. If it sounds too good to be true, it probably is!

James Arnold, the editor of the stock market advisory letter, *The Primary Trend* (700 North Water Street, Milwaukee, Wisconsin 53202) succinctly summed up the whole secret of successful investing: "The secret of successful investing is so simple, it is derided by those who claim to have all the answers... the secret is to avoid disasters." The multiple-asset allocation concept is the single best method for ensuring that you avoid the disasters in your own portfolio.

The popularity of the asset allocation approach has led to the creation of mutual funds that practice it. Some funds you may want to investigate include Blanchard's Permanent Portfolio, USAA Cornerstone, the BB&K Diversa Fund, and the American Funds Capital Income Builder.

---

10 Top-Performing Investment Advisory Newsletters
2/28/85 through 2/28/90

* 1) MPT Review (average)
* 2) OTC Insight (average)
* 3) Zweig Forecast
+ 4) The Mutual Fund Strategist
* 5) California Technology Stock Letter

* 6) Zweig Performance Ratings Report
* 7) The Princeton Portfolios (average)
o 8) Systems & Forecasts
* 9) Telephone Switch Newsletter (average)
* 10) Dessauer's Journal

    o   Unchanged from previous edition
    *   New appearance on list
    +   Moved up from previous edition
    −   Moved down from previous edition

Source: Hulbert Financial Digest

Conservative Permanent Portfolio

Type IV

1. 20% U.S. stocks
2. 20% international stocks
3. 20% long bonds (10-year or longer Treasuries)
4. 20% money market funds
5. 5% gold (mutual funds diversified into North American mines and bullion)
6. 15% real estate (REITS, RELPs, or wholly owed)

Aggressive Permanent Portfolio

Type II

1. 20% U.S. stocks
2. 20% U.S. bonds
3. 20% money market
4. 10% REITs or wholly owned RELPs
5. 20% international securities (15% stocks, 5% bonds)
6. 5% managed futures accounts (a tangible play)
7. 5% gold (mutual funds diversified into North American mines and bullion)

Conservative 1990s Dynamic Portfolio

Type III

1. 20% money market
2. 20% U.S. stocks
3. 15% international securities
4. 15% real estate (REITS or RELPs wholly owned)
5. 5% gold
6. 25% U.S. bonds

Aggressive 1990s Dynamic Portfolio

Type I

1. 15% money market fund
2. 20% U.S. stocks
3. 25% U.S. bonds
4. 20% international securities
5. 10% real estate (REITs or RELPs) or wholly owned
6. 5% gold
7. 5% managed futures account (play on tangibles)

CHAPTER 24

TEACHING CHILDREN ABOUT MONEY

A GLANCE AHEAD

In this chapter, you will learn
- *How and when children find out about money*
- *How to teach your children the importance of money's role in society*
- *When to encourage your children to consider optional investing opportunities*
- *To teach your children that money helps meet our needs for tommorrow*

A Lesson in Value

When Ben was just four years old his grandfather gave him a silver dollar on his birthday. Ben was barely able to carry on a conversation with Grandpa much less appreciate the value of the gift. Grandpa somehow made Ben understand just how special the old silver dollar was and Ben's dad showed him how to put it away in a place where it would be safe but also where he could go to look at it.

On Ben's fifth birthday, his grandfather gave him another silver dollar, like the first, minted at the turn of the century. And by the time Ben was nine years old, he had six fine old silver dollars.

By this time, Ben had grown familiar with money and especially with what money could buy. And even though he thought his silver dollars were beautiful, shiny things, they no longer meant quite as much to him unless he could buy something with them. Another year went by and his coin collection grew to seven.

On his tenth birthday, Ben had a few questions for his grandfather and for his dad.

"Grandpa, are you going to keep giving me silver dollars on my birthday?"

"Well, Ben, just as long as I'm around," said grandpa.

"Dad, when are you going to let me spend them?"

"Son, those silver dollars are worth a little more than you might think. They're very old, and the truth is, the older they get, the more they're worth."

"Yes, Dad, but they aren't doing me much good just laying around. I'd sure like to spend them."

"Tell you what," offered his grandfather. "I'll buy those silver dollars back from you and give you an extra 25 cents for each one."

"Now, Pop," said Ben's dad. "Don't you think you ought to give Ben a little time to think about it?"

"I have thought about it," said Ben eagerly. "It's a deal, Grandpa."

Ben received $8.75 from his grandfther and gave up the silver dollars. He went to the store and bought a new baseball bat and spent the change on baseball cards and bubblegum.

During that school year, Ben got a little shock. He learned one day that the kind of silver dollars his grandfather had been giving him were worth far more than ordinary dollars, much more.

On his eleventh birthday, Ben met his grandfather as he drove up to the house.

"Hi, Ben!" his grandfather called. "Got another silver dollar for you. Maybe you can start fresh."

"Yes, maybe, Grandpa. But you know, that was kind of dumb for me to sell you those silver dollars."

"Think so," smiled his grandfather slyly. "Why?"

Ben told his grandfather what he's learned in the last year.

When he was finished, his grandfather opened the trunk and retrieved a small velvet bag. He gave it to Ben.

"Silver dollars?" asked Ben.

"You bet. All seven, or eight of them," smiled his grandfather.

"But you owe me ten dollars."

"It's a deal," said Ben. "And thanks."

Some parents have a hard time relating the importance of money matters to their children. There are pitfalls and false starts that can hinder a child's progress toward an understanding of financial matters and of the responsibility that goes with them. Some parents tumble by using money as a disciplinary tool and others by failing to help their children set realistic goals. Worst of all, some simply ignore the issue. Refer to the goal-setting strategies outlined in Chapter 3; and read The 10-20-70 Money Management Tips discussed in Chapter 4.

It is a mark of wisdom to teach children about money at an early age. Give your four-year olds different coins so they can learn their values. By the time they are entering first grade, assign new challenges and tasks so they learn to relate to the real value of money and to earning. When they're a little older, take them to a bank to open their personal account. Give your kids the freedom to make their own deposits and draw attention to their passbooks which will show how savings grow.

Be careful not to link money with punish-ments, rewards, or chores. The idea is to teach kids the value of money rather than the sway it holds over our lives.

An Allowance Makes it Real

Children will most likely come into their first contact with money at play, fingering shiny coins and learning that they can be fun in themselves. They will learn—and sometimes the hard way—just which coins are worth what.

Some experts believe that when a child knows how to count, he or she should be ready to handle small sums of money. It may not be advisable to start allowances before ages six to eight. This will depend on the child's maturity. Remember most children under ten do not have a grip on time. And time is an important influence on money., Regardless, it's a lesson that can be learned using some of the basic compounding principles taught in chapters 4 & 5.

A good way to teach an easy lesson in deferred gratification is to give your child a small amount of cash and ask that it be kept until a couple of days later when something at a favorite store can be purchased. This thoughtful approach to spending will help curb natural impulsive behavior, a very difficult value for most parents to teach.

Settling on the size of the allowance is usually the parents' first consideration. While the size of an allowance will vary owing to the constraints of individual family incomes, the sum can be apportioned so that part must be used for school lunches and supplies, another part for after-school snacking, with some left over to be used as the child sees fit. It can be spent on a treat or saved toward purchasing a favorite toy or an article of clothing (put-and-take). This is embryonic budgeting. It's good to have a little "play money," money to spend freely and without parental judgement.

Older children will soon be able to learn how to work within a budget, to "allocate" money for the expenses they know need to be met each day. For example, one weekly allowance might cover school lunches, bus fare, and telephone calls, and some left over for fun. Later on, into those turbulent years of adolescence, the allowance becomes more of a stipend given by the good graces of parents.

It's important to instill the working concept of budgeting early in the teens. It's a lesson that may have to be learned the hard way. This lesson can be lost if you give in to your son or daughter each time he or she blows a weekly allowance before his/her weekend activities begin. A pout from a suppliant daughter may tug at your heart strings, but don't let it draw your purse strings.

Remember, the real purpose of an allowance is to reinforce the fact that funds, in whatever family context, are limited. Money is to be spent but spent prudently, and when it runs out, there isn't any more—at least not immediately.

Earn and Learn

Allowances can work well to familiarize your children with hard cash, but, as virtual handouts, they seldom garner the respect that the products of earning power do. When kids begin to equate remuneration in money form with a commensurate working endeavor, they begin to understand the most abstract aspect of money: its value. If your teenage son conveys his desire to you to earn a little extra money for the weekend, let him wash the car, or spruce up the landscaping. Younger kids may present more of a challenge. Some kids can fold clothes and even do laundry. They can sweep sidewalks and clean the yard, wash the dog or stack wood. All of these can be done "for hire" from time to time and need not become a regimen.

But beware. The concept can be taken a little too far. Many kids have a tendency to take advantage of the "for hire" concept by petitioning for fiscal recompense for regularly shared family chores, like bed-making, picking up toys, feeding pets, or setting the table.

Remember, It's Still Their Money

While children need the benefit of sound guidance, they should also be able to make very real decisions about spending their own money. While a parent may not always be very pleased with the spending decision, it's a good way to build trust.

Child development specialists often agree with financial advisors that children should become more acquainted with how to spend before learning how to save.

Parental Example

The way parents handle money imperceptibly molds their children's attitudes—fears and desires. Many parents have difficulty themselves with their own needs and those of the family. Each member of the family has different priorities and each feels his/her needs are important.

Parents have sacrificed for the needs of their families almost as a tradition. Today, most families look at the needs of all family members and since many moms are in the work force, they have clothing and professional needs that must be met. Have you known of a parent who went without getting their own teeth fixed so that their child could have music or dance lessons? This is not so extreme. It is natural for parents to want to sacrifice for their children, to give them a fulfilling and better life.

Some have a value conflict with the demands of today's teenagers and their expectations for name-brand clothing, cars, ski trips, etc. How do parents balance all the demands of today within the family and yet execute a workable financial plan that addresses retirement and college needs as well?

The principles of using the 10-20-70 plan are referred to over and over, but the lesson of permission to spend and permission for each family member to have "spending money" is imperative. In your 20% PUT AND TAKE budget, subaccounts can be formed; one for Dad as his "toy account," one for Mom as her "clothing and personal allowance," and one for each child. These PUT AND TAKE funds are as simple as the piggy bank or your credit union account. The point is that money must be accessible for spending on your "NOW NEEDS," but limited to a responsible percentage of take home pay.

Family counselors tell us that at least 85% of the arguments in young marriages are over money. Using the PUT AND TAKE concept with pre-agreed allowances takes a lot of the conflict out of money management for parents and kids. Try this as an idea. Each person will gain a pride in his own account and each person in the family will be responsible for meeting his/her own short-term needs. This technique also teaches that money managed with freedom to spend with a predetermined limit frees the rest of the budget for living expenses and PUT AND KEEP (investment) funds.

Like teaching any skill, your child needs to learn the very basic principles of spending controls within limits and with your permission. You can set some guidelines and standards that require responsible behavior on the part of your child. Should money from his/her PUT AND TAKE fund be unwisely spent, don't replace it. Stay on budget. People become responsible with money when they develop discipline. The concept of PUT AND TAKE makes it fun.

Good management principles show in the financial statements of families. It isn't surprising that those who have a plan for investing, saving, spending, and overall goals, seem to achieve even more than families who may have much larger incomes. When you pay attention to money behavior, you'll achieve your objectives. A family without that discipline and without predetermined objectives and goals will find that they struggle with power over money and accountability within the family. These power struggles will pass on to the children and can have long-lasting emotional consequences.

The Wisdom of Saving

There is a fable of Aesop's about an industrious, foresighted ant, and a happy-go-lucky, spend-thrift grasshopper fond of fiddling away the warm, secure summer days. Again and again, the ant, loaded with forage, trudged slowly in the hot sunlight past the recumbent, snoozing grasshopper in the shade to deposit its stores safely.

"Wake up, grasshopper!" shouted the tiny voice. "Old Man Winter's around the bend."

But the complacent grasshopper answered back, "Why should I?" I've got plenty to eat all around me. The grass is green and thick, and the crickets still sing at night. Be on your way, you silly ant!"

Everyone knows what happened when the snow flew. The ant had saved and survived. The grasshopper had squandered and perished.

For your children, it's a little easier for them to think not so much as how saving can protect, but rather how it can work to attain the objects of one's desires. A parent can arouse this powerful motive by identifying one of his child's longings: a trip to the Big City, a bicycle, a new camera. Then take it from there: figure out the cost and availability or scheduling; plan how much money must be set aside each week to pay for it (put-and-take).

About That Job...

If your children have an awareness of money values and have learned a work ethic, you will be pleased when your teenager comes home after school and says, "Dad! I got a job!" Your child may be excited at that sense of independence. Imagine their own money. You may hear dreams of a new car or the latest electronics, but it's a good idea to limit those jobs to about 20 hours per week. For some students work hours should be even less than 20, especially if they are struggling with academics or their hours leave little time for rest.

During the school years, again comes that challenge of what a child has a right to be paid for and what he does not.

For example, don't give your children money just because they behaved like perfect ladies and gentlemen during a family reunion; or slip them ten dollars for every "A" inked on their report cards. It's okay to reward performance from time to time in a monetary way. But, some parents find themselves trapped in a money vs. behavior routine.

A Lesson in Investing

In the middle of the 1980's more than two million people between the ages of 10 and 19 in the U.S. owned stocks or shares in mutual funds. Their approaches differ. Some like to take the money they earn from odd

464   TEACHING CHILDREN ABOUT MONEY

jobs and summer employement and invest it. With the close guidance of parents, others convert windfalls like inheritances of gifts and accumulate a good amount of mutual fund shares.

The question is, how can parents encourage children to consider the advantages of making their money grow? Not everyone is a Wall Street wizard, however easy managed mutual funds make investing. It's good to teach the value of the more distant reward. It's an idea realized only through systematic investment, putting away a few dollars each month. Simple self-discipline. Simple patience. And often, so simple to learn. (see Chapter 5: Dollar Cost Averaging.)

A good way to show how money can grow is to use the example of a growth mutual. The chart below assumes that a growth mutual fund was purchased with an initial $250 in December ten years ago. Each month $150 was invested systematically for the following ten years. Note that the total invested was $18,250. The ending balance was $42,062, an annual internal rate of return of 15.9%.

Some parents have used the dollar-cost-averaging approach to accumulate college funds. This is part of their financial planning. They have also given their children the opportunity to join with them as an investment partner using the PUT AND KEEP concepts and investing part of their child's allowance allocated for this purpose. The child's portion may be $50.00 and mom and dad match with $100.

There is a tremendous sense of pride and

SYSTEMATIC CONSTANT DOLLAR INVESTMENTS
Growth Mutual Fund
$150.00/month - 10 years

| --------------Cash Inflows and Outflows-------------- | | | | | | ----Holding---- | |
| | | ----------Dividends---------- | | | Taxes | Market | |
Invest	Withdraw	Income	Cap Gns	Reinvest	Due	Value	Shares
250						250	66
1,800	0	36	0	36	0	2,390	503
1,800	0	101	0	101	0	5,370	859
1,800	0	171	16	186	0	6,636	1,216
1,800	0	240	499	739	0	9,955	1,720
1,800	0	209	1,196	1,405	0	13,675	2,238
1,800	0	379	4,237	4,616	0	16,857	3,595
1,800	0	440	891	1,331	0	24,480	4,200
1,800	0	385	2,705	3,091	0	30,959	4,953
1,800	0	768	4,337	5,105	0	32,041	6,013
1,800	0	792	629	1,421	0	42,062	6,522
18,250	0	3,522	14,509	18,031	0	42,062	6,522

Ending Market Value Attributable to Principal:	21,286	3,301
Income:	3,895	604
Capital Gain:	16,881	2,618
Annual Internal Rate of Return:	15.9%	

Source: CDA Technologies

an enormous wealth of learning when this technique is used. Remember that in our earlier chapters we talked about the reduction and management of risk. Follow the chart from the first years through the tenth year. See how time as a risk reducer and dollar-cost-averaging work so very well together. Try this idea.

Tax Facts for Children with Their Own Income

Some taxpayers are disturbed with the new "kiddie tax" as well as the "old age tax", both recent changes since the Tax Reform Act of 1986. The kiddie tax is a special set of tax rules that affect children under 14 who have investment income. Earned income is taxed at their tax rate. Mom and Dad get stuck with the paperwork and a lot of parents are getting confused. Adding dividends, interest and capital gains, it is quite easy for a child's total unearned income to exceed $500 and that's enough to trigger the tax. Signing your child's tax return properly takes some careful thought. The correct way, the IRS says, is: Janet McCann by Dianna McCann, parent (or guardian) for a minor.

The Internal Revenue Service claims that of the thousands of returns filed for minors most involved incomes of less that $5,000. Since tax rules for children used to be simple (they filed for investment income only over $1,000 and anything over that was taxed at their rate, usually only 11%) the new rules seem very complex.

Now only the first $500 of a child's investment income isn't taxed. The next $500 is taxed at the child's rate (usually the minimum of 15%). Any additional, unearned income is taxed to the child, but at the parent's rate.

To figure the tax, parents need to do their own return first, then their child's. They will compute the kiddie tax using instructions on IRS Form 8615. This form is filed with the child's return.

Things get more complicated: You must sign your child's return or you may not represent your child without a power of attorney if the child's return is audited. Also the child is responsible for any penalties or interest assessed by the IRS because a return for your child wasn't filed. According to a recent *Wall Street Journal* report, Michael

---

PLANNER'S TIP

If a parent or grandparent were to reach age 59 1/2 by the time the child reaches college age, you might consider saving for college through an annuity (fixed or variable). An annuity defers the tax until the funds are withdrawn. If you're not sure how responsible or serious your child will be at age 18, the annuity gives you control—you do not have to disburse funds until you decide to do so. Uniform Gift(s) to minors's accounts are the children's property at majority.

Savage, A New York tax attorney was quoted, "That is, children pay for the sins of the parent."

Beginning in 1989, parents have the option of reporting a child's income on their own returns or filing one for their child if three conditions are met:

1) The child has only interest and dividend income

2) The child's income is over $500 but under $5,000

3) No estimated payments or back-up withholding were paid under the child's name and Social Security number.

Ways to Avoid the Kiddie Tax

You can avoid the kiddie tax in a number of ways. One of the most common routes is to set up a simple trust: the trust pays the tax, not the child. The child is beneficiary of the trust. This works as long as the money isn't distributed to the child. The trust will pay a 15% tax on all income up to $5,000. After that it will be taxed at 28%.

If you have several children in the family, you can set up the trust to "sprinkle or spray" income to the over 14-year-old children. The trust would not pass income or assets to younger children until they pass age 14. The trust idea isn't for everyone. It becomes a math problem since the greater benefit is a tax rate of 28% versus a personal rate of 33%. If you are transferring assets to young children or are thinking about it, you may want to reconsider your investment program. You might decide to use Series EE U.S. Savings Bonds, with a tax on the interest postponed until the bonds are cashed, or municipal bonds where there's no tax on the interest. You might consider growth mutual funds where dividends are low because the investment emphasis is on growth through appreciation of the shares, however capital gains are taxed. Another investment concept usable for older people is to use the Annuity or life insurance products that shelter income. Remember, too, that you are allowed to gift money to anyone at $10,000 per beneficiary per year without estate or gift-tax consequences.

Summing Up

Many of the concepts and beliefs we have as adults regarding money were learned consciously and subconsciously during our childhoods. Money has been used as punishment and reward. Neither is the best way money can be used. People who grew up with conflict over money have trouble with money as adults. Mixed messages may plague an adult involving money fears and insecurities—the fear of losing or being abondoned.

Let's get back to some basic psychology... recall former chapters when we talked about "near-term gratification needs" and "deferred gratification needs."

In Chapter 4, you learned how to use the 10-20-70 BUDGET for cash flow planning for yourself.

Use the same principles for your kids. You might consider, for a small child, two piggy banks: one for their "put-and-keep" account, and one for their "put-and-take" account. An allowance of dollars can be divided with permission to spend and enjoy the "put-and-take" money and a lesson in deferred gratification needs by saving the second piggy bank for longer-term plans. This money could be invested in a money market fund ($25.00 or more) for compounding or by using a growth mutual fund with a minimum monthly deposit of $10.00 to $50.00 for college education. Parents can match the child's deposit and grandparents can help too.

The bottom line resides in the significance of the lesson we try to teach our children: that money is to enjoy as well as to meet our needs tomorrow.

Since parents in the past have used money to punish as well as to reward, it is important that you do ot use money to manipulate your children emotionally, but rather to teach sound money habits.

A little child psychology may help. No one wants to wait for pleasure... especially a kid.

Notes

_____

_____

_____

_____

_____

_____

_____

_____

_____

_____

_____

_____

_____

CHAPTER 25

SURVIVING THE FINANCIAL MARKETS IN THE 1990s

A GLANCE AHEAD

In previous editions of J.K. Lasser's Personal Investment Planner, *this chapter was devoted to economic and investment forecasts by a panel of nationally recognized financial planners and investment advisors. However, numerous considerations made that approach impractical for the current edition.*

As we were nearing the completion of this year's update, Iraq invaded Kuwait. The resulting crisis, and the fact that as we went to press there appeared little likelihood of a prompt settlement satisfactory to all parties, made the very difficult job of forecasting even more treacherous than usual. Two weeks after the initial invasion, it was clear that there was little consensus among leading experts about the potential effects the 1990 Middle East crisis would have on the economy and investment markets.

In situations such as the Iraq invasion, there is a tendency to focus solely on that event to the exclusion of other important factors. It would be costly to ignore other major domestic and international events such as the Savings & Loan (S&L) fiasco in the U.S., the planned 1992 economic integration of Western Europe, the freeing of Eastern European countries to pursue independent political and economic aspirations, and the unification of Germany. Each or all of these events have profound financial implications in their own right.

In our opinion the early 1990s represent a significant transition period from the high flying decade of the '80s. It is critical to the financial well-being of investors that they understand that times are changing. Flexibility is a key characteristic of any successful investor. What worked in the 1980s, may not be as successful in the next decade.

In the pages that follow we have tried to give you a broad overview of key domestic and world developments and how they may affect your investment decisions. We discuss each asset class with reference to international developments particularly in Europe and domestic prospects. In addition we have provided guidelines to assist you in understanding economic changes and how they may affect your investments.

Many investors make the mistake of withdrawing totally into cash or cash equivalents when crises develop. Keep in mind that crises also represent opportunities.

In this chapter you will learn:
- *How multiple-asset diversification enables you to take advantage of world events while limiting your losses if your forecast is wrong.*
- *The economy's prospects by late 1990 and what indicators to watch to tip you off on its future direction.*
- *What developments in Europe mean to you and how you might take advantage of them.*
- *How to put together a simple portfolio designed to perform better than average with lower risk.*

WHAT'S PAST IS PROLOGUE:
The 1980s

As we mentioned above, it is a mistake to assume that what worked before will necessarily work now. In other words, every investment has its cycles. To the best of our knowledge there is no perfect investment. The key to long term investment success is recognizing this very simple principle and adjusting your investment portfolio accordingly. Take a longer term perspective though. For example, even though stocks were big winners during the 1980s, there were certainly periods of six to 12 months in which stocks lagged behind other assets. However, over the ten-year-period, few investments outperformed common stocks.

During the 1980s, stocks and bonds were the big winners. In the 1970s, gold, silver and other tangibles were the most profitable investments. Below we have detailed the performance of major investments for the decade of the '80s:

Japanese Stocks (in U.S. dollars)	956%
Impressionist art	771%
International Stocks (in U.S. dollars)	449%
U.S. stocks (S&P 500)	376%
American paintings (pre-WWII)	335%
Growth & Income stock funds	320%
Chinese ceramics	317%
Growth stock funds	310%
Balanced funds	262%
Long-term Treasury bonds	232%
Intermediate Treasury bonds	200%
Money market funds (taxable)	150%
Municipal bonds	138%
Diamonds (rough cut)	76%
Real estate (single family, median)	65%
Inflation (Consumer Price Index)	64%
Gold	- 21%
Farmland	- 24%
Oil	- 34%
Silver	- 83%

Source: USA TODAY

THE GREAT CRASH REVISITED

Even three years later, the great stock market crash of October 1987 still weighs heavily on the minds of investors. Despite rallying to new highs in 1990, evidence of the damage done to investor psyches is easy to find. Trading volume in the (Standard and Poors) S&P 500 futures index and the S&P 100 OEX options markets collapsed following the crash and never fully recovered. Institutional volume as a percentage of total volume is even greater now than before the crash as individual investors continue to shy away from buying stocks directly, opting instead for mutual funds.

One significant change the crash did initiate was a greater acceptance of the benefits of multi-asset diversification. After the crash, "asset allocation" became a hot buzz word in financial circles. By 1990 there were 39 asset allocation funds being offered to the public.

It is not difficult to understand the attraction for investors. In the year of the crash, 1987, a number of asset allocation funds significantly outperformed the stock market as measured by the S&P 500 Index (+5.23%). For example, Dreyfus Capital Value climbed 34.45%, Permanent Portfolio was up 13.15%, and Blanchard Strategic Growth posted a 16.37% gain. Asset allocation funds include:

Fund	Load/ No Load	Phone
AMEV Asset Allocation	L	(800)872-2638
BB&K Diversa	NL	(800)882-8383
Blanchard Strategic	NL	(800)922-7771
Calvert Social Invest-Mgd Growth	L	(800)368-2748
Dreyfus Capital Value	L	(800)645-6561
Flex Growth	NL	(800)325-3539
Flex Income & Growth	NL	(800)325-3539
Integrated Total Return	L	(800)821-5100
Lowry Market Timing	L	(800)645-0027
MIMLIC Asset Allocation	L	(800)443-3677
Monitrend	L	(800)251-1970
Morison Asset	L	(800)325-9244
Nat'l Strategic Allocation	L	(800)223-7757
Oppenheimer Asset Allocation	L	(800)525-7048
Paine Webber Asset Allocation	L	(201)902-8314
Permanent Portfolio	NL	(800)531-5142
Primary Trend	L	(800)443-6544
Pru-Bache Flexi - Aggres.	L	(800)225-1852
Pru-Bache Flexi - Conservative	L	(800)225-1852
USAA Cornerstone	NL	(800)531-8000
Rightime	L	(800)242-1421
Rightime Blue Chip	L	(800)242-1421
Schield Aggressive Growth	L	(800)826-8154

Schield Value	L	(800)826-8154
SFT Asset Allocation	L	(800)523-2044
Shearson Multiple Opportunities	NL	(800)368-3863
Strong Investment	L	(800)368-3863
Strong Opportunity	L	(800)368-3863
Strong Total Return	L	(800)368-3863
Vanguard Star	NL	(800)662-7447

ECONOMIC OUTLOOK: RECESSION AHEAD IN THE 1990s

As the decade of the '80s pulled to a close, economists argued whether the historical business cycle had finally been repealed. Would the Federal Reserve be able to engineer a "soft landing"? A "soft landing" is considered an economy that grows at a slower pace, generally below 2% per year. Theoretically this would engender a moderate rise in unemployment. Such a slowdown, it was argued would prevent an overheated economy from falling into a recession (negative economic growth) with all the associated adverse consequences that would entail.

Despite widespread predictions that an economic recession would follow the stock market crash of October 1987, the expansion continued to chug ahead. However, by late 1990 it was evident that the record-long peacetime expansion was getting long in the tooth. Gross National Product (GNP) growth averaged an anemic 1.3% in the five quarters ending the second quarter of 1990. The sharp deceleration began in the spring of 1989. No quarter in this time period was 1.7%. That compares to the long-run average potential growth of 2.5%.

While such slow growth fell within the definition of a "soft landing," rather than a recession, a look at the details of GNP figures reveals serious problems. For example, if production that went into inventories is excluded for the second quarter 1990 figures, final sales actually fell by 1.5% in the quarter. In other words, no part of the economy—consumer spending, business investment, construction, nor even exports—contributed any real strength to the economy in the spring of 1990.

That falls far short of the more sought after "soft landing." The August 1990 invasion of Kuwait by Iraq came at the worst possible time. The invasion boosted oil price (from the $20 level to over $30 in a few short weeks). That increase in energy prices will slow economic growth even more. Higher energy prices will lead to rising inflation eventually due to the pervasive nature of energy costs for virtually every production and distribution process. Higher energy costs increase the operating costs for many companies and further hurt businesses that depend on car travel and on consumer spending. Even before the invasion there were strong signs that consumers had cut back on their spending.

Perhaps most ominous for long term economic consequences is the probability of an increase in U.S. budget deficits as a result of slowed (or negative) economic growth. This would mean that tax revenues would decline at the same time the demand for social services paid for by government increases.

Rising inflation and a larger budget deficit could push interest rates higher. That would further slow the economy and increase government and business expenses when both are stretched to the limit.

On August 14, 1990 *The Wall Street Journal* reported the results of its survey of 34 leading economists on the prospects for the economy following the Iraqi invasion of Kuwait. Prior to the invasion, the consensus of this distinguished group of analysts was that the expansion was not in danger of ending. In June, 35 out of the 40 economists surveyed felt that the expansion would continue for at least another 12 months. Two weeks after the Iraqi invasion, 34 of the economists updated their forecasts, with only 19 predicting that the economy would grow for another 12 months.

The average economic forecast in the August 14 survey was for a 0.3% rise in the GNP for the second half of 1990. They expected a 1% increase in the first half of 1991. Those figures are down considerably from the consensus forecast in June which called for a 1.6% growth in the second half of 1990 and 1.8% growth in the first half of 1991.

Saddam Hussein's actions also brought about changes in average forecasts on inflation. The consensus forecast for inflation as measured by the Consumer Price Index rose to 5.4% for the second half of 1990 versus projections of 4% in the June survey.

Unemployment estimates also rose from 5.5% to 5.8% by November and 6.1% by May 1991. On the other hand, slow economic growth was expected to benefit the bond markets as the forecasts for the yield on three-month Treasury bills declined from 7.56% to 7.2% at year-end 1990, and 7% from 7.43% by mid-1991. The yield on 30-year Treasury bonds was expected to fall to 8.25% (up from 8.16%) by year-end 1990 and under 8% (from 8.1%) by mid-1991.

Interpreting the Data

It is usually best to go with the current trend until there is evidence of a need to be more defensive. However, the data by late 1990 tended to indicate that the U.S. economy was sliding into a recession in terms of harm to consumers and businesses regardless of whether the statistics met the technical definition of "recession." The real danger is whether a slowdown in economic growth may be exacerbated by a collapse of the huge debt pyramid that has built up over the past decade. Such a domino effect could have dire effects on the economy. (See our discussion below.)

In our last edition we noted that only seven of the 38 economists who responded to *The Wall Street Journal's* June 1989 survey predicted negative growth for the next 12 months. For the third consecutive year the consensus proved correct. However, we urge readers to proceed with great caution into the first half of the decade of the '90s.

While a trend in motion tends to stay in motion, it is also a truism that in the investment arena most people are on the wrong side of a market trend at turning points. When people are most enthusiastic about the stock market (like they were in August 1987) is when the market will usually turn. Everyone, even the public at large, can be right for awhile. But the tendency for investors to get carried away and drive markets to extremes prior to major reversals is well documented. As Marie Antoinette is rumored to have observed: "The key to success is keeping your head, while all around are losing theirs."

There are a number of indicators that will give you an early clue to a coming recession (and its severity). When these indicators flash their signals (and some had already been triggered by late 1990) it is time to take a defensive stance in your investment allocations. It is time to move to defensive allocations:

- If the leading economic indicators turn down for three consecutive months.
- If consumer confidence as measured by either the monthly survey of the University of Michigan or the Conference Board Survey of Consumer Confidence is lower for three straight months.
- If industrial production turns lower for three consecutive months.
- If the inventory to sales ratio climbs over 1.5. However, the trend is more important than the absolute number. A rising number indicates that inventories are rising relative to sales which is an early warning indicator of consumer sales problems.
- If consumer spending contracts for three consecutive months. Consumer spending fell in the first quarter of 1990 but picked up again the second quarter. Consumer spending accounts for two-thirds of the GNP. Minor changes have important implications for the health of the economy.
- If protectionist trade legislation rears its ugly head once again, expect the worst. Protectionist measures, just when Europe is freeing its markets and exports are playing an ever larger role in the U.S. economy, could be a critical blow to the economy that will take many years to overcome.
- If gold rallies and stays above $450 an ounce, look for rising inflation to once again play a role in the U.S. economy. In this case, raise your precious metals allocation to the upper range and exit bonds.
- If the stock market drops below 2200 on the Dow Jones Industrial Average (DJIA), look for a fall to 1600.
- If corporate earnings consistently fall below forecasts look for a weaker stock market.
- If the National Association of Purchasing Management's Index falls below 50% for three consecutive months, its signals a stagnant economy.

Don't expect to get ALL the above conditions occurring concurrently. However, by monitoring these indicators and using a "weight of the evidence" approach, you can improve your overall returns while minimizing risk. If you wait until all the evidence is in, you will miss much of a market's move. Gradually shift your allocations among various asset categories as evidence mounts. Waiting for conclusive proof usually means you will make your moves just when the markets are preparing to turn once gain.

A common mistake made by nonprofessional investors is that they tend to be either all invested or all out. There are distinct advantages to gradually building or selling your investment positions. Since no one knows with certainty what the future holds, it does not make any sense to take an "either or" investment stance.

A defensive strategy should include the following:

- Buy defensive stocks (utilities, food, tobacco, liquor) to the minimum allocation levels suggested.
- Increase cash equivalents to the upper end of the recommended range. Hold at least 50% in three-month T-bills or in money market funds that invest solely in T-bills.
- Buy gold coins with a portion of your precious metals allocation.
- Pay down debt as quickly as feasible.
- Buy only the highest grade bonds. Hold at least 50% of your fixed income portfolio in intermediate term Treasury bonds.
- Emphasize liquidity. Stay away from highly leveraged real estate or long-term commitments over 12 months.

THE 1990s: DOMESTIC TRENDS
A Look Back: Innovations in the 1980s

The 1980s have been variously and accurately termed the Decade of the Deal, the Decade of Debt, and the Decade of the Financial Innovation. The face of the financial world was changed during the 1980s. Many financial products that are now commonly accepted investment alternatives were barely known ten years ago.

In 1979, banks offered a measly 5 1/2% on their passbook savings, the most they could pay by law. By December 1982, bank deregulation had shifted into high gear.

Banks could pay higher rates on a new type of account. In 1983, banks were allowed to set rates on Certificates of Deposit (CDs) and sell them in smaller denominations.

By 1990 savers had placed over $1.6 trillion in money market deposit accounts and CDs of less than $100,000. Traditional passbook accounts mounted to $405 billion.

Perhaps the most important innovation of all was the rise of money market funds. While they made their first appearance in the 1970s, they became mainstays for savings in the '80s. At the end of 1979 there were 2.3 million money market accounts with total assets of $45.2 billion. By 1990 there were over 20 million accounts with assets of over $600 billion.

Another innovation in the 1980s developed as a direct result of changes in the tax law. The 1986 Tax Reform Act phased out the deduction for consumer interest. The law left only interest on loans secured by homes as tax deductible. As a result "home equity credit lines" emerged as the fastest growing area for bank lending.

High mortgage rates in the late 1970s and early 1980s priced many buyers out of the real estate market. Lenders developed adjustable rate mortgages (ARMs) with lower first-year rates which then float in accord with a specific formula. It made sense for banks because ARMs enabled them to shift part of the risk for rising interest rates to borrowers. Over 25% of outstanding mortgages are now adjustable.

Other tax-driven innovations included the widespread use of IRAs. In 1982 Congress made IRAs available to all workers. It enabled tax payers to put away money for retirement that would earn money tax free. While the 1986 Tax Reform Act restricted the tax deductibility of IRA contributions, it left IRAs as a method for tax payers to benefit from tax-deferred compounding on their retirement funds.

In 1978, tax laws first allowed employers to set up 401(k) retirement savings plans. The plans enable employees to invest pretax dollars in self-directed investment plans. In 1982 only 2% of major corporations offered them to their employees. By 1990 almost 95% of the Fortune 500 companies offered 401(k) plans to their employees. Today, total 401(k) assets amount to over $450 billion.

What to Expect in the 1990s

The fast and furious pace of financial product innovation has probably crested. To many analysts the financial product explosion of the last decade was actually detrimental for investors. While we certainly do not agree with that perspective, there is little question that the vast array of new and complex products made it more difficult for average consumers to understand all the possible alternatives they had available.

The flood of investment innovations offers many new choices and new opportunities, but at the same time, it opened the doors wider for con artists to insinuate themselves. Leveraged precious metals scams involving "bank financing," options, options on futures, and other esoteric vehicles cost investors millions of dollars.

Perhaps the most widely debated financial development of the 1980s is already undergoing substantial changes: the junk bond market. At the beginning of the decade, junk bonds were a very minor part of the financial landscape. By 1990 they had mushroomed into a $200 billion market. At the same time, uses and abuses of the bonds led to the downfall of one of the most powerful Wall Street brokers: Drexel Burnham Lambert. Caught in the net were many prominent investment professionals including Ivan Boesky and Michael Milken.

The collapse of the junk bond market in 1989 and 1990 probably spells the end of the rapid growth of junk bonds. As highly leveraged deals such as the Campeau fiasco begin to pull apart, the markets will see a return to equity financing. Huge debt loads will hurt many companies who were caught up in the debt frenzy for many years to come.

Junk bond defaults soared to $6 billion in 1989, with projections that that figure could rise to $15 to $20 billion in 1990 without a recession! By 1989 the volume of junk bond new issues had dropped to $50.9 billion, a 22% decline from the peak year of 1986 when $65.5 billion of junk bonds were issued.

At the same time though, this very factor offers astute investors a golden opportunity. During the 1980s, debt as a percent of total capital at nonfinancial companies grew to 49% from 34%. An even scarier statistic is the decline in interest coverage: the multiple by which corporate cash (defined as earnings before interest and taxes) exceeds interest payments. A multiple of less than one means that the company is not generating sufficient cash to meet its interest obligations. In 1980, nonfinancial companies had an interest coverage ratio of 4.6. By mid-1990 that number had dropped to 3.3.

Properly used, debt boosts a company's return on shareholders' equity. Tax policy also encouraged the heavy use of debt. Interest payments on bonds are tax-deductible to the corporation. Dividends paid to shareholders are not. That tax break makes debt a much cheaper way to finance growth.

While debt seemed to be the cure all for corporate financial needs, all too many companies failed to understand that there are limits. As a company increases its borrowing, it also increases its risk of default if continuing operations are unable to generate sufficient cash flow to service the debt. When times are rosy, when the economy is expanding and demand rising, all is well and good. However, during the inevitable slowdowns overleveraged companies suddenly find that the tax benefits of debt are not sufficient to overcome the detrimental business consequences of too much debt.

It is our feeling that the overleveraging of American corporations will take years to straighten out. Many leveraged deals are already headed into bankruptcy and many more will undoubtedly drift into Chapter 11 before it is all over. We expect the number of leveraged buyouts (LBOs) and hostile takeovers to shrink considerably in the 1990s. The October 12, 1989 190 point crash in the stock market due to problems with the United Airline (UAL) buyout probably signaled the end of the LBO era. Of course, there will continue to be mergers and acquisitions, but we doubt that we will ever see such frenzied, nonsensical biding wars in our lifetime.

Taking Advantage of the Debt Crisis

To take advantage of this changing environment, we recommend that your sights be set on ferreting out low-debt companies with strong positions in industries that are generally loaded down with debt. It is impossible to include a comprehensive list due to the everchanging nature of the stock market. However, representative examples of companies in mid-1990 that fit this criterion include American Airlines and Delta in the airline industry. In retail, hard hit by the Campeau disaster, May Department Stores and Liz Claiborne fit the bill.

Look for companies which have a market value less than or equal to cash and other current assets minus current liabilities and long-term debt. Don't fall victim to the simplistic idea that all it takes to find that hidden jewel is to compare cash on hand with market value. Some companies have a lot of cash, but are also loaded down with debt.

If you are very conservative and only want to deal with larger capitalization and better known companies, look for blue chippers which have more cash than average. A company with 10% to 12% cash and cash equivalents to market value represents a relatively liquid company. In late 1989, Ford had a 29% cash to market value ratio.

Locating such companies can be done by yourself by studying S&P's Stock Guide or Value Line Investment Survey. Barron's also publishes useful data every week. Some computer databases supply the right information. You merely need to devise the screen you want to employ.

Another idea is to focus on companies with substantial overseas exposure. With the freeing of European markets (see section on international opportunities), those U.S. companies which are well situated can take advantage of overseas opportunities. Stick with multinational companies in industries such as drugs, health care, foods, tobacco, electrical equipment, and computer systems.

We believe that investors in the 1990s will prize financially solid companies which make good use of equity financing in conjunction with debt to pay for their growth. The junk bond market will be shaky for years to come. That means that traditional lenders such as banks and insurance companies will once again take the upper hand in lending. Look for tighter money and tougher terms, especially in the first five years of the decade, as the debt problem is sorted out.

The Changing Face of Banks and Brokers

L. William Seidman, Chairman of the Feder-al Deposit Corporation stated in 1990 that in all likelihood the S&L industry is dead once the bailout finally winds down. S&L will become banks. The banking industry is in the throes of major change. The worsening real estate market and the overhanging problem of bad overseas debt will rock the banking industry in the 1990s. Expect to see substantial consolidation as smaller, poorly managed institutions are gobbled up by larger concerns.

Look for a rise in bank failures. In 1988, the Federal Deposit Insurance Corporation (FDIC) reported its first loss in 50 years. It is widely acknowledged that the FDIC's reserves are simply not sufficient to bail out a large bank. This combined with the $500 to $750 billion S&L bailout will put the final nail in the coffin of the $100,000 federal insurance on deposits. We expect to see that insurance limit lowered. Another idea which is being bandied about as more politically acceptable is maintaining the same $100,000 limit, but including a deductible such as 20 or 25%.

The 50 largest U.S. banks will go on a buying spree as smaller banks find themselves at a competitive disadvantage not only with U.S. banks but with foreign institutions such as Japanese banks as well.

Look for banks to develop cash management accounts to compete with those offered by major brokerage houses. The differences between services that brokers and bankers can offer will diminish with time.

Both brokers and banks are devising new and creative ways to assess account fees. Much as Swiss banks currently charge for each individual service (e.g., bank statement fee, per check fee, deposit fees, etc.), American banks are exploring ever more ways to extract fees from their customers. Look for fees to be assessed on virtually every transaction. It will become vital to know and understand your bank's fee structure. Once again, money market mutual funds may offer realistic alternatives to the banks.

Brokerage firms have also stepped up their fees in the last fee years. Some firms are charging fees to open a stock account, fees for getting into mutual funds, fees on top of commissions, and even fees on "inactive" accounts.

For example, Bear, Stearns & Co. charges

clients a $2.50 per-transaction handling charge on top of its regular commission. Others doing the same thing include Merrill Lynch and Kidder Peabody.

Shearson Lehmen Hutton charges a $50 annual fee on accounts which are inactive for six months. Cash management accounts offered by most major brokerage firms carry fees ranging upwards from $50 per year.

We expect that banks will offer many services now thought to be the domain of brokerage firms. Already many banks sell various investments. Watch for more banks to start selling stock and bond mutual funds. By mid-1990 there were 435 bank-advised funds with assets totaling $71 billion. Only 88 of the largest banks actually manage the funds themselves. Others contract with mutual fund companies to sell outside funds in bank offices, often under a bank name.

The Move to 24-hour Trading

In June 1990 the New York Stock Exchange (NYSE) announced its intention to begin trading during the night by 1991. In an attempt to regain trading volume in NYSE-listed stocks from foreign markets (especially London and Tokyo), the NYSE plans to conduct auctions on each listed stock at 8 p.m., midnight, and 5 a.m. Each stock will trade only once during each auction. All trades will be combined at whatever price can be agreed upon.

Not to be outdone, the American Stock Exchange, the Chicago Board Options Exchange, and the Cincinnati Stock Exchange announced an alliance with Reuters Holdings of Britain to offer nighttime trading. The after-hours trading system is primarily designed for options trading. However, plans call for it to accommodate trading in most Big Board issues in the S&P 500-stock index.

Other changes will inevitably follow. A report released in 1990 by the Office of Technology Assessment, an independent Congressional agency, sharply criticized the specialist system used by the NYSE and Amex to trade stocks. The report stated that rapid changes in the marketplace, including growing trading volume and large block trades "may make the specialist system obsolete in the foreseeable future."

The futures markets also came in for sharp criticism: "Futures markets may not be able to accommodate the pressures of increasing volume and foreign competition without further automation. They already have demonstrated the difficulty of controlling fraud and consumer abuse in their present manual trading procedures."

The report also suggested that jurisdictional problems between the Commodity Futures Trading Commission (CFTC) (charged with regulating the futures markets) and the Securities and Exchange Commission (SEC) (charged with regulating the securities markets) may hamper effective regulation during times of market stress.

That very point reached fever pitch in 1990 with the Bush Administration proposing that the SEC be given responsibility for overseeing stock index futures trading. That would entail taking jurisdiction away from the CFTC. As this is being written, early indications are that some compromise is in the works. The most often suggested alternative is for the CFTC to maintain its role overseeing stock index futures trading, but that the Federal Reserve should set margin requirements.

If the SEC does get jurisdiction, many industry observers believe that it will be only the first step in a long term campaign to have the SEC take over regulation of the futures markets. The most likely first step the SEC will take would be raising the margin requirements.

For example, margin requirements for the S&P 500 Future Index in 1990 ran about 11% of the value of the contract. If the index was at 300, the value would be $150,000 ($500 per point). The margin would be approximately $16,500. Talk on the street is that the SEC would raise the initial margin requirements to as much as 20%. That would eliminate many individual investors, though it probably would not affect institutional investors who are responsible for the vast majority of the volume in the S&P index.

The SEC is generally considered more conservative. If jurisdiction passes to the SEC, many observers feel that the rate and range of innovative products would be hampered.

This all came about as a result of the October 1987 stock market crash. After that, the government moved to put various "circuit breakers" into place. These safety valves got their first real test in October 1989, when the market went into a 190 point freefall in the last hours of trading on October 13. The circuit breakers failed to stem the tide. In fact, many observers felt that the mechanisms actually exacerbated the drop.

THE 1990s: THE EUROPEAN DECADE?

Foreign investment in the United States gets most of the headlines in our own media. Yet, the fact is, U.S. citizens are very heavy investors abroad. During 1989, Americans bought a record $220 billion in foreign stocks. That was a 45.7% increase over 1988. The previous high was $190 billion in 1987.

In 1989, purchases exceeded sales by $13.7 billion. The largest share of net purchases, over $10.5 billion, went to Europe. It is not hard to understand why. With totalitarian regimes in Eastern Europe crumbling and Western Europe on the verge of economic integration by 1992, the prospects for dramatic growth in the Old World never looked better.

Much of this growth is the direct result of the increasing internationalization of the world's economies. Mutual funds designed to invest in overseas markets have experienced explosive growth over the past five years. In the first quarter of 1990 alone, sales of international mutual funds soared to $2.5 billion from $400 million in the comparable period one year earlier.

We believe that the changes now taking place in the world economy point to Europe and the Pacific Rim nations becoming leaders in the world's economic growth in the 1990s. As we have indicated above and elsewhere in this book, the U.S. economy appears to be slowing as we enter the '90s. Slowed by budget deficit problems that will certainly be aggravated by the huge expenses of the Middle East armed forces expedition, weakening consumer spending, record debt levels, and declining consumer confidence, at least for the first half of the '90s, growth prospects appear much greater for

foreign economies.

There are numerous ways for you to take advantage of these developments. When selecting companies for your domestic stock portfolio, look for those firms which have strong positions in foreign markets, either through exports or via foreign subsidiaries. For example, Coca-Cola is rapidly establishing a presence in Eastern Europe in the short time that that market has been open to foreign companies. Other companies include Phillip Morris, Merck, IBM, Boeing, and Sears.

While many commentators lament that the American economy is weak and uncompetitive (you no doubt have read much about the U.S. as the "world's largest debtor nation"), the facts belie this simplistic analysis. The Federal Reserve concluded in a report released in 1990 that "The United States continues to enjoy an absolute price and cost advantage over its major trading partners.... U.S. labor costs in manufacturing are more than 15% below those in other major industrial countries."

These advantages show up in the trade figures. U.S. merchandise exports have climbed more than 50% since 1987 to over $364 billion in 1989. Meanwhile imports growth is less than half that rate. These figures do not include the service export earnings where the U.S. enjoys a substantial trade surplus.

The 1990s will be a critical transition era for America. The U.S. economy will be led by export growth for the first time in its history. Americans will be making more of their livelihood selling to foreigners! Many analysts seem to think that the U.S. is somehow poorer because the rest of the world has grown more prosperous. Nothing could be further from the truth.

Look at tourism for example. Last year foreigners spend $1.2 billion more in America than we spent abroad. No one thought that kind of turnaround would ever happen. Foreigners were "too poor" and the U.S. was too expensive!

In 1990 over 42 million foreigners will visit the United States spending a net of $2 billion dollars. By 1991 experts project an increase to over 436 million visitors.

The most important single export from America is intellectual. U.S. university education for foreign students is a leading service export. Royalties and fees on U.S. inventions earned a net of $1.3 billion in 1989. That number is increasing steadily. For example, the royalties on Texas Instruments' patent on the integrated circuit (the basis of the computerized world!) was only recently recognized by Japan. Annual royalties could run to $700 million a year in the 1990s.

Intellectual wherewithal is sold in our most important service exports. Motorola's cellular telephone design has been accepted as standard by Japan. U.S. computer and software exports total nearly $14 billion. While costs for raw material such as those that go into a computer disk are only pennies, the knowledge on those disks is worth thousands of dollars.

U.S. labor cost advantage is not a result of low wages, but rather is due to the highest output per employee in the world. Productivity in manufacturing is growing at historic rates. Yet many observers continue to lament America's "decline" as an international economic power.

These observers fail to understand the significance of the transition to an export-led economy. Historically the U.S. has not depended on foreign trade as much other countries such as Japan or West Germany. During the 1980s, the U.S. imported far more than it exported. This trade imbalance helped other nations to prosper. The U.S. paid out billions of dollars and wound up borrowing back some of that money in the form of Treasury security sales.

Now as export sales become increasingly important to U.S. industry, it means that consumer spending will grow more slowly in the '90s than in the '80s. Offsetting this slowdown and maintaining employment levels to some extent will be a pickup in production (including production by foreign companies in the United States).

Since WWII U.S. economic strength has helped to bring peace and prosperity to Western Europe. Now peace and freedom is spreading to Eastern Europe and even the Soviet Union. As revolutionary changes sweep over Europe, you can see that other Western countries such as West Germany are in a position to supply funding for rebuilding the economies of the East! The U.S. is not weaker simply because others are more prosperous. The whole world economy will experience more balanced growth and everyone will benefit from the resulting peace and prosperity.

Investing Overseas

If we have convinced you of the wisdom of investing in foreign stock markets, it is now necessary for us to drop the other shoe. Prepare for a wild and wooly ride! While stock price swings in U.S. markets have led to complaints by many investors, a look at foreign markets shows that the American market is actually one of the world's least volatile ones.

U.S. stock prices have been less volatile over the past five years than prices in Japan, West Germany, Britain, and France, according to data compiled by Morgan Stanley Capital International. Over the 12 months ending in June 1990, the U.S. market was less volatile than 18 of the 19 other markets included in the firm's survey. Only Canada was calmer.

At the same time however, most other stock markets offered higher returns in dollar terms over the last five years. The U.S. market, in fact, ranked next to last in total return among the 18 markets with five-year records (New Zealand's market is relatively new and five-year data is not available).

Over the 12 months ending in June 1990, the U.S. market's return of 16.9% pales in comparison to Austria's 115%, Germany's 62%, or Switzerland's 49%. Below we have included a table listing the 12-month and five-year (ending June 1990) performance measured in U.S. dollars and volatility of the world's 17 leading stock markets (ranked by 5-year performance):

Country	Performance		Volatility	
	12 month	5 year	12 months	5 years
Belgium	19%	471%	14%	18%
Sweden	27%	456%	18%	19%
Austria	115%	431%	14%	18%
Spain	10%	411%	16%	21%
France	44%	345%	17%	20%
Italy	40%	332%	14%	23%
Japan	-14%	310%	23%	23%
Norway	40%	286%	22%	26%

Denmark	50%	284%	17%	32%
Germany	62%	256%	21%	23%
Switzerland	49%	236%	19%	19%
Netherlands	29%	234%	15%	18%
United Kingdom	21%	187%	17%	20%
Australia	9%	173%	19%	25%
Hong Kong	18%	168%	33%	30%
Singapore	22%	129%	18%	25%
United States	17%	121%	13%	19%

Source: Morgan Stanley Capital International

Given the dramatic changes taking place in Europe, we believe that this trend will continue into the '90s. A very important consideration for multi-asset investors is the fact that foreign price movement is not closely correlated to U.S. stock price moves. This means that adding foreign stocks to your portfolio mix can actually reduce the overall volatility of a portfolio that was invested exclusively in U.S. stocks.

For example, in the 1980s, investors with 70% of their money in U.S. stocks and 30% in international issues, earned a higher return and had lower overall volatility than investors with 100% of their funds in U.S. stocks.

Don't forget though that when you invest in foreign issues you are making a twofold bet. First, you are betting that the foreign market will go up. Second, you are betting that the foreign currency will at least hold steady or possibly appreciate against the dollar. If the dollar's value increases more than the market rises, you may actually lose money despite a correct call on market direction!

Finding the Right Foreign Stock Fund

The revolutionary changes taking place in Europe have led to an explosion in stock fund offerings. In 1989 alone 24 country funds were launched or registered with regulators, triple the number in 1988. That brings to 50 the number of country funds that are listed in New York or London. The funds now account for several billions of dollars in assets.

The vast majority of these funds are closed end. A closed end fund issues only a fixed number of shares which are publicly traded like any other stock. Shares in a newly issued fund typically sell at a premium to the value of the fund's underlying portfolio. However, most funds eventually fall to a discount. For example, a 15% discount means that you can buy $1 in assets for only 85 cents.

This premium/discount feature of closed end funds represents a significant difference with the more common open end funds. It also means that the funds tend to be quite volatile. For example, for most of 1989 the single country closed end funds sold at premiums to the value of their underlying portfolios. At one point the Spain Fund sold for an unheard premium of over 100%! Historically, though, closed end funds sell at discounts. By mid-1990 most closed end funds were once again selling at discounts.

When evaluating closed end funds it is important to consider the premium or discount. However, do not make the mistake of assuming that simply because a fund is selling at a sharp discount that it should be bought. As with any mutual fund purchase, you should thoroughly research the track record of the fund's manager.

In June 1990 a number of funds oriented to the European markets were selling at discounts of over 10%. These included:

Fund	Discount
Alliance New Europe Fund	14%
Emerging Germany Growth	16%
Future Germany Fund	12%
Growth Fund of Spain	14%
Irish Investment Fund	19%
Scudder New Europe Fund	15%
United Kingdom Fund	14%

Source: Lipper Analytical Services

What About Japan?

1990 proved to be a tough year for Japan's stock market. Even before the Iraqi invasion of Kuwait, the stock market was dropping sharply. Fundamentals have changed from the very bullish conditions existing when there were low interest rates, low inflation, rapidly growing economy, and strengthening yen.

Double digit increases in the money supply, a worsening labor shortage, record low inventories, rising exports, and growing backlogs of orders have fired inflation fears. Closely related to inflation fears are worries about higher interest rates. When the central bank raised rates in March 1990, it was the fourth increase since May 1989. The Middle East crisis renewed fears that the Bank of Japan will raise rates once again.

Following the Iraqi invasion, the 225-stock Nikkei average hit a 1990 low of 26,176. That was down 33% from its all time high at the end of 1989. Even reports by leading economists that Japan's economy stands to lose only 0.1% of its growth this year if oil prices stabilize at $25 a barrel or lower failed to stem the selling.

A major problem is that expectations of capital gains based on very low interest rates are no longer practical. Competing financial investments, such as fixed income securities, are drawing money from stock investments. As we have written in the last two editions of this book, the Japanese stock market is overvalued by almost any measure. Average P/E (Price/Earnings) ratios of over 50 seem pricey by any standard.

The Japanese market has been one of the strongest for most of the 1980s. All markets go through cycles and it appears that the time has come for the Tokyo market to settle back into a slower growth pattern while the Japanese economy digests the massive changes it is undergoing.

However, we are believers in the long term vitality of the Japanese economy and its stock market. Japan has managed to lessen its reliance on Mid East oil since the terrible blows it suffered in the 1970s. Evidence of the difference was the reaction of the Yen. Immediately after the Iraqi invasion, the yen dropped sharply. However, it soon began to rally back. Energy costs account for only 4.7% of the consumer price index in Japan compared to 7.6% in the U.S. We believe that Japan is in much better shape to weather the 1990s Middle East crises than it was in the 1970s.

We would be buyers of Japanese stocks on pull backs up to 25 to 30% of your international stock allocation. A drop to the 22,000 level on the Nikkei Index would offer excellent long term values. We recommend that you participate in the Japanese market through mutual funds that specialize in that market.

Why We Like the Prospects for Europe

Beginning in 1992, the 12-member European Community is supposed to drop all internal barriers to trade and start to function as one integrated economy. European stock markets should benefit from decreased regulation which will enable companies to merge to compete more effectively with international competitors. In addition, freer markets and growing outside investments from American and Asian interests will push some of Europe's traditionally secretive corporations to disclose more of their strengths in an effort to attract investors. Such disclosures may uncover true "hidden values."

European economic growth rates are substantially above those of the United States. For example, West Germany GDP (equivalent to our GNP) is growing faster than 3.5% after adjusting it for inflation. France's growth is almost as good. Both countries are experiencing a capital spending and export boom. With trade increasing within the European community itself, they are less dependent on the U.S. markets. That is particularly important if the U.S. slips into a recession in the early '90s.

What Happens in 1992?

There is much confusion over what exactly "Project 1992" will mean. Since 1968, members of the European Community (formerly the Common Market) have traded without tariffs. However, there have been many other barriers to trade. Shippers experience long delays with customs. Taxes are inconsistent. Air travel is very expensive. Also each country imposes national product standards such as Germany's famous beer standard rules.

In response to these problems, the European Community adopted the Single European Act, which sets 1992 as the target date for full economic integration of the members economies. Theoretically at least, that should mean freer movement of goods, services, and capital among the member states.

We want to caution you against getting caught up with some of the more blatant hyperbole of European promoters. Some people are saying that the integration will mean two million more jobs, drops in consumer prices, savings in business costs, more equitable taxation, and open competition for government contracts. We will believe it when we see it!

How to Take Advantage

Our preferred method for investing in Europe is mutual funds. We have covered this alternative in some detail both in this chapter and in Chapter 15 on "International Securities." Another approach is to consider American Depository Receipts (ADRs).

The ADR market is expanding. The New York Stock Exchange offers 37 European ADRs from six countries. The OTC (over the counter) market features another 48 ADRs from eight countries.

ADR companies are established, more stable, better known companies. It is possible to assemble a diversified portfolio of ADR issues by both industry and country.

As this is being written, the situation in Eastern Europe is unsettled and it will be a while before foreign investors can participate directly. Currently, the best way to get a foot in the door is to buy stock in Western European mutual funds which buy companies that will benefit from trade with eastern Europe.

CONCLUSION

The 1990s represent a change from the wheeling-dealing days of the 1980s. The international community has already demonstrated a new cooperativeness as evidenced by the reaction to the Iraq invasion of Kuwait in August 1990. However, as always there exists a wide range of opinion on how to best take advantage of the situation.

Regardless of your final decisions on allocating your investment dollar, we can state with some certainty that those investors who diversify their portfolios over at least three and preferably five or more asset categories will suffer less volatility in the value of their portfolios than those who concentrate all their funds in one basket or asset class.

If the quickly changing events such as the Middle East crisis, the S&L fiasco, the European economic integration, the ever changing face of former communist countries, high stock market volatility, changing tax laws, etc. make you nervous, shade your portfolio allocations to the conservative side. Keep more of your funds in money market funds. Maintain a balanced exposure in the balance of your asset classes.

If you are more confident in your forecasting ability, or in the ability of your chosen advisor(s), then don't hesitate to concentrate slightly more of your assets in the direction you feel is correct. But don't become so enamored with your forecasts that you forget that the most important tool of all for building net worth is the long term: diversification!

Bailard, Biehl & Kaiser (BB&K) has been one of the pioneers in researching and employing sophisticated asset allocation techniques in managing their clients' money. Larry Biehl, one of BB&K's founders, has previously participated in our "experts" panel. He is fond of emphasizing the "power" of diversification. A properly diversified portfolio hedges against all probabilities. BB&K's own approach to determine what weighting to use for each asset category is based on a thorough analysis of the probabilities of each of a number of different economic scenarios occurring.

All investors must make a decision concerning their desire for stability versus the risk of high volatility. It is easy to see market tops and bottoms in retrospect, but "market timing" on a real time basis is subject to many errors. We believe that taking lower overall risk by diversifying over a select number of asset classes will achieve returns comparable to single asset (such as stocks) over the long term. In fact, the BB&K Diversified Portfolio Index, which is a measure of the performance of a portfolio diversified over cash equivalents, common stocks, domestic bonds, international securities, and real estate, has approximately the performance of the stock market over the last 20 years with only about half the volatility.

APPENDIX A: GLOSSARY OF PERSONAL FINANCE

Account executive. See **Registered representative.**

Accountant's opinion. The document issued by an independent accountant after his or her examination or audit of an organization's financial records.

Accredited investor. A designation used by the Securities and Exchange Commission (SEC) to define an investor having sufficient income and/or assets to accept the risk of participating in a private limited partnership. The investor must have a net worth of at least $1 million, or an annual income of at least $200,000, or a net worth at least five times his or her investment in the partnership, assuming that interest is $150,000 or greater.

Accrual basis. A method used by accountants to record and apportion expenses and income at the time they are incurred, regardless of when they are paid or collected. See also **Cash basis.**

Accrued dividend. When a dividend is considered earned but not declared or payable, it is added to the value of the asset.

Accrued interest. The interest that has accrued on a bond since the last interest payment. A buyer pays the market price of the bond and any accrued interest.

Accumulation plan. A strategy in which mutual funds are purchased via regular investor contributions and the reinvestment of dividends and capital gains distributions.

Acquisition fees. The fees and commissions paid to affiliates and nonaffiliates of the general partner in connection with the purchase of property for a real estate limited partnership (RELP). They may include real estate commissions, development fees, selection fees, and nonrecurring management fees, but do not include loan fees paid for brokerage services.

Acquittance. The document issued on the discharge or release from a financial obligation.

Actuary. A statistical mathematician responsible for calculating the premiums, dividends, reserves, and pension insurance and annuity rates used by an insurance company or other program involving financial risk.

Actuarial tables. The tables devised by an actuary to determine mortality rates, based on the company's history of claims and other general and statistical data. Generally used to determine insurance policy rates and annuity payments.

Adjustable rate mortgage (ARM). A mortgage whose interest rate is tied to a floating index, such as U.S. Treasury bills. Premiums are raised or lowered at predetermined intervals to reflect changes in the prevailing interest rates.

Adjusted basis. The price on which capital gains or losses are calculated at the time an asset is sold.

Adjusted gross income (AGI). The calculation of personal income tax liability that reflects adjustments made for moving expenses, employee business expenses, payments to an individual retirement account (IRA) or Keogh plan, penalties on early withdrawal of savings, alimony paid, and marital deduction for a working couple. Not included are itemized deductions, the standard deduction, charitable contributions, and personal exemptions, all of which are subtracted from the AGI to determine taxable income.

Adjuster. The person responsible for investigating insurance claims and determining the amount of settlement.

Administrator. The person or institution appointed by the court to distribute the estate of a decedent when there is no will or when the will fails to name an appropriate executor.

Affidavit. A written statement sworn to before a person authorized to accept an oath or affirmation, such as a notary public.

After-tax value or cost. The effective value or cost of an investment once the loss or credit is taken into account.

Aggressive growth fund. A mutual fund that primarily provides capital gains, often by investing in more volatile stocks, instead of current dividend income.

Alternative minimum tax (AMT). A device used by the IRS to make certain that individuals, trusts, and estates are not able to escape from tax liability through tax preference strategies.

American depository receipt (ADR). An instrument sold by banks allowing investors to trade in foreign currency exchanges without the usual delays, currency exchange rate fluctuations, and other complications.

Amortization. A banking practice used to reduce a debt gradually through regularly scheduled payments. Or an accounting procedure by which the purchase price of an asset is reduced over time to reflect its declining resale value.

Annual percentage rate (APR). The interest rate applied to a consumer loan.

Annual renewable term insurance. Term life insurance with guaranteed annual renewability, regardless of health considerations.

Annual report. A year-end summary of an organization's business activities and financial condition, with balance sheet, income statement, and information for shareholders on dividends declared on outstanding shares.

Annuity. A contract, usually with an insurance company, for guaranteed periodic payments for life or for a predetermined number of years.

Appreciation. The amount an asset grows or increases in value.

Appreciation participation mortgage (APM). A mortgage in which the lender reduces the interest rate in exchange for a percentage of the equity in the property to be paid when the loan is retired.

Arbitrage. The practice of buying and selling commodities in two separate markets to take advantage of price differentials existing between the markets.

Asset. Any item that may be sold or exchanged by its owner.

Audit. An examination of the accounting and financial documents of an organization by an independent accountant for accuracy, consistency, and adherence to legal and accounting principles.

Back-end load. A commission or sales charge paid when an asset is sold, transferred, or otherwise disposed of.

Balance sheet. A detailed statement of the assets and liabilities of an individual, family or business organization at a given moment in time.

Banker's acceptances. A type of letter of credit, developed to aid international trade by providing a third-party guarantee of payment.

Bankruptcy. The inability of an individual or organization to pay due debts, as determined by a federal court.

Basic asset category. One of six fundamental groupings of assets, including near-money and money market investments; U.S. equities (individual stocks or stock market mutual funds); U.S. fixed income (interest-bearing debt investments); real estate limited partnerships (RELPs); real estate investment trusts (REITs); international securities, such as international mutual funds; and precious metals and tangibles, such as stock in mining companies, metal bullion, or coins.

Bear market. An investment market marked by generally declining prices.

Beta coefficient. A statistical measurement of a stock's volatility determined by comparison to the Standard & Poor's 500 Index. A stock that rises and falls faster than the S&P 500 Index has a beta greater than 1; those which fluctuate more slowly have betas less than 1.

Black Friday (Monday, etc.). A term generically used for any sharp drop in a financial market. The original "Black Friday" occurred in 1869 when a group of financiers tried to capture the gold market and set off a business panic and depression. On a Friday in 1873, another panic set in. The Black Monday of October 19, 1987 was also preceded by a Black Friday.

Black Monday. On October 19, 1987, the Dow Jones Industrial Average fell 508 points for a loss of $500 billion; most of the drop was blamed on program (computerized) trading and the previous over-valuation of stocks. Although it was percentage-wise the second greatest single-day drop in the history of the stock market, Black Monday has as yet had no apparent lasting effect on U.S. or global economies.

Blue-chip stocks. Stocks issued by companies with a long history of proven earnings records, stable management, and nonvolatile stock prices. Ideal for risk-averse investors.

Bond. A long-term debt instrument issued by a corporation or government entity evidencing the issuer's promise to repay interest at a guaranteed rate on a specified maturity date.

Book value. An accounting calculation that subtracts from the original cost of an asset its accumulated depreciation.

Bracket creep. The inflationary trend that moves taxpayers into higher tax brackets even as their real income remains stable. Indexing, which was introduced by the IRS in 1985, was designed to eliminate bracket creep by raising the brackets, personal exemptions, and standard deductions each year to keep pace with the cost of living.

Broker-dealer. A person or firm registered with the Securities and Exchange Commission to buy and sell securities.

Budget, 10/20/70. A budget strategy commonly used by financial planners to help families create three distinct accounts: for (1) long-term savings; (2) consumer spending; and (3) household expenditures.

Bullion. Uncoined gold or silver in the form of bars or plates.

Business cycle. The recurring rise and fall of markets as they pass through expansion and contraction, as measured by changes in the **gross national product (GNP)**. Traditionally, business cycles have lasted for about 30 months.

Call option. An option to buy 100 shares of a security at a guaranteed price by a specified date.

Capital gains (or losses). Profits or losses resulting from the exchange or sale of an asset. Long-term capital gain (six months or longer) is taxed at a rate lower than the taxpayer's full income tax rate; short-term capital gains are taxed at the full rate.

Capitalization rate (cap rate). A method of evaluating the sales price of income property based on its current net income.

Cash equivalents. Investment products that are highly liquid and that may be guaranteed, from savings accounts and interest-bearing checking accounts to money market funds and repurchase agreements.

Cash flow. The difference between monthly income and monthly liabilities.

Cash surrender value. The amount the insurer will pay the insured on cancellation of the policy.

Cash value insurance. An insurance policy that accumulates a cash surrender value.

Certificate of deposit (CD). A loan from an investor to a bank or thrift institution for a specified period of time at a set interest rate.

Certified Financial Planner (CFP). Financial planners who have met the educational, experience, and ethical standards established by the International Board of Standards and Practices for Certified Financial Planners, Inc. (IBCFP).

Certified Public Accountant (CPA). A license granted by a state board of accountancy to individuals who have passed the Uniform CPA Examination and have met other educational and professional requirements.

Closed-end investment company. A company that issues a fixed number of mutual fund shares. The shares are traded on the open market, but are not redeemable by the issuing company. See **Open-end investment company.**

Collectibles. Nonfinancial physical objects found in limited supply that provide esthetic, psychological, or practical value to the owner. They are expected to appreciate as a result of inflation or through increased recognition of their rarity.

Commercial paper. A short-term promissory note usually issued by banks and other corporate borrowers, bearing a variety of maturity dates and backed by bank lines of credit.

Commodities. Any hard asset, such as grains, foodstuffs, livestock, oils, and metals, that is traded on the national exchanges.

Common stock. A security representing an ownership interest in a corporation. Holders of common stock share in the success or failure of the issuing company through dividends and the changing value of the stocks in equity markets. Stockholders also participate in management decisions via the voting rights conveyed by their shares.

Community property. A form of co-ownership, used in seven states, that declares that the assets of a married couple are owned jointly, except for, property acquired by one partner by will, inheritance, or gift.

Compound interest. Interest that is calculated on the principle and previously paid interest; it may be computed daily, monthly, quarterly, semiannually, or annually.

Consumer Price Index (CPI). A figure calculated each month by the U.S. Department of Labor, based on the cost of about 400 items in major cities. The resulting number indicates the relative rise and fall of prices of consumer goods nationally.

Convertible. A corporate bond or preferred share that may be exchanged for a certain number of the issuing corporation's common stock.

Coupon. Certain bonds include "coupons" that are redeemed periodically for the appropriate interest payment. Originally, coupons were attached to the bonds but now most coupon redemptions are accomplished via computer.

Current ratio. The relationship between current assets and current liabilities, expressed as a ratio.

Custodial account. An account established in a bank, brokerage firm, or mutual fund on behalf of another, particularly an account established by a parent for a child.

Dealer. An individual or firm acting as a principal rather than an agent. Dealers generally buy securities for their own account and sell to individuals.

Debenture. A promissory note that is unsecured by a lien on any specific property but that is backed by the general credit of the borrowing corporation.

Debt-to-equity ratio. In a household, the relationship between what is owed and what is owned.

Deferred annuity. An annuity where benefits are scheduled to begin in the future on a specified date.

Deflation. The economic condition that exists when the cost of goods and services is decreasing.

Demand deposit. Any bank account that may be drawn on without prior notice via check, cash withdrawal, or electronic transfer between accounts.

Depreciation. The practice of accounting as a non-cash expense the cost of an asset over time, even though the asset may, in fact, be appreciating in value.

Depression. An exaggerated and extended recession in the business cycle: a period of time in which prices fall, purchasing power diminishes, unemployment rises, production declines, supply exceeds demand, inventories expand, and business activity in general decreases. The mood of the population is generally fearful and cautious. (Colloquially, a *recession* is when your neighbor is out of work; a *depression* is when you are out of work!)

Discount. The difference between a bond's par, or face, value and its current market price.

Discretionary income. Money that's available to be used for investing after one's bills have been paid.

Distribution. In estate law, distribution is the disposal of the decedent's assets according to the will. In mutual funds and closed-end investment companies, it is the payout of capital gains to investors.

Diversification. The allocation of investment dollars into a variety of instruments, vehicles, or basic asset categories to compensate for natural market fluctuations; the opposite of the "all the eggs in one basket" philosophy.

Dividend. A payment made from corporate net profits to shareholders, on the vote of the board of directors. Common share dividends usually fluctuate according to profit levels; preferred shares usually pay fixed dividends.

Dollar-cost averaging. The systematic purchase of securities by investing a set number of dollars at regular intervals; the investor buys more shares when the price is low, and fewer when prices rise, which has the effect of decreasing the cost per share.

Domestic equities. Equity shares in a corporation chartered under the laws of the United States.

Dow Jones Industrial Average (DJIA). Dow Jones & Company publishes four sets of stock indicators daily. The Dow Jones Industrial Average (commonly known as the "Dow") follows the value of 30 leading industrial stocks; the Dow Jones Transportation Average (DJTA) tracks 20 airline, railroad, and trucking stocks; The Dow Jones Utility Average (DJUA) monitors 15 gas and electric utility stocks; and the Dow Jones Composite ("Dow 65") combines all three averages.

Durable power of attorney. A provision that allows one person to make legal and financial decisions on behalf of another. Usually employed to designate a responsible party in case of an anticipated or feared disability.

Earnings per share. The net earnings of a corporation—once taxes have been paid and dividends to preferred shareholders and bondholders have been made—divided by the number of outstanding shares of common stock.

EE bonds. U.S. Government savings bonds sold at a 50% discount off face value and redeemed in full in 11 years.

Employees Retirement Income Security Act (ERISA). A law established in 1974 that regulates the operation of most pension and retirement plans.

Entitlement. Benefits received from a program in which an individual establishes eligibility, such as Social Security.

Equity. The market value of a property or a business, less liens and other claims against it; the owner's interest in an asset.

Equity participation mortgage. See **Appreciation participation mortgage.**

Estate planning. The strategy for protection and disposal of one's assets at death. Includes writing a will, establishing trusts, naming an executor, etc.

Eurodollars. U.S. currency that is held in foreign banks.

Ex-dividend. Meaning "without dividend"; refers to a stock that has been traded after the record date for dividends, so the price excludes any declared dividend and the dividend is paid to the seller.

Executor. The person named by will to carry out the wishes of the decedent.

Face value. The primary, or stated, value of a note, bond, or contractual obligation. The issuer guarantees to repay the lender the face value of the obligation at maturity.

Federal Deposit Insurance Corporation (FDIC). A quasi-governmental entity that insures the deposits in federally chartered banks.

Federal Home Loan Bank System. A system of 12 regional Federal Home Loan Banks that issue bonds and notes to raise funds to provide credit for savings and loans, cooperatives, and other mortgage lenders. Institutions borrow from the system based on the amount of collateral they can provide.

Federal Home Loan Mortgage Corporation (FHLMC, or Freddie Mac). A government-sponsored corporation owned by shareholder savings institutions. Freddie Mac buys residential mortgages from its members and repackages them into mortgage-backed securities, selling them on the open market.

Federal Housing Administration (FHA). A federally sponsored agency that insures lenders against losses on residential mortgage lending.

Federal National Mortgage Association (FNMA). Known as Fannie Mae, this publicly owned government-sponsored corporation purchases FHA- and Veterans Administration-insured mortgages, repackages them, and sells them as mortgage-backed securities to be sold on the open market.

Federal Reserve System. The central bank of the United States; it regulates the supply of money to the economy, establishes reserve requirements for banks, and acts as a clearinghouse for funds transactions.

Federal Savings and Loan Insurance Corporation (FSLIC). A federal agency that insures the deposits in member savings and thrift organizations.

Financial planning. A process of money management that may include any or all of several strategies, including budgeting, tax planning, insurance, retirement and estate planning, and investment strategies. In effective financial planning, all elements are coordinated with the aim of building, protecting, and maximizing net worth.

Fixed expenses. Those household expenses that do not vary from month to month.

Floating exchange rate. A nonfixed foreign currency exchange rate that fluctuates according to natural marketplace processes of supply and demand.

401(k) plan. A profit-sharing plan that allows employees to reduce their income by investing a portion of their income, which is often matched by the employer. Earnings compound tax-free, and the employee contributions are excluded from federal income tax.

Futures option. An agreement to buy or sell a specified commodity or financial instrument on a future stipulated date at a price negotiated between the buyer and the seller. The buyer may choose whether or not to exercise the option by the agreed-on date.

Futures contract. Same as a futures option, but the buyer is obligated.

General partner. In a limited partnership, the individual (or individuals) responsible for the management of the partnership and having full liability for its debts and obligations.

Glamor stock. Any stock that enjoys wide popularity among private and institutional investors.

Government National Mortgage Association (GNMA or Ginnie Mae). A government-sponsored agency that purchases mortgages from private lenders. The mortgages are repackaged and sold on the open market as mortgage-backed securities.

Gross national product (GNP). The value of all goods and services produced in a nation. In the United States, the GNP is calculated quarterly by the U.S. Department of Commerce.

Historic rehabilitation. A subcategory of the real estate market in which tax credits are allowed for the rehabilitation of historic properties for investment purposes.

Holographic will. A hand-written will. Holographic wills are valid only in some locations and if state "witnessing" requirements are met.

Hot hands fallacy. An emotional illusion that mistakenly assumes that past performance of an investment or advisor is an indicator of future performance.

Imputed interest. The theoretical income, as calculated by the Internal Revenue Service, earned each year on a zero-coupon bond; a means of converting capital gain to ordinary income for taxation at a higher rate.

Income splitting. A tax-planning strategy in which income is transferred from the ownership of a person paying a higher tax rate to one paying a lower rate; usually a parent and child.

Income statement. A detailed summary of the total income and expenses of an individual or organization (in a business, often known as the "profit and loss" statement).

Index fund. A mutual fund designed to emulate the performance of one of the major stock indexes, such as the Standard & Poor's 500 or the Dow Jones Industrial Average.

Index of Leading Indicators. An index of 12 components of economic activity, which are monitored by the U.S. Commerce Department's Bureau of Economic Analysis and compiled to create a forecast of ups and downs in the business cycle.

Individual retirement account (IRA). A retirement savings program that allows certain individuals to make tax-deductible contributions; earnings are not taxed until the funds are withdrawn, usually during retirement.

Inflation. An economic condition marked by generally rising prices, often attributed to the overexpansion of the money supply and demand for goods at or near full employment and industrial output. Measured in the United States by the **Consumer Price Index** (CPI), among others.

Initial public offering (IPO). A corporation's first offering of stock to the public.

Insider trading. Illegal securities trading based on knowledge of the market not available to the general public.

Inter vivos trust (living trust). A trust created during the grantor's lifetime.

Intestate. The condition created when a decedent does not leave a will, leaving disposition of the estate to state law.

Irrevocable Trust. An **inter vivos trust** in which the grantor gives away all rights of ownership and that may not be revoked. See **Revocable trust.**

Joint tenancy. Ownership of a piece of property by two or more people. On the death of one, the survivor(s) assume the decedent's interest.

Junk bond. A bond rated BB or lower by an investment-rating service. Junk bonds are riskier than bonds rated BBB or higher (investment-grade bonds) and pay higher yields.

Keogh plan. A retirement savings plan for individuals who are self-employed. Annual contributions are tax deductible and earnings accumulate tax free until withdrawal, usually at retirement.

Krugerrand. A popular and frequently traded gold bullion coin minted by the Republic of South Africa.

Lease. A contract between a lessor (property owner) and lessee (tenant) detailing the conditions by which a tenant may occupy and use the property.

Leverage. In investing, the use of borrowed money for investment purposes; in business, the relationship between debt and equity.

Leveraged buyout (LBO). The takeover of a company using borrowed funds, usually secured by the assets of the target company.

Liabilities. All financial claims against a business or individual.

Lien. A creditor's claim against property; a mortgage is a lien against a house, and a bond is a lien against a company's assets.

Limited partner. An investor whose liability in a partnership is limited to the amount the individual invested. See **General partner.**

Limited partnership. A form of business organization that allows small investors (limited partners) to pool their funds and participate in programs otherwise available only to investors with larger sums. Profits, losses, and deductions are passed through to the limited partners.

Liquidity. The ability to easily exchange an asset for cash.

Load fund. A mutual fund on which a sales charge is levied by the agent or broker. See **No-load fund.**

Lump-sum distribution. The one-time disbursement of the complete proceeds of a profit sharing or pension plan, an annuity, or similar account.

Macroeconomics. The aggregate performance of a nation's input and output markets, measured by such indicators as GNP, stock prices, unemployment, inflation, and the supply of money.

Margin. Refers to an investor's equity in a securities account against which he or she may borrow to purchase additional securities.

Marital deduction. Created by the Economic Recovery Tax Act of 1981 to allow the assets of one spouse to pass, tax-free, to the other on the death of the first.

Maturity. The date on which a debt instrument, such as a loan or bond, becomes due and payable.

Mental accounting. The tendency to mentally segregate money into separate accounts, each with its own specific purpose; i.e., consumer spending or retirement.

Microeconomics. The study of individual elements of the economy such as firms, households, and specific industries.

Modern portfolio theory. The underlying strategy of asset allocation theory, which holds that diversification of investments among more than one type of vehicle or asset class will help maximize return and minimize risk.

Money market. The market that exists for short-term debt instruments such as negotiable certificates of deposit (CDs), commercial paper, banker's acceptances, Treasury bills (T-bills), and other short-term instruments characterized by safety and liquidity.

Money market fund. A mutual fund that invests in short-term instruments.

Money supply. The total amount of money in the U.S. economy including currency, demand deposits, commercial bank time deposits, and thrift deposits. It's measured weekly by the Federal Reserve, which has the power to expand and decrease the money supply, thus manipulating interest rates and, ultimately, the growth of the economy.

Moody's Investors Service. Moody's is a subsidiary of Dun & Bradstreet and is a major financial publisher and investment- rating service.

Mortgage. The debt instrument by which a borrower obtains money by granting a lender a claim against real property used as security. The borrower has use of the property, and the lien is removed when the loan is repaid.

Mortgage-backed security. A security issued by government agencies and backed by home mortgages.

Multiple-asset allocation. See **Diversification.**

Municipal bond. A long-term promissory note issued by a state or local government. Usually, interest is exempt from federal income tax and state tax within the state where the bond is issued.

Mutual fund. A fund created by a management company in which the money of many individual investors is pooled to purchase a diversified portfolio of securities. New shares continue to be sold, and outstanding shares are redeemed on demand.

NASD Automated Quotation System (NASDAQ). A centralized system of providing brokers and dealers with up-to-the-moment securities price quotes; operated by the National Association of Securities Dealers.

National Association of Securities Dealers (NASD). A self-regulatory organization empowered by the Securities and Exchange Commission to oversee the brokers and dealers who operate in the over-the-counter market.

Negative amortization. When payments on a promissory note are insufficient to meet current interest charges, the unpaid interest is added to the outstanding principal. Future interest is calculated on the new balance, and the unpaid balance of the note is increased rather than reduced.

Net asset value (NAV). The price at which a mutual fund redeems its shares. It is calculated daily by dividing the net market value of the fund by the number of outstanding shares.

No-load fund. A mutual fund that charges no sales commissions to the purchaser, although other management or penalty charges may be levied.

Negotiated order of withdrawal (NOW) account. An interest-bearing checking account.

Offering circular. See **Prospectus.**

Open-end investment company. An investment company that redeems (buys back) its shares, and that usually offers new shares to the public on an ongoing basis. See **Closed-end investment companies.**

Over-the-counter (OTC) market. A market administered by the National Association of Securities Dealers (NASD) for the exchange of securities that are not listed on the organized stock exchanges. Trades are conducted by telephone and over a computer network.

Par value. The face, or denomination, value of a bond.

Passive investment. Under the 1986 Tax Reform Act (TRA), a passive investment is one in which an investor does not "materially participate." Material participation requires regular, continuous, and substantial involvement in the operation.

Passthroughs. A tax term for the losses generated by a limited partnership and passed through to the limited partners, who use it to shelter income created by passive investments.

Point. In commercial lending, the amount paid to the lender as a loan fee, or 1% of the total principal. In bonds, a point represents a 1% change in relation to the bond's face value. Also used interchangeably with *basis point*, or one-hundredth of a percentage point of yield. In stocks, a $1 price fluctuation.

Portfolio. A group of investments held by an individual or an institution. A portfolio implies holdings of more than one stock, bond, commodity, or real estate investment for the purpose of diversification.

Power of attorney. A means by which one person grants to another the right to perform on his or her behalf. As opposed to durable power of attorney, the activities granted may be limited.

Preferred stock. A class of stock that has claim over a company's earnings before payment is made to the holders of common stock.

Present value. The discounted value of future payments. The discount assumes a specified interest for a specified period of time.

Probate. The period of time during which a court supervises the affairs of a decedent, including the disbursement of assets.

Prospectus. A document offering a new issue of securities to the general public and providing information necessary to make an informed decision about the security. Mutual funds and limited partnerships publish prospectuses as well.

Proxy. A shareholder's written authorization allowing another party to represent him or her in voting his or her shares at a shareholders meeting.

Put option. An option to sell 100 shares of stock at a specified price within a set period of time. The buyer pays a forfeitable premium that is lost if he or she chooses not to exercise the option.

Put-and-keep account. The 10% portion of a 10/20/70 budget designated for long-term savings and investments.

Put-and-take account. The 20% portion of a 10/20/70 budget allocated to consumer spending.

Qualified retirement plan. An IRS-approved pension, profit-sharing, or deferred-income plan established by an employer for the benefit of the employees. Employees pay no current income tax on employer contributions, contributions accumulate tax free until withdrawal, and contributions are a deductible business expense for the employer.

Random walk theory. An aspect of modern portfolio theory that holds that the "random walk" of stock prices gives no single trader an advantage over another, regardless of track records.

Real estate investment trust (REIT). An investment company whose holdings are in real estate.

Real estate mortgage investment conduit (REMIC). A corporation, partnership, or trust that holds a fixed pool of mortgages.

Recession. A severe contraction in the economy, generally defined as two consecutive quarters of decline in the gross national product.

Red herring. Slang for a preliminary prospectus published to determine interest in the offering. The term derives from the statement printed in red ink on each page that the contents may change.

Registered representative. An employee of a firm that is a member of a stock exchange or of a broker-dealer who acts as an account executive on behalf of his or her clients. Said representative meets the requirements of the exchange regarding background and knowledge of securities, acts as a customer's broker, and receives commissions for his or her services.

Repurchase agreement (REPO). A money market agreement in which the seller warrants his or her willingness to buy back the securities for a higher price on a fixed date.

Return. The pretax profit on an investment.

Risk. The measurable possibility of loss or no gain on an investment. Differs from uncertainty, in that **risk** is measurable.

Rollover. The ability to move funds from one investment vehicle to another similar vehicle without incurring a gain or loss; usually refers to the transfer of retirement funds from a qualified retirement plan into a rollover IRA or to the gains from the sale of a principal residence that are used to purchase a new home.

Rule of 72. A method for calculating the number of years an investment will take to double at a given compound interest rate: To determine this value, divide the interest rate into 72.

Securities and Exchange Commission (SEC). The federal regulatory and enforcement agency that oversees investment trading activities.

Simplified Employee Pension Plan (SEP-IRA). A qualified retirement plan under which employees establish their own individual retirement accounts, to which the employer may make contributions.

Standard & Poor's. An investor's services and financial publishing firm best known for the **S & P 500**, a weighted index of 500 widely held stocks, 400 industrials, 40 public utilities, and 20 transportation stocks.

Short selling. The sale of stock or a commodity futures contract that's not owned by the investor but that has been borrowed from a broker in anticipation of a drop in the stock's value. If the stock's value declines, the investor buys it at the lower price to make up the loss; if the price increases, the investor takes a loss.

Subchapter S corporation. A corporation that, for tax purposes, chooses to be treated as if it were a partnership; this allows profits and losses to pass through to individual shareholders.

Tangible asset. Also known as hard assets: An asset that is physical and material, such as cash or property, as opposed to intangible assets such as trademarks and licenses.

Tax bracket. The range of taxable income taxed at a certain rate.

Tax credit. Certain dollar-for-dollar deductions in tax liability allowed for expenses such as child care, residential energy improvements, and foreign taxes.

Tax deduction. An expense that is deducted from a taxpayer's adjusted gross income to determine taxable income. Examples include medical expenses, interest paid on the mortgages on first and second homes, and charitable contributions.

Tax-deferred investment. An investment whose earnings are not taxable until they begin to be withdrawn.

Tax-exempt security. A security whose interest is exempt from local, state, or federal income tax, such as a **municipal bond**.

Tax shelter. An investment which provides tax savings by creating losses that offset taxable income.

Tenancy by the entirety. A joint tenancy between spouses with the right of survivorship.

Tenancy in common. Co-ownership by two or more people, each of whom owns a defined percentage of the whole.

Term life insurance. Life insurance that is issued for a limited time period as specified in the contract.

Testamentary trust. An irrevocable trust created by a descendent's will.

Time diversification theory. Embraces the concepts of dollar-cost averaging and multiple-asset allocation: to reduce risk, investments should be held through a complete market cycle generally lasting four to six years.

Treasury bill. A short-term U.S.-government paper sold in minimum denominations of $10,000 at auction through the Federal Reserve Banks; maturities range from 13 to 52 weeks.

Treasury note. U.S. Government paper with a maturity of not less than one year and not more than 10 years; issued in denominations of $1,000 and $5,000.

Trust. A legal entity created by an individual in which one other person or an institution holds and manages property for a third party, known as the *beneficiary.*

Universal life insurance. Life insurance that consists of a term portion and a cash accumulation portion. It provides for current rates of interest and flexible premium payments that are not fixed in either timing or amount.

Veterans Administration mortgage. A residential mortgage that is guaranteed by the Veterans Administration.

Vesting. The amount of time necessary for an employee to become a participant in a qualified retirement plan.

Volatility. The tendency of a security or a market to fluctuate in price. See **Beta coefficient.**

Warrant. A certificate giving the holder the right to buy a number of shares of common stock at a set price, which is usually higher than the market price, within a specified period or in perpetuity; usually issued with a bond or with shares of preferred stock.

Whole life insurance. Life insurance that provides for regular premiums, regular death benefits, and cash values. The cash values may be borrowed against or withdrawn when the policy is surrendered.

Yield. Another way of expressing investment return, usually expressed as a percentage of the market price of a security.

Zero-coupon bond. A bond sold at a deep discount from its par, or face, value. These bonds appreciate rapidly but pay no payments of interest until maturity. The annual accrued appreciation on a zero-coupon bond is taxable unless it's a municipal bond.

APPENDIX B: MONEY MANAGEMENT ATTITUDES

BASIC FAMILY INFORMATION

Name _____ Birth Date _____

Age _____ Social Security Number _____ Birth Place _____

Residence Address _____

_____ Residence Phone _____

Business Address _____

_____ Business Phone _____

Highest Academic Degree _____ Institution _____

Other Colleges _____

Employer _____

Position _____

Spouse's Name _____ Birth Date _____

Age _____ Social Security Number _____ Birth Place _____

Family Name _____ Marriage Date _____

Highest Academic Degree _____ Institution _____

Employer _____

Position _____

Employer Address _____

_____ Employer Phone _____

If not employed, how long out of labor force _____

Specific Skills _____

Trusts: _____ Date of: _____ Fed. I.D. #: _____

Children:

Name	Birth Date	Sex	Health	Birth Place	Married	Soc. Security #
1.						
2.						
3.						
4.						
5.						

Other(s) Dependent on You (Parents, Brother, Grandchildren, etc.):

Name	Birth Date	Birth Place	Soc. Security #
1.			
2.			

Any former marriages _____ Are you paying alimony _____

Alimony amount _____ Children by former marriage _____

If so, ages _____ Support obligation _____

BASIC FAMILY INFORMATION
(Continued)
ADVISORS

Attorney _____

  Address _____

  Phone _____

Accountant _____

  Address _____

  Phone _____

Bank Officer _____

  Address _____

  Phone _____

**Insurance
Agent** _____

  Address _____

  Phone _____

**Insurance
Advisor** _____

  Address _____

  Phone _____

Broker _____

  Address _____

  Phone _____

Trust Officer _____

  Address _____

  Phone _____

Physician _____

  Address _____

  Phone _____

**Other
Advisors** _____

  Address _____

  Phone _____

BASIC FAMILY INFORMATION
(Continued)
DOCUMENTS
Location

Your Will _____

Spouse's Will _____

Copy of Last
Instructions _____

Trust Agreements _____

Mortgages _____

Property Deeds _____

Car Titles _____

Stock Certificates _____

Stock Purchase
Agreements _____

Bonds and C.D.'s _____

Bank Statements _____

Savings Account
Passbooks _____

Insurance Policies _____

Contracts _____

Retirement
Agreements _____

Pension or Profit
Sharing Plans _____

Birth Certificates _____

Marriage Licenses _____

Divorce Papers _____

Notes Receivable _____

Notes Payable _____

Employment Contracts _____

Income Tax Returns _____

Gift Tax Returns _____

Military Documents _____

Financial Surveys _____

Other Records and
Valuables _____

_____

MONEY MANAGEMENT ATTITUDES

Financial planning and personal money management are not exact sciences. Not only must you make decisions based on your understanding of the economy and how it affects your financial situation, but these decisions are made within a framework composed of your attitudes toward and experiences in managing your money. The following questionnaire will help identify your financial attitudes, needs, and goals. Complete the following pages quickly. Write down your immediate reactions, respond—don't reflect!

IDENTIFYING FINANCIAL CONCERNS

Review each of the following concerns to see which apply to you. Place and X under the number which comes closest to how important each concern is to you.

	Most Important 1	2	3	4	Least Important 5	6
____ Safety						
____ Liquidity						
____ Income if disabled						
____ Income for loved ones if you die						
____ Growth of Assets						
____ Recession Protection						
____ Diversification						
____ Professional Management						
____ Tax Profection						
____ Inflation						
____ Emergency fund						
____ Education funding						
____ New Home purchase						
____ Retirement funding						
____ Medical Care costs						
____ General investment funding						
____ Estate Planning						
____ Vacation funding						
____ Debt reduction						

1. Next to how many items did you place a 1 or 2? _____
2. In the **last six months,** what steps have you taken to achieve the objectives you identified as the most important?

   _____

   _____

   _____

3. During the **next six months** what steps are necessary to achieve your most important objectives?

   _____

   _____

MONEY MANAGEMENT ATTITUDES AND EXPERIENCE

1. Everyone should keep the equivalent of _____ months' income in a savings account for emergencies.

2. People buy life insurance for the following reasons
   _____ To save money
   _____ To replace the breadwinner's income
   _____ Other reasons:
   _____
   _____
   _____

3. My biggest financial worry is _____
   _____
   _____

4. The best investment I ever made was _____
   _____
   _____

5. The worst investment I ever made was _____
   _____
   _____

6. Five years ago I wish I had invested in _____
   _____
   _____

7. My attitude about my current tax situation is _____
   _____
   _____

8. I consider myself to be (answer yes or no)
   _____ A good money manager
   _____ A conservative investor
   _____ Aware about what tomorrow might bring
   _____ Prepared for tomorrow
   _____ A risk taker
   _____ Financially successful
   _____ Able to recover from financial losses
   _____ In control of my financial affairs
   _____ Controlled by my financial affairs
   _____ Happy with my accumulation of assets relative to the income I've
   earned during the last 10 years

FINANCIAL PLANNING GOALS

There's a saying: "The whole world steps aside for the people who know where they are going." What about your goals? Do you know where you are going? This is the most important step in the entire financial planning process. You must know all of your goals—hopes, dreams, commitments, and obligations.

The next few pages will give you a chance to think through and write down exactly what your goals are and when you want to achieve them. Give yourself adequate time to think them through and discuss them with everyone concerned with their achievement.

Retirement

1. At what age do you plan to retire? _____
2. How much spendable monthly income do you want at retirement in today's dollars? _____

Give your estimate of the income you will recieve from the following when you retire:

     Social Security _____

     Company retirement plans _____

     Other retirement plans _____

     Estimate any lump-sum distributions you will receive at retirement _____

     Estimate the rate of return on your financial security investments _____

     Estimate the rate of return on your education investments _____

     Estimate the rate of return on your retirement funds _____

     Once you have achieved your goal, what is your estimate for the income-producing rate of return

         (1) on your financial security investments? _____

         (2) on your retirement investments? _____

Estimate your average tax bracket when you retire _____

Financial Growth Expectations

1. Based on the investment risk you are willing to assume, what is a reasonable rate of growth to expect for your investments? _____%
2. Over the next 10 years, what do you expect the rate of inflation to be? _____%
3. If you had to live off the earning from your savings and investments without undue risk, what rate of return would you expect? _____%

Income Replacement

1. How much monthly income does it take for family maintenance currently? $ _____
2. Does anyone in the family have any special needs that are of a continuing nature? How much monthly? $ _____
3. Do you have the care of or do you contribute to the support of parents or others? How much monthly? $ _____
4. Is anyone in the family the beneficiary of any trusts, or does anyone expect any inheritances? If so how much and when? $ _____
5. In the event of death or disability of the primary "breadwinner," will the surviving spouse work?
_____

     If so, in what type of occupation? _____

     How much income potential? $_____ monthly.

     Will any retraining or education be needed? _____

Education

1. Do you plan to contribute to or pay the entire cost (circle one) of higher education for any family members? If yes, list members by name, number of support years, and expected amount of annual support.

Name	Date to Begin College	# of Years	Current College Fund	Annual Amount ($)	Total Amount Needed

Short-term Goals

Goal   Dollars needed for each year (non-budget items only)

	Year: 1	2	3	4	5	Beyond
Vacations						
Second home						
New autos						
Home repairs						
Redecorating						
Recreational vehicle						
Education costs						
Totals						

In order to accumulate funds for both your short- and long-term goals, are you in a position to devote any more of your current income to savings or investments? _____
If yes, how much more on a monthly basis? _____

Estate Preservation Goals

1. How important is it to you to preserve for the surviving spouse the value- and income- producing ability of your estate at death? _____

2. How important is it to you to preserve for your children or other heirs the value of your estate at the death of the surviving spouse? _____

3. How concerned are you about avoiding or reducing probate costs? _____
   Estate taxes? _____

4. Do you have any charitable interests you want to benefit from your last estate? If so, which charities? _____

NET WORTH—ASSETS

Use this section of the questionnaire to record what you own. The first part of the form asks for a description of the asset, the owner code (C=Community, J=Joint, SP=Separate Property, T=Trust), the current value of the asset, its current income, the date the asset was bought, its purchase price, and the reason that you have this asset (G=Growth, I=Income, L=Liquidity, T=Tax Advantage). The second part asks for a subset of information. Include the cash value of your insurance here. These data will be used in assessing your net worth, an analysis of your investments, and establishing your gross estate. Use an additional sheet of paper if necessary.

	Description	Owner Code	Current Value	Current Income	Purchase Date	Purchase Price	Objective
Cash							
Checking							
Savings							
Money Market							
Cert. of Deposit							
Life Ins. Cash Value							
TOTALS							
Liquid investments							
Mutual Funds							
Bonds							
Stocks							
Other							
TOTALS							
Notes receivable							
TOTALS							
Personal Property							
Auto							
Furnishings							
Art, Antiques							
Furs/Jewelry							
Other							
TOTALS							

NET WORTH ASSETS, cont.

	Description	Owner Code	Current Value	Current Income	Purchase Date	Purchase Price	Objective
Real estate							
	TOTALS						
Residence(s)							
	TOTALS						
Retirement funds							
Pension,Keogh							
Deferred Comp.							
IRA,TSA							
Profit Sharing							
	TOTALS						
Other investment							
Limited							
Partnerships	TOTALS						
Business Equity							
	TOTALS						
Pending Inheritances							
	TOTALS						
Collectibles/ Coins							
	TOTALS						
Other							
	TOTALS						
TOTAL ALL ASSETS							

NET WORTH—LIABILITIES

Use this section of the questionnaire to record what you owe. Describe what you own, the ownership code, how much you owe, and the interest rate you are presently paying on the amount. Don't include any loans against insurance policies here. Instead, list them under life insurance policies. This information is used in assessing your net worth and your gross estate. (C=Community, J=Joint, SP=Separate Property, T=Trust)

	Description	Owner Code	Current Balance	Monthly Payment	Internal Rate	Purchase Price	Due Date
Residence Mortgages	_____	_____	_____	_____	_____	_____	_____
	_____	_____	_____	_____	_____	_____	_____
	_____	_____	_____	_____	_____	_____	_____
Real Estate Mortgages	_____	_____	_____	_____	_____	_____	_____
	_____	_____	_____	_____	_____	_____	_____
			_____	_____		_____	
Credit Cards	_____	_____	_____	_____	_____	_____	_____
	_____	_____	_____	_____	_____	_____	_____
	_____	_____	_____	_____	_____	_____	_____
	_____	_____	_____	_____	_____	_____	_____
	_____	_____	_____	_____	_____	_____	_____
	_____	_____	_____	_____	_____	_____	_____
			_____	_____		_____	
Installment Loans	_____	_____	_____	_____	_____	_____	_____
	_____	_____	_____	_____	_____	_____	_____
	_____	_____	_____	_____	_____	_____	_____
	_____	_____	_____	_____	_____	_____	_____
	_____	_____	_____	_____	_____	_____	_____
	_____	_____	_____	_____	_____	_____	_____
			_____	_____		_____	
Personal Loans	_____	_____	_____	_____	_____	_____	_____
	_____	_____	_____	_____	_____	_____	_____
	_____	_____	_____	_____	_____	_____	_____
	_____	_____	_____	_____	_____	_____	_____
			_____	_____		_____	

Go to the next page to draft your personal Balance Sheet. It will summarize the Asset & Liability information you have just completed.

PERSONAL BALANCE SHEET

NAME: _____   **DATE:** _____

ASSETS			LIABILITIES & NET WORH		

ASSETS

CASH
Cash On hand	_____
Checking account	_____
Savings accounts	_____
Money-Market Funds	_____
Life Ins. Cash Values	_____
Notes/Acc.Receivables	_____
Total:	_____

MARKETABLE SECURITIES
Stocks	_____
Bonds	_____
Government Securities	_____
Mutual funds	_____
Other	_____
Total:	_____
Total Current (Liquid-Assets):	_____

PERSONAL PROPERTY
Automobiles	_____
Household Furnishings	_____
Art, Antiques, Collectible	_____
Clothings, Furs	_____
Jewelry	_____
Other Posessions	_____
Total:	_____

REAL ESTATE
Residence	_____
Other Properties	_____
Total:	_____

PENSIONS
Vested Pension Benefits	_____
IRA/Keogh	_____
Tax-Sheltered Annuity	_____
Total:	_____

LONG TERM ASSETS
Equity in Business	_____
Pending Inheritances	_____
Other	_____
Total:	_____
TOTAL ASSETS:	$ _____

LIABILITIES & NET WORH

CURRENT DEBTS: Due w/in 12 months
Rent/Mortgage	_____
Utilities	_____
Charge accounts	_____
Insurance Premiums	_____
Education	_____
Tot. Loan Pmts.Due (P&I)	_____
Other	_____
Total:	_____

TAXES: Due w/in 12 months
Federal	_____
State	_____
Property Taxes	_____
Social Security	_____
Total:	_____
Total Current Liabilities:	_____

MORTGAGES: Prin.Due>12 Mos.
Residences	_____
Other Property	_____
Total:	_____

OTHER LOANS: Prin.Due>12 Mos.
Auto	_____
Education	_____
Home Improvement	_____
Life Insurance	_____
Other	_____
Total:	_____

TOTAL LIABILITIES	$ _____
*TOTAL NETWORTH**	$ _____
TOTAL LIAB. & NET WORTH	$ _____
*CURRENT RATIO ***	_____
*NET WORKING CAPITAL ***	_____
*DEBT TO EQUITY RATIO ***	_____

*   (Net worth: Assets less liabilities)

**   See Chapter 4

INCOME SOURCES

Use this section to record your current and projected income. Indicate whether you or your spouse received the income. Use last year's tax return for the taxable items. Use your current records for the year to date, then estimate what the income will be for the rest of the year, and the following year. This information will be used to analyze your current income/expenditures, your current tax situation, and your income, expenditure, and tax-planning projections for the next three years. (Use income codes as follows: (T=Taxable, TF=Tax Free, TD=Tax Deferred, P=Passive).

	Description	Earner	Last Year	Current Year to Date	Estimate for Rest of Year	Next Year	Tax Code	Notes
Earned Income								
Salary (1)								
Salary (2)								
Self Employ (1)								
Self Employ (2)								
Portfolio Income								
Interest								
Dividends								
Royalties								
Cap Gain/Loss								
Annuities								
Pension								
Passive Income/Loss								
Partnership (1)								
Partnership (2)								
Other Passive								
Other Income								
Real Estate								
Minors Unearned								
Social Security								
Retirement Plan								
Lump Sum Dist.								
Misc.								
INCOME TOTAL:			$	$	$	$		

EXPENDITURES

Use this section to record your current and projected expenditures. This section is very similar to the last section on income except that it also asks for your estimate of your expenses at retirement.

	Description	Last Year	Current Year to Date	Estimate for Rest of Year	Next Year	Tax Deductible Y or N	Amount at Retirement
Housing							
Real Estate							
Taxes							
Transportation							
Medical							
Hshld. Repairs							
Housekeeper							
Utilities							
Insurance							
Child Care							
Education							
Food							
Clothing							
Travel							
Entertainment							
Hshld. Furnshgs.							
Pers. Allowance							
Miscellaneous							

Expenditures (continued)

	Description	Last Year	Current Year to Date	Estimate for Rest of Year	Next Year	Tax Deductible Y or N	Amount at Retirement
Installment Credit							
Credit Cards							
Auto							
Furniture							
Real Estate							
Taxes							
INSURANCE							
Life							
Health							
Auto							
Homeowners							
TAXES							
Federal							
State							
Social Security							
RETIREMENT PLAN							
Contributions						Y	
Pension						Y	
IRA/TSA						Y	
Keogh						Y	

	Description	Last Year	Current Year to Date	Estimate for Rest of Year	Next Year	Tax Deductible Y or N	Amount at Retirement
Business expenses	_____	_____	$_____	_____	_____	_____	$_____
	_____	_____	$_____	_____	_____	_____	$_____
Business interest	_____	_____	$_____	_____	_____	_____	$_____
	_____	_____	$_____	_____	_____	_____	$_____
Moving expenses	_____	_____	$_____	_____	_____	_____	$_____
	_____	_____	$_____	_____	_____	_____	$_____
Other adjustments	_____	_____	$_____	_____	_____	_____	$_____
	_____	_____	$_____	_____	_____	_____	$_____
Interest paid (Personal)	_____	_____	$_____	_____	_____	_____	$_____
	_____	_____	$_____	_____	_____	_____	$_____
						_____	
Charitable contributions	_____	_____	$_____	_____	_____	_____	$_____
	_____	_____	$_____	_____	_____	_____	$_____
	_____	_____	$_____	_____	_____	_____	$_____
	_____	_____	$_____	_____	_____	_____	$_____
Miscellaneous deductions	_____	_____	$_____	_____	_____	_____	$_____
	_____	_____	$_____	_____	_____	_____	$_____
Other discretionary expenditures	_____	_____	$_____	_____	_____	_____	$_____
	_____	_____	$_____	_____	_____	_____	$_____
TOTAL:	$_____	$_____	$_____	$_____		$_____
Number of exemptions	_____		_____	_____		
						_____

Filing status for income tax purposes _____

PERSONAL INCOME STATEMENT FOR YEAR

NAME: DATE:

AMOUNT

ANNUAL INCOME
- Salary & Wages $ _____
- Interest & Dividends _____
- Capital Gains _____
- Other Investment Income _____
- Other _____

                         TOTAL: $_____

LESS TAXES
- Federal _____
- State _____
- Social Security _____

                         TOTAL: $_____

       TOTAL ANNUAL DISPOSABLE INCOME: $_____

           MONTHLY DISPOSABLE INCOME: $_____

COMMITTED EXPENDITURES
- Housing (incl. Mortgage) _____
- Transportation _____
- Medical _____
- Household Repairs _____
- Insurance _____
- Utilities _____
- Misc. Debt Repayment (P&I) _____
- Housekeeper _____
- Other _____

                         TOTAL: $_____

MANAGEABLE EXPENDITURES
- Food _____
- Clothing _____
- Travel/Entertainment _____
- Household Furnishings _____
- Contributions/Gifts _____
- Education _____
- Personal Allowances _____
- Misc. _____
- Other _____

                         TOTAL: $_____

           TOTAL ANNUAL EXPENDITURES: $_____

                 MONTHLY EXPENDITURES: $_____

                   ANNUAL NET INCOME $_____

                 MONTHLY NET INCOME $_____

     LESS AMOUNT TO SAVINGS (ANN.): $_____

     LESS AMOUNT INVESTMENTS (ANN.): $_____

           NET INCOME AVAIL. YEARLY $_____

         NET INCOME AVAIL. MONTHLY $_____

APPROPRIATE SPENDING LEVELS
AS A PERCENTAGE OF NET INCOME

ANNUAL INCOME

Earnings from Employment	$ _____	_____%
Investment Income (Interest & Dividends)	_____	_____%
Gifts, Inheritances	_____	_____%
Alimony, Child Support, Other	_____	_____%
Miscellaneous _____	_____	_____%
TOTAL INCOME: $ _____		100%

ANNUAL EXPENSES

Housing	$ _____	_____%	_____% *
Loan Payment	_____	_____	_____
Food	_____	_____	_____
Hobbies/entertainment	_____	_____	_____
Child care	_____	_____	_____
Out of Pocket (miscellaneous)	_____	_____	_____
Transportation	_____	_____	_____
Utilities/phone	_____	_____	_____
Clothing	_____	_____	_____
Savings	_____	_____	_____
Pension	_____	_____	_____
Medical	_____	_____	_____
Education (including student loans)	_____	_____	_____
Gifts/contributions	_____	_____	_____
Vacation	_____	_____	_____
Insurance	_____	_____	_____
Personal Care	_____	_____	_____
Dues/subscriptions	_____	_____	_____
TOTAL EXPENSES:	$ ===========		

☞ * In Column 3 GO TO page 58 to find the general guideline for appropriate spending levels. Are you within the averages: What needs to be adjusted?

Go To...

INSURANCE/ESTATE PLANNING

Use this section to record the different aspects needed to assess your insurance and your estate taxes. Begin by compiling an insurance policy information sheet.

Property Insurance
Policy type _____
Agent's name _____
Renewal date _____

Company _____
Phone _____
Location of policy_____

Life Insurance
On life of _____
Policy type _____
Agent's name _____
Renewal date _____

Company _____
Phone _____
Location of policy _____

On life of _____
Policy type _____
Agent's name _____
Renewal date _____

Company _____
Phone _____
Location of policy _____

Auto Insurance
Car #1 _____
Policy type _____
Agent's name _____
Renewal date _____

Policyholder _____
Company _____
Phone _____
Location of policy _____

Car #2 _____
Policy type _____
Agent's name _____
Renewal date _____

Policyholder _____
Company _____
Phone _____
Location of policy _____

Health Insurance
Policyholder #1 _____
Policy type _____
Agent's name _____
Location of cards _____

Dependents covered _____
Company _____
Phone _____
Location of policy _____

Policyholder #2 _____
Policy type _____
Agent's name _____
Location of cards _____

Dependents covered _____
Company _____
Phone _____
Location of policy _____

Estimate of Amount Required

	You	Spouse
Funeral	_____	_____
Administrative	_____	_____
Current bills	_____	_____
Emergency fund	_____	_____
Mortgage*	_____	_____
Education	_____	_____
Other expenses	_____	_____

*Estimated contributions and actual/
estimated gifts and taxes*

Charitable contributions from estate	_____	_____
Taxable gifts made after 1976	_____	_____
Gift taxes paid on post-1978 gifts	_____	_____

Estimate of the percent that current living expense will be reduced if you die _____

Estimate of the average tax bracket your spouse will be in _____

Death benefits of retirement programs _____

Value of personal assets your spouse could convert to cash _____

Estimate of your spouse's employment income if you should die ** _____

Estimate of any other income your spouse may receive _____

* Does not need to be paid off
** Because of the situation, it may not be the same as the current employment income

Congratulations! By completing this book you have in effect:

* Analyzed your current financial situation
* Set your financial goals
* And developed a budget to achieve them.

COORDINATE

Now that you have a general plan, you will probably need advice and assistance from your financial advisor, a lawyer, an accountant, or a certified financial planner.

As you went through this you probably noticed that many financial questions are related to each other.

* Your investment choices are affected by tax considerations and your goals.

* Your will and your life insurance are closely related since both affect the disposition of property at death. If your estate is large enough, tax questions will also have an impact on these areas.

* Your budget, of course, is the central arena for most of these areas.

As you implement your plan by working with your financial advisor, you'll want to pay attention to how the various areas—tax, investment, and insurance—are related to each other.

MONITOR

Even after you've inplemented your financial plan, the job is not done. Financial planning is never done. Your financial situation changes constantly, so you need to constantly monitor it. Evaluate your goals at least once a year. Update for changes in your objectives, the economic situation and other events that affect you financially.

* Is your Estate Planning appropriate for your needs?

* Have you established your 10-20-70 Budget?

* Are you satisfied with your insurance planning to date?

* Are there tax saving ideas you should consider?

* Are your investments still appropriate for your goals?

As usual, you should consult with your financial advisors, since they will have up-to-date information about legislative changes or new products in their areas of expertise.

ACTION PLAN

	Target Date	Completed Date	By Whom

Cash Flow Management

1. Establish a budget using the Personal Cash
   Flow Management System provided
   a) _____ _____ _____
   b) _____ _____ _____

2. Risk Management/Casualty Insurance
   a) _____ _____ _____
   b) _____ _____ _____

3. Estate Planning (Will, etc.)
   example—

   a) See an attorney and update will & durable
      power _____ _____ _____
   b) _____ _____ _____
   c) _____ _____ _____

4. Tax Planning
   a) CPA and/or Financial Planner
      review of last year's return _____ _____ _____
   b) _____ _____ _____

5. Investment Planning
   a) _____ _____ _____
   b) _____ _____ _____
   c) _____ _____ _____
   d) _____ _____ _____
   e) _____ _____ _____
   f) _____ _____ _____

6. General Goals
   a) _____ _____ _____
   b) _____ _____ _____

ACTION STEPS

List 10 specific steps you will take during the next year to implement your personal financial plan.

_____

_____

_____

_____

_____

_____

_____

_____

Record Of Security

Name of Security _____

Symbol _____

Traded on _____

CAPITALIZATION

Common _____

Preferred _____

Long-Term Debt $ _____

Year Ends _____

WORKING CAPITAL

Current Assets $ _____

Current Liabilities $ _____

Working Capital $ _____

Type of Business _____

Dividend Rate _____ Paid _____ Dividend Paid Since ____

Conversion Privileges _____ Callable at _____

Broker _____ Representative _____

Address _____ Tel. _____

EARNINGS PER SHARE

Year	1Q	2Q	3Q	4Q	Year	Est.
	$	$	$	$		

Year	Price Range	$ Sales (000)	$ Earnings (000)

PURCHASES Stock Dividend, Splits or Rights					SALES					GAIN OR (LOSS)		BALANCE			
Date	Broker or Certif. #*	# Shares	Key	Gross Amount Unit	Date	# Shares	Key	Cost	(Net) Selling Price	S or L		# Shares	Key	Unit Cost	Amount
			1					$	$	$					$
			2												
			3												
			4												
			5												
			6												
			7												
			8												
			9												
			10												
			11												
			12												
			13												
			14												

Source: *J.K. Lasser Institute*, "Stock and Mutual Fund Owners Record Book and Planner" ©1988 Simon and Schuster, Inc.

FUTURE VALUE OF $1.00 AT THE END OF VARIOUS PERIODS

Example: $10,000 would be worth what in 10 years at 10% interest?
Find the appropriate factor; 2.5937 x $10,000 = 25,937.00.

Period	1%	2%	3%	4%	5%	6%	7%	8%	9%	10%	12%	14%	15%	16%	18%	20%	24%	28%	32%	36%
1	1.0100	1.0200	1.0300	1.0400	1.0500	1.0600	1.0700	1.0800	1.0900	1.1000	1.1200	1.1400	1.1500	1.1600	1.1800	1.2000	1.2400	1.2800	1.3200	1.3600
2	1.0201	1.0404	1.0609	1.0816	1.1025	1.1236	1.1449	1.1664	1.1881	1.2100	1.2544	1.2996	1.3225	1.3456	1.3924	1.4400	1.5376	1.6384	1.7424	1.8496
3	1.0303	1.0612	1.0927	1.1249	1.1576	1.1910	1.2250	1.2597	1.2950	1.3310	1.4049	1.4815	1.5209	1.5609	1.6430	1.7280	1.9066	2.0972	2.3000	2.5155
4	1.0406	1.0824	1.1255	1.1699	1.2155	1.2625	1.3108	1.3605	1.4116	1.4641	1.5735	1.6890	1.7490	1.8106	1.9388	2.0736	2.3642	2.6844	3.0360	3.4210
5	1.0510	1.1041	1.1593	1.2167	1.2763	1.3382	1.4026	1.4693	1.5386	1.6105	1.7623	1.9254	2.0114	2.1003	2.2878	2.4883	2.9316	3.4360	4.0075	4.6526
6	1.0615	1.1262	1.1941	1.2653	1.3401	1.4185	1.5007	1.5869	1.6771	1.7716	1.9738	2.1950	2.3131	2.4364	2.6996	2.9860	3.6352	4.3980	5.2899	6.3275
7	1.0721	1.1487	1.2299	1.3159	1.4071	1.5036	1.6058	1.7138	1.8280	1.9487	2.2107	2.5023	2.6600	2.8262	3.1855	3.5832	4.5077	5.6295	6.9826	8.6054
8	1.0829	1.1717	1.2668	1.3686	1.4775	1.5938	1.7182	1.8509	1.9926	2.1436	2.4760	2.8526	3.0590	3.2784	3.7589	4.2998	5.5895	7.2058	9.2170	11.703
9	1.0937	1.1951	1.3048	1.4233	1.5513	1.6895	1.8385	1.9990	2.1719	2.3579	2.7731	3.2519	3.5179	3.8030	4.4355	5.1598	6.9310	9.2234	12.166	15.916
10	1.1046	1.2190	1.3439	1.4802	1.6289	1.7908	1.9672	2.1589	2.3674	2.5937	3.1058	3.7072	4.0456	4.4114	5.2338	6.1917	8.5944	11.805	16.059	21.646
11	1.1157	1.2434	1.3842	1.5395	1.7103	1.8983	2.1049	2.3316	2.5804	2.8531	3.4785	4.2262	4.6524	5.1173	6.1759	7.4301	10.657	15.111	21.198	29.439
12	1.1268	1.2682	1.4258	1.6010	1.7959	2.0122	2.2522	2.5182	2.8127	3.1384	3.8960	4.8179	5.3502	5.9360	7.2876	8.9161	13.214	19.342	27.982	40.037
13	1.1381	1.2936	1.4685	1.6651	1.8856	2.1329	2.4098	2.7196	3.0658	3.4523	4.3635	5.4924	6.1528	6.8858	8.5994	10.699	16.386	24.758	36.937	54.451
14	1.1495	1.3195	1.5126	1.7317	1.9799	2.2609	2.5785	2.9372	3.3417	3.7975	4.8871	6.2613	7.0757	7.9875	10.147	12.839	20.319	31.691	48.756	74.053
15	1.1610	1.3459	1.5580	1.8009	2.0789	2.3966	2.7590	3.1722	3.6425	4.1772	5.4736	7.1379	8.1371	9.2655	11.973	15.407	25.195	40.564	64.358	100.71
16	1.1726	1.3728	1.6047	1.8730	2.1829	2.5404	2.9522	3.4259	3.9703	4.5950	6.1304	8.1372	9.3576	10.748	14.129	18.488	31.242	51.923	84.953	136.96
17	1.1843	1.4002	1.6528	1.9479	2.2920	2.6928	3.1588	3.7000	4.3276	5.0545	6.8660	9.2765	10.761	12.467	16.672	22.186	38.740	66.461	112.13	186.27
18	1.1961	1.4282	1.7024	2.0258	2.4066	2.8543	3.3799	3.9960	4.7171	5.5599	7.6900	10.575	12.375	14.462	19.673	26.623	48.038	85.070	148.02	253.33
19	1.2081	1.4568	1.7535	2.1068	2.5270	3.0256	3.6165	4.3157	5.1417	6.1159	8.6128	12.055	14.231	16.776	23.214	31.948	59.567	108.89	195.39	344.53
20	1.2202	1.4859	1.8061	2.1911	2.6533	3.2071	3.8697	4.6610	5.6044	6.7275	9.6463	13.743	16.366	19.460	27.393	38.337	73.864	139.37	257.91	468.57
21	1.2324	1.5157	1.8603	2.2788	2.7860	3.3996	4.1406	5.0038	6.1088	7.4002	10.803	15.667	18.821	22.574	32.323	46.005	91.591	178.40	340.44	637.26
22	1.2447	1.5460	1.9161	2.3699	2.9253	3.6035	4.4304	5.4365	6.6586	8.1403	12.100	17.861	21.644	26.186	38.142	55.206	113.57	228.35	449.39	866.67
23	1.2572	1.5769	1.9736	2.4647	3.0715	3.8197	4.7405	5.8715	7.2579	8.9543	13.552	20.361	24.891	30.376	45.007	66.247	140.83	292.30	593.19	1178.6
24	1.2697	1.6084	2.0328	2.5633	3.2251	4.0489	5.0724	6.3412	7.9111	9.8497	15.178	23.212	28.625	35.236	53.108	79.496	174.63	374.14	783.02	1602.9
25	1.2824	1.6406	2.0938	2.6658	3.3864	4.2919	5.4274	6.8485	8.6231	10.834	17.000	26.461	32.918	40.874	62.668	95.396	216.54	478.90	1033.5	2180.0
26	1.2953	1.6734	2.1566	2.7725	3.5557	4.5494	5.8074	7.3964	9.3992	11.918	19.040	30.166	37.856	47.414	73.948	114.47	268.51	612.99	1364.3	2964.9
27	1.3082	1.7069	2.2213	2.8834	3.7335	4.8223	6.2139	7.9881	10.245	13.110	21.324	34.389	43.535	55.000	87.259	137.37	332.95	784.63	1800.9	4032.2
28	1.3213	1.7410	2.2879	2.9987	3.9201	5.1117	6.6488	8.6271	11.167	14.421	23.883	39.204	50.065	63.800	102.96	164.84	412.86	1004.3	2377.2	5483.8
29	1.3345	1.7758	2.3566	3.1187	4.1161	5.4184	7.1143	9.3173	12.172	15.863	26.749	44.693	57.575	74.008	121.50	197.81	511.95	1285.5	3137.9	7458.0
30	1.3478	1.8114	2.4273	3.2434	4.3219	5.7435	7.6123	10.062	13.267	17.449	29.959	50.950	66.211	85.849	143.37	237.37	634.81	1645.5	4142.0	10143.
40	1.4889	2.2080	3.2620	4.8010	7.0400	10.285	14.974	21.724	31.409	45.259	93.050	188.88	267.86	378.72	750.37	1469.7	5455.9	19426.	66520.	*
50	1.6446	2.6916	4.3839	7.1067	11.467	18.420	29.457	46.901	74.357	117.39	289.00	700.23	1083.6	1670.7	3927.3	9100.4	46890.	*	*	*

FUTURE VALUE OF $1.00 AT THE END OF VARIOUS TIME PERIODS

Example: If you sold your home on a private contract at 10% interest for 20 years for $100,000, what would its present value be worth today? Find the appropriate factor: .1486 x $100,000 = $14,860 today. Knowing this, is the contract a good decision since the time value of money principle teaches that a dollar today is worth more than a dollar tomorrow?

Period	1%	2%	3%	4%	5%	6%	7%	8%	9%	10%	12%	14%	15%	16%	18%	20%	24%	28%	32%	36%
1	.9901	.9804	.9709	.9615	.9524	.9434	.9346	.9259	.9174	.9091	.8929	.8772	.8696	.8621	.8475	.8333	.8065	.7813	.7576	.7353
2	.9803	.9612	.9426	.9246	.9070	.8900	.8734	.8573	.8417	.8264	.7972	.7695	.7561	.7432	.7182	.6944	.6504	.6104	.5739	.5407
3	.9706	.9423	.9151	.8890	.8638	.8396	.8163	.7938	.7722	.7513	.7118	.6750	.6575	.6407	.6086	.5787	.5245	.4768	.4348	.3975
4	.9610	.9238	.8885	.8548	.8227	.7921	.7629	.7350	.7084	.6830	.6355	.5921	.5718	.5523	.5158	.4823	.4230	.3725	.3294	.2923
5	.9515	.9057	.8626	.8219	.7835	.7473	.7130	.6806	.6499	.6209	.5674	.5194	.4972	.4761	.4371	.4019	.3411	.2910	.2495	.2149
6	.9420	.8880	.8375	.7903	.7462	.7050	.6663	.6302	.5963	.5645	.5066	.4556	.4323	.4104	.3704	.3349	.2751	.2274	.1890	.1580
7	.9327	.8706	.8131	.7599	.7107	.6651	.6227	.5835	.5470	.5132	.4523	.3996	.3759	.3538	.3139	.2791	.2218	.1776	.1432	.1162
8	.9235	.8535	.7894	.7307	.6768	.6274	.5820	.5403	.5019	.4665	.4039	.3506	.3269	.3050	.2660	.2326	.1789	.1388	.1085	.0854
9	.9143	.8368	.7664	.7026	.6446	.5919	.5439	.5002	.4604	.4241	.3606	.3075	.2843	.2630	.2255	.1938	.1443	.1084	.0822	.0628
10	.9053	.8203	.7441	.6756	.6139	.5584	.5083	.4632	.4224	.3855	.3220	.2697	.2472	.2267	.1911	.1615	.1164	.0847	.0623	.0462
11	.8963	.8043	.7224	.6496	.5847	.5268	.4751	.4289	.3875	.3505	.2875	.2366	.2149	.1954	.1619	.1346	.0938	.0662	.0472	.0340
12	.8874	.7885	.7014	.6246	.5568	.4970	.4440	.3971	.3555	.3186	.2567	.2076	.1869	.1685	.1372	.1122	.0757	.0517	.0357	.0250
13	.8787	.7730	.6810	.6006	.5303	.4688	.4150	.3677	.3262	.2897	.2292	.1821	.1625	.1452	.1163	.0935	.0610	.0404	.0271	.0184
14	.8700	.7579	.6611	.5775	.5051	.4423	.3878	.3405	.2992	.2633	.2046	.1597	.1413	.1252	.0985	.0779	.0492	.0316	.0205	.0135
15	.8613	.7430	.6419	.5553	.4810	.4173	.3624	.3152	.2745	.2394	.1827	.1401	.1229	.1079	.0835	.0649	.0397	.0247	.0155	.0099
16	.8528	.7284	.6232	.5339	.4581	.3936	.3387	.2919	.2519	.2176	.1631	.1229	.1069	.0930	.0708	.0541	.0320	.0193	.0118	.0073
17	.8444	.7142	.6050	.5134	.4363	.3714	.3166	.2703	.2311	.1978	.1456	.1078	.0929	.0802	.0600	.0451	.0258	.0150	.0089	.0054
18	.8360	.7002	.5874	.4936	.4155	.3503	.2959	.2502	.2120	.1799	.1300	.0946	.0808	.0691	.0508	.0376	.0208	.0118	.0068	.0039
19	.8277	.6864	.5703	.4746	.3957	.3305	.2765	.2317	.1945	.1635	.1161	.0829	.0703	.0596	.0431	.0313	.0168	.0092	.0051	.0029
20	.8195	.6730	.5537	.4564	.3769	.3118	.2584	.2145	.1784	.1486	.1037	.0728	.0611	.0514	.0365	.0261	.0135	.0072	.0039	.0021
25	.7798	.6095	.4776	.3751	.2953	.2330	.1842	.1460	.1160	.0923	.0588	.0378	.0304	.0245	.0160	.0105	.0046	.0021	.0010	.0005
30	.7419	.5521	.4120	.3083	.2314	.1741	.1314	.0994	.0754	.0573	.0334	.0196	.0151	.0116	.0070	.0042	.0016	.0006	.0002	.0001
40	.6717	.4529	.3066	.2083	.1420	.0972	.0668	.0460	.0318	.0221	.0107	.0053	.0037	.0026	.0013	.0007	.0002	.0001	*	*
50	.6080	.3715	.2281	.1407	.0872	.0543	.0339	.0213	.0134	.0085	.0035	.0014	.0009	.0006	.0003	.0001	*	*	*	*

SOCIAL SECURITY ADMINISTRATION

Request for Earnings and Benefit Estimate Statement

To receive a free statement of your earnings covered by Social Security and your estimated future benefits, all you need to do is fill out this form. Please print or type your answers. When you have completed the form, fold it and mail it to us.

1. Name shown on your Social Security card:

First   Middle Initial   Last

2. Your Social Security number as shown on your card:

3. Your date of birth: Month   Day   Year

4. Other Social Security numbers you may have used:

5. Your Sex: ☐ Male ☐ Female

6. Other names you have used (including a maiden name):

7. Show your actual earnings for last year and your estimated earnings for this year. Include only wages and/or net self-employment income subject to Social Security tax.

    A. Last year's actual earnings:
    $ _____ , _____ . 0 0
    Dollars only

    B. This year's estimated earnings:
    $ _____ , _____ . 0 0
    Dollars only

8. Show the age at which you plan to retire: _____

SOCIAL SECURITY ADMINISTRATION
SALINAS DATA OPERATIONS CENTER
100 E. ALVIN DRIVE
SALINAS, CA 93906

9. Below, show an amount which you think best represents your future average yearly earnings between now and when you plan to retire. The amount should be a yearly average, not your total future lifetime earnings. Only show earnings subject to Social Security tax.

   Most people should enter the same amount as this year's estimated earnings (the amount shown in 7B). The reason for this is that we will show your retirement benefit estimate in today's dollars, but adjusted to account for average wage growth in the national economy.

   However, if you expect to earn significantly more or less in the future than what you currently earn because of promotions, a job change, part-time work, or an absence from the work force, enter the amount in today's dollars that will most closely reflect your future average yearly earnings. Do not add in cost-of-living, performance, or scheduled pay increases or bonuses.

   Your future average yearly earnings:
   $ _____ , _____ . 0 0
   Dollars only

10. Address where you want us to send the statement:

Name

Street Address (Include Apt. No., P.O. Box, or Rural Route)

City   State   Zip Code

I am asking for information about my own Social Security record or the record of a person I am authorized to represent. I understand that if I deliberately request information under false pretenses I may be guilty of a federal crime and could be fined and/or imprisoned. I authorize you to send the statement of my earnings and benefit estimates to me or my representative through a contractor.

▶ Please sign your name (Do not print)

Date   (Area Code) Daytime Telephone No.

ABOUT THE PRIVACY ACT
Social Security is allowed to collect the facts on this form under Section 205 of the Social Security Act. We need them to quickly identify your record and prepare the earnings statement you asked us for. Giving us these facts is voluntary. However, without them we may not be able to give you an earnings and benefit estimate statement. Neither the Social Security Administration nor its contractor will use the information for any other purpose.

SP ☐

INDEX